Contents

A detailed list of contents precedes each chapter. Selections of A level questions and guides to further reading and study can be found at the ends of chapters. In addition to Chapters 1, 2 and 21, Chapters 3, 6, 9, and 17 can be read for their high theoretical content.

iii

To Marie and Saisha, and to the memory of Charles Wright Mills

Thomas Nelson and Sons Ltd
Nelson House   Mayfield Road
Walton-on-Thames   Surrey
KT12 5PL   UK

51 York Place
Edinburgh
EH1 3JD   UK

Thomas Nelson (Hong Kong) Ltd
Toppan Building 10/F
22A Westlands Road
Quarry Bay   Hong Kong

Thomas Nelson Australia
480 La Trobe Street
Melbourne   Victoria 3000
Australia

Nelson Canada
1120 Birchmount Road
Scarborough   Ontario
M1K 5G4   Canada

By the same author
New Introductory Reader in Sociology, ISBN 0-17-448140-3

A New Introduction
to Sociology

M

F

S

Nelson

SECTION D Work, Organisations and Alienation

SECTION E Social Order, Public Power and Personal Potential

and Voting • Non-class Variables and Voting • Liberal-
pluralism • Marxist and Elite Theories • Recent Research
on Ideology and Voting Behaviour

SECTION F Sociology, Knowledge and Social Policy

Foreword

This revision of Dr O'Donnell's highly successful *A New Introduction to Sociology* reflects the aims of the first edition. His continued involvement in teaching A level students in the five years that have elapsed since the original publication facilitates both the readability and relevance of the text to students on such GCE courses, while not being limited to that group of students alone. My own students, for instance, on initial and in-service teacher education courses have used the first edition and will benefit from this revision.

Inevitably, over a period of years, the world changes and the way in which sociologists and others perceive the world changes too. The updating that has taken place in both of these senses would be sufficient to justify a new edition. There are, however, two additional changes which merit attention. Syllabus revisions are, rightly in my view and that of the author, rediscovering the importance of demographic considerations and this is fully reflected in the new edition. Most important, perhaps, is a new emphasis on matters of social policy.

The relationship between a dispassionate examination of social structures and processes on the one hand and intervention in society on the other has been an area of controversy in the social sciences for a very long time – as long as there have been social sciences. The debate shows no sign of going away. Dr O'Donnell retains his claim to 'libertarian socialism' professed in the first edition. Importantly, however, this is coupled with a thorough and sympathetic treatment of alternative views, which is especially welcome.

There is, in fact, substantial concern with the policy implications of 'findings' which stresses the relevance of sociology to matters of public interest or, for that matter, public passion. This does not, of course, mean that the study of society from a sociological perspective has any necessary value implications, simply, that such a study is likely to make for more informed judgements than might otherwise have been available and it is in this spirit that the new emphasis should be understood.

In my foreword to the first edition I remarked that were I 'faced with several hundred A level scripts each year' I had 'little doubt' that this book would make that task more rewarding. As it has transpired I have resumed examining sociology at GCE A level and my prediction has been, I'm happy to say, justified.

I am confident that my enthusiasm over this revised edition will also be justified and commend it to A level students and others who want a well written, serious and comprehensive introduction to sociology.

TONY MARKS
Formerly Chief Examiner
GCE A Level Sociology
Associated Examining Board
June 1986

Preface: How to Use this Book

In September 1980 I wrote in the preface to the first edition of this book of the lack of suitable sociology textbooks at this level. That is hardly the case now. As it turned out, this book is one of several choices. In this edition, I have again sought clarity and relevance as well as a full coverage of the major syllabuses and I hope that these are, in fact, distinctive features of this book. I hope, too, that I have managed to spark in the reader some of the interest I have enjoyed in writing it.

The main purpose of the second edition is to add chapters on the newer AEB syllabus topics of development/underdevelopment, population, social policy and health. The new material should also better answer the needs of other syllabuses, particularly London and Oxford. The theoretical content, if not the precise topics, should also be relevant to the JMB syllabus. Several sections of the first edition have been replaced or revised and I have added brief concluding sections to many chapters – usually to make some current comment. Work on my recent book, *Age and Generation*, has prompted me to revise the chapter on that theme very fully. In particular, a section on childhood has been added. In addition, there has been considerable updating although where a diagram does not lend itself to updating but still makes its point effectively, I have left it. The chapters on stratification and deviance are relatively unchanged but I have taken a current look at these areas in Chapter 22.

'Topics' in sociology are, to some extent, arbitrary and overlap greatly. There is no need to read this book in any particular order: chapters and sections are self-contained. The index is an essential part of the book. Some themes are followed through several chapters and the index signposts where. In addition, ample cross-references are given within chapters. In the first edition, I stressed that this book is written mainly for the 'A' level student. This remains true although I hope that this edition will, like the first, prove of interest to a wider audience. The early chapters are somewhat simpler than the later ones. Sections E and F are theoretically quite demanding although this may be marginally less true of the chapters on health and educational policy. The new policy chapters in Section F give a different balance to this edition. They break from the perspectives approach, more closely reflecting established political divisions, and represent a clear commitment to relevance. The tension between the supposed 'objectivity' of sociological theory and the 'subjectivity' of political ideology punctuates these chapters. The second edition of this book matches more closely to its companion, *A New Introductory Reader in Sociology*, especially in the newer topic areas. However, although the books complement each other, they can be used quite independently.

Bias and uncontrolled subjectivity are always spoilers and readers must guard against them; I also ought to say where I myself stand both sociologically and politically. Sociologically, I cannot conveniently place myself squarely within a single major perspective: a combination of conflict-structuralism and interpretive perspectives seems to me to offer the best possibility of a coherent understanding of society. As I make clear in the last chapter, I take no joy in the theoretical fragmentation currently characterising sociology, and I make some suggestions towards a single unified sociological paradigm. By all means let the thousand flowers bloom, but let us arrange them in some sort of order. Politically, I am a libertarian socialist. This may explain why the themes of democracy and equality recur through the various chapters of this book. I have kept in mind, however, that a textbook should present all relevant information and opinion with absolute fairness. I hope that, if I had not stated my own opinions and values, they would not otherwise have been too obvious.

Finally, this textbook is not a substitute for doing sociological research. It is quite true that 'you cannot find out about society from a book.' You must go out and examine it for yourself, with the sociological tools you have at your disposal. All I aspire to do in these pages is to guide you on the way.

MIKE O'DONNELL, *February 1986*

Acknowledgements

I would like to thank Anne Vellender for typing, correcting and, sometimes, improving this book. My thanks also to Dorothy Montague for the typing she did. Caroline Riddel and Gina Garrett gave constant advice and encouragement: it can be truly said that 'without their help this book would not have been written'. I am very grateful to Howard Newby for his advice on Chapter 6, Stan Cohen for his detailed comments on drafts of Chapters 17 and 18, and Tom Bottomore for looking over the chapters on stratification and politics. Through vigorous debate and criticism, Jim Pey has helped to clarify my presentation of educational sociology, for which I am now grateful. Tony Marks gave helpful advice over a range of matters. My thanks also to Helen Huckle and Diana Giese of Harrap for their editorial guidance.

For the second edition, Sandra den Hertog, Karen Laws and Marie Brown met my typing needs rapidly and cheerfully. David Lee, Juliette Hunting and Pat Mayes have offered advice and suggestions which have materially improved this edition and I sincerely thank them. For the rest, I take full responsibility.

MIKE O'DONNELL

Section A **Perspectives: Theory and Method**

How to Use this Section

Students often begin a textbook with the feeling that they must carefully read it from cover to cover. That is not the spirit in which to approach this section.

The intention here is both to *introduce* the theory and method of sociology and to provide a *point of reference* for theory and method to which the students can return as necessary for fuller information about given points. Thus, if you come across a reference to Marxism in Chapters 3 or 4 and want to check back to Marxist theory in general, then, using the index if necessary, it would be a simple matter to refer to the relevant pages in Chapter 1. Similarly, if you meet a reference to the method of enquiry known as *participant observation* in a later chapter, you might want to return and re-read the detailed description of it in this section. So, the initial way to approach this section is to read it for a *general impression*. Get a 'feel' for how sociologists go about their work rather than trying to learn in detail about it. At a later point, possibly about half-way through the course, it will be necessary to give closer study to Chapter 2, though, by then, the contents of Chapter 1 will probably have already been fully absorbed.

We can liken sociology to a mansion full of a variety of valuable things. At the moment, you are outside the mansion and will remain so for a short time. In front of you lies a map and some implements used in the construction and decoration of the building. Examining these things may be less interesting than touring the house but being familiar with them helps in appreciating it. Understanding the blueprints and implements used in any enterprise or craft is bound to deepen our knowledge of it. In the case of sociology, Chapter 1 *(perspectives, theory)* can be thought of as 'the map' of the subject and Chapter 2 *(theoretical concepts, methods)* can be regarded as 'the tools of the trade'. Some will spend longer studying Chapters 1 and 2 at this stage than others. This does not matter, but every one should at least read Chapter 1 now.

Beyond this section lies the varied *content* of sociology. This includes information and analysis of the family, race, deviance and so on. Every subject can be divided into the way people go about doing it (theory-method) and what they find (content). Subjects are often presented to the general public only in terms of their content – it is assumed that only 'the expert' can 'do' them. By contrast, this book attempts to present the content of sociology, to describe how to practise the discipline and to examine the relationship between the two. The final chapters of this book deal with many of the issues raised in this section at a higher level.

1 The Making of Sociology: Sociological Theory and Method, Part 1

Why Study Sociology?

Sociologists, like Socrates, the Greek sage, are sometimes accused of corrupting youth. This accusation is usually based on a vague anxiety that they have the power to implant dangerous and subversive ideas in the minds of the young. It is almost as if they are regarded as sorcerers who can charm others from the paths of virtue. Indeed, within education something resembling 'witch hunts' of sociologists do occasionally occur when attempts are made to undermine the prestige and influence of the subject. Like Socrates, sociologists are inclined to defend themselves by replying that their aim is not to corrupt, but to enlighten – not just the young but anybody who will listen and take part.

But 'enlightenment' is perhaps a pompous way of putting it. What sociology can do is to provide the means or the tools to understand society better than would otherwise be likely. To understand society better is to know a little more about what is happening to you, thereby, perhaps, gaining more control over your own life. For example, to appreciate how and why advertisers try to persuade you to buy their products – especially the leisure and fashion products popular in the teenage market – arms you against exploitation. Similarly, to know why qualifications are worth less in the job-market than they used to be, should help you to evaluate your own prospects more clearly.

There are many other important ways in which sociology can improve your understanding of your own life. It can show you how society works, including how people manage to get along with one another. It may help you to be more independent and avoid being manipulated by others. Perhaps that is what the opponents of sociology really mean when they say it is corrupting. They may prefer that you conform without understanding why you do: that way, life is easier for those in power, who are reassured in their own opinions. For students who require a practical as well as an intellectual motive for studying sociology, the subject provides a useful background for training in many careers, as will become apparent during the course of this book.

Understanding yourself and society better will not happen, magically, in a moment. Learning any worthwhile skill takes some time. But the early stages of learning are usually the worst. Take learning to ride a bicycle or to drive a car: there is no need to describe how frustrating and demoralising both can be. But they are worth it in the end. So is sociology.

The Continuing Importance of Marx, Durkheim and Weber

You will probably have noticed that so far I have indicated some of the things that sociology can do for you without quite defining the subject. Nor do I intend to do so immediately. A better way of approaching the discipline is firstly to appreciate some of the problems sociology attempts to analyse. This is where *Marx* (1818–1883), *Durkheim* (1858–1917), and *Weber* (1864–1920) are relevant. They were among the first to look at society in what we have come to think of as a specifically sociological way. Far from being out of date, their work and influence is greater now than it ever was. To say no more, Marxism as a method of understanding how society works and as a way of life has captured half the world.

The continuing relevance of the work of these three 'founding fathers' is a result of two things. First, some of the problems they attempted to understand are the same as, or similar to, major problems of today. Second, the frameworks of social analysis and explanation or *sociological perspectives* that they worked out have not been replaced by anything better, although they have been greatly developed and modified.

The early nineteenth century was a period of rapid change every bit as great as today's. Industrial and political revolutions, sometimes known as the 'dual revolutions', tore apart the fabric of society. The agricultural revolution forced peasants off the land, and the industrial revolution provided jobs for them in the cities. Often, the new industrial workers – and, at first, these included women and children – lived and worked in conditions of squalid exploitation. By contrast, the manufacturing, commercial and financial middle class prospered in an industrial boom. The traditional landed aristocracy also generally thrived, partly because of its great hereditary wealth and power, and partly because many of its members managed to 'get in on' industrial expansion.

Politically, the new middle class struggled successfully to share power with the aristocracy. In Britain, it managed to acquire the vote and other political rights without revolution, but France and other European countries experienced almost a century of political turmoil. As the century progressed, the claims of the working class for political rights and social justice were more and more strongly asserted. Europe was swept by revolution in 1848. In this, the working class and its supporters played a prominent part. Marx himself participated in an unsuccessful uprising in Germany in that year.

Marx, Durkheim and Weber were interested in and wanted to understand the major changes that were occurring in Europe during their own time. Even though they were of different nationalities, Marx being German, Durkheim French and Weber Austrian, the scale and scope of change was such that they were confronted by much the same problems. Our interest arises from the fact that our own period is a direct continuation of theirs and society today can be partly explained by past events and developments. Ours is an industrial, urban society in which, at last, the working class and women have political rights, but in which class conflict is by no means dead. The nineteenth century was a battleground between the old regime and the new, the traditional and the modern. Along with the study of class relations, the contrast and conflict between the traditional and the modern remains an axial consideration of sociology. Britain is still cloaked in tradition: witness the continuation of the monarchy and the House of Lords. Further, the conflict between traditional, rural society and modern, industrial society has been partly 'exported' from Europe to the wider world, in which the developing countries are the new battleground. Marx, Durkheim and Weber's writings are of relevance to all these matters.

But the founding fathers of sociology wanted to do more than just tell the tale of their times and perhaps offer a few unsystematic interpretations of events. They went deeper than that in their search for explanations and, in doing so, created the foundation of a new discipline, sociology. Separately, they attempted to develop ways of examining society and social change which would account not only for how their own societies functioned and changed but which would explain the nature and functioning of society itself. They believed that a scientific approach would assist them greatly in this enterprise. Indeed, perhaps they put too much faith in science, and many sociologists have since argued that, as well as being affected by society, men also help to create it – perhaps to a greater extent than Marx and Durkheim, though possibly not Weber, allowed. In their faith in science, the founding fathers reflected the spirit of their period. Charles Darwin's exciting new scientific theory of evolution seemed to offer a biological explanation of the origin of man and Marx, Weber and Durkheim sought to explain social life in similarly scientific terms. They were aware, however, that human consciousness and creativity raise issues that do not occur in the non-human sciences and we return to these later. Marx and Durkheim, in particular, built up distinctive perspectives or general models of how society works. Since their deaths, other perspectives have been developed within sociology, some of which address themselves more specifically to the problems of the individual in modern society. We mention these shortly. In what immediately follows we will tend to emphasise the differences rather than the similarities between the perspectives of Marx, Weber and Durkheim. However, we attempt to convey the common central concerns of sociology by examining their perspectives in the form of answers to a number of fundamental sociological questions. Sociology is better understood as a series of questions on the nature of society with no set answers, than as a set of agreed findings.

Sociological Theory: Structural and Interpretive Perspectives

At this stage, all that we mean by sociological theory is the body of ideas, tested and untested, making up sociological thought.

We can best understand the disagreements among contemporary sociologists, many of which have their roots in the thought of Durkheim, Marx and Weber, by examining some basic questions of sociological theory to which, in one way or another, all three gave answers. It would not be possible to construct an adequate sociological perspective without answering the following questions, although other major questions could also be asked:

1 **How is society constructed?**
2 **How does society 'operate' or function?**
3 **Why are some groups in society more powerful than others?**
4 **What causes social change?**

5 Is society normally in orderly balance or in conflict?
6 What is the relationship of the individual to society?
7 What is the primary purpose of sociological study?

The different (though not entirely different) answers given to these questions by Durkheim, Marx and Weber helped to produce three distinct traditions of sociological thought or perspectives: *Functionalism* which owes much to Durkheim, *Marxism* (Marx), and *Social Action Theory* (Weber). We will examine separately these three traditions and the answers they give to the above questions of theory. All three of these sociological perspectives are *structural* in nature. Structural sociology is primarily concerned with how society affects individual and group behaviour, rather than with how individuals and groups create society. Thus, the sort of issue a structural sociologist would be interested in, is how the class and family background of an individual (the individual's *social-structural position*) affect his chances of doing well at school and getting a good job. Functionalism is referred to as *consensus* structuralism because it emphasises the central role that agreement (consensus) between people on moral values has in maintaining social order. Marxism and Social Action Theory, on the other hand, stress *conflict* in society rather than consensus. It is a further crucially important feature of the structuralist theories that they tend to seek scientific or *positivist* explanations of social behaviour.

Interpretive sociology, in contrast to structuralism, is primarily concerned with how individuals and groups create, find meaning in, and experience society, rather than in how society affects them. Examples of the kind of matters that have interested interpretive sociologists are what it 'feels like' to be labelled a 'criminal' or 'mad' or, simply, 'not very bright' at school work. Interpretive sociology is, in part, a reaction against the scientific or positivist approach associated with the structural perspectives. We further explain interpretive sociology later in this chapter. Immediately, we describe the structural sociologies of Functionalism, Marxism and Social Action Theory by reference to the seven key questions stated above. It can be seen that the answers given to the questions by the various perspectives differ, sometimes to the point of contradiction.

Structural Perspectives: Functionalism: **Consensus Structuralism: Durkheim**

1 How is society constructed?

Society or the *social system* is constructed of various *institutions*, the most basic of which is the family. A social institution is a group of people organised for a specific purpose (or purposes) – the nuclear family, for example, is organised in order to produce and rear children. As societies develop, the number and complexity of social institutions increases. This process is referred to as *differentiation*. The civil service and industrial corporations are examples of complex, modern institutions. They developed, respectively, from the King's adviser and small-scale cottage industries.

Institutions are grouped together into four sub-systems:—
a Economic (factories, offices)
b Political (political parties)
c Kinship (families)
d Cultural and Community Organisations (schools, churches)

2 How does society 'operate' or function?

Functionalists consider that society 'operates' in a way comparable to the functioning of a biological organism. This comparison is referred to as the *organic analogy* (or *organismic analogy*). So social institutions function in combination with one another and for the benefit of society as a whole just as the various parts of the human body function in relation to one another and to the whole body. For example, schools function in relation to work because they prepare people for work. And, like the human body, society is more than the sum of its individual parts.

Although the *structure* and *functioning* of society can be separated for the purpose of theoretical consideration, in reality they are inseparable. Obviously, a society or organisation has to exist (have structure) before it can do anything (function).

3 Why are some groups in society more powerful than others?

The question of power in society has tended to interest Marxists and *social action theorists* more than functionalists. The latter tend to assume that *it is practically necessary that some individuals and groups be more powerful than others, because only a limited number*

9

can take important decisions. Thus, they argue that there must be leaders in organisations and in society, otherwise there would be chaos.

4 What causes social change?

According to functionalists, *social change occurs when it is functionally necessary for it to do so.* For example, in modern societies educational systems tend to expand because such societies require a more literate and numerate population than less advanced societies.

Change may occur through adaptation or integration. Adaptation occurs when an existing institution readjusts to meet new needs – as in the example given in the last paragraph. Integration occurs when a society adopts a new element and makes it part of itself. Thus, a society may successfully integrate (or fail to integrate) a group of immigrants.

Functionalists tend to think of change as *evolutionary,* (gradual) not *revolutionary.*

5 Is society normally in orderly balance or in conflict?

Functionalists consider that order and equilibrium (balance) are normal to society. Disequilibrium (civil war, for example), is an abnormal social state. They compare disequilibrium in society to sickness in a living organism.

The basis of social equilibrium is the existence of *moral consensus.* Moral consensus means that everybody, or nearly everybody in a society shares the same values. Thus, a high level of consumption of goods might be a value in American society, but not in many economically and technologically more 'primitive' societies. As we shall see in a later chapter, functionalists stress the importance of the effective teaching of social values in maintaining order and conformity. The role of parents and teachers in passing on values to the younger generation is stressed.

6 What is the relationship of the individual to society?

Functionalists regard *the individual as formed by society* through the influence of such institutions as the family, school and workplace. They leave little room for the view that the individual can significantly control his own life, let alone change society. Durkheim stated that, for him, the individual is the point of arrival, not of departure. In other words, in his view sociology is not about the individual. As we shall see, not all sociologists agree with this.

7 What is the primary purpose of sociological study?

The primary purpose of sociology is to *analyse and explain the normal (and abnormal) functioning of society*. This involves studying the relationship of the different parts of society to one another, and of the parts to the whole. Thus, the relationship between education and work is studied but so, too, is the (necessary) contribution of both to the functioning of the social system as a whole. Durkheim insisted that sociologists should discover and explain the relationship between *social facts*, just as natural scientists do with physical facts.

Marxism (Conflict Structuralism I)

1 How is society constructed?

According to Marx, *society is constructed from classes. In all societies except the most simple, there are two major social classes. It is people's relationship to the means of production that determines which class they are in.* The most powerful class is that which owns the means of production (land, factories) and the least powerful is that which has to sell its labour in order to make a living. In capitalist society (a society based on a private enterprise economy), the *capitalist class* or *bourgeoisie,* as Marx called it, is the ruling class and the *working class* or *proletariat,* the subordinate class. In other words, in his view, business controls labour.

2 How does society 'operate' or function?

In Marx's view *society operates mainly through class conflict. Each class normally pursues its own interest, and this brings it into conflict with other classes.* In particular, he argued that in capitalist society the bourgeoisie and proletariat are fundamentally opposed. This point is developed and explained later.

3 Why are some groups in society more powerful than others?

For Marx, class is the basis of power. *Some classes are more powerful than others because they own more property and wealth, and this*

11

gives them the means to defend and keep what they hold. Unlike functionalists, Marx did not consider that this state of affairs is inevitable and necessary. He believed that socialism could achieve a more equal sharing of power, property and wealth.

4 What causes social change?

Social change occurs as a result of class conflict. Class conflict is the dynamo of history. In the later middle ages, there was conflict between the landed aristocracy and the rising bourgeoisie, and in capitalist society the major conflict is between the bourgeoisie and the proletariat. The victory of a new class introduces a new historical period. Thus the rise of the bourgeoisie introduced the *capitalist epoch.*

5 Is society normally in orderly balance or in conflict?

Society is in a state of fundamental conflict between the classes. Marx recognised, however, that periods of social order and equilibrium can occur, in which class conflict is temporarily submerged. He argued that such periods benefit the rich and powerful more than others.

6 What is the relationship of the individual to society?

There are two major schools of thought amongst Marxists about the relationship of the individual to society, and these reflect an ambiguity in Marx's work itself. One tradition of Marxist thought tends to see *the individual as powerless to affect either his own life or that of others.* Those who hold this view regard class conflict and socialist revolution as inevitable regardless of what any single individual may do. Some Marxists, however, see a much greater role for the individual in society even though they still see the prime source of individual identity as coming from class membership (Chapter 21, pp. 607–8).

7 What is the primary purpose of sociological study?

The purpose of sociology is *to describe, analyse and explain class conflict.* Nearly all Marxists also want to change the world in a Marxist direction.

Social Action Theory (Conflict Structuralism 2): Weber

1 How is society constructed?

Society is created through social interaction. Social interaction is the behaviour of people consciously relating to one another. In the process of interaction, people form institutions. Although people create institutions such as schools, factories and churches, these institutions in turn influence people. This is partly because pressure exists to observe the rules and procedures of institutions.

Weber felt that Marx overemphasised the importance of class groupings. He recognised that classes are important but considered *political parties* and *status groups* (social and friendship groups) to be further powerful and important forces in society, not necessarily dependent on class (as Marx contended they essentially were). This major point of difference between Marx and Weber is explained fully in Chapter 9. Weber also stressed the power of large organisations or *bureaucracies* over the life of the individual.

2 How does society 'operate' or function?

Again. Weber's answer to this question shows his keen awareness of both the individual's influence on society and of society's influence on the individual. On the one hand, he stresses that *the ideas and feelings people have do sometimes inspire action and affect history.* For example, he argued that certain powerful and dynamic figures. or *charismatic* leaders as he called them, such as Christ and Napoleon, really can change the course of events. On the other hand, he realised that *most people's lives are formed and limited by the society they live in, and particularly by the immediate institutions they come in contact with, such as schools and places of work.* He was personally concerned that large-scale institutions of modern societies (factories. government bureaucracies for example) would limit the scope of individual freedom and creativity. It seems to worry Weber more than the strict functionalists that many people are no more than 'small cogs in large machines' as far as their work is concerned.

13

3 Why are some groups in society more powerful than others?

Power is one of Weber's central concepts. He combines elements of consensus and conflict sociology in his treatment of this matter. He agreed with the functionalists that for society to function efficiently some people have to have more power than others. He pointed out that *in modern bureaucratic organisations (the civil service, for example) there are always more powerful people at the top, and less powerful people at the bottom; that is, bureaucracies are organised hierarchically.* But Weber also accepted with Marx that those groups that do gain a powerful position in society tend to use it primarily in their own interest. Thus, in medieval society the king and nobility used power for their own ends, even though they may also have sometimes used it for the general good as well.

4 What causes social change?

Weber considered that social change can occur for many reasons, or, more technically, his analysis of social change was *multifactoral. Ideas, new inventions, war, the rise and fall of power groups, influential individuals and other factors all contribute to, and are part of, historical change.* In insisting on the possible variety of causes of change, Weber wished to distinguish his position from that of Marx, whom he thought overemphasised class conflict as an explanation for change.

5 Is society normally in orderly balance or in conflict?

The issue of equilibrium and conflict in society is posed to contrast functionalism and Marxism and is of less central concern to social action theorists. Weber considered that society is not normally either in balance or in conflict – the state of society varies from case to case. *A society may be untroubled for centuries and then be plunged into decades of turmoil. Weber preferred to study specific cases rather than make sweeping generalisations about what is 'normal'.*

6 What is the relationship of the individual to society?

The relationship of the individual to society is of central importance in social action theory. Although Weber fully realised that individuals are affected by social institutions such as the family, school, the workplace and the mass media, he did not consider analysis of the operation and effect of these influences to be the only or primary purpose of sociology. It is more important, in his view, *to understand the meanings that individuals experience in their own social lives than simply to analyse what 'causes' or 'influences' them to act as they do.* Although Weber appreciated that individual social action is uniquely experienced by the social actor he still felt able to *generalise* about *social action,* because in practice there are widely-shared patterns of social behaviour. For instance, people may act *rationally, emotionally* or *idealistically,* and it is possible to categorise and generalise their actions accordingly. Despite Weber's emphasis on *interpreting* the quality and potential variety of individual experience and meaning, he was, therefore, committed to scientific sociology. Nevertheless, although we have termed him a *conflict structuralist* in this section, he was also a founding father of interpretive sociology. The interpretive approach has become popular, and has developed in a number of forms in the twentieth century.

7 What is the primary purpose of sociological study?

The purpose of sociology is *to understand and explain the meaning of social action and interaction.*

Interpretive Perspectives: Phenomenological Approaches: Symbolic Interactionism and Ethnomethodology

The meaning of the above terms is much simpler than their length and clumsiness might suggest. The sociological approaches they describe are all primarily concerned with *the interpretations and meanings that actors in social situations give to events* rather than imposing interpretation and meaning on them by use of scientific or mathematical techniques such as statistical analysis. Thus, it is how *you*, the student, are experiencing school (bored? interested?) rather than merely *what is supposed to be happening to you* (being taught Maths or Geography) that the phenomenologist tries to discover. (As we shall see, this approach requires different research methods from traditional, scientifically-oriented sociology). We will use the terms *phenomenology* and *interpretive sociology*, more or less interchangeably, to cover sociological perspectives of this kind. Sometimes, too, we will employ the term *interactionism* to refer to the same approach. These terms do have specific roots, but within general sociology they are virtually synonymous. Phenomenology has its origin in the philosophical approach of Edmund Husserl (1859–1938). Alfred Schütz (1899–1959) took Husserl's central point that interpretation must be based on the meanings of actors, and applied it to sociology. *Symbolic interactionism* and *ethnomethodology* are the major examples of perspectives that can be grouped under the broad heading of phenomenology (or interpretive sociology).

We will defer more detailed consideration of symbolic interactionism until Chapter 3. This is because the symbolic interactionist perspective is best introduced within the specific context of socialisation. Indeed, the founding father of symbolic interactionism, the American, George Mead (1863–1931), was as much a psychologist and philosopher as a sociologist. He was very interested in the processes by which children are integrated into, and learn to participate in, society.

Although Mead's approach was quite different from Weber's he shared certain underlying concerns. Firstly, both believed that society is the product of social interaction and that social action has meaning in so far as human beings intend it to have. Thus, Mead cited *language* as the prime example of meaningful communication, but he believed that most aspects of human social behaviour bear the stamp of *conscious purpose*. This is true of comparatively unimportant actions such as deciding not to go to school or work on a particular day, and of important ones such as assassinating a Prime Minister. Secondly, both Weber and Mead considered that it was a major part of the social scientist's task to understand the purpose and meanings of social action.

Despite his widespread influence, Mead himself wrote comparatively little. Since the Second World War, symbolic interactionism has been developed by a number of sociologists, mainly American. It is largely through its application to crime and deviancy theory that symbolic interactionism has recently progressed (for details, see Chapters 17 and 18). Interactionists argue that *it is part of the sociologist's task to understand the point of view and experience of, say, the criminal, the juvenile 'delinquent' or the football 'hooligan', as well as of the authorities that label these people deviant.* They insist that it is not the sociologist's role to decide what is right or wrong in society, but rather to understand how the power to decide operates and how decisions about what is, and is not, deviant affect people.

Ethnomethodology is an attempt to describe *how individuals make sense of their social experience.* This is a rather different emphasis from the concern of symbolic interactionists with *shared meaning.* Indeed, ethnomethodologists point out that different individuals can experience the same situation and yet give a quite different *account* of it. We can illustrate this with the example of witnesses at a car crash. All have their 'story' to tell and all may very well be telling the 'truth' – but it is the truth as they see it. One witness may blame the driver of the blue saloon, another the driver in the red sports car, yet another may find fault with a pedestrian and so on. Now, undoubtedly this tendency to relate and interpret the same situation differently does widely exist. To take another example, you might very well find that the account that two students give of the same class or lecture is quite different not only in the way they evaluate it, but also in terms of the sort of occasion it was, and the nature of the events that took place. What ethnomethodologists seek to do is to explain how individuals arrive at their accounts of events. Further, they argue that sociological accounts of events are essentially no different from the commonsense accounts that everybody makes of them. In that sense, everybody is his or her own sociologist. Ethnomethodologists try hard to 'see beneath the surface' of their own societies – they believe that only by taking *nothing* for granted will they see more clearly how people act. (Chapter 21, pp. 511–14).

The variety of social life means that generalisations are dangerous and ethnomethodologists, in contrast to structuralists, tend to prefer small-scale, detailed and specific studies. Thus, they would rather study crime in a single area than, say, national criminal trends. Later, we examine just such a study by the American criminologist Aaron Cicourel (Chapter 18, pp. 511–12). Finally, ethnomethodologists issue a warning to sociologists themselves. Given that sociologists, too, have their own 'commonsense' values and beliefs, it is important that they be critically aware of this when doing their work. If not, confusion can result – as Cicourel and Douglas show in Chapter 18.

Sociological Perspectives and Values, Personal and Political

So far, we have described the sociological perspectives as though they are nothing less than attempts to describe the social world exactly as it is. To varying degrees this is the intention of some sociologists. The substantial differences between the perspectives, however, indicate that they are *a combination of the way given sociologists perceive the social world and its actual 'reality'*. The perspectives differ because sociologists perceive society differently. To some extent this is inevitable although sound sociological research can establish some theories to be, to various degrees, correct, and others not. Here we will avoid the question of *why* sociologists perceive the social world differently and instead concentrate on the practical question of *what kind of values (or, bias) tend to influence them to perceive the world in given ways*. The student needs to know this. In reading a person's work, it often helps to be aware of what his values and beliefs are. Fortunately, it is easy to show, in a broad way, what values tend to underly the major sociological perspectives.

Values and the Sociological Perspectives

	Functionalism	Marxism	Social Actionism	Interpretive Theories
Essence of Perspective	Consensus	Conflict	Conflict	Individual Interaction
Underlying Value	conservative	Marxist (socialist/ communist)	socialist/liberal	

The above diagram contains great oversimplifications, but if it enables you to get an early 'feel' for the perspectives, and to appreciate that they represent different viewpoints, not just 'collections of facts', it will have done its job. Functionalists are often conservative although most live in countries (notably the United States and France) in which no party called Conservative exists. It is therefore easier to think of their conservativism as personal, rather than specifically political: crudely, they are 'conservative types'. The link between Marxist sociology and Marxist politics is much more direct. Jibing at arm-chair theorists, Marx said 'philosophers have tried to understand the world, the point is to change it'. Probably all Marxist sociologists want a more communist and socialist world, though they may disagree about precisely what such a world would be like.

The link between the remaining perspectives and values, political or personal, is extremely loose indeed. Nevertheless, a number of sociologists, whose work we shall, in due course, discuss, seem to have turned to Weber's social action theory in order to find a conflict perspective other than Marxism. A.H. Halsey and David Lockwood are among them. Politically, such writers often tend towards socialism, but would not want to call themselves Marxists. Interpretive sociology often reflects a highly individualistic and liberal view of social life. The term 'liberal' here means a stress on personal freedom and creativity. Such an outlook does not easily translate into political terms, but often interpretive sociologists are libertarian – that is, they identify with civil and political rights and the right to be personally 'different'. In Britain, work reflecting a fusion of Marxist and interpretive perspectives has recently appeared.

Sociological perspectives are not merely collections of opinions that 'float in the air', relatively untouched by what actually happens in society. *Perspectives are bodies of theories and concepts which must, as far as possible, be tested against the findings of research.* Sociology is extremely rich in its research methodologies – as, indeed, it needs to be – given the complex nature of its subject matter, human beings.

2 The Making of Sociology: Sociological Theory and Method Part 2

Theory, Method and the Perspectives

Whereas the last chapter was concerned to present the major sociological perspectives, this one is mainly devoted to describing the concepts and methods of sociological research. Now that you have a general blueprint (or blueprints) of the subject, we concentrate on how it is done at the practical research level. Basic sociological research methods are not difficult to understand, and you may well want to do some research yourself.

However, it is important to start this chapter with an awareness of the links between perspectives, theories and methods. We consider sociological theory and method under two headings: the *scientific* or *positivist*, and the *interpretive*. These divisions flow directly from those adopted in the previous chapter to describe the perspectives: functionalist, Marxist and social action perspectives tend to adopt a more scientific approach and symbolic interactionist and ethnomethodological perspectives an interpretist one.

Before separately analysing scientific and interpretive theory and methods, we must present some terms that occur throughout sociological practice.

Theories and Concepts

Concepts are general ideas or generalisations. They are necessary to describe types of phenomena (objects, physical or mental). 'Car' and 'House' are concepts, because they describe a type or category of object and have an abstract or 'ideal' existence in our minds and in verbal communication. Two sociological concepts are 'class' and 'role'. It can be seen from these examples that concepts are infinitely variable in the scope of what they represent. Without concepts specific to the discipline, it would be impossible to practise sociology or for sociologists to communicate effectively about their discipline. Along with research

21

methods, concepts are the basic tools of the trade. Nevertheless, sociologists sometimes disagree about the precise meaning of a given concept. Fortunately, however, their disagreements about concepts are probably less than those about general perspectives. An example of a difference in conceptual usage is the term 'role'. Functionalists tend to describe roles as socially given 'things', behavioural patterns that *have* to be performed, whereas interpretive sociologists stress that roles can be 'played' (or interpreted) differently by different people. Thus, functionalists tend to see the role of worker as one in which a job is done, whereas interpretive sociologists try to understand the worker's individual responses to, and feelings about, the job. The notion of a role as a 'thing', on the one hand, and as a part to 'play', on the other, encapsulates the difference between scientific and interpretive perspectives.

The key concepts used in this book include social structure (social division as well as integration); interaction; power and authority; culture and ideology; community and alienation. You probably already have some idea of what these concepts mean and we will define them in more precise sociological terms in relevant contexts later. The point to grasp here is that these concepts are part of the essential substructure of sociology. For example, 'what is the *structure* of society?' is the first sociological question we asked in the last chapter. The concept of structural stratification or division provides the conceptual framework for Chapters 9 to 14 and the concepts of interaction and culture recur throughout this book (in addition Chapter 20 is devoted to cultural issues).

The above concepts are commonly used as analytical tools by all sociologists. For example, Robert Nisbet uses three of them – community, alienation and power (or, more precisely in his terms, authority) – as what he calls 'unit ideas' in sociology. In this author's view, Nisbet's illuminating work, *The Sociological Tradition*, is flawed by its failure to include structure, particularly structural conflict, as a unit idea or fundamental concept of sociology. So sociologists can disagree about the relative importance of the various concepts. Other important concepts, many related to the above, are introduced throughout this book.

Theories are propositions about the relationship between specified phenomena. They may be *unproven* or, on the basis of research or testing, *proven*. An example of a theory is that educational attainment correlates with (is closely linked to) social class origins. By now, research has virtually proved this theory. We will discuss how theories are 'researched' and tested shortly. Concepts play a part in the construction of all theories. Take, for instance, Marx's theory of class conflict, which combines the concepts of class and conflict. In isolation, concepts explain nothing; it is only in their concrete application to the analysis of problems that they become useful.

We will now examine the relationship between theories, concepts and perspectives. It helps to think of *the perspectives as made up of bodies of related theories and concepts*. Thus, Marxism contains concepts and theories such as class, class conflict and many others which, together, help to make up the perspective. Concepts of consensus, integration, adaptation and others characterise functionalism. Those of meaning and interaction are commonly found in phenomenology. It is perhaps too sweeping to think of disposing of a whole perspective by 'proving it wrong', but theories and concepts associated with given perspectives must be open to testing. Thus, despite the tendency of given perspectives to use some concepts more than others, the major sociological concepts are the 'common currency' of the discipline.

Although interpretive sociologists do produce theories, they tend to be rather less concerned with testing them than structural sociologists. Often description and understanding are the limited but not easily achieved goals of interpretive sociologists.

Explanatory and Descriptive Research: A Precise Distinction?

Explanatory research seeks to explain why something happens. An example would be an attempt to find the causes of levels of educational attainment. *Descriptive research is aimed at finding and presenting facts (for example, about poverty) or at describing social processes (for example, how a gang operates).* We need to be wary, however, of the distinction between explanatory and descriptive work both in principle and in practice. To describe 'the facts' involves selecting what is and what is not important. Facts do not choose themselves. By implication, therefore, some interpre-

23

tation is implied in selection. In practice, most researchers prefer to take the responsibility of interpreting their own findings. Peter Townsend, for instance, in his book on poverty in Britain presented massive factual findings on the subject, but he also included explanations of why it occurs. Researchers are usually in the best position to explain their own findings – if left without guidance, others may misunderstand or misuse them. We now turn to the problem of sociological method.

Scientific Sociology

Science

This section offers a simple introduction to the nature of science. More problematic issues are considered in the final chapter of this book. *Science is concerned with the accumulation of verifiable (capable of being proved true) knowledge.* It has traditionally used two methods: *observation* and *experimentation.* For reasons outlined below, laboratory experimentation is often considered the most accurate and, therefore, ideal method of testing a theory. In practice, all the sciences also use observation. Biologists observe, record and attempt to explain aspects of organic life. The same applies to astronomers in respect of their field of enquiry. It is important that observations are precisely and accurately made. To establish the truth of an observation, it helps to repeat it. Sociologists make full use of observation but very little of the laboratory experiment. Instead, they have developed a battery of methods of their own. How these compare to the laboratory method we consider below.

Scientific research of an explanatory kind often involves *establishing whether the scientist's initial idea or hypothesis is true or false. The research is the means by which the hypothesis becomes a proven theory.* Thus, we can very simply present the process of explanatory scientific enquiry in three stages:

1 *The generation and formulation of a hypothesis (unproven theory)*
2 *Testing the hypothesis by research (method)*
3 *Analysing the data and researching a conclusion (proven theory)*

The most common method used by natural scientists such as chemists or physicists to test a hypothesis is the laboratory-controlled experiment. We discuss this method now because the precise findings it gives and the relative lack of its use in sociology are often cited to undermine its scientific claims.

The Laboratory Experiment

Natural scientists, like social scientists, often want to measure the effect of one 'thing' on another. A biologist might want to measure the effect that being deprived of light has on the growth of a plant; a sociologist might want to measure the effect of class background on educational attainment. Let us see how a biologist might set up his experiment. He may hypothesise that light deprivation will slow growth, but is not sure by how much. He is likely to use two plants that for reasons of precise comparability are as similar as possible. One will be deprived of light and the other (the control) will not. Here we must introduce the concept of a *variable,* something that varies. Relevant variables that can affect plant growth are moisture, heat, soil quality and, of course, light. All other variables apart from light must be *held constant* between the two plants. This means that both plants must receive the same amount of moisture, heat and so on, but not, of course, light. If this were not so, it would be impossible to tell whether light variation or some other variable accounted for the difference in growth. Another way of putting this point is that the conditions in which the experiment takes place must be *controlled.* In this experiment, light is referred to as the *independent variable* (because it is assumed to be the causal factor, not the affected factor, in the experiment) and growth is the *dependent* variable (because it is affected by the independent variable). The biologist can calculate the result of the experiment by measuring the difference between the plants. He will then be able to confirm, discard or rephrase his original hypothesis in more precise theoretical terms. A reliable and valid experiment is *repeatable* and so its findings are open to further *verification* (proof). A repeatedly verified experiment adds to the growing body of scientific knowledge.

Bearing the above in mind, we now turn specifically to the problem of how sociologists pursue their own discipline. We divide this into two sections. The section on scientific sociology is itself divided into the production of original or primary data and the use of existing or secondary data.

Scientific Sociological Methods 1

The Systematic Production of Original Data (Primary Research)

a THE EXPERIMENT Despite the popularity and undoubted usefulness of the laboratory method in the natural sciences, it is almost never used in sociology. The reasons are both practical and moral. Two major practical problems may be noted. Firstly, the kind of processes sociologists study, such as the effect of family background on educational attainment, often occur over too long a time-span to be artificially 'set up' and observed in a laboratory. Secondly, people would not behave as they normally do in such an artificial environment. Psychologists are often better served by the laboratory method because they tend to study very specific and limited aspects of *individual* behaviour. Any moral objection to experimentation involving humans must depend on the nature of the particular experiment. For instance, most social scientists would find it morally abhorrent to test by laboratory experiment the effects of, say, extreme and prolonged overcrowding on human social behaviour. Such experiments were conducted by the Nazis during the Second World War and were widely condemned as being against natural law. Biologists and psychologists, however, are able to experiment with animals in this way without, apparently, greatly offending public opinion. Scientists experimenting with plants and inanimate matter do not, of course, face the same moral issue.

Sociologists have, however, used experimental techniques in broader, if less controlled contexts than the laboratory. Many of these, such as testing the effects of media violence or sex on attitudes and behaviour have tended to be psychological rather than sociological in nature (see Chapter 20). When testing the effects of such material it is helpful to set up a *control group* (a group not to be exposed to the material) as well as an *experimental group*. The control group should be as similar as possible to the experimental group, so that any differences in attitude or behaviour that develop after the experimental group has, for example, seen the films the effect of which the researcher wishes to test, can be reliably attributed to that fact.

The sociologist's 'laboratory' could be said to be society itself. S/he wants to study how people actually behave, not how they might behave in a laboratory. But scientific concepts such as the concept of the variable have been of immense use in educational and other social research. Further, in examining the relationship between variables (say, a social class variable such as parental income and educational attainment), sociologists, often use mathematical and statistical techniques. This, however, applies to the *processing* rather than the *production* of data. To produce data, scientifically-inclined sociologists typically use social survey rather than experimental methods. We now discuss this method of data production.

b THE SYSTEMATIC PRODUCTION OF ORIGINAL DATA BY USE OF QUANTITATIVE METHODS Quantitative methods are virtually synonymous with *the social survey*. When a sociologist wants to produce his own statistical data, he invariably conducts a social survey. Social surveys are not used only for academic social research, however. They are used by the government (for example, the Census), in market research (for example, to test public response to a new product), and in public opinion research (for example, election polls). Used properly, the social survey is one of the most useful tools produced by social science.

It is helpful to think of a social survey as being undertaken in three stages:
1 *The Selection of a Sample*
2 *The Collection of Information from the Sample*
3 *The Processing of the Information*
A census is a survey of the whole of the group or *population*, as it is technically termed, that the sociologist is interested in. He usually has neither the time nor the money to conduct a census. He must therefore, obtain a *representative* sample. As M. D. Shipman ironically remarks, monkeys caged in a zoo are unlikely to provide data representative of the behaviour of humans. There are two basic types of samples: the *purposive* (or judgemental) sample and the *random* (or probability) sample. A *purposive sample* is one selected for its appropriateness by the researcher himself. Thus, when John Goldthorpe, David Lockwood and their colleagues wanted to study the affluent (well paid) manual worker, they selected a group of workers in Luton, because it is a prosperous town likely to contain the kind of workers they were looking for. This was a good choice because it ensured that the sample chosen was

representative of the group Goldthorpe *et al.,* were interested in (for a fuller account of their research see Chapter 10, pp. 267–71). Within the purposive sample, quota sampling may occur. The characteristics of the target group are specified and a quota selected by the data-collector.

A *random sample* allows each member of the group being sampled an equal chance of being selected. Thus, a sample of fifty students from a total of five hundred could be randomly selected by putting the names of the whole group into a hat and drawing out fifty. It is more usual, however, to take a *systematic sample.* This involves selecting names at regular intervals, depending on how big the sample is to be. In the case of our 500 students a school or college list could be used from which every tenth name would be selected up to the five hundredth to get a sample of fifty. The same technique could be used in the case of electoral registers or other lists appropriate to particular areas of research.

Sometimes the population or target group chosen for survey is *stratified,* or divided, into separate groups to facilitate specialised study. Thus, if 75% of a population is immigrant and 25% non-immigrant, it can be divided into two strata of the same percentage proportion. It is then possible to survey the strata either randomly or by the quota method (in which the choice of respondents lies with the researcher or interviewer).

Once the sample has been selected, and if the sociologist has decided what questions he wishes to ask, the survey can be implemented in a variety of ways. Which way is chosen to implement the survey will have an effect on the extent and the quality of the sample *response.* However, the researcher would be foolish to rush into the full-scale survey at this stage. Instead, it is desirable to test systematically the various features of the survey design by means of a *pilot study.* This is not a haphazard process. C. A. Moser and G. Kalton compare it to the final dress rehearsal of a play – a lot of work has preceded it. The analogy breaks down only in that a pilot-study is on a smaller scale than the main survey, but contains all its essential features. Thus in a questionnaire survey, a pilot study should establish which questions elicit imprecise (or angry) answers.

We can now consider problems relating to the main survey. Generally, the least satisfactory way to administer a questionnaire (list of questions) is through the post. The possibility of large numbers being lost or ignored is considerable. Response rate can be improved if either the researcher or an assistant visits the places to which the questionnaires have been sent. This also enables difficult or misleading questions to be explained (though in a well-designed questionnaire, there will not be any). Alternatively, the questionnaires may be personally presented either at the respondents' front doors, or even in the street. In such circumstances, however, answers may not always be well thought out. Sometimes the best alternative is to deliver a questionnaire personally, explain its contents, and arrange to pick it up at a later date.

The completely formal interview technique with standardised questions and restricted answer-options in which the interviewer merely records the answers, is sometimes adopted for ease of quantification. The more standardised the answers (a choice of 'yes' or 'no' would be the most standardised), the simpler it is to quantify them for analysis – possibly with the help of a computer. Sociological data that are to be processed by a computer must be able to be given a numerical value. This means it must be possible either to quantify it (for example, 20 'yes's', 80 'no's') or to *codify* it. To codify means to put something into numerical form for the purpose of statistical analysis.

A problem with formal interviews and, indeed, with questionnaires is that respondents often feel frustrated that they cannot elaborate on or qualify their answers. At worst, they may consider that their real 'feelings' have not been expressed at all. In such cases, a respondent may give angry, silly or humorous answers, and so invalidate (as far as the researcher is concerned) the findings. Many researchers accept that feelings and subtle shades of opinion cannot adequately be expressed in statistical form and for that reason informal and unstructured interviews are sometimes preferred (see below).

The problems faced by social survey researchers in achieving scientific precision are considerable. Things can go wrong at the sampling stage if the sample selected is too small or unrepresentative, at the stage when information is collected, or, finally, at the various stages of processing, analysing and interpreting information. The random sample is always subject to the laws of chance: a small unstratified survey of a black ghetto could always 'catch' the few whites living there and only a disproportionately small number of blacks.

Even so, social survey methods of investigation have become steadily more sophisticated and a well designed survey can expect to overcome all these problems. But even a successful survey can only achieve a limited amount compared to a scientific experiment. The difference in the kind of results achieved by the experimental and social survey methods is as much a function of the difference in the subject matter (non-human/ human) of science and social science as in the methods themselves. A successful social survey will give an accurate measurement of attitude and opinion *at the time the survey is conducted*. A fact of life that sociologists have to live with is that once surveyed, human beings change their minds and chemicals do not. It would, however, be misleading to give the impression that social surveys never discover repeated patterns of human behaviour. They do. For instance, every large-scale survey on voting behaviour has shown that the working class in Britain *tends* to vote Labour and the middle class *tends* to vote Conservative. In particular, social surveys have been able to show how given variables *tend to influence* human behaviour. Thus, a number of independent surveys have shown that the variables of maternal interest in a child's education and the material quality of the home *tend* greatly to affect a child's educational performance. *Longitudinal* surveys (studies over a period of time) can be used to monitor the effect of a given variable or group of variables over a period of time. The famous television survey *7 Up* is an example in point. A group of children from different social backgrounds have been interviewed at regular intervals of seven years (so far, the group has been interviewed at seven, fourteen and twenty-one). It is quite clear that *social class* has had a great effect on the life of these children and particularly on their educational career and cultural opportunities. Social surveys, can, then, help to establish regularities or *tendencies* in human behaviour, but not social scientific laws. Taken together, established tendencies provide a basis for the cumulative (gradually increasing) development of social scientific theory and knowledge, just as scientific experiment and law provides a similar basis for science.

We need, finally, to establish a connection between the large or *macro* level theorising and research of the structuralists, and the more limited or *micro* research of social surveys. Social survey methods can provide means to test aspects of general structural theory. Thus, the hypothesis, at one time unconfirmed, of many sociologists that a disadvantaged social class background is likely to affect adversely the life opportunities of even an intelligent child has now been confirmed by many social surveys. Whilst it is true that the confirmation of this hypothesis could have been predicted by commonsense, this does not apply to many of the *detailed* findings of these surveys.

It can be said that social science research as a whole is faced with two categories of problems. Firstly, there are a variety of difficulties associated with the design and implementation of research and the analysis of findings. Secondly, there are problems that arise from the unpredictable nature of the subject matter itself – human beings. Underlying both these difficulties is a third: the fact that the social scientist is himself an example of the species he is researching into. We discuss in a later chapter the problems of bias and lack of perspective that this can produce. Despite these problems, however, logical and rational methods of procedure are available to 'scientifically-minded' social scientists. If these fall short of producing results comparable to those obtainable in a laboratory, they are still far better than mere guesswork.

Scientific Sociological Methods 2

The Systematic Use of Secondary (Existing) Material

There is, of course, a vast fund of existing information about human society available to the sociologist. This includes historical documents, contemporary records and statistical sources. Weber and, particularly, Durkheim, offered detailed guidance about how secondary material can be properly used by sociologists. As the material already exists, neither quantitative nor qualitative methods are needed to produce it. If anything, this means that it must be used even more critically and carefully than freshly produced data.

Both Durkheim and Weber advocated the use of the *comparative method as an alternative to the experimental method.* Thus, in trying to explain the rise of capitalism (the private enterprise economic system) in certain European countries, Weber found it useful to compare conditions in these countries with China. As both the Chinese and the Europeans were relatively advanced technologically Weber was able to deduce that some factor other than technology was likely to have triggered capitalist development in Europe. After extensive comparative research he concluded that those countries or areas in which the Calvinist religion was strongly established were predisposed to develop capitalist economies. (Chapter 20, pp. 566–8).

The *historical method* is often closely linked with the comparative. Indeed, Weber's previously mentioned study of the rise of capitalism was historical as well as cross-cultural (comparing more than one culture or society). Sociologists, like historians, are interested in explaining social change and development. Durkheim actually went as far as trying to classify societies according to their 'stage of development'. Although his scheme is not widely used now, it is good practice, when comparing societies, to be aware that they may be at a different developmental or evolutionary stage. In Chapter 9, for instance, stratification (the division of society into different social layers) is described in traditional (pre-industrial) and modern (industrially developed) societies. Even a general framework such as this imposes some order and coherence which otherwise would not exist on sociological material.

Durkheim, Marx and Weber all hoped that by systematic study of an historical and/or comparative kind they would be able to demonstrate *regularities* in the operation of society. *A regularity meant that a recurrently causal relationship between two factors was established.* For example, Durkheim believed that his research on suicide established a causal connection between high suicide rates and low levels of community support and identity (or low levels of community *integration* as he referred to it). Again, given that the laboratory is closed to the sociologist, disciplined, comparative social research provides an alternative way of establishing regular patterns of social behaviour. Both Durkheim and Marx were extremely optimistic that they would be able to establish a high level of causal explanation of social events. Let us follow Durkheim further in his attempt to do this in respect of his explanation of suicide.

Durkheim wanted to find out what causes suicide. Or as he put it, he wanted to discover what *social facts* cause suicide. For reasons already given, the laboratory method was not open to him. He could hardly experiment with people using in turn a number of variables (isolation, loss of income and so on) to see which made them commit suicide! Indeed, he could not control in any way the social conditions in societies whose suicide rate he wished to compare. All he could do was compare the official suicide rate in various societies and observe what *seemed* to be the most frequent factor which correlated with a high rate of suicide. This is exactly what he did. We examine his methods and findings and various criticisms (mainly from an interpretive standpoint) in Chapter 18, pp. 501–4. The general point to note here is that Durkheim sought to establish the causal relationship between social facts such as community integration and suicide. Although social scientific research methods have greatly improved in the half-century since Durkheim's death, they still do not produce results that are as precise, repeatable and which provide so sound a basis for prediction as those of the natural sciences.

Max Weber also offered an original contribution to sociological method with his concept of the *ideal type* which he also used widely in comparative research. An ideal type has nothing to do with ideals or perfection in, for instance, the religious sense. *An ideal type is merely a theoretical model which is made up of the typical characteristics of the species or general category that it represents.* Thus, Weber gave an ideal type definition of *bureaucracy* (large-scale, modern organisation) which contained such characteristics as hierarchy (top to bottom structure of authority); appointment on the basis of experience and qualifications; promotion through merit and vertical (top to bottom) lines of communication. What is the use of such an ideal type model? The answer is that ideal types, like other concepts, help to guide and structure research, particularly comparative research. By knowing *precisely* what he was looking for, Weber was able to describe, analyse and compare the similarities and differences in the growth of government bureaucracy in a number of different countries. Like any sociological model and concept, ideal types must be tested against social reality – they are of little use if they are imprecise. Once tested, they help the sociologist to arrange his findings in an orderly and meaningful way, as did Weber's ideal type model of bureaucracy.

One of Weber's better known applications of the ideal type is to the concept of social action (see Chapter 1, p. 15). Among his major types of social action were the rational, the emotional and the idealistic. His typology of action was useful in the systematic or, broadly, the scientific study of human behaviour.

Obviously, the rational action of a bureaucrat will be different from the idealistic action of a freedom fighter and to be able to categorise them helps analysis. Weber did not consider that his interest in the meaning of action prevented the scientific study of it and its consequences. Indeed, this was his prime concern.

Marx also attempted to study society as scientifically as possible. However, his concern was not to establish factual correlations, as was Durkheim's, but to develop what he thought of as a scientific theory of society. Among his major theoretical concepts were class and class conflict, and we shall see that he used these in combination with other concepts to build-up a theory of how capitalist society (society with an economy based on private business) operated and changed. There is widespread disagreement about how scientific Marx's sociological approach is. A particular problem is that Marx himself was openly critical of capitalist society and wanted to change it. His motives were as much political as analytical and this has brought the charge of bias against him. A fuller perspective on these matters will be presented in the course of the book (see especially Chapter 21, pp. 606–9).

At this point we must add another name to the trinity we have just been considering. It is that of Auguste Comte (1798–1857), who is often considered to be the first genuine sociologist. He believed that man's behaviour can be explained by the laws of 'cause and effect' in the same way as the behaviour of matter. This approach is known as positivism. Comte argued that positivistic sociology would eventually provide a complete explanation of human social life. Today, positivism is widely regarded as a narrow approach to science. To a greater or lesser extent, however, the founding fathers were all positivists. Comte had a major influence on his fellow countryman, Durkheim, who was thoroughly committed to the positivist approach. Indeed, Durkheim dedicated himself to the study of the relationship between social facts and to their effect on man. Of the founding fathers, Weber was perhaps the most modest in his expectations of the level of scientific precision, explanation and prediction that sociology could achieve. He thought it could establish regular patterns of causal connections but rarely, if ever, social laws. Marx is still thought by some to have discovered the laws of social change but, for all his insight, we can take it that this claim is far too optimistic.

Comte equated the positivist approach with science itself, but a broader definition of science is simply that it is the systematic pursuit of knowledge. This definition includes both the observational and interview methods of sociology discussed below but as these have, in addition, the particular purpose of interpreting meaning rather than merely explaining behaviour, we treat them separately.

Interpretive or 'Qualitative' Sociological Methods

There are three types of interpretive or qualitative methods of sociological research: the *in-depth interview, non-participant observation and participant observation. These methods are employed in order to observe accurately and record faithfully the quality of social experience that the social actors themselves feel.* Their purpose is to provide description and human understanding rather than causal explanations. As we shall see, in some instances, these methods come closer to artistic rather than scientific forms of understanding social behaviour. It hardly needs to be said that qualitative methods and interpretive theory complement each other. Given that precise observation is an acceptable scientific research method, *qualitative research can also be considered scientific.* Certainly, it can add to our stock of knowledge about human social behaviour. Perhaps the point to emphasise, however, is that it is the *quality* of human experience rather than its causes that interpretive sociologists wish to explore – though the two motives are frequently combined.

The In-depth Interview
The in-depth interview is often lengthy, sometimes extending to several hours. Frequently, *several separate interviews with the same person or group will be necessary,* as was the case with Elizabeth Bott's study of twenty families of varied class background. In-depth interviews are usually unstructured, though the interviewer will generally have a clear idea of the ground that needs to be covered and can gently direct the interview accordingly. Often the researcher will have a schedule of questions corresponding with areas to be covered in the interview, as did Hannah Gavron in her interviews with ninety-six housewives, the results of which were published in her study *The Captive Wife.*

35

Nevertheless, as has commonly been recognised by social scientists, the main value of this type of interview is that it provides the respondents with the opportunity to say what *they* want rather than what the interviewer might expect. This intention contrasts strongly with the much more limited aim of the formal interview. The major danger with the unstructured interview is that the interviewer will unduly influence the respondent. This is particularly likely, if the interviewer has strongly preconceived ideas about what his findings might be.

Non-participant Observation

Non-participant observation involves the sociologist in an exclusively observational role in relation to the subject of his research. At least, that is the theory. In fact, however, one of the earliest examples of the use of observational technique showed how difficult it is for the researcher to remain entirely separate from his subject. This was in Elton Mayo's Hawthorne Experiment of 1924. Mayo and his team were asked to examine the effects of various changes in working conditions on the productivity of the work force at the Hawthorne factory. Mayo found that virtually any change in working conditions – even those that made conditions worse than they were originally – seemed to result in an improvement in productivity! At last, he was forced to conclude that what caused the improvement in production was the presence of the research team itself. It must have stimulated the workforce to greater efforts! The Hawthorne experiment provides a strong warning to sociologists to be aware of the effect they themselves can have on their findings. Taking their cue from Mayo's experience, some sociologists have preferred to 'factor out' the effect of their own presence by observing their subject matter secretly. (Chapter 16, pp. 441–2).

Participant Observation

Participant observation involves the sociologist taking part in the social events which he seeks to describe and understand, so that he may do so more effectively. It is a more commonly used method than non-participant observation and has been particularly widely employed since the nineteen sixties by interactionists and ethnomethodologists. The origins of participant observation within social science go back, however, to the earlier part of this century. It was in anthropology that participant observation became popular. It was employed, in particular, by Bronislaw Malinowski and Margaret Mead (see Chapter 14 for further reference to Mead's work). One of the societies that Malinowski examined was the Trobriand Islanders of the Western Pacific. Malinowski used participant observation for the same purposes as more recent sociologists. He wanted to 'grasp the natives' point of view', to 'realise (their) vision of the world' and observe them 'acting naturally'. To do this he had to remain with them for over a year. In order for the participant observer to give people the opportunity to adjust to his presence and to show a typical range of behaviour, he must often be prepared to spend lengthy periods of time with them. It is crucial for the participant observer to win the confidence and acceptance of the people he is studying if they are to behave naturally.

More recent participant observational studies have often been of specific subcultures. In particular, there have been a large number of participant observational studies of gangs and other youth subcultural groups. One of the earliest and most influential of these was William Foote Whyte's *Street Corner Society*. Whyte studied a gang in a poor, largely Italian immigrant part of Chicago. He described himself as 'seeking to build a sociology based on observed interpersonal events'. The following quotation from Whyte states a major justification for the participant observational approach:

> As I sat and listened, I learned the answers to questions that I would not even have had the sense to ask if I had been getting my information solely on an interviewing basis.

In other words, participant observation teaches the social scientist what questions to ask as well as providing some of the answers.

A more recent study of a gang is James Patrick's *A Glasgow Gang Observed*. Keeping his identity as a researcher secret, Patrick joined a Glasgow gang. The result is a fascinating study of gang behaviour and particularly of gang hierarchy and ritual. But was Patrick justified in keeping his identity secret? According to the author's own account, the members of the gang did not think so and would happily exact revenge on him for misleading them. No general moral rule can be laid down on this question of privacy: each sociologist must make his own judgement on the matter.

The very involvement that is the basis of the deepened insight that participant observation can give, may itself become a disadvantage. Again, William Foote Whyte puts the issue well when he states that although he began as a participant observer, he ended up as an 'observing participant'.

If the sociologist comes to identify strongly with the subject of his research, his account may be biased and offer little in the way of a general contribution to the research area. Ronald Frankenburg, himself the author of a celebrated participant observational study of life in a Welsh village, has usefully suggested three stages of research for the participant observer. Each of these stages involves a different degree of involvement with the subject matter. Firstly, the research project must be set up – a relatively objective process. Secondly, the sociologist becomes subjectively (personally) involved with those he wishes to study. Thirdly, he withdraws to consider and assess his experience and findings.

The relatively small amount of space given to explaining interpretive methods of research should not mislead the student into thinking that they are less important than scientific methods. This is a matter for each sociologist to decide for himself or herself. It happens that interpretive methods are best understood in the context of specific pieces of research. In addition to those examples mentioned above, several more are included in later chapters (see especially Chapters 7, 16 and 17).

The Relationship Between Theoretical Perspectives and Method

Having established that a simple and typical connection exists between theoretical perspectives and method, we must now introduce qualifications.

Firstly, the relationship between general theoretical perspectives and applied sociological method is, in practice, much looser than might be expected. This is especially the case in respect of the structural perspectives. A major reason for this is that the various sociological perspectives are so *general* that it is virtually impossible conclusively to prove or disprove them by testing their content in research. Thus, functionalists have been able to maintain their view about the 'normality' of social order and consensus, and Marxists have held their position on social conflict partly because it is not feasible to mount a survey wide enough in scope to prove one or other view correct. Further, propositions of this degree of generality are both likely to have some basis in fact and so it is easy to select evidence to support either of them. Whether we like it or not, therefore, general theory tends to have a life of its own!

This may sound very unsatisfactory. Surely, sociology is concerned with proving things about society and not just disagreeing about them? It is certainly true that if investigation does strongly suggest that a particular proposition of general theory is incorrect, then it should be discarded. It is, however, helpful to look at the sociological perspectives in a different light from this. Here we come to a further explanation for the loose connection between sociological theory and method, and one which perhaps does partly justify what might otherwise seem too flabby a relationship. Instead of regarding theoretical perspectives merely as something to be proved or disproved, it can be more useful to think of them as a *guide* to examining and understanding society. The perspectives can help the sociologist to order his concepts and direct his detailed research. Thus, because of the nature of their respective perspectives, Marxists typically direct their attention to class conflict whereas functionalists are more interested in how harmony and consensus are produced in society. In studying industrial relations a Marxist would regard tension and dissatisfaction at work as normal, whereas a functionalist would consider them to be 'dysfunctional' (the opposite of functional). The perspectives literally do give perspective, context and overall meaning to detailed research. Regarded in this way, the various perspectives provide wide-ranging models or, to use a more technical term, *paradigms* within which sociologists can arrange and make overall sense of their concepts and research. Nevertheless, in those areas in which the perspectives basically contradict each other the effort to reconcile them should continue.

There is a second reason for qualifying the clear connections between theory and method described in the first paragraph of this section. Although, as previously stated, a strong tendency exists for specific perspectives to be associated with complementary methods, this relationship is by no means invariable. In particular, much of the best of what would be broadly categorised as interpretive sociology is, more precisely, something of a theoretical and methodological mix. Stanley Cohen's book, *Folk Devils and Moral Panics,* contains elements of interpretive and structural analysis and employs both quantitative and qualitative research methods as well as a technique termed *content analysis* which has elements of both (for an analysis of this work see Chapter 18, pp. 495–6). *Content analysis involves examining what is contained in, say, various newspapers or media programmes to determine their interest in and treatment of a particular issue.* Thus, to choose an obvious example, the *New of the World* contains a high percentage of material on sex and crime (which it appears to disapprove of). Another work that employs a variety of theoretical perspective and method is Paul Willis's *Learning to Labour: How Working Class Kids Get Working Class Jobs.* Willis employs observation, participant observation and taped interviews and interprets his material from within a Marxist perspective which still manages to do justice to the feelings and opinions of the 'lads' he is writing about (see Chapter 5, pp. 101–2). Students should not, therefore, feel either overwhelmed by the variety of sociological theory and method or that they must work rigidly within the boundaries of perspectives.

'Doing' Sociological Research

It is no doubt the purpose of a textbook to describe and explain rather than to inspire. Nevertheless, perhaps enough interest has been raised to suggest the possibility that the student should attempt to do some of her or his own research. By far the best way to find out the advantages and disadvantages of a particular research method is to try it. Indeed, someone embarking on research for the first time will probably find that he learns more by trying to construct a well designed piece of research than from the results themselves. If original research is attempted, it is only fair that selected 'guinea pigs' should not be unduly inconvenienced. For obvious reasons, more students have been the subject of research than probably any other single group. Yet sociology students should think twice before deluging their particular school or college with questionnaires. When faced with a sudden outbreak of questionnaires, the patience of staff and other students can wear thin. This does not help the rate or quality of response! Most local communities offer opportunities to carry out research which challenges the student to think more widely than school-based research and relieves the school of the burden of too much enthusiastic attention from would-be sociologists. Research into certain areas, such as attitudes to local public amenities, could be positively useful. If well done, such a piece of research might deserve to be published in the school magazine, if not the local press.

Guide to Further Reading and Study

Two useful, contrastingly presented books at our level, are Murray Morison, *Methods in Sociology*, (Longman, 1986) and Patrick McNeill, *Research Methods* (Tavistock, 1985). Chris Brown's *Understanding Society* (John Murray, 1979), is also to be recommended as an introduction to theory.

Rather more advanced coverage than the above – really second year sixth form level – is provided by several articles on *theory and method* in Meighan, Shelton and Marks, *eds, Perspectives on Society* (Nelson, 1979). Other collections of readings on theory are generally more suited to students in higher education. Nevertheless, given the high standard and competitiveness of 'A' level nowadays one of the more comprehensible of these is worth mentioning. Cuff and Payne, *eds, Perspectives in Sociology* (Allen and Unwin, 1984) covers the various perspectives in greater detail than is necessary at 'A' level, but for those students who are prepared to stick with it, it clears up many problems that often remain obscure and confusing at 'A' level.

A very useful, clear and comprehensive book on *method* is M. D. Shipman's *The Limitations of Social Research* (Longman, 1981). Emphatically for the more advanced student only, is Bell and Newby, *eds, Doing Sociological Research* (Allen and Unwin, 1977). This collection of readings tends to the anecdotal (the sociological equivalent of 'travellers' tales'), but for those who have thoroughly grasped the basics, it illustrates well the variety of sociological methods available and the part that personality and human relations can play in research. Otherwise, the student is best referred to the methodological appendices of some of the better known recent works of sociology published in popular paperback editions in Penguin, Pelican, Paladin or other almost equally cheap and accessible labels. The section 'Appendix: How the Research was Done', in Young and Willmott's famous study *Family and Kinship in East London* (Pelican, 1962) is strongly recommended. This study employed a variety of social survey techniques, interviews and participant observation. Although quite different in style and content, Stanley Cohen's *Folk Devils and Moral Panics* (Martin Robertson, 1981) also contains an appendix which succinctly and clearly describes a wide range of sources of data used by the author. The late Hannah Gavron's appendices on method to *The Captive Wife* (Pelican, 1970) is recommended as a guide to the advantages and pitfalls of the interview method. The place to find brief descriptions of sociological method is at the back of books of original sociological research. If the student dislikes what s/he finds, there is no shortage of alternative choice.

Questions

A selection of questions on theory and method from Past 'A' Level Papers will be found at the end of Chapter 20. The following questions are more suitable for students *starting* an 'A' level course, and don't require essay-length answers.

1 What were some of the questions about society that interested Durkheim, Marx and Weber? Are they still of interest to us?

2 Can society be usefully compared to a living organism? Criticise this analogy from other perspectives.

3 Compare and contrast Marxist and social action sociological perspectives.

4 In what sort of research situations might you prefer qualitative to quantitative methods?

5 What are the major links between the theoretical perspectives and research methods?

6 'Comparative study is to sociology what the experiment is to natural science'. Explain and discuss. (London, 1985).

Section B **Self, Socialisation and Society**

How to use this Section

As with Section A, the reader should use this section as is convenient. Some may prefer to move straight into study of the family and education, leaving the more theoretical material on socialisation and culture in Chapter 3 until later. In fact, Chapter 3 and Chapter 20, 'Culture and Ideology: Religion and the Media', are closely linked and could usefully be read together. However, for those who wish to stay with it there is a logical progression in this section.

Broadly, the plan of the section is to *proceed from the micro-level of self and family through an analysis of the educational system, to a consideration of some major macro-issues of social order, conflict and change at the urban/regional, national and international levels.* The initial theme of self and society is continued throughout the section. It is important not to lose sight of the individual as we review the influence on him/her of ever larger institutional systems – family, community, educational system, region, nation and global system. To let this happen would be a form of sociological alienation. Society does not exist apart from people. That is why Durkheim's advice to treat social facts as though they are 'things' (in order to establish relationships between them) must be treated with the utmost caution. People *make* society and if this is the basis of their freedom, it is also their burden of responsibility. If it is possible to forget this when considering only our own relatively stable society, it is less easy to do so when surveying the West's uncertain relationship with the Third World. There is a large and growing number of individuals 'out there' and, increasingly, they are part of us.

An important point must be noted about Chapter 4, 'The

Family and Community'. Developments in feminist analysis of social (particularly family) policy and in the sociology of childhood make it essential to refer to the relevant sections of other chapters where indicated.

University of Chester, Seaborne Library

Title: Understanding modern sociology /
Wes W. Sharrock, John A. Hughes and
Peter J. Martin.
ID: 01117783
Due: 05-12-14

Title: Sociology: a new approach [Book]
ID: 00982315
Due: 05-12-14

Title: A new introduction to sociology / Mike
O'Donnell ; foreword by Tony Marks.
ID: 90012301
Due: 05-12-14

Total items: 3
14/11/2014 11:12

Renew online at:
http://libcat.chester.ac.uk/patroninfo

Thank you for using Self Check

4

3 Self, Socialisation and Culture

Introduction

An overview of the concepts of self, socialisation and culture gives an idea of the scope of sociology itself. The self refers to the conscious individual; socialisation, to the process by which the individual learns behaviour; and culture, to the way of life of a society or group. Socialisation continues throughout life, though we generally learn most rapidly in childhood when the main means of cultural communication – language – and basic patterns of behaviour are acquired. The major *agencies* of socialisation are the family, education, work, religion and media.

The common distinction between *primary* and *secondary* socialisation was perhaps first introduced by Charles Cooley. He defined primary groups as 'those characterised by intimate

45

face-to-face association and co-operation', of which the main examples are the family, childhood peer groups and neighbour-hood and community groups. Secondary groups provide more impersonal and specific goal-orientated contexts for socialisation and major examples are the educational institution and work situation. The complexity of modern life has led to an increase in secondary socialisation notably in the expansion of education and work training. The concepts of informal and formal socialisation somewhat parallel those of primary and secondary socialisation. Formal socialisation refers to the organised and specific teaching of behaviour and informal socialisation to behaviour learnt, often unconsciously, in everyday, unplanned interaction. The term 'informal' suggests the fluid nature of socialisation and usefully cuts across the rather too tight primary/secondary distinction: informal groups and interaction occur in nearly every context, even the most formal. Thus, informal groups of anti-school children can greatly affect what occurs in school regardless of the formal intentions of teachers, parents and government (see pp. 101–2).

Functionalist and Social Action Theory

A central problem in interpreting human behaviour is to decide what emphasis to give to choice and what emphasis to give to social conditioning. There is no final agreement on this issue and different writers and perspectives strike the balance differently.

Emile Durkheim left a legacy to Functionalism which reflected his view that society has enormous power to form and direct the thought and behaviour of its members. Durkheim argued that sociology is the study of a 'category of facts (which) consists of ways of acting, thinking, and feeling, external to the individual, and endowed with a power of coercion, by reason of which they control him'. So for Durkheim, sociology was largely about establishing what the 'rules or norms of a society are and how behaviour is controlled by them. He considered that the resulting order is essential for society to function well. He acknowledged that individuality exists but stated that it is not the object of sociology to study it. Rather, sociology is the study of the effect of social conditions on behaviour: such as economic crisis on the rate of suicide (see pp. 631–2).

In contrast to Durkheim, his contemporary, Max Weber, did

not attempt to separate the study of the individual from the study of society. Indeed, he would have considered such a separation impossible because in his view, the individual and society exist not independently but in a state of interaction in which they can change each other. People's values and ideas are influenced by society but they also change society. His theory of *social action* posits that the starting point of sociology is *meaningful* action. Weber's study of organisations (pp. 438–40) shows his appreciation of the power of what Durkheim called 'social facts' to structure people's lives, but equally his analysis of charismatic figures such as Luther and Napoleon indicates that he believed individual personality and ideas could have a major impact on society.

Talcott Parsons is the founder of modern Functionalism (Durkheim and Weber did not use the term to describe their orientations). His social systems theory attempted to synthesise Durkheim's social structural and Weber's social action perspectives together with the insights of other social scientists, notably Freud. Parsons considered that people learn basic *values*, *norms* (rules) and *roles* through socialisation. He saw the successful *internalisation* of society's values, norms and roles as a precondition of social order, and the failure to learn or accept them as a problem of deviance (see pp. 467). Despite his attempt at synthesis, Parsons is widely considered to have produced a model of society which tends much more to the social structuralism of Durkheim than to the social action emphasis of Weber. Whatever his intention, Parsons treats values almost as though they are 'things' socially imposed upon the individual rather than partly the product of his or her own considered choice. As the diagram below indicates values are presented predominantly as the property of systems rather than of individuals and groups. (For an example of Functionalist analysis of values, see Bert Hoselitz, pp. 189–90.)

The diagram of Parsons' social system model requires brief explanation. The four sub-systems fulfil four functional imperatives (requirements) of social life. The economy meets the imperative of *adaption* (i.e. material needs); the political sub-systems or *polity* provides an institutional framework for collective *goal attainment*; kinship institutions provide *pattern maintenance* (of accepted ways of behaviour) and *tension management* (of emotions); and the cultural and community sub-

Society as a Social System

Instrumental Functional Imperatives (Practical Needs)		Expressive Functional Imperatives (Creative/Emotional Needs)	
Economic Sub-System made up of	Political Sub-System made up of	Kinship Sub-System made up of	Cultural and Community Sub-System made up of
Institutions eg Factories, Trade Unions... made up of	Institutions eg Political parties Civil Service... made up of	Institutions eg Family, Marriage... made up of	Institutions eg Schools, Churches, Media... made up of
Roles eg Assembly line worker, shop steward	Roles eg MP, Minister	Roles eg Wife, husband	Roles eg Teacher, Pupil
Norms (define roles) eg Hard Work	Norms eg Public support for Government	Norms eg Mutual Affection between kin	Norms eg Respect for Authority

Norms (and whole system) Supported by Fundamental Values such as Loyalty

systems provides *integration* (co-ordination and control of the various parts of the system).

From our point of view, the integrating function of the cultural/community sub-system is particularly important. This is achieved by reinforcing values and socially acceptable behaviour – familiar functions of church and school. These values, of course, permeate the whole system and are the basis of the social *consensus* that underpins social order. For Parsons, as for Durkheim, society is a moral entity which requires conformity from its members to function effectively. Like his influential contemporary, Edward Shils, Parsons sees a major role for the elite of society to maintain the 'central value system'. Their tendency to equate elite values with society's values has been criticised by conflict theorists who point to class, racial and other opposing values between groups. This and other points of criticism of Functionalist cultural analysis are explored below.

Marxist and Conflict Perspectives

Functionalist perspective on the individual and society is based on the assumption that social order and consensus is natural to society, just as a general state of equilibrium is natural to biological organisms (the organic analogy). Marxist historian, E. P. Thompson, and cultural critic, Raymond Williams, both insist that elements of conflict, particularly class conflict, as well as consensus are normal and natural aspects of culture and society. Culture, then, refers to 'a way of life' in all its variety.

To understand Marxist perspective on cultural socialisation, we need to introduce the concept of ideology. As Stuart Hall says, whatever the different definitions of ideology, they all agree that the term refers to the role of ideas (and is thus more specific than the more general term, culture). Two main and fairly distinct usages of the concept occur in Marxist writings. First, ideology is used to refer to the ideas and beliefs that reflect the 'interests' of a particular class: thus socialism is considered to reflect the interests of the working class and capitalism that of the capitalist class. Second, ideology refers to the *single* belief system shared by all classes but which, in the Marxist view, really reflects the interests of the dominant class (this usage bears comparison with the Functionalist concept of the central value system). The term 'dominant ideology' best expresses this usage. Thus a slave who accepts slavery or a worker who accepts capitalism are incorporated into the dominant ideology. Marx described such acceptance as 'false conciousness' although, as the following quotation shows, he fully appreciated the power of the ruling class to persuade others of the rightness of their system:

> The ideas of the ruling class are in every epoch the ruling ideas: i.e. the class which is the ruling material force of society is at the same time its ruling intellectual force. The class which has the means of material production at its disposal, has control at the same time over the means of mental production. . . .

Examples of the 'means' of mental production are the church, media and educational system.

Despite the suggestion of social determinism about the above statement, a representative summary of Marx's analysis of ideology would be that classes can develop ideologies in opposition to the dominant one, which may help to overcome the system, but that the control exercised by the dominant ideology is often so great that the development of alternative ideologies can be very difficult.

The Italian Marxist, Antonio Gramsci, and the French Marxist, Louis Althusser, have both examined the role of ideology in capitalist society. Gramsci's term hegemony refers to the powerful cultural and ideological dominance that the ruling class sometimes achieves. It occurs when the ideas of the ruling class are generally seen as right and incontestable by the majority. Perhaps the essentially similar ideologies of Reaganism and Thatcherism achieved near hegemonic dominance in the early nineteen eighties. As Gramsci said, however, hegemony is a 'moving equilibrium' and can be made to change. Althusser usefully introduced the term ideological state apparatus (ISA) (Marx's means of 'mental production') to refer to the various means by which the dominant class controls thought and opinion. He considered that the educational system has replaced the church as the main means of state ideological control and his colleague Bourdieu has expanded upon this (see pp. 97–101 for a critique of this analysis). Althusser's framework may seem open to the charge of structural determinism, i.e. ideology merely reflects productive (class) relations. However, his concept of the 'relative autonomy of the superstructure' (i.e. of cultural life) suggests he believes that ideas do play a somewhat independent role in social change.

The Weberians, John Goldthorpe and David Lockwood made a useful ideal-type comparison of working and middle class beliefs, values and attitudes. The former typically believed in the social order divided into 'us' and 'them', the later in a hierarchy of differentially rewarded positions; their values differed on the basis of collective or group solidarity versus individual effort; and their attitudes on a range of cultural, political and economic issues, reflect these underlying differences of belief and value. However, along with many other commentators, Goldthorpe and Lockwood appreciated that cultural and ideological patterns were changing in the post-war era, not least among the working class. Lockwood later (1975) introduced a typology differentiating three working class 'images of society' generated through various work and local community experience. First, is the *traditional proletarian*, typified by miners and other occupational communities of workers. This group corresponds to the one described in the above ideal type comparison but it is now clearly seen as a declining part of the working class. A classic study of traditional working class community life is Dennis, Henriques and Slaughter's *Coal is Our Life*. As the mines close down year by year the way of life goes with them. Lockwood's second group is the *traditional deferentialist*, typified by the conservative and respectful rural worker described in Howard Newby's *Deferential Worker* but who also crops up in other areas of employment where the paternalist authority of 'the boss' is strong. Third, is the *'privatised'* affluent worker who is family and home rather than community orientated and who votes for instrumental (self-interested) motives rather than out of feelings of traditional loyalty.

Frank Parkin produces a similar analysis of working class ideology to Lockwood but perhaps his most interesting observation is that given the power of the elite to mould attitudes and values, one would normally expect the working class to conform to the elite's viewpoint. What partially stops this is the 'shielding' effect of working class occupational and community life which generates experience that can lead to criticism of and even opposition to the *status quo*. Again, it is worth noting that as traditional industries decline, so this protective shield may erode (for further analysis of Goldthorpe and Lockwood see pp. 267–71; and Parkin, p. 529).

It is this last point that Howard Davis fruitfully develops in *Beyond Class Images*. He suggests that 'the processes of (economic) rationalisation are leading to the ascendancy of the technical system of work over the occupational system'. In other words, the almost universal trend to mechanise and automate production – farm, factory, mining and office – may begin to flatten out the differences between class experience and ideology based on occupation. If so, other factors may become relatively more important in influencing the way people perceive class and society. Davis suggests the media as one of these and the education and training system also merit consideration. However, Davis seems to imply that these agencies tend to reduce awareness of distinct class identity, whereas the old patterns of work and community had sharpened it. These developments are open to a variety of interpretations. Liberals such as Daniel Bell and Ralf Dahrendorf do see them as an indication of the decline of class conflict in industrial society whilst Marxists find that they complicate and obscure but do not remove the fundamental causes of that conflict.

Differences of race and gender, as well as of class, also generate cultural and ideological differences. Indeed, all three play a part in most, if not everybody's life – whether or not this is recognised. These are connections we seek to trace during much of the rest of this book.

Socialisation, Culture and the Development of Self: Interactionist Perspective

So far, we have stressed the power of institutions such as family, school, the peer group and the work place, to form values, attitudes and norms: this involved an emphasis on *structural influences*. In turn, we now examine the process of socialisation and development of self from a specifically *interactionist perspective* and with close reference to the work of the American social psychologist, George Mead. He describes two general stages in the development of the self: the *play* and *game* stages. Prior to these stages the child's relationship to others is one of imitation without conscious awareness of the meaning of actions.

At the play stage, the child begins to try out certain familiar roles such as parent, teacher or doctor. The child's 'let's pretend to be ...' is a powerful in-built learning device. It is, however, a limited one. At this stage, the child does not see beyond individual roles to a more generalised view of social situations. He or she only attempts to perform the roles of certain *significant others* seen at first hand or perhaps through the media. It is as if in the early stages of learning a play, the child 'gets to know' some leading parts but has little sense of the 'plot' as a whole.

The game stage involves virtually a double progression. Firstly, in Mead's words, 'the child must have the attitude of all the others involved in that game' or situation. Perhaps children play team games so badly because they have not fully developed an awareness of the various roles in the team or a competent way of fitting in with other roles. Gradually, the child becomes more socially aware, not only at games, of

course, but in other group situations such as meals and outings. However, the full development of self depends not only on
the awareness of all other roles in a situation but on the
further ability to realise that the group, community or society
as a whole 'exercises control over the conduct of its individual
members.' In this sense, Mead refers to the group as a whole
as the 'generalised other'. Only in so far as the child learns to
take the attitude of the other does he become a full member of
society. Essentially, Mead is saying the same thing as Parsons.
Both recognise the need for the child to learn 'the rules of the
game' or of society. Crucially, Mead gives more emphasis to
the capacity of the individual to *'play* the game' actively and
creatively. This is apparent in the aspect of his thought to
which we now turn and which complements the above.

Mead divided the self into the *'I'* and the *'me'*. The 'I' is the
active part of the self whereas the 'me' is passive, that is, the
'me' is the part that others (significant and generalised) act
upon (see diagram below). Cooley used the term 'looking-glass
self' to describe how we see an image or get an impression of
ourselves through the responses of others. As the individual
becomes aware of the 'me', he or she is also able to act upon
him or herself, by controlling it. As Mead put it, the individual
becomes an object to him or herself. More than Cooley, Mead
wanted to stress that the 'I' can control or direct the self not
only to conform but to act independently. As he put it: 'The
"I" gives the sense of freedom, of initiative'. Mead noted that
the dynamic 'I' often dominates over the conformist 'me' in
highly creative people such as artists and brilliant sportsmen
but that we all have moments of originality (or, at least,
moments that feel original). In providing a framework of

**Symbolic Interactionist Model of Socialisation (and Social
Experience Generally).**

analysis in which the social actor could, indeed, be conceived of as *acting*, often unpredictably and with uncertain consequences, Mead made an outstanding contribution to social science.

Mead's awareness of both the constraints on (controls and limits) and creativity of, social interaction is apparent in his analysis of language – a central feature of symbolic interactionism. Language is the major vehicle of social communication. Its purpose is to express meaning. Of necessity, the young child is, at first, only the object of linguistic communication, but gradually begins to use language for his or her own purposes. Mead strenuously rejects the notion that language is simply a matter of imitation (except, he concedes, in the parrot). Nearly all the meanings that an individual could want to express are available in the stock of words of most languages but, even so, scientists and poets operating at the limits of available meaning and language do create new words and linguistic forms. That is what language is for: to provide meaningful symbolism. When necessary, new verbal symbols are created. Because the main concern of symbolic interactionists is with meaningful communication they have a primary interest in language. Interactionists frequently stress that (by means of language), people *negotiate* the various social roles they are expected to play. This means that they bargain with others, often those in authority, about how exactly they will perform them. This suggests the further concept of *negotiated order*. For example, certain students or workers may be able to 'get away with' doing less work than others because, over time, they have managed to establish or 'negotiate' a lower level of performance with whoever is in charge. Others may also try to do so but for some reason fail. Order exists but it reflects the complexities and negotiations of interaction. Similarly, interactionists note that different individuals *interpret* the same role in different ways. Roles are seen as less binding than functionalists suggest. Thus, as a glance around your classroom or lecture hall will verify, the role of student can be interpreted in many different and contrasting ways.

Before concluding this section, we need to be clear about how interactionists approach the analysis of social institutions. For them, an institution is not a 'thing' separate from the people that make up its structure, but is considered as the product of interaction; this is true of the family, the school, the peer group. Indeed. any institution can be viewed as the product of the interaction of the people of whom it is composed. As we shall see when we examine specific topics, such as education and work, this perspective is extremely fruitful. It can, however, be criticised as incomplete. Interactionists persistently disregard the very real power of institutions to mould and limit individual and group action. This criticism is developed at some length in the conclusion to the chapter on Deviance and Social Control (Chapter 18).

The nature of modern symbolic interactionist theory is well illustrated by the metaphors interactionists use to describe social life. Erving Goffman has compared social interaction with the dramatic action of a play, and Eric Berne, the founder of transactional psychoanalysis, entitled one of his books *Games People Play*. For Goffman, the main difference between acting in a play and 'acting' in life is that there is more scope for role interpretation in life itself; nor is the social actor tied to a formal script but can improvise freely. He recognises that social change greatly depends on such original and creative 'improvisation'. Yet, the essential similarity between drama and life remains and Goffman adopts a *dramaturgical* model of social interaction. Social life, like a play is 'made up': it is a human construction that has the meaning and 'reality' that human beings give it.

Conclusion: Self, Actualisation and Society

The strength of symbolic interactionism is that it links the individual and social groups in a two-way, mutually influential and changing flow of interaction. The fluidity of the model corresponds to the fluidity of society. Sometimes interaction involves choice and creativity, and sometimes it is highly rigid and uncreative, even destructive.

To an extent, therefore, symbolic interactionism provides the necessary social psychology to link self and society. However, there are many other perspectives and models which contribute to our understanding of this linkage, including phenomenology and existentialism. The term 'humanistic' is more or less applicable to them all as they all seek to explain society as a human enterprise. The humanistic psychology of Abraham

Maslow will be used in this book as an occasional touchstone by which to review the impact of people on institutions and vice-versa.

Maslow gives a comprehensive theory of human needs and motivation. He suggested that behaviour is centred upon a series of needs which can be arranged as a hierarchy. These are:

1 Physiological needs, e.g. food
2 Safety or security needs, e.g. shelter
3 Social needs, e.g. human interaction
4 Esteem or egoistic need, e.g. status
5 Self-actualisation needs, e.g. the expression of a personal talent or creative ability

There is some similarity between Maslow's model and the concept of functional needs discussed above. However, Maslow allows for much greater play of individuality than does the Functionalist model. He does not tie the meeting of needs as closely to particular institutions as do the Functionalists. In the last resort, Maslow considers that human will, imagination and intelligence are capable of reaching beyond the prescriptions of society and of criticising and changing it. Maslow's scheme is used to provide positive critical perspective in the chapters on work and leisure (15), social policy (22), and educational policy (24). Whilst few people may be well in touch with the apex of Maslow's hierarchy, it does provide a relatively comprehensive view of human and societal potential. In any case, self-actualisation, like social life, is a process, not a destination.

Questions

1 Compare and illustrate primary and secondary socialisation
2 Discuss the view that socialisation can create consensus or conflict
3 Define and illustrate the concept of ideology
4 Critically discuss interactionist perspective on socialisation.

4 The Family and Community

The Family: Definition of Terms

There are two basic family systems: the *nuclear* family and the *extended* family. A nuclear family is comprised of mother, father and child or children, whether natural or adopted. The nuclear family is also sometimes referred to as the *conjugal* family. Usually, members of a nuclear family share the same household. The extended family consists of the nuclear family and at least one relative living in the same household. The extended family is also sometimes referred to as the *stem* family. The classic extended family in Britain was a couple, their eldest son, and his wife and children living in the same household. It is helpful, however, to broaden our conception of the extended family. Often relatives such as grandparents or elderly aunts live near a given nuclear family and participate in fairly intense social interaction with it. It is useful to think of such a situation as an *extended family type structure*. We also include various communal structures within this broad description. *Kinship* is social relationship based on real or assumed (adopted) consanguinity (blood relationship).

Different forms of marriage affect family structure. *Monogamy* allows one wife to one husband and is usually the only legally permitted form of marriage in societies in which the Christian tradition has predominated. *Polygamy*, which allows a person to have more than one spouse is common in some traditional societies. Polygyny, where a man has more than one wife, is more

common than polyandry, where a wife has more than one husband. The former is common in some tribes but is also practised by some modern Muslims. It also occurs as a result of
Mormon religious belief, particularly in the North American
State of Utah. Polyandry occurs as a matter of practicality in
parts of Tibet. It operates as a form of birth control in poorer
regions. However many husbands a woman has, she is limited
by nature to a certain number of children.

Perspectives on the Family

For many, the family seems a familiar and comfortable institution. It can be a 'haven in a heartless world', a refuge from
the impersonality and stress of work or school.

Sociologists have never accepted as adequate this simple and
romantic view of the family. They have always considered that
the influence of society penetrates deeply into the family and
some have argued that the family, in turn, can substantially
influence society. Nevertheless, until quite recently the sociology
of the family occupied a predictable niche in sociology. Broadly
speaking, the literature dealt with the functions of the family in
relation to society as a whole or to the various social subsys-
tems. The functionalist approach has now been challenged from
various directions. Even so, functionalist analysis of the family
provides perhaps the clearest and easiest to understand application of this perspective.

a Functionalist

Functionalists regard the family as an important 'organ' in the
'body' of society. It is what the family 'does' or the functions
of the family that most interest them. George Murdock, an
early functionalist, considered the four basic functions of the
family to be the sexual, the reproductive, the socialising and
the economic. Although these functions can evolve, he considered them to be 'universal'.

We can take *sex* and *reproduction* together. According to functionalists, marriage and the nuclear family provide the best
opportunity for the socially controlled expression of the sex
drive. More importantly, they provide the necessary institutional stability for the reproduction and nurture (bringing up)

of children. The bringing up of children requires considerable time and effort: human maturation takes longer than that of any other species relative to life-span. To be brought up effectively, children usually require the help of more than one person (for practical if not emotional reasons). In most societies the two people who produce a child are expected to take responsibility for its upbringing. Family work is usually divided into domestic and economic. Practical commitment to children based on shared involvement and responsibility exists in polygamous as well as monogamous marriages. In polygamous Muslim societies a man is not expected to marry more wives and produce more children than he can afford.

To argue that the nuclear family is a socially useful institution is not to say, as some functionalists do, that it is biologically necessary and inevitable. Margaret Mead seems correct in contending that the nuclear family is *culturally created*, not *biologically given*. Comparisons with similar species by no means provide conclusive evidence, but males of other primates often do not remain with the female they have made pregnant. The fact that the human male usually does so is probably because this arrangement conveniently provides a secure context for the lengthy child-rearing necessary to our species. Another pointer in this direction is the fact that whilst many societies have allowed considerable sexual freedom before marriage, the widespread tendency is to curtail or abolish it afterwards. This, again, is a question of practicality not biology: it focuses energy and attention on spouse and children and, in particular, prevents the male from having more children than he is able to look after. Historically, the taboo (social disapproval) on sex outside marriage is a protective device for children and, to that extent, the human species. This argument loses much of its practical, if not emotional, force, however, in the age of the pill.

The family's role in laying down the basis of culture through socialisation is universally stressed by functionalists, as seen in Chapter 3.

The basic *economic* function of the family is to provide food and shelter for its members. In pre-industrial societies many families produced much of what they consumed. Now, individuals work for wages but the family remains an important unit of consumption of industrially produced goods.

As explained in the first chapter, functionalists see each social institution in terms of its role within its own social sub-system and in terms of its relationship to society as a whole. The model below illustrates this point in respect of the modern family.

The Interchange between the Nuclear Family and the Functional Sub-systems of Society

Nuclear Family	Wages ← Labour → Goods ← Family Assets →	Economy
Nuclear Family	Leadership ← Loyalty → Decisions ← Compliance →	Polity
Nuclear Family	Support ← Group- Participation → Identity ← Adherence →	Community
Nuclear Family	Specification of standards ← Acceptance of standards → Approval ← Conformity →	Value System

Source: Adapted from *Bell and Vogel,* 1960.

The figure is very simple to interpret. It shows that the family gives 'something' to and gets 'something' from each sub-system. Take the example of the economy. The family provides labour for which its members get paid. Money is then 'recycled' back into the economy through the purchase of goods which the family needs and through family savings. Thus, the family is seen as both dependent on and contributing to the economy. It is the same with the political system. In return for loyalty and obedience (compliance), family members get leadership from politicians (however confusing this may sometimes be!). From the community comes support and identity in return for participation and commitment (adherence). The only aspect of the model that might cause difficulty is calling the fourth sub-system the value system, rather than kinship. The family is, of course, part of the kinship system and reflects and passes on the values of society. Other institutions are involved in value socialisation, but the family's role is primary.

Despite great recent criticism of functionalist analysis, this model has a certain commonsense usefulness. However, as D. H. Morgan points out, Murdock's analysis suffers from a failure to consider whether other institutions could take over the functions he associates with the family, but later functionalists such as Parsons have explored this issue. Further, Murdock rather too readily assumes that the nuclear family functions harmoniously. More contemporary functionalists, N. W. Bell and E. F. Vogel, as well as radical phenomenologists R. D. Laing and David Cooper, have shown that the modern family can contain frightening tensions. Recent functionalists, however, still tend to assume a 'fit' between the nuclear family and society as a whole, even though they may concede that it may be internally under stress. Arguably, they are overinfluenced by the harmony implicit in the organic analogy in making this assumption. We examine functionalist analysis of how the family has 'adapted' to the 'needs' of industrial society in a later section (Chapter 4 pp. 71–7).

b Marxist, other Class-based and Feminist Family Analysis

Marxists also adopt a structural perspective on the family. They do not, however, regard the nuclear family as a universal feature of human society, but put it in the particular context of capitalist society and, particularly, the class nature of that society.

Friedrich Engels' (1820–1895) *The Origin of the Family: Private Property and the State*, remains the starting point for most Marxist analysis of the family and of gender relations. Engels examines the emergence of the nuclear family and male dominance in an historical context. He hypothesised that in the nomadic stage of man's social development there was a substantial measure of sexual equality. Neither exclusive sexual possessiveness nor much private property existed. People and things were held in common although mothers had an immediate involvement with young children. Gradually, the male sphere of activity became more specialised and distinct: cattle breeding, mining and trade were added to their primary responsibility of hunting. This leads to the central point of Engels' argument. As men acquired greater control over wealth and property, they sought means to ensure that it stayed within their personal possession and was passed on to their offspring. To do this they had to know who their offspring were! This meant that the free sexual relations of the horde had to be replaced by monogamy, and a system of inheritance based on blood introduced. In a male-dominated society, the eldest male was established as inheritor. The state, also male-dominated, gave powerful legal support to male control over the family, women and private property. Thus, in Engels' analysis, the growth of private property and male dominance evolved together.

As Rosalind Delmar puts it, the major contribution of Engels was to assert 'women's oppression as a problem of history, rather than of biology.' She uses the word 'assert' rather than 'prove' because the details of Engels' historical account are thought to be wrong. The precise historical truth on this issue is probably beyond proof but the point to appreciate is that Engels concluded that as the monogamous nuclear family and female subordination had developed historically *they were capable of being changed.* This is the basis of Marxist and most socialist analysis of the family. The opposite view, that the sexual division of labour which consigns the woman primarily to the home and the man to economic labour, is founded on the analysis that such an arrangement is biologically rooted and virtually immutable (unchangeable). It is the basis of the more crude functionalist analysis of the nuclear family.

Although the patriarchal (male-dominated) nuclear family pre-dated capitalist society, Engels, and Marx too, considered that it fitted the needs of capitalism particularly well. Capitalist society was based on the accumulation of private wealth and property mainly controlled by men. Accordingly, a patriarchal family structure linked to a system of primogeniture (in which the eldest son inherits) suited it very well. Primogeniture was primarily of significance among the upper and middle classes: the working class had little to pass on anyway. Marx and Engels did argue, however, that capitalism provided a limited opportunity for women to escape domestic bondage by finding employment outside the home and thus acquiring an independent source of income. Even so, they considered that, ultimately, the liberation of women depended on a change of social system from capitalism to socialism. Private property would then be abolished and the organisation of child-rearing and socialisation would be a matter for the community as a whole to determine.

More recent Marxist and socialist writers – particularly feminists – have tended to be sceptical of the supposed improvement in the status of women that more direct involvement in the economy brings. Blackburn and Stewart point out that women often play the kind of 'service' role in the work situation which can be regarded as an extension of their low domestic status rather than an improvement on it. Further, Engels has been somewhat criticised for a 'waiting for the revolution' approach to the solution of gender exploitation. Contemporary Marxist and socialist feminists such as Juliet Mitchell and Ann Oakley tend to be much more diligent than he was in the search for immediate improvements in gender relations towards that larger end (see Chapter 12, pp. 313–15 where non-Marxist feminist perspectives on gender are also discussed).

Some Marxists regard the sexual possessiveness of marital partners as just one expression of the possessive and, in their view, selfish, individualism of capitalist society. Marx himself claimed that marriage 'is incontestably a form of exclusive private property'. The female 'gives' sex in return for the economic security her husband provides. She gets the worst of the arrangement because she is the more dependent. Engels suggested that her position is one of glorified prostitution. Perhaps the cultural stereotyping embodied in such phrases as 'she's a real gold-digger' and 'she's out to get her man' bear out the view that the economic dependency of women under capitalism can undermine their dignity.

Marxists consider that the family can socialise children to conform, even though, in the case of the working class, it is against their interests to do so (see Chapter 3, pp. 49–52). On the other hand, experience of exploitation can produce feelings critical of the system among the *proletariat* (working class) and these may also be passed on through the family as well as through workmates and friends. As we shall see, Marxists generally consider that the socialising and other functions of the nuclear family could, at least, be pared down and done more effectively by other institutions such as state nurseries.

It would be wholly wrong to think that only Marxists are aware of the major influence of class on family life and, especially, of the way the family socialises children to 'belong' to a particular class. On the contrary, since the war a vast body of largely empirical work has contributed to our knowledge of the links between family and class. The writings of A. H. Halsey and J. W. Douglas are examples. Through the research of these and other scholars we later study the relationship between family, education and class, and that section (Chapter 5, pp. 96-105) should be regarded as a direct continuation of this chapter. Indeed, class pervades not only the family but virtually all aspects of social life. The experience of class, however, begins in the family. (For an analysis of Feminist Family Policy Contributions, see Chapter 22, pp. 665–8).

Is the Nuclear Family Universal or can it be Replaced?

The Debate between Functionalists and Marxists

We must now put to the test the partly conflicting functionalist and Marxist claims about the family. We do so mainly by examining various attempts to modify the family along broadly socialist lines and by discussing a celebrated example of a society which did not appear to have a nuclear family, the Nayar case.

Although Murdock's arguments are now regarded as oversimple, modern functionalists still accept that the nuclear family is universal. They, of course, recognise the widespread existence of the extended family but see the nuclear family as its essential core. Literally, the extended family is an *extension* of the nuclear family. The same argument is applied to polygamous families. One person may make several marriages but each separate coupling and offspring is regarded as a nuclear family.

Two quite distinct arguments are presented to support the contention that the nuclear family is universal. Firstly, the universality of the nuclear family is seen as a result of its unique practicality and usefulness in meeting certain basic human needs. A few functionalists take this to the point of claiming that man is biologically predisposed towards the nuclear family. Secondly, the accumulation of historical and cultural material is taken to show that, as a matter of empirical fact, the family is universal. We now examine these two arguments in turn.

We have already discussed the first argument: that the family is universal because it is functionally necessary. In the next section we look at how these functions have evolved – particularly under the impact of industrialisation. Here it only needs to be added that functionalists stress that it is only the family which *combines* the four basic functions mentioned above. Other institutions can perform some of them but only the family is so effectively *multi-functional*. The basic functions of the family are to a greater or lesser extent concerned with one matter – the maintenance and regeneration of the species – and it is efficient and convenient that they should be integrated into a single institution.

A useful way to test the second functionalist argument that, as a matter of *fact*, the family is universal, is by finding and evaluating possible alternatives to it. This we do below.

The Nayar Case

It can be argued that the Nayars of Malabar offer an example of a society in which the nuclear family did not exist. Until about the mid-nineteenth century, when their traditional social system began to break up under the impact of the British, the Nayar produced and reared children without the aid of the nuclear family. No direct institutional link existed between sex and reproduction and the rearing of children. Once a woman had undergone a sexual initiation ritual, she could have sexual intercourse with any man she wished. As a result, paternity was often uncertain. In practical terms this did not matter, as the mother's brother, not the natural father, was responsible for looking after her and her offspring. When this was not possible the next nearest male relatives on the mother's side were responsible.

The Nayar case is surely an exception to the familiar nuclear family pattern. Kathleen Gough's point that a special and socially recognised tie existed between a woman and the man who first initiated her sexually does not affect the argument at all. The 'couple' certainly did not constitute the basis of a nuclear family in that the nuclear 'unit' had no continuous social existence. Further examination shows, however, that there was a sound functional reason for the Nayar form of child-rearing. The Nayars were a very warlike people. The women were able to assist each other during the frequent absences of the men, and in the event of one male relative being killed, there would still be others left to provide for the woman and her children. The Nayar system of child-rearing was, then, *functionally well adapted* to the needs of that particular society. Regarded thus, it is quite consistent with functionalist perspectives about the need of children for a stable social environment. Perhaps this is more significant than the literal fact that the Nayar case does represent a rare exception to the 'universality' of the nuclear family.

The Kibbutzim
There have been few attempts in modern society to abolish the nuclear family outright but many efforts to replace it partially by other institutions or to merge it within a larger extended family-type structure. Perhaps the best known attempt to supplement the family by providing alternative institutions to assist parents with childrearing is the Israeli *Kibbutzim*. In the early days of the Jewish settlement in Israel, the Kibbutzim stressed the collective values of the whole community against the more concentrated, limited, and, it was thought, selfish ties of the family. It was also part of the beliefs (or ideology) of the movement to release women from child-rearing and to enable them to have as much time for work and leisure as men. Young infants were taken to special Children's Houses after only a short time with their parents. They grew up together and were looked after by specially trained nurses (or metapalets) and teachers. They were allowed to see their parents for a few hours only each day, and slept in the Children's Houses and not their parents' residence. Women were therefore free to do any work on the same terms as men. Gradually, these patterns are changing: the separation between parents and children is less complete; in many Kibbutzim, children return to spend the night at their parents' flat, and women are more involved than men in traditionally feminine roles such as working in the communal kitchen or laundry.

Despite this partial return to nuclear family norms, the Kibbutzim still thrive and are now well beyond the experimental phase. It is significant that children of the Kibbutzim and adults from Kibbutzim backgrounds are as psychologically well adjusted as others. Not unexpectedly, however, many have acquired values that express the importance of the group rather than individual achievement. The charge by Bruno Bettelheim that adults brought up in the Kibbutzim lack the capacity for leadership has not been found to be true, however. It does seem, therefore, that the role of the family in rearing children can be successfully reduced, as long as other *effective* institutions exist to do the job.

The Sixties Commune Movement

A much less organised effort to breach the limits of the nuclear family was the commune 'movement' of the late nineteen sixties. Communes of one kind or another have existed for thousands of years – religious communities are one example – and will no doubt continue to exist, although they have a tendency to be short-lived. An interesting example of communal idealism which illustrates the fragility of the movement was the plan of the poets Wordsworth, Coleridge and Southey to establish a *utopia* (perfect society) in miniature on the banks of the Sussquehannah River in the United States. Like most people's dreams of returning to nature this one, too, remained a dream although Wordsworth and Coleridge did go to live in the more accessible English Lake District.

The ideological theorising which inspired many of the communes of the nineteen sixties was rarely as well thought out as that of the Kibbutzim pioneers. Ideas of 'togetherness' and of 'sharing things, feelings and experience' were enough to persuade thousands of young people, at one time or another, to spend a few weeks or months in a commune. Others pursued the ideal of alternative living more rigorously and attempted to live self-sufficiently, practising communist principles in respect of property. In many communes nuclear families or, quite often, single-parent families simply fitted in – sometimes benefiting from the help that single adults or childless couples gave them with their children. In others, more organised attempts to bring up children communally occurred and in such cases these arrangements were often consciously thought of as alternatives to the nuclear family. Likewise, serious attempts were sometimes made to share the burden of domestic work equally between men and women.

Even at its peak in the late nineteen sixties the commune movement was never more than a marginal challenge to conventional family structures. The nature of modern society tends strongly to undermine the extended family type structure of communes. Geographical mobility – often caused by occupational change – is so great that the chances of the same group of people finding it convenient to stay together over a long period are small. Unless modern society itself breaks down and we return to a more localised agricultural pattern of living, communes seem likely to remain peripheral. Yet, for certain groups, especially students and young, unmarried adults, communal living can offer an enjoyable and practical social framework. It is also not uncommon for groups of one-parent families to live either together or close to one other in order to benefit from mutual cooperation and assistance.

Similarly, the relatively few examples of homosexual or lesbian 'families' are best seen as an accommodation to circumstances by an interested minority, rather than as a challenge to the nuclear family. Research evidence indicates that children brought up by a couple of the same sex are no more likely to be homosexual than children raised by a heterosexual (sexually mixed) couple. Again, this suggests that other institutions besides the nuclear family are capable of bringing up children successfully.

The Soviet 'Experiment'

There has been only one attempt by a government seriously to undermine the nuclear family. This happened in the Soviet Union in the period immediately following the Revolution of 1917. Marriage, divorce and even abortion were made available on almost a casual basis. The ideological inspiration behind this attempt to undermine the family was the Communist ideas of Marx, Engels and Lenin. They considered that in capitalist societies the family both expressed and helped to perpetuate the unequal and repressive nature of the system itself. In particular, they considered that the domination of husband over wife in the family reflected that of the capitalist manufacturer over the wage-labourer in economic and social life. But it was not simply ideology that motivated the Communist revolutionaries. Practically, they wanted to release more women from domestic toil to enable them to assist in reconstructing the country's economy which had been badly damaged by revolution and civil war. To help achieve this, communal facilities were established for bringing up children, though at first these were quite inadequate.

In the mid nineteen thirties, the government substantially changed major aspects of its policy towards the family. In 1935 a new law was passed, making parents legally responsible for the misbehaviour of their children. In 1936 much stricter marriage and divorce legislation was passed. This was partly because the previous approach had helped to produce considerable social problems, including a high rate of infant mortality and neglect and juvenile delinquency. In addition, the government was now keen to increase the birth rate and this was thought to require a stable family structure and fewer abortions. It is significant, however, that a progressively extending network of maternity homes, nurseries and kindergartens was also established both to assist population expansion and to allow women more freely to enter and remain in the labour force.

As Professor Bronfenbrenner says, conditions were so unstable in post-revolutionary Russia that it would be unwise to regard the Soviet experiment to undermine the family as a serious test of whether it is possible for a society to do without the family. Nevertheless, certain less general conclusions do suggest themselves. Firstly, the Soviet experiment again makes it obvious that the crucial functions concerning the reproduction, nurture and socialisation of children, traditionally fulfilled by the family, cannot just be left to chance. If the family does not perform them, then some other institution or institutions must. Secondly, where adequate alternative institutions are established, they can, at least in part, replace the family. The Soviet Union, and indeed other Communist countries, have recognised the need for planned alternative facilities for child-rearing if the traditional functions of the family are to be reduced. The Soviet Union, East Germany and China are much better equipped with nursery and pre-school facilities than Britain. In addition, the Soviet Union runs a state system of boarding schools which bring up millions of children and so frees their parents, particularly their mothers, from the need to do so.

It is clear that the nuclear family is outstandingly well-equipped to perform the basic functions of the reproduction and rearing of children although in many traditional societies it only functions efficiently as part of an extended kinship system. It is historical fact that in almost every society the nuclear family has been the basic social unit. It is equally obvious from the above comparative cultural survey, however, that it is possible to reduce the functions of the family as long as additional supportive institutions are established. Whether any government or given group of people wants to increase or reduce the role of the family in society is a question of *judgement* and *value*. As such, it is beyond the strict limits of sociological consideration. Those who wish to maintain or extend the role of the nuclear family and ensure its prestige as a social institution often do so because they value the strength and intensity of the personal relationships that they believe characterise it: the husband-wife and mother-child relationships are perhaps especially valued. By contrast, many Communists and other radicals consider that the nuclear family is a narrow institution which fosters selfish individualism and helps to maintain the corrupt capitalist system. In particular, they argue that the family prevents women from fulfilling their true personal and social potential. (For a discussion of the one parent family as an alternative to the nuclear family, see pp. 90–1).

The Family and Community in Britain from Pre-Industrial to Modern Times

It used to be thought that the extended family was typical in pre-industrial England and that the nuclear family became predominant as a result of industrialisation. It was argued by Goode and Parsons that the industrial economy requires a more mobile population and that this tends to break up extended families; in particular, the urban, industrial areas drew in younger people. Historical and sociological research has shown this to be too simple a view. Nevertheless, as Edward Shorter and others argue, this new knowledge need not fundamentally change our perception of the difference between local community life in pre-industrial and modern times. Even though family structure has changed less than was thought, its relationship to the wider community has changed. We will divide our study of changes in the family into three historical phases: the pre-industrial, the early industrial and the modern.

1 The Pre-Industrial Family

Peter Laslett has shown that, in fact, the nuclear family was the norm in pre-industrial Britain and other research strongly suggests that the same was true for North America. It is quite likely, however, that the extended family was more common in continental Europe, at least in the East. One important exception to the nuclear family norm existed in Britain. It was usual for the eldest and inheriting son and his family to remain in his parents' home. This was to mutual benefit: the ageing parents could receive help from their eldest son who was able to live in and look after the property he would eventually inherit. Although other children usually moved out of the parental home at marriage, they normally lived close by.

An interesting suggestion emerging from the new research on the family further refutes the functionalist view that the nuclear family was the result of industrialisation. Harris argues that the very fact that non-inheriting children had to make their own way in the world helped to provide a mobile labour force and to foster the values of hard work and achievement necessary for capitalist activity. Seemingly, it was not necessary for the family to 'adapt' greatly to the early industrial society as functionalists maintain. On the contrary, the single inheritance system may have helped foster industrialisation. The same system of inheritance exists in Japan and may have had a similar effect.

Talcott Parsons has emphasised the multi-functional nature of the pre-industrial family. Whereas the modern nuclear family typically receives much assistance from the state in performing its basic functions, the pre-industrial family had to be more self-sufficient. At times of crisis, considerable help was often provided by kin and neighbours. If this help was essentially informal, it was also expected and needed.

Then, as now, the family was the major institution of sex, reproduction and nurture. As far as socialisation was concerned, the family, supported by church and community, taught traditional behaviour and morality. For the great majority, there was no formal schooling and most could neither read nor write. Skills, including farming skills, were normally learnt through practical application, usually under the watchful eye of family or kin. The major economic function of most families was to produce enough for their members to survive – if possible, comfortably. The better off and more successful produced a surplus which could then be sold in market towns – mainly for consumption by the urban minority. The function of *job-placement* was more often performed by the family in pre-industrial times, than now. This means that older members of the family would frequently place younger members in work.

Whatever the precise size and structure of the pre-industrial family, Edward Shorter seems to be right when he suggests that both kin and community had greater control and influence on individual and nuclear family life before the nineteenth century, than now. This observation fits in with the functionalist view that family and community 'did' more for their members then than today.

2 The Early Industrial Family

With industrialisation and the movement of population to the towns, major changes began to take place in the functional relationship of the family to society. But just as sociologists have exaggerated the extent of the extended family in the pre-industrial past, so they have often over-stressed the speed and extent of the change to the nuclear family in industrial, urban areas. Obviously, if the nuclear family was the predominant form *before* industrialisation, there could hardly have been a massive shift towards it *after* industrialisation. There is some evidence that in industrial working class areas the extended family was, in fact, more common than in rural areas. This was the pattern found by Anderson in his research into households in the cotton-manufacturing town of Preston and a rural area nearby, in the mid-nineteenth century. Peter Willmott and Michael Young's famous study of working class family life in Bethnal Green in the nineteen-fifties showed the strength of extended family type structures at that time and it is likely that this pattern had existed for several generations. The usefulness of extended family type structures to the working class in the nineteenth century is apparent. Older women could help out domestically when the younger married ones went out to work. Kin arriving from the rural areas would often stay with relatives, not only out of immediate necessity but in the hope of

picking up tips about jobs or even getting a specific recommendation and placement. Extended families in contemporary
immigrant communities play much the same role.

There were also sound personal and social reasons for middle class families to stay close together in Victorian England.
In particular, the old still depended on their kin for help and
companionship. The welfare state is a twentieth century
phenomenon. Quite often, the large, three-floor Victorian middle class house was the home of three generations.

Despite the considerable amount of evidence that there was
no marked change from the extended to nuclear family form as
a result of industrialisation, it is likely that *over a long period of
time*, say, from the early nineteenth into the twentieth century,
the *further* development of the nuclear family at the expense of
the extended occurred. As Goode and Parsons stipulate, this
was partly the result of the geographical mobility that a free
labour market tended to stimulate. As the service sector
increased and people with specific educational qualifications
were demanded, it became more likely, particularly for the
middle class young, to leave their home locality to work elsewhere.

Even so, the pattern painted by modern scholarship is of
more continuity between pre-industrial and early industrial family structure and life than has been previously noted. The
extended family and supportive community was often needed as
much in industrial areas and dockland as it had been in rural
areas. The middle class Victorian septuagenerian had no more
taste for living alone than had the aged country gentry. The
real change in family and community life occurred much closer
to our own time.

3 The Modern Family

a CHANGING FUNCTIONS The twentieth century, our third period
for consideration, has seen substantial changes in the size of the
family and in its relationship to society. Largely as a result of
improved methods of birth control and the resultant decrease in
the fertility rate, families tend to be much smaller than in Victorian times. A family of four, parents and two children, has
become typical of both the working and middle classes. Change
in family size has probably had as much effect on family life as
any supposed change in family structure. Nevertheless, it can

be said that the post-Second World War period is the one in which the nuclear family has overwhelmingly predominated over the extended. Indeed, in 1979, the majority of households contained only one or two people – a fact which suggests that even the nuclear family is suffering some fragmentation. According to functionalists such as Talcott Parsons, the modern nuclear family has adapted to fulfil more *specialised* functions. Finally, the relationship of family to community has changed.

The basic functions of the modern nuclear family remain those that the family has traditionally fulfilled. To a greater or lesser extent, however, all four functions have been modified. As the basic functions have tended to be reduced, the family has, arguably, acquired a still greater role in personal and emotional life. There has been a parallel decline in the involvement of the local community with the individual. Often there is a wall of privacy between family and neighbourhood community.

For the majority, marriage is still the main outlet for sexual activity and some consider it to be the only morally acceptable one. Many others, however, no longer exclusively associate sex with marriage. Michael Schofield's work shows a growth in permissive attitudes to sex before marriage among young people. In America the Hite Report suggested that many women no longer regard sexual expression exclusively in terms of their marital relationship. If marriage is not as exclusively the outlet for sexual expression as in the past, is still provides the most popular basis of companionship and mutual assistance.

Reproduction still occurs predominantly within a two-parent family context despite a noticeable increase in illegitimacy in recent years. There has been a corresponding rise in the number of children taken into local authority care, but most of these still received early nurture and socialisation within some sort of family situation, however unstable.

The state has come increasingly to intervene in child socialisation, particularly from the age of five when children usually start school. Even infants and, for that matter, unborn children can benefit from a variety of advice and assistance available from central and, sometimes, local government sources. A state system of pre-school nurseries is not, however, provided in Britain and the responsibility for early child-care and socialisation falls more squarely on the family than in the Communist countries of Eastern Europe. Functionalists stress the continuing central importance of the family as the agency of primary socialisation. Here they are not merely referring to informal socialisation, which functionalists have always seen as necessary to passing on the values and norms of society, but to formal teaching too. Fletcher notes that more teaching and learning take place in the family now than in the past. We live in a complex world in which the three 'r's' are necessary rather than optional. Many parents play a large part in teaching these and other skills.

The protection and assistance traditionally afforded by kin and community is now commonly provided by the state. Muriel Nissel goes so far as to say that: 'Supplementary benefit, not the family, must remain the safety net for people faced with poverty.' The National Health Service plays a major role here. So, too, do the contributory national insurance schemes covering sickness and unemployment payments and the social security system which, as its name implies, is supposed to be the ultimate 'security' against poverty if all else fails. Some have seen the apparent loss of the family's welfare function and its assumption by the state as an example of the growing impersonality of the modern world. Even caring for one's fellow man has been taken over by 'big brother.' Strugglers are assisted by salaried social workers rather than friends. This is too simple a view. Firstly, the welfare state provides many services, including necessary medical services to the poor, that people would not otherwise obtain. Secondly, help from family and friends does and, indeed, should supplement and overlap that provided by the welfare state. The state cannot usually supply the human and emotional support that people undergoing material or emotional crisis often need, although many social workers make remarkable efforts to do so. The administration of social security payments has, however, often been obtusely bureaucratic – hardly a bracing recipe for 'clients' often already dispirited and suffering.

The family is rarely now a unit of economic production, although it is an important unit of consumption. Many goods, such as refrigerators, washing machines, and three piece suites are manufactured largely for the family market. It hardly needs to be said that, without this market, there would be economic collapse. In addition, families collectively produce and maintain the labour force. Finally, the investment of family money in banks, building societies, unit trusts and stocks and shares provides necessary loan capital for industrial investment.

Talcott Parsons emphasises the importance of the contemporary family in 'stabilising' the adult personality. It provides a relatively secure and personally meaningful context for self-fulfilment, in contrast with the frequently stressful and impersonal nature of work. Parsons considers that the family has shed some of its less necessary functions and has adapted to become more specialised in two tasks: that of socialisation, and 'tension' or emotional management. Marxists are sceptical of this claim and, as we shall see when we examine the evidence for stresses on the family, they are not without ammunition for their cause.

b PRIVATISATION Michael Young and Peter Willmott make some interesting observations on changes in family roles and relationships in their book *The Symmetrical Family*. Much of what they say continues and develops earlier British research on the family, including their own. In the nineteen fifties, for instance, Elizabeth Bott found that, on the basis of an admittedly small sample (twenty families), working class spouses tended to divide tasks sharply whereas the opposite applied to the middle class. Thus, she describes these as, respectively, *segregated* and *joint conjugal* role relationships. Willmott and Young found that, by the time they did their research in the early nineteen seventies, joint conjugal role relationships had become quite common among the working class, too. For one thing, far more women had joined men in the labour force. So impressed were Willmott and Young by this development that they used the term 'symmetrical' in the title of their book to indicate the trend to greater role sharing. Feminists have strongly criticised Willmott and Young for exaggerating this trend and we shall air their criticisms later (see Chapter 12, p. 322).

Willmott and Young also echo a point made about family life by John Goldthorpe and David Lockwood in their 'affluent worker' study. Goldthorpe and Lockwood noted a tendency towards family – rather than community – based social life both among their main sample of affluent manual workers and the smaller, control group of white collar employees. Spouses spent time together inside the home rather than in visiting friends and neighbours. Goldthorpe and Lockwood termed this trend the *privatisation* of family life.

There are several reasons for the development of the privatised nuclear pattern of living. An underlying factor is the movement of population caused partly by the operation of a free labour market and government policy to disperse population from the declining inner city areas. This has undermined community and extended family type social networks. Important, too, is the massive post-war boom in home-based, leisure consumer items such as televisions and hi-fi's. Many married people, as well as aspiring to a high material standard of living, have great expectations of their marital relationship as well. Unlike many Eastern societies in which marriages are arranged by parents, Western societies allow people to marry for love and romance. Even after the first flush is over, couples tend to expect and demand much of each other, both in terms of everyday companionship and deeper emotional and physical commitment. With this in mind some commentators have referred to modern marriage as *companionate marriage*.

Christopher Lasch, a radical American intellectual, gives a depressing view of the nuclear family in capitalist society. He puts quite a different value on family consumerism and even on the marital relationship from that of functionalists. He argues, as do many Marxists, that the family market is manipulated by capitalist advertisers and producers. People are persuaded to buy the 'latest' item even when they neither need nor want it: this spending keeps the wheels of the capitalist economy turning. The stresses of a materialist society which lacks deeper spiritual or human values shows in marriage – and divorce. For Lasch the family in 'bourgeois' society has ceased to be a private refuge. Its walls have been breached by relentless waves of media propaganda, its members are awash like flotsam in an uncaring sea. We look more closely at these and like observations in the following section.

c FAMILY, CLASS, CULTURE AND COMMUNITY Middle and working class cultures remain distinct despite the invasion of almost every home by the consumer durables of the 'mass' market. Here we further explore differences between working and middle class cultural and community life or 'social networks', to use Margaret Stacey's term.

Already Richard Hoggart's painstakingly detailed description of traditional working class life in Leeds has a curious old fashioned snap-shot quality. But the fact that traditional working class community is breaking up does not mean it never existed. Some recent commentators, failing to find thriving working class communities of the kind described twenty years ago by Willmott and Young and by Hoggart seem almost to assume that the whole phenomenon is a romantic fiction.

Coates and Silburn's generally excellent study of the lower class St Anne's district of Nottingham falls a little into this trap. The fact that they find St Anne's to be a fragmented community does not mean it was always so. As they, in fact, well illustrate, the decline of community was due partly to urban renewal policies – a factor also emphasised by Willmott and Young in their Bethnal Green study well over a decade previously.

Apart from those working class people who have chosen to leave inner city areas, many had to leave because of compulsory clearance orders and were offered public housing elsewhere. This was part of a national plan (which had considerable local variations) to divert industry and population away from the inner cities, which could then be used as the location for office blocks, major shops and stores, and as the centre of the leisure and entertainment industry. Public housing makes up well over a quarter of residential property, and generalisations need to be made carefully. However, a consensus has emerged, which includes even their original designer, that high rise flats have been a failure as a major means of providing cheap mass-accommodation. Incidents such as the collapse of the Ronan Point block, and the suicide jump from her high-storey flat of a depressed Birmingham mother, with her baby, have created the worst publicity, but myriad problems of design and functioning, such as block entrances leading out into garbage zones or lifts perpetually breaking down, have provided a daily diet of irritation and frustration for thousands. Nevertheless, it is, of course, a major contribution that the material conditions of living provided by many of these developments are vastly superior to that of the old-fashioned terraced houses they have often replaced. But this improvement can be achieved equally in smaller, low rise developments or still other kinds of accommodation at less cost to communal life. As potential communities high rise flats have limited possibilities. Living off the ground is not conducive to shared activity and most corridors in high rise flats do not provide an environment that encourages friendly conversations with neighbours. Even Frank Lloyd Wright's imaginative idea of high rise developments as 'vertical streets in the sky' with various shops, facilities and meeting places strategically scattered on all levels to facilitate interaction and communication seems expensive and artificial, though clearly the concept is an improvement on the human filing cabinets that some blocks have become.

Working class housing estates make up most of the rest of public housing. These are often located on the outskirts of urban areas and replace traditional, more centrally situated housing. Living conditions on post-war, mainly working class housing estates vary from almost as bad as in the worst of the high rise flats to very good indeed. John Stedman's estate at Corby and the prize-winning Handley Green development at Laindon, near Basildon, are spacious, well-designed and attractive. But in general, people have to travel to work from public housing estates and shopping, too, can require a journey. The separation of these basic functions is not conducive to an integrated community life in the old style. A seldom remarked-on effect of the decrease in the fertility of working class mothers is that fewer children exist to establish inter-family social links and this must further reduce the numbers of friends within the neighbourhood. Community centres, which are a feature of some recently established estates, often fail to draw people together for leisure activities though teenagers do frequently use them. Even so, the streets and open areas of estates are often preferred by adolescents – especially by 'tougher' boys. Perhaps it is through their activity and that of younger children who still like to 'play out' that we see a glimpse of at least one continuous strand in the pattern of working class neighbourhood life.

Despite the complexity of the overall picture, most middle class owner occupiers still tend to live in suburban neighbourhoods. The term suburban neighbourhood can cover a wide spectrum from, for instance, areas of inter-war semi-detached property, with upper working as well as lower middle class residents, to areas of high status, often detached property occupied mainly by professional, managerial and business groups. Generalisations therefore need to be cautious.

In dormitory suburbs, the very fact that people live and

work in separate places is not conducive to the development of integrated community life. But if work is not a shared activity as in a mining or docking community, it can provide a conversation topic for middle class people who already know each other or want to get to know each other. 'What do you do?' is a favourite opening question at middle class dinner parties. Though social life in the immediate suburban neighbourhood is less intense than in a traditional working class community, networks of friends and acquaintances tend to be spread more widely. The middle class are more ready to join clubs and associations requiring commitment to activity beyond the immediate neighbourhood. For instance, middle class parents are more likely to participate in organisations and activities concerning their children's educational welfare such as Parent-Teachers Associations or school open days.

The privatisation of middle class family life is highly compatible with extended friendship networks and relative lack of involvement in the immediate neighbourhood. Social life is more organised and friends are not expected to 'pop in and out' as they might do in a traditional working class neighbourhood. A telephone call can courteously pave the way for a visit but it can as easily do instead if one of the parties is occupied. Privacy and control of time can be virtually a necessity if work brought home from the office and children's homework is to be properly done. The home, with all its modern amenities, can serve as a place of almost self-sufficient retreat.

Mutual concern with children is what brings middle class people most readily together. In their book about the Canadian suburb of 'Crestwood Heights', Seeley and his co-authors argue that the major institutional focus of the community is on child-rearing. Interfamily social life is organised, mainly by mothers, around this central concern from the time when turns are taken to give children's tea parties, to when offspring depart for higher education. At this point the female parent often returns to work.

Despite the above contrasts, family and community life is more similar across the middle and working classes than, say, fifty years ago. Then, the majority of the working class was forced to live in rented accommodation. Now, the majority live in public housing and an increasing proportion own their own houses. Indeed, a majority of families in Britain now own their own homes. This fact, in combination with the movement out of the urban areas means that the suburban ideal cuts across class lines to a considerable extent. A house of their own out of town, is what most families seem to want and many have already achieved it. Add to this the even more general processes of family privatisation, consumerism and, more controversially, symmetrical gender role-playing already noted and a very real *convergence* in family life-style between, particularly, the lower middle and upper working class is apparent. Yet, as we shall see throughout the book, class and status differences still divide these groups and even more, those groups at the social extremes.

Stresses on Marriage and the Modern Family

The evidence that the modern family is under considerable stress is substantial, though whether things are now 'worse than they were' is, like all such generalisations, highly debatable. The rise in the divorce rate is the most striking indicator of family stress. It is important to note, however, that many thousands of broken marriages end in separation rather than divorce. The divorce figures, therefore, underestimate the extent of family and marriage break up. In 1961, 32,000 divorce petitions were filed and in 1984, 179,000. For every three to four marriages there was one divorce. Children were involved in the majority of divorce cases. A detailed picture of the *rate* of increase in divorce can be seen from the table below.

The Increase in the Divorce Rate* 1961–1983

1961	1971	1976	1979	1980	1981	1982	1983	1984
2.1	6.0	10.1	11.2	12.0	11.9	12.1	12.2	12.0

*The divorce rate is the rate of divorces per thousand of the married population.
Source: *Social Trends*, 1986.

Indicators in respect of child welfare also suggest that the family is not fully coping. In 1976, the number of children in local authority care passed 100,000 and has since remained at about this figure. It has frequently been shown that the majority of boys in care develop antisocial behaviour patterns but it was thought that girls were damaged less. Recent research suggests, however, that girls in care are also often profoundly disadvantaged. In 1979 'the year of the child,' the number of 'latch-key' children was declared by a concerned charity to be at a record figure – well in excess of 600,000. Whoever is to 'blame' for this, the many thousands of unsupervised children in the five to fourteen age-group involved in road accidents gives pause for thought on the matter. It is now apparent that child abuse is a major problem. The matter received wide publicity in both Britain and the United States in 1985 when a series of severe cases of violent or sexual abuse were reported (see pp. 360–3). It remains to be seen whether this concern will lead to effective action. A still more emotional issue is that of abortion. Opinions vary from the view that it is a murderous way to escape from parental responsibility to the conviction that only a woman has 'the right to choose' whether or not to have a child. The 1967 Abortion Act made abortion on the National Health easier to obtain. As a result legal abortions went up from 50,000 in 1969 to 111,000 in 1973. The total dropped slowly to 103,000 in 1977 and rose again to 112,000 in 1978. The rise continues and in 1984 the number of legal abortions was 146,000. Moral dilemma and personal agonising characterise many cases behind these hard figures. Finally, the steady increase in juvenile delinquency since the War and the more recent steep increase in heavy drinking among the young is considered by some to be partly related to the breakdown of family authority. Others, however, would see these factors as symptoms of a much wider crisis of social values and norms.

Is it possible that there is an underlying crisis in the family which explains the above, admittedly mixed, though generally depressing, collection of facts? We will start answering this question by examining the causes and some consequences of divorce.

Divorce: Reasons for and Implications of the Increase

a CHANGES IN CULTURAL ATTITUDES Changes in cultural attitudes towards marriage have created a climate of public opinion in which it has been possible to pass laws which have made it increasingly easy to opt out of marriage. The long-term background to the erosion of marriage as a permanent and binding commitment is the decline in formal religious belief. Marriage is less often seen as a sacred, spiritual union, but more as a personal and practical commitment which can be abandoned if it fails. This attitude to marriage has resulted in a series of changes in the law, making the grounds for divorce less strict and the administrative procedure for obtaining it less complicated and time-consuming (in 1977 it became possible to get divorced by post in some circumstances). The Divorce Law Reform Act of 1969 (actually implemented in 1971) established that it was enough merely to prove 'irretrievable breakdown of marriage' to obtain a divorce. The 'irretrievable breakdown of marriage' was made the sole cause for it. The phrase is general enough to be interpreted to include virtually all conceivable reasons for divorce. Although there was an increase in the divorce rate following the Act, it would be crude to think of the Act as 'causing' this increase. Deeper reasons for it must be sought in the broader cultural factors mentioned above. Viewed in longer perspective, the statistical trend is that of a gradual increase in divorce with occasional sharp jumps when enabling legislation was passed. In addition to the 1969 Act, another such instance was the 1949 Legal Aid Act which enabled women seeking divorce to obtain financial assistance in doing so.

As well as the decline of religion, another cultural factor that explains the fragility of modern marriage is the rise of individualistic and romantic values that have replaced the traditional values referred to in the previous paragraph. The question of romantic marriage must be seen against the background of a steady decline in family and community control of choice of partner, courtship and marriage. Traditionally, couples married (or had their marriages arranged) for down-to-earth material reasons such as, to take a middle class example, joining two family estates or businesses together. Courtship was supervised closely, if more or less informally, within the community. For a period of about two hundred years, however, people have been increasingly marrying whom they want rather than whom they are told to. As Edward Shorter points out, the danger in marrying for mainly romantic reasons is that when romantic love and attraction disappear, so, too, might marriage.

A further factor to consider in relation to our own time is the sexual revolution of the post-Second World War period. The pill provided a safe opportunity to have sexual relations with more than one person after marriage as well as before it. However much most people say they disapprove of such behaviour, more and more seem to be indulging in it (though needless to say reliable statistics are not available on so personal and sensitive a matter).

Edward Shorter suggests that the underlying factor which ultimately explains why so many marriages now end up in the divorce courts is the nature of capitalist industrial society itself. Capitalism broke up traditional communities and set their populations 'free', in the limited sense that they could come to towns and compete for work. But they were free also from traditional family and community control, freer in personal and sexual relations with whom they wished. In the long-term, this freedom evolved into the virtual right to choose and, within ever more generous limits, get rid of one's spouse. Of course, there is a price to pay for this freedom, particularly in terms of anguish and, frequently, material deprivation to children of broken families. There is, however, evidence from several sources that children with divorced parents show fewer signs of mental stress and delinquent behaviour and have a better adjustment to their parents than children from intact but unhappy homes. It seems that keeping an 'empty shell' marriage together 'for the children's sake' can backfire. The wide belief that divorce is 'bad for' children cannot, then, be simplistically accepted.

b PROBLEMS OF INTER-PERSONAL COMMUNICATION A cluster of other factors – most of which are fairly self-evident – correlate with divorce. Partners who are dissimilar in culture, social background, or religion, or who are of very different age are more prone to divorce, as are those who marry young and may still be developing personally and emotionally. Barbara Thomas and Jean Collard in a recent publication, *Who Divorces*, suggest that for these and other divorced couples a common underlying problem is often poor inter-personal communication. Consistent with Willmott and Young, they note that the small conjugal family has increasingly become the principal and, sometimes, sole source of deep emotional expression, and that this can put a strain on the marriages of those who have communication problems.

C THE CHANGING STATUS OF WOMEN Some observers associate the increase in divorce with the changing status of women. The female share of divorce petitions has generally outnumbered that of men in both Britain and the United States, and recently there has been a striking increase. In Britain the female share was about seventy per cent in the late nineteen seventies. It may be that, as more women have entered the labour market, they have acquired the necessary economic independence to opt out of an unsatisfactory marriage if they choose to do so. Further, going to work also enables them to meet more prospective partners than if they remained full-time housewives. Interestingly, according to the U.S. Bureau of Census Report (1972), better-paid female divorcees are more likely to delay remarriage or remain single than are low-paid ones. Whether women will be able to maintain their limited gains in the contracting labour market of the early eighties remains to be seen.

FAMILY AUTHORITY Among the mixture of facts used to illustrate the supposed decline in parental authority within the modern family, the increase in juvenile delinquency is often mentioned. Specifically, the charge made is that the family is failing to act as an effective agency of social control. This accusation however, could equally be made against the schools and police. The causes of juvenile delinquency must, therefore, be sought in the wider society rather than in the failure of any single institution such as the family. This we do in Chapter 17. Here, it need only be said that the more permissive and democratic ideals of the post-war period reduce the credibility of physical punishment as a means of maintaining control both within the family and within society. Reason may often be preferred to force as a matter of principle and humanity, but it is an instrument that takes time and patience and, unfortunately, is no more guaranteed to succeed than cruder methods of control. Similarly, there are no easy solutions to the problems of children that arise because their parents divorce or because both work. Socialists want more state aid for the family so that, in particular, women can go to work in peace. Conservatives generally would like to see families (and particularly mothers) resume what they feel to be their traditional responsibilities to children more fully.

ABORTION The abortion issue highlights the extent to which matters relating to the family and especially the role of women within it are politically, socially and morally sensitive. On the day these lines are being written, massive demonstrations and counter-demonstrations for and against a bill to curb the availability of abortion, as laid down in the 1967 Act, are taking place in London. Some see the bill as a first step in an attempt to restore traditional family stability and responsibility. Others consider that, to the extent that it forces women to have children they do not want, it will have the opposite effect. For the modern world, moral disagreement and confusion characterise matters relating to the family as they do so much else.

THE DYNAMICS OF FAMILY VIOLENCE: RADICAL PSYCHIATRY One of the cult figures of the nineteen sixties was radical psychiatrist, Ronald Laing. His analysis of the family illustrates aspects of the phenomenological perspective. His primary concern is with the 'self' but he does not separate the life of the self from that of others. For him 'madness' is not a personal deficiency but must be interpreted as a way of making sense of experience. Thus, he spoke of schizophrenic families rather than schizophrenic individuals – if the self is forced into fantasy escape it is because there is something to escape from. Although Laing's primary focus of analysis is the micro level of group interaction, the tension and psychological 'violence' he sees in family life persuaded him to look at the wider world:

> Concerned as I am with this inner world, observing day to day its devastation, I ask why this has happened.

If he finds an answer to this question it is that the violence of the outside world – the Vietnam war was particularly in his mind – fuses with and reinforces the potential for violence within us. Corpses on a dead television screen are unreal, but slowly we learn not to care about them or each other, or the human consequences of what we do. The family cannot cope with all this or give it meaning. He suggests that for some, personal madness is a retreat from 'madness out there.' This recalls the pained cry of poet Allen Ginsberg: 'I have seen the best minds of my generation driven mad.'

David Cooper, a colleague of Laing's, goes beyond the latter in taking explicitly political attitudes. His approach owes much to Marx, but, unlike him, Cooper wants to abolish the family itself – at least, as a hard and fast biological unit. Cooper's basic criticism of the family in bourgeois society is the peculiarly limiting and constraining role it plays:

> The child, in fact, is taught primarily not how to survive in society but how to submit to it. Surface rituals like etiquette, organised games, mechanical learning operations at school replace deep experiences of spontaneous creativity, inventive play, freely developing fantasies and dream.

That, perhaps, is the nub of Cooper and Laing. They want a freer, less repressive society – always provided that what is freely expressed is love rather than selfishness or hate. Cooper's belief that spontaneous, 'wanted' relationships should take preference over biological and legal bonds is what leads him to attack the traditional family.

In retrospect, Laing and Cooper's contributions have been less in the directly social and political dimension of their work than in nudging their sizeable audience, particularly among young, educated adults, further in the direction of experimental permissiveness in relationships, not only with children, but with each other. To that extent they are not entirely out of tune with the genial liberal advisor on childrearing of the fifties, Dr Spock – although they might regard that comment as an attempt to bury rather than praise them.

Another commentator on the family, anthropologist Edmund Leach, seems to capture the essence of the above criticisms of the family in his own description of it as 'a prison.' Although Leach intends the analogy to be derogatory there is a sense in which the family must inevitably constrain the individual. Society itself is also sometimes compared to a prison and for the same reason: it limits total freedom. If functionalists accept the need for social control too uncritically perhaps the radical psychiatrists underestimate the potentially dangerous as well as positive effects of its absence.

IS THE FAMILY BREAKING UP OR MERELY CHANGING? We have examined impressive evidence of stress on the family. This does not mean that the family is breaking up, or to use David Cooper's more dramatic word, 'dying.' Marriage remains highly popular. Well over ninety per cent of the population gets married. Moreover, the remarriage rates of divorcees are high, both in Britain and the United States, where three quarters of divorced women and five sixths of divorced men remarry. At current remarriage rates in Britain, nearly one in five born around 1950 will have been married twice by the time they are fifty. True, statistics from Britain, the USA, and Sweden show that young people are living together for more lengthy periods than previously, but most established couples do eventually get married. So stress on the family does not result in either marriage or the family being unpopular – they are not.

When people divorce they are giving up a particular partner, not the idea of marriage. In any case the majority of the population still does not get divorced but remains committed, more or less happily, to one partner for life. If present trends continue, however, a large minority will experience a different marital pattern from the traditional one. This pattern has been called *serial monogamy*. This means having more than one spouse, but at different times. Less frequently, individuals have more than one family.

The above change can give little obvious comfort to those who favour the extended family type structures. The modern family is typically small and second families especially so. No satisfactory general alternative to the nuclear family seems to exist. The nature of modern society works against extended family structures – attractive though these may be in principle. A less mobile, more localised society would no doubt produce a family system woven into kin and community but, for the moment, that is not the kind of society we have. Nevertheless, the minority pattern (serial monogamy) just described does not seem an especially functional social adaptation. Rather, it represents what a large number of people seem to want or, at least, accept as sometimes necessary regardless of considerable inconvenience. A United Kingdom survey in 1977 found that as many as sixty per cent of young people considered that divorce was something that might happen to them. So a recognition of the potential impermanence of marriage and even family commitment is now part of our cultural outlook.

If marriage and the family remain very much alive, the radical criticisms of them nevertheless deserve to be taken seriously. Edmund Leach has drawn attention to the often huge gap between the ideals of family and marriage and reality. In particular, women are often sold misleading images of romance and motherhood through the media, and suffer much when hard truth dawns. It may even be that the ideal of exclusive love of one person for life is selfish, restricting and, in the modern world, unlikely to be achieved. Of course, insecurity and emotional emptiness in relationships are no replacement for personal romance and love. An alternative might lie in less possessive and wider relationships of the kind communal movements aspire to but find so difficult to attain. Here, however, we have left sociology for moral speculation.

Conclusion

In fact, there are more one-parent families in mid-nineteen eighties Britain than extended families or communes. In 1983 about one in six families were of this type. Divorce forces many – mainly women – to live, for a time at least, as single parents. The steep increase in the percentage of non-marital births from 6% (1961) to 17% (1984) has also swelled the number of one-parent families. As its title suggests, Ellis Cashmore's *Having To: The World of One-Parent Families* is about those who were coerced by circumstances into single parenthood – often battered wives. Frequently, these families cope successfully against the odds and there is no evidence that the children are damaged as a result of being brought up by one parent (although how they will fare as teenagers remains to be seen). Jean Renvoize's *Going Solo: Single Mothers by Choice* deals with a very different group of single parents: mostly middle class who can afford the family style of their choice. They want children and believe they can rear them as effectively as two parents. Again, so far they have not been proved wrong. Further, some women feel that the well-established (though difficult to quantify) risk of male violence to wives and children is best avoided. Generally, one-parent families function more effectively if the single parent is comfortably off or if some external support system exists. For instance, one-parent families headed by women of Afro-Caribbean extraction often get support from female relatives – usually their mothers – and as a result some are able to do paid work. In Sweden and the Soviet Union adequate national nursery systems meet the same need. In a review of the above books, Margaret Foster suggests that if the one-parent family 'trend continues, the fabric of our society is already radically altered . . . a new script is being written for the family. It is not a bit of good blaming feminism or anything else. If men want to alter this script they had better be quick'.

Is the trend, then, marital and family change or continuity? Conservative critics, such as Ferdinand Mount, tend to stress continuity, particularly the continuing appeal of privacy and independence *together* rather than individually. Initially, radicals such as Leach and Laing, and more recently feminists, have lifted the nuclear family's veil and found much worthy of change or rejection. No doubt, Robert Chester's comment indicates the truth in both perspectives:

> Altogether it is clear that there have been many changes in family behaviour in Britain. . . . But there is a strong framework of continuity.

The personal point, though, is perhaps to choose what is right for you.

Guide to Further Reading and Study

Adrian Wilson's *Family* (Tavistock, 1985) is a clear introduction to the topic. It covers the main issues and is aimed specifically at 'A' level students. Somewhat more demanding is Mary Farmer's *The Family* (Longman, 1979) – this includes a useful series of chapters taking a life-cycle approach. C. C. Harris, *The Family and Industrial Society* (George Allen and Unwin, 1983) is a concise summary of much research on the topic (including Laslett's) and is an excellent teacher's crib. Ronald Fletcher's *The Family and Marriage* (Penguin, 1973) gives a functionalist analysis of the family which substantially departs from that of Talcott Parsons. Ferdinand Mount's *The Subversive Family: An Alternative History of Love and Marriage* (Counterpoint, 1982) is a similarly robust defence of the family. More critical accounts of the family are E. R. Leach *A Runaway World?* (BBC Publications, 1967) and R. D. Laing and A. Esterson *Sanity, Madness and the Family* (Penguin, 1970). A useful Marxist perspective on the family is Sidney Peiris's 'The Family – a Marxist View' in R. Meighan *ed, Perspectives on Society* (Nelson, 1979). Eli Zaretsky's brief book *Capitalism, the Family, and Personal*

Life (Pluto, 1976) blends Marxist and feminist analysis and is worth the effort it takes to read. A similar perspective is taken in Rosalind Delmar, 'Looking Again at Engels' "Origin of the Family, Private Property and the State" ' in Juliet Mitchell and Ann Oakley *eds*, *The Rights and Wrongs of Women* (Penguin, 1976). The recommended readings sections at the end of Chapters 12 and 22 contain feminist references relevant to the family. Michael Young and Peter Willmott's three books on the family are useful for their methodological appendices, as well as their contents: *Family and Kinship in East London* (Penguin, 1962); *Family and Class in a London Suburb* (Mentor, 1967), and *The Symmetrical Family* (Penguin, 1975).

Past Questions

1 'The picture of the family as functional both for its members and for society has come under strong criticism'. Outline the functionalist analysis of the family and discuss major criticisms of this analysis. (AEB, 1982)

2 Examine the major causes and social consequences of the increasing frequency of divorce. (OLE, 1983)

3 'The phrase "the typical British family" is stereo-typical and is misleading.' (a) Why is this so? (13 marks). (b) What are the consequences of the use of this stereotype? (12 marks). (AEB, 1984)

4 'The argument that families change from "extended" to "nuclear" in the process of industrialisation is inadequate because it assumes that all families move towards the same structure and roles, regardless of such factors as class and ethnicity.' Discuss and illustrate. (London, 1985)

5 In what ways have feminist writers challenged earlier sociological accounts of the family? (AEB, 1985)

(See also Chapter 22, pp. 665–8)

5 Education

The Relationship of the Educational System to Society

This chapter and the next should have personal relevance to all students who read them. The educational system claims a large portion of your life – a minimum of eleven years and probably thirteen or more, given that you are reading this book. It is certainly worth knowing what the educational system is 'doing' to you.

A major issue in the sociology of education is that of equality, particularly why working class children *generally* attain less (in terms of examinations) than middle class children of similar measured intelligence. For instance, J. W. Douglas compared the attainment level of high ability students from different social backgrounds and found that success at 'O' level was directly and very strongly correlated with class: 77% of upper middle, 60% of lower middle, 53% of upper working and 37% of lower working class were successful. He found the difference between intelligence and attainment was even greater among pupils of less measured intelligence from a similar wide range of social backgrounds. Social class, then, makes a substantial contribution to academic attainment. A number of sociologists, including the American, Jencks, have raised another important question of educational inequality. They argue that even when children of different social backgrounds do achieve similar levels of attainment, their life-chances, in terms of careers and acquiring wealth, are not equalised as a result: higher classes still do better.

Both functionalists and Marxists agree that education socialises people 'into' society by formal and informal processes. Because Marxists are opposed to capitalist society, however, they are highly critical of the ways in which young people are socialised to conform to it. Functionalists tend to take conformity for granted as normal. A third perspective occurs within educational sociology. It is a distinctly liberal one and reflects the reforming political orientation (inclination) which, as we noted in Chapter 1, characterises some sociologists. Liberal sociologists take their stand on the principle that everybody should have equal educational opportunity, even though they accept that fair competition will still result in inequality in examination results, and in career opportunities and rewards. Nonetheless, they want equality at the starting line, not at the finishing tape. The attempt to achieve the limited goal of equal opportunity has involved much political campaigning and legal change. The abolition of the 11+ examination in many areas owed something to the analyses and efforts of liberal sociologists. Both Marxists and liberals see the source of inequality of educational opportunity in socio-economic background differences, but liberals tend to be much more optimistic that this inequality can be reduced by reform at the educational level itself, whereas Marxists argue that real change in the educational system requires a much more fundamental change in the structure of society. Thus, if there were more equality of income and if workers had more control of the places they work in, they would be able to afford to keep their children at school longer and also pass on greater confidence and experience to them.

The above perspectives should be regarded as 'ideal-type' descriptions rather than labels: reality is usually more complex than any description of it. Sociologists do not like being neatly labelled, any more than anyone else does. For instance, many functionalists take a liberal attitude to educational reform. Similarly, some Marxists carefully support certain educational reforms, even though these do not go as far as they might like. There are, also, other strands in the sociology of education as important as the ones so far mentioned. These include the interactionist perspective, and a growing body of work on the curriculum (school courses) itself. We return to these later.

1 Education, Socialisation and Cultural Reproduction:

Durkheim and Marx

Both Durkheim and Marx fully understood that in order to survive, societies need to socialise their young to accept dominant norms and values. If the existing culture is not passed on, it must die. The contemporary French Marxist, Pierre Bourdieu, has stressed the same point in referring to the need of capitalist society to 'culturally reproduce' itself. Reflecting the realities of his time, Marx himself concentrated relatively more on the role of religion in reinforcing cultural conformity whereas present day Marxists see a greater role for education. Interestingly, some of the major contemporary contributions to the sociology of education owe substantial debts to both Marx and Durkheim: this is particularly true of Althusser and Bourdieu.

We begin with Durkheim partly because of the importance and detail of his work in this area and partly because of his continuing influence. The following quotation illustrates how great he considered the power of education over the individual to be:

> . . . each society, considered at a given stage of development, has a system of education which exercises an influence upon individuals which is usually irresistible.

Although Durkheim considered that the individual can hardly resist the effect of the educational system, his own historical studies of educational systems show that he also regarded the educational system itself as open to wider social influences. Basically, it must pass on society's values. For example, he argued that the competitive examination system came about precisely because modern society is itself individualistic and competitive. He contended that such a system would have been positively dysfunctional (disruptive) in the middle ages, when people generally inherited their social status. For the aristocracy to have to compete with others to maintain their social position would have risked overthrowing the whole social order so such an idea was not entertained.

We need to give more practical illustration of what Durkheim meant by the role of the educational system in producing conformity. Most obviously, teachers 'tell' pupils formally what to do. Formal socialisation can cover a great deal, such as telling pupils how to eat, dress and speak, as well as what values they should hold. Durkheim particularly emphasised the role of ritual in forming patterns of behaviour and in reinforcing values. Thus, school assemblies might involve rituals in which national patriotism is expressed and strengthened. He was also aware of the less obvious or 'unconscious' ways in which pupils are socialised. For example, schools are very hierarchical institutions (power is concentrated in the hands of a few people), and it is precisely because hierarchy is assumed to be beyond question that children come to accept it as inevitable. They learn that some people, such as headmasters, can command more respect, politeness and obedience than others and, as a result, they are prepared to accept the same situation in society generally.

Althusser, Bourdieu and Bernstein

The Marxist structuralists, Althusser and Bourdieu, have absorbed much of Durkheim's approach to analysing education, as well as that of Marx. It is worth explaining briefly how this dual influence has come about. Durkheim was, of course, French. His influence was passed on to Althusser and Bourdieu partly through a philosopher called Lévi-Strauss, the founder of a school of thought known as *structuralism*. An important aspect of structuralism is that by *unconsciously* (without conscious awareness) learning ways and structures of thought, feeling and behaviour, people 'automatically' carry on the culture into which they have been born. Really, this is to say little more than that people are socialised to conform, except that it emphasises the extent to which this process occurs unconsciously. Now, the socialisation of the unconscious mind has been stressed by Durkheim and, via Lévi-Strauss, it surfaces again in the work of Althusser and Bourdieu. It is to their work that we now turn.

It must be remembered that although Althusser and Bourdieu reflect the influence of their compatriots, Durkheim and Lévi-Strauss, they are also Marxists. Marx's thought, therefore, figures prominently in their writings. Following him, Althusser considers that the functioning of the educational system is largely determined by the needs of the capitalist socio-economic system. As far as the working class is concerned, this means that it must also be socialised to accept its position in the class system and the kind of work it has to do. It is the second of these points which we concentrate on in this section – we examine the first in detail shortly. What must be grasped is that, to Althusser, the educational system serves the needs of capitalism. Bourdieu has made a specialist study of education in capitalist society and, particularly, in France. It is in his writings that we see most clearly the convergence (coming together) of certain concepts of Marx and Durkheim.

Whereas Durkheim emphasised that certain aspects of a common culture (for example, patriotism) are passed on to all members of a society, Bourdieu concentrates on how middle and working class cultures are reproduced. He analyses particularly the role of the educational system in this process. Like Althusser, he argues that schools are middle class institutions, run by middle class people (teachers), in which, in general, middle class pupils succeed. Working class culture does not fit well into the demands of such an educational system. In support of his case, he is able to point to substantial empirical evidence to show that both in the United States and the Western European countries, middle class children tend to achieve better qualifications and to get better jobs than working class children of equal measured intelligence. He explains this further by use of the term *cultural capital*. He argues that because the educational system is middle class, middle class children come into it better equipped to do well. Their values, attitudes and behaviour correspond more closely with teachers' expectations and the demands of the examination system than those of working class children who, in that sense, suffer a cultural deficit (see Chapter 3, pp. 49–52 for a general view of class cultural differences). This observation does not mean that Bourdieu has a low opinion of working class culture, but that he regards it as largely non-academic. For instance, a working class novelist is a contradiction in terms because any such person who writes a novel employs middle class patterns of thought and expression and therefore starts to become middle class.

The work of Basil Bernstein on class culture is highly complementary to that of Bourdieu. Bernstein is particularly noted for his contribution to the analysis of the relationship between class and language. He has suggested that working class children speak in what he calls a *restricted code* and middle class children in an *elaborated code*. This means that the former tend to talk about particular cases or examples whereas the latter express themselves more conceptually and are more inclined to make abstract generalisations. Thus, a working class child will understand from concrete experience what it means to be 'diddled' or 'done' by paying too high a price in a shop or supermarket, but he will be less prepared than the middle class child to understand and talk about, say, the concept of the inequalities of the capitalist system. According to Bernstein, this is not just a matter of unfamiliarity with the relevant vocabulary – although this must play a part – but it is due, more fundamentally, to lack of practised competence in elaborated (or conceptual) codes of thought.

Bernstein's hypothesis has been criticised by the American sociologist, William Labov, amongst others. Labov interviewed a number of black working class children and found that, once they felt confident and at ease with him, they were perfectly capable of expressing themselves in abstract conceptual terms, albeit in dialect rather than standard English. Interestingly, from the point of view of the effect of research method on findings, Labov stresses the importance of establishing an interview situation in which the subjects can behave normally. He suggests that formal interviews can sometimes have the opposite effect and produce misleading data. In defence of Bernstein, it still remains quite possible that middle class children have more practice in conceptual thought and expression. Further, to take Labov's point at face value, differences of dialect, whether based on race or class, would tend to disfavour working class children and to favour middle class children in communicating with middle class teachers. Both points are acceptable within Bourdieu's broad capital-deficit model of cultural reproduction. He himself relates his scheme to the whole range of cultural expression: it is not just the language and modes of thought but also the style and manners, sentiments and forms of emotional expression of teachers that accord better with those of middle class children. For example, behaviour that seems 'nice and well-mannered' to a middle class child may seem 'posh and snotty' to a working class child. Neither view is more correct than the other, but the former provides a more stable basis for a productive school relationship than the latter.

Bourdieu regards the examination system primarily as a formal and ritual ('ceremonial') occasion, of which the already reproduced cultural ascendancy of the middle class child is ratified and *legitimised* (made to seem generally just and acceptable). The 'success' of middle class children and the 'failure' of working class children is certified. The examination system is not a fair competition although it *seems* to be as there is a surface appearance of neutrality. Because it is accepted as fair by the middle and working class alike, it serves to legitimise (justify) what Bourdieu regards as the fundamentally unequal process of cultural reproduction. As a result, the middle class is generally considered to have earned its superior rewards and status and the working class, likewise, to have gained its deserts. Bourdieu sums up the means by which this 'illusion' is achieved in the term *symbolic violence*. It is a powerful phrase and it means that the middle class cultural ascendancy and privilege is conserved and reproduced not by physical force but by a commanding superiority in the field of communication – particularly language. Thus, expertise in manipulating cultural symbols and forms such as literature, art and logic in a way acceptable to the middle class is a weapon in the class struggle, whether consciously used as such or not. Untrained and inexperienced in this skill, working class children are often overawed and 'mystified' by it. The almost physical sense of injury and loss undoubtedly suffered by many working class 'failures' perhaps justifies Bourdieu's savage metaphor of symbolic violence. At any rate, to him, it provides the answer to the question of how working class people are ideologically persuaded to fit into their often boring and relatively unrewarding roles.

Bourdieu has been criticised both by more orthodox Marxists and by liberals. Of the former, Raymond Boudon argues that Bourdieu overstresses the cultural or, as he calls them, the primary effects of stratification to the point of virtually ignoring the secondary, or material and practical, effects. Boudon considers the secondary effects more important. These affect older working class pupils, who may find that they simply do not have enough money to stay on at school, or who may leave school just because their friends do. Boudon gets qualified support from the British sociologist, A. H. Halsey, whose refutation of Bordieu we turn to shortly.

Bourdieu and his colleague, Althusser, are also sometimes accused of a mechanical or deterministic view of cultural reproduction. Bourdieu, in particular, is arraigned as a 'cultural determinist.' (This is not a simple issue and the student need not worry if he or she fails to understand it here. We return to it in Chapters 20 and 21). Basically, the charge of determinism means that Bourdieu is thought to believe that class culture is inevitably passed on from generation to generation, changing only in response to deeper developments in the economic substructure (or base) of society. Thus, he would recognise that changes in economic production, such as wide scale automation, might affect the way of life and the educational training of working people but, or so the accusation goes, he would not allow the possibility that working class people could change their own social position or cultural awareness outside the framework of such technological and socio-economic development. This charge seems broadly to be valid, although in defence of Bourdieu, he does allow that the educational system (and the cultural system generally) can operate in a 'relatively autonomous' (free) way. In other words, teachers, artists and other intellectuals and creative people have some freedom of thought and action. Bourdieu makes two major qualifications of this, however. First, such 'autonomy' does not ultimately change the class system; indeed, it may even provide a safety valve for it. Second, teachers and artists, like other people, are in any case socialised 'into' the class system and, consequently, most unlikely to think beyond it. Such freedom as exists is, therefore, very limited for most individuals. Althusser's position is similar to that of Bourdieu, although he uses different terminology to present it. We return to him in a later chapter (Chapter 20).

How Working Class Kids Get Working Class Jobs: An Observational Study

Paul Willis' book is entitled *Learning to Labour*, but its real concern is manifested in its sub-title: *How working class kids get working class jobs*. Willis describes a harsh collision between the tough working class 'lads' who are the subject of his study and the highly middle class world of the educational system. The 'lads' seldom even begin to struggle for examination success which not only requires a kind of mental discipline foreign to their experience but is unlikely to be of much use in the kind of manual jobs most of them expect to get. The lads tend to find the conformist behaviour of the 'lobes', as they call more hard-working pupils, a matter for mockery and amusement.

The school experience of the lads fails significantly to alter the course of their lives. Schools are middle class institutions in that they are run by middle class people (teachers) and because success in them requires conformity to middle class values, such as academic commitment, and middle class goals, such as a career. Comparing the lads to the lobes, Spansky, one of the lads, says:

> I mean, what will they remember of their school life? What will they have to look back on? Sitting in a classroom, sweating their bollocks off, you know, while we've been . . . I mean look at the things we can look back on, fighting on the Pakis, fighting on the JA's (Jamaicans). Some of the things we've done on teachers, it'll be a laff when we look back on it.

School seems to be good for a 'laff' and not much else. Judging by the following reactions of the lads to a lecture on the need for discipline at school and work, they obviously see little connection between school and the type of work they will do.

> *Spansky*: He makes the same points all the time, Fuzz. He's always on about if you get a job, you've got to do this, you've got to do that. I've done it. You don't have to do none of that. Just go to a place, ask for a man in charge, nothing like what he says.
> *Joey*: It's ridiculous . . .

Paul Willis notes that in later years, some of the 'lads' do come to regret their failure to realise that education did offer a possible escape from life as a manual labourer. But to what extent does the school system give the 'lads' a fair chance? Basically, Willis sympathises with their spirited rejection of the label of 'failures'. He appreciates, far more than Bourdieu seems to, that, in terms of their own class position, their way of life makes sense. It does so because most of them will, in fact, remain working class.

A. H. Halsey's Critique of the Theory of Cultural Reproduction

A. H. Halsey is one of the leading post-war British sociologists. His recent work draws heavily on a survey study of social change in Britain between 1913 and 1972, known as the Oxford Mobility Study. The original sample was of 10,000 men between the ages of 20 and 64.

Before describing the points on which Halsey differs from Bourdieu, it is important to be clear on their fundamental points of agreement. They are at one in stressing and lamenting the fact that many working class children do not reach anything approaching their full educational potential and, therefore, get jobs below their capacity. Both want to change this situation, although they have different views about how this might be done (see next chapter).

A substantial and important point of emphasis, rather than a total disagreement, divides Halsey and Bourdieu. To explain this, we need first to introduce the difference between material and cultural factors affecting educational attainment. Material factors are physical and environmental, such as the standard of housing, clothes and food. Virtually, they amount to 'the things money can buy.' Cultural factors refer to less tangible matters of values, norms and attitudes. We have already seen that Bourdieu argues that it is the possession of 'cultural capital' which accounts for the educational success of middle class children; school merely plays a part, albeit an important one, in the reproduction of cultural advantage. In his major work, *Origins and Destinations*, with A. F. Heath and J. M. Ridge (1980), Halsey tends to emphasise material rather than cultural factors in explaining class differences in educational attainment. He makes a number of points. Firstly, drawing on data from the Oxford study, he shows that there has been a substantial and progressive tendency for children to improve on the formal educational attainment of previous generations, and that even in state selective schools (mainly grammar schools selecting at 11), the 'overwhelming feature' was that the majority of pupils came from social backgrounds in which neither parent had an education of grammar school quality. Clearly, therefore, these first generation 'selected-school' pupils could not have inherited their cultural advantage from parents who did not have it to pass on.

A second point in Halsey's case is his critique of Jackson and Marsden's *Education and the Working Class,* a piece of research that seems to support Bourdieu's thesis. Out of a sample of 88 working class boys who went to grammar school, Jackson and Marsden found that a much higher number (34) than would have been expected purely on the basis of chance, came from 'sunken' middle class backgrounds. By 'sunken' middle class, they mean working class families with middle class relatives or families whose head had previously owned a small business. Halsey's data, however, forces him to work with a slightly different definition of sunken middle class; even so, his findings lead in the opposite direction from Jackson and Marsden's. His evidence is that the relative chances of obtaining selective education declined for those from educated backgrounds, and that this was true of the sunken middle class as well as others. The group of middle class children that *did* benefit disproportionately from selective education did not have selectively educated parents, and so could not have inherited cultural capital in this way. Finally, although Halsey fully accepts that working class children are educationally disadvantaged, he makes much of the fact that those who did get places at grammar school *and* survived there to take 'O' levels did almost as well as children from middle class backgrounds. The problem, of course, as Halsey recognises, is that relatively few working class children got into grammar schools in the first place.

Although Halsey emphasises material rather than cultural factors in explaining the educational under-attainment of working class children, he is not conclusive on the issue. Indeed, he has to concede that class cultural, as well as material factors, may account for the fact that, under the tripartite system, a much higher proportion of middle class children sat 'O' levels. Disadvantage took effect particularly at the 11+ examination which prevented a large number of able working class children, as well as 'border-line' children from all classes, from obtaining an academic education.

Halsey is aware of the need to take into consideration the change in the secondary system from tripartite to comprehensive in explaining the relatively low attainment of working class children. In doing this, he uses the terminology of Raymond Boudon, who categorises the educational effects of class stratification into the primary and the secondary. As interpreted by Halsey and applied to British education, primary effects are cultural and material differences that hamper educational success in early schooling, and secondary effects are those that govern performance at secondary school level. Halsey suggests that, under the tripartite system, primary effects probably predominated, but that with the widespread abolition of the 11+ examination and the introduction of comprehensive education, secondary effects may be more potent. Their operation could well prevent the improvement in educational opportunity and attainment of working class children that comprehensivisation was widely expected to bring about (see next chapter).

Halsey stresses that class is 'a major' factor affecting educational attainment, but he avoids sweeping generalisation in favour of closely reasoned argument supported by detailed evidence. The following quotation, taken from one of his reviews, perhaps reveals his complex spirit:

> Life, including the life of the . . . examination room, is understood better by gamblers than by mechanistic theoreticians. The dice are loaded – by class, by sex, by date of birth and even, perhaps . . . by genes. Among these, the force of class is a major one: it affects deeply the structure of opportunity. The force of stratification is still wider and deeper. But neither make it possible to deduce automatically the fate of particular individuals.

2 Education, The Economy and the Preparation of a Labour Force

The preparation of a labour force requires not only the teaching of specific skills, such as the three 'R's,' typing or computing, but also the more general socialisation of individuals to accept the discipline of work and, to some extent, their own likely place within the occupational structure. We will begin this section by presenting a functionalist perspective on these points, and then introduce Marxist and liberal refutations.

Functionalism, Occupational Selection and Social Mobility
Talcott Parsons gives a highly functionalist description of how he considers the educational system operates in relation to the

occupational structure. He suggests that elementary (primary) schools sort out pupils according to their general level of ability (capacity), that secondary schools establish the more specific abilities and, accordingly, direct some to work and others on to further education:

> Very broadly we may say that the elementary school phase is concerned with the internalisation in children of motivation to achievement. The focus is on the *level* of capacity . . .
>
> In approaching the question of the types of capacity differentiated, it should be kept in mind that secondary school is the principal springboard from which lower-status persons will enter the labour force, whereas those achieving higher status will continue their formal education in college, and some of them beyond.

Parsons, then, believes that the educational system actually does what is generally claimed for it – that is, selects people according to their ability and qualifies them accordingly. He and other functionalists tend to assume that there is a rough correspondence between individual intelligence, individual attainment (a pupil's measured performance) at school, and the job he eventually gets. Parsons sees the allocation of occupational status on the basis of 'achievement' as strongly characteristic of modern capitalist societies and particularly of the United States. More traditional societies allocated people to occupations on the basis of 'ascription' (by birth). Ralph Turner also considers that genuine and intense competition operates in the American educational system through comprehensive high schools, and he calls the resulting social mobility (movement up and down the social scale) 'contest' mobility. By contrast, he regards mobility of talented lower class children in Britain as 'sponsored' – through the grammar school system. This distinction, made in the nineteen fifties, has been blurred as a result of comprehensivisation in England and Wales. In any case, Turner's argument is severely weakened by the fact that he failed adequately to consider that lower social class membership substantially hinders social mobility in both countries.

The Relationship between Functionalism and the Hereditary View of Intelligence

It is clear that the functionalist case rests on whether intelligence, academic attainment and occupational position do, in fact, correlate strongly with one another. In particular, if intelligence and occupational status do not correlate strongly, then the functionalist model is largely discredited and the possibility must be examined that other factors are more relevant in determining occupational status. The functionalist position has recently acquired support from the work of a number of psychologists on both sides of the Atlantic though, as these scholars are not sociologists, it would be misleading to think of them as functionalists when their work merely complements the functionalist position. In Britain, Hans Eysenck is the foremost of these and, in the United States, Arthur Jensen and Carl Bereiter have been prominent. Before briefly summarising their major points, something must be said about what is meant by intelligence. Intelligence refers to general cognitive ability, or the ability to reason, comprehend and make judgements. It is produced by heredity and environment. Psychologists do not agree on the precise relative importance of these two factors: some put the influence of heredity as low as 50%, whilst others put it at 80%, or even slightly higher.

As one might expect, those psychologists who consider that intelligence and occupational status strongly correlate, estimate the hereditary element of intelligence at the high end. The 'high-estimate' viewpoint received a blow when it was demonstrated that the methodology of Sir Cyril Burt, on whose work the hereditarian case partly rested, was unscientific. Nevertheless, the debate continues. The psychologists who stress heredity – we may call them 'the hereditarians' – explain the fact that the children of parents of high occupational status also tend to achieve similar status in terms of their relatively higher level of inherited intelligence. The same applies, in reverse, to people of low social origin. Of course, although the hereditarians argue that there is a strong link between the level of intelligence of parents and children, they accept that this correspondance is not complete. For the minority of less intelligent middle class children and more intelligent working class children, the possibility of downward or upward mobility, respectively, occurs by reason of the level of their intelligence. The hereditarians regard the fact that there is only a fairly small amount of long-range upward or downward mobility in either Britain or the United States as evidence for, not against, their argument. Like functionalists, the hereditarian psycholog-

ists consider that the educational system 'does its job.' It qualifies people according to their ability and directs them towards
appropriate occupations.

Marxism, Occupational Selection and Social Mobility

To date, the major refutation of the above argument comes
from the American Marxists, Herbert Bowles and Samuel Gintis. We will present their refutation first and then describe the
broader theoretical context of their position. On the basis of
detailed statistical analysis, Bowles and Gintis show that, in the
United States, the probability of obtaining economic success is
considerably greater for those born of parents of high socio-
economic status than for those of high intelligence. Put plainly,
socio-economic background is generally a much more significant
factor in obtaining economic success than is intelligence. They
show that a man born in the bottom decile (tenth) in terms of
socio-economic background has only 4.2% probability of being
in the top fifth of income distribution, whereas a person born
in the top decile in terms of socio-economic background has a
43.9% probability of being in the top fifth of income distribution as an adult. That this extreme inequality of outcome is
due to socio-economic background and not to the differential
distribution of intelligence is shown by a further sophisticated
statistical calculation. This calculation is hypothetical (rests on
supposition) and demonstrates how income *would* be distributed
on the basis of measured intelligence only. Because the general level
of measured intelligence is somewhat higher for those born into
higher socio-economic backgrounds, those born into the top
decile have, in this hypothetical model, a *marginally* better
chance of reaching the top fifth of income distribution than
those born into the bottom decile on the basis of 'the genetic
inheritance of I.Q.' (Bowles and Gintis). Those born in the
bottom decile would have an 18.7 probability of being in the
top fifth in income, and those born in the top decile a 21.4
probability on the basis of differences in intelligence alone.
These figures are so far from the actual patterns described
above that we have to agree with Bowles and Gintis' insis-
tence on the unimportance of I.Q. and the prime importance of
socio-economic background in explaining economic success. The
best hope for obtaining high income, then, is to be born into a
high socio-economic background. As Bowles and Gintis say suc-

cinctly: 'The power and privilege of the capitalist class are often inherited, but not through superior genes.'

Another American, Christopher Jencks, has also written with authority in this area. He sums up the matter effectively when he writes that although the heredity-environment argument is likely to rage indefinitely, the best evidence

> ... does not, however, suggest that variations in cognitive skill account for much of the inequality among American adults.
>
> There is nearly as much economic inequality among individuals with identical test scores as in the general population.

Jencks further points out that schools themselves cannot make an unequal and hierarchial society equal. For that to happen, income, wealth, cultural opportunity and status would have to be more equally distributed. This observation is obvious but nonetheless true.

It is a strength of Bowles and Gintis's case that they use their opponents' data on the relationship between heredity and intelligence. Other authorities also see this relationship as less strong than Jensen and Eysenck do and point out that not only does the relative level of educational attainment of a child vary over time but so do scores in intelligence tests. Indeed, it is actually possible to prepare successfully for intelligence tests, so they can hardly be regarded as neutral instruments of measurement. J. W. B. Douglas, whose work we refer to above, regards intelligence tests in this more sceptical light. He argues that scores achieved in them, as well as academic performance, are considerably influenced by social background.

A Reformer's Response to Marxists and Functionalists: A. H. Halsey

Halsey rejects what he sees as the pessimism of Marxists and the conservatism of many functionalists. Yet, in arguing that educational reform can facilitate upward mobility from the working class, he has to work hard with the facts produced by his own research and that of his colleagues. The data he presents in *Origins and Destinations* largely confirms the established view that in Britain, as in America, the offspring of the middle class have a very much greater chance of remaining middle class than the offspring of the working class have of becoming middle class, (over six times greater, depending on precisely how middle and working class are defined). What is more, this situation did not substantially change between 1913 and 1972. What *did* happen is that because of the expansion of the service sector and the contraction of the industrial sector of the economy, more middle class jobs became available. All classes benefited, but the working class did *not* do so any more than others. Indeed, in the years following the immediate post-Second World War period, it did relatively less well.

In the face of such evidence, Halsey is determinedly hopeful rather than optimistic. He conceded that, so far, the middle class has benefited proportionately more from the expansion of state education than the working class, but he argues that this would be unlikely to continue if *further* expansion took place. Given that middle class youth is now largely catered for, an additional increase in educational opportunity would be bound to benefit the working class. He also hopes that as (and *if*) the comprehensive system becomes better established, it will reduce class inequalities in education. His own research, however, does not provide data on whether or not this is happening (see Chapter 24). The section of Halsey's book on future educational policy is, inevitably, more speculative than the rest of *Origins and Destinations*. Perhaps its implied corollary is that, in his view, there is, in any case, no practical alternative to reform.

Marxism, Economy, Education and Class

Marxists do not consider that the educational systems of advanced capitalist societies effectively and fairly match people to jobs. They believe that education in capitalist society contributes to the continuance of the class system and class inequality; in particular, it reproduces a labour force which is socialised to accept its lot and has, in any case, no adequate alternative means of survival. By 'socialised' we mean that the majority of working class children who 'fail' academically tend to accept their own 'failure' and the 'success' of most middle class children as legitimate. The fact that a small minority of working class children do 'make it' helps to foster the illusion that the educational system is fair and 'neutral,' and a highly unequal society presupposes that most children will fail academically and fill the lower occupations. In a sense, these matters become 'facts of life' for them, although, for many, an underlying sense remains that circumstances could be different.

Like Bourdieu, Bowles and Gintis give many examples of how social relationships in the educational system echo those of the economic system and thus prepare children for working life. They stress especially that educational institutions, like factories and offices, are intensely hierarchical. Like workers, pupils are expected to obey authority and have little or no control over the content of their work. This results in a feeling of non-involvement in, or *alienation* from, work. Only a minority of mainly middle class children go on to experience relative freedom and responsibility in study: fewer still are educated for leadership.

The American Marxist, Harry Braverman, has expanded interestingly and controversially the analysis that, far from being primarily involved in teaching working class children specific occupational skills, it is one of the hidden functions of schools to prepare children for the tedium of work (by being tedious themselves!). Braverman's critique, however, is more complex than this suggests and deserves fuller presentation. He sees the educational system as subordinate to the economic, but not, perhaps, as might be anticipated. He makes a powerful argument that most unskilled, semi-skilled and even many so-called skilled manual and non-manual jobs can be done with little or no skill at all (see Chapter 15). He therefore eliminates occupational training as a major function of education for the majority. Indeed, it is true that most jobs at these levels are learnt at work itself, not at school. He agrees that the three basic communication skills of reading, writing and arithmetic are learnt in schools, but he considers these to be necessary in the general context of modern life, rather than specifically at work (where, of course, they also help!) Braverman's thesis is supported by estimates that in Britain between two and five million adults are not fully literate; yet they obviously manage to do their jobs, despite this handicap. He also differentiates between the kind of work just described and professional, managerial and other work of a similar level, for which lengthy training is necessary. Some critics have suggested that even with these occupations, the length of time spent in studying in institutions could be profitably shortened. Thus, Robert Dore suggests that engineers could be well trained through a combination of supervised experience 'on-the-job' and part-time or short, full-time courses.

What, then, are the functions that Braverman thinks schools do perform? He considers that they socialise and 'child mind' whilst parents are at work. He points out that the raising of the minimum age for compulsory education has coincided with the increase in the numbers of working mothers. His comments on the relationship between educational expansion and the rate of unemployment are interesting and are echoed by the British social historian, Harold Silver. They both claim that, in the nineteen thirties, this relationship served to reduce unemployment amongst the young by removing large numbers of them from the job market. In addition, it provides jobs in teaching and administration for many thousands of middle class people. The increase in those staying on for further education in Britain during the late nineteen seventies and early eighties similarly 'mops up' some of the unemployed. However useful or not qualifications may be, the pursuit of them occupies the time and energy of young people. Significantly, provision has been made increasingly for less qualified sixteen year olds, who are the weakest in the job market, to stay on in education. Braverman's rather exaggerated remark that 'there is no longer any place for the young in society than school' refers to the role of schools generally, but it has a particular application to those of school leaving age.

Braverman not only argues that few job-specific skills are learnt in pre-sixteen education, but also that the 'qualification paper-chase' is in itself unnecessary and futile. Whilst there is empirical support for the first position, the second depends very much more on point of view. It is true, however, that pupils and the general public are sometimes unaware of the extent to which the job-market value of qualifications has become substantially less now that more people have them at all levels. To take two examples, teacher training and librarianship; the GCE qualifications required for entry into both these courses have risen. This does not guarantee that the people now entering them will be better than in the past or that they will do the job more effectively, but they will appear more impressive on paper. Braverman suggests that employers use qualifications as a screening device to ensure a minimum quality of entrant and, to maintain the same standard over time, they tend to adjust their requirement upwards. He cites some interesting survey evidence from Berg that there is now chronic over-qualification in many areas of unemployment, particularly at the clerical level. Berg's data also showed that over-educated employees tended to do a worse job, and to be more dissatisfied than the less well qualified.

Although the functional relationship between the educational and economic systems in Britain and America is, in some respects, rather obscure, its importance should not be underestimated. Modern nations require, at the least, a highly educated minority, particularly in the areas of scientific and technological research, and a generally literate and numerate population. Accordingly, education is a major item of government expenditure in all such societies. Some critics have suggested that the educational system in Britain ought to be more closely directed to serve the needs of the economy. In many other countries, the government insists on closer control: the Soviet Union is an example. Its planned economy is dependent on the government's knowing in advance the number, quality and variety of skills of the country's labour force. Japan is another country that has had a recent tradition of centralised planning in education: its 'economic miracle' would not have been possible without the efficiency of its educational system. Great emphasis is placed on the development of mathematical and scientific skills; although this has achieved results, it has often been at the price of putting extreme pressure on teenagers.

Factors Influencing Educational Attainment

The various factors that influence educational attainment are interconnected and, to a greater or lesser extent, social class, including class cultural experience, probably always plays some part in an individual's educational career. The factors we discuss here are social class and culture, intelligence, the quality of schools, gender and race. The educational policy of central and local governments also plays a role in providing the resources for educational success (or failure), and that issue is dealt with in the next chapter.

1 Social Class, Class Culture and Intelligence
As the above points have been discussed extensively in previous sections of this chapter, they need only to be briefly reviewed

here. There is a virtual consensus among sociologists that social class has a major effect on educational attainment, although a number of functionalists and 'hereditarian' psycologists give greater emphasis to intelligence which they argue, or sometimes appear to assume, is overwhelmingly (about 80%) hereditary. There is a growing debate among those sociologists who stress the influence of social class on educational achievement about the relative importance of cultural and material factors. It may be, as Halsey himself implies, that it is simply not possible to separate the two entirely. In any case, the family is seen as the primary medium through which class factors, cultural and material, are focused, with the school taking an important secondary role. Despite current debate, Morrison and McIntyre's summary, published in 1971, of cultural and material aspects of home environment, which researchers had consistently found related to academic success, remains a useful check-list:

1   Parental Attitudes to Education
2   Educational Level of the Home
3   Family Size (it is generally an educational disadvantage to be a member of a large family)
4   Quality of Maternal Care of Young Children
5   Material Prosperity of the Home
6   Social Disorganisation
7   Abnormal Family Background (for example, a 'broken' home)

Working class children are more disadvantaged than middle class children in respect of the first six factors, (though family size is of much less significance, as a general tendency for families to be smaller was apparent in the nineteen seventies). The seventh factor is increasingly likely to affect children of all social backgrounds, owing to the rapid rise in the divorce rate between the mid nineteen sixties and late nineteen seventies. It is worth adding that the precise way in which each of the above factors influences educational attainment varies, not only between the classes, but from individual to individual.

The two tables printed opposite summarise differences in educational qualifications by social class and by sex. The differences between the educational qualifications of the sexes has diminished noticeably among younger people, but the data given below presents a useful overview of the total population. The degree to which higher social classes are better formally

Highest educational qualification by social class, males,* Great Britain (percentages)

	Social class (R.G.(S.E.)70)						
	1	2	3	4	5	6	All
Degree or equivalent	60	10	11	Ø	Ø	1	8
Higher education below degree	20	15	13	4	1	1	8
G.C.E.† A level or equivalent	9	10	13	8	3	1	8
G.C.E.† O level or equivalent, or C.S.E.§ grade 1	4	18	20	12	7	4	13
C.S.E.§ other grades/ commercial/apprenticeship	1	10	7	20	9	5	13
Foreign and other	3	5	5	3	4	2	4
None	2	31	32	53	75	85	47
Social class of sample	7	16	18	41	15	4	100

*Economically active, aged 20–69, not in full-time education.
Data for 1977 and 1978 combined
†G.C.E. = General Certificate of Education
§C.S.E. = Certificate of Secondary Education
Ø = Less than 1 per cent   N = 15,327

Highest educational qualification by social class, females,* Great Britain (percentages)

	Social class (R.G.(S.E.)70)						
	1	2	3	4	5	6	All
Degree or equivalent	67	7	4	Ø	Ø	–	3
Higher education below degree	12	13	15	2	1	1	8
G.C.E. A level or equivalent	3	4	4	2	1	Ø	3
G.C.E. O level or equivalent, or C.S.E. grade 1	6	15	19	9	7	3	13
C.S.E. other grades/ commercial/apprenticeship	2	11	16	8	7	5	12
Foreign and other	5	6	4	3	3	2	3
None	6	44	39	75	81	89	58
Social class of sample	1	5	50	18	27	10	100

*Footnotes to above table apply to this table also
N = 10,549

Source: From Ivan Reid, Social Class Differences in Britain, Blackwell, 1981, tables 6.2 and 6.3 (devised from table 6.5 General Household Survey 1978, 1980).

qualified is very marked. Compare, for instance, the data on degrees and social class.

2 Schools, 'Labelling' and Cultural Reproduction

We have already seen how the Marxists, Bourdieu and Bernstein, see the educational system as a middle class agency which helps to reproduce middle class cultural ascendancy. A number of interactionists, in Britain and America, have reached similar conclusions. Their theoretical focus is, however, in some cases narrower than that of the Marxists, and their method of research, likewise, is on a smaller scale and largely participant-observational.

A pioneering study in this area is David Hargreaves' *Social Relations in a Secondary School*. The secondary school in question was an all boys' secondary modern school in which Hargreaves took on the participant observational role of teacher. His study was concerned with the factors *within* the school context which contribute to the creation of two sub-cultures, 'the academic and the delinquescent.' He emphasises how academic streaming greatly affects the membership of these two sub-cultures. Those who were placed in the lowest ('E') stream were the most likely to become part of the delinquescent (or delinquency-prone) sub-culture, whereas those in the 'A' stream tended to conform. Hargreaves attributes the formation of these peer-group sub-cultures directly to the school's policy of streaming which, he claims, results in an increasing feeling of inferiority on the part of the lower stream boys as they progress into the third and fourth forms. We can, then, conveniently think of the streaming process as a form of *labelling* which, in this instance and presumably often, has unintended consequences. It must be said that other sources show that social class factors mediated through the home and neighbourhood also contribute to the formation of youth peer-groups, although these were beyond the practical limits of Hargreaves' research.

Colin Lacey's *Hightown Grammar* is a precise parallel study to that of Hargreaves, concerned with the effect of streaming in a grammar school. His findings complement those of Hargreaves and he adds the observation that when frustrated expectations at school coincide with problems at home, 'the worst cases of emotional disturbance occur.'

In Paul Willis' study, *Learning to Labour*, the role of the school, including the labelling of working class 'lads' and the formation of what he calls *anti-school sub-cultures*, is put in a much wider socio-economic context. In pointing out that the academic failure of the 'lads' provides new recruits to manual labour, and so helps to maintain the capitalist system, Willis shows himself to be a structural sociologist as well as a detailed ethnographer (a social scientist who studies cultural activity through detailed observation).

Like Willis, Nell Keddie draws on both interactionist and structural perspectives in her detailed examination of how cultural reproduction occurs in the classroom through the labelling process. She argues that sometimes intelligent working class children may be labelled, or mis-labelled, stupid because of 'troublesome' behaviour. This label can become a 'self-fulfilling prophecy,' if the child accepts it and loses the motivation to compete academically. Keddie distances herself, however, from Bourdieu and Bernstein by rejecting any implication that working class culture is inferior: she refers to this view as 'the *myth* of cultural deprivation.' She argues that the educational system should build on working class culture rather than ignore or repress it – a view that Bernstein himself accepts as having clarified his own position. One problem is that nobody has yet explained in detail what a curriculum based on, or even substantially reflecting, working class culture might be like, or how it would help working class children to function better in capitalist society (if, indeed, that were its aim). The way of life of the 'lads' seems to defy the limits of any curriculum outside that imposed by the experience and discipline of work. We return to these issues in our discussion of educational policy in the next chapter.

3 The Quality of Schools

A piece of research which contrasts markedly with those described in the previous section is that of Michael Rutter *et al.*, *Fifteen Thousand Hours*. Rutter's methods were highly empirical and statistical and both his methods and his findings have attracted strong criticism, but he has stood by his main conclusions. *Fifteen Thousand Hours*, published in 1979, summarised several years' research into the performance of twelve inner London secondary schools. The aim of the research was to discover why some schools 'succeeded' and others did not. The team looked at four factors: attendance, academic achievement, behaviour in school, and the rate of delinquency outside it.

Rutter found that schools obtained very varied ratings on all the above counts, even when difference in social class background and intelligence in intake was allowed for. Those schools that scored well on one factor tended to do well on others. What, then, on Rutter's evidence, makes for a successful school? Pupil performance on the above four points is associated with a certain school 'ethos' of which sound teaching and professional behaviour is the keynote. Teachers who are punctual, well-organised, patient, encourage pupils, share extracurricular activities with them, and can inspire by example, are likely to get the best from pupils. Whatever the teacher's style and values, consistency helps. This applies as much to senior staff as to junior, and Rutter adds that an established system of rewards and punishments improves pupils' performance. Because some schools were successful on all four points, the researchers sought an underlying reason. These successful schools varied in their approach from the traditional to the progressive but the researchers concluded that what they had in common was a consistent commitment to their own values and rules. This consistency created an atmosphere or ethos that was secure and purposeful and in which effective work could take place and good human relationships prosper.

Fifteen Thousand Hours was initially well received both by the press and by many influential academics. Like many books that elicit such a response, it clarified and built upon a body of sentiment that had been growing for some time. In the mid-nineteen seventies, a concern for academic standards and quality in education, which had been simmering for some time, rose to the surface. The Bennet Report of 1976, comparing various kinds of teaching methods in primary schools found, amongst other things, that whatever method of teaching was used, the ability, experience and commitment of the individual teacher was a crucial variable. Formal and informal teaching methods could both be successful – *provided* that they were done well. Again, themes of consistency and commitment are stressed.

We can divide Rutter's critics into those who attack the quality of his research in its own terms and those who argue that, in addition to the limitations of his methodology, he also asks inadequate, if not wrong, questions. Of the former, several are especially concerned with the limitations of his statistical method. Amongst these, particularly, are Anthony Heath and Peter Clifford of Oxford University, who argue that the effect on performance which Rutter attributes to secondary school factors might well have been caused by the carry-over effect of primary schooling or by the interest of parents. In brief, Rutter has not controlled for the various non-school factors that are well known to affect children's school attainment.

The second group of Rutter's critics put their criticisms of his methodology within a broad critique of his whole theoretical approach. Michael Young rejects the assumption that social relations in school can be adequately understood on the basis of a model that assumes value consensus within the school. He finds it inconceivable that a school could 'function' or be properly analysed without reference to class, gender and racial divisions. To him, it is ludicrous to applaud consistency without raising the question of 'consistency in the pursuit of what purposes?' Rutter's answer to Young was that his research was only concerned with school performance in relation to the four factors mentioned above.

A further criticism of the report is that it tells us nothing about the fate of the children when they leave school. Rutter does not even present data on the question of whether, because children in some schools do better in public examinations than others, their occupational prospects are improved – a point which cannot be assumed, given that most of the children in the study were highly disadvantaged and that even 'the examination successes' were moderate by national standards.

Perhaps Rutter cannot be condemned for asking a particular set of questions, but clearly these questions are limited in scope and context and, to judge by the current state of debate, the answers to them require to be treated with caution. Even so, it is worth recalling in the heat of argument that, if interpreted cautiously and in the light of other relevant data, Rutter's findings appear neither startling nor particularly original. Writing in 1968 of lower manual working class pupils, J. W. Douglas said:

> Although (they) . . . are at a disadvantage relative to the middle class in all types of school, those at schools with a good record are far less handicapped.

4 Gender

Despite the changes that the women's movement has helped to bring about, certain social roles in our society tend to be allocated to men and others to women. It still remains true that, in a family context, the man is expected to be the 'main breadwinner' and the woman to take care of her home, even if she also works outside it. This division of labour, based on sexual difference, has become more blurred but it remains strong.

Education plays a major role in preparing males and females for their traditionally different social roles and therefore helps to maintain a division of labour based on sexual differences. The table (p. 115) shows how relatively ill-equipped woman are, in terms of formal qualifications, to compete with men. This is especially true of working class women. Why is there such inequality of educational attainment between the sexes? At the most obvious level, girls tend to study subjects such as needlework or home economics which will help them either in housework or in certain 'female' occupations, rather than subjects such as woodwork or technical drawing which are considered 'more suitable' for boys. Although it is now illegal, under the terms of the 1975 Sex Discrimination Act, for schools to discriminate on grounds of gender in offering school subjects, advice and guidance often steer pupils in predictably traditional directions. As long as society as a whole tends to assume that the pattern of a person's life is largely determined by sexual identity, this is, perhaps, inevitable. It is the 'hidden curriculum' of sexist assumption rather than formal discrimination that operates against girls.

In an interesting article, 'Why are there so few women scientists and engineers?', Tessa Blackstone and Helen Weinrich-Haste offer some detailed analysis of female under-achievement in education. They argue that girls 'learn' to under-achieve. In particular, there is some evidence that parents and teachers expect and even demand academic success for boys, but not so much for girls. They point out the problem of sex *stereotyping* in which girls are expected to do certain kinds of subjects and boys others. At the most general level, sciences are sometimes thought of as hard, masculine subjects concerned with physical realities, and the arts as the opposite. They mention clear evidence that stereotyping has more powerful effect in mixed than in single-sex schools. In the latter, girls are more likely to choose and do well in maths and sciences. It seems that the very presence of boys has a negative effect on girl pupils' (and perhaps teachers') educational expectations. At least, this is so in England. Research on the comparative educational performance of West Indian boys and girls suggests that the strength of the matriarchal family tradition in the West Indies and amongst West Indian immigrants in Britain seems to give the girls a positive and 'coping' attitude to work, including school work, and they do better than West Indian boys.

The gender problem in secondary education is not lower female achievement but their concentration in subjects that ultimately tend to bring lower status and rewards and the smaller proportion choosing to go to higher education. In fact, the average performance of females at 'O' level is better than males and for the first time, in 1985, a higher proportion achieved at least one 'A' level pass. Yet at degree level male advantage is still marked – in 1982 there were 59,000 male and 34,000 female graduates. Further, the great majority of graduates in law, science and mathematics degrees which tend to lead to careers in better-paid professions – are men. Women still tend to be concentrated in arts, education and social science departments. When we look at the situation of non-advanced courses in further education, the picture is quite different. Rather more females than males are involved in a wide variety of non-advanced courses in major establishments of further education (*Social Trends*, 1986). Post-16 education for women is, then, generally at a lower level than for men. We can suggest two reasons why this is so.

Firstly, society as a whole, including many, if not the majority of women, has lower career expectations of women than of men. This inevitably means lower educational expectations as well. As we shall see later (Chapter 12), these lower expectations are fully reflected in career as well as educational performance. Although individual teachers may dislike this situation, schools in general probably reflect society on this issue. Secondly, and very importantly, the structure of society still supports a division of labour in which men are the 'main breadwinners' and women look after the children and home. As we shall see in Chapter 12, there have been significant but not fundamental changes in this situation. Again, the educational system tends to mirror dominant attitudes on gender. Blackstone refers to the 'caution and lower aspirations' girls show in their career choices. If this is 'realistic' in terms of the way society is, then, perhaps, the challenge is to change further the dominant social attitudes towards gender, and not merely the educational system that reflects them. It may be that the cliché, 'education cannot change society,' applies as much to gender as to class inequality.

5 Race

The problem that race presents in education is vividly shown in the table below.

Percentage of Pupils fully educated in the UK placed in Upper Quartile on transfer to Secondary School
(in the Inner London Education Authority)

	English	Mathematics	Verbal reasoning
West Indian origin	9.2	7.4	7.2
Asian origin	19.3	20.2	21.2
Indigenous	25.0	22.9	19.8

Source: Alan Little, 'Schools and Race', in *Five Views of Multi-Racial Britain*, 1978, p. 61.

The performance of children of Asian origin is comparable to those of indigenous or British origin and does not, therefore, constitute a major problem. The performance of children of West Indian origin is much worse than that of both the other groups and does, therefore, constitute a considerable problem. Comparably low performances have been found for black children in the United States. The evidence of the school performance of West Indian children is not all depressing, however. A study by the National Children's Bureau showed a noticeable improvement in the achievements of *second generation* British West Indian children, although they remained below Asian and British. There is also some evidence that the secondary school performance of West Indian children is relatively better than their primary school performance. One very limited survey of school leavers in five multi-racial inner-city schools shows that

West Indian boys and, especially, girls achieved results that were generally better than those of English boys and girls. The author of this research, Geoffrey Driver, attributes the success of West Indian girls to the strength derived from the matriarchal tradition in Jamaica and carried over, out of practical necessity, to England. A major problem with Driver's research is that he does not control for social class variables and it may be that he is comparing groups of white and black children of different socio-economic background. In any case, he himself counsels against generalising from his research and we must pitch our discussion on wider and more pessimistic findings.

For those who consider that black people are genetically less intelligent than Caucasian (Indo-European) people, no problem is presented by the evidence of their comparatively low achievement. Jensen, for instance, believes that the fact that negroes score, on average, 12 to 15 points less on general intelligence tests than whites is a clear indication that they are innately substantially less intelligent. From his point of view, the kindest course would be to accept this and to cease trying to make them achieve levels of academic attainment that are generally beyond them. A variety of arguments can be cited against Jensen's view, but here we will concentrate exclusively on the environmental factors which might affect the performance of blacks in attainment and in intelligence tests.

The first environmental factor to consider is the child's home and family. A disproportionate number of immigrant families relative to the indigenous population live in old, often inner city houses which lack basic amenities. Partly because of the stresses brought about by slavery, the black family in the United States, the West Indies, and now Britain, tends to be less stable than that of whites or Asian immigrants. In particular, there is a higher proportion of one-parent families among West Indians than the indigenous population. We know that children from one-parent families are often the most disadvantaged of all. Another cultural heritage from the West Indies is the stricter, 'power-based' discipline of many West Indian homes. It has often been noted that this is poor preparation for the liberal climate of many British schools. Sometimes, when West Indian children do not find the authoritarian form of discipline they expect, they threaten the orderly running of classes and even schools.

A further example of clash between West Indian sub-culture and indigenous culture is language usage. The school is the major arena (one might almost say 'battlefield') in which this clash occurs. The difference between the form of English used by most West Indians and 'standard' English is great enough to cause some difficulty in communication between West Indian pupils and their (mainly) white teachers. This difficulty is often seen in terms of a language 'problem' of the West Indian students rather than one caused by cultural differences between pupils and teachers. In fact, the form of English used by most West Indians is a *dialect* of English, containing grammatical features which reflect various West African languages. Thus, *'he stand still'* and *'six boy'* are usages that occur regularly in the writing of West Indian children. A further point is that black sub-culture in both Britain and, especially, the United States has been extremely rich in the production or reworking of words. Thus, 'pop' words like 'hippie,' 'cool' and 'high' have their origin in black sub-culture. Sometimes black teenagers employ their distinctive linguistic forms and vocabulary deliberately to cut themselves off from white society which they feel has, in any case, rejected them. Given the above circumstances, it is not surprising that black children generally perform less well than whites on vocabulary tests.

The problems Asian pupils have in learning English as a second language have been recognised and, to some extent, met. It is only recently that the extent of the difficulties facing West Indian pupils has been appreciated and measures to accommodate them started. In fairness to Jensen, his case does not rest primarily on the fact that blacks perform worse on vocabulary tests than whites. The evidence is also that blacks score lower on tests of non-verbal reasoning – a major aspect of general intelligence tests. N. J. MacKintosh's response to Jensen is that non-verbal reasoning may itself be an ability which develops better in some environments than others. Groups that lack experience in the sort of abstract thinking measured by non-verbal reasoning tests might be expected to do worse at them.

Finally, there is much disturbing evidence that the *self-image* of many West Indian children is low. Low self-esteem undermines the learning process. In trying to do something, it certainly helps to believe that it can be done. Often, West Indian children appear to have lost confidence in their ability to succeed educationally. In the course of research in the Southern United States, Robert Coles noted that the drawings of black children contained some strange features. They tended to picture themselves as small, dowdy and, sometimes, with various features missing, whereas they portrayed white children in a large and positive way. Even the weather and landscape on the pictures depicting the white children were better! More recently, Bernard Coard came across a similar phenomenon in Britain (*Urban Education*, 1971). No doubt black self-image is undermined partly by the depressing position of blacks historically (since slavery), and in most present-day industrial societies. In addition, teachers themselves can unwittingly damage the confidence of black children. A particularly harmful example would be to decide prematurely that a West Indian child is 'not academic' and to place him in a bottom stream, although there are many less obvious ways of slighting a child than that.

We have not, in this section, refuted Jensen's arguments about black intelligence directly nor in the highly technical terms in which he presents them. Instead, we have simply described the alternative possibility that environment and cultural interaction (between black and white) produce profound problems likely to affect the attainment levels and, quite possibly, 'intelligence' scores achieved by black pupils. Until these problems have been more fully understood and fairly and sensitively accommodated, there can be no serious talk of black inferiority. Indeed, to do so might seem more like an example of further ideological discrimination than of scientific observation.

Sociology, Ideology and Policy

The recurrent issue in this chapter is that of wasted potential. The relative under-achievement of many working class children, girls and young blacks needs more than analysis: it begs for solution. Such is the strength of feeling generated by these issues that opinion and values always threaten to break through the posture of objectivity and scientific neutrality adopted by some researchers. Sociologists have, of course, every right to support their values and beliefs with research findings provided that they do so with honesty and with appropriate caution. In chapter 24 we examine some practical educational policy issues in which sociologists have been much engaged.

Guide to Further Reading and Study

Starting in the late nineteen seventies, the British educational system began to undergo considerable changes and will almost certainly continue to do so through the end of the eighties. When change, controversy and conflict are the order of the day, it is not easy to provide an outline of the state of the subject area! The reading guides at the end of the chapters on youth (14) and educational policy (24) are intended to capture the commitment and urgency of debate. Here I have decided to disregard any concern with reading level and simply make suggestions that either cover established fundamental matters or important contemporary issues. Writing in 1986, the basic questions still seem to me to be the ones presented in this chapter and the following books are central to our understanding of them: Samuel Bowles and Herbert Gintis *Schooling in Capitalist America* (Routledge and Kegan Paul, 1976); M. F. D. Young *ed, Knowledge and Control* (Macmillan, 1971); A. H. Halsey *et al, Origins and Destinations* (Oxford University Press, 1980); C. Ball *Beachside Comprehensive: A Case-Study of Secondary Schooling* (Cambridge University Press, 1981); and Rosemary Deem *Schooling for Women's Work* (Routledge and Kegan Paul, 1980). The issue of the educational under-achievement of black children is covered in the *Rampton Report: West Indian Children in Our Schools* (HMSO, 1981) and urban and racial issues are also dealt with in Frank Field *ed, Education and the Urban Crisis* (Routledge and Kegan Paul, 1977).

More general readers and texts include B. R. Cosin *ed, School and Society* (Routledge and Kegan Paul, 1977); Frank Musgrove *School and the Social Order* (John Wiley, 1980); and Jack Demaine *Contemporary Theories in the Sociology of Education* (Macmillan, 1980). The following books cover specific issues: curriculum – Geoffrey Whitty *Sociology and School Knowledge: Curriculum Theory, Research and Politics* (Methuen, 1985); the examination system – John C. Matthews *Examinations: A Commentary* (Allen and Unwin, 1985);

vocational education – Inge Bates *et al*, *Schooling for the Dole: The New Vocationalism* (Macmillan, 1984).

Past Questions

1 'The major role of the education system is to prepare children for adult occupational roles.' Discuss. (OLE, 1983)

2 Assess the influence of 'the adolescent subculture' upon educational achievement. (OLE, 1983)

3 Evaluate the major sociological explanations of why some social groups are disproportionately represented among the 'failures' of the education system. (AEB, 1984)

4 It is argued that formal education is directly related to the maintenance of social inequality. Using examples from more than one society, discuss the evidence for this argument. (London, 1985)

6 Community and Urbanisation; Development and Population

Guide to Further Reading and Study 154–5

Past Questions 155

In this section we have so far moved through progressively larger areas of personal experience – first, primary (family) then, secondary (education). This chapter reverses this procedure and examines some of the major factors that affect not just personal but also national and global life. Its perspective is predominantly structural. Topics analysed are the nature of traditional and modern societies; urbanisation; development and underdevelopment; and, finally, population and related problems. Class is an underlying reality behind all these themes. We refer to it continually but do not deal with it specifically until the next section.

From Rural Community to Urban Society

There have, of course, been great changes in Western society in the last two hundred years. Crudely, we can say that Western society has moved from the traditional to the modern. Poorer societies – nearly all of them in the southern hemisphere – are today going through a similar process of change even though many are trying to control, interpret or even resist it in their own way. What we seek, therefore, are concepts and theories that explain and illuminate this near-universal pattern of change.

The shift from traditional to modern is probably the most fundamental development in world history. Raymond Aron, the French sociologist, remarked that it was not until he visited India that he realised that the significant division in the world was not between communism and capitalism but between the modern, industrially-advanced states and those which remained industrially underdeveloped. Over-simplified or not, this comment at least helps to knock aside the cultural blinkers which often obscure the way Westerners see the world.

Community Defined

It is frequently observed that over the past few centuries there has been a 'loss of community.' This comment is often expressed with the sentiment that, in a human rather than material way, life was better 'then' than 'now'. Before any assessment of the validity of this feeling can be made, we must be clear about what is meant by community. Three major usages can be discerned.

1 The term community is employed to describe *locality* (*a given geographical area as a basis of social organisation*). Thus, a traditional rural village where people are born, live and die close to each other fits this usage.

2 Community is used to refer to a *local social system or set of relationships that centre upon a given locality.* Margaret Stacey suggests that, from a sociological point of view, it is the concentration of relationships, rather than the geographical factor that matters. Stacey would prefer to drop the term community in favour of *local social system.* This has the advantage of implying nothing at all about the nature of relationships in a locality but simply designates them as the topic for study.

3 Community is also used to describe a *type of relationship* which produces a strong sense of shared identity. This usage does not depend on physical whereabouts or even on people having met each other. Thus, it is possible to refer to the Catholic or Jewish community in a neighbourhood, town, country or, even, throughout the world. The Argentinian nation had every appearance of being a community at the moment of their team's World Cup Final victory of 1978. In fact, their President referred to the popular involvement in the team's progress as 'an experience in collective unity.' Similarly, this author recalls a newscaster's comment after Manchester United won the European Cup in 1968 that 'this was not only a victory for Manchester United fans but for the British people as a whole.' As Howard Newby points out it is 'loss of community' in terms of shared identity and accompanying experiences that accounts for much of the usage of the phrase.

We will consider how useful and accurate the notion 'loss of community' is when we have reviewed the major literature comparing traditional and modern society.

Ferdinand Tönnies and Emile Durkheim: Gemeinschaft/Gesellschaft and Mechanical/Organic Solidarity

Tönnies and Durkheim sought to understand the change from traditional to modern society. Their major writings on this matter were published before the turn of the century and their focus was European rather than global. Nevertheless, their theories have influenced more recent thinkers, particularly those of a functionalist perspective, who have had a major interest in world development.

Tönnies in *Gemeinschaft and Gesellschaft* (1887), and Durkheim in *The Division of Labour* (1893), contrast the social life of traditional rural communities with that of rapidly developing, industrial urban areas. On the one hand, they stressed family and community as sources of identity and support and, on the other, their relative weakness in the urban context where a more individualistic and impersonal way of life was developing. Tönnies used the terms *gemeinschaft* and *gesellschaft* to describe this broad sweep of social change. *Gemeinschaft* means community and *gesellschaft* can be translated either as society or association. He considered *gemeinschaft* relationships to involve the whole person and to be typical of rural life. Because people related more *fully* to each other, and not simply in respect of their specific functional roles (shopkeeper, policeman, teacher), greater mutual involvement and caring existed, and so a stronger community was formed. Thus, a policeman was not merely somebody who did a given job but a friend or, at least, an acquaintance who had a *general* concern for the order and welfare of the community. The difference is summed up in the admittedly rather exaggerated and idealised contrast between the 'friendly, village bobby' and the modern, panda-car policeman.

Gesellschaft relationships are seen as associations or transactions for practical purposes, with little informal content. Thus, a policeman appears on given occasions and for specific purposes; otherwise, in our privatised and individualistic society, he is likely to be considered as 'nosey' or 'interfering.' Terms that are virtually interchangeable with the rather cumbersome phrases *gemeinschaft* and *gesellschaft* relationships are, respectively, *holistic* (full) and *segmental* (partial) relationships. Tönnies used his key terms not only to describe relationships but also organisations. *Gemeinschaftlich* ('community-like') organisations such as the church are stronger in traditional societies, whereas *gesellschaftlich* organisations, such as big businesses, are stronger in modern societies. Churches have a moral and emotional influence, whereas businesses predominate in the practical and

economic spheres. These examples illustrate the deep change
perceived by Tönnies from the moral/emotional quality of traditional life to the practical/rational quality of modern life.

Durkheim's analysis in *The Division of Labour* concentrated
rather more systematically on the problem of how societies
achieve social order and cohesion or, to use his term, social *solidarity* than did Tönnies. Nevertheless, his terms *mechanical* and
organic solidarity overlap and complement Tönnies' *gemeinschaft*
and *gesellschaft*. He described solidarity in traditional societies as
mechanical and in industrial societies as *organic*. Mechanical solidarity is the product of a uniformly accepted and strictly
enforced system of belief and conduct and is facilitated by a
small, homogeneous (similar) population. Classically, it occurs
in primitive or traditional societies in which everybody shares
the same religiously inspired beliefs and habits. In such
societies, a person would not think of rejecting the moral consensus: personal fulfilment and identity are gained by identifying with the whole group and not through a separate sense of
individuality, as to a large extent they are in modern societies.
A different basis of order and cohesion – organic solidarity –
develops as societies become more complex. Organic solidarity
is a product not of common beliefs but of shared material
interests and practical *interdependence*. To understand this, we
must first describe what Durkheim meant by the division of
labour. The *division of labour* means that work is broken down
into specialised tasks performed by different people. It is a particular feature of modern society, and assembly-line production
may be considered the prime example of it. Organisationally
and humanly, the division of labour divides men but it also
makes them more dependent on one another. Thus, a single
group of workers, say, toolsetters, can bring an assembly-line to
a halt by taking disruptive industrial action. Interdependence is
broader than this example might imply and encompasses the
whole of a modern society – a strike in the gas or electricity
industries might bring other forms of industrial production to a
halt. Durkheim himself succinctly reconciles the paradox of
increased job or role specialisation with increased solidarity:

> This (organic) solidarity resembles that which we observe among
> the higher animals. Each organ, in effect, has its special
> character and autonomy; and yet the unity of the organism is as
> great as the individuation of the parts is more marked. Because

of this analogy, we propose to call the solidarity which is due to the division of labour, 'organic.'

Although Durkheim commented on the strength of organic solidarity, he felt that the ultimate stability of modern society depended on finding a new *moral* basis of solidarity in addition to practical interdependence. He argued that without moral and normative consensus in society, people tend to suffer from *anomie* – a sense of normlessness or lack of moral guidance to behaviour. In such circumstances, deviant activities such as crime and suicide tend to rise. We examine Durkheim's theory of anomie and deviance in greater detail in Chapters 17 and 18

The work of Georg Simmel, (1858–1918), echoes many of the sentiments of Tönnies and Durkheim. More than they, he attributed most that is characteristic of modern life, including 'lack of community,' almost solely to the growth of the city. His stress on the impersonality and isolation of city life parallels Durkheim's concern with anomie. Simmel's particular interest in the effect of the urban environment on the individual – eloquently expressed in his essay 'The Mind and the Metropolis' – places him as much within the tradition of social psychology as sociology. This essay and his work on dyads (two people) or tryads (three people) have led some to claim him as a founding father of interactionism, which is the sociological perspective that gives most attention to individual psychology.

Yet Simmel also had a strong sense of structure, as his analysis of the characteristics of urban life shows. He designated urban life as *rational* in the sense that it involves quick, logical and calculating reactions. This is because of the many practical, money-based relationships that city life depends upon. He contrasted this to the slow, habitual quality of rural life. Quite simply, he argued that the mind became more agile in the city through sheer overstimulation. Crudely, we could say that he gives academic clothing to the popular stereotypes of 'city slicker' and 'country bumpkin.' There is no doubt, however, that like Tönnies and Durkheim, Simmel is on the side of what he sees as a receding rural past, rather than the emerging urban present. He regards the blasé and reserved attitudes necessary to cope in the city as poor change for the involvement and community of rural life, despite the greater material wealth and cultural sophistication of the city. Within it, the values of the market-place so predominate that people often treat others as things or mere bearers of commodities and services. Like Durkheim, Simmel had great influence on the Chicago School of urban sociologists, whose work we consider shortly. Several comments and criticisms can be made about the community/society model. Firstly, it is suffused with conservative romanticism about the past. As a result, it tends to minimise the *repressive* nature of traditional community and perhaps exaggerate its satisfying aspects. Secondly, the model largely disregards class conflict, or reduces it to the level of mere 'disequilibrium' in society. There were immense differences in wealth, power, life-style and prestige between people before the industrial revolution, as well as after it. The fact that the privileged position of the nobility was sanctioned by custom, tradition and religion never *did* convince all the peasantry that such glaring inequalities were either natural or justifiable. Thirdly, a bi-polar or two part, model of change is too simple. Durkheim himself constructed a more complex scheme of comparative change but rather than describe this in detail now, we will go on instead to consider more recent and, often, more complex, theories of order and change.

Talcott Parsons' Pattern Variables

Parsons' attempt to analyse the transition from traditional to modern society owes something to both Durkheim and Weber. His lists of pattern variables (which categorise *pairs* of contrasting values and norms) can be regarded as an expansion of Durkheim's mechanical-organic axis of comparison. Accordingly, we can present them as follows:

Pattern Variables 'A': characteristic of Traditional Society	Pattern Variables 'B': characteristic of Modern Society
Ascription: The status etc. a person is given at birth, for example, king	*Achievement:* The status a person acquires through his own efforts, for example, a soccer star
(Role) Diffuseness: relationships are broad or gemeinschaftlich (see above)	*(Role) Specificity:* relationships are for specific purposes or *gesellschaftlich* (see above)

Particularism: people treat each other in a *personal* way, so a farm-labourer asks 'the squire' to give his son a job

Universalism: the same rules, principles or laws apply to everybody equally, as in appointing a person to a post in the civil service

Affectivity: the expression and satisfaction of emotions is felt to be important, so criminals are publicly punished so that the community can express its vengeance

Affective Neutrality: the affective or emotional side of man is controlled so that it does not interfere with 'the job in hand', so a bereaved person must control his grief rather than share it with colleagues

Collective Orientation: shared interests are most important, for example, with the family or community

Self-Orientation: individual interest is most important, as in the pursuit of personal success even if it distances an individual from his family

At this stage, it is enough thoughtfully to read through Parsons' pattern variables paying as much attention to the examples as to Parsons' tongue-twisting terminology itself. Having presented his pattern variables as a contrast between traditional and modern society, we must, in fairness, immediately complicate the picture. First, Parsons fully recognised, as did Tönnies and Durkheim, that there can be considerable overlap between the two types of society. Indeed, it makes sense to think in terms of a graded rural-urban *continuum* (development) of which pattern variables 'A' and 'B' are extreme poles, which, in practice, are more likely to appear together in various 'mixes.' Further, he considered that though modern society is more rational and affectively neutral, people do, of course, have feelings which they need and want to express. These feelings or *expressive functional imperatives,* as Parsons rather gruesomely called them, find their main outlet in the kinship and cultural community sub-systems (see Chapter 3). Still, what we want to emphasise here is the continuity of Parsons' model of societal types with those of Durkheim and Tönnies. As such, it hardly does more than offer a useful comparative check-list for locating given societies on a traditional-modern continuum. Thus, a primitive tribe would 'score' high under 'A', a modern state high under 'B', and an industrially developing country, such as Saudi Arabia, would show a mix. We will further evaluate Parsons' pattern variable model in the section on *development* later in this chapter.

The Urban and Community Studies of the Chicago School of Sociology

The Chicago school of sociology established an international reputation between the two world wars. Durkheim was a major influence on the urban sociology for which the school became renowned. This showed itself in two ways: first, in the clean cut contrast made between rural, 'folk' society and urban society and also in the use of the organic analogy to describe the processes of urban life.

Louis Wirth followed Durkheim closely in making a firm distinction between rural and urban society. He defined the city in terms of three fundamental features: population *size, density* and *heterogeneity* (Wirth, 1938). These characteristics meant that though the city dweller would experience more human contacts than the rural inhabitant, he would also feel more isolated because of their emotionally 'empty' nature. Social interactions typical of the city, those required to obtain goods and services, were seen by Wirth as impersonal, *segmental* (narrow in scope), superficial, transitory, and usually of a purely practical or instrumental kind. These kinds of interactions were referred to as *secondary* contacts. Wirth considered that secondary contacts had increased at the expense of *primary* contacts, that is total relationships involving emotional as well as practical content, such as those within a family. Like Durkheim, Wirth saw a partial solution to individual atomisation in the rise of voluntary associations, representative political institutions, industrial organisations and other collective or corporate organisations. However, he too did not think these provided the quality of emotional self-expression characteristic of primary group relations.

It is in the work of another urban sociologist of the Chicago school, S. W. Burgess, that we find the most faithful application of functionalist theory to the physical and social development of the city. Burgess describes urban processes 'as a resultant of organisation and disorganisation analagous to the anabolic and katabolic processes of metabolism in the body.' More usually, Burgess draws on plant ecology rather than human biology as a model for understanding urban processes. He writes of 'urban ecology' almost as if it is an impersonal and natural phenomenon, rather than man-made and susceptible to control.

Burgess presents a model or, as he referred to it, ideal construction, of the tendency of urban areas to expand radially from the central business district. The centre circle of the series of concentric circles in the model is the main business area. Next comes the zone of transition containing the slums and ghettos of the lower working class and immigrant groups. This zone is also characterised by cheap hotels and lodging houses and the easy availability of drink and sex. Other descriptions of this zone used by Chicago sociologists still sometimes employed are 'twilight zone' and 'zone of deterioration.' Later we shall look in some detail at the analysis of lower class 'deviance' within this zone developed by sociologists at the University of Chicago (Chapter 18, pp. 489–90). The next zone contains the homes of more successful and respectable working class people: it is an area of escape from the ghetto. Beyond are the higher class residential areas which make up the next zone. Finally, there is the commuter zone interspersed with countryside and farmland and merging into predominantly rural areas.

In his own day, Burgess' model was far from universally applicable – even in the United States. Since the Second World War, residential patterns have become still further complicated, particularly in countries such as England and Holland, where public housing projects have often been built outside the central urban zones. As a guide to the physical location of particular social groups and as a way of understanding why these groups inhabit particular areas, Burgess's work is inadequate. It does make the point, however, that social groups are cut off from one another both spatially and in their way of life or culture. Other urban sociologists, including Hoyt, have argued that a sectoral model provides a more accurate description of the patterns of neighbourhood layout. More recently, B. T. Robson's carefully researched study of residential patterns in Sunderland found that Hoyt's model applied closely to the south of the city and Burgess', somewhat less precisely to the north.

Sociologists now consider other issues to be more important than the relationship between space and residential patterns as such. One such issue is to explain how physical and spatial environments affect people's social and cultural opportunities and the nature and quality of their interactions. We can refer to this type of analysis as *socio-spatial*. A further sociological concern is to identify the factors that enable some social and ethnic groups to live in 'desirable' neighbourhoods and which force others to live in slums. A major criticism of the sociologists of the Chicago school is that they largely ignored this problem. Their work is descriptive rather than explanatory. Instead of examining how the free-market system in land and property affected socio-spatial systems, they assumed these effects to be 'natural' and therefore did not analyse what caused them. Because they did not adequately examine how the control of wealth and power affects residential patterns and community life, their work can be said to be clearly limited by their own belief in, or ideological commitment to, capitalism. As with Tönnies, Durkheim and Parsons, what they took for granted masks vital issues of social justice both in relation to what might be considered a fair distribution of material resources (property ownership) and in respect of the differential availability of cultural opportunities (educational facilities) between people living in different areas. The Chicago school failed to refine and develop significantly the thinking of their mentor, Durkheim. In addition to the points made above, they underestimate both the survival of the community in the city and the ability of people to develop means of self-expression other than within primary groups. It is to the issue of 'loss of community' that we now turn.

Criticisms of the 'Loss of Community' Thesis

The works we have so far discussed have been at the level of 'grand theory.' Perhaps the best way of testing the ideas presented in them is by means of the community study. Of course, it is impossible to go back and examine at first hand what community was once like but, at least, the persistent stereotype that community has declined can be measured against real cases. In addition, the world offers many examples of traditional as well as modern communities and these can be studied for comparative purposes. Our first case-study is of just such a kind.

SOME CASE STUDIES In the nineteen thirties, Robert Redfield published a study of social life in Tepoztlan, a Mexican village. He found a stable, well-integrated and harmonious community. In 1949 an account of the same village appeared, written by Oscar Lewis. He discovered a tense, divided and distrustful community. It seems highly probable that some of the apparent 'change' lay in the eyes of the beholder rather than in the social life of the people of Tepoztlan. More precisely, the two researchers approached the village with different expectations and theoretical perspectives: Redfield was predisposed to find community, and Lewis was conscious of the degradation that poverty can produce in traditional societies. Howard Newby, who has a keen eye for the relationship between sociologists' personal values, their choice of theoretical and methodological approach, and their ultimate 'findings,' describes the discrepancy between the reports of Redfield and Lewis as 'unnerving.' It reminds us that, despite sociologists' impressive battery of research apparatus, they, like others, sometimes end up seeing what they want to see. With due caution, therefore, it can only be said that Lewis further opened up the doubts about the *gemeinschaftlich* qualities of traditional communities.

Studies of urban life, however, have raised questions about the *gesellschaft* side of the comparative model. Herbert Gans' *The Urban Villagers* describes the lively, 'village-like' ethnic and working class communities of Boston's West End and New York's Lower East Side. The individual is seldom isolated, but supported by informal groups of family, kin and friends. We have already referred to Willmott and Young's Bethnal Green study which was published in 1957. Some seventy years after Tönnies mourned the passing of community, Willmott and Young found a thriving community in an inner city industrial area. They emphasise especially how 'mum' figures are at the centre of local interactions, functioning as combined information exchanges and transit-depots. The key link in the traditional working class extended family is the relationship between mother and daughter. This continues when the daughter is married because of the likelihood that the newly married couple

139

will live close to the female's family of origin or, in the early days of marriage, actually in her parents' home. Traditionally, men spent much of their leisure time separately from women in pubs and Working Men's or Labour Clubs. This pattern of segregation has long been breaking down, though there are still public bars in some areas where 'respectable' women would not drink, even in male company. Although there are enthusiastic exceptions, watching and playing football is largely a male monopoly and this is even more true of the declining sports of dog-racing and 'pigeon fancying.' As looking after the home is now quicker and easier, older working class women often turn to bingo to pass the time. Working class children of all ages tend to be left to get on with their own lives much more than middle class children and 'playing out in the backs' or 'on the streets' can be a major activity until well into adolescence, especially for boys. Any 'mischief they get up to' is likely to be met with rougher parental justice than a middle class child would normally expect to receive. Traditional working class community is woven in a web of 'talk' and 'gossip' and in the passing of time together in ways more or less amusing or practically useful. There are reserved areas of personal and family privacy but the whole is or was, essentially open, collective and social.

The waning of the above pattern of life might be regarded as a second phase – and, perhaps, a more genuine one – in 'loss of community.' Already Richard Hoggart's painstakingly detailed description of working class life in Hunslet has the quality of an old snapshot about it. But the fact that traditional working class community is breaking up does not mean it never existed. Some recent commentators, because they no longer find thriving working class communities of the kind described twenty five years ago by Willmott and Young and by Hoggart, seem almost to assume that the whole phenomenon is a romantic fiction. But one of the reasons for chronicling traditional working class life was an awareness of its imminent decline.

Coates and Silburn's excellent study of the lower working class St Anne's district of Nottingham falls somewhat into this trap. The fact that they find St Anne's to be a fragmented community does not mean it was always so. As they well illustrate, the decline of community was due partly to urban renewal policies – the effects of which had been emphasised by Willmott and Young in their Bethnal Green study well over a decade before. By 1970, St Anne's was a classic example of a working class community in decline. We attempt to explain the causes of the widespread decline of working class community later (but see also Chapter 4).

Another development that has undermined any simplistic rural-urban contrast is the fast growth of commuter villages. In *Urbs in Rure* (The City in the Countryside), R. E. Pahl draws our attention to the commuter invasion of rural areas. Some villages are almost wholly occupied by people who work elsewhere. Pahl has also written of the culture clash between indigenous village inhabitants and commuters. The irony is that in their search for community, commuters sometimes destroy what they are looking for. Other studies have shown that class division, business rationality and many of the problems of isolation and anomie frequently associated with urban life also occur in rural Britain.

In addition to the above case studies, it is worth recalling that historical enquiry has also thrown doubt on notions of traditional community, at least in so far as they depended on the predominance of the extended family (see Chapter 4).

SOME GENERAL POINTS OF CRITICISM OF 'THE LOSS OF COMMUNITY' THESIS The empirical data discussed in the previous section provides a tentative basis from which to make some general criticisms of the 'loss of community' thesis.

Firstly, it is an oversimplification. At both 'ends' of the continuum we have found evidence to contradict the model. Secondly, a related point: the model seems to underestimate the capacity of people to rebuild community in new circumstances after the break-up of their old communities. Thirdly, the *ideological* limits of the model need to be criticised. It is characterised by conservative nostalgia. As a result, it tends to miss or minimise the unpleasant aspects of traditional society. From this limited perspective, a crucial theoretical flaw emerges – which brings us to our fourth point. The model has no use for class or class conflict in the analysis of community life. It takes as a 'given' the capitalist system instead of examining how this system shapes social life. More recent work has sought to rectify this imbalance. Indeed, it has tended to argue that it is precisely what the above critics ignored – capitalism and resultant class divisions – that account for the lack of community which so concerned them. Before examining these conflict-based approaches, however, we will briefly review the new towns movement in Britain which, among other things, represented a 'search for' better communities than had developed in the urban environment of industrialism.

THE NEW TOWNS: AN EXAMPLE OF 'THE SEARCH FOR COMMUNITY' The New Town concept, first popularised around the turn of the century by Ebenezer Howard, was an attempt to plan social idealism into reality. Howard's 'bread and roses' idealism aimed at providing the city dweller with improved housing in less crowded neighbourhoods with conveniently available facilities, but he also advocated sacrosanct agricultural areas around the town, and wanted to erode class barriers by introducing socially mixed neighbourhoods. Welwyn Garden City, one of the early new towns (1920), probably came closest to the fulfilment of Howard's dream but more recent new town developments tend to have been less ambitiously conceived. Notwithstanding the inevitable crop of mistakes and complaints there is no doubt that, in terms of basic amenities provided, the new towns are a vast improvement on what they replaced. One woman in Milton Keynes said: 'It's like being in paradise compared to where I used to live.' There is no doubt, despite her choice of metaphor, that she was thinking in terms of such things as an upstairs bathroom, spacious lounge, perhaps central heating, and having a toilet which belonged to her own house and which worked properly. Against the backcloth of inner city decay (which we examine shortly), the New Towns represented a substantial improvement in the standard of life of most who moved to them. Nevertheless, contrary to what is often imagined, only a small percentage of migrants from the inner city have gone to New Towns. Crucially, from the point of view of the decline of the inner city, these have often been skilled or semi-skilled workers and their families.

As an attempt to tinker with the class system by introducing 'socially balanced' neighbourhoods, the new towns have been less successful. A useful piece of research in this area is B. J. Heraud's *Social Class and the New Towns* – a detailed study of social class in Crawley. One of Heraud's crucial findings is that movement out of the originally mixed social class areas was usually to social-class defined communities. This was especially true of middle class families. The original balanced areas tended to become socially more working class whereas the middle class moved into the new subsidised housing areas. As Heraud points out, however, the commitment of the town's Urban Development Corporation to social balance seemed to weaken progressively, and it is possible that a more sustained experiment would be more successful.

In the middle nineteen seventies, as the total population went into slight decline and it became clear that the inner cities were, if anything, under- rather than over-populated, New Town developments have tended to slow down or be abandoned. Stonehouse, which was to have been near Glasgow, and the planned central Lancashire New Town, reputedly to have been named Red Rose, will probably stay on the drawing board. It may be that this slackening in momentum will provide opportunity to adjust to, and improve on, the changes that have already taken place.

The New Towns, therefore, have provided materially better communities than elsewhere, but not socially very different ones. In particular, they, too, are characterised by class division. Given that they exist in a predominantly capitalist society, this is probably inevitable.

Conflict-based Models of Urban-rural Analysis

a THE SOCIAL EFFECTS OF CAPITALISM It is not only Marxist critics who find the ultimate cause of both urban and rural inequality and decay in the nature of capitalism, but the roots of such an analysis are certainly to be found in the writings of Marx and, his colleague, Engels. Unlike Durkheim and Tönnies, Marx's starting point for understanding society was not community or lack of it, but class. Marx believed that national and international community would be part of a socialist world but he did not consider that such community was possible under capitalism: competition and class conflict prevented it. Only *within* classes did he consider that community and *solidarity* (a sense of unity and mutual support) were normal, although he fully recognised that the capitalist ruling class would seek to produce a 'false' sense of national community so as to reduce class conflict and consolidate its own interests (see Chapter 3).

The contemporary Marxist, Manuel Castells, contextualises his analysis of urban life within a broad critique of capitalism. He sees almost every aspect of urban life as a spin-off from the capitalist system's need to have a readily-available pool of workers concentrated in the city. Because the education, housing and maintenance of these workers is not generally a profitable business, it is left to government to provide them. Sufficient resources are rarely allocated for these purposes. Castells sees the inefficiency and inadequacy of the welfare state and the dissatisfaction this produces as a potential weakness and conflict point in the 'system.' For Castells, there are no isolated problems of urban life: mothers inconvenienced through lack of nursery facilities, homelessness, and environmental negligence, are all explicable mainly in terms of a system concerned with private profit rather than public need. Thus, when a large national or multinational corporation decides to close a plant in a given area, the social effects can be enormous. For example, thousands became unemployed when Courtauld's closed down in Skelmersdale. After a few days an event like this ceases to be news, but the effect on people's lives can last for years.

A brilliant, if controversial, exploration of the relationship between the capitalist economic system and its social effects is John Rex and Robert Moore's *Race Community and Conflict*. Specifically, they examine how the *housing market* operates. In particular, they wanted to know why coloured immigrants occupied a disproportionate number of old, run-down inner city houses (either as tenants or, less often, as owner-occupiers) and relatively few council houses. The answer given was their weakness in the housing market. Low income often prevented them from obtaining mortgages and the length of residence requirement disqualified them from council housing (though this now applies to far fewer immigrants than when Rex and Moore wrote). Rex and Moore's theoretical framework perhaps owes more to Weber than Marx. Like Castells, however, their perspective is socio-economic rather than narrowly social. Recently, Rex has given more attention to the position of black immigrants in the job market and educational system, as well as in the housing market (see Chapter 13).

b THE SOCIO-SPATIAL EFFECTS OF CAPITALISM The separation here of the social and socio-spatial effects of capitalism is purely for the purposes of presentation and in recognition of the fact that the use of space has been of particular interest to sociologists in recent years. Clearly, the amount and quality of space people occupy and otherwise enjoy is a major feature of their social life. The spatial question is, therefore, essentially a social rather than a physical issue as far as we are concerned. 'Space' is rather an abstract word, but what is meant is that identifiably different groups of people occupy different 'bits of territory' within a given society. Thus, as we saw, coloured immigrants are over-represented in inner-city areas as, for that matter, are poor whites. The middle class predominates in suburbia, although, as Herbert Gans has shown, this is something of an oversimplification as far as the United States is concerned. What sociologists seek to do is to explain *why* some groups occupy *more* and *better* space (both environmentally and in terms of amenities) than others. Put as simply as possible, why do some people live in bigger and better houses and less crowded and more attractive neighbourhoods than others?

The answer given to the above question by the social geographer, David Harvey, is the same as that offered by Castells and by Rex and Moore. The problems associated with the city – housing, environmental decay, poverty, crime – are not caused by the city as such, but by the way the socio-economic system affects the city. In other words, the problems are *societal* rather than essentially urban in nature. It is the unequal way in which the employment, housing and consumer markets work *nationally* (and *internationally*) that is the main cause of these problems. Logically, therefore, these problems can also occur outside the urban environment in places where the capitalist system favours some at the expense of others. As we have seen, R. E. Pahl's appropriately titled *Urbs in Rure* makes exactly this point: high-income commuters and 'second-house' weekend visitors introduce new class divisions and material and status inequalities into rural society. Raymond Williams, however, makes the point that class divisions, including the glaring juxtaposition of ostentatious wealth and humiliating poverty, have long been a feature of rural life. He stresses that the capitalistic development of agriculture has often been as hard on the peasantry as industrial development has been on the urban proleteriat.

Indeed, originally it was partly because the peasantry were dis-possessed of their land by the agricultural revolution that they spilled into the cities in search of work. This sort of systematic socio-economic analysis is far from either the static concentric circles model of Burgess, or the simple rural-urban continuum of Tönnies.

C CLASS AND GROUP CONFLICT IN THE URBAN CONTEXT: CAPITAL, POLITICIANS, PLANNERS AND CITIZENS We now discuss the urban context in terms of groups which have power and those which have little or none. The groups we will consider are business-men, politicians, miscellaneous 'gate-keepers' and the citizen-ship as a whole. Although this section will mainly be descrip-tive, two conflict theories should be noted. First, is the pluralist, rooted in Weber, which regards multi (plural) group conflict as essential to liberal democracy. Second, is the Marxist, which places group conflict in the, for them, profounder context of class conflict (see pp. 234–9).

Businessmen have power to affect the lives of other people. Investment provides work and a basis for prosperity, and lack of it causes unemployment and social hardship. The fact that we tend today to think of business in terms of large national and international companies and institutions may make economic power *seem* more impersonal, but the effects of it are real enough. If Henry Ford were to decide to switch car pro-duction to a European or American factory, there is relatively little that British Ford workers could do about it. It is true that trade unionists are beginning to respond to the inter-national nature of many large companies by organising inter-nationally themselves, but they often lack the resources and experience to do so effectively. In any case, the harsh truth is that, if private enterprise declines, withdraws or fails to invest in a given area, that area tends to decline socially as well as economically. The poverty and social deprivation of parts of the North East during the depression of the interwar period vividly demonstrates this.

National and local politicians are a second group whose power affects others. As elected representatives of the people, their policies ought to benefit the public though this does not always seem to happen. Let us look at local government first. Joe Chamberlain, as mayor of Birmingham in the eighteen seventies, was an early urban reformer who successfully sought to improve the public amenities and standard of health of his city. His achievements were a model for other local politicians concerned with the standard of public amenities in their areas and were the prelude to great advances in civic provisions. Not all local authorities, however, have matched what he helped to inspire. Theoretically, government should be 'above' sectional interest and seek to serve the common good. This involves placing checks and controls on the activity of business. There is always a danger, however, that government may favour business 'development' at the expense of others. Sometimes it even happens that the immense revenues controlled by local authorities which are the practical basis of their power and patronage are mis-spent. Much of the design and construction of public works such as the building of roads and houses is contracted out by local authority officials to private companies of builders and architects. Inevitably, this sometimes leads to corruption. An example is the case of T. Dan Smith, the leading politician on Newcastle's Labour-dominated Council in the early nineteen seventies. Smith was found guilty of giving contracts to architect John Poulson in return for bribes and favours. Such clear-cut cases of corruption are rarely proven but sometimes Council contracts do seem to favour the interests of commercial developers rather than the public. After the Second World War, most working class people as well as most politicians believed that a new Council residence was worth the destruction of their old house. Now, doubt and suspicion have not infrequently come to replace trust and optimism.

A third 'group' which has power in the city is made up of planners, architects, state and local authority bureaucrats, welfare workers, and managers of banks and building societies. We include them together mainly as a matter of convenience. The important thing that these various people have in common is that their decisions can profoundly affect the lives of ordinary citizens. Because of this power they are sometimes referred to as 'gate keepers'. They can open or close the door to valuable resources such as public housing, social security payments and help from the social services. More than that, some of these agencies have great power to interfere in, and even radically change, the course of people's lives. Payment of social security will often be made dependent on a visit from an investigator who will ask a range of questions that in normal circumstances would be regarded as constituting an invasion of privacy. In some circumstances, investigation can continue in a secret and lengthy manner. Social security 'fiddling' is, understandably, not popular with the majority of the public and so the pryings of officialdom tend to be grudgingly accepted in this area by the tax-paying majority.

Planning policy, by contrast, is an example of bureaucratic power that has frequently provoked widespread condemnation. With the support of the politicians who employ them and who often depend on them for detailed advice, planning officers can make use of wide legal powers to require people to quit their houses which can then be destroyed. A number of key positions which regulate access to various resources controlled by private enterprise ought also to be mentioned here. In particular, money lending institutions of various kinds, notably banks and building societies, can make decisions that affect people's lives radically. For instance, acquiring a mortgage may mean the difference between independence, security and comfort for a family and the opposite. Yet often a remote 'expert' will assess a mortgage claim on the basis of prescribed rules with little idea, or perhaps even thought, about the human consequences of his decision.

We now discuss the most important group mentioned above, the citizenship as a whole. Actually, the phrase 'citizenship as a whole,' like 'the average man,' hides more than it reveals. What we really want to talk about are the varied individuals and groups who live or work in urban areas. For many of these people – and this is one of the most important observations in this book – the problems they have faced in the post-war period have caused them to adjust their practical understanding of democracy. Classically, democracy in Britain involves voting for a representative with, perhaps, occasional communications thereafter. Increasingly, people have become more aware of the possible conflict between their own interests and the policies of government and its official representatives. Sometimes the 'threat' seems to come from an alliance of government and business. Let us give an example.

Bridgtown is a small suburb of the town of Cannock in Staffordshire. In 1976, the Bridgtown Redevelopment Inset Plan stated that 'the redevelopment of the area for industrial purposes will ultimately necessitate the removal of all residential property.' The opposition to this plan in the 1,500-strong community was considerable, and much of it was challenged through the Bridgtown Residents' Action Group. A newspaper report quotes one particularly uncompromising resident, a Mr Tart, as follows:

> 'They'll have to carry me out of here. I'm staying.'

Another observed:

> This place was built because of industry, we have learned to live with it. There is no need to mow us down.

In response to the opposition, the chief planning officer produced the circular argument that the development of more industry in Bridgtown would lead to a further deterioration in the district as a residential area and that it was therefore in the best interests of the residents to be rehoused over a period of years.

It would take much more space than is available here to establish the merits of this conflict. What is important is to appreciate the organised response to a perceived threat of members of the Bridgtown community. Although their roles are not examined in the above brief account, it is clear that industrialists – who would supply some of the resources for 'development' – and politicians – who have the power to pass the plan into law or not – are as deeply involved as the planners in the conflict. Although the Bridgtown example is a particularly graphic case of community power politics, similar conflicts are reported almost daily in the press.

Communities are created and recreated in a crucible of power. Decisions taken by businessmen, politicians and planners affect the lives of individuals and communities. C. Wright Mills sought passionately in his writings to make people aware of the relationship between 'private' troubles and 'public' or' political issues. It is largely in an attempt to control, or at least to influence and make more accountable, the above powerful groups that community action movements began rapidly to develop in the nineteen sixties. These movements vary widely in kind and purpose. Tenants' Associations are concerned with practical matters of self and group interest such as rents and living conditions. They bear a similar relationship to community life as do trade unions to work: they aim to protect the interest of their members. More *ad hoc* groups may organise around an issue affecting a particular local area at a given time. An example from the provinces is the protest group in Preston's suburb of Ashton, which organised against a plan to drive a road through an avenue of birches in Haslem Park.

Where an issue is general rather than local – such as homelessness – a movement with a wider geographical base of support may develop. For instance, there were some 30,000 estimated squatters in the Greater London area in 1977, many of whom received some assistance from the London Union of Squatters. Their case was that London's many homeless should be matched with the even greater number of empty residential properties in the area. Against this is the legal argument that they do not own the property they squat in and the administrative one that they should wait their turn in the official queues for public housing.

In the nineteen eighties, a crisis occurred in the public life of many of Britain's urban areas of a kind that citizens – however they organise – cannot easily hope to solve. There are four obvious aspects to this crisis. First, there is the growing inequality between the inner urban 'have nots' and the suburban and county 'haves'. Second, the poorer urban areas can rarely raise the revenue to deal with their problems – a difficulty intensified by the reduction in the rate support grant by central government. Third, the increasing centralisation of economic power in the hands of large, often multi-national companies makes the urban economy very vulnerable. Fourth, and not unconnected with the above, a major problem of public order developed in Britain's inner cities in the nineteen eighties.

In the light of this crisis it is worth considering the viability of the two models of political conflict referred to earlier. How realistic a description of current urban politics is the liberal model of pluralist democracy? As far as the city is concerned, particularly the city poor, is liberal democracy working? On the other hand, is there now a basis for an effective traditional, socialist coalition in urban areas? De-industrialisation, the numerical decline of the manual working class and union membership, and the growth of the lower (under) class are some problems such a coalition would face as, indeed, the Militant-led Liverpool Labour Council did.

(For a discussion of liberal, Marxist and Elite political theories, see Chapter 19).

The Inner City: An Example of Conflict Analysis

This section is about the inner city not as a physical entity but as the focal point of the activity of groups of people, the most powerful of whom are probably businessmen, politicians and top civil servants. Sometimes these groups act in concert and sometimes in conflict, but their major decisions affect the lives of the rest of us. More abstractly, we want to show how the capitalist system operates on the inner city – always bearing in mind that government can try to act as a checking or, to use Galbraith's term, *countervailing power* to control business as well as to smooth its path.

Since the Second World War the inner city or, more precisely, the inner city ring (the area *around* the business centre) has been inhabited by low income groups and beset by social problems. Once-thriving manufacturing areas were hit by the decline of such staple industries as docking, shipbuilding, textile production and heavy manufacturing. Manchester, Liverpool, Glasgow, Belfast, Newcastle and Inner London all developed 'inner city problem areas.' For instance, the break-up of traditional working class community in East London (see above, Willmott and Young) was due to the decline of the docks and the associated service and distribution trades. In addition, advanced technology and large scale industry made the craft industries and other small scale production units of the East End obsolete and uncompetitive. People moved out in droves. Between 1961 and 1971, almost 100,000 people left the single borough of Tower Hamlets. Those that remained in inner London were drawn, disproportionately, from the old, socially disadvantaged, unskilled and semi-skilled workers. They were joined by coloured immigrants who were prepared to do unskilled and semi-skilled work in the inner city of a kind that many whites wished to avoid.

It would be quite misleading to 'blame' individual businessmen for the above situation. Many of them also suffered as a result of the decline of Britain's traditional industrial base. The point to pursue is a quite different one. It is that when capitalism falters or fails – even if only in the process of change rather than collapse – it is incapable of rectifying the resultant adverse social consequences. The capitalist system works on profit, not philanthropy, and when it fails it is left to the some-times reluctant hand of government to pick up the pieces.

We now look more closely at occupants of the inner city (and in part, the centre city) to show that class factors like income and education mean that people in the same geographi-cal zone lead radically different lives. Inner city occupants can be divided into various disadvantaged groups: immigrants, 'cosmopolites,' and some members of the upper class. We have already explained why the disadvantaged and immigrants are disproportionately represented in the inner city, and we will have much more to say about them later (see Chapters 10 and 13). 'Cosmopolites,' to use Gans' term, include students, artists, writers, musicians, entertainers as well as other intellec-tuals and professionals. Though some may be quite poor, this is not the definitive feature of life that it is for disadvantaged groups: for them the city is meaningful because it provides opportunity for self-expression and experience. The fact that dif-ferent social groups can live in close physical proximity, yet socially in different 'worlds', is still better illustrated by refer-ence to the very rich who keep a town residence (often in the centre rather than inner city) as well as, often, a country home. A member of the upper class may live a stone's throw from a poor community but is sealed off from its occupants by wealth, privilege and power. The urban environment may be the physi-cal limits of the poor man's world but the rich man is much more geographically mobile: he can escape to the 'country' or abroad, almost at will. On the whole, the upper class do not live or spend time in the countryside to seek community except in some cosmetic or whimsical sense. Their residences are usu-ally well secluded from those of nearby inhabitants, although traditionally-minded landed aristocrats and gentry may still pride themselves on being 'part of the local community,' how-ever cushioned their position may be by privilege and by the deference afforded to them. In fact most of these, like the nouveaux riches who have bought into rural real estate, tend to have friends of similar social status who, in the nature of things, are unlikely to live close by. The upper class, however, can afford to travel and visits and meetings are easily arranged. Friendship networks are likely to be national or international and may seem to have an unreal, 'starry' quality to those outside the charmed circle. Members of the upper class know each other but others only know of them. Recently, upper middle and middle class people have bought property in some previously working class areas in the inner city. This process is sometimes referred to as 'gentrification.' It has added to the jigsaw-like quality of the social patterns of residence of many of Britain's cities.

The role of national government in helping to create the above social and demographic (population distribution) patterns is important. In the post-war period, government and industry co-operated to disperse industry and population away from the old industrial areas. The new town movement was part of this policy. The centre and inner city zones were redeveloped as office and service areas. Some of the new housing, including high rise flats and large estates, was of poor quality and design. 'Living in the sky' made community virtually impossible and caused families great practical problems. Even so, the new housing was generally a material, if not an aesthetic, improvement on what was left undemolished of the old inner city housing stock. Most of this came to be occupied by those groups who, for reasons already mentioned, did not participate in the new 'out of city' expansion. Welfare state expenditure tends to be relatively high in inner city areas although this is a palliative, not a solution to the basic problem. Various government schemes have been adopted to encourage the economic development of these areas. As in similar schemes in the United States, money has tended to disappear without much seeming to happen. Perhaps this is because the basic economic and planning trends described above tend to be 'inevitable.'

The above account of the inner city is intended to illustrate the inequalities and potential conflict caused by the capitalist system. Whether government is seen as the handmaiden of capitalism or the saviour of its 'victims' is a matter for personal assessment, but what is undeniable is their mutual involvement in inner city processes.

Conclusion: Perspectives, Politics and Policy

Both Marxists, such as Castells, and Weberians, such as Rex, consider that the conditions, for good or ill, of modern Western

153

cities are generated by capitalism rather than industrialisation or urbanisation. This analysis gained further credibility in the nineteen eighties, when it became even more clear that industrial investment is the key factor in prosperity, not only on an urban, but on a regional, national and global basis. Most contemporary conflict theorists consider that only central government can hope to control capital and deal with its social consequences. The *gemeinschaft-gesellschaft* model of Tönnies and the rural-urban framework of Wirth now seem rather antiquated or, at least, inadequate to deal with contemporary urban issues.

Unemployment, poverty, racial conflict and public disorder, have increased the urgency of the debate on urban policy. This debate is part of a wider disagreement about the kind of economy and society Britain might become. The Conservatives believe that only free enterprise – large-scale and small – can provide a secure basis of jobs and prosperity. To varying degrees social democrats argue that the state must step in where private enterprise fails and, indeed, sometimes take initiatives in its own right. They certainly consider the condition of the inner cities as a suitable issue for substantial intervention. Marxists argue that capitalism is inherently inegalitarian and capricious and seek to attack urban problems along socialist lines. In any case, few scholars, these days, find it a priority to make elegant comparisons between rural and urban life. The heat of ideological and policy debate is intense and the inner city is at the centre of the furnace.

Guide to Further Reading and Study

For those who want an overview of tradition rural/urban theory without returning to the original sources, Michael P. Smith's *The City and Social Theory* (Basil Blackwell, 1980) is recommended. This book also contains a chapter on capitalism and urban political conflict. Two books which suggest similar processes are at work in the countryside and the city are Howard Newby, *Green and Pleasant Land? Social Change in Rural England* (Penguin Books, 1980) and Raymond Williams, *The Countryside and the City* (Paladin, 1975). The latter has a penultimate chapter which compares rural and urban devlopment within societies to the relationship between the developed and underdeveloped 'worlds'. David Lee and Howard Newby's *The Problem of Sociology* (Hutchinson, 1983) presents with authority and insight a variety of 'schools of thought' on industrial society.

The condition and problems of some of Britain's inner cities is such as to make this topic one of considerable interest and urgency. Andrew Friend and Andy Metcalf's *Slump City: 'The Politics of Mass Unemployment'* (Pluto Press, 1981) does justice to these sentiments. Equally relevant and written in a lively, involved style is David Robins and Philip Cohen's *Knuckle Sandwich: Growing up in the Working-class City* – a book which can be cross-referenced to youth culture. There are a number of readings on urbanisation in the Third World in Hamza Alavi and Teodor Shanin *eds, Introduction to the Sociology of 'Developing Societies'* (Macmillan, 1982). Several readings relevant to urbanisation are given at the ends of Chapter 8 and 13.

Past Questions

1 Examine sociologists' contributions to our understanding of *one* of the following:
a) suburban communities
b) inner city areas
c) towns and cities in developing countries. (AEB, 1982)
2 'The paradox of the sociology of community is the existence of a body of theory which constantly predicts the collapse of community, and a body of empirical studies which finds community alive and well.' (Abrams: *Work, Urbanism and Inequality.*) Explain and Discuss. (AEB, 1983)
3 Either (a) the problems of the inner cities are essentially those of poverty and unemployment; the problems would therefore disappear if poverty and unemployment were eliminated. Discuss. or (b) What factors determine the pattern of residential segregation in cities? (OLE, 1983)

7 Comparative Demography: Population and Development

Introduction

The term 'comparative demography' is a rather high-sounding description of the material covered in this chapter. Demography is the study of the statistics of population. As the *Shorter Oxford English Dictionary* puts it, 'demography . . . treats of the statistics of births, deaths, diseases, etc. . . .;

I will not deal here with the methodological problems of the discipline or with the issues relating to the social construction of statistics (for this, see pp. 510–15). The chapter will present demographic data, generally accepted as reliable, and examine some demographic trends. It will focus mainly on comparative population structure and change and particularly analyse birth and death rates (definitions below). How population trends affect education and employment will be examined in Chapter 8, as will a number of related policy issues. As Philip Abrams says, population statistics provide 'maps' of certain problems and therefore inform policy discussion: consequently, no 'maps', no coherent discussion.

There should be no need to justify coverage of demographic trends and issues in a global rather than merely a national context. The affluent West has been too parochial and complacent in its response to the problems associated with world population growth and of the linked issue of Third World underdevelopment. As the Brandt Report points out, in a highly interdependent world, even self-interest requires broader understanding and policies.

Terminology

The *birth rate* and *death rate* are key determinants of population size. The birth rate is the number of live births per year per 1,000 people and the death rate is the number of deaths per year per 1,000 people. The *fertility rate* is the number of live births per 1,000 women of child-bearing age (15-44). The *infant mortality rate* (IMR) is the annual rate of death of infants 0–12 months per 1,000 live births. The IMR varies internationally mainly according to the quality of child care and makes a critical contribution to the overall death rate. The difference between the birth rate and death rate gives the *rate of natural population increase* and, if we adjust for net immigration and emigration, we get the *rate of population growth*. The concept of *dependent population* is very important. It refers to non-producing members of the population. The *dependency ratio* is arrived at by dividing non-producers by producers.

Population Trends

World Population Trends
The diagram below shows the increasing rate of world population growth:

The Growth of World Population

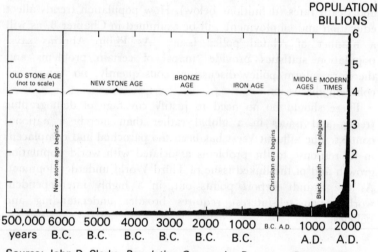

Source: John D. Clarke, *Population Geography*, Pergamon Press, 1976, p. 155.

In many parts of the world, population growth has outstripped available resources. Millions have died through starvation or ill-health caused by malnutrition. Until recently, forecasts suggested that there would continue to be an increase in the rate of population growth. It was feared that the crisis of global over-population would escalate beyond control early in the twenty-first century. However, the *State of World Population Report*, published by the United Nations (1982), indicates that a drop in the rate of population increase has at last occurred and that population will level off at about 10.5 billion in the year 2110.

Between 1950 and 1975, the average growth rate was 1.9% a year. By 1978, it had decreased to 1.81% and by 1980 to 1.73%. The decrease is due to an overall fall in the birth rate. In poorer countries this reflects some success in the policy of governments and Third World agencies (see below). In countries at an intermediate level of development, parents themselves often opt for smaller families, largely to secure living standards. In any case, these global figures conceal an average rate of growth of about 2.5% in poorer countries compared to 1% in developed countries.

The Report makes the following estimates of the world population at given times:

1950	1980	2000	2110
2.5 billion	4.4	6	10.5

If the current trends are proved correct, the world should be able to maintain its people adequately if resources are developed, distributed and used for this purpose. That is a big 'if'. The exploitation of resources to create private wealth or their diversion into armaments build up are alternatives.

Regional Population Trends

The above trends are of concern to the whole species. This section examines briefly specific regional trends.

Population will stop growing and stabilise first in the industrially developed areas of the world. According to the United Nations Report, this will happen first in Western Europe in about 2030 when its population will be about 400 million. Next will be North America, levelling off at 320 million, soon followed by the Soviet Union at 380 million.

There has been concern in the European Parliament about the combined effects of a falling birth rate and a low death rate. The danger perceived is that there will not be enough workers to cope with the burden of dependency caused by an ageing population. The population of the ten countries which make up the European Community was 8.8% of the world total in 1950 but is estimated to be 4.5% in the year 2000 and 2.3% in 2025. European women had an average of 2.79 children each in 1964, and 1.68 in 1982 – well below the population replacement rate of 2.1. A Presidency paper argued that 'this situation is disturbing'.

There are arguments against adopting policies to increase the Community's birthrate. First, Europe, and particularly Britain, is far from employing all of its present population of working age. Secondly, many older people are quite capable of doing productive work should they be required and want to do so. Thirdly, the working population of Europe could be increased indefinitely by changing immigration policies. In view of the continued expansion of population in the Third World, the latter might be a particularly effective policy.

Continued population expansion in the Third World puts Europe's problems in proportion. The biggest increase in population will come in the world's poorest continent, Africa. It is the only region in which the rate of population increase is not slowing down. Africa, where millions already die or are disabled through malnutrition, is expected to quadruple its population by the year 2110. That of South Asia is expected to treble to 4.2 billion, a figure not far short of the present population of the world.

Latin America, which is generally better able to support its people, is also expected to treble its population. East Asia, however, will level off quickly, rising from 1.2 to 1.7 billion. This is largely because of the success of birth control policies adopted in China.

REGIONAL POPULATION AGE STRUCTURES The following chart gives key demographic data about seven countries from underdeveloped and developed regions of the world (1978).

	Birth rate	Death rate	Infant mortality rate (per 1,000)	% of population under 15	% of population over 64
Tanzania	47	22	167	47	2
Vietnam	41	19	115	41	4
China	22	8	65	33	6
El Salvador	40	8	55	46	3
Australia	17	8	14	28	8
USA	15	9	15	24	11
UK	12	12	14	23	14

Source: World Health Organisation

In demographic terms, Tanzania and Vietnam are reasonably representative of the less developed countries of the Third World. The data on both indicate three major problem areas. First, the gap between the birth and death rate shows rapid population growth; second, the infant mortality rate is appallingly high; third, in both countries, over 40% of the population is under the age of 15. This puts a heavy burden of dependency on the adult population, even though many older children in Third World countries contribute to family income. The low death rate in China and El Salvador is a result of success in reducing the rate of infant mortality and to the relatively youthful age structure of their populations. The percentages of the population under 15 are far higher than in advanced industrial countries. However, this situation is rapidly changing in China because of the success of its one child per family policy.

Australia, the USA and the UK are at a similar stage of demographic development. In 1978, the birth and death rates in the UK were actually in balance. The problem of age dependency for Britain and, to a lesser extent, the USA, is with the group 65 or over – the opposite end to where the problem lies for countries such as Tanzania and Vietnam.

The three charts below contrast the population composition of Mexico, the USA and West Germany. The age structures of South

Comparative Population Composition: Age and Sex.

Rapid Growth
Mexico

Slow Growth
United States

Negative Growth
West Germany

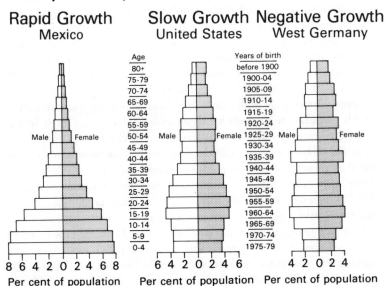

Sources: Censuses of Mexico, the United States and West Germany (The Population Institute, Washington D.C.).

Asia, Latin America and Africa are fairly similar to that of Mexico, and that of the Soviet Union to the USA. The populations of Western Europe are the oldest, and the region has about 5% fewer aged 14 or younger than both the USA and USSR. The problem of old age dependency is, therefore, at its most acute in Europe, though it will also be felt sharply in the USA early next century.

British Population, Trends and Age Structure, (Compared to the Third World)

The purpose of this brief section is twofold: first, to establish the historical development of the British population from a demographic point of view; second, to indicate the main demographic issues facing contemporary Britain. Because demography cuts into so many other topics, the reader will be sign-posted elsewhere in this book for detailed discussion of specific points.

Broadly, the population growth of Britain has followed the pattern indicated in the figure on p. 165 (part 1). It is not possible to say precisely when slow population growth gave way to more rapid increase but slow growth, interrupted by occasional natural disasters, occurred throughout the middle ages. More rapid growth preceded the industrial revolution but the improvements in public health and nutrition which underlay the increase became more marked in the nineteenth century, especially the latter part (see pp. 680–2). These improvements reduced the death rate but the birth rate barely fell until the last quarter of the nineteenth century: thus, the rapid population growth for the preceding century. Indeed, a high birth rate was necessary to maintain a stable population in traditional society. Given a very high infant mortality rate, families had to have several children to ensure the survival of two or three. Children functioned as breadwinners and later as protectors of their parents, should the latter reach old age. Fertility was regarded as a blessing and had religious sanction. Similar factors explain the persistence of high birth rates in the Third World, especially in poorer, more traditional societies. There are two crucial differences, however. First, Britain's period of rapid population growth was supported by and essentially caused by an even greater increase in wealth and resources. Comparable development is not occurring in the Third World. On the contrary, the population boom in the Third World was partly triggered by the entirely artificial factor of Western medicine, particularly in the control of infectious diseases, which destroyed 'natural' population balance. As a result, poor Third World countries with booming populations tend to become highly dependent on the West. Second, and more optimistically, the modern family planning methods, which only became widely available in the West well after its population boom had passed its peak, are currently available to the Third World. Arguably, however, the best stimulus to population control is development itself (see pp. 167–9). The diagram below compares population growth in the developed and underdeveloped world between 1975 and 2000 (projected).

25 Years of World Population Growth

In millions

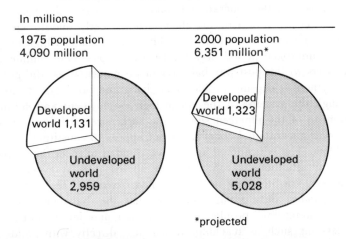

1975 population
4,090 million

2000 population
6,351 million*

Developed world 1,131

Undeveloped world 2,959

Developed world 1,323

Undeveloped world 5,028

*projected

Source: The Global 2000 Report to the President, a report prepared by the Council on Environmental Quality and the Department of State, USA.

Three main issues present themselves concerning the structure of the British population. Each focuses on a particular generation: the old, the middle-aged and the young.

The elderly have become an issue because of the sheer increase in their numbers which was fivefold between 1901 and 1983 (pp. 383–4). The percentage of people aged 65 or over is expected to remain at about 15% until the end of the century, but within the age group there will be a substantial increase in those aged 85 or over. This will result in heavier demand for health and social services and possibly for care within the family. The latter point raises issues of policy and gender. If a policy of de-institutionalisation of the old is pursued, will sufficient resources be channelled to those who care for them? Will the carers still be overwhelmingly women (often daughters), as they have traditionally been? Already, a woman caring full-time for her senile mother has successfully taken the British government to the European Court and received a ruling requiring it to help pay for her caring work. Beyond the matters of dependency and resources, it is possible that the majority of active and relatively healthy elderly will challenge current negative stereotypes of old age. A Harris poll (1975) of elderly Americans seemed to show that they have much more positive images of themselves than do the general public.

Members of the generational cohort of 1945 (i.e. those born in that year) are now entering their forties – early middle age. In Britain and the United States the birth rate remained high for an almost unbroken period between 1945 and 1964. One commentator refers to the post-war baby boom phenomenon as 'the pig in the python' – causing problems for itself and others as it moves through the system. In the era of high employment and cultural optimism of the nineteen sixties, the sheer size of the immediate post-war generational cohorts did not appear to constitute a great problem. The educational system was funded to meet their needs and the situations vacant columns offered jobs at every level. However, Ira Steinberg in *The New Lost Generation: The Problems of the Population Boom* (1982), suggests that the 'babyboomers' are now running into problems of promotion and job mobility. In professions such as teaching, which deal directly with children, their difficulties are exacerbated by the much lower birth rate, starting in 1965. Simply, they have a smaller clientele. The results of this were seen in both countries in the closing down and amalgamation of primary and secondary schools and in voluntary redundancies. Several effects of job and promotional scarcity seemed noticeable: a quickening of competitiveness in some cases, a loss of morale in others and a tendency for the teaching profession to come more into conflict with government.

The above review indicates that generational problems must be understood in the historical contexts in which they occur. Size is only one, albeit an important factor, and is itself influenced by others. Indeed, Richard A. Easterlin in *Birth and Fortune: The Impact of Numbers on Personal Welfare* (1980) argues that economic factors have a major effect on the birth rate. Thus, the economic prosperity of the post-war period encouraged larger families and the ensuing more austere period, smaller ones.

The younger generation – let us say, those born after the peak year for births, 1964 – come, as teenagers, into what seems a tougher world than the sixties. First, following the 'pig in the python' must be for many a stultifying experience. The sixties generation, 'beautiful people' and all, are typically clinging to their jobs – like their parents before them. Inevitably this is at the expense of the would-be upwardly mobile young. Second, mass generational unemployment darkens the future of today's young. This situation is not the fault of the now middle-aged, but is caused by factors – international competition, new technology, and arguably government policy – which affect the whole population. However, the young are particularly hard hit and I have devoted a section at the close of this book to the issue of youth education and employment.

Finally, a sobering thought is that when what is left of the

Comparison of Population Growth in 'Developed' and 'Developing' Countries

Part 1 Developed Countries

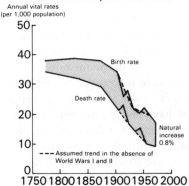

Annual vital rates
(per 1,000 population)

In developed countries death rates declined slowly beginning in the late 18th century. Birth rates followed closely. Population growth rates rarely exceeded 1.5% per year.

Part 2 Developing Countries

Annual vital rates
(per 1,000 population)

In developing countries birth and death rates remained high through the first decades of the 20th century. Then death rates began to drop. Birth rates stayed high and populations grew at 2.5, 3.0 and 3.5% or higher a year. Since the mid-1960s some countries' birth rates have begun to decline.

Source: United Nations

165

former baby boomers are, at last, old timers, it will fall largely to today's young to care for them. Having contemplated the 'pig' from below for two generations, they will be expected, at last, to cherish its rump!

Perspectives on Population Growth

I will review briefly four approaches to population growth and control. The first, that of Thomas Malthus, can fairly be termed a theory on the basis of the historical and comparative evidence he accumulated in support of it. The others concentrate as much on advocating forms of control as on explaining growth and are strongly tinged with ideology. The separation between this section (on perspectives) and the next (on policy) is not precise – there is a particularly large overlap in relation to perspectives (ii) and (iii).

(i) Malthus

Malthus (1766–1834) argued that 'population, when unchecked, increases in a geometrical ratio. Subsistence only increases in an arithmetical ratio.' Thus population increases as follows – 1, 2, 4, 8, 16, 32 . . . – and food – 1, 2, 3, 4, 5, 6. At the sixth point in this progression, population increase has run ahead of the increase in food production by over 500%. Malthus may not have been precisely correct, but there is no doubt that he observed a general tendency. The one solution he offered to the resultant misery was moral restraint, including postponement of marriage, coupled with pre-marital chastity until the partners could afford to support a family. Malthus's policies of control have not proved popular, but his analysis of population control remains influential. R. K. Kelsall suggests that as far as many Third World countries are concerned 'the factors in the situation are basically those to which he drew attention', i.e. population growth out-running food supplies.

(ii) Neo-Malthusianism – Family Planning

A second approach is sometimes referred to as Neo-Malthusianism. It broadly accepts Malthus's analysis but argues for the adoption of birth control within marriage. Today, many of those involved in the practical urgencies of population policy advocate birth control whenever necessary with little concern for theoretical reference. Malthus did not adequately anticipate the effect of birth control on population growth, nor did he fully appreciate the extent to which improved crop fertilisation and production could sustain larger populations. In fact, human invention in the fields of birth control, health and nutrition and agriculture has produced a pattern of population growth outlined in the diagram below, rather than repeated cycles of growth and decline back to a stable figure as Malthus indicates.

The theory of population transition presented below (see also Part 1 of the figure on p. 165), developed at the United Nations, should not be over-generalised. It applies well to most modern societies but it may apply less well to Third World societies if the factors that reduced population growth in the West fail to do so there (see Part 2 of the figure on p. 165).

Type	Birth rate	Death rate	Population growth
1	High	High	Stable
2	High	High/declining	Slight increase
3	High	Low	Large increase
4	Falling	Falling	Falling
5	Low	Low	Low and stable

Type 1 would describe many simple societies unaffected by modern factors and type 5 most modern societies. It should be possible to pick out various types in the chart from the previous section.

In summary, then, the second approach covers those who advocate modern techniques of birth control and improved crop fertilisation to reduce population and improve nutrition in the Third World. The assumption that technology is the key to progress in population control complements one version of modernisation theory (see pp. 188–9).

(iii) Redistribution of Resources and Population Stabilisation

We now turn to a third approach. Susan George, in *How the Other Half Dies: The Real Reasons for World Hunger*, (Penguin, 1977, p. 59) sharply attacks attempts to deal with the problems of Third World countries primarily in terms of population control. She states her own position clearly:

The first thing to realise when trying to think straight about

167

population/food is that hunger is not *caused* by population pressure. Both hunger and rapid population growth reflect the same failure of a political and economic system.

George finds a grossly unequal distribution of wealth in world and, in most cases, national terms. Hunger and population growth are symptoms – one is not the cause of the other – of this inequality. Couples have many children because *only* children will protect them against poverty. Population decrease tends to follow decrease in poverty. The abolition of poverty is, therefore, what should come first and the resources are there to achieve it. Belabouring the poor about birth control is to appear to blame them for problems that are not of their own making.

In the following quotation, George summarises some of the evidence for her case:

> The Overseas Development Council report *Population* quotes a 1971 study by William Rich showing that where decrease in birth rates is concerned, variations between UDCs (UDCs is short for Underdeveloped Countries) with similar gross national products per capita result primarily from differences in the *distribution* of this GNP. In more equalitarian countries, birth rates tend to decline rapidly, and vice versa. These conclusions are also borne out by the comparative figures for five UDCs published by the *New Internationalist* . . .
>
> This (data) shows that if you want to get your natural birth rate from 41 down to 26 (Taiwan) or from 45 to 30 per thousand (Korea), the best way to go about it is not to distribute condoms and IUDs and hope for the best, but to give people effective land reform and more income. They will reward you with fewer babies. (George, *How the Other Half Dies*, p. 63).

Very importantly from the point of view of practical policy-making, a study by staff of the World Bank and of the Institute of Development Studies at the University of Sussex came to conclusions similar to those of George. First, they argued that the main goal of development should not merely be growth but 'redistribution with growth'. They noted that growth could occur without the majority benefiting. Instead they argued for development strategies that would meet the needs of the majority. This became known as the 'basic needs approach'. Second, they tended to regard population control as secondary to and dependent on more egalitarian policies of development (see below). Incidentally, this marked a sharp departure from the assumptions of the modernisation theorists who believed that the general population would almost automatically benefit from growth. Consequently, they rarely addressed the issue of the redistribution of resources.

(iv) Population Laissez-faire

A fourth, quite different perspective on world population growth comes from the political right. It reflects the free-market view that became popular in the late seventies and early eighties. One example of this approach is a draft position paper prepared in the Presidential White House for the United States delegation to the UN International Conference on Population (August 1984; source, Harford Thomas, *Guardian*, 3 July 1984, p. 21). It argues that population growth is, in itself, as asset. It became dangerous only because in developing countries 'economic statism' interfered with the natural mechanisms of economic incentives and rewards which would have adjusted population growth to rising living standards. The draft document then goes on to argue that the USA 'does not consider abortion an acceptable element of family planning programmes.'

Although presented as theory, this approach is highly ideological and speculative. Supposing reduced population control results in population increase rather than decrease? Free-market population policies may be no more effective in reducing population than free-market economics has so far been (1984) in reducing unemployment in Britain. Perhaps a free-market 'experiment' in the area of population would be too risky.

My own view favours a policy combining a redistribution of resources (as Susan George argues) and continued efforts to extend birth control (an up-dated version of approach (ii)). Though George's case is well sustained, there is evidence that birth control does have an independent effect in reducing population. In *Human Numbers, Human Needs,* Paul Harrison and John Rowley point out that, in the industrialised world where 70% couples of reproductive age are using contraception, birth rates are low at 16 per 1,000 whereas in underdeveloped countries where less than 20% are practising conctraception the average birth rate is 34 per 1,000 – twice as high. Estimates suggest that if unwanted births were prevented in Bangladesh, Colombia, Jamaica and several other countries, population growth rates could be halved.

Population Policy and Development

(i) Problems and Policy Overview: Ozzie Simmons

As the previous section suggests, the precise relationship between the rate of population increase and development (and vice-versa) is contentious. Fully aware of this, Ozzie G. Simmons, nevertheless, attempts to summarise the relationship between rapid population growth and development in the light of existing research. In his article, 'Development Perspectives and Population Change', he briefly examines this relationship in respect to several key areas: health, education, labour absorption, food and income distribution. Broadly, his perspective reflects the assumptions of (ii) and especially (iii) of the previous section.

On the matter of health, Simmons observes that high fertility rates have a direct effect on the cost of services 'since obstetric and paediatric care constitute a large part of total demand for health services'. However, he emphasises that there are other causes of inadequate health care of comparable importance in the Third World. In most less developed countries (LDCs), health care tends to be concentrated in the urban areas and available mainly to the urban elites and middle class. He argues for a change from expensive, high-technology, hospital-based medicine to a primary care approach carried out by larger numbers of accessible, though less fully and expensively trained, paramedics (for a fuller discussion of this issue, see pp. 642–7).

The provision of education facilities is the factor which Simmons sees as most negatively affected by rapid population increase. Quite simply, an age structure weighted towards children and teenagers tends to raise the cost and decrease the quality of the educational system. On the matter of labour absorption, he considers rapid population growth to exacerbate rather than cause unemployment and under-employment. He advocates meeting the problem by improving the skills and access to productive assets of the majority (a basic needs approach) and through labour intensive development (see also pp. 217).

The scale of hunger and starvation in the Third World needs to be indicated before we discuss Simmons' comments on food. About 40 million people die each year from hunger, almost half of them children. Of the 122 million children born in 1981 – the International Year of the child – one in ten died within a year, mainly from malnutrition. The Ethiopian famine made world hunger and starvation a major issue of public concern and conscience in 1985. Tens of thousands of personal contributions helped to meet an immediate need though it remains to be seen whether public opinion will pressure national governments and the United Nations to make the fundamental changes necessary substantially to reduce world hunger. As Ozzie Simmons points out, the world can produce enough food to meet forseeable needs, taking into account estimates of population growth. However, this calculation depends on the food surplus produced by the developed countries (DCs) which is expensive for LDCs to buy. Alternatively and preferably, Simmons suggests that the LDCs should try to achieve the 3.5% to 4% increase in food production required to meet their needs and which is physically, technically and economically possible. He concludes that to be successful, this policy would need to be accompanied by income redistribution which would both enable people to buy food and probably reduce population growth (see George above). In short, he sees the food problem primarily as one of production and distribution rather than as a function of over-population.

Simmons considers that there is a tendency for rapid population increase adversely to affect income distribution in two main ways. First, in the absence of growth, the more people there are, the more thinly resources – health, education, land – tend to be spread. Second, high fertility increases inequality of income between families because the poor tend to have larger families. Despite hazarding these two points, Simmons stresses that the state of research in the area does not support generalisations. He comments that it is 'just as likely' that inequality causes high fertility among poorer, less educated sections of the population as the reverse.

Simmons concludes by arguing that both population control and poverty-focused development strategies are necessary and, carefully pursued, almost certainly complementary. Finally, his emphasis is on eliminating what he refers to as 'the underlying causes of poverty':

> The real solution lies in structural change, in changing the distribution of productive wealth and thus the distribution of economic power, and in increasing the participation of the poor in decision-making and thus enabling them to exercise political power.

He offers no detailed blueprint for population policy or

development strategy because the factors involved vary and require different responses in different societies. Similarly, he sees no single political road to change – continued resistance to change, reform and revolution are all possible.

Population Policy in the Third World with Particular Reference to the Young

Two issues relating to population are discussed below: the reduction of the fertility rate and infant and child mortality and disease, i.e. child health. These issues, particularly the second, are so urgent that they require immediate response. However, in discussing them, the analysis already made in this section needs to be remembered. These are issues not merely of population policy, but of the development and distribution of resources – both within Third World societies and globally. The education and employment of the young of the Third World is discussed in the next chapter (pp. 217–20).

(a) THE REDUCTION OF THE FERTILITY RATE A reduction in the fertility rate is historically a major factor in reducing the rate of population increase. However, a variety of factors make this a more complicated matter than one of contraception education. There is resistance to birth control for both practical and cultural reasons in many Third World societies and, in any case, expert opinion in the West is not certain precisely how key variables such as female education and more equal income distribution affect the fertility rate.

The main practical reason for producing large families in the Third World, is to provide enough workers to run the family's property and to ensure care and protection for parents in their old age. In the absence of a welfare state this makes sense and even more so given high infant mortality rates among the very poor – 3 out of 10 children die before they reach the age of 5. The cultural complement to this is the high status normally associated with having a large family and religious disapproval of 'unnatural' interference with reproduction. For these reasons, it is usually both crude and ineffective for outsiders to impose birth control or to try to bribe people to use it (although China itself seems successfully to have enforced its own one-child per family policy).

A better way is to discover, and where practical, to create the conditions that are associated with a decline in the fertility rate.

One commonly found correlation with a decline in the fertility rate is a prior decline in the rate of infant mortality. This relationship occurred in Britain and other European societies as they developed (see pp. 165) and in virtually all Third World societies in which the fertility rate has decreased. A decline in infant mortality, then, seems almost a precondition of a decline in the rate of fertility although the former can occur without the latter. The logic of this correlation appears to be that when there is a high likelihood of children surviving, there is less need to have so many of them. This brings up a second factor associated with fertility decline which is also strongly associated with a decline in the rate of infant mortality: an increase in the income and resources of the poor. Robert Repetto's *Economic Equality and Fertility in Developing Countries* demonstrates that the more equal the total distribution of income in a society, the lower the overall birthrate will tend to be. Again, this appears to establish a crucial link between development and a reduction in the rate of population growth.

According to Ozzie Simmons, the effect of female education on fertility is less certain than is commonly thought. He suggests that '(p)erhaps the most widely accepted generalisation is that of the inverse relationship between education and fertility', i.e., the educated tend to have fewer children. However, in countries with the *lowest* rates of female literacy, education is likely to increase fertility possibly by simply increasing the ability to have live births. Otherwise, education is associated with a decline in fertility, especially the education of women and particularly in urban areas. Simmons also claims that a fourth factor, the paid employment of women, is ambiguous in its effect on fertility. He cites a range of studies of female work status and fertility in Latin America which show no consistent inverse relationship between female employment outside the home and fertility. However, the recent World Fertility Survey covering the period from 1972 to the mid-eighties appears to re-establish the general connection between both the education and paid employment of women and low fertility. Three fifths of the world's illiterate are women and this provides an added reason for doing something about it.

Finally, the effect of family planning programmes on fertility remains to be considered. The debate centres on the issue of whether family planning programmes are effective in the absence

173

of development and in the presence of strong cultural resistance to them. The balance of opinion is that such programmes tend to be more effective where at least some development has occurred, but in some cases they may also help independently to reduce fertility. The following example of a successful family planning programme was implemented in a society, Indonesia, which had experienced some development.

With an estimated population of 150 million, Indonesia seems a prime case for an effective planning policy. Its population has been increasing by 2.9 million per year and each year 2 million more jobs are needed. In the face of these trends, Indonesia has achieved a 'success story unrivalled in family planning history', according to demographers Terence and Valerie Hull, and Masri Singarimbun.

The setting up of the National Family Planning Co-ordination Board in 1970 indicated firm commitment to family planning. Initial funding came from the Indonesian government ($1.3 million) and foreign donors ($3 million). Now the programme's annual budget is over $50 million. The programme has helped to bring down population growth rate from 2.4% in 1964 to around 1.9% in 1981. In the Bali region, for instance, the birth rate fell an astonishing 34% between 1970 and 1975. A lower rate of growth still is the target.

The major reason for the success of the programme is that it has been well organised and implemented. The programme is effective down to the village level. Local part-time field workers and prominent members of the community operate the programme and simple clinics have been established. It is local people, rather than outside experts, who have succeeded in persuading and explaining about birth control. Backing up the field workers are thousands of local volunteers who have helped to set up over 30,000 community family planning posts. Efficient communication between the local administrators and the Planning Board is crucial. The Board evaluates incoming data and advises local workers accordingly.

The success of the above programme goes some way towards undermining the view that there is almost overwhelming cultural resistance to birth control in many traditional societies. Perhaps resistance in the past has been the fault of insensitive administrators, ignorant of local feeling and custom. The Indonesian case suggests that there is another way. Certainly, the case for combining family planning programmes with anti-poverty development strategies seems strong.

(b) REDUCING INFANT AND CHILD MORTALITY AND DISEASE Statistics are not, in themselves, 'appalling' but the misery and deprivation behind the figures of infant and child mortality and disease certainly are. The basic or absolute poverty which underlines them is perhaps the major human and social problem in the world today. Only two other issues of survival – the nuclear and environmental – are of comparable importance. It may help to illuminate the personal experience of childhood poverty and starvation if we concentrate briefly on two aspects of it – mental illness and physical disablement – rather than attempt a global coverage.

It is a myth that mental illness is a 'luxury' of materially rich societies. Different cultures produce different illnesses, but overall, mental illness seems to be as common in the underdeveloped as in the industrialised world. It is not hard to see why. Poverty produces stress and depression; malnutrition can lead to apathy. People in the Third World are more subject to natural disasters, bereavements, rising but often frustrated expectations, enforced migrations and wars than Westerners. All of these are typically emotionally stressful occurrences.

War, of course, causes unequalled physical and emotional damage. The following is a report from Berry Brazleton on a number of Kampuchean children most of whom had been orphaned by war. He is writing about an orphanage in Phnom Penh:

Most infants in these overcrowded orphanages lie around all day, flat on their backs, their heads flattened and the hair worn off the backs of their heads.

The orphans are being physically salvaged in Phnom Penh, but the quality of their future lives is far from assured. We know now that unless a baby is stimulated by his environment to learn and to experience the excitement of learning, he will not be able to learn later. The combination of an under-nourished brain coupled with a non-stimulating environment can be critical deprivation to an immature developing child.

We are not sure how long such deprivation must last or how severe it must be to affect a child's future potential, but the combination of nutritional and functional deprivation is much more severe than either one alone.

In Phnom Penh and the Thai border camps the babies are well nourished, but the girls taking

175

care of them have been through too much themselves to be able to respond to the psychological needs of small dependants. Everyone in the orphanages means well and they would insti- tute the same kinds of interactive experiences that I did, but they have not thought of them. Their own lives have been too sparse, and they have barely recovered from a mass depression.

From Berry Brazleton, 'Games that Children Play for Survival,' *Guardian*, 18 December 1981, p. 7.

There are about 200 million disabled children in the world, most of them in underdeveloped countries. Malnutrition is a major cause of disablement in the Third World. For instance, every year 250,000 children become blind through lack of vitamin A. Prevention can cost as little as three or four pence per person. In 1979, a survey in the villages of Camp Tinio and Mananac in the Philippines showed that 119 out of 568 children under the age of six were to some extent disabled – over 20%. Of those impaired, 80% were found to be mal- nourished. The following is an extract from a report by Teresa Tunay on the low cost community-based care programme that followed the survey. It is particularly worth noting the reasons why she thinks the programme was effective.

Today, only a few months later, 46 per cent of those chil- dren have shown very significant improvements.

The original survey also found Josefina, a 10 month old baby girl who was a victim of Down's Syndrome. In other words, she was a mongoloid child. When her home was visited by one of the survey team, Josefina was virtual- ly a wilting head of lettuce in her mother's arms. Her body appeared boneless. She could not even hold her head up. Her eyes were lifeless and she responded to neither the sound of a voice nor to a smiling face.

Today only 16 weeks later, Josefina has put on weight, runs around the house in a baby walker, plays enthusiastically with a string of coloured beads, and is just as responsive as any normal child of her age.

Josefina's 'therapy' did not re- quire institutionalisation or gadgetry. Her mother was shown how and where to 'tickle' her baby to exercise the muscles. The treatment progressed through gentle kneading of the child's limbs to a daily ritual of ther- apeutic exercise. Soon, the child began to make steady and con- tinued progress. . . .

The key to low-cost but dramatic improvements in the lives of the majority of the disabled lies in releasing the care and support which is latent in the family and the community. And it was from that point that the 'Reaching the Unreached' programme began. Two young researchers, one trained in occupational therapy and the other in pre-school education, went to live in the village, renting a small hut at a nominal rate, from the village or 'barangay' captain.

In discussion with the community, they agreed to concentrate their efforts on children under the age of six, not only because the young child is the most vulnerable, but also because the earlier the help the more potential there is for improve-ment and the less damage is done to the normal processes of child development.

Village volunteers were trained. Non-technical indicators were listed for the detection of impairments. And the community as a whole was involved in finding impairments in their children, in discussing their attitudes towards it, and in planning and carrying out the rehabilitation programmes themselves.

From Teresa Tunay, 'Miracles for the Many,' *New Internationalist*, No. 95, p. 13.

Conclusion: Population Policy and Politics

As the above discussion of world population problems and policy progressed, the political issues that underlay all policy decisions should have become increasingly apparent. As Susan George emphasises, at the centre of the political debate about population is development. Birth control policies may help – international aid helps – but development is essential to solving the problems of the Third World's people. However, there are deep political and ideological disagreements about how development best occurs. These disagreements are not merely about the 'mechanisms' of development but reflect profound differences of value and preference. At its widest, this debate is about what kind of future world community we will make. To this issue, we now turn.

Guide to Further Reading and Study

R. K. Kelsall's *Population* (Longman, 1975) is a standard basic introduction to the area. Paul R. Ehrlich's *The Population Bomb* (Ballantine Books, 1968) is now considered alarmist but did put the issue firmly on the agenda. Susan George's *How the Other Half Dies: The Real Reasons for World Hunger* (Penguin, 1977) analyses population as part of the wider problem of development, as do several other books indicated at the end of the next chapter. Some useful points are made on the teaching of population in Roger Gomm and Patrick McNeill's *Handbook for Sociology Teachers* (Heinemann, 1982), for which the index is the best access.

Past Questions

1 (a) Explain why there has been a 'population explosion' in underdeveloped countries. (b) Examine some of the consequences of such a 'population explosion' (AEB, 1982)

2 Compare and contrast the population increase of Britain in the nineteenth century with that of underdeveloped countries in the twentieth century. (AEB, 1983)

3 What do you understand by the 'dependency ratio'? Assess the major changes in the dependency ratio since 1945 and their social consequences. (OLE, 1983)

4 The major influences on variations in the birth rate since 1900 have been changes in the level of economic activity, not developments in method of contraception. Discuss. (OLE, 1983)

5 What are the causes and consequences of an ageing population? Illustrate your answer with reference to *one* society. (AEB, 1985)

6 Analyse the cause of any *two* major demographic changes in any one society you have studied. (London, 1985)

(For Questions 5 and 6, see also Chapter 14.)

8 Social Change: Development and Underdevelopment

Conclusion: Issues and Future Trends

Guide to Further Reading and Study

Past Questions

Terminology

Social change includes both development, undevelopment and underdevelopment. Development implies some positive progress in a society's condition whereas underdevelopment implies decline or stagnation. Underdevelopment is a term used especially by Marxists to indicate that the operation of international capitalism tends to prevent or retard development in the Third World. What is viewed as development varies somewhat from society to society. The goals of socialist societies are not the same as those of capitalist ones. The former tend to stress egalitarian and communal objectives, whereas the latter put greater emphasis on individuality and personal freedom. Nevertheless, there are some aspects of development on which in practice there is near-universal agreement. These are mainly technological, economic and educational. Nearly all societies seek to improve their technology, increase their wealth and develop the skills of their people. How this should be done and who should most benefit from development are, of course, matters of wide disagreement.

Once we move beyond quantifiable and measurable matters of wealth and technique to consider political and cultural issues, disagreement about what constitutes development becomes more marked. The Western democracies tend to want 'developing' societies eventually to adopt the political and civil liberties common in the West. By contrast, the Soviet Union and China look to the Communist Party – theoretically the organ of the working class or peasantry – as the means of political decision and expression. Even so, a number of 'developing' societies have, at different times, attempted to combine Western-style political institutions and civil liberties with broadly socialist programmes of economic development. Jamaica under Michael Manley's leadership and Chile under Salvador Allende are examples.

There is even less agreement about what constitutes a developed cultural life than about political development. This applies both to the level of popular culture, i.e. the quality of everyday life, and to 'high' culture – literature, music and the rest of the arts. Unsurprisingly, capitalist images of 'socialist man' and socialist images of 'capitalist man' tend towards the uncomplimentary. In capitalist society, socialism is often depicted as producing mass, wooden conformity from which only a few brave writers and artists successfully break. For their part, socialist societies often present capitalists as greedy and manipulative. Yet, both at the ordinary and exceptional level, there is much successful cultural interchange. Many citizens of the First and Second Worlds seem capable of getting on well with each other and the best of Socialist and Western art is appreciated in both cultures. Both at the level of the mundane and the uniquely creative, shared values and concerns exist. If literature and art illuminate the common ideals and hopes of humanity, then they may provide a better guide to developmental goals than the ideological utterances of politicians.

The terminology of social change reflects a variety of ideological perspectives, some of which have been indicated above. The term development tends to reflect an optimistic liberal-capitalist view that world 'progress' is likely, whereas that of underdevelopment has clearly negative overtones. To avoid the polarisation of these terms, some prefer more developed countries (MDCs) and less developed countries (LDCs). As J. K. Galbraith suggests, the terms rich and poor nations are probably the simplest and truest. The widely used terms, First, Second and Third World are useful providing no hierarchy is assumed. The First World is the United States and Western European capitalist democracies, the Second World is the Soviet Union and its communist bloc allies, and the Third World is the poor or relatively poor countries.

Not all countries fit neatly into simple categories. The diagram below shows three groups of countries at different levels of development according to income and type of production. A large service sector is usually taken as an indicator of advanced development; such economies, for example the United States, are sometimes referred to as post-industrial or post-modern though Marxists prefer the terms capitalist/socialist/communist. The diagram also gives data about the employed population (usually a smaller proportion of the total population in poorer countries).

Breakdown of Employment in Selected Countries:

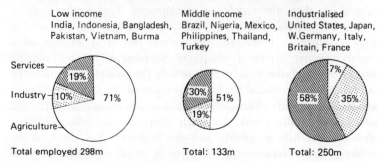

Low income India, Indonesia, Bangladesh, Pakistan, Vietnam, Burma	Middle income Brazil, Nigeria, Mexico, Philippines, Thailand, Turkey	Industrialised United States, Japan, W.Germany, Italy, Britain, France

Services — 19%
Industry — 10% 71%
Agriculture

30% 51%
19%

7%
58% 35%

Total employed 298m   Total: 133m   Total: 250m

Levels of Development

Note. The percentages refer to levels of employment in given economic sectors.

Source: *The Economist*, February 24, 1979, p.32.

The West and the World: Historical and Contemporary Overview

Many of the problems and issues of the contemporary world are the product of the impact of the Western powers on the rest of the globe. This impact began in the fifteenth century, intensified in the nineteenth and remains very strong. Of course there is nothing new or modern in imperial expansion. The Greeks and Romans established large empires which radically changed the economic, political and cultural lives of their subject peoples. The modern European empires have done no less. The major difference is that between them the Western European powers settled, occupied or subdued virtually the rest of the world. The result is that even today world politics, economics and even cultural relations take place within a framework largely created by Western Europe. On the whole, the societies of what we now call the Third World have been put in a reactive position, few have attained power and influence comparable to that of the Western nations. Put more technically, the causes of change in Western European societies – particularly, Britain – were largely endogamous (generated from within) whereas in the Third World they were and are predominantly exogamous ('imported' or imposed from outside). It would be difficult to exaggerate the shock of many traditional and primitive societies as they struggled to re-orientate or even survive (for instance, the American Indians) under the impact of the West.

Three phases of Western influence and domination can be indicated. First, is the period of exploration, trade and conquest beginning in the fifteenth century and which included the 'discovery' of the Americas. Second, is the period of the formal empires – when most European colonies were established – of the nineteenth and first half of the twentieth century. Third, is the post-Second World War period during which the formal European empires were broken up. Politically, the United States and the USSR have become the dominant world powers although they have usually tried to avoid (often unsuccessfully) establishing formal occupations of societies they seek to dominate. The world economic power of European corporations (and especially now American) continues, however. The term neo-colonial is widely used to describe a situation in which one country is actually, though not formally, controlled by another (the term can refer to either economic or political control). Finally, during the post-war period, Japan has developed into an economic power of global significance.

What, then for good or ill, has the Western impact on the Third World been? The arguments that surround this question are the substance of the rest of this chapter. Certain key points should be noted here. Economically the issue is whether the West has tended or, at least, tried to stimulate development (economic growth) or whether it has more typically exploited and underdeveloped the Third World. Politically, interest now focuses on the struggle between the USSR and the United States and the systems they represent and advocate. Previously, the European powers had been caught in the contradiction of supporting nationalism and democracy at home but not always in their subject territories. Eventually, however, all of them acquiesced to the political independence of their colonies. Many ex-colonies adopted political systems reflecting the originally European ideologies of liberalism and socialism. The cultural impact of Europe on the rest of the world defies summary. Christianity, liberty and democracy (liberalism), equality (socialism), the idea of linear progress itself, all spread from the West. Currently, the domination of the West, particularly the United States, of the entertainment media raises profound issues of value, and of cultural independence, creativity, quality and taste. The image of members of a Chinese peasant commune avidly watching Western films (shown in the documentary 'Heart of the Dragon') focuses the issue nicely.

Contemporary Contexts and Issues

It is not possible to make much sense of the development/ underdevelopment debate presented below without knowing the basic institutional framework of post-war political and economic life. After the defeat of Germany and Japan, two new power blocs emerged: the North Atlantic Treaty Organisation (NATO) of the United States and most of Western Europe, and the Warsaw Pact which included the Soviet Union and most of the countries of Eastern Europe. These alliances operate mainly in Europe and on a global scale the independent activities and rivalry of the USSR and the United States are most obvious. The 'cold war' began almost before the Second World War ended.

The United Nations was established as part of the post-war settlement in an attempt to provide a forum in which international problems and emergencies could be discussed and to some extent acted upon. In practice, the UN was so constituted that the major victorious powers surrendered none of their independence or sovereignty. Nevertheless, the UN is a unique focus of world opinion and cannot be ignored by the major powers. It has frequently been used by representatives of Third World nations – either individually or in concert. It has also fulfilled important, though, in the total world context, minor functions in such areas as health, education, research and peace-keeping. If these kind of issues are ever to be tackled primarily through a world agency, then the United Nations and its predecessor, the League of Nations, will be seen as the embryo of this approach.

The post-war world was also divided into two main economic blocs paralleling the political. The General Agreement on Tariffs and Trade (GATT) established the framework of international commerce for most of the world. The Soviet Union opted out and instead introduced Comecon for the Eastern European bloc. In practice, there is a significant amount of trade between blocs. Many Third World nations argue that GATT favours the manufacturing interests of the First World rather than their own agricultural and extractive indutries and have sought changes in the Agreement to accommodate this view.

The monetary system established after the war reflected the emergence of the United States as the world's leading economic power and the relative decline of Britain. The dollar became the world's major reserve currency – because much international trade was now conducted in dollars it became necessary for most countries to keep reserves of dollars if they wanted to buy Western products. The lending institutions related to the United Nations, the World Bank and International Monetary Fund, (IMF) reflected the dominance of the United States and Britain. The role of the World Bank, whose full title is the International Bank for Reconstruction and Development, was to provide loans for development projects in Europe or elsewhere following the destruction of war. In recent years its lending has been concentrated in the so-called Third World developing countries. The International Monetary Fund had a much wider brief to provide loans for countries in major economic difficulty, including balance of payment deficit, (i.e. when the value of imports exceeds exports.) Loans are provided at interest and subject to the borrowing recommendations for economic recovery laid down by the Fund.

The countries of the Third World, then, struggle for political, cultural and national identity and for economic development in a world not of their own making. Indeed, some of them, such as Nigeria, were literally put together by Western nations. Others, such as Iran, still cherish aspects of traditional culture as old or older than Western European civilisation. Even apologists for Western imperialism agree that some of the peoples of the Third World have suffered greatly (as well as, in their view, benefited) at the hands of the West. The slave trade alone proves the point. It is hardly surprising that intense and conflicting feelings of hatred and admiration, rejection and imitation, and of disgust and envy are freely expressed about Europe and the United States in the Third World. No doubt, if history had been different, and Western Europe had itself been occupied, its inhabitants would have felt similarly about their conquerors.

It will be obvious from the above survey that economic, political and ideological factors are highly related in the process of world change and development. Few Third World powers develop free from the economic and/or political influence of the Soviet Union or the United States although some, such as India, do seek an

185

independent or non-aligned position in relation to the superpowers. The diagram below summarises the main economic and political division in the contemporary world.

	Developed	**Underdeveloped**
Communist	USSR EASTERN EUROPE NORTH KOREA	CHINA, VIETNAM, CUBA
Capitalist	USA, EEC, JAPAN, AUSTRALIA, SOUTH AFRICA	CAPITALIST THIRD WORLD eg INDIA

Theories of Change

Neither theorists nor policy-makers agree on why some regions develop and others do not. I have divided the following theoretical section into four parts: development or modernisation theories; Marxist theories; two liberal theories – new conservative (free-market) theories and social democratic theories; and a feminist account of change. Many important issues are raised within the theoretical discussions but a number of key themes are further analysed in the next section.

Development (Modernisation) Theory

Developmentalists or modernisation theorists argue that the pattern of historical change has been from simple to complex, or modern, societies. They differ in their explanations of change but are in agreement in rejecting the Marxist model (see below). Many developmentalists also subscribe to convergence theory, i.e. they contend that the advanced industrial societies, whether socialist or capitalist, are growing more alike. Again, this differs from Marxists who see socialist and capitalist societies as radically different. Many of the concepts of modernisation theorists can be found in the earlier work of Spencer, Durkheim and Weber.

Spencer, Durkheim and Weber on Change
The view that social development has broadly evolved towards the

more complex, is apparent in the work of several of the founding fathers of sociology, notably Spencer and Durkheim. Ronald Fletcher usefully distinguishes between the descriptive and explanatory in their work. Thus, Spencer's descriptive criteria were: the simple society; the compound society (clans, tribes); doubly compounded (city states, kingdoms); and trebly compounded (empires, modern nations and federations). His explanatory typology consisted of the military and industrial types of society. He explained the change from the one to the other partly by the very success of military societies in establishing the conditions for the peaceful development of industry and welfare. Durkheim's descriptive criteria are very similar to Spencer's: the horde; the clan; simple polysegmental; polysegmental simply compounded (confederations of tribes); polysegmental doubly compounded (nations and federations). His explanatory typology proposes an increasing differentiation of society from the mechanical to the organic (see pp. 132–4) and has much more currency among contemporary sociologists than the now largely disregarded typology of Spencer.

Both Spencer and Durkheim were influenced by the strong nineteenth century interest in biology and, in particular, the tendency to find parallels between biological and social evolution. Both employed the concept of structural differentiation to indicate that as society develops more functions it becomes structurally more complex. This perspective has been elaborated more recently by Talcott Parsons (see below).

Max Weber's contribution to understanding change does not lie in the development of formal descriptive or explanatory frameworks. Yet, in his 'dialogue with Marx' (see below) he made several observations about the nature of social change which have influenced more recent modernisation theorists and liberal historians. First, Weber stressed the importance of ideas and choice in the process of change (see pp. 566–7). In this respect, Weber is sometimes described as a 'voluntarist'. Second, a related point, he rejected what he took to be Marx's overemphasis on the economic causes of change. Instead of economic 'determinism', he offered a multi-factoral approach to understanding change in which ideas played a major role. Third, he rejected Marx's analysis of class conflict and revolution. Change could be gradual as well as revolutionary and there were other important sources of change than class conflict. Fourth, although he recognised the inequality of capitalist society, he did not attribute it essentially to capitalism. Rather, he thought that large, rational organisations or bureaucracies, including the capitalist corporation, were necessarily hierarchical and unequal. He anticipated that as socialist societies developed large scale industrial and governmental bureaucracies, they would be characterised by inequality. Again, modernisation theorists and liberal thinkers have tended to accept and build on this analysis whilst, in some cases, arguing for the mitigation of the extremes of inequality in their own and other societies. One can see in Weber's analysis of bureaucracy in modern society, the seeds of convergence theory.

Developmental (Modernisation) Theory

This section gives examples of modernisation theory. They differ mainly in the extent to which they stress the *diffusion* (spread) of technology or of ideas as the primary stimulus to development.

Walt Rostow's emphasis is on the role of technology, though not exclusively so. Rostow's influential work *The Stages of Growth* was first published in 1960. He argued that it 'is possible to identify all societies, in their economic dimensions as lying within one of five categories'. These are:

(i)   traditional society
(ii)   preconditions for take-off
(iii) take-off
(iv)   drive to maturity
(v)   age of high mass-consumption

There is a broad similarity between Rostow's categories and the descriptive evolutionary frameworks of Spencer and Durkheim. However, he is openly little interested in what he calls traditional societies. He uses the term as a catch-all to describe those societies whose productivity is 'limited by the inaccessibility of modern science'. For Rostow, modern science and its practical application in technology is the key to the 'take-off' into development. In Europe the scientific and technological preconditions for take-offs were developed internally, elsewhere it was the 'intrusion by more advanced societies' which 'shocked the traditional society' and began or hastened its undoing and opened the way for change, especially 'economic progress'. In the take-off phase, growth becomes the 'normal condition'. In traditional society, take-off requires not only the availability of capital and technology but the emergence of a modernising, political elite. The 'drive to maturity' is characterised by a high percentage of national income reinvestment 'to extend modern technology over the whole front of its economic activity'. Once this economic infrastructure is laid down, leading economic sectors 'shift towards durable consumers' goods and services'. Higher personal income and greater leisure time stimulate this process. Rostow also notes that in this stage, money available for welfare expenditure increases.

On the relationship between development and democracy, Rostow acknowledges what in a later publication he refers to as 'an important and painful truth' (1971): that it is possible for development to occur under totalitarian leadership. In *Stages of Growth* he devotes a full chapter to attacking Communism although he also refers to the Meiji Restoration in Japan and Ataturk's Turkey as non-communist forms of 'peculiarly inhumane . . . political organisation capable of launching and sustaining the growth process'. However, he seems to reveal that his primary concern is with communism rather than totalitarianism as such when he argues the need for a partnership between the Western powers 'in association with the non-communist politicians and peoples' to achieve growth and democracy. To be consistent in opposing totalitarianism, he should have written 'non-totalitarian' rather than 'non-communist'. In fact, it has been a criticism of American post-war international policy that its government has been too ready to work with and support right-wing totalitarian regimes merely to oppose communism, as in the case of the Shah of Iran and President Diem of (formerly) South Vietnam. Frequently, the underlying problem is that there is little or no democratic tradition in Third World countries. This raises the question of whether supporting 'democracy' against communism is a viable basis of political policy in societies in which it has few roots. We return to this controversial and ideologically charged question later.

Talcott Parsons and Bert Hoselitz conceptualise modernisation within a functionalist framework. Following Weber, they stress that the diffusion of ideas and values from the West outwards is the underlying dynamic of modernisation rather than the spread of technology emphasised by Rostow. However, the two approaches are not incompatible. According to Parsons, as society evolves in a more complex direction, so its institutions change and adapt and become more functionally differentiated. Thus, in more modern societies, many of the more formal aspects of socialisation are carried out within the educational system rather than the family. In *Sociological Factors in Economic Development* (1960), Hoselitz draws on Parsons' typology of pattern variables (see pp. 134–5) and uses it as a means to analyse the social factors that contribute to economic growth. He concluded that the values of achievement, universalism and specificity (particularly as applied to the division of labour) are conducive to growth, and those of ascription, particularism and diffuseness to stagnation. Interestingly, he finds that the former three values have accompanied growth in the Soviet Union as in the West thus indicating some convergence between the two types of society (see below). Finally, he suggests that 'deviant' elites may be more effective agents of modernisation than traditional ones.

The social psychologist David McLelland has also examined the attitudes conducive to development. His work is more empirical than that of Hoselitz. McLelland set out to test whether the need for achievement, or Nach as he termed it, is related to development. Using tests he devised for the purpose, he attempted to relate increases in Nach in a given culture to increases in the production of certain relevant commodities. His tests included both historical and contemporary societies and seemed to establish the positive correlation he had hypothesised. Since this was so, McLelland recommended greater socialisation in achievement motivation in Third World countries.

McLelland's work is an interesting piece of cross-cultural social psychology but politically naive. To those Third World societies struggling against often acute economic difficulties and, as some of them see it, imperialist exploitation, the advice to take achievement courses must have seemed, if not arrogant, ludicrous. A second criticism is that the correlation he establishes between increases in achievement motivation and production need not be causal. For instance, both could occur as part of a much wider imitation of the West or, in certain cases, both could be imposed by Western powers.

The practical effect of modernisation theory – in so far as it can be gauged – was to underpin a rather simplistic approach to aid and development on the part of the Western powers in the twenty years following the world war. 'Modernisation' turned out to be a much less predictable and neutral and a more political process than these theorists seemed to anticipate.

Critique of Modernisation Theory

In retrospect, perhaps the most damaging criticism of modernisation theory is its ethnocentrism, i.e. it assumes the necessity of 'modern' (in effect, American and to a lesser extent Western) values to Third World societies with little consideration of their own cultures. The notion that Third World societies might want to balance modernisation with traditional culture or even reject aspects of modernisation is not adequately appreciated. Instead 'modern man' or rather 'American man' is the presumed ideal goal. What now seems a naive belief in progress supported these chauvinistic attitudes. Second, the grand models of the developmentalists lack the feeling and meaning of historical reality: we are presented with a succession of stages rather than with people acting out of a variety of motives with a variety of results. Third, and related to the second point, modernisation theorists fail to explore the variety of class and national conflicts which radically effect development/underdevelopment (see section on underdevelopment theory). The issue of inequality has deeply concerned many in the Third World but an appreciation of its profound importance is not apparent in developmentalist writings until the nineteen seventies. Marxists particularly criticise diffusionists for not appreciating that the motive of economic exploitation is the key to understanding capitalist expansion.

Fourth, there is a clear tendency to deterministic thinking in modernisation theory both in its more technological and in its more 'value-functionalist' versions. This tendency is at its strongest in convergence theory which is fully presented in the next section. Weber's original emphasis on values was, of course, intended to give due importance to subjectivity and choice. However, Hoselitz's treatment of values, framed within Parsons' pattern variable pairs, makes them appear prescriptive and restrictive. Ironically, this is probably the oppositive of Weber's intention although he too struggled systematically to reconcile value subjectivity with the objective effects of social institutions.

Finally, mainstream developmentalist thinking both in United Nations development institutions and elsewhere has been steadily moving away from the assumptions of modernisation theory for almost twenty years. In particular, within the World Bank, it is no longer taken for granted that economic growth will benefit all social groups within the society it occurs. There is now much more concern to find strategies for development which immediately meet the basic needs of the poor (see pp. 168–9). However, modernisation theory remains of great interest as an example of how social science can play an ideological role – in this case the support and justification of American liberal capitalism – even to the point where, sadly, social science and ideology appear barely distinguishable.

Convergence Theory

Convergence theory is closely related to modernisation theory. It is usually applied to more industrially developed societies which by virtue of certain technological and organisational imperatives (needs) are seen as moving closer together. In particular, the comparison is made of the United States and the Soviet Union. Thus, Raymond Avon, the French sociologist remarked that it was not until he visited India that he realised that the significant division in the world was not between communism and capitalism, but between modern states and those which remained industrially undeveloped. However, the models of development surveyed above imply an asumption of convergence on an even larger scale, which all societies undergo as they 'modernise'.

Convergence theory focused a number of themes in American and, to some extent, European liberal-social democratic thought during the late nineteen fifties/early sixties. Together, these themes cohered into a mood which considerably influenced politicians and policy makers. A key work stimulating this climate of opinon was Ralf Dahrendorf's *Class and Class Conflict in an Industrial Society* (1959). Dahrendorf argues that there has been a decline in the 'old' militant working class and in the 'old' individualistic, capitalist class and in traditional class conflict (see pp. 271–2). He observes instead a managed or organised society in which solutions to social (no longer class) problems are technical rather than ideological in nature. Daniel Bell, who acknowledges Dahrendorf's influence, makes this point the central theme of his *The End of Ideology: On the Exhaustion of Political Ideas in the Fifties* (1961). Bell strongly contends that ideological and political 'extremism' such as fascism and communism, are not merely redundant but dangerous: their contempt of compromise and intolerance leading almost certainly to inhumanity and bloodshed. He believed he saw a prudent consensus emerging in the West in which the institutions of liberal democracy were accepted as the most mature and realistic means of political expression. With Bell, as with other modernisation thinkers, it can be difficult to disentangle what he believes is happening from what he wants to happen. Although Dahrendorf and Bell's expectations of immediately convergent trends referred mainly to the Western capitalist democracies, it is arguable that the sharply polarised ideological politics of the sixties and eighties (in the West) directly contradict even this limited thesis.

Clark Kerr *et al, Industrialism and Industrial Man* (1959) is probably the most comprehensive statement of convergence theory. Like Dahrendorf he considers that it is the industrial rather than the capitalist nature of modern society which gives it many of its basic characteristics. The same industrial technology produces similar occupational and stratificational systems and in Kerr's view mature industrial society requires higher levels of managerial, technical and labour skills than early industrial society. Both arguments have come in for sharp criticism. John Goldthorpe's view that stratification in socialist 'industrial' societies is produced primarily by political rather than technological or market factors is presented later (pp. 299–301). The view that advanced industrial society requires a more skilled labour force was refuted in the United States by Harry Braverman and, more recently, in Britain, by Paul Thompson. They argue that 'deskilling' of the industrial labour force has occurred partly because of the deliberate selection by capitalists of forms of technology and organisation that require low levels of worker skills and intelligent participation (and in some forms of production little or no worker involvement at all). No doubt the overall situation is complex. It may be that a highly skilled occupational elite has developed but that the experience of the majority is closer to what Braverman and Thompson suggest.

Kerr envisaged that industrial society would be marked by increasing wealth and leisure. This trend has occurred but Marxist and many other critics point out that capitalist society does not ensure a growing equality of wealth distribution and that the ability to enjoy leisure is likely to be correspondingly unequal. However, as Kerr assumes that industrial society is hierarchical this presumably is not a problem for him. Like Bell and Dahrendorf, he argues that, contrary to Marx, protest will not increase in later industrial society: 'Rather, turning Marx on his head, protest tends to peak early.' This is partly because increasing general affluence and the welfare state remove the incentive for protest, particularly based on class. In this case, the 25 years since Kerr wrote do not tend to bear him out. Rather, perhaps what has happened is that in Western Europe and the United States, a substantial and growing minority of unemployed and low-paid are not sharing in the now not so general affluence (see Harrington pp. 641–3). Perhaps the urban riots of the nineteen sixties (USA) and eighties (Britain) are a form of protest.

Finally, again echoing Bell, Kerr links industrialism with the development of *liberal pluralist democracy* and with the *consensus* about basic values, including a belief in compromise, necessary for it to work. Thus, industrial society 'develops a distinctive consensus which relates individuals and groups to each other and provides a common body of ideas, beliefs and value judgements integrated into a whole'. In comment, whilst a general commitment to liberal democracy and values persists in the West, the broader liberal consensus of the fifties has been split to the left and right (see pp. 654–6). Social and political life in the West has proved less settled and less easily manageable than Kerr and his liberal contemporaries imagined.

Kerr is somewhat ambiguous in committing himself to the view that either the Soviet Union or countries of the Third World will evolve essentially as the Western industrial democracies have done. Less cautiously, Rostow refers to communism as a 'disease of transition' which popular demand for consumer goods and political freedom (i.e. capitalist democracy) would eventually undermine. So far this development has simply not occurred and there certainly does not seem to be an inevitable convergence. Convergence theory seems even less easily applicable to the Third World. Diversity at all levels – technological, economic, stratification, political and cultural – exists to an extent that now makes any thesis of global convergence look highly speculative.

A most formidable criticism of modernisation/convergence theory has been made by Marxists. They argue that the major impact of the capitalist West on the Third World has not occurred through the diffusion of technology and ideas but through economic and political exploitation. The lack of consideration of this perspective – even in a marginal way – among modernisation theorists does seem a remarkable failure of imagination. That such a viewpoint is widely held, particularly in the socialist Third World, was made forcefully apparent by the North Vietnamese in the nineteen sixties and by the socialist Sandanista government of

Nicaragua in the conflict with the Reagan administration in the nineteen eighties.

Marxist Theories

Marx and Lenin

Like the other founding fathers, Marx attempted to describe and explain historical change. His descriptive categories are primitive communism, the Asiatic mode of production, the ancient form of society, feudalism, capitalism, and communism (with socialism as an intermediary stage between the last two). Primitive communism is a simple form of hunting and gathering society in which goods are held in common and there is no class stratification. The Asiatic mode of production occurred mainly in Asia and was not a necessary stage in historical change: it was characterised by state exploitation of labour. The ancient form of society emerged out of primitive communism through tribal warfare; successful tribes established cities and enjoyed the surplus produced by conquered slaves. The Greek and Roman empires are examples. A more recent case of a slave society is the plantation society of the southern United States. Feudalism is characterised by control of the land by the minority who exploit the labour of the serfs or peasant majority. Capitalism signals the rise to dominance of the manufacturing middle class over the landed nobility. Marx anticipated that capitalism would be replaced by communism when the urban proletariat overthrew the capitalist class and took over the means of production.

Marx's explanation of historical change is based on class conflict. As he put it, 'the history of all hitherto existing society is the history of class struggle'. He saw class conflict as a 'dialectic' or process which generates change. As the above description indicates, the dominant class is always the one that owns the main means of producing wealth and the exploited class is the one that provides the labour to work these.

Marx was well aware of the role of imperial expansion in causing change. He observed that 'modern industry has established the world market'. He appears to have thought that the impact of capitalism on the non-capitalist world though brutal was necessary to its industrial development. However, his own efforts were directed towards analysing capitalist society rather than capitalism's impact on the world.

195

In his essay, *Imperialism, the Highest Stage of Capitalism,* Lenin offers a more detailed global analysis. Even so, he is primarily concerned with the internal dynamics of capitalist society which generate imperialism rather than with the detailed effects of imperialism on non-capitalist societies (on, for instance, their class structures). He argues that up to about the last quarter of the nineteenth century, the main purposes of capitalist imperialism were to acquire raw materials and open up markets for manufactured products. From then on – rather earlier for Britain – the nature of imperialism began to change to the extent that a new form – finance imperialism – was already dominant by the First World War. Finance imperialism involved the export and investment of capital in poorer countries. This provided income and cheap labour.

Lenin regarded finance capitalism as an aspect of a new stage in capitalist development, monopoly capitalism. Monopoly capitalism occurs when production is concentrated increasingly into a few, large-scale enterprises. Lenin cited considerable evidence to suggest that the banks control monopoly capital because they finance it – thus finance capitalism. Much 'surplus capital' is 'exported' abroad where profits are often highest: 'Thus, finance capital almost literally . . . spreads its net over all countries of the world'. According to Lenin, there develop 'international capitalist monopolies which share the world among themselves'. Supporting this economic 'exploitation' of 'small, or weak nations' is the political activity of 'capitalist' governments who eventually complete the 'territorial division of the whole world'. Lenin referred to the mutual involvement of the state and monopoly capital as 'state monopoly capitalism' and foresaw it as an increasing trend.

In summary, Lenin states: 'If it were necessary to give the briefest definition of imperialism, we should have to say that imperialism is the monopoly stage of capitalism.' Lenin may have under-estimated the continuing need for raw materials and commodity export markets in motivating imperialism but his analysis does accommodate the vital and growing role of the large, international corporation in the world economy – to the extent that he foreshadows the much later commentator, Andre Gunder Frank.

Baran and Sweezy, and Gunder Frank

Like Lenin, Paul Baran and Paul Sweezy describe monopoly capitalism as a world system of exploitation. In their book, *Monopoly Capitalism*, they state:

> From its earliest beginnings in the Middle Ages, capitalism has always been an international system. And it has always been a hierarchical system with one or more leading metropolises at the top, completely dependent colonies at the bottom, and many degrees of superordination and subordination in between.

They are equally succinct about the purposes of the 'multinational corporations which dominate American policy':

> What they want is monopolistic control over foreign sources of supply and foreign markets, enabling them to buy and sell on specially privileged terms, to shift orders from one subsidiary to another, to favour this country or that depending on which has the most advantageous tax, labour and other policies – in a word, they want to do business on their own terms and wherever they choose. And for this what they need is not trading partners but 'allies' and clients willing to adjust their laws and policies to the requirements of American Big Business.

According to Baran and Sweezy, because of these 'privileged terms' the multinational companies frequently make a much higher profit on investment abroad than in the United States. Accordingly, between 1946 and 1963, foreign direct investments of American corporations increased more than five times. A key concept used by Baran and Sweezy is economic surplus ('the difference between what a society produces and the costs of producing it'). The multinationals make more surplus in foreign than domestic investment, most of which they then repatriate, thus depriving the producing country of its use.

An interesting feature of Baran and Sweezy's analysis is their view that 'the rise of a world socialist system as a rival and alternative to the world capitalist system' has occurred. Twenty years after they wrote, it is clear that world socialism is less integrated and united than they assume. In particular, deep Sino-Soviet divisions are now apparent. Further, they under-estimate the expansionist ambitions of the Soviet Union – certainly in Eastern Europe but also elsewhere (as the invasion of Afghanistan in 1979 demonstrated). Again, with the benefit of hindsight, their analysis of socialist Cuba seems similarly unbalanced. It is fair of them to stress the attempts of the United

States government to undermine and overthrow the Cuban regime (US supported Bay of Pigs invasion, 1961) but they fail even to consider the international socialist ideology of Fidel Castro and Guevara already apparent in the early sixties. More recently we have seen thousands of Cuban troops and advisors in various Latin American and African countries. Baran and Sweezy, therefore, do not fully follow the logic of their view that there are two competing systems, capitalist and socialist. Whichever bloc is the original aggressor, both now have a substantial record of foreign conquest and intervention. To present the Soviet Union as no 'threat' borders on the naive.

The two major contemporary analysts of capitalism as a world system are Immanuel Wallerstein and André Gunder Frank. Both argue that the 'dependency' produced by world capitalism has typically created 'underdevelopment' in the Third World. 'Development' is a myth which obscures the reality of exploitation: rhetoric aside, the capitalist powers have never seriously intended to give up their economic domination of the Third World. Here I will present only Frank's perspective in detail, occasionally supported by authors of similar views.

Frank's earlier work concentrated on the history of capitalist 'exploitation' – both imperial and neo-colonial – and in laying down the framework of his analysis of contemporary capitalism. As he put it, his 'approach rests on two fundamental pillars, historicity and structural unity', both of which he attributes to Marx. His historical analysis leads him to the conclusion that wherever capitalism impacts, it transforms the local society by forcing it into the capitalist system – in a dependent capacity. Such is the power of capitalism that other forms of social systems such as slave or feudal systems cannot survive independently of it. Thus, following the black Marxist historian, Eric Williams, he rejects the idea that slavery in the South of the United States, the West Indies, and Brazil was pre-feudal and terms it 'capitalist slavery'. He goes on to say:

> It extracted immense riches from Africa where the slaves came from, from America where the slave-produced goods came from, and from the slave trade itself, all of which, while serving an undoubtedly important source of the . . . accumulation of capital in the metropoli, not only decapitalised the populations of peripheral countries but implanted the social, economic, political and cultural structure of underdevelopment among them.

Similarly, he wrote of Latin America, his major area of detailed analysis, that whatever previous forms of social organisation existed – primitive or feudal – 'they were turned to the (capitalist) metropolitan outside, produced for the outside and were controlled by the outside' (my brackets).

Frank's historical analysis indicates the nature of his model of the capitalist world system as a unified structure. The basic system is comprised of the core and the periphery, more usually referred to as the metropolis–satellite relationship. Thus the capitalist metropolis of the United States has many dependent satellites in Latin America, including, for instance, Honduras and Mexico. Within both the metropolis and the satellite, further bi-polar relationships occur. Thus, London is a metropolis for Britain and Mexico City for Mexico. They enjoy a surplus extracted from the rest of the country. This surplus is syphoned up through regional and local metropolitan centres which also take a share of it. For Frank as for Baran and Sweezy, then, accumulating a surplus – crudely, a profit – is the major purpose of capitalism.

Although the key metropolis–satellite relationship is between the capitalist and Third World countries, the role of the major Third World metropolis in facilitating capitalism is also vitally important. The multinational companies seek a relationship with the central political-military and business elites in the satellite country which enables them to enjoy favourable economic conditions. Thus, in order to attract multinational investment some countries, such as Mexico and the Philippines, provide tax-free trade zones. Often, Third World elites become wealthy on the basis of such collaboration. Largely to service the needs of the elite and those of rich foreign nationals, a small urban middle class also develops. The majority – overwhelmingly peasants – remain poor in a situation of 'uneven' development (see pp. 694–6 for health inequality). Frank refers to the total process of Third World 'exploitation' as 'the development of underdevelopment'.

Frank has sometimes been accused of making too rigid a contrast between development and underdevelopment. He goes some way towards meeting this criticism in his twin-volumed study *Crisis: In The World Economy* (1980) and *Crisis: In The Third World* (1981). In the latter volume he introduces a category of 'intermediate, semiperipheral, or subimperialist economies' of Brazil, Mexico, Argentina, India, Saudi Arabia, Iran, Israel and

South Africa. Two varying characteristics describe these countries. First, they are generally wealthier than the majority of Third World countries. Most of them practised – with some success – a policy of 'import substitution' by which they replaced First World imports with their own manufactures. Second, these powers sometimes function as control 'intermediaries' between central metropolitan and peripheral areas, such as South Africa on the African continent and Israel in the Middle East. However, Frank emphasises that all these powers are themselves still dependent: several have chronic balance of payment problems, massive debts, or rely on the metropolitan powers for arms – in some cases all three.

The dynamic nature of Frank's analytical framework is further illustrated by his comments on developments among the metropolitan powers. He suggests that Japan, Germany and Russia may be seriously challenging the economic and political dominance of the United States. Mindful of Britain's loan under severe conditions (from the International Monetary fund in 1976), he comments: 'The British economy is now threatened by an absolute decline to semi-peripheral or even underdeveloping near-peripheral status.' No doubt the rise of unemployment in Britain from less than one million to over three million since he wrote would help confirm him in his observation.

In *Crisis: In The Third World*, Frank surveys a range of major Third World problems within the above theoretical framework. He examines what he calls the 'superexploitation' of Third World labour by multinational enterprises, the enormous debts of many Third World countries, 'political-economic' repression and the role of the state, the international arms trade and warfare in the Third World, and the efforts of certain Third World countries to combine in order to maintain the price of exports – as the Organisation of Petroleum Exporting Countries (OPEC) did with oil. Here these points are discussed as an interconnected piece rather than separately.

The common thread behind these themes is the relentless pursuit of profit by multinational corporations – supported, on occasions, by metropolitan government pressure or military action. Thus, the drive for profit results in the 'superexploitation' of many Third World workers by which Frank means they are paid at less than subsistence level and are kept alive by assistance from relatives and friends who work in the traditional sector of the economy. Profit also accounts for the billions of dollars of arms sold to Third World countries. Sometimes these are used to quell unrest – as in South Africa; sometimes in nationalist wars, which ruin economies and maintain dependency, as in the Iran–Iraq war. Often these arms are sold to states which, far from being democratically representative, need them precisely because they are not. Thus, Britain sold arms to the undemocratic, neo-Fascist Argentine junta led by General Galtieri, despite its presumed abhorrence of the regime. There are many examples of this kind which lead Frank to conclude that profit is a stronger motive than democracy in the capitalist West. On the same issue, Teresa Hayter claims that 'the majority of governments supported by the West are authoritarian, often military regimes of a brutally repressive nature'.

Such is the power of Western capital within the capitalist world system that Frank holds out little hope that OPEC-like strategies could effectively redistribute wealth from the rich to the poor world. He comments that even 'the oil bonanza has been relatively short lived and very localised in a few OPEC countries'. Certainly, in the mid-eighties it is clear that the capitalist countries have been able to diversify or develop their own sources of energy. Further, according to Frank:

> The few OPEC countries that have had a balance-of-payments surplus recycled their money to and through the Western banks and financial markets. The deficit counterpart of the first post 1974 'OPEC surplus' was shifted to the non oil-producing Third World countries, where the state and the bourgeoisie obliged the masses to bear the burden of the higher costs of the world's oil.

In other words, the West raised the money to pay for the increase in the price of oil by lowering the price paid for commodities from poorer, less well-organised Third World countries. Frank suggests that if this was the result of a Third World grouping combining to control the production and marketing of oil – one of the most favourable commodities for such action – the chances of doing better with another commodity are slight. However, he advocates trying.

Two other aspects of Frank's analysis which illustrate the power and pervasiveness of world capitalism require mention. First, in contrast to Baran and Sweezy, he does not see the Soviet Union (or China) as providing the basis of a genuinely alternative *socialist* world system to capitalism. Indeed, he cites the growing trade links between the First and Second Worlds as evidence of one world market, not two. He further argues that the profit the Soviet Union gains in exporting rather less sophisticated and cheaper manufactured products to the Third World provides it with the capital to buy more sophisticated items from the West – again illustrating the single market system. Second, Frank is pessimistic about the chances of a New International Economic Order (NIEO), demanded by Third World Governments in the United Nations, ever being accepted by or, still less, pressured upon the West. The NIEO would seek to improve the economic and trading situation of the Third World in a variety of ways. However, if anything Frank sees a tendency to First World protectionism rather than an opening up of its markets. In any case, he regards NIEO as an attempt of the Third World bourgeois elites to gain a more secure position in the capitalist world system rather than as a genuinely egalitarian and popular movement.

Frank refers to the huge debts of many Third World countries as 'bondage'. These debts are so enormous that there is no forseeable prospect of paying them. Indeed, quite frequently debtor nations have to borrow to pay the interest on their debts – as Argentina did in 1985. Some of these debts are owed to international 'development' agencies such as the World Bank but increasingly to private Western banks which charge higher rates of interest. Lenin's concept of finance imperialism would seem applicable here, though Frank does not use it. Frank notes that several of the intermediate level economies have tried to 'grow' their way out of debt dependency by amassing substantial balance of payments surpluses. Several years after Frank wrote, this policy seems to be faltering badly (see the diagram below).

When, as often happens, Third World countries are unable to pay their debts, they usually turn to the International Monetary Fund to borrow money to do so. In many cases the conditions the IMF imposes for the loan are severe and cause unrest. The left-wing critic, Anthony Sampson, describes the case of the socialist government of Michael Manley in Jamaica.

> At first Manley's government kept away from the IMF, but by 1977 they had to ask for help. The fund offered them the biggest loan (per head) in its history, but conditions as usual were strict. After drawing the first loan Jamaica soon failed its 'performance test' and had to negotiate again. The finance minister resigned, the Jamaican dollar was drastically devalued, and in 1978 average

wages fell by thirty-five per cent. Wherever their drastic remedies had been applied (one Fund official was quoted as saying) they had either led to the death of democracy or the overthrow of the government. There were riots and demonstrations (or 'social tensions' as the IMF called them), while new disasters visited the island, including floods and the higher oil-price. The only really thriving industry was marijuana. The government showed no signs of being able to meet its next test, and it had to go back to the Fund. ... (Anthony Sampson, *The Money Lenders: Bankers in a Dangerous World*, Hodder and Stoughton, 1981, p. 339.)

In her bitterly titled book, *Aid As Imperialism*, Theresa Hayter makes an analysis of the aid relationship which seems supportive of Frank's perspective on Third World financial dependency. Government aid is usually 'tied' to the purchase of items from the lending country and aid channelled through United Nations institutions is often available only for approved projects which sometimes have more appeal to, for instance, World Bank economic experts than those of recipient countries. Hayter argues that most aid neither reaches the people who really need it nor goes into the kind of projects likely to ensure long-term development. Instead, it sticks in the hands of Third World governmental and business elites to whom it acts as a kind of bribe to pursue policies compatible with the interests of Western

Debtors' Weakening Trade Balances

Source: Morgan Guaranty Trust Co. and *New York Times*, 13 June, 1985

multinationals and governments. Even an apparently successful programme such as the 'green revolution' in India, which greatly improved crop yield, made many rich landowners – some of whom were leading politicians – richer and disenfranchised many poorer peasants from the land.

What solution does Frank advocate to the pessimistic world situation he describes? His answer is socialism, though he finds little to enthuse about in the Soviet model. He is also acutely aware of the danger of socialist societies being incorporated into the capitalist world system. For instance, he believes that in the period following North Vietnam military victory over the United States, the Vietnamese leadership actually sought such economic connection. Which group or groups, then, are the possible agencies of socialist revolution? Here, Frank differs from orthodox Marxists though consistently with his own analysis (see below). He believes that the development of socialist movements in the West does not provide the best model for the Third World. Marx considered the industrial working class to be the agency for change in advanced capitalist societies but in many Third World countries this group is numerically small. Frank argues that capitalism has been imposed on the Third World from the outside and that the peasantry – many of whom are wage workers – are a potentially anti-capitalist revolutionary force. He hints that a world revolutionary alliance between the Third World peasantry and the Western urban proletariat might be possible. He advocates development independent of the world capitalist system to those countries that achieve socialist revolution. He also favours mutual co-operation between socialist societies. At no point does he suggest that any of this is either inevitable or easy. The 'crisis' of capital accumulation (a falling rate of surplus) he considers characterises contemporary capitalism may be resolved as others have been. He offers not prophecy, but struggle.

Modes of Production Theory (Critique of Frank)

From the point of view of Marxist theory, there is an obvious and major inadequacy in Frank's analysis. In treating capitalism primarily as a market system – a means of exchange – he fails to deal with it systematically as a mode of production. Indeed, the concept of production – fundamental to Marx's theory of change and class structure (see pp. 234–5) – is generally of peripheral importance in Frank's work.

An early and perhaps still the most effective critique of Frank along these lines was Ernesto Laclau's essay, *Feudalism and Capitalism in Latin America* (1971). Laclau demonstrates that there are *various* modes of production existing in Latin America and elsewhere in the Third World. What this means in terms of class structure and for the prospects and strategies for change needs to be examined in detail, case by case. It cannot be taken for granted that the peasantry are a new global revolutionary proletariat. Significantly, however, Laclau agrees with Frank that there is *one* world capitalist system. What he insists on is that different modes of production occur within this world system and this makes for much more complex analysis both in particular cases and globally than Frank achieves in his over-simplified scheme.

Two more recent works deal further with points raised by Laclau. In *From Modernization to Modes of Production*, John G. Taylor argues that to understand Third World economic systems and social formations (his preferred term to 'societies'), the imposition of the capitalist mode of production on non-capitalist ones is the appropriate framework for analysis. Capitalist imperialism impacting on the non-capitalist world results in economic, social and political effects not found in the West where capitalism developed indigenously. Typically, this produces a highly differentiated, even fragmented, class structure in Third World societies. Thus, the capitalist class is divided into the 'comprador' class supported by multinational money and a 'national' capitalist class seeking more independent development. Sometimes the latter is sufficiently 'progressive' to draw substantial support from the peasantry and urban proletariat. Such a coalition sustained the Christian Democratic government of Edward Frei in Chile between 1964–70. It broke up when the peasantry became sceptical about Frei's proposed land reforms, leading the way for the formation of Salvador Allende's Marxist minority government in 1970. Laclau's account ends here but we can continue it. Allende was overthrown in 1973 by a military coup led by General Pinochet. According to Nathaniel Davis, US Ambassador to Chile, 1971–73, the United States' Central Intelligence Agency spent at least $6 million on covert operations during Allende's period in office. Pinochet calls his regime an 'authoritarian democracy' – an otherwise non-existent term. It is, in fact, a military dictatorship.

As Taylor's example indicates, the complexities of Third World class formations are mirrored in the political and ideological spheres. Instability and unpredictability seem to be a general result of the 'imperial' connection. In a similar vein, Ian Roxborough in *Theories of Underdevelopment* comments on the weakness of the domestic bourgeoisie in Third World societies. They are generally unable to achieve the bourgeois liberal revolution that the much stronger bourgeoisie brought about in Western societies in the nineteenth century. Instead, Third World societies are vulnerable to the power play of elites which are themselves frequently under pressure from outside forces.

The conclusion of the above debate between Frank and his Marxist critics would seem to be that Third World societies must be analysed in terms of internal and external factors or, in Taylor's terms, the interaction between the two. This brings us rather close to the proposition at the beginning of this chapter that change can be analysed in endogamous and/or exogamous terms. Does this mean that the millions of words written on the 'Frank controversy' were a waste. The answer is 'no' because the theoretical and empirical details that have emerged in the debate have led to a fuller understanding of the complexities and unpredictability of change. Simplistic formulas have crumbled and, amid the ruins, the idea that people make history is discernible. They do not do so in circumstances of their own choosing but nevertheless in circumstances that can be changed.

Two Liberal Theories

(1) Old Liberalism: New Conservatism

Nineteenth century liberal capitalism has made a revival in the late twentieth century in the new conservatism of Thatcherism and Reaganism. The label is different but the ideology is essentially the same. Adam Smith's *The Wealth of Nations* (1776) was the most influential early statement of capitalist economics. Milton Friedman, the contemporary American economist, refers to Smith's writings often and enthusiastically in his own work, *Free to Choose*. Like Friedman, the British development economist, Peter Bauer has been a significant intellectual influence on the new conservatism. Bauer's book, *Dissent on Development*, is also committed to private enterprise and the free market as the means of development, although he does not return to Smith's classical principles to the extent of Friedman.

Friedman wants (virtually) to exclude government from economic life. He cites four functions for government, the first three of which are given by Adam Smith: defence, law and order, the provision of those necessary public works that private enterprise does not find it profitable to provide, and the protection of members of the community who cannot be regarded as 'responsible' individuals. Bauer sees a wider range of functions for government, including 'the provisions of basic health and education services' but the only economic function he mentions is the 'management of the monetary and fiscal system'. Both regard the production, distribution and exchange of goods and service and investment as best left to private rather than public enterprise. Following Smith, Friedman argues that as long as economic exchange is voluntary both parties can benefit because 'no exchange will take place unless both parties do benefit', i.e. people pursue their own interests. Both Friedman and Bauer seem to believe that this principle operates both between individuals and between nations. In addition to their theoretical arguments, they cite empirical illustrations of the success of the free-market system in stimulating growth. Friedman gives Hong Kong as 'perhaps the best example'. It has no tariffs and virtually no other restraints on international trade and, according to Friedman, the role of government is interpreted rather narrowly within the 'four duties'. Despite the natural disadvantages of small size and dense population, it has one of the highest standards of living in Asia 'second only to Japan and perhaps Singapore'.

Friedman and Bauer's enthusiasm for private enterprise is matched by their opposition to central planning and aid as means to development. Bauer states: 'Comprehensive planning has thus not served to raise general living standards anywhere. There is no analytical reason or empirical evidence for expecting it to do so. And in fact both analytical reasoning and empirical evidence point to the opposite conclusion.' Although this point is made in a typically assertive and authoritative manner by Bauer, it is open to dispute. If we take growth rather than increase in living standards as the basis of assessment, then it is clear that the Soviet Union has successfully developed under central planning in the post-war period when its rate of growth has generally been greater than that of the United States. Much of this growth has been in the military sector but there is no theoretical reason why it could not occur in the consumer section of the economy. There are signs that this is beginning to happen. A second example which may be regarded as disproof of Bauer's statement is Sweden – only mentioned once and in passing in Bauer's book. It is not clear whether Sweden represents an example of 'comprehensive planning' as indicated by Bauer but it is certainly one of the more planned mixed economies. In the post-war period, it has had as high if not a higher average living standard than that of the United States. The state also played a major role in the industrialisation of Japan and Germany. One of the most notable features of societies with comparably high living standards to the United States – such as Switzerland, Luxembourg, Japan and West Germany – is the relatively small proportion of the economy devoted to armaments production.

Both Friedman and Bauer are emphatic in their opposition to aid. Aid here refers not to emergency assistance, as in the Ethiopian famine, but aid as a regular strategy for development. They consider it distorts the free market process. As Bauer puts it, if the conditions for a viable development project are present then it will be possible to raise money on the commercial market, if not, the project should not be undertaken. Needless to say, this assertion of freemarket principles would not be considered axiomatic by either socialists or social democrats. A second point made by Bauer is that aid often ends up in the wrong hands and benefits the wealthy rather than the needy. The Marxist Hayter makes the same point. Criticism of aid policies from various quarters suggests a need for radical review. However, there is little support, even among conservatives, for Friedman and Bauer's precise position. Rather, what has happened under President Reagan is that aid has been more closely tied to political goals. Thus, an aid programme for Carribean countries was made contingent on the political and economic suitability of recipients. Similarly, aid was sent to the Contra rebels in Nicaragua whilst an American trade embargo was set up to undermine the governing socialist party, the Sandanistas. Aid is the carrot, whilst the embargo and, more usually, the activities of the CIA are the stick.

Finally, both theorists make a point which demands serious consideration as the core of their socio-economic philosophy. Friedman makes it most succinctly: 'Economic freedom is an essential requisite for political freedom'. Or conversely, comprehensive central planning is a 'sure recipe for tyranny'. Bauer takes to task the Swedish social scientist, Gunnar Myrdal, on the same issue. In his book, *Asian Drama: an Inquiry into the Poverty of Nations* (1968), Myrdal comes out in favour of strong central planning as a means to 'modernisation'. Bauer is able to show that Myrdal at least implies that the price of such policies is likely to be a decrease in political and civil freedom. Smelling the beginnings of the canker of totalitarianism, Bauer severely condemns Myrdal for believing that the conditions for development can or should be imposed. In comment, it is a major challenge of modern socialism to reconcile equality and freedom much more effectively than, say, the Soviet Union has done. Many social democrats, as well as conservatives such as Bauer and Friedman, make this reservation and consequently choose not to be socialists.

Despite Bauer's criticism of the ideological bias of other development theorists, the conservative perspective seems equally ideological. Friedman's view that it is human nature to pursue one's interests individually seems neither philosophically nor historically more valid than the view that interests can be pursued collectively. Further, their use of illustrative example is highly selective and both seem to employ the near unprovable generalisation as freely as the Marxists and social democrats they oppose.

(2) Liberal/Social Democratic Perspective on a 'New' World Order

By the late nineteen seventies, a large number of politicians and intellectuals throughout the world were convinced that the huge gap between the rich and poor countries was both morally wrong and politically dangerous: morally wrong because of the poverty and suffering in the Third World, politically dangerous because want made these countries susceptible to 'extremist' political ideologies. This mixture of humanitarianism and pragmatism is what inspired the liberal reform movements in Britain and other Western European countries earlier in the twentieth century. Just as social reform ameliorated the condition of the working classes in the advanced industrial societies, so now certain adjustments in the world trade, finance and aid could help the Third World. These policies were to be implemented within the framework of the world capitalist system of trade and finance which they were partly intended to strengthen. The best known expressions of this spirit of liberal reform are the two reports of the Independent Commission on International Development Issues under the chairmanship of Willy Brandt: *North-South: A Program For Survival* (1980), and *Common Crisis: Cooperation for World Recovery* (1983). It is important to add that many of the recommendations of the 'Brandt Reports' are supported by the politically various 'Group of 77' (now closer to 150) Third World nations established in Algiers in 1967. The view of many in the Group was that the Brandt package, though not ideal, was the best likely to be offered and worth uniting around (see below).

Both 'Brandt Reports' argue that the rich North and the poor South share mutual interests on which to base co-operation. The North needs the raw materials of the South and the South needs the manufactured products of the North. As the South develops more heavy industry, the North can turn more to high technology and services. More 'equitable' prices for Third World products would fuel the ability of the poorer countries to trade with the richer ones. Protectionism would reduce world trade and have a generally damaging effect.

The recommendations of the two Reports are a mixture of idealism and practicality with *Common Crisis* tending more towards the latter. *North-South* states that 'there must be an end to mass hunger and malnutrition' and suggests more international financing of agricultural research and development in the South. Co-operation to avoid the waste of common global resources and of 'irreversible ecological damage' is urged. The Ethiopian famine of 1985 was partly caused by ecological breakdown and underlines the urgency of this issue. Shrewdly, *North-South* recommends both population control *and* anti-poverty programmes. The Report also urges an end to the arms race and a reduction in armaments production, instead resources should be transferred to production for peaceful purposes including the reduction of world poverty. The peace-keeping role of the United Nations would be increased.

Both Reports make recommendations on industrial development, trade and finance. Finance is perhaps the key issue because without it development is not possible. It is the major focus of *Common Crisis*. Essentially, the detailed suggestion for reforms of the IMF and the World Bank amount to more and easier credit for developing countries. More participation in these institutions for Third World countries is recommended. The hope is expressed that, given a lead, the private banks will follow suit. Aid-giving countries were urged to double their contributions by 1985 (although, in fact, Britain reduced its official aid). Beyond these suggestions, *Common Crisis* indicates that a revision of the post-war settlement of the world trade and financial framework at Breton Woods is required largely with a view to strengthening the currently weak and dependent position of the Third World. The free-trade perspective of the Reports has already been mentioned and the above financial initiatives were perceived as complementing this approach.

In reality, the liberal-conservatism described in the previous section has tended to dominate the world economic scene in the eighties rather than the liberal reformism of the Brandt Reports. Whatever the prestige and eloquence of the Commission, power lies in the hands of national governments, particularly the United States, and the international corporations and no consensus has developed among them to adopt the bulk of the Brandt proposals. The dependency theorist, Wallerstein's comment that capitalism is more dominant at world than national level because of the absence of significant restraining checks, seems especially true of the nineteen eighties. The Brandt Reports offered some voluntarily introduced restraints and a marginal redistribution of power and resources. If its major proposals are not adopted, a further polarisation of the world into capitalist (democratic or otherwise) and socialist camps seems likely.

In 1985 a report was published claiming both to 'defend' and 'extend' the reasoning of the above two reports. It was the Report of the Socialist International Committee on Economic Policy, chaired by Michael Manley, titled *Global Challenge: From Crisis to Co-operation; Breaking the North South Stalemate.* Although firmly based on social democratic principles, the Report was more radical than its predecessors. It declares monetarism dead and calls for an application of updated Keynesian principles to tackle the needs of the global economy. In addition it demands 'a major redistribution of resources'. *Global Challenge* is sharply critical both of the failure of the United States to pursue fundamental reforms to deal with the debt crisis of the Third World and of much of the United States' foreign policy. Although the Report's 'main proposal is for a multilateral solution to the North-South' problem, it also suggests that others should proceed without the United States if that country's leaders are unwilling to move

211

ahead. Certainly, one of the Report's most challenging statements will not easily be accepted by any foreseeable United States government: 'Without disarmament there can be no genuine development.'

Gender and Development

The established perspectives on development, including even underdevelopment theories, tend to ignore both the impact of development on women, and the importance of their labour before it. As for strategies for future development, it is only in the area of population control that adequate appreciation of women's role is beginning to occur (pp. 172–7). As Aidan Foster-Carter ironically comments, in development theory, women are 'the satellite that is no-one's metropolis'.

Leghorn and Parker's *Woman's Worth: Sexual Economics and the World of Women* provides a feminist framework for analysing development. For them the main gender issue is simple:

> In virtually all existing cultures, women's work, though usually invisible to the male eye, sustains the economy and subsidises the profits, leisure time and higher standard of living enjoyed by individual men, private corporations, and male dominated governments. In spite of this, women live almost universally without the corresponding economic, political and social control over their lives that such a crucial role should mean. How does this happen?

An attempt is made to grapple with the issue of why men generally have more power than women (patriarchy) in chapter 12. Here, the question is the relationship between development and gender. Leghorn and Parker provide three categories which they describe as 'an alternative women-centred way of looking at and understanding the economic organisation of cultures throughout the world'. They are
1. Minimal power. This involves minimal access to crucial resources, low valuation and freedom in reproduction, high violence against them, and few occasions to share experiences, support and resources. Examples are: Ethiopia, Peru, Algeria and Japan.
2. Token power. This is a more variable situation in relation to the areas indicated in (1) and includes 'some freedom to create

networks, though these networks may be undermined when they become effective bases of change'. Examples are: USA, Cuba, the USSR and Sweden.

3. Negotiating power. This involves greater access to resources which may be different to men's and enough economic power to provide a bargaining tool, high valuation and support for reproduction and highly developed networks. Examples are: China (post-revolutionary), Ewé and Iroquois cultures.

It may come as a shock to the reader that the modern societies of the USA, the USSR and Sweden appear only in the second category. In this respect, Leghorn and Parker receive some support from Ivan Illich, though their positions require distinguishing. Illich argues in *Gender* that in many pre-industrial societies male and female roles were often complementary in what he refers to as 'the regime of gender'. Development imposes a cruder sexual division of labour in which patriarchal domination increases. Leghorn and Parker are less inclined to romanticise gender relations in pre-industrial societies and show, for instance, that in many such societies women have been physically mutilated (foot-binding in traditional China, infibulation in parts of Africa – a severe form of female circumcision) as well as socially subordinated. They, therefore, discriminate between those pre-industrial societies in which women have more power (3) than in industrial societies and those which have less (1).

Leghorn and Parker offer no grand theory of gender and development. The impact of development on each society varies. They do argue, however, that:

> Because women's role was secondary in virtually all cultures before colonialism (whether these assumptions and values were overt or subtle), the existing norms and institutions made it possible for western-based forms of sexual oppression to be superimposed.

Thus, the impositon of colonial taxes on indigenous inhabitants would often break up the family, requiring the male to work in the urban-industrial economy and leaving the women to do domestic and agricultural work (including what had been the work of their spouses). The assumption that men are 'naturally' better suited to modern industrial and agricultural work has also reinforced the subordination of women. Thus, whilst women in Africa do 70% of the agricultural work, almost all the agricultural aid has gone to men. Most education and training funds also go to men.

They point out that there are occasions when women's status improves as a result of Western influence. Thus, access to work outside the home in Algeria and Japan broke women's traditional seclusion and improved their chances of acquiring some economic and social independence. In Africa, infibulation, although still widespread, is now typically done in more sanitary conditions. Of course, Western female norms are not always accepted wholesale by traditional societies. For instance, women in Iran have long struggled to balance traditional Muslim belief with what they see as the more desirable aspects of Western female behaviour.

It would be a mistake, in any case, to imagine that liberation, female or otherwise, has been a prime purpose of the Western nations in relation to the Third World. Although not dealt with by Leghorn and Parker, the working conditions of certain women employed by Western corporations illustrates highly patriarchal attitudes. Thus, in the Phillipines, Mexico and elsewhere young women are sometimes employed (until they are 'burnt out') in such areas as assembling electronic components or textiles. The personnel manager of one multinational presented the following recruitment criteria:

> I choose people with elegant figures and thin hands because they are more agile . . . I take physical appearance into account; you can tell if people are aggressive by the way they look, so I try to choose people who seem more docile and can be managed more easily.

A businessman from the United States showed a similar level of enlightenment:

> There's no welfare here. You can push Mexican workers. Also there's the 48 hour week. You don't see any horsing around here, no queues for the water-fountain or the bathroom. These girls work.

It is businessmen, remember, along with government and the military, who are mainly responsible for the dealings of the West with the Third World. The people they deal with are usually rich, unrepresentative male elites. As Teresa Hayter says, 'The majority of governments supported by the West are authoritarian.' It is perhaps little wonder that some feminists believe that women would make a better job of running the world than men and that they merit a chance to do so.

The Iroquois cultures of the eighteenth and nineteenth centuries are among those in which Leghorn and Parker consider women have negotiating power. Significantly, women had considerable economic power both in the production and distribution of food. Further, descent was matrilineal and residence upon marriage was the home of the wife's mother. The leading women, the matrons, exercised an indirect political power in selecting the male council of elders. Women worked collectively and had ample opportunity for 'networking' – a process of mutual support which Leghorn and Parker greatly emphasise.

They conclude that despite differences in women's lack of power across cultures, women are a global caste. They record their impression that within each of their three categories, women overwhelmingly carry the burden of family care and receive a comparably limited amount of time and money from their male partners. They urge women to organise on the basis of a matriarchal concept of power, reflecting values of creativity, co-operation and caring. Institutions would reflect those values and would be organised in a decentralised and collective way rather than hierarchically and individualistically.

Strictly, Leghorn and Parker's view of women as a caste is not reconcilable with the socialist view that the primary category of social analysis is class (see pp. 313–14). However, the values and institutional frameworks they advocate are remarkably similar to traditional libertarian socialist ideals and as such are as applicable to men as to women. Leghorn and Parker recognise this but are not prepared to wait for men to act accordingly. In time, perhaps men will change, but in their view, the immediate task is for women to liberate themselves. In the Third World many feminists are, of necessity, less separatist than Leghorn and Parker and pool their feminist principles in movements of national liberation and socialism. The goals of national independence and combating poverty may take immediate precedence over reforming patriarchal structures within a society, as they did in China. Even so, women often acquire new roles, experience and confidence in these movements and in this practical way the principle of gender equality is asserted.

Development Themes

Urbanisation, industrialisation, employment and education are key themes in development. Those of health and poverty are given extensive analysis elsewhere (pp. 694–6 and pp. 167–9) and are implicitly further considered here. The themes of change and conflict, inequality and exploitation are, of course, the main content of this chapter and occur again here.

Urbanisation and Industrialisation

The urban populations of the Third World are expanding much more rapidly than those of the First and Second where, indeed, the numbers resident in many major cities are decreasing. By the year 2000, it is likely that only a couple of Western cities will feature in the ten most populous cities of the world. By then, Mexico City may well have over 30 million residents. What has caused this phenomenal increase?

First, it is instructive to note a factor which generally has contributed little to the increase in urban population – industrialisation. This is in stark contrast to what occurred in the developing West, where accelerated urbanisation was largely the result of industrialisation. In the Third World there is usually only a scant industrial base to sustain the expanding urban masses, though this is less true of some countries at an intermediate level of development such as South Korea, Brazil and Argentina. However, most migrants to the city do not get a (relatively) high paying industrial job. Push as well as pull factors account for the move to the cities. First, population increase means fewer jobs to go round in the traditional agricultural sector. Second, where agriculture is modernised an absolute reduction in jobs typically takes place. Of the pull factors, the strongest is the prospect of making a better living than as a rural peasant. Cities, especially international ones, have large formal and informal economies in which the determined or inventive can survive and, in some cases, even prosper. Even begging and the odd official handout are likely to produce a better income in the city. Second, facilities such as clean water and drainage are more likely to be available in the city, as are odd bits of unwanted or 'spare' material with which to build or shelter. Third, is the cultural attraction of the city – the glamour of the 'modern' way of life. John Roberts in *The Triumph of the West* emphasises the fascination and charisma of Western culture and it is in the cities of the world that the artifacts of the West are most temptingly displayed. No doubt what appeals most is Western wealth and lifestyle, but perhaps, too, there is a deeper desire to 'become' Westernised – to think and feel like us. Modernisation theorists might regard this process as liberating and Marxists as the very trough of ideological dependency but Roberts is surely right that it is wide spread (as, it must be said, is the resistance to it).

Neither governments nor the private housing sector in most Third World countries can hope to house all the people flooding into the city. In any case, many could not afford to rent, still less, buy accommodation. What can work well, is the provision of loans, aid or material by the government or voluntary agencies, for people to build their own houses. In general, however, how people make out in the city, including where they live, depends on what they can earn.

Employment and Education

There has been a severe crisis of unemployment in the advanced capitalist countries, especially among the young. Ironically, in Britain this crisis has coincided with policies to make education more vocationally relevant. Unemployment, particularly youth unemployment, in the Third World, is on a far greater scale than in the capitalist West. There are several reasons for this.

Population increase is, of course, a major factor in global unemployment. During the 1970s the size of the labour market in the Third World increased by 200 million. It is estimated that by the year 2000 another 500 million will have joined the labour markets. More than 30 million new jobs per year will be needed to absorb this increase. A second important factor contributing to unemployment is lack of investment in agriculture and industry. Many Third World countries are deeply in debt to Western banks and cannot afford extensive development investment. This observation raises the issue of whether the world trading system is so weighted against the Third World that prospects of significant development and higher employment are remote. We will return to this point shortly. Thirdly, economic development in the Third World, as in the capitalist West, often results in a reduction rather than an increase in employment. This is because some projects are capital rather than labour intensive: machinery replaces people. In such cases, increases in production and profit are likely to benefit the few who own businesses rather than the majority. Frequently, the owners of businesses in the Third World are Western multinational companies who are attracted by the lower wages they can pay, usually unorganised workforces, lack of legal restrictions, and developing markets. Sometimes multinational companies use Western employees in their Third World operations to avoid the expense of training Third World workers in more technical tasks and to ensure a compliant workforce.

Despite the above difficulties and the fact that employment in the Third World remains overwhelmingly rural, growing opportunities for work exist in the cities, not least in the informal sector:

> Many Africans migrating to the cities found themselves without jobs, or unable to get those they aspired to. Some accommodated themselves to a socially disapproved existence as pimps, touts, prostitutes, or thieves, living often at the margins of subsistence or preying, like parasites, on what few pickings a capital city of an impoverished country can offer. Others swelled the ranks of those who staff the industries, small trades and services that blanket the landscape of any African city. This sector of the urban economy, described often nowadays as the 'informal sector', in fact accounts for a considerable degree of urban employment. . . . The conditions of employment can be extremely harsh. For three or four years apprentices are bound to their masters in a condition resembling that of servitude. A space on the workshop floor is living accommodation, and pocket money barely covers the means of survival, while the El Dorado to the apprentice, namely a workshop of his own, is difficult to finance and may indeed never materialise. (Robin Cohen, 'The Emergence of Wage Labor' in C. Allen and G. Williams *eds., Sociology of Developing Societies: Sub-Saharan Africa* (Macmillan, 1982, p. 39).

Tens of millions of people survive in the 'twilight zone' of the informal sector. Uncomfortable though governments may be about the existence of this kind of enterprise, for many it is likely to be the only work available in the foreseeable future. Even in the West, the failure of the formal economy has forced millions to seek informal means of supplementing their incomes in the so-called 'black economy'. Third World governments and development planners would do better to accommodate the working and living needs of workers in the informal sector rather then viewing them as a temporary phenomenon.

Workers in the informal sector are not the bottom of the urban 'heap' in the Third World. As Robin Cohen puts it, 'there exists a group of genuinely unemployed workers, 'job applicants' by self description, but in fact a lumpen-proletariat proper'. A lumpen-proletariat is an ill-defined mass of individuals without any regular employment. One of the major historical causes of the drift to the city in many countries was the seizure of land by white settlers as happened in Kenya and South Africa. Today, rural overpopulation and the hope for material advancement that the city symbolises are important factors.

Increasingly, migration in search of work is not merely internal, but international. The international migrant population of the world is well over 20 million and still increasing. Several millions of these workers are Eastern Europeans who have found temporary jobs in Western European countries. Generally, they receive low pay for doing some of the least attractive work, and do not enjoy the rights of citizenship. In the Third World, migrants across international boundaries frequently do not even find work. Their situation is perilous and many exist in absolute poverty. Their vulnerability was illustrated in Nigeria in 1983. Nigeria is the most prosperous country in West Africa because of its oil and other resources. It attracts many illegal migrant workers. However, it was particularly badly hit by the world recession of the early 1980s because of the drop in the world price of oil. It ordered illegal migrant workers out of the country. As a result, hundreds of thousands had to return to their impoverished homelands.

Many in the Third World see education as the main hope of escaping from the kind of problems we have been discussing. They are probably right, yet the relationship both between education and individual achievement and between education and development is problematic and unclear. First, there is the question of what priority to give to the various sectors of education. There is a strong correlation between development and an extensive primary (and to an extent secondary) system of education. In other words there is a case for concentrating on mass numeracy and literacy, although typically it is secondary and higher education that gets favoured treatment. Second, there is curriculum content and particularly the question of relevance to development needs. In many ex-colonial countries spectacular examples of irrelevance occurred with youngsters becoming more expert in the history and literature of the former colonial power than their own – an example of cultural neo-colonialism and self denigration at the heart of the socialisation process. In higher education, irrelevance has often taken the form of over-concentration on classical subjects and liberal professional training, such as law or medicine, when the greater need was for practically-trained graduates. Thus, there is a surplus of barristers in the West Indies and of doctors in

India but a shortage of trained business people and engineers in both. Curricula can also be over-academic at the secondary level. Thus the promise that all Zimbabwean children would have the opportunity to take 'O' levels came back to haunt the government not only because of its impracticality but because of its irrelevance to the country's economic needs. Third, the principle that 'those who have shall get even more' applies as much to education as to other matters. The offspring of the wealthy can buy an education which will equip them for elite membership whilst distancing them from the struggles and feelings of the great majority. Even so, some elite members educated in the West seem responsive to the principles of democracy and social justice for all, while others seem quite resistant to them.

Conclusion: Issues and Future Trends

A character in the science fiction film *Blade Runner* suggested that only three questions 'really' matter: 'Where did we come from? Where are we going? How long have we got?' The social scientific perspective is perhaps not usually consulted to provide answers to these questions but it does have a particular contribution to make. I shall look at the three questions in turn. This chapter has largely been an attempt to answer the first one – in developmental and historical terms. We have come through a period in which the West has indelibly left its imprint on the world. Everywhere one looks, the impact of the West is apparent.

South Africa

Take South Africa, for example. The whites are there because their Dutch and British forebears occupied the territory. Over time they established a system of racial domination and segregation – apartheid – only paralleled in modern history by the plantation slavery of the pre-civil war southern states of North America. An aspect of apartheid has been the setting up of so-called 'homelands' for blacks, by which the majority of people are required to reside in a fraction of the country's generally less desirable territory. However, as black labour is needed throughout the country a system of residency permits, personal passes and heavy policing and bureaucracy allows blacks restricted access to 'white' areas. Over a million black workers have become migrants within their own land. European, particularly British, and American economic and commercial links with South Africa remain strong but some companies have cut or reduced them, apparently in response to increased black militancy within South Africa and growing international protest against apartheid, especially among students. Once dependent upon imports for its key military hardware, the South African government now relies mainly upon its own arms industry which is producing an increasingly formidable array of weaponry both for internal and external sale. Opposition to apartheid both within South Africa and Africa as a whole is such that it seems safe to say that force is now the major legitimising factor underpinning the present South African regime. State violence is not new, but the scale seems to be increasing. For instance, in 1976 many black school children were killed as they protested the imposition of the Dutch-derived Afrikaans language as the official medium of learning. Is, therefore, the use of violence against the regime justified? Both Nelson Mandela, the country's best known political prisoner, and the banned national liberation party, the African National Congress (ANC) believe so. The ANC is now trying to take its struggle into the white suburbs. In 1985 there were hundreds of deaths in South Africa as a result of violent political conflict. Some have predicted a bloodbath in South Africa, although a less dramatic but more protracted steady flow of blood is also possible. The only other way is the announcement by the government of a serious programme and timetable for political, social and economic reform – but the chances of this seem small.

One test of the relevance of the colonial history and theoretical interpretations presented in this chapter is whether they help us understand real issues such as South Africa. First, however, it must be stated that the South African situation is not a typically post-imperial one. In most ex-colonies the newly independent country is taken over by the indigenous majority and the occupying forces, government and administration withdraw and mostly return to their homeland (often the process of withdrawal and achievement of independence is gradual). Sometimes white settlers remain as a minority (Zimbabwe) or, more rarely, as a majority (North America). In South Africa, the difference is that the remaining white minority have retained power, long after Holland and Britain have given up the formal imperial connection. Nevertheless, the problems of South Africa are largely the product of empire even though they are particularly acute and intractable. Both Weberians and Marxists can find support for their theories in South Africa. Weberians can argue that ideas and beliefs – particularly of racial superiority – partly explain apartheid and that South Africa is a caste society in which stratification is based on race rather than class. The former point is illustrated by the use of Calvinist doctrine of predestination by some South Africans of Dutch descent to explain and justify apartheid (though to outsiders a less impressive cause than apartheid for the argument 'God is on our side' may seem hard to imagine). Weber himself does not crudely argue that ideas 'cause' socio-economic systems or vice-versa but that ideas and interests (such as the advantages gained from racial exploitation) can occur concomitantly, i.e. they complement and reinforce each other. Presented in this way, Weber's analysis of the social role of ideas is not incompatible with certain Marxist interpretations of ideology. Marxists stress that racist ideology can obscure economic exploitation and divide the black and white working class: although it is recognised that a simple application of this analysis to South Africa is not appropriate partly because the white working class itself can be considered in a neo-colonial relationship to blacks and richly enjoys the surplus created by black labour. Marxists universally stress the commercial and financial links of international capital with the South African regime. Whilst many capitalists would prefer to deal with a liberal democracy rather than a racist autocracy in South Africa, historically they have tended to tolerate apartheid. Some, including the pro-capitalist Reagan government, have argued that trading and diplomacy – 'constructive engagement' – could be used to 'soften' apartheid. However, in 1985 a strong Congressional lead persuaded him to accept limited sanctions.

The theoretical debates reflect and illuminate the real circumstances and issues of South Africa. Marxist analysis of oppression and inequality usually leads to support for socialist policies and there are Marxists within the black liberation movement in South Africa just as there were in Angola, Mozambique and Zimbabwe. Thus, the ANC as well as seeking a democratic, non-racist South Africa also intends a redistribution of wealth and the nationalisation of mines, banks, monopolies and land. Indeed, it seems that the longer colonial powers or white settler minorities try to delay national independence, the more likely are the liberation movements to move towards Marxism. Perhaps with these precedents in mind, the capitalist democracies of the West are increasingly urging South Africa to go down the road of liberal reform. Probably all or most of the modernisation theorists, liberal conservatives and liberal social democrats we have mentioned would favour this approach and would view with concern the emergence of socialism in South Africa, particularly if supported by the Soviet Union. So behind the central issue of racial struggle, profound political and social issues remain to be resolved in South Africa.

Futurology

The second question asked at the beginning of the section was: 'Where are we going?'. It is no job of the sociologist to predict the future, though some have tried. What sociologists can do is establish trends which, other things being equal, may lead in certain directions. This more modest exercise is justified and necessary. It is based on existing statistical data and informs public debate and policy. We have already seen something of the application of demographic trends to policy. Two other sections of this book deal in tentative futurology in relation to work/stratification (Chapter 15, pp. 429–33) and culture (Chapter 20, pp. 581–5). Here I will confine myself to the theme of development/underdevelopment of the last three chapters. The two books chosen to focus our discussion are Alvin Toffler's *The Third Wave* and John Naisbitt's *Megatrends*.

Toffler indicates three 'waves' of historical change: the period of agricultural settlement; the industrial period; and an emerging age of new technologies and social organisation – the third wave. The dynamo behind the third wave is 'accelerating breakthroughs' in areas such as quantum electronics, information theory, molecular biology, oceanics and the space sciences. Currently, we are in a transitional period in which the technologies and social forms of the second and third waves are in collision – with all the gains and losses, triumphs and anxieties that implies. A little more precisely than Toffler, but consistent with him, John Naisbitt argues that post-industrial society is the 'information society'. He cites data to show that nearly all the rapid expansion in the service sector in the United States since the nineteen fifties has been in the information area. In 1950 about 17% worked in information jobs whereas in 1983 more than 65% worked with

223

information as programmers, clerks, teachers, secretaries, accountants, managers, technicians etc. Echoing Toffler, he gives a three-word 'history of the United States' – 'farmer, labourer, clerk'.

As far as the developed societies are concerned, Toffler and Naisbitt present attractive pictures of what is emerging. A constant refrain in both books is how the old centralised, hierarchical, mass society is breaking up into smaller units of production (small business), power (participation/networking) and individuality (of roles and life-style). Toffler even coins a term – 'prosumer' – to describe a common type of the new age. The central characteristic of the prosumer is self-help and his or her time may be divided between working for someone else and producing independently for personal or market consumption. Utilising the potential of the new technology, the prosumer may do much work at home. In a section titled 'the child-free culture', Toffler implies that, if not always choosing to be childless, prosumers are likely to be concerned primarily with their own work and leisure. Naisbitt's observations are generally compatible with Toffler's although he is less convinced that the 'cottage-office' will be quite so popular. He believes that people will continue to want to work together and that in medium and higher level occupations, at least, the potential for more communication (networking) and participation in decison making is greater than in the past. Naisbitt also stresses the new political independence of voters whose variety of opinion, lifestyles and interests is no longer reliably reflected in one party or the other. He sees the emergence of a more issue-oriented politics for which more participatory mechanisms such as referenda are necessary.

Two areas receive fairly scant treatment by Toffler and Naisbitt: poverty in the developed countries and the situation of the Third World in relation to the new developments. Toffler recognises that there will be casualties as the second and third waves collide but devotes no space to discussing them. The words 'poor' and 'poverty' are not even listed in Naisbitt's index although it is unlikely that he assumes they will cease to exist in the information society. Both do devote a few pages to the Third World. Naisbitt's position is almost identical with that of the Brandt report which he cites approvingly. He considers that the trend to the information society in the West and Third World industrialisation are complementary and that increased aid should be directed to stimulate this tendency. Toffler concentrates mainly on the issue of what productive technology Third World countries might best adopt, given their frequent need for labour intensiveness and the nature of their social systems. He suggests that decentralised, smaller-scale third wave technology may be less disruptive to these societies than second wave technology has been. Thus, given the new technology, a country like China could become 'industrialised' without most of its population having to urbanise. This is imaginative stuff but overall it is easy to find Toffler's section on the Third World far too vague and cosy.

Quite simply, what is missing in Toffler's and Naisbitt's books is a willingness to face clearly that there will almost certainly be many groups for whom the new age will bring major problems. Peter Hall's article 'The Social Crisis' focuses on the issue. He sees a potentially disastrous consequence in the new technology. He argues that it is possible that the point has now been reached when the loss of jobs due to technological innovation 'is occurring so fast that no amount of further product innovation – the development of new industries – can compensate'. The result would be levels of unemployment more or less permanently as high as they are now in most of Western Europe and, of course, much higher ones in most of the Third World. Some conservative thinkers, such as Milton Friedman, have suggested reducing welfare to force current recipients into low-paid jobs. Indeed, the low paid sector has recently expanded in both the United States and Britain (another factor not considered by Toffler and Naisbitt). Hall cites an alternative approach presented in the Australian Barry Jones' visionary book *Sleepers Wake!* His solutions:

> ... involve changes in economic measurement to include domestic, informal and DIY work; a vast increase in educational spending to give working class children the same opportunities for higher and further education as their middle class counterparts, with general tertiary education available to everyone; a guaranteed income scheme for all; and legislation to guarantee full and appropriate employment for all those willing and able to work.

Such state intervention is, however, a long way from the liberal capitalism that Toffler and Naisbitt assume.

The potential problems of poverty and starvation in the Third World do not even surface in the two works under discussion. This surely reflects a tunnel vision of the future. The world is not going to be inherited exclusively by the rich and comfortable. To think so is not only inhumane, but probably unwise.

How Long is the Future?

The third question is: 'How long have we got?'. Nobody, of course has the answer to that question. What is new in modern society, however, is that we have the means to destroy ourselves, and access to those means is spreading. Therein lies probably the greatest danger of a nuclear disaster – that nuclear weapons will finally come into the hands of those willing to use them other than as an option of last resort. Alternatively, and even more horrendously, one of the major nuclear powers may, by intent or accident, actually start a holocaust. It may be that the end of our species is as inevitable as the end of our individual lives but it seems desirable to put it off as long as possible and certainly to avoid self-destruction. For this to be achieved the armaments race and the global proliferation of nuclear weapons must at some point be checked and reversed. Once agreed, this would involve the setting up of an international inspection system, perhaps under the aegis of the United Nations.

If the energy and intelligence that has been used in the creation and development of nuclear weapons could be released and channelled into economic and social projects, there is no reason why the conditions of poverty and misery described in the last chapters could not be greatly improved. We saw an international outpouring of constructive concern over the famine in Ethiopia in 1985. Yet it would take the 'moral equivalent of war' to deal with the problems of hunger and poverty on a global scale. Even Bob Geldoff, the inspiration behind Bandaid, at last complained of 'moral exhaustion' after a period in Africa overseeing the distribution of aid. Something more organised and sustained than an occasional outpouring of charity, however intense, is necessary to meet the problems we have described. It is not for me to suggest an action agenda for the coming generation, but dealing with the nuclear issue and world poverty must surely be close to the top.

Guide to Further Reading and Study

There are now a number of topic books which suitably cover development/underdevelopment for students. One of these is Wendy Bradford's *Development* (1984, available from the Association for the Teaching of Social Sciences (ATSS) Resources Exchange, University of York, Department of Sociology, Heslington, York). My *A New Introductory Reader in Sociology* (Nelson Harrap, 1983) has a full section of readings on development/ underdevelopment, as does Peter Worsley *ed, Modern Sociology* (Penguin, 1978).

The major statements of theoretical positions covered in the text tend to be heavy going. However, there are a number of books covering specific issues which are quite accessible. Among these are Susan George, *Ill fares the land: Essays on Food, Hunger and Power* (Writers and Readers Publishing Co-operative, 1985) and Teresa Hayter and Catherine Watson, *Aid: Rhetoric and Reality* (Pluto Press, 1985). From a quite different perspective but with an oddly similar title, P. T. Bauer's collection of essays *Reality and Rhetoric: Studies in the Economics of Development* (Weidenfeld and Nicolson, 1984) is a lucid introduction to conservative thinking in the field. The two reports produced under the chairmanship of Willy Brandt contain a mass of useful data and information. They are *North-South: A Programme for Survival* (1981) and *Common Crisis: Co-operation for World Recovery* (1983) both published by Pan. Tougher, and more urgent and radical, is: *Global Challenge: from Crisis to Co-operation: Breaking the North-South Stalemate*, the report of the Socialist International Committee on Economic Policy, chaired by Michael Manley (Pan, 1985). For an account of a Third World country torn by a series of disasters and the West's response, read William Shawcross *The Quality of Mercy: Cambodia, Holocaust and Modern Conscience* (Fontana, 1985). The book concludes with a chapter, 'Ethiopia, 1985'.

Past Questions

1 Examine the major competing explanations for some societies remaining 'underdeveloped'. (AEB, 1982)

2 'Modernisation theory is based on false assumptions and has served as a justification of the dominance of Western capitalism over the rest of the world.' Explain and discuss. (AEB, 1984)

3 Examine sociological explanations of the persistence of marked inequalities between developed and underdeveloped societies. (AEB, 1985)

4 What explanations do sociologists offer for social conflict and social change. (AEB, 1985)

Section C **Stratification**

How to Use this Section

The thematic unity of this section is too obvious to be laboured: it is that of *stratification*. The six chapters specifically about stratification are the cornerstone not only of this section but of the whole book. The major stratificational divisions of class, gender, race and generation drive wedges between the lives of us all. The study of them is essential to our understanding of the structure and operation of our society and of our own social experience. Chapters 10 to 14 deal with the main areas of stratification; the other, Chapter 9, is a simple introduction to the basic theory of the area. Because although stratification explains so much about society it, too, must be explained. Definitions of class differ, but the immediate origins of stratification lie in the relationships people have to economic production and in the way work is organised. For this reason, Chapter 10 begins with a review of recent economic development in Britain, and its effect on stratification.

9   Introduction to Stratification

Definition and Importance of Stratification

Stratification is the division of a society or group into layers. In modern societies the most important of these layers is social class. As was explained at the beginning of the previous chapter, class must be understood within the economic context of society. This point is further pursued below. Stratification occurs in almost infinite variety: height, weight, physical attractiveness, prowess at sport, academic attainment can all be used as a basis for stratification although they might be relevant only in specific contexts – height, for example, in selecting a basketball team.

The division of society into layers, or *strata* (stratum – singular), as they are more frequently called, is often compared to geological formation. But to compare social stratification to layers of rocks, one on top of each other, suggests more rigidity in social structure than is usually found. If we remind ourselves that the relationship between geological strata can shift and change, the simile begins to tell us more about the dynamic relationship between social strata. Further, just as in certain cases, where there is extreme tension between geological strata, an earthquake can erupt and change the structure of the land, so, too, extreme social conflict, in the form of revolution or invasion, can overturn social orders.

It would be a small-minded contemporary sociologist who failed to recognise wider units of stratification than those within the nation-state: most conspicuous is the division of the world into rich and poor nations. As we saw in the previous chapter, the wealthy nations are themselves divided into two major blocs – the Soviet, and United States/Western European blocs. These two blocs vie for influence in the poor or Third World, using as their means both 'aid' and, in some cases, military intervention.

The term social *differentiation* is often found in the context of stratification, although it has a wider application. *Differentiation refers to that which makes an individual or group separate and distinct:* thus differentiation provides a basis for categorisation and comparison. For instance, within class strata, occupation, income, and education provide criteria for differentiation, classification and comparison. Given adequate data, it is possible to place every individual in a given class within the social class struc-

231

ture – that is, to differentiate individuals and groups from one another.

We will introduce the concept of *social mobility* only briefly here, as a full section will be devoted to it in the next chapter. *Social mobility refers to movement either up or down the social hierarchy to a different social status or position.* In industrial society this is usually brought about by occupational change.

Stratification in Pre-Industrial Societies

There are two major reasons for comparing traditional, or pre-industrial, forms of stratification to industrial, class-stratified society. Firstly, traditional societies continue to exist in what we arrogantly call 'the modern world'. Indeed, even those societies, which are the most basic and 'under-developed' continue to survive in parts of Africa, Australia, South America, and elsewhere. There are many areas of the world in which the traditional and the modern come into contact and, invariably, conflict. Thus, the modernisation programme of the Shah of Iran, aided by Western expertise and technology, so enraged traditional Muslim believers (not least over the question of female emancipation) that a popular backlash developed which forced him to leave the country in early 1979, and threw into doubt the future direction in which the country would move. As we shall briefly consider later, the recent history of India can also be seen in terms of the coming together of the traditional and the modern – often with conflicting results.

A second reason for surveying forms of stratification in traditional societies is that a comparative perspective may enable us to see more clearly what the origins and causes of stratification are. This enquiry implies the additional question: is stratification universal – does it occur in all societies? The answer, in turn, prepares the way for what is, in a sense, the 'sixty-four thousand dollar question' about stratification: is it inevitable? We attempt to answer this question in Chapter 12, pp. 304–307.

Estate and Caste Societies
Estate systems date back to the ancient Roman Empire, but the European feudal system may be taken here as the most relevant example of this form of stratification. In an estate system,

the people of the various strata were identified by the rights they had and the duties they were expected to perform. These rights and duties were enforceable by law or by military might. At the top of the feudal hierarchy in medieval England were the king, nobility and clergy. The gentry, free tenants, and serfs followed in order of descent. A most important right, from the king's point of view, was that of being able to summon the nobility to provide soldiers for him. This was established when they took their oath of allegiance to him. It was generally believed that the feudal system was 'sanctioned by Almighty God'.

In general, there were therefore strong legal barriers against social mobility in estate systems. Exceptions could occur, however. The king could ennoble a given individual. The church provided an avenue of social ascent for some able individuals – as, indeed, it was intended to do. The growth of a powerful commercial and industrial class, and with it the increasing demand for economic and political rights, contrary to feudal law and practice, eventually undermined the feudal system in Europe. Even so, its influence lingers on – perhaps most conspicuously in the survival of the House of Lords.

Another form of stratification is the *caste system*. A pure caste system is a form of stratification rooted in religious belief, involving rigid ranking according to birth, and restrictions on occupation and marriage. The Hindu caste system of India comes closest to matching this definition. The term 'caste' has also come to be used more widely to refer to any hereditary and exclusive social group. In caste societies, social mobility is open to groups but not to individuals. This is because every individual, from the highest to the lowest, is considered to be divinely predestined to fulfil the role into which he has been born. In India, the caste system has been undermined, but by no means destroyed, by Western influence: caste and class exist uncomfortably side by side.

Sometimes more change took place in estate and caste societies than was officially admitted. A major reason why estate and caste societies seem rigid and unchanging is that those groups who benefited from the *status quo* did not want to accept or sometimes even acknowledge change. They managed to pursuade themselves and, to a remarkable extent, the 'lower orders' as well, that society was best as it was.

The above brief description of stratification in pre-industrial societies does not deal with major theoretical debates and, in fact, is closer to Weber than to Marx. Marx viewed all such societies, apart from 'primitive communist', as class societies in the sense that they each had a ruling and subordinate class, the first of which owned productive resources and the second of which worked these resources. Weber, however, considered that other factors than property relations produce systems of stratification including military power (the feudal system) and cultural beliefs (the Indian caste system). This disagreement is pursued below in the specific case of capitalist society.

Stratification in Industrial Societies

This section is mainly concerned with describing the theories of stratification put forward by Marx and Weber. Much briefer mention is made of Durkheim's contribution. This is because, as we saw in Chapter 6, Durkheim and other functionalists are much more concerned with social solidarity than with social class. Important mention is made of the elite/masses theory of the Italian sociologist, Mosca. We also present a number of attempts to stratify people on the basis of occupation, of which the most widely used is the Registrar General's occupational scale. Finally, a working model of class stratification is put forward in which I attempt to pull together elements from some of the previously described models.

Marx's Theory of Stratification (Class Conflict)

THE ECONOMIC ROOTS OF CLASS CONFLICT Marx argued that conflict between social classes is inevitable because of their different relationships to the means of production. This much has already been explained. Here, we will describe Marx's theory of stratification mainly in relation to modern capitalistic society. To recap briefly, in capitalist society the two major classes are the capitalist, or *bourgeoisie,* and the industrial working class, or *proletariat.* As far as Marx was concerned, estate and caste societies were just as much class stratified societies as are capitalist societies. The landed nobility of feudal Europe and the wealthy higher castes of traditional India he simply regarded as ruling classes. He considered as mere convenience (or as mere ideology) their claims that their social position was divinely sanctioned – whether they recognised this themselves or not.

In Marx's view, class conflict, rooted in the economic realities of differential relations to the means of production, flowed into every aspect of social life, including work, politics, education, family and religion. With particular reference to capitalist society, let us analyse what he meant by conflict in the economic context a little further before describing how it operates in other areas. Marx contended that those who own the means of production always try to make a profit on the commodities (goods, services) produced by those who work for them. The lower the wages paid, the higher the profits made by the capitalist. The difference between the wages and the price of commodities (goods, services) produced by those who work for the capitalist class, Marx called *surplus value*. The interest of the capitalist class is to maximise surplus value and thus increase profits. Marx's contention, that the economic relations of production produce the framework for social relations, is aptly illustrated by the startling facts of economic inequality. Even in our own day, the richest 1% own over 25% of personal wealth and the bottom 80% rather less than 20%. In Marx's time inequality was even greater. He and his friend, Engels, commented bitterly on the low wages, poor housing, insanitary living conditions, and lack of medical care of the working class (see Engels' *The Condition of the English Working Class*, 1844).

THE BASE AND SUPERSTRUCTURE In order to explain how Marx considered class conflict operates, it will be helpful to introduce a simple, two part classification of the social system which he put forward – the division of society into the *base*, and *superstructure*. In effect, we have already described what Marx meant by the base: it is the economic system and the bi-polar (two part) class system that economic relations produce. The superstructure refers to all other major aspects of society, such as politics, education, intellectual and religious life and so on. Marx argued that the base influences and even determines the nature of the superstructure, although there is much argument about how complete he considered this determination to be. He certainly thought that class relations are lived out in all major areas of social activity. The superstructure can be roughly divided into the *state* (government, civil service, judiciary) and *ideological institutions* (e.g. the educational system, the church, the media).

Marx considered that, in a capitalist society, control of the state is in the hands of the economically most powerful class, the bourgeoisie. This does not mean that he thought that capitalists and businessmen held all, or most, of the top positions in politics, civil service, or in the legal profession themselves. He meant that the power of the bourgeoisie as controllers of wealth and production is so great that it limits the power of other groups effectively to act against the capitalist system and the capitalist class. For Marx, therefore, economic power is the key to political power: the economically most powerful class is also the ruling class. We will examine in detail, later, Marx's controversial analysis of the relationship between economic and political power (Chapter 19, pp. 544–545).

Marx is as clear and consistent, within the terms of his own analysis, about the relationship between class and ideology as he is about that between class and state. He believed that, in any age, the ruling ideas (the predominant and most generally accepted) are those of the ruling class. For example, in the feudal period most people believed that the monarchy was, in some sense, divinely approved. A Marxist would argue that this idea became widespread because it suited the practical interests of the monarchy that it should be. If people believed that the monarchy was 'hedged in with divinity' they would be more likely to respect and accept it. Today, when the monarchy is no longer powerful, few believe that it is a divinely inspired, rather than a purely human, institution. The same analysis is applicable to 'bourgeois' ideology. Marx described the ideology of the capitalist class as *bourgeois liberalism* or *bourgeois individualism*. As far as he was concerned, this meant little more than the liberty of the bourgeoisie to pursue private gain and wealth. Bourgeois ideology, like bourgeois society, emerged out of feudalism. In feudal society people were expected to keep to their station and there was legal restraint on individual initiative, particularly in the area where the bourgeoisie most wanted it – the economic. The bourgeoisie achieved their aims through parliamentary pressure, refusing to pay certain taxes, and by civil war. Marx pointed to socialism, which emphasised collective action and greater material equality, as an alternative to bourgeois liberalism. In his analysis of the spread of bourgeois ideology to other sections of the population besides the capitalist class, he was particularly concerned to explain how some sections of the working class came to adopt a bourgeois liberal ideology rather than socialism, which he considered to be more in their interests. How modern Marxists consider people are socialised to conform has already been described in Chapters 3 and 5, and we examine this issue further in Chapters 19 and 20.

CONFLICT AND CHANGE So far, our account has tended to stress Marx's analysis of how the ruling class establishes and maintains its position. We know, however, that he considered *change* and *conflict* to be at the heart of the social process. He argued that the position of the working class in the economic structure placed it in conflict with the capitalist class. Trade unions are the organisational means by which the working class seek higher wages and better working conditions. Marx also stressed the need to establish a revolutionary party of the working class, with socialist and communist ideals. He observed several *contradictions* and developments in the capitalist system which, he felt, would promote the rise of revolutionary class consciousness. A major contradiction in the capitalist system which he suggested was that, in order to make as much profit as they could, the bourgeoisie would pay as low wages as possible to the working class and thus *emiserate* them (make their situation miserable). The precise meaning of Marx's so-called *emiseration hypothesis* is the subject of scholarly debate, but we can take it that he expected the working class to suffer economic exploitation, and that this would provide a stimulus to revolutionary discontent. This has not happened in capitalist society and may well never do so.

In retrospect, Marx's analysis of the contradiction that can develop between the *relations of production* (the formal and legal framework governing the relations of workers and capitalists) and the *forces or means of production* (machinery/technology), seems a more important and lasting contribution to sociological theory. He meant that technological developments can make out of date, and so help change, the relationships of social classes to one another, even to the point where the established system breaks down. (A clear example of technological change producing profound, if not 'break-down' social effects, is apparent in our own time in the impact of the micro-chip 'revolution'.) Marx argued that the capitalist class itself rose to power because it controlled *capital* (money) and productive machinery, and that these became even more important than the old basis of wealth and power – *land*. A revolution in both the forces and relations of production constituted a change in the *mode of production*, a term encompassing both concepts. Marx believed that the development of large-scale production would eventually make it a reasonably simple matter for the working class to take over control of industry, if they were to consciously organise to do so.

A factor that facilitated the development of working class consciousness of its own power and interests was that its members were increasingly crowded together in urban areas and factories. This gave them the opportunity to react collectively to collective grievances and to organise against them. Marx expected that the factors promoting the creation of revolutionary consciousness among the working class would prove stronger than those persuading them to accept capitalist society. He did not, however, assume that this would happen without the conscious efforts of committed individuals and groups to bring about change and revolution.

OTHER SOCIAL GROUPS (PETIT-BOURGEOISIE, PEASANTRY, LUMPEN-PROLETARIAT) So far, our analysis of Marx's account of social class in capitalist society has referred to only two social classes: the bourgeoisie and the proletariat. This fairly reflects Marx's own emphasis. Nevertheless, he recognised the existence of other groups. He referred to small businessmen and, sometimes, to professionals as *petit-bourgeois*. He considered that, as the conflict between the bourgeoisie and the proletariat developed, the petit-bourgeoisie would be forced into one side or the other of the class struggle. At the bottom of the social stratum are two further groups: the *peasantry* and the so called *lumpen proletariat*. Marx considered that, in an industrial and urban society, the peasantry would become smaller, less powerful and less relevant to the central class conflict of the capitalist order. The lumpen proletariat refers mainly to the unorganised working class: it includes those in low-paid and irregular employment and those who, for one reason or another, are virtually unemployable. Many of these are poor. Marx rightly considered that the lumpen proletariat was much less powerful than the industrial proletariat.

We will deal with various criticisms and revisions of the above aspects of Marx's class analysis in the appropriate parts of this book. Conveniently, Max Weber addressed himself fully to several important issues raised by Marx, and it is to Weber's analysis of stratification that we now turn. Before doing this, those looking for a summary of recent developments in Marxist thought will find it in Chapter 21.

Max Weber: Power and Stratification

CLASS, PARTY AND STATUS For Weber, as for Marx, the public life of a society is largely concerned with *power conflict*. Whereas Marx saw stratification and power conflict in terms of an exclusively class-model of society, Weber described two additional dimensions of stratification – *party* and *status*. Weber used these terms to refer to three separately distinguishable but greatly overlapping areas of stratification: the economic (class), the political (party), and the social (status). It is much easier to differentiate these factors in theory than in practice, but Weber was keen to distance himself from Marx's view that party and status are merely functions of class.

Although Weber did not attach the absolute importance to class that Marx did, he still considered it to be a most important aspect of stratification. He differed from Marx, however, on the precise definition of class, making a distinction between *economic class* and *social class*. He defined economic class as a person's situation in the economic market; both the commodity market (buying/selling) and the employment market (providing or seeking jobs). Social class includes economic but, in addition, members of the same social class share similar chances of social mobility (thus people from a low social background would tend to have a poor chance of upward mobility). Members of a given social class, therefore, share a common socio-economic situation. This difference in the definition of class led to a fundamental disagreement between Weber and Marx about the class structure of capitalist society.

CLASS: THE 'WHITE COLLAR CLASS' Weber described four major social classes. He agreed with Marx that the most powerful class in capitalist society is that of the owners of property and wealth – the upper class. Again, like Marx, he recognised that, in rare cases, education could provide entry to the upper class from lower down the stratification hierarchy. He also agreed with Marx that a second class, the petit bourgeoisie, was likely to become of less importance and that the growing strength of the third group, the manual working class, gave it great potential importance. Contrary to Marx, however, Weber gave great emphasis to what he considered was a distinct and numerically expanding class: propertyless white-collar employees. He referred to them as 'technicians, various kinds of white-collar employees, civil servants – possibly with considerable social differences depending on the cost of their training.' It is Weber's view of the role and importance in capitalist society of this class that fundamentally distinguishes his class analysis from that of Marx who was far more interested in the industrial proletariat. Weber regards white-collar employees as middle class. What distinguishes their market situation is that they sell mental or intellectual labour and skill rather than manual. In general, these skills are rarer than manual skills; thus the market situation of the middle class tends to be stronger than that of the working class. Obviously, this applies to some more than to others: it is more true of a top civil servant than of a clerk.

PARTY (POLITICAL POWER) We now consider Weber's view of the role of parties in the stratification system. As we have seen, Marx contended that economic control was the source of political power in capitalist society. Weber disagreed. He regarded political power as a distinct dimension of stratification and not merely as a function of economic factors.

In contrast to Marx, Weber did not regard political democracy as mere 'window dressing', designed to obscure the fact that the capitalist class had the real decision making power and influence. He felt that once the working class had won the vote, it could be used as a powerful lever to achieve social change. He considered that policies such as nationalisation, redistributive taxation, expansion of the welfare state and public education, adopted by political parties supported by the working class, could help to provide new economic and social opportunities for the working class. For Marx, of course, these policies were no substitute for socialist revolution and 'real' change.

Weber insisted that, although economic factors could certainly affect political ones, the reverse was also true. For instance, the policy of nationalisation favoured, in some degree, by most European Socialist parties of Weber's own day, was likely to have profound economic consequences. In the chapter on political sociology (Chapter 18), we will look much more closely at the relationship between economic and political power. For the moment, it is enough to be aware of the major issues involved in Marx and Weber's 'great debate' on power.

STATUS (SOCIAL PRESTIGE) A status group provides a shared life style or similar level of social prestige for its members. Status is symbolised in *patterns of consumption* and habits of behaviour. Thus, to give three examples: wearing a bowler hat, sticking pins through one's nose and dressing in smart 'mod gear' are status symbols of (some) businessmen, punks and mods respectively. *Ascribed* status is the status a person is born with, and *achieved* status is acquired during the course of life. Weber argues that ascribed status rapidly declined as a means of access to economic and political power in modern societies. In the political area, for example, the titles and functions of royalty and aristocracy have generally become of symbolic significance only – they are certainly no longer an automatic passport to national or local leadership. Similarly, he regards economic and career opportunities as increasingly open to competition. He can be criticised for not considering sufficiently whether this 'free' competition is, in fact, equally open and fair to all classes. He perhaps did not fully realise that the decline of status and the rise of class meant that one form of inequality replaced another.

Later we will apply the concept of status to the analysis of both race and youth. Here, however, we will draw our detailed example of status stratification from traditional society, because Weber considered that status stratification is strongest in this type of society. He argued that the Hindu caste system was (and to some extent remains) a form of status stratification

241

which helped the upper castes to control society and led to the exclusion from wealth and privilege of the lowest castes, particularly the 'untouchables', who were considered to be outside the caste hierarchy. It must be said that, despite the efforts of recent Indian national leaders to discredit caste taboos against the untouchables, traditional attitudes persist strongly, especially in rural areas. In 1978, a young British educated Indian doctor, who happened to be an untouchable, felt that to return home to practise a calling forbidden to his group might mean persecution and even death. He was willing to risk this martyrdom, not only to provide needed medical skills, but also to undermine what he saw as repressive traditional beliefs. It would be difficult to find a more vivid example of the operation of status distinction.

It needs to be said again that Marx regarded status distinctions primarily as a function of class stratification. Certainly, the overlap between the three dimensions of stratification – which Weber himself stressed – is particularly obvious in the case of status. In modern societies, an individual's status is usually derived from his economic or class situation. The wealthy generally adopt the status symbols they can afford, as do other groups. Even though Weber accepted this, he also believed that the chain of causation can operate in the other direction: status group membership can give access to economic and political power and advantage, as he argued it did in the caste system. Later, we further examine Weber and Marx's disagreement about the importance of the concept of status in the context of our analysis of race and youth.

Although Weber is rightly seen as a conflict theorist, he deliberately set out to qualify Marx's extreme stress on conflict. He argued that party and status identities could cut across class lines and thus blur the edges of class conflict. In rejecting Marx's polarised analysis of the class structure and replacing it with a more finely graded version, he attempted to undermine further Marx's theory of stratification. Yet, the basis of Weber's perspective *is* power-conflict. Throughout society he sees individuals and groups competing for power and control and the wealth and prestige that often accompanies them. In this fundamental matter, he and Marx were in agreement.

Durkheim and Stratification

Durkheim, like later functionalists, regarded stratification as necessary and universal. He assumed that very important or particularly demanding social roles would naturally be allocated more status and rewards than would less functionally important ones. Thus, even in relatively unstratified primitive society, the power, duties and wealth of, say, a chief or medicine man would differentiate him from others.

Partly because Durkheim tended to take stratification for granted, he did not give it the detailed analysis that we find in Marx and Weber. It is only in the work of the later functionalists, Talcott Parsons and, notably, Davis and Moore, that we find fuller justification of the view that stratification is necessary and universal. We examine functionalist arguments about stratification and the reply of a number of conflict theorists to them at the end of Chapter 11.

Durkheim himself regarded the problem of social solidarity and stability as more important than that of stratification (see Chapter 6, pp. 132–3). His analysis of stratification tends to become subsumed in this more urgent concern. Stratification stresses the divisions and conflicts in society and this was not the emphasis Durkheim wished to make. For him, it was normal for society to function harmoniously just as it was normal for the human body to do so. Indeed, in a most interesting reference to class conflict, he stated that 'nothing comparable to this can be observed in the (biological) organisms.' It is worth adding that, like Weber, he considered that social mobility could moderate class conflict.

The Concept of Elite in Stratification Theory

The concept of a governing elite was partly developed as an alternative to Marx's ruling class theory. *A governing elite is a group of people who rule.* Whereas Marx argued that the basis of the power of the ruling class is economic, elite theorists contend that the power of the ruling elite (as they prefer to call it) may be primarily military, political, economic, or whatever. As originally presented by Pareto (1848–1923), elite theory was undemocratic. He argued that although elites 'circulated' (replaced each other in power), an elite ruling during a given period was generally unrepresentative of the people it controlled. Mosca (1858–1941) argued, however, that it is quite possible for elites

243

to exercise power in a representative and democratic way – as he believed they did in parliamentary democracies. Mosca was the first to distinguish systematically between the elite and the mass (the rest) – a framework of analysis that has been influential not only in political sociology, but also in cultural analysis. To some extent, the term 'masses' was intended to supersede 'classes' – again with the intention of presenting an alternative to the Marxist model of society. Although elite/masses theory has not been primarily developed by functionalists, Mosca's version would be acceptable to most.

Social Class and Occupation: The Registrar General's Scale

THE USES AND LIMITS OF CLASS SCALES DETERMINED BY OCCUPATION

The Registrar General has the unenviable task of categorising over 20,000 occupational titles into five social class categories. The occupations included below are merely amongst the most common examples:

Typical Occupations by Social Class

Social Class	Examples of Occupations Included
I Professional etc.	Accountant, architect, chemist, clergyman, doctor, lawyer, surveyor, university teacher
II Intermediate	Aircraft pilot or engineer, chiropodist, farmer, nurse, police or fire-brigade officer, school teacher
III Skilled non-manual	Clerical worker, draughtsman, sales representative, secretary, shop assistant, telephone supervisor, waiter
III Skilled manual	Bus driver, butcher, bricklayer, carpenter, cook, electrician, miner (underground), railway guard, upholsterer
IV Partly skilled	Agricultural worker, barman, bus conductor, fisherman, machine sewer, packer, postman, telephone operator

| V | Unskilled | Kitchen hand, labourer, lorry driver's mate, messenger, office cleaner, railway porter, stevedore, window cleaner |

Whereas Marx defined class in terms of a person's relationship to the means of production and Weber defined it in terms of a person's market position, most recent attempts to construct detailed hierarchies of stratification have been based on occupation. In Britain, the best known of these is the Registrar General's scale of social classes. Social class scales based on occupation tend to reflect the thinking of Weber more than Marx, although Marxists have found it quite possible to use certain information categorised within this framework. In the next section, we discuss in detail the problem of constructing a single, simple and easily applied model of class stratification from among the various existing models.

On the basis of what criteria does the Registrar General classify occupations by social class? Occupations entered in a given class are, as far as possible, of comparable general standing in the community, although changes in classification have occurred from time to time. Educational and economic factors are of great importance in deciding to which class a particular occupation is allocated, although income itself is not of overriding importance. It is true, however, that in order to guess a person's income or educational attainment the single most useful piece of information to know is his social class. To put it in more technical terms, the three factors *correlate* strongly. In 1971, the division of social class III into non-manual and manual was officially adopted. This may have misled some into thinking that the classes above III non-manual are also non-manual, and vice-versa for manual. In fact, only class I is exclusively non-manual and class V exclusively manual. Classes II and IV are mixed, although the former is predominantly non-manual and the latter predominantly manual. It is also worth noting that persons whose basic occupational status is class IV or V, but who are of foreman or managerial status, are allocated to class III (foreman and manager, class V occupation), or II (manager, class IV occupation).

In official surveys, married women and dependent children are allocated to the class of their husband or father. The

245

majority of married women are not in full-time work and of those who are, few are in occupations of higher status than those of their husbands. To a considerable extent, therefore, class categorisation by male occupation reflects a family based social system. There are those who feel that this system of classification illustrates and underlines the inferior position of women in British society. This is a point we will return to later.

Although the Registrar General's scale is the most widely used, others exist. Indeed, a government department, that of Employment and Productivity, uses two different occupational classifications in its research and publications. Another classification widely used by sociologists (other than the Registrar-General's) is the Hall-Jones scale. A criticism of the scale is that the sample of opinion that Hall and Jones used in helping them to construct it was biased towards the middle class. As this illustrates, the difficulties in establishing a sufficiently objective basis for occupational classification are considerable. We will discuss one of these problems later – the fact that 'objective' and 'subjective' social class do not always coincide. The scale adopted by the National Survey of Health and Development is worth mentioning because it was not based solely on occupation. As well as occupation, the educational and social class background of the father- and mother was considered relevant in determining the class of the children involved in the survey. Finally, the important study of social mobility made at Oxford University (1972) adopts a complex definition of occupation based on comparing the market and work situations of various groups (see Chapter 10, pp. 279–281).

THE USES AND LIMITS OF CLASS SCALES DETERMINED BY OCCUPATION Simply to know a person's class suggests a very great deal of other information about him or her. Ivan Reid, in his useful book *Social Class Differences in Britain* (1981), does not overstate the case:

> We can state that middle class people, in comparison with the working classes, enjoy better health; live longer; live in superior homes, with more amenities; have more money to spend; work shorter hours; receive different and longer education, and are educationally more successful; marry later in life; rear fewer

children; attend church more frequently; belong to clubs more often; have different tastes in the mass media and arts; are politically more involved – to mention only a few examples.

Much of this book is concerned with the operation of social class in specific contexts such as the family, education, and work. It would be quite wrong, however, to think that class predetermines the nature of family, education, work or any other experience in a crudely causal way. As will become clear, we often do not know precisely how class differences operate. Merely collecting facts about class will not necessarily tell us why the facts are as they are. Sometimes, of course, empirical data does suggest explanations about the nature of the internal relationship between facts. That numbers of the upper class tend to send their children to private schools is obviously related to the fact that they can afford to do so. Yet, even here, we cannot say wealth *causes* the upper class to send their children to private school: indeed, some do not.

Sometimes 'the facts' do no more than supply ammunition for theoretical argument. Many of the more interesting questions about social class do not lend themselves readily to simple, factual proof. Examples of such questions are: is class conflict inevitable? Why do large numbers of lower class people conform to societies in which they are relatively deprived? Do schools reduce or increase the influence of class factors on educational attainment? There is certainly an empirical element in the answer to all these questions, but considerable theoretical construction is also required to provide adequate answers to them. In addition, as well as quantifiable facts, it is necessary to know something about the everyday life or culture of classes and groups before presuming to generalise about them.

Stratification and Culture

All the sociologists referred to in this chapter would agree that the work a person does tends greatly to affect his way of life or culture. For a start, occupation largely determines income which, in turn, determines what we can buy, including the size and quality of our house, car and other consumer items. Work influences our choice of friends and, as we have seen, leisure habits. In fact, the long list of class correlatives (factors associated with class) on the previous page vividly illustrates how class affects almost all aspects of cultural life.

Marx sees a particularly strong connection between class and culture (Chapter 3, Marxist Perspective). Marxists often use the term *class culture* to refer to the way of life – physical and mental – and behaviour typical of a given class. The Marxist historian, E. P. Thompson, defines the concept in terms of human experience, not as a collection of statistical correlations. The following quotation from Thompson deserves a close reading:

> The finest-meshed sociological net cannot give us a pure specimen of class, any more than it can give us one of deference or of love. The relationship must always be embodied in real people and in a real context. Moreover, we cannot have two distinct classes, each with an independent being, and then bring them *into* relationship with each other. We cannot have love without lovers, nor deference without squires and labourers. And class happens when some men, as a result of common experiences (inherited or shared), feel and articulate the identity of their interests as between themselves, and as against other men whose interests are different from (and usually opposed to) theirs. The class experience is largely determined by productive relations into which men are born – or enter involuntarily. Class-consciousness is the way in which these experiences are handled in cultural terms: embodied in traditions, value-systems, ideas and institutional forms. If the experience appears as determined, class consciousness does not. We can see a *logic* in the responses of similar occupational groups undergoing similar experiences, but we cannot predicate any *law*. Consciousness of class arises in the same way in different times and places, but never in just the same way.

Weber did not think that culture was quite so closely connected with class as do Marxists. Indeed, he often used the term *life-style* rather than culture, which has a deliberately more individualistic sound to it. For him, the working class person with middle class values, friends and leisure pursuits is a relatively common exception requiring no special explanation. People develop their own cultural habits which can easily cut across class lines. For Weber, a middle class pigeon fancier or a working class member of a yacht club would be within the predictable range of human variety. He tended to refer to groups of people with similar life-styles, such as members of a youth sub-culture, as *status groups*.

Functionalists, including Durkheim, tend to regard it as the major role of culture to unite rather than to divide society (see Chapter 3, Socialisation and Social Consensus). In particular, Durkheim was concerned to bridge the rift between capitalist and worker. He suggested that they join together for mutual benefit in industrial associations. As we have seen, he also regarded the educational system as a means for socialising children into cultural conformity. Marx regarded this process as ideological exploitation.

Towards a Working Usage of Class

This framework is in addition to, and not instead of, those already referred to. We will later discuss the merits of established theories of stratification in the light of recent social change, but meanwhile an easy and uncontroversial reference point for the understanding of class is necessary. Detailed though the Registrar General's scale is, it does not provide an adequate basis for theoretical analysis of class. In particular, it cannot be used to understand either the upper class or the poor. The framework offered here is as follows:

Upper class
Upper middle class
Lower middle class
Upper working class
Lower working class
The poor

As we shall see, the four classes between the upper class and the poor are defined, quite conventionally, in terms of occupation. The upper class and the poor, however, are defined in terms of their wealth and income (or lack of them). This definition can be justified in respect of the upper class, because it is largely inherited and otherwise unearned wealth, rather than occupation as such, which is the more important to its members. Wealth is the basis of the privileged cultural life and status of the upper class, although it is possible to be rich and yet excluded from it on the basis of, say, lack of connections, education or social graces.

Whether the upper class approximates to Marx's bourgeois or capitalist 'ruling' class is a matter for analysis in due course (see Chapter 19, pp. 446–8). It needs, finally, to be noted that many members of what we have termed the 'upper class' appear as 'middle class' in some official occupational scales. Our contention here, however, is that it makes more sociological sense to consider, say, a millionaire school master first as a millionaire and then as a school master.

Our description of the upper and lower middle class is taken from A. H. Halsey, with the difference that what is called here 'the upper middle class' he refers to as 'the middle class'. The upper middle class, then, is composed of professional, managerial, and administrative occupational groups and higher technicians. The lower middle class is composed of non-manual employees, small proprietors, self-employed artisans and also lower grade technicians and supervisors of manual workers who might be thought of as a 'blue collar elite.' Halsey describes the working class as 'industrial manual workers and agricultural workers whether skilled, semi-skilled or unskilled.' We will take the line between skilled manual workers and those 'below' them as the rough divide between the upper and lower working class.

Who, then, are the poor? The following groups are particularly liable to poverty: the old, the low paid, the unemployed, the chronically sick and disabled, and one-parent families. A disproportionate number of immigrant families is also poor. It will be obvious why we do not follow the convention and categorise this group according to occupation. Many of them do not have a regular occupation, and some do not have an occupation at all. Whether the poor can correctly be called a 'class' is to some extent an academic point. They are a group of several millions identified by the common experience of poverty. There can be no argument that they merit separate consideration in the stratificational hierarchy, although we must remember to examine the possibility that the reasons why some people are poor may be related to the reasons why others are very rich.

No claim is made here that the above usage of class would satisfy the sociological purist, or even that it is internally consistent. The student should, however, find it comprehensive and useable until such time as he decides for himself which theory or combination of theories about stratification he finds most convincing.

Class and Other Forms of Stratification

It is not intended here to return to the debate between Marx and Weber on whether stratification is best viewed exclusively in class terms or should include party and status as well. Rather, the aim is to remind the reader briefly that other forms of stratification exist besides class; amongst which gender, generation, and race are considered to be the most important in modern society. Superficially, these three categories can be seen as forms of status stratification. Male and female, young and old, black and white are allocated different degrees of status, apparently on the basis of sex, age, and racial differences. In fact, in all three, class cuts across, although it does not obliterate, the lines of status differentiation. For instance, a working class woman may find it easier and more practicable to make common cause with working class men than with middle class women – even though all women may be victims of discrimination on grounds of their sex. A young, middle class white person may have much more in common with his parents than with a working class 'street kid'. A black labourer may identify with his workmates of all colours and find little in common with the 'black bourgeoisie'. The relationship between these forms of stratification and class is a matter for careful consideration later in this book.

Guide to Further Reading and Study

Tom Bottomore's *Classes in Modern Society* (Allen and Unwin, 1965) is highly recommended as a brief, succinct introduction to class stratification. His *Elites and Society* (Penguin, 1964) has the same virtues, although the topic is perhaps better pursued in detail under political sociology, later in the course. Ivan Reid's *Social Class Differences in Britain* (Open Books, 1981) is certainly not a theoretical introduction to stratification theory, but is an excellent collection of empirical data about class differences. The Tavistock Key Sociologists series has titles on *Marx and Marxism* (Peter Worsley), *Max Weber* (Frank Parkin) and *Emile Durkheim* (Kenneth Thompson). Anthony Giddens's

The Class Structure of the Advanced Societies (Hutchinson, 1981) is useful but demanding.

For questions on Class Stratification see the end of Chapters 10 and 11.

10 Class Stratification in Britain

The Issues

For the sake of simplicity, this chapter and the next have been broken down into syllabus oriented sub-sections, but it is important not to lose sight of the central theme of social equality. We examine stratification primarily in Britain but also, more briefly, in a wide comparative context. As far as Britain is concerned, the major issue explored is whether it has become a more or less equal society since the last war. This involves looking at changes in class structure, class culture and in the rate of social mobility. The first two are analysed together as part of our examination of each class, and the third separately – but they are all part of the same general inquiry. The data presented enables us to answer the future question of whether Britain remains a deeply class-divided society – as it certainly has been historically. An issue that is particularly discussed is whether post-war affluence and certain other factors have resulted in a decline of traditional working class attitudes and culture. Is it true that 'we are all middle class now' or that 'there is no such thing as class any more'? Finally, it is essential to remember that whereas Marxists regard political and status issues as rooted in class, for Weberians these are relatively separate aspects of stratification. We allude to these two perspectives on a number of occasions in this chapter, although both the political and status aspects of stratification are discussed fully elsewhere.

At this stage, we need only distinguish two basic concepts of equality: the *socialist* and the *liberal*. Ironically perhaps, neither means *absolute* (complete) equality. Socialists do characteristically believe, however, that there should be a substantial degree of *material* equality (for example, in income and housing) and that this will partly pave the way to equality of cultural opportunity. Only a minority of socialists are Marxists, but Marx's own epigram on this issue has wide appeal: 'from each according to his ability, to each according to his need'. The Marxist ideal of a classless society need not be taken to imply complete equality although Marx certainly considered that there would be much greater material equality in communist than in capitalist society. This is rather general but it is probably safe to say that most socialists and, certainly, all Marxists, favour a greater degree of material equality than exists in Britain today.

Marxists consider the achievement of stable equality to be dependent on the abolition of the major forms of private property (for example, private enterprise) but other socialists, including many members of the British Labour Party, tend to favour a mixed economy (part nationalised, part private) and rely on redistributive taxation and heavy government expenditure on public services to bring about greater equality. They further contend that the public provision of better material and cultural services such as libraries and educational facilities will provide equal cultural opportunity for all. This is, of course, quite different from saying that, given equal cultural opportunity, people will express themselves in the same way; that is an absurd idea.

The liberal view of equality is that every individual should have equal opportunity to *compete* for wealth, power and status. This view was developed by Adam Smith and John Stuart Mill among others, and took firm hold in the nineteenth century. It has tended to appeal, in varying degrees, to politicians across the three major parties. The outcome of such competition would almost certainly be a society of great inequality – but, at least, it would be an inequality based on *merit*, not inheritance and privilege (which conservatives defend). It is possible to test whether equal opportunity does exist by examining the rate of social mobility and the extent to which the talented rise and the untalented fall. This we do later. In practice, most modern liberals would wish to reduce even 'natural' inequality resulting from 'fair' competition. They would do so by a limited redistribution of wealth, mainly through taxation. The 'middle-of-the-road' liberal and 'middle-of-the-road' socialist meet halfway between the two philosophies of equality.

The Economic Context of Class Change

Economic and occupational change is the background against which developments in the British class system must be understood. It is worth summarising these changes here: since about 1900 there has been a steady expansion of the service sector and a parallel growth of female employment; there has been a move from small to large-scale production and corresponding expansion of bureaucracy (large, hierarchical organisations), and a growth in public corporations at the expense of small-scale private businesses. Class is produced primarily in the work situation and changes in the class system can only be understood in the context of economic and occupational change. This summary statement is intended to include the Marxist view that changes in the means of production (for example, technology) will affect class relations. For instance, a rapid increase in automation could affect the class position of millions. Class is not, however, exclusively defined in terms of work. Class consciousness (awareness of class identity) and class culture are part of class although they cannot be properly analysed without reference to the economic and occupational structure within which they are generated. For that reason, class structure and culture are considered together. For the purposes of presentation, social mobility is considered separately, although in reality it is also inextricably intertwined with class structure. Movement up or down the social structure is bound to change it.

The importance of the effect of changes in the occupational structure on class is worth pursuing in more detail. These developments also have profound implications for gender relations because they have changed the working and domestic lives of both sexes. The following chart shows the number of people working in different sectors of employment from 1960 to 1978. The two charts show the industries in which men and women work, and how the numbers in each group of industries have changed over time.

One of the most important developments in the occupational structure has been the increase in the number of women employed in the service sector; a massive 2¼ million since 1960. We give this development fuller analysis in a separate section (Chapter 12, pp. 326–9), and make only brief comment here. There has also been a less spectacular increase of male employment in the service sector: by half a million. Overall, therefore, it is the expansion of the service sector that is the outstanding feature of change in the structure of employment since 1961. Other data shows that a remarkable 71% of the *increase* in service sector employment between 1961 and 1975 occurred in the areas of central and local government, although the economic cuts of the late nineteen-seventies and early eighties stopped this trend. In general, women have tended to fill lower status and men higher status service sector jobs. In 1976, approximately one in five men were professionals, employers or managers compared to one in twenty women. Over a much longer period than that covered by the chart, the growth of a managerial 'class' has been a feature of the British and other advanced economies. Whether managers have replaced owners as the dominant force in industry is a key issue discussed later.

Employees in Employment: by Industry

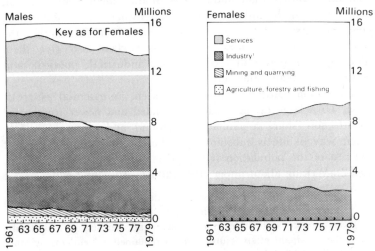

Males   Millions   16

Key as for Females

Females   Millions   16

☐ Services
▩ Industry¹
▧ Mining and quarrying
▦ Agriculture, forestry and fishing

1961 63 65 67 69 71 73 75 77 1979

¹ Includes manufacturing: gas, electricity, and water; and construction industries: and for females also includes agriculture, forestry and fishing; and mining and quarrying.

Sources: Department of Employment and *Social Trends*, 1981.

Industry remains the major area of male employment, although to a somewhat lesser extent than previously. Between 1901 and 1978, the decline in the industrial sector was about 1½ million men. Female employment in industry fell by half a million over the same period. Partly because of technological advancement (it is largely unskilled jobs that have been lost) and partly because of the way industrial jobs have been regraded, the proportion of skilled to semi-skilled and unskilled occupations in industry has dramatically increased. Again, this applies much more to men than women.

1 Class and Change in Britain: Change in Class Structure and Culture

The Upper Class and the Managerial Elite
The upper class consists of the few thousand wealthiest and most

culturally privileged businessmen and property owners in the country. We also consider the very top of the upper middle class in this section because they often work closely with the upper class and are highly privileged themselves. By upper middle class is meant people like managing directors of large companies rather than middle level management; chiefs of staff rather than high ranking officers; top rather than middle level civil servants, and so on. The important issue is whether the wealth and opportunities of the upper class also give them much greater power and control over industrial, political, and cultural life than other groups.

A common culture is, as we have seen, an essential aspect of class. To a large extent, traditional landed and newer commercial wealth now share a similar background and cultural outlook. Their way of life is substantially different from that of most of the rest of the population (Chapter 3, partly illustrates this, pp. 49–52). Writing about upper class culture, Anthony Giddens says:

> The most striking characteristic of the British upper class in the latter half of the nineteenth century is the mutual penetration of aristocracy and those in commerce and industry ... Certainly the dominant ethos (cultural tone) remained a 'gentlemanly' one, facilitated by the entitlement of industrialists, or at least of their offspring; but the very creation of the notion of the 'gentleman' was in substantial degree the product of the nineteenth century, and the rise of the public schools was the milieu (cultural context) for effecting this peculiar fusion of the old and the new. In this manner there came about that 'blend of a crude plutocratic (power based on money) reality with the sentimental aroma of an aristocratic legend' which R. H. Tawney described as the feature of the British upper class. *(All brackets author's).*

We now consider the wealth and economic and industrial power of the upper class. The wealth of the upper class has diminished as a percentage of total wealth but remains formidably large. Wealth is much more unequally distributed than income, mainly because of the importance of inherited wealth. According to Lord Diamond's commission, in 1923 the top 1% owned 61% of all private wealth. In 1974, this had dropped startingly to 22% but, by 1976, had risen to 25%. The increase between 1974 and 1976 was due mainly to the rises in share prices during that period. Under the first Thatcher administration, the top 10% became relatively slightly wealthier and the bottom 50% relatively slightly poorer – a trend which sharpened in 1983/4.

Not unexpectedly, the wealth of the very rich tends to be made up differently from that of other people. They are much more likely to own shares and sizeable amounts of property – including land – than others: they are also more likely to own art treasures, precious metals and jewels. The preservation and creation of substantial wealth gives the upper class a shared material basis for class identity and sets them apart from the majority. Upper class exclusiveness can be partly explained as an attempt to maintain and defend its common interest.

Few of the wealthy depend on earned income as a major source of their wealth. The share of all national incomes of the top 1% of income earners in 1981/82 was 4.6% – a small figure compared to the percentage of wealth owned by the 1% most wealthy. Many major shareholders draw salaries as directors of the company or companies in which they have holdings. Usually, however, the day-to-day running of large companies is in the hands of paid managers who are not usually extremely wealthy people in their own right. This raises the crucial issue of *where* industrial power lies in contemporary capitalism – with owners (or, at least, large shareholders) as Marx argues, or with managers. It should be noted that the new, managerial class, is just as well established in central and local government and in nationalised industries as in private enterprise.

Ralf Dahrendorf has made a significant contribution to the debate about where power lies in modern societies. He argues that with the development of large scale joint stock companies which enable the general public to buy shares in a company, much control is exercised by top salaried managers and less by capitalist owners. He refers to this process as the decomposition of capital. Following Weber rather then Marx, he goes on to argue that, in *advanced* industrial societies, power operates through large organisations rather than through a few very rich individuals (those who make up the capitalist class). Managers of organisations, unlike old-style capitalists, cannot pursue their own interest alone, but must answer to shareholders, perhaps government, and even the general public. According to Dahrendorf, this applies still more to the managers of publicly owned companies and to top civil servants. Dahrendorf, there-

fore, sees modern societies as 'managed' societies. To understand modern societies, 'capitalist' or socialist, it is necessary,
therefore, to come to terms with their institutional (organisational) nature (see Chapter 16 for the development of this
point). He further contends that the rise of managers has produced considerable potential for conflict within the economic
elite (that is, between owners and management). He considers
that whereas owners tend to be interested in profit, managers
are more concerned with the long-term productivity and security of the corporation which they see both as in their own
interest, and in that of its shareholders, small and large. Again,
managers are regarded as more constrained (controlled) by the
rules of the large organisations of which they are a small part
than the tycoons of early capitalism ever were. It is part of
Dahrendorf's thesis that management is also constrained by the
powerful organisations of the working class, mainly unions, as
well as, to some extent, by government.

Anthony Giddens criticises Dahrendorf sharply on two
counts. First he points out that, even though the growth of
joint stock companies has broadened the basis of ownership,
profit remains the purpose of capitalist enterprise: thus, the system is still a capitalist one. In addition, only a minority still
gains substantial profit from shareholdings. There is a huge difference between multi-millionaires, like Sir James Goldsmith,
with majority holdings in several major companies and somebody who owns, perhaps, a few hundred pounds of shares.
Giddens's second point is related to his first. He suggests that
far from there being a conflict of interest between capitalists
and top managers, there is more likely to be a *close identity of
interest*. They are both primarily concerned with the success and
profitability of the company. As far as companies having a
public 'conscience' is concerned, there is no guarantee of this,
although some do. We examined in Chapter 6 several examples
in which companies put their own welfare before that of the
general public, if the latter is considered to include workers
(made redundant) and local communities (variously neglected
or abused).

Giddens' contention that owners and top management – the
economic elite – share common goals, suggests the important
wider question of whether the upper and upper middle class
dominate the other major institutional elites, as well as the

economic elite, of the country. Drawing on a study of elites, carried out at Cambridge, he concludes that at least half the top positions in *all* major institutional sectors in Britain, including the economic, the military, the armed forces, the judiciary and the church, are filled by people from public school backgrounds (see Chapter 18 for details). In other words, a majority of those in top positions in this country come from a privileged and, more or less, wealthy upper or middle class background. Whether these people can be called a ruling class is an issue we also discuss in Chapter 19, pp. 446–8).

The importance of the Dahrendorf–Giddens disagreement bears emphasising. It is, after all, about who controls our society, how they do so and in whose interest. This must surely matter to all of us. Do capitalists manipulate our world in their own interest or is power mainly located in large organisations which, almost impersonally, run our lives? We can agree with Dahrendorf that we live in a society of large organisations run by 'experts' and with Giddens that there is still a rich and powerful upper class with a distinctive culture. How and to what extent these two points can be reconciled we leave for further consideration (see especially Chapters 16 and 19).

The Middle Class

The middle class is a huge group. Although some of the developments we discuss have affected the class as a whole, a preliminary distinction must be made between the upper and lower middle class. According to figures cited by A. H. Halsey in 1978, 20.1% of the population are upper middle (Halsey prefers simply to call them 'middle') and 24.9% lower middle class. The term 'white collar employee (or worker)' is sometimes used to refer to the salaried middle class in general, but we have tended to use it to describe the lower levels of this group.

a THE UPPER MIDDLE CLASS The upper middle class is composed of professional, managerial, and administrative occupational groups and higher technicians. Karl Renner first referred to it as the 'service class' and the term has been adopted by Halsey and others. Although the word 'service' is somewhat ambiguous, the term may well become standard. The very top of this group we considered in the previous section because of its links with the upper class. Most members of the upper middle class do not, of course, achieve any national power or prominence but, locally, many have significant influence and status. They often participate in voluntary organisations, become magistrates, or stand for local government. Comparatively speaking, they are well off. Typically, they might earn one and a half to two and a half times as much as the average national wage, and enjoy substantially more than average fringe benefits. They earn strikingly more than their lower middle class counterparts. In 1980, the average pre-tax wage of a doctor was well over twice that of a school teacher. Even so, their income has tended to decline relative to that of most other groups, particularly manual workers. Since 1913–14, higher professional workers' salaries have gone up 26 times, whereas those of unskilled manual workers have gone up 54 times – over twice as much.

The relative decline in the living standards of some of the groups that comprise the middle class has led them to take a more militant attitude towards their employers. This happened particularly among those, such as doctors, employed predominantly by the state. This same process has also occurred among lower middle class groups, such as teachers, social workers, nurses and, for that matter, clerical workers in the civil service. As far as this development is concerned, the middle class can be considered as a whole. There has been considerable recent sociological interest in this trend which is given full coverage in Chapter 15, pp. 409–11.

b THE 'WHITE COLLAR' CLASS: LOWER MIDDLE OR WORKING CLASS? Office workers and salespeople make up the majority of the lower middle class. This group has rapidly expanded during this century and in 1971 made up 24.9% of the working population of which rather more than half were clerks. At the top of the lower middle class are the so-called semi-professions of teaching and nursing. The 'typical' white collar figure is the clerical worker about whom there have been a series of studies since the war. The reason for this interest is clear and centres upon a disagreement about the class position of white collar employees. Marxists argue that their relationship to the means of production is that of wage-workers and that they are, therefore, part of the working class. Marxists, however, also recognised that they are non-productive workers whose class consciousness is likely to be less advanced, from a socialist point of view, than that of industrial workers. As we have seen, Weber regarded this group as middle class: he sometimes referred to it as 'the new class'. It was 'new' in that it was largely created by the needs of big business and central and local government for office workers and other white collar staff.

C. Wright Mills published the first major post-war analysis of the white collar employee, in 1951. He drew almost exclusively on American data but the basic developments he comments on are also a feature of British society. His work reflects the influence of both Marx and Weber. The influence of Marx is apparent in Mills' distinction between the old, *property owning* and *self-employed middle class* and the new, *salaried white collar class*. He includes in the latter group managers, paid professionals, salespeople, and office workers (a wider but comparable definition to our own). Even in 1940, this group outnumbered the old middle class and now does so overwhelmingly. Thus, the United States has gone from a nation of small capitalists to a nation of hired employees. A similar process has occurred in most advanced industrial countries. In this sense, what Zweig calls *debourgeoisement* has certainly taken place. Whatever we call the 'new class' it is certainly not identical with the old bourgeoiseie and petit-bourgeoisie.

Mills recognised that, in terms of their class situation, source and size of income (often relatively small), the white collar group could be considered working class – but he hesitated to classify them as such. In fact, he tended to refer to them as the *new middle class* for reasons which recall Weberian stratification theory. He claimed that the white collar group had higher *status* than manual workers among all sections of the public. Historically, this was largely because of the 'borrowed prestige' they acquired from working in close proximity to ownership and management. This 'reflected' status has become less common with the growth of separate, often relatively large-scale 'office areas', many of which seem closer to the factory floor than the boss's room. More recently, it is the better 'perks' associated with white collar work and the continuing belief that non-manual work is more prestigious than manual work that gives the white collar class a status edge over manual workers.

Mills observed that the white collar class is uncertain of itself and insecure about its future position relative to that of well

263

paid manual workers. The high wages and comfortable standard of living of the affluent manual workers challenged its marginal superiority, sometimes causing what Mills referred to as 'status panic'. He saw several possible directions of development for the white collar class. These were:

It might become part of the working class

It might establish itself more securely as part of the middle class

As it increases in number and power, it might form a buffer between labour and capital and so blunt class conflict

It might become a distinctive class, separate from others

A study of clerical workers, published in 1958 by David Lockwood amply illustrates the 'ambiguity' of the work and status situation of clerks. Lockwood drew his material from Britain: he examined the social position of clerks under the model of stratification presented by Weber. He analysed their market position, work situation and status situation. It will be remembered that, according to Weber, the major indicator of class is market position. Lockwood was in no doubt that the market situation of clerks is substantially better than that of the manual worker even though the average wage of skilled workers is higher than that of clerks. Clerks have more job security, better prospects of occupational mobility (into management) and, generally, better pension rights and fringe benefits, such as cleaner, more comfortable work conditions and longer holidays. More recent data comes from Lord Diamond's Commission on the Distribution of Income and Wealth. In 1977, employee benefits added the equivalent of 20% of the value of their pay for white collar workers, compared to only 14% for the blue collar workers. The value of these benefits is, however, increasing fast for both groups. Lockwood also emphasises the higher wages of clerks as compared to manual workers although this is now less true than at the time he wrote.

Lockwood extends Weber's conceptualisation of class to include the work situation of clerks. Again, he argues that, historically, clerks have tended to be closer to, and more influenced by, management than labour. He points out, however, that in large, modern mechanised offices identification with 'the boss' is less apparent. Developments since Lockwood wrote show a furthering of this trend. In particular, a rapid unionisation among white collar employees hardly suggests either deferential or snug attitudes to employers. In 1970, white collar union membership was 38%, an increase of one third over 1964. It is significant, however, that unionisation has been much more a feature of the public than the private sector. In 1970, the former was 80% unionised, and the latter only 10%. Willingness to organise for economic defence and advancement does not mean that public sector white collar employees are politically radical, but it is obviously a trend which might seem promising to Marxists as well as socialists of a milder ideological hue who wish to claim the political support of this group. A very much higher proportion of the lower middle class than the upper middle class vote Labour, though in no election has a majority done so.

Lastly, Lockwood examines the status situation of clerks. He remarks that the differences in class and work situations between clerk and manual worker continue to provoke status rivalry. At worst, clerical 'snobbishness' is answered by 'working class' contempt, although such stereotypical attitudes are probably less common now than at the time of Lockwood's research. Any clerical affectation is probably due as much to what Mills refers to as 'status panic' about the growing ambiguities of their social position than any real sense of superiority.

A third study we can briefly refer to is by David Weir. In the late nineteen sixties, he conducted a survey of 98 male clerks in large *private* sector firms. He tended towards the conclusion that clerks had a *distinctive* group consciousness. He contrasted their attitudes to social mobility with those traditionally associated with the middle class – that is, that society is a 'ladder' which anybody can climb up if they make the effort and have the ability. He summarises his findings succinctly:

> The replies ... taken together indicate a pattern that seems incompatible with the perception of the class structure as an open one, affording opportunities to all who possess the appropriate motivation to move upwards!

Yet, despite this, clerks, particularly those in the private sector, are far less inclined to 'us and them' attitudes than the manual working class. A majority, however, do not *personally* expect to be upwardly mobile although most recognise the possibility of upward mobility in *general* terms. Weir has also commented interestingly on the position of female white collar workers who

265

occupy a majority of the lower status positions of this kind of work. They often do routine jobs, such as filing or operating machines, which are quite similar to factory work. Yet they are less militant than men and more likely to think of themselves as middle class. They are also less likely to be union members although this is beginning to change.

Finally, Howard H. Davis's sensitive analysis of interviews with 19 senior clerks merits our attention. Although the clerks invariably call themselves 'middle class' they are, nevertheless, reluctant to define themselves as 'not working class' because many of them 'came up' from the working class and consider that opportunities of mobility still exist. To a much greater extent than the traditional working class they believe in the effectiveness of individual action in career terms and also in making social relationships not necessarily bound by ties of class.

In conclusion, the research evidence shows that the subjective class consciousness of white collar employees tends to be ambiguous in conventional class terms or, more precisely, in Weber's terms to show a distinctive awareness of their own interests. The increase in unionisation among this group, and the substantial minority of them that regularly vote Labour, gives some support to the hopes of Marxists, such as Westergaard and Resler, that they will eventually identify their 'true' proletarian interests. Meanwhile they use unions to pursue their own interests as they see them, not in the spirit of proletarian solidarity or, still less, as a means to achieve radical social change.

The Working Class
In the decade between 1961 and 1971, Britain employed 12.5% fewer people in the manufacturing sector. By contrast, Japan employed 21% more and West Germany 2% more. The British working class is shrinking in size. Nevertheless, it still remains the largest class. In 1972, 55% of adult males were working class. The total percentage of working class people was somewhat greater as working class men tend to have larger families, although this is now a diminishing trend.

a THE AFFLUENT WORKER: 'EMBOURGEOISEMENT' OR CONVERGENCE?
The 'embourgeoisement' hypothesis, first presented in the late

nineteen fifties, sparked off one of sociology's classic debates. The issue is about what is happening economically, socially, politically and culturally to the upper end of the working class. Are they, as Zweig suggested, becoming more middle class – that is, experiencing 'embourgeoisement'? Or, is what is happening more complex than this rather glib term suggests?

The 'embourgeoisement' hypothesis seemed particularly persuasive in the aftermath of the decisive defeat of Labour in the 1959 general election. As with the 1979 election, twenty years later, there was a swing against Labour among the working class. D. E. Butler and R. Rose suggested that Labour might be experiencing particular trouble in holding the affluent working class vote. The response of A. R. Crosland, a leading Labour politician, was to suggest that Labour should try to widen the basis of its political support to include as many middle class people as possible, rather than rely too exclusively on its traditional working class support.

In this atmosphere of rather speculative and politically charged debate, John Goldthorpe, David Lockwood and their collaborators decided to put the embourgeoisement hypothesis to empirical test. Their inquiry, which spanned several years in the early nineteen sixties, is considered something of a model of sociological research but is not beyond criticism. Their initial assessment was that the embourgeoisement thesis was probably an oversimplification. In order to avoid bias, however, they followed the scientific procedure advocated by Karl Popper and sought to *disprove* their own expectations. This meant choosing an area and sample as favourable as possible for the validation of the embourgeoisement thesis. (A *selected* sample of this kind is termed a purposive sample.) Luton, a prosperous and expanding town, qualified well as a suitable locale. It had the particular advantages of having a substantially migrant labour force – clearly willing to move to find better paid work – and of being without a strong Labour tradition. The research was based primarily on 229 manual workers and, for comparison, 54 lower level white collar workers. The former were drawn from three high wage paying local manufacturing firms. They were also all married men, as the researchers had a particular interest in examining family life-style, although this meant that the sample was not representative in terms of marital status and age.

Goldthorpe and Lockwood questioned their respondents under

three major headings: economic, relational (community relationships), and political (mainly their voting behaviour). They found that the high wages of the men in the sample did put a middle class standard of living within their reach. They shared many of the consumer items enjoyed by the middle class, such as televisions, refrigerators and automatic washing machines. Apart from this, their economic situation was largely different from that of the middle class. Firstly, their high wages were usually gained only at the cost of overtime: the average working week was 40 to 50 hours. Moreover, 75% of the sample were on shift work. A 'normal' background of overtime and shift work could put pressure on family and social life of a kind rarely experienced by the lower middle class. Secondly, promotional prospects were appreciably worse than for non-manual workers and this was fully realised by the majority of both groups sampled. The manual workers appreciated that any economic advances they made were likely to be *on the basis of their present economic role* and through collective bargaining, with the help of their trade unions. The non-manual sample typically entertained more hope of personal progress but they, too, have become more unionised, though less so in the private sector. Thirdly, as already mentioned, the lower middle class generally benefited from greatly superior fringe benefits. Fourthly, and perhaps more important, most of the manual workers expressed much lower levels of intrinsic satisfaction (pleasure in the job for itself) than did the white collar sample.

Goldthorpe and Lockwood's second category, relational aspects, may be thought of as cultural and community life. Not surprisingly, given the nature of the sample, few of the men studied shared the traditional pattern of community life often found among urban industrial workers and their families. Equally lacking, however, was any evidence that middle class company and life-style was sought, as might have been expected if 'embourgeoisement' had taken place. Kin still played a relatively prominent part in the social lives of the couples studied. This was particularly true of the (approximately) 50% of the sample whose kin lived mainly within a fifty mile radius of London, but it still applied to many of the rest. 41% of the former and 22% of the latter named kin in response to the question 'who would you say are the three people that you spend most of your spare time with?' (apart from spouse and children). Otherwise, *close neighbours*, rather than selected individuals from within the larger community, provided most friends. Interestingly, white collar couples had more contact with friends who were not neighbours, even though they also spent still more time with kin (probably because their kin were generally nearer).

Only 7% of the couples sampled deviated from the above relational pattern to the extent of having predominantly and unambiguously middle class friendship networks. Generally, affluent working class couples associated with those whose presence in their lives was largely 'given', such as kin, close neighbours and workmates. Relations were usually informal. They were, for instance, much less likely to have people round for dinner than the white collar groups. They were also far less likely to belong to formal organisations and those they did participate in, such as working men's clubs, tended to be solidly working class.

The changes in relational patterns that did typify the sample were not in the direction of embourgeoisement. The difference between them and the traditional working class could be explained by reference to major objective factors of their existence, such as work and geographical and residential mobility. Their relatively high level of consumption was explicable in terms of their hard work and relatively high pay. Their family *centredness* or *privatisation* can partly be explained in terms of new leisure facilities in the home and lack of traditional community links. In these limited aspects the life-style of the affluent worker *converges* with that of the lower middle class.

Goldthorpe and Lockwood's findings under their third heading, the political aspect, are dealt with in Chapter 19, and we summarise them only briefly here. They concentrated particularly on the voting behaviour of the main sample. On the basis of what they admit is limited data, they found a negative correlation between working class affluence and Conservative voting. In other words, the affluent worker is less likely to vote Conservative than less affluent workers. Again, they explain this by reference to the social, and not merely economic, realities of the affluent worker's life. Employment in large-scale industry, high union membership (87%) and frequent life-long membership of the working class are factors cited. It is interesting, however, that Goldthorpe and Lockwood make little of a *margi-*

nal trend away from Labour among affluent workers. This trend was apparent in their own data, assessed on the basis of the way members of the sample had voted in 1959 compared to their *intended* votes for 1964. Certainly, the *long-term* tendency since 1945 has been for the Labour vote to drop as a percentage of the total vote, and much more recent data than that available to Goldthorpe and Lockwood suggests that 'defections' among affluent workers have contributed to this trend. They themselves comment that the strong Labour vote among affluent workers was based on *instrumental* (practical self-interest) thinking rather than traditional emotional *solidarity* (identification) with the party. This important finding left open the possibility that they would change their vote if it seemed to suit their interests to do so.

We summarise the previous two sections from a comparative middle and working class perspective in the section immediately below.

b MIDDLE CLASS AND WORKING CLASS CONVERGENCE? In place of the 'embourgeoisement' hypothesis, Goldthorpe and Lockwood offer the observation that some *convergence* is occurring between the upper working and lower middle class. Instead of the upper working class becoming more like the middle class, both classes are *in some respects* developing a number of common characteristics. As we have seen, convergence is not much apparent in the political and social relational areas. It is, however, occurring in the field of economic *consumption*. Both groups seek a good standard of living, particularly in furnishing their homes with modern amenities. Given this, it is logical that *home and family centredness* should be a feature of members of both groups. Outside the family, their patterns of social life continue to be distinct. Money is the basis on which the consumer-family life style exists and it is not surprising that, in pursuit of it, *collectivisation* in the form of unionisation has been increasingly adopted by the salaried middle class as well as by the working class. The areas of convergence are, then, *economic consumption, family centredness and privatisation,* and *instrumental collectivism.* A. H. Halsey adds the observation that, in addition, status distinction between the middle and working classes has become less obvious and less important during this century and especially since the last war. He attributes this primarily to increased rates of

270

social mobility. With so many more first generation middle class people about, spotting the 'right' accent or the 'right' dress becomes a more precarious way of identifying status. But Halsey is aware of the relative superficiality of this. Just as important for him in making for a fairer and more equal society are the political and legal rights (mainly of association, such as the right to join a union) only acquired or consolidated by the majority during this century and discussed elsewhere in this book (see, especially Chapter 19). Even so, he cannot be accused of underestimating the extent of continuing inequality. The middle sections of society may have converged but the vestiges of status no longer cover the continuing huge discrepancies of wealth and poverty at the social extremes (see next chapter).

c THE TRADITIONAL WORKING CLASS AND ITS CULTURE: FRAGMENTATION OR RECONSTRUCTION? Before deciding whether the traditional working class is fragmenting or perhaps even disappearing, we need to know its composition. Defined most broadly, the traditional working class means manual workers, whether in or out of work, and their families. In addition, the term has special reference to workers in the now generally declining basic industries such as shipbuilding, mining, docking and heavy manufacturing. The phrase *traditional working class culture* refers to their way of life, based on work, community, a strong sense of solidarity and support for the union movement and the Labour party. (see Chapter 3, pp. 49–52, and Chapter 4, pp. 78–82 for further detail.) These people are the core of the working class, and it has been suggested, mainly by a number of liberal writers, that the working class is falling apart from the centre. In Ralf Dahrendorf's terms there has been a 'decomposition of labour' just as he believes there has been a 'decomposition of capital'. He argues that, in advanced countries, the working class has developed into three fairly distinct groups. First, are skilled workers such as miners – well paid and enjoying relatively high status and jealously ready to defend their position through their unions. All this is rather less true of semi-skilled workers such as bus conductors and they have something to protect and are generally organised through unions to do so. Much more precarious is the position of unskilled workers, such as kitchen hands. Because they are less well-paid, more easily replaced and usually less well organised, unemployment and poverty are often a real threat to them and they make up a relatively large proportion of the unemployed. Marxists would not deny that there is an empirical basis to the above description of the contemporary working class. As we shall see, however, they argue for a different *interpretation* of the facts from Dahrendorf.

Undoubtedly, certain developments have occurred which have greatly affected the traditional working class. First, because of the expanding service sector, more people of working class origins 'made it' into the middle class in the post-war period than at any previous time. Meanwhile, the manual working class itself declined in size, though it remains the largest class. Further, the decline of Britain's basic industries located in the inner cities, coupled with the housing clearance and renewal policy, and patterns of migration, have dispersed traditional, concentrated, working class communities. Now, a smaller working class is residentially more widely dispersed, and this has weakened community life. Few 'Bethnal Greens' remain, and if something like traditional community can re-emerge on public housing estates, patterns of privatisation and generally less intense neighbourhood relations militate against it. The continued popularity of 'Coronation Street' is probably as much an exercise in nostalgia as realism: or, if the characters are perceived as 'real', they are seen as part of yesterday's reality rather than today's.

Prosperity is a second development that is sometimes assumed to have eroded traditional, militant working class consciousness. Even if the word 'affluent' is too generous to describe the living standards of most of the working class, the vast majority are materially far better off than their counterparts of two or three generations ago. Although our analysis of the 'affluent worker' shows that new forms of militancy can replace the old, group self-interest expressed through unions falls short of traditional class solidarity. The Welfare State is also often considered to contribute to a more comfortable and therefore less discontented life for the working class. In 1980, however, there occurred significant reductions in real terms of welfare benefits to several groups and this served as a reminder that minimum standards can be lowered as well as raised. What effect this may have on working class attitudes is not yet clear.

The above developments have brought about a change in working class cultural life and attitudes. We can now see that the surge of interest in working class culture in the nineteen fifties and sixties was an attempt to capture in art a way of life that was already in retreat. A number of so-called 'Kitchen sink' novels, plays and films celebrated the toughness, humour, vitality and closeness of traditional working class life. The best of them such as *Saturday Night and Sunday Morning, Look Back in Anger, Chicken Soup with Barley* and *This Sporting Life*, still live on because they successfully convey aspects of this culture. Yet, for all their authenticity, they begin to seem positively nostalgic. Now, at a time when most own their own houses, many in suburbia, it is clear that these works describe times past.

What new norms, values and patterns of behaviour are replacing traditional working class culture? The liberal progressive view is that, just as the material standard of life has generally improved, so have levels of cultural opportunity and achievement. A much more pessimistic view is based on the theory of mass culture. Historically, elite-masses theory has had more appeal to conservative than to left-wing critics, but C. Wright Mills has given the concept a radical gloss. He agrees with liberals that affluence and consumerism have blunted material discontent but he savagely attacks the 'cultural trivialisation' of the media which he thinks distracts working people from seriously considering the nature of the society they live in and their own position within it. If they were able to do so, they would appreciate that they are still controlled and exploited at work and stunted in educational and cultural opportunity. Instead, he sees the majority of working and new 'middle' class people as processed mass. It may be remembered that we discussed Christopher Lasch's similar sentiments in Chapter 4, p. 78.

There is some similarity between Mills' observations and the cultural aspects of Goldthorpe and Lockwood's convergence thesis, but there is also a vital disagreement. They, like Mills, recognise the growth of consumerism and of privatised leisure across the classes, but whereas he sees little hope of a resurgence in working class consciousness and political activity, they are by no means so pessimistic. A basic difference of context is that Mills is writing of America where trade union activity has always been much weaker than in Britain, and which has never had an effective socialist party. Goldthorpe and Lockwood do observe a possible erosion in traditional working class support for the Labour party (see Chapter 19) and in active union involvement, but also stress that a new, if more critical and demanding, possible basis of support for the left exists among instrumentally oriented workers.

More orthodox Marxists than Mills, if, indeed, he can be called a Marxist, tend to reject the mass society model. They see culture in terms of classes, not masses. Thus, Raymond Williams states:

> There are in fact no masses: there are only ways of seeing people as masses.

He means that to lump people together as a mass is to miss the variety of individuals and groups. Nevertheless, Williams like other Marxists, is profoundly concerned that the media in capitalist society tends to make people passively satisfied with the mediocre. Remember, the Marxist ideal is fulfilment for all and they see little prospect of this in contemporary capitalist society.

Marxists analyse working class culture within the framework of the changing relations of the working class to the means of production. Richard Johnson makes the point in slightly broader terms:

> The conditions of existence of classes profoundly shape class cultures, less by specifying 'interests', more by supplying a kind of agenda with which the culture must deal. It is a matter of historical record that working class culture has been built around the task of making fundamentally punishing conditions more habitable.

The need to struggle for a comfortable survival through unions and political action, will continue to be 'on the agenda' for working class people in the foreseeable future. But Marxists recognise that in material terms the need for this struggle is not equally great throughout the working class. Dahrendorf's division of the working class into three broad groups –the skilled, semi-skilled and unskilled – is perhaps crude but some such distinction is necessary. At any rate, it clearly cannot be assumed that a skilled craftsman, say, a fitter, and an unskilled worker, will recognise much identity of interest even though Marxists consider that they share the common experience of exploited labour. Not only are there significant economic differences between such groups, but their social outlook or 'consciousness' varies considerably. The Weberian, David Lockwood, uses another term, 'social image', to describe general social attitudes and we have already met two of the major 'types' he finds among the working class. These are *proletarian* or *traditional* 'them and us' attitudes of groups such as miners and *instrumental* attitudes such as those exemplified by the affluent car-workers. He finds a second type of social image among the traditional working class which he terms *traditional deferential*. This attitude is common among individuals who work close to their bosses and involves respectfully 'knowing their place'. A considerable body of research on social images exists in addition to that of Lockwood. Howard H. Davis, amongst others, has pointed out that the social consciousness of craftsmen tends to be quite distinctive. The self and occupational images of the maintenance fitters of his own study were based on a strong sense of individual merit and achievement. It is worth remarking that these attitudes are not unlike those frequently attributed to middle class professionals! Serge Mallet, the French Marxist, has examined the attitudes of a quite different group of workers, those in automated industry. He finds evidence that they might unite with technicians and lower level management with whom they frequently deal against top management and ownership. Thus, he takes the view that developments in the occupational structure have created a 'new' working class with considerable potential for radical change. Certainly, we are beginning to build up a complex picture of social consciousness among the working class.

Marxists bring some order to the above complexity by reference to basic Marxist theoretical concepts and perspective. Firstly, they point out that, whatever their differences, the working class share a common relationship to the means of production. Braverman has made the more specific observation that capitalism has developed in a way that has progressively removed control of work out of the hands of more and more workers. Most workers – manual and non-manual alike – play small roles in large organisations. Secondly, and related to this, they argue that a common relationship to production is the basis of a common class interest. Thirdly, they contend that this common class interest can be best expressed in the socialist movement aimed at stopping capitalist exploitation and establishing a more equal society. The fourth part of this chain of thought is *how* this change will happen. Here the link is uncertain because Marxists disagree on the matter themselves. Simplifying somewhat, structuralists such as Althusser contend that the working class in general will only become aware of, and energetically pursue, its common interest in socialism when capitalist society begins to collapse and ceases to produce prosperity. Other Marxists, notably E. P. Thompson, stress that, within limits, working people have made their own history, and will make their own future. This leads to an emphasis on the need to 'raise the level of consciousness' among the working class by socialist propaganda and organisation. Despite their disagreement, both Althusser and Thompson make the important point that social consciousness is not static, but open to change. Because the working class is divided and even fragmented today does not mean it will be so tomorrow. It is also relevant to point out here that if white collar employees are included within the working class, as they are by many Marxists, then the numerical strength of the working class is much greater and so, therefore, must be its *potential* political strength. It is likely that a revival of working class politics would be based on some sort of 'coalition' extending from white collar unionists, through the employed manual working class, and embracing many of the growing numbers of unemployed. Such a 'coalition' would be based not only on mutual interest but also on a sense of moral solidarity by which the stronger shoulder some of the burden of conflict for the weak.

There is a wide range of agreement among sociologists of various perspectives and ideologies that the contemporary working class is internally highly differentiated both in terms of living standards and cultural outlook. But whereas liberals such as Dahrendorf tend to regard such divisions as a fact with which it is futile to argue, Marxists point to the continuing underlying common structural situation of the working class and regard the varying, and in some cases 'low', level of socialist consciousness among different groups of workers as a 'problem' to be wrestled with rather than as an immutable reality. If this comment makes sociology seem uncomfortably close to politics, it does not mislead.

2 Social Mobility

Terminology and Factors Associated with Social Mobility
We have already defined the concept of social mobility as
movement up or down the social class hierarchy. Mobility
may be *long-range* (from social class v to social class I) or, what
is much more common, *short-range*. *Individual* and *stratum* mobility can occur and the former is considered to be generally more
possible in modern than in traditional societies. *Ascribed status*
refers to social position which is predetermined by others and is
usually acquired at birth on the basis of the social standing of
the individual's parents. *Achieved status* refers to the social position individuals acquire in their own lifetime, whether higher or
lower than the one they had at birth. Again, the possibility of
achieving a change in social status is considered to be greater
in modern than in traditional societies, although most people
remain in the class of their birth. The word 'achieved' is slightly misleading in this context, because merit is not necessarily
implied in a change of social status.

The terms *status of origin* and *status of destination* provide a
more neutral alternative to describe the same phenomenon.
*Status of origin refers to the status into which a person is born and
status of destination to the one he or she acquires. Intragenerational
mobility* describes the situation when an individual acquires a
different social status from the one which he previously held.
Intergenerational mobility describes social mobility between
generations and it is our main concern here. Finally, the terms
vertical and *horizontal* mobility are frequently used. Vertical
mobility is simply another way of referring to upward or
downward mobility and horizontal mobility involves a change
from one occupation to another of equal status. Strictly
speaking, horizontal mobility refers to occupational rather than
social mobility as it involves no change of social status.

Status and class differences usually coincide, but rapid social
mobility can cause them to be 'out of joint'. For example, a
public school 'type' who finds himself having to do, say, a
manual job may find the symbols of middle class status, such
as accent and dress, something of an embarrassment. The same
can happen to the working class 'lad' who suddenly 'makes it': he
may appear to lack the polish of the more established rich. *Status
dissonance* is the term used to describe this kind of occurrence.

It should be remembered that most people remain in the class into which they are born. This can be *partly* because their life-style effectively cuts them off from other groups. For example, the traditional working class were often culturally very 'inbred'. Parker has referred to this as *social closure*.

We now give a list of the major factors associated with social mobility – simply as a checkpoint: they are explained later in the section. It is scarcely possible to separate the overlapping factors affecting group and individual mobility. Broadly speaking, however, those affecting groups come first:

1 *Substantial Change in Occupational Structure*
2 *Differential Fertility*
3 *Educational Opportunity (Qualifications)*
4 *Social and Cultural Factors*
5 *Intelligence and Talent*
6 *Marriage*

All these are explained and illustrated below in our detailed analysis of social mobility in England and Wales.

Social Mobility in England and Wales: A Test of the Liberal Ideal of Equality of Opportunity

There have been few more important public issues in twentieth century Britain than that of equality of opportunity. For Britain to be the 'open society' of liberal ideals, a society in which equality of opportunity exists, a good deal of social mobility must take place. More precisely, people must be able to compete for occupational position, on equal terms, regardless of their social class background. Many liberals of various political persuasions have regarded equality of opportunity as a precondition of a fair society. Of course, equality of opportunity does not guarantee equality of outcome: it means that people will achieve jobs suitable to their intelligence and talents, regardless of social background. As we have seen, Marxists want a different kind of equality from this: they want resources to be distributed in terms of need rather than competition. Others, again, are influenced by both views. Here, however, we examine how far the classic liberal ideal of equal opportunity is achieved in Britain. To do this, we must analyse the extent of social mobility in this country.

a STUDIES OF SOCIAL MOBILITY IN BRITAIN There have been two major studies of social mobility in England and Wales, the first led by David Glass in 1949 and the second conducted by a team of sociologists at Nuffield College in 1972. The latter is known as the Oxford Mobility Study. Ideally, the findings of the two surveys would be directly comparable, and it was certainly the intention of the Oxford group to achieve this as far as possible. In fact, they do not attempt precisely to *replicate* Glass's methodology partly because of a number of criticisms that have been convincingly made against it. The major effect of the flaws in Glass's methodology is that he may have underestimated the rate of social mobility, particularly long-range upward mobility. As one of his important findings was that there was little long-range mobility, either upwards or downwards, the methodological criticisms are significant. Glass also found that family and social background had a major effect on social status and that most people remained at a similar level to their fathers.

Our analysis of the 1972 findings will be assisted by reference to the following table although by no means the whole of the following discussion emerges from the data presented there.

Inter-generational class mobility: adult males, England and Wales, 1972

	Destinations (Ten years after entry to work)		
Origins	Middle class %	Lower Middle %	Working class %
Middle class	7.0	3.7	2.6
Lower Middle	7.0	9.9	13.9
Working class	6.1	11.3	38.5
Total	20.1	24.9	55.0 100

Source: A. H. Halsey, *Change in British Society*, p. 114. (slightly adapted).

This table repays detailed study. The vertical readings of the grid describe inter-generational inflow to three destination classes. The horizontal readings describe inter-generational outflow from origin classes. The diagonal reading from top left to bottom right describes those who were still in their class of origin ten years after starting work. A further key piece of information is that in terms of their class of *origin*, 13.3% of the sample were middle class, 30.8% lower middle class and 55.9% working class. These figures contrast interestingly with their 1972 *destinations* which were respectively, 20.1%, 24.9% and 55.0%.

Broadly, the findings of the Oxford Study confirm two popular clichés. The first is that the chances of improving one's social status got better in the post-war period, and the second – perhaps more a sociologist's than a layman's cliché – is that is is still much easier to *retain* high social status once born to it than it is to *achieve* it in the first place. Let us take these points in order.

Because of the expansion of the middle or service class since the war, there has been more opportunity for the lower middle and working class to move upwards. John H. Goldthorpe, a major contributor to the Oxford Study, rejects the thesis that a significant degree of 'closure' exists at the higher occupational levels of British society. Writing of the upper end of the middle class (the top 8% occupationally) he argues that the survey data shows 'a very wide basis of recruitment and a very low degree of homogeneity in its composition'. In other words, people from a great variety of social origins are members of this class (recruitment), and by that very fact its members are in many ways dissimilar (lack homogeneity). A particularly interesting illustration of this is that, in 1972, marginally more members of social class 1 came from working class backgrounds than from upper middle class backgrounds. This shows a very much higher rate of long-range upward mobility than Glass found. If we return to Halsey's table, we can see that what Goldthorpe says of class 1 is true of the middle class as a whole. Indeed, in 1972, almost two thirds of it were made up of people of non-middle class origin.

The lower middle class, too, is highly penetrable from below. It contains more people of working class origins (11.3%) than of lower middle class origins (9.9%), although relatively few middle class people (3.7%) are downwardly mobile into it. Concluding this point, then, opportunity for upward mobility substantially increased in post-war Britain. There is, however, quite another way of looking at the findings of the Oxford Study and we must adopt this perspective now.

The chances of a class 1 son remaining in class 1 compared to the chances that a working class son has of reaching class 1 have changed little over recent generations. Again, referring to the table, the proportion of sons of middle class origin who retained middle class status is more than 1 in 2, whereas only about 1 in 9 working class sons achieved this status. What has happened is that increased opportunities have been shared more or less equally between the classes: there have been rather more opportunities for all. But if the chances of upward mobility for working class sons have improved, the shrinkage of working class jobs and the expansion of middle class ones has protected the middle class against downward mobility. Overall, therefore, relative mobility rates have changed remarkably little. Goldthorpe concludes that the pattern of inter-generational mobility in recent decades has been one of stability or even marginally increasing relative inequality.

It needs to be said that the Oxford Study does not address itself directly to the Marxist concern with the upper class. Other data shows that there is much more self-recruitment to this group than to the much larger class 1 as a whole. It is also quite probable that those of non-upper class origins who do become members of it tend to adopt the values and attitudes of that class. Marxists are also able to interpret what is happening to the working class in a way quite consistent with their perspective. The working class is the most closed class and despite the differences between them, its members remain relatively disadvantaged. These factors may provide a sound basis for solidarity and collective action.

b FACTORS EXPLAINING THE RECENT PATTERN OF SOCIAL MOBILITY IN BRITAIN We now turn to discuss the factors that account for the pattern of social mobility described above. First, the increase in upward mobility has been largely due to a substantial shift in employment from the industrial to the service sector. Men have particularly benefited because lower status white collar jobs have been filled mainly by women, and men have been able to fill most of the new professional, technical, administrative and managerial posts. The increase has had little, if anything, to do with government policy. Indeed, in so far as the relative class rates of mobility have not changed, government policy to achieve greater equality of opportunity can be said to have failed.

Historically, differential fertility rates between the middle and working classes (that is, middle class families have produced fewer children) has created 'space' into which some working class people could move. Quite simply, the middle class did not produce enough children to fill all the middle class jobs available. This has been especially true in the rapid expansion of the service sector in the post-war period. Since the mid-nineteen sixties, there has been a tendency for family size to fall throughout the social classes, and although differences remain, differential fertility is now less important in explaining upward social mobility. The slight general increase in the birth rate in 1978 and 1979, even if sustained, is not likely to change this.

We have already examined the effect of educational expansion on social mobility and there is no need to rehearse the contents of this lengthy section here (see Chapter 5). In summary, Halsey *et al*'s research on the tripartite system and various less extensive studies of the comprehensive system show little *relative* change in the educational success and career achievements of children of different class origins in the post-war period. The middle class has taken as much, if not more, advantage of state education as the working class and has virtually sole access to the privileged private sector. Gamely, but not entirely convincingly, Halsey argues that a *further* expansion of educational opportunity must, by reduction, disproportionately benefit the working class. There may be no liberal alternative than but to try this, but history warns against excessive optimism about the likely results.

The influence of social and cultural factors on both educational and career opportunities does not need to be laboured here. It has been a constant theme in earlier chapters. The material disadvantages of a lower working class background are obvious, but the cultural disadvantages, if any, remain open to debate despite Halsey's sophisticated statistically-based attempt to show that they are much less than Bernstein and Bourdieu have argued.

However much intelligence may be helped or hindered by social environment, there is no doubt that the possession of high intelligence can be of assistance in upward mobility, and that low intelligence is a near fatal bar to it. Obviously, this factor applies virtually exclusively to the lower classes. It requires no intelligence at all to be born into the upper classes (although it usually requires, at least, the intelligence to appoint a good accountant to stay there). Lipset and Bendix have suggested that high intelligence may help working class children to recognise middle class attitudes and norms and to see the advantage of imitating them.

Traditionally, exceptional talent in either entertainment or sport has been an avenue to the top for a few working class people and, particularly in the United States, for some black people. But for most, this possibility is just a dream. There are not many Sophia Lorens or Muhammad Alis. A further miscellaneous group of factors, such as character, looks and luck can no doubt play a part in mobility but they are too unpredictable and personal to require more than brief acknowledgement here.

Of more sociological importance is the fact that women achieve upward mobility by marriage more often than men. This is a result of their generally inferior economic position and earning power. 'She's a gold digger' can be understood more sympathetically in the context of a society in which women depend heavily on men for material comfort and social status. This dependency is not the fault of individual women but lies in the nature of our sexually unequal society (see chapter 12).

If the recent past is a good guide, the prospects for upward mobility in Britain depend on the further expansion of the service sector. In the early nineteen eighties, the medium term prospects are for less employment in this area. Clearly, expansion cannot go on for ever. If higher status and better paid jobs are not available, a better academically qualified population will go to waste at the dole queues. There has so far been quite remarkably little thought about this possibility and what is to be done about it.

Britain is still a class divided society. Wealth remains concentrated and relative poverty persists. Social mobility out of the working class has increased but middle class children have as good a chance as ever of maintaining the status inherited from their parents. Both of these factors are due to the expansion of the service sector and not to the success of government policies aimed at bringing about greater equality of opportunity. There is more 'room at the top' (or, more precisely, in the middle) but the class origins of those who 'make it' are roughly in the same proportion that they were fifty years ago. And in the future, it is quite possible that upward access will become more difficult. In 1980–81, for instance, thousands of civil service jobs were lost. Already the most rapidly expanding 'occupational' group in British society is the unemployed. Practically and culturally, the country is largely unprepared for this – that is, neither the policies, nor attitudes and ideas to deal with it are much in evidence.

For the working majority, however, a degree of *situational convergence* has occurred. White collar employees at all levels tend more frequently to work in large organisations and, like the manual working class, have to haggle in the market place to maintain and defend their pay and working conditions. To do so more effectively they have become more unionised. According to Goldthorpe and Lockwood, *instrumental collectivism* increasingly characterises the attitudes of most employees – whatever the colour of their collar. Whether common economic experience and response will ever provide a basis of a shared political approach among unionists is a matter for speculation. Union membership has become a *less* reliable factor in predicting voting behaviour. Specifically, a greater number of trade union members vote Conservative or Liberal than twenty years ago. It may be, however, that in a time of economic crisis in which white collar as well as manual working class security is threatened, a more unified political approach will emerge among unionised employees.

Convergence has also partly occurred at the cultural level, although what is said here must be balanced against the emphasis we have already given to cultural inequality and difference. Traditional working class culture has declined but so, too, has the aura of respectability and status that used to envelop the middle class. Certainly, the symbols of status have diminished in importance to the point where they can easily seem quaint or ridiculous – the cloth cap or 'plummy' accent of the comic's joke. People seem to value others and themselves in terms of *consumption* rather than traditional status. Yet, consumption is frequently not ostentatious: indeed, much of it is privatised and family based. One television set is much the same as another. The thrill of owning the first colour television among one's peer group can only be brief – the machinery of mass production sees to that.

Assessments of modern culture are too various to catalogue in detail here. For some, the cultural profile of corporate capitalist society is flat and uninteresting. Others, however, see a burgeoning of individual expression in increased leisure activity and regard the variety of electronic based entertainments now possible within the home itself as a great improvement in the quality of life. What cannot be doubted, however, is the privatised nature of our culture.

Guide to Further Reading and Study

The third edition of A. H. Halsey's *Change in British Society* (Oxford University Press, 1986) is an invaluable introduction to most aspects of stratification in contemporary Britain though it leaves one wanting more on gender divisions. J. Westergaard and H. Resler, *Class in Capitalist Society: A Study of Contemporary Britain* (Penguin, 1976) covers similar ground from a Marxist perspective. J. H. Goldthorpe *et al, The Affluent Worker in the Class Structure* (Cambridge University Press, 1969) is a classic piece of research into a social group of great significance in the post-war period. Also standard on the cultural side, is Richard Hoggart's *The Uses of Literacy* (Penguin, 1966). Nicholas Abercrombie and John Urry, *Capital, Labour and the Middle Classes* (George Allen and Unwin, 1983) fills a gap in this area. The main sources for the capitalist class/managerial elite reviewed earlier in this chapter are R. Dahrendorf, *Class and Class Conflict in Industrial Society* (Routledge and Kegan Paul, 1959) and R. Miliband, *The State in Capitalist Society: The Analysis of the Western System of Power* (Quartet Books, 1973). More recent is John Scott, *Corporations, Classes and Capitalism* (Hutchinson, 1985). A. F. Heath's *Social Mobility* (Fontana, 1981) is a useful overview of that topic; highly authoritative but demanding is J. Goldthorpe *et al, Social Mobility and Class Structure in Modern Britain* (Oxford University Press, 1980).

Past Questions

1 'The thesis of the white collar workers becoming proletarian should be viewed as sceptically as that of the manual worker becoming middle class.' In the light of the available evidence, do you agree? (AEB, 1980)

2 'It is now more realistic to talk about "the middle classes" than the "middle class".' Discuss. (AEB, 1982)

3 'In contemporary Western societies the major influence upon the class structure is the distribution of productive capital.' Discuss (OLE, 1983)

4 Describe the major trends in the rate of social mobility since 1945. What are the major factors determining rates of social mobility? (OLE, 1983)

5 (a) Examine the problems sociologists face in studying social mobility. (12 marks). (b) Discuss whether the study of social mobility should be of central concern to sociologists. (13 marks) (AEB, 1984)

6 'A new occupational sector composed of managers, intellectuals and professionals has developed in advanced industrial societies.' Consider the implications of this view for theories of social stratification. (AEB, 1985)

7 Outline *one* general theory of stratification. What evidence would you submit in support of the theory? What criticisms could be made of it? (JMB, 1985)

(Refer also to Chapter 9)

11 Wealth, Poverty and the Search for Equality

The Issues

This chapter is about the extremes of inequality in Britain and in the contemporary world. Focusing mainly on Britain, it deals primarily with the brute facts of material inequality and attempts to explain them. Our brief consideration of poverty in the Third World should be considered as a supplement to the sections on Development and Underdevelopment and Population at the end of Chapter 7, in which the reasons for the relative inequality of the developed and underdeveloped countries are discussed. Inequality of cultural opportunity usually goes hand in glove with material inequality. We do not explore this matter here, as it was a major theme of Section B and appears again prominently in Chapter 19.

Material equality is a socialist and communist rather than a liberal ideal. Yet many holding these views would shy back from committing themselves to the principle of complete equality. It is worth recalling that even the Marxist ideal of a classless society does not necessarily imply *complete* equality even in material matters. Nevertheless, the majority of socialists and communists seek a much greater measure of equality than exists in Britain and the contemporary world. We briefly examine the search for greater equality in the case of four societies. Finally, and partly in view of the difficulties experienced by these societies, we ask whether equality is possible or desirable.

Wealth and Poverty: Some Facts

We can usefully begin our examination of the extent of inequality in Britain by looking at the distribution of income and wealth. This will give us a clear picture of relative inequality. The difference between income and wealth as economic assets needs to be made clear. Income is, generally, 'money in the hand' and, within the limits of a person's commitments, can be spent as he wishes. Wealth includes other assets besides cash savings. Income enables a person to consume, whereas wealth, as well as doing this, gives long term security and status. We look at income first.

Comment on the table divides into two. Between 1949–76 there was relatively little overall change: the change that did occur was notably at the expense of the top 1% and in favour of the group *between* the top 10% and the bottom 50%. From 1976–77 'the gap between the rich and the poor ... widened substantially' – to quote the *Guardian* (9.1.86) which cited additional data to that given below.

The Distribution of Income in the U.K. after Tax

Income share of the	1949	1976/77	1981/82
top 1%	6.4	3.5	4.6
top 10%	27.1	22.4	25.6
next 40%	46.4	50.0	49.2
bottom 50%	26.5	27.6	25.2

Sources: Adapted from the *Report of the Royal Commission on the Distribution of Income and Wealth*, and *Social Trends*, 1985.

As we saw in the previous chapter, wealth is much less evenly distributed than income. The very rich are invariably wealthy because of what they inherit, not because of what they earn. Despite the gradual trend towards a redistribution of wealth in the post-war period, the top 1% are still about 25 times richer than average, and the gap between the richest and the poorest is almost unimaginable. In concrete terms, it is the difference between sleeping in a louse-infested bed in an East End doss-house and sleeping in the world's best homes and hotels. It is the middle class that has primarily benefited from wealth redistribution – largely as a result of the increase in home-ownership. Statistical experts warn us against the incompleteness and inadequacy of official figures on the distribution of income and wealth. In particular, the exclusion of *non-marketable* assets, especially state and other pension rights, tends to exaggerate inequality. On the other hand, massive upper class family wealth is sometimes obscured in official figures (partly because of tax-avoidance strategies such as making 'gifts' to relatives). In any case, the pattern of fundamental inequality is clear.

Both the statistics and human reality of poverty in the Third World are a challenge to our imagination. In 1978, the world spent 120 billion dollars on arms while 17 million infants died of malnutrition, bad water or preventable disease before reaching their fifth birthday. As Westerners seek to make marginal economies to cope with the energy crisis, over 600 million families in the Third World struggle on incomes which would not pay half the cost of the average Western family's annual heating bill.

Finally, without being sanctimonious, a different kind of poverty should be mentioned. Cultural critic Jeremy Seabrook calls it 'the poverty within us'. He means the constant obsession with material things that thinly obscures the lack of values and humanity in Western society. Things have become more important than people. The claim to be, if not poor, at least 'stretched' is common. Yet we live in a period of great wealth. Seabrook suggests that in the West, the common plea of 'poverty' is actually a cry from the impoverished spirit rather than the empty stomach. Of course, it cannot be suggested that this is true of those in genuine material need.

The Poor

This section examines the extent and causes of poverty in Britain and, more briefly, in the Third World. First, however, we consider what it is like to be poor.

THE MEANING OF POVERTY (A PHENOMENOLOGICAL PERSPECTIVE) Most people reading this book will not *know* poverty because they will never have experienced it. The poor do not, on the whole, go in for further education and read books like this. The stunting of educational and cultural opportunity is the consequence of poverty. Some who read this book will have *seen* poverty: some may have even seen the absolute degradation of poverty in, say, Calcutta. But seeing poverty is not the same as *being* poor. It is very easy to close your mind to poverty that is merely observed. In India, the visiting Westerner will, at first, often give to the poor, but endless requests for alms become an irritation. Excuses not to give come readily to mind: 'They're taking me for a ride'; '*This* one doesn't look hungry'; 'He'll spend it on drink'; 'They're using the baby to make me feel sorry for them'; 'Anyway, surely the abolition of poverty is the responsibility of the international community, not of an individual', and so on. In fact, neither personal charity nor the efforts of relief agencies have solved the problem, although that does not mean either should cease.

The main effect of poverty is to cause human pain and suffering. This may be physical, such as rickets or the failure of the brain to develop fully, or mental, such as demoralisation and despair. In so far as there is enough wealth in the world to abolish poverty we can say that this pain and suffering is needless. Let us look at two cases of poverty in Britain. Both involve children of single parents. They may seem slight in comparison with starvation in the Third World, but a little imagination will show what distress underlies them. First:

> Being poor means being sad on the first day of school. My little girl shan't have a uniform. The head teacher says it won't be covered by the Department of Health and Social Security or the education authority as it is not compulsory. The fact remains that the only children without one are from families that can't afford it.

Second:

> Being poor meant finding a flat for £10 and having the DHSS refuse to pay more than £6, so your child is removed into care and you are lodged in a doss house with no bathroom.
>
> (*The Times*, 24th December, 1979)

Human statistics are meaningful primarily in terms of the personal experience they attempt to record. Think of the following statistics in those terms. In Britain in 1978, 500,000 children lived in families whose income was below the official poverty line even though one or both parents were in full-time work. Almost 1,000,000 lived in families dependent on supplementary benefit because the head of the family was physically or socially incapacitated in some way. Over 100,000 were in the care of local authorities, and about 300,000 were left alone either after school or during holidays, often because both parents worked. It is not, however, only child poverty that should be perceived in human terms but all poverty.

DEFINITION AND EXTENT OF POVERTY AND INEQUALITY Before the extent of poverty can be estimated, we must define what we mean by the term. Poverty can be thought of as either *absolute* or *relative*. Absolute Poverty is insufficiency in the basic necessities of existence: in practical terms, this usually means being without adequate food, clothing or shelter. Absolute poverty is a rarity in Britain but commonplace in the Third World. In Runciman's terms, relative poverty or *deprivation* is not being able to afford what one's *reference group*, or group of comparison, enjoys. In his recent (1979) authoritative survey on poverty, Peter Townsend described relative poverty as the inability to participate in the community's style of living. Thus, a person who cannot afford the record player that all his friends have is relatively deprived. Understandably, some social commentators feel that this concept can be taken too far. It is one thing to feel deprived at the lack of a record player, but are these feelings justified in respect of, say, coloured televisions or video-recorders? In principle, however, the concept of relative deprivation is applicable to any such situation.

How, then, do we draw the poverty line as far as Britain is concerned? Obviously absolute poverty is a rarity although many still eat less well than they should and live in unhealthy conditions. Peter Townsend offers several different approaches to measuring poverty. He starts with the government's own definition embodied in the *supplementary benefit* scale. The scale determines a minimum level of income for claimants who are unable to work, and whose other sources of income, if any, are inadequate to meet their needs. Supplementary benefits are paid for out of general taxation and are quite separate from *contributory benefits* such as old age pensions and unemployment and sickness benefits. Supplementary benefits are *means tested*, which is to say that they are given only to those whose own resources are below a certain level. Means testing necessarily involves an intrusion into privacy. The value of supplementary benefits in real terms has tended to increase, but the value relative to the average wage has not changed greatly.

In 1969, there were about 5 million people in Britain claiming supplementary benefit, that is 9% of families below the official poverty line. Both J. C. Kincaid and Frank Field have argued that this grossly underestimates the numbers in poverty. There may be as many as 2 million people or more affected by the non-taking up of benefits. This includes some workers whose jobs pay wages that are below the income that supplementary benefits would provide for a worker's family. Astonishingly, some have regarded this as an argument for reducing benefits rather than raising the wages of the low-paid. To 'earn' poverty is a grim irony and not exactly an incentive to work. Some authorities have claimed that a realistic point at which to draw the poverty line would be 20% or even 40% above basic supplementary benefit rate. The Supplementary Benefits Commission does sometimes allow special grants to be made up to this level, although discretionary grants may eventually be reduced. 'The supplementary benefit plus 40%' point would put 12½ million in poverty.

The above definitions are all based on varying levels of material deprivation. Townsend's use of the concept of relative deprivation, which produced a total of 14 million in poverty (22.9% of the population), adds a consideration for how people feel when they lack the means to get what their friends and acquaintances have. People who are clearly unable to meet the demands and expectations inherent in their social relationships are relatively poor. We recall the child whose single parent could not afford a school uniform. In terms of sociological jargon, her distress was relative, not absolute, but no less personally felt for that. Some of the Conservative press attacked Townsend's broad concept of poverty as hopelessly unrealistic and there is no doubt that, a socialist himself, he sees no solution to poverty without a fundamental redistribution of wealth.

Townsend's massive empirical survey (1200 pages!) was carried out in 1968–69. We have to ask if his findings are still applicable. Writing in 1979, A. N. Atkinson, himself an expert in the area, argued that, during the decade between Townsend's research and its publication, the overall relative position of the poor was no better. For instance, the earnings of the lowest paid 10% of male workers improved by a mere 1% of the median between 1968 and 1978 (from 66 to 67%); unemployment trebled in that period, and there was a substantial increase in the number of one parent families. All these trends continued into the 1980s except that the earnings of the lowest paid fell to 64.1% of the national average (1983). Which groups, then, make up the 15 million poor? The rising numbers of unemployed (3 million families) and low paid (3 million families) from the late 1970s increased the size of these categories. One-parent families are particularly at risk. Though no longer the most vulnerable to poverty, still over 3 million pensioners are poor, as are about 150,000 sick and disabled (see Chapter 22, pp. 643–5).

The Causes of Poverty and Some Policy Solutions

There is a variety of possible explanations of poverty. Not all are equally applicable to all groups. We discuss suggested causes and policy solutions of poverty together.

POVERTY AS MORAL INADEQUACY A popular nineteenth century view of poverty was that it was the result of laziness or even moral inadequacy. Hard work was considered to be the virtue that ensured prosperity and those who did not practise it were felt to deserve poverty. Few would see laziness as the major cause of poverty in contemporary Britain; the facts disprove this point of view. About a quarter of the poor are old people, and more than a third are actually in work but are poorly paid. The occasional panic about social security 'scroungers', orchestrated by elements in the media, is disproportionate to the size of the problem. There are far more who fail to claim benefits to which they are entitled than who claim dishonestly. The small percentage (about 5% of claimants) who actually get more from social security than they would from work are generally unskilled workers with large families. This anomaly of the system perhaps· reflects more discreditably on a society that tolerates such low pay than on the individuals concerned. (For more on this perspective, see pp. 629–31).

POVERTY AS MISFORTUNE A second explanation of poverty is that it is often due to personal misfortune or need, rather than the result of individual moral failing. This view is associated with progressive liberal or social democratic political ideas, and it inspired much of the reforming legislation that set up the framework of the twentieth century Welfare State. First, contributory old age pensions and then insurance for employees against sickness and unemployment were introduced by government. The Welfare State was consolidated and extended by the first post Second World War Labour government. Two important measures were the setting up of the National Health Service, and of the National Assistance Board. The purpose of the latter was to provide help for those who remained unemployed after their unemployment benefit had been exhausted, or who were otherwise without income. The role of the NAB has since been taken over by the Supplementary Benefits Commission.

The reformer's view that poverty 'hits' certain identifiable groups, who must therefore be helped, is enticingly simple, yet poverty stubbornly persists despite the Welfare State. It is a severe disappointment to the many politicians and intellectuals, who hoped that the Welfare State would virtually abolish poverty, that millions are in receipt of social security in the early nineteen eighties. Such was certainly not the intention of Lord Beveridge whose official report was largely responsible for the structure of the NAB. He hoped that a low unemployment and high wage economy, coupled with a better system of unemployment insurance, would mean that the supplementary function of the NAB would substantially decrease rather than increase. There are other criticisms of the way the Welfare State operates. One is that it fails significantly to redistribute wealth from the better off to the poor. This is because the middle class make more use of the Welfare State than the poor. Thus, they keep their children in education for longer, and, often, use the health service more. Further, as middle class people, from clerks to Principal Secretaries (top civil servants), run the Welfare State, it is *in a sense,* an employment subsidy for them. Often, the bureaucratic way in which welfare is administered confuses or 'mystifies' those who need help. Long waits, form-filling and questioning may or may not be the norm, but they happen frequently enough – particularly in the administration of social security – to intimidate some.

Reformers still hope to improve and extend the Welfare State. Some, such as the late Richard Titmuss, would like to see the abolition of *means tested benefits* (those given after income and other support has been assessed) in favour of the universal right to a minimum standard of living for all – that is, the triumph of the principle of *universalism* over *selectivity.* More recently, Peter Townsend has been involved in campaigning to reduce the extent of dependency on supplementary benefits and the humiliating means tests that go with them. He was an influential figure behind the state pensions scheme introduced in 1978. This should gradually reduce the number of old on supplementary benefit. Others call for the improvement of administrative techniques and better co-ordination of public and voluntary welfare agencies. Marxists, however, believe that reform is not enough and, as we shall see in considering the fourth explanation of poverty, regard it as the inevitable product of capitalist society. In any case, it should not be assumed that the Welfare State will expand indefinitely, or even that

295

welfare expenditure is never reduced. Indeed, after six years of Labour rule in which very little redistribution of wealth to the poor occurred, cuts in welfare expenditure were implemented by the Conservative government, elected in 1979. Social services had an effective 9% cut imposed on their projected expenditure for 1980–81 and, as a result, planned cuts in such services as home helps, meals on wheels and old people's homes.

THE CULTURE OF POVERTY THESIS A third explanation of poverty is that it is generated and regenerated by the cultural attitudes and life-style of the poor. This is the 'culture of poverty' theory, one which tends to be adopted by conservative social critics. It often involves 'trait analysis' of the life-style of the poor. These traits, or characteristics, are said to include present-centredness, a sense of resignation and fatalism, and a strong predisposition to authoritarianism. At its most extreme, this interpretation sees the poor as inadequate and pathological. Edward Banfield describes the 'lower class individual' as follows:

> Although he has more 'leisure' than almost anyone, the indifference ('apathy' if one prefers) of the lower class person is such that he seldom makes even the simplest repairs to the place that he lives in. He is not troubled by dirt and dilapidation and he does not mind the inadequacy of public facilities such as schools, parks, hospitals and libraries; indeed, where such things exist he may destroy them by carelessness or even by vandalism. Conditions that make the slum repellent to others are serviceable to him.

Given that Banfield regards the cause of poverty as rooted in psychological attitudes, he is dubious about easy solutions aimed at changing the way in which people live. Cultural attitudes tend to undermine imposed reform.

An earlier study by Oscar Lewis puts the concept of the culture of poverty in a wider context. The conditions in which it flourishes include a low-wage, profit-oriented economy and inadequate government assistance for the poor. These are frequently to be found in Third World areas which are undergoing 'development' by foreign capital and, more locally, in inner-city areas almost anywhere in the world. Given this wider context, the culture of poverty thesis loses its conservatism and becomes, generally, more useful.

Sir Keith Joseph's concept of the 'cycle of deprivation' has some similarity to the 'class culture' approach but it lays greater stress on the effect of material factors, such as poor housing and low income, in undermining prospects for self-improvement from generation to generation. Among cultural factors, he particularly emphasises the inadequacy of parental upbringing and the home background. The logical conclusion of this is to help and strengthen the family. Whether this can be done on a piecemeal basis is highly debatable. In any case, research, led by Michael Rutter, has shown that most poverty is not intergenerational. Even if the 'cycle' were broken for those who supposedly suffer from it, the majority of those who are in poverty would remain so.

STRUCTURAL EXPLANATIONS OF POVERTY Finally, we come to the analysis of those who regard the rough consensus of the major parties around the Welfare State solution to poverty as misguided. Most of these critics are socialist and some Marxist. They consider the cause of poverty to be in the structure of the capitalist system itself. Profit, not human need, is the basic principle of capitalism. The Welfare State merely patches up the wounds caused by exploitation and greed – and not very effectively at that. J. C. Kincaid concludes his influential book *Poverty and Equality in Britain* with the following remarks:

> Poverty cannot be abolished within capitalist society, but only in socialist society under workers' control, in which human needs, and not profits, determine the allocation of resources.
> For the immediate present, the urgently needed reform of the Welfare State remains contingent on the mobilisation of the working class as an independent force in British politics.

Kincaid's last sentence indicates that even within capitalism some reform is better than none. The alleviation of suffering and deprivation cannot be left to await 'the revolution'. The alternative to such a programme may be that a new 'underclass' of the poor and powerless will develop. A virtual halt to national economic growth, high unemployment, and a labour movement only half-heartedly committed to the needs of the poor, is the type of scenario that could enable this to happen. (For more on this perspective, see pp. 639–45.)

Stratification in Socialist Societies: The Search for Equality

Convergence Theory

Stratification in Socialist societies is of interest for two major reasons. Firstly, a large number of societies, particularly in the Third World, have been so attracted to the ideal of socialist equality that they have based their socio-economic system on socialism. This is one of the chief world developments of this century. The second point is of more specific sociological interest. The socialist societies present us with an empirical testing ground of the practicality of social equality – as defined in socialist terms. We must be careful, however, not to reach simplistic and uninformed 'verdicts' on the practical possibility of equality on the basis of the experience of socialist societies so far. In the sheer struggle to survive, in a hostile world, many socialist regimes have pursued policies far from their own preferred ideals.

One of the most formidable criticisms of the efforts of the Soviet Union and other industrialised Communist countries to achieve greater equality than exists in the West, is implied in *convergence theory*. This view argues that the nature of modern industrial technology requires the same range of skills wherever it is used, and that people of different abilities and education will attract correspondingly different rewards. This classic functionalist argument was applied to the Soviet Union by American liberals Daniel Bell and Clark Kerr in the early nineteen sixties, partly to demonstrate that the egalitarian hopes of the Soviets were destined to flounder before the 'logic of industrialism'. J. H. Goldthorpe, in the spirit of diligent empirical research for which he is widely respected, decided to 'test' whether the system of stratification operating in the Soviet Union was in fact substantially similar to that of advanced capitalist countries. We consider his and other relevant findings on this matter in the context of a broad survey of stratification in the Soviet Union. We then move on to examine convergence theory as applied to Sweden, a socialist democracy. Finally, we briefly look at stratification in two Third World countries: China and Tanzania.

The Soviet Union: Equality or Convergence?

The first socialist society was the Soviet Union. After the Bolsheviks (Communists) came to power in 1917, vigorous efforts were made to reach a much greater degree of social equality than existed in Tsarist Russia. Wage differentials between blue and white collar workers were greatly reduced, and rapid expansion of the social services occurred. Further, from the nineteen twenties the Soviet Union provides us with a classic example of a society in which structural change opened up the opportunity for substantial upward social mobility. The change in this case was due to the rapid rate of industrialisation, which provided higher status jobs for former peasantry. The expansion of administrative, managerial and political posts enabled a limited number to achieve mobility to a higher status range. No great credit redounds to government policy for the increase in upward mobility, although peasants and workers were favoured over the middle class. A rapidly modernising country tends to experience an increased rate of upward mobility – regardless of whether it is communist or capitalist. The same happened in the United States during a period of comparable expansion.

For a 25 year period, up to the death of Stalin in 1956, the process towards greater equalisation tended to be reversed, except in respect of increased social mobility and even this took place in a society that was becoming more and more stratified. This was due to Stalin's belief that the country needed firm leadership both for internal development and in foreign affairs – he feared Germany – and partly because of his own authoritarian personality. Liberty – civil, political and economic, such as workers' control of, or participation in industry – declined, as did equality, during Stalin's dictatorial rule.

More recently, there has been a partial return to the ideal of material equality in the USSR, although substantial differentials exist. What is important from the point of view of comparative stratification, however, is not the precise ebb and flow of inequality but *how* it is produced. On this basis Goldthorpe rejects convergence theory, and argues persuasively that the *underlying basis* of stratification is different in the Soviet Union and other centrally-controlled Communist countries from the capitalist West. He contends, that whereas market forces produce *class* stratificiation in the West, they are not allowed sufficient operation to do so in Soviet-type regimes. In Soviet society, Communist Party control produces a *politically based form of stratification.* Top politicians ultimately have the power to determine and to change the structure of status and rewards (that is, there is stratification hierarchy). Following the logic of Goldthorpe's argument, it is more precise to refer to this group of top people as a *ruling political elite* rather than a ruling class.

Goldthorpe is surely correct to see stratification in Soviet-type countries and the West as *generically* different (of a different type). Frank Parkin also makes a point based on the distinction between a market and a politically controlled economy, adopted by Goldthorpe. He is able to illustrate that the allocation of rewards, in the form of income and status, is somewhat different in Russia and other East European countries from that in the West. In particular, manual workers tend to be better paid than lower white collar workers, who also tend to receive fewer fringe benefits than in the West. In Marxist countries there is a tradition of allocating higher status to manual work whereas, in the West and perhaps particularly in Britain, the opposite tendency prevails (Chapter 10, p. 265). Nevertheless, an educated elite of much better paid employees also exists. Parkin found, however, a somewhat narrower range of income than in the West, though it has been argued that the privileges of politicians and top bureaucrats perhaps partly cancel this out. Parkin found a higher rate of social mobility in the East European countries than in the West and, significantly, more long-range mobility. He considers that the large number of recruits to the 'intelligensia' has helped to prevent the development of a distinct culture and style among this group comparable to that of the English upper class or French *haute bourgeoisie.* As Parkin is aware, the high rate of upward mobility in Russia was probably due more to the rapid expansion of that country's service sector than to deliberate policy (though this played a part). The same process has occurred in England in the post-war period. In both countries upward mobility will almost certainly decline if this expansion stops and in the absence of government policies to maintain it.

Although Goldthorpe and Parkin do make important distinctions about the causes of stratification in advanced Western and East European countries, they both recognise that substantial material inequality still exists in Russia. Speculatively, David

Lane raises the possibility that this inequality *may* be part of a transitional phase after which true Communism will be achieved. This speculative optimism is not shared by Yugoslav former politician and writer Milovan Djilas, who was one of the first to offer a critique of the nature of stratification in Soviet and other East European Communist Bloc countries. He argued that a new ruling elite or class (the distinction is not always clearly made) of *political leaders* and *bureaucratic officials*, as distinct from an economic ruling class, had emerged in these countries. His thesis has become a familiar one and has, more recently, been applied to China and other non-European countries. Most socialist societies, European or otherwise, do produce a sizeable bureaucratic class which generally operates *under* the control of the political elite. History has shown that both politicians and bureaucrats can threaten the liberty and living standards (they are expensive non-producers!) of the majority of the people whose 'servants' they are supposed to be. The two groups are highly interdependent and it is not surprising that they sometimes have a sense of shared interests against 'the masses'. As Tom Bottomore suggests, the term *power elite* rather than *ruling class* better describes the political, rather than economic, basis of the power of the ruling minorities in the East European Communist countries.

Although Goldthorpe and Parkin undermine convergence theory, it remains possible that, as functionalists argue, there is a deeper *general* reason for the widespread, if not universal, occurrence of stratification, which neither convergence theory nor Goldthorpe or Parkin explore. We return to this issue in the next section. Yet, Goldthorpe and Parkin do open the door to the possibility that men can adapt systems of stratification to fit in with their own political and ideological beliefs. Alvin Gouldner, the American radical sociologist, goes further, and passionately argues that both Eastern Communist and Western capitalist countries could be both more equal and more democratic. With this in mind we now examine convergence theory in the context of Sweden.

Sweden: Corporatism and Convergence

The concept of the corporate state is often associated with convergence theory, though the concepts are distinct. Corporatism involves a high degree of co-operation and consultation between government, business and trade unions in 'managing' the industrial state and in reducing internal conflict between capital and labour. J. K. Galbraith has been a particular exponent of this concept and regards a degree of corporatism as necessary to the efficient running of an advanced society and implies, therefore, that some form of corporatism will be universally adopted in such societies. Sweden is often considered to be a prime example of a corporate state. We will give a brief description of Swedish society and then comment more theoretically.

Swedish socialism is of great interest because it is the only example of 'socialism' in an advanced Western society which can be said to have gone 'beyond the Welfare State'. The well-funded and comprehensive Swedish Welfare State was largely the product of an alliance between the Swedish Social Democratic Party and the unions. The Swedish Welfare State has achieved a far higher degree of equality and security among the country's citizens than in Britain. Of course, the price to pay is a much more redistributive system of taxation (Sweden has the most redistributive system of taxation in Europe). The policies of the partnership between the Social Democrats and unions promise to breach the divide between capital and labour to the extent that, within half a century, the former may even be absorbed by the latter and one socialist community created. Already Sweden has an advanced system of industrial democracy (see Chapter 15, pp. 422–3) and a proposal adopted by the LO (the Swedish TUC) for 'employee investment' within companies would, if accepted by the government, eventually result in the socialisation of the Swedish economy. Of course, this may not happen and, indeed, in 1979, the Social Democrats went out of office for the first time in 44 years. Nevertheless, Sweden provides a credible example for those who argue that socialism in advanced societies can be achieved via 'the long, hard march through the institutions', rather than through the frightening gamble of revolution.

The Swedish case suggests that convergence theory is both too generalised and based on highly elitist assumptions. Sweden combines a degree of equality as great if not greater than, that of Soviet-type societies and enjoys at least as much civil and political equality as Western, capitalist societies. Swedish society certainly has its problems but its achievements suggest that greater equality, democracy and participation are possible than convergence theory implies. It lends support for Gouldner's belief that to a significant extent men and women can 'run' society rather than 'be run' by it: neither technocratic nor undemocratic political elites are inevitable.

The Struggle for Equality in the Third World: Tanzania and China

Space does not allow for a detailed account of the struggle of many underdeveloped countries to achieve development through socialist means but the matter should at least be briefly dealt with here (see also Chapter 8, pp. 209–12). We will make the tension between democratic and elitist tendencies within such societies our major focus for consideration.

The case of Tanzanian socialism provides an example of how the idealism of a leader and the enthusiasm of the masses can be frustrated by a gamut of problems including the emergence of an *indigenous* (home-produced) system of stratification. Here we only have the space to contrast the democratic and participatory ideas which Julius Nyerere, Tanzania's president, aspires to, with what several admittedly critical Tanzanian intellectuals argue has actually happened. Nyerere has said:

> Socialism is a way of life, and a socialist society cannot simply come into existence. A socialist society can only be built by those who believe in, and who themselves practise, the principles of socialism.

Critics point out that, in practice, the power of party and state officials has expanded rather than contracted since Nyerere made this statement in 1967. I. G. Shivji calls the rulers of Tanzania a 'bureaucratic bourgeoisie'. This includes the cabinet, top civil servants, industrial leaders, party officials and army officers. Meanwhile, he suggests, Nyerere's scheme of village democracy and economic development flounders. As Nyerere himself realises, his ideas are destined to survive only on the printed page until the industrial proletariat and much larger peasant class can learn to apply them. For him, this remains the full and, as yet, unachieved ideal of socialism. Nevertheless, he defends the take-over of power from colonial rulers, the control of the 'commanding heights' of the economy by the state rather than by foreign capital, and the (sometimes) democratic rural development schemes, as a start and as certainly better than the colonialism that preceded his regime.

China is, perhaps, the socialist country that has most consciously attempted to grapple with the problems of centralised political and bureaucratic power, and the threat to liberty and equality this presents. Its recent history shows the problems involved in that struggle. Commentators have generally been more favourable in their assessment of Chinese than of Soviet efforts in this matter although the balance sheet has varied at different times since 1949 when Mao's Communists took power. The trend towards greater popular participation and social equality in the late nineteen sixties was largely due to the convictions and leadership of Chairman Mao. Such *charismatic* (personal) interventions cannot, of course, be relied on, nor are they always successful in the face of the vested interest of privileged politicians and bureaucrats, and the sheer difficulty in making participation work effectively. After the death of Mao a trend towards elitism in government and organisation asserted itself, but whether this will threaten the democratic and participatory goals of the Chinese Revolution, it is still too early to say.

Is Equality Possible or Desirable?

In describing stratification in necessarily rather formal terms, we may have made inequality seem rather an abstract matter. The human realities associated with inequality are, however, not in the least abstract. They are concerned with great wealth and the life-style, power and opportunity that go with it; also with poverty and all that goes with that. In global terms, the gap between the rich and the poor nations is increasing. In Britain itself, great inequality persists despite a growth in the numbers of families within the middle income bracket. Is inequality, then, part of the 'nature of things' or can it be much further diminished or even abolished?

Let us begin to answer this question by examining the arguments of those who consider stratification to be inevitable. Within sociology, this view has always been associated with functionalist theory. The definitive functionalist presentation of this issue was by Davis and Moore (1956), but the roots of the functionalist position can be traced to Durkheim and Herbert Spencer. Both of them considered that as societies evolve and

grow more complex a greater variety of social roles and functions develop. One of the first examples of role differentiation
in the evolution of most societies is that of tribe or band
'leader' or 'priest', or perhaps a combination of both. Now differentiation need not lead to stratification if equal power, status
and rewards are attached to all roles but, in practice, this
rarely, if ever, occurs. Indeed, Durkheim and Spencer assumed
the opposite – that key or particularly demanding roles, such as
leader or chief, would be recognised as having more status than
functionally less important and demanding ones. Since role differentiation, in a factory or bureaucracy, for instance, is so
much a part of modern life, so must stratification be. A complex system of stratification is seen by functionalists as a
necessary product of a complex society.

Davis and Moore extend some of the arguments of earlier
functionalists and add a number of their own. They contend
that some positions in the social system are more important
than others for the functioning and stability of society. Thus,
the position of 'chief' or managing director are both relatively
crucial in these respects. Functionally important positions
require talented people to fill them and there are only a limited
number of such people in a given population. Even talented
people must undergo long periods of training if they are to
execute such key roles as surgeon, air pilot or research scientist.
In return for undergoing lengthy training and for the qualifications and skills thus acquired, they require more pay and 'perks'
than less able and less well trained people. In addition, they
would also expect their occupations to carry high status. The
existence of a group with greater access to material and status
rewards than others means, in effect, that a system of stratification also exists. As such a group is necessary to all societies, it
follows that stratification must be inevitable as well as functional.

Marxist scholars have been notably energetic in revealing and
attacking the assumptions behind the arguments of Davis and
Moore. Recently, Bowles and Gintis have pointed out that, in
the United States, intelligence is less associated with economic
success (and thus with career success) than the socio-economic
status of a person's parents (see Chapter 5 for details of this
argument).

Tom Bottomore, writing several years before Bowles and Gintis, firmly refutes the contention that the occupational hierarchy is a true reflection of innate 'talent' or ability:

> The major inequalities in society are in the main social products, created and maintained by the institutions of property and inheritance, of political and military power, and supported by particular beliefs and doctrines, even though they are never entirely resistant to the ambitions of outstanding individuals.

Bottomore has further argued that this state of affairs is only mitigated, not abolished, by increased educational opportunity and more open competition in the job market.

Davis and Moore have also been attacked by Tumin for failing to appreciate the great wastage of talent and potential amongst the lower classes that stratification can cause. Because of social background disadvantages there is not, in his view, equal opportunity. Tumin also stresses the human cost of stratification in terms of the frustration and sense of failure that quite able, but less privileged, members of society can feel.

Marxists seem able to cite enough evidence to demonstrate that stratification benefits some at the expense of others and that it persists, not merely because it is useful, but at least partly because the rich and powerful wish it to. Marxists, however, tend to overlook the possibility that *as well as* benefiting the rich and powerful at the expense of the less advantaged (as most systems of stratification certainly do), stratification may exist for other, more necessary reasons. We will return to this point shortly.

Marxists themselves believe that stratification exists because of the unequal ownership of private property. They consider that if private property is abolished and communism established, class stratification will cease to exist. This is easier to assert than to prove: after all, historically and in the contemporary world few, if any, clear examples of non-stratified societies can be cited. Attempts to 'engineer' more equal societies have given doubtful cause for optimism. The communist revolution in Soviet Russia may have produced more economic equality than exists in most capitalist countries but few would deny that political power in the Soviet Union remains very highly centralised. There does seem to be a widespread, genuine commitment to equality in Communist China but the continuing ideological ferment there means that the principles on which the new social order rests are still not entirely clear. Stratification, therefore, seems so universal that as well as being seen as a frequent mantle for exploitation, it can also be argued that it must be functional.

The essence of the functionalist position, then, is that *somebody* must do the more difficult and skilful tasks and will, as a result, expect higher rewards and status. This argument could still be true, whatever the social origins of those who came to occupy the top occupational positions. It would be sustainable even if children of lower class origins were disproportionately successful (instead of the opposite). The Marxist reply to this would be that, *if* people were rewarded according to need rather than on the basis of the nature of work they performed, no material or status inequality would result from differences in occupation. In a communist society, all property would be held in common and the product of all human labour would be shared on a rough basis of equality, with variations depending on individual circumstances and requirements. In addition, as far as possible, jobs would rotate so that more people had an opportunity to do interesting work and escape being permanently trapped in boring and unhealthy occupations.

In an ideal sense, Marx's vision – for it is a visionary's dream – of a classless society is 'better' (if we may speak for a moment in moral terms) than the stratified societies that we are more familiar with. But is such a society possible? It is, perhaps, easier and more possible to answer this question in terms of 'degrees' of equality rather than in any absolute sense. Certainly, it is not beyond human imagination and ingenuity to construct more equal societies and a more equal world – even if complete equality remains elusive. It is merely very difficult. Perhaps, as Frank Parkin reluctantly accepts, a more equal world would be functionally less efficient. When the jealousy and the conflict that inequality causes is weighed in the balance, however, it may be that a more equal society would be less torn by strife, and less wasteful of human energy, than highly stratified societies are. Whether we shall ever know what the reality of social equality means is an open question, but it is an issue likely to remain alive for a long time yet.

Guide to Further Reading and Study

Several of the books mentioned in the 'Guide' of Chapter 10 deal, to a varying extent, with wealth and poverty. A very basic source of information on income and wealth as well as on other matters of social interest is *Social Trends*, published annually by HMSO. A more detailed source is the Royal Commission on the Distribution of Income and Wealth, *Report, No 7, 1979* under the Chairmanship of Lord Diamond. On poverty, J. C. Kincaid's *Poverty and Equality in Britain* (Penguin, 1973) is still a useful introduction despite numerous developments since its publication. J. Mack and S. Lansley's *Poor Britain* (Allen and Unwin, 1985) and Bill Jordan's *Mass Unemployment and the Future of Britain* are current and show the concern their subjects merit. (For further books on poverty, see the end of Chapter 22.)

The issue of equality in socialist societies is well covered in David Lane's *The End of Social Inequality: Class, Status and Power under State Socialism* (Allen and Unwin, 1982). Useful contributions to the study of comparative stratification are Frank Parkin's, *Class, Inequality and Political Order: Social Stratification in Capitalist and Communist Societies* (Paladin, 1971) and John D. Stephens' *The Transition from Capitalism to Socialism* (Macmillan, 1979). A recent anti-Functionalist essay is Philip Green's *The Pursuit of Inequality* (Martin Robertson, 1982).

Past Questions

1 Examine the view that social stratification and social inequality are permanent, necessary and inevitable features of human societies. (AEB, 1983)

2 'Far from having faded away, social inequality has actually increased as society has got more complex.' Assess critically the proposition that as societies enter the advanced stages of industrialisation, social inequalities diminish. (London, 1984) (See also Chapters 12, 13 and 14.)

3 Examine the implications of permanent high unemployment rates for any *two* theories of social stratification. (London, 1985)

4 'Sociological explanations of poverty have increasingly focused on structured social inequality rather than on the cultural

characteristics of the poor.' Explain and discuss with reference to any *one* society. (AEB, 1985)
(See also Chapter 22.)

12 Gender

The Meaning of Gender

Ann Oakley makes a useful distinction between sex and gender. *Sexual differences* are biological in nature, whereas *gender differences* are culturally produced. This distinction has the further implication that sex differences are more or less unchangeable, whereas gender differences are very much open to change and adaptation. The definitive sexual difference between males and females is based on the parts of the body concerned with sex, procreation and nurture: the genitals and breasts. An example of a difference in *gender behaviour* occurs in Muslim society. Frequently women veil their faces, whereas men do not. Clearly, there is nothing natural about this. Because of the greater cultural influence of the West in Kuwait than in Saudi Arabia, this custom is somewhat less prevalent there.

The major preliminary problem in the sociology of gender is in deciding which aspects of male and female behaviour are biologically and which culturally based. Real behaviour cannot be separated out into two categories labelled 'biological' and 'cultural' – a fact which vastly complicates research into the matter. Authorities vary on whether, and to what extent, women are naturally (biologically) different from men, for example, more or less passive or more or less competitive than men. We cannot hope to solve this matter here although readers with an interest in biology or psychology may well wish to pursue it further using the recommended reading at the end of the chapter. Our perspective (and practical way of resolving the problem) will be to examine *particularly* major cultural influences on the behaviour of females and males. Comparative cultural studies of gender behaviour help here. They tell us that almost any kind of gender behaviour is possible. Witness, for instance, the following pattern in the Wahiba, a Bedouin tribe of central Oman in the Persian Gulf:

> The men live with their mothers, apart from their wives, whose huts may be as much as 50 miles away, and just visit them

311

occasionally. Both men and women share the work of making the home but wives then have sole ownership.

In general, work is equally divided, with goats and sheep being the responsibility of the women while the men tend the camels . . .

One of the traditional tasks of the men is the cooking . . .

(*Observer* magazine, 19 November 1978)

Examples of this kind which explode our assumptions about 'normal' gender behaviour are easily found. They make it clear that *gender identity* is more various, and, therefore, presumably, more adaptable to change than is often thought. This view is supported by various cross-cultural studies which show a wide range of gender behaviour. In particular, Margaret Mead's work demonstrates that there is no universal 'masculine' or 'feminine' personality. For example, in her fieldwork in the South Pacific she found that both sexes of the Arapesh conform roughly to our traditional stereotype of 'feminity', and both those of the Mundugumor to our 'masculine' stereotype. We will, therefore, assume nothing about supposed 'natural' differences between males and females, apart from the obviously physical, the most important of which is that *women bear children*.

Perspectives on the Origins and Nature of Gender Differentiation and Stratification

There are various theories about how the pattern of gender differentiation and stratification familiar in western industrial societies came about. Some critics stress the sexual basis of stratification, but others, mainly Marxists and socialists, see sexual stratification as very much within the context of class stratification. Most accept, however, that female subordination occurs within a class-divided society and the practical problem of analysis is largely in balancing the two elements of gender and class.

One of the first attempts at a general explanation since that of Engels in 1844, was Kate Millett's *Sexual Politics*, published in 1970. Theoretically, the book did little more than argue persuasively that the dominance of men over women occurs in every sphere of western social life. She contended that *patriarchy* (male dominance) is social rather than biological in origin, but did not really establish why, if this is the case, it is so wide-spread. Nevertheless, in her argument, Millett established the approach adopted by most later theorists of gender oppression, who pursued structural explanation in more detail. An exception, however, is Shulamith Firestone whose book, *The Dialectic of Sex*, was published about a year after Millett's.

Firestone finds the origins of sexual inequality in the basic reproductive unit of female, infant and male: in other words, in the family. The result of bearing and nurturing children is to make women dependent on men for the material necessities of life and protection. She, therefore, writes of 'sex class' as an additional category to 'economic class.' She argues that the liberation of women depends on the abolition of the family and the 'power' relationships and psychology that its unequal structure breeds. It is probably true to say that, as a result of Firestone's work, many feminists recognise more clearly the problems that can result for women from their reproductive roles, but rather than abolition of the family, they look for other solutions, including, more equal sharing of domestic work.

We now examine some feminist literature influenced by Marx and Engels (it is worth recalling Engels' analysis of the family at this point (Chapter 4, pp. 62–4).

Juliet Mitchell's *Women's Estate* (1971) is a Marxist-feminist attempt to analyse the nature of female oppression, particularly in capitalist society, and to explore how to combat it. She rejects a simple biological explanation of the sexual division of labour in the sense that women 'have to' bear and produce children. Instead, she points to the superior physical power and ability to coerce, of men. The point is that men have been able to make women do almost whatever they wanted. In her words 'Women have been *forced* to do women's work.' And 'women's work' can be almost anything. Thus, in many zones of tropical Africa women still perform many heavy 'customary' duties, such as carrying loads. The richness of Mitchell's analysis is, however, that she does not exclusively emphasise any one factor in explaining male domination. She considers that repression can operate in any of the three interconnected 'structures' of the family – the sexual, the reproductive, and the socialising – and also in the sphere of economic production. Accordingly, she urges that the 'fight' for liberation must be directed at all these structural levels, with particular reference to whatever is weaker at a given time. She considers that birth control has given women a basis of control over reproduction and sex – they are no longer 'slaves' to them – but her particular interest is in the area of gender socialisation. She seeks to explore how women come to accept, believe in and even want dependency and inferiority. She sees the production of *oppressive ideology* in structural terms:

> What does our oppression within the family *do* to us women? It produces a tendency to small-mindedness, petty jealousy, irrational emotionality and random violence, dependency, competitive selfishness and possessiveness, passivity, a lack of vision and conservatism. These qualities are *not* the simple produce of male chauvinism, nor are they falsely ascribed to women by a sexist society that uses 'old woman' as a dirty term. *They are the result of the woman's objective conditions within the family* – itself embedded in a sexist society. You cannot inhabit a small and backward world without it doing something to you.

In examining the ideological role of the family under capitalism, Mitchell calls upon Freud as much as Marx. Psychoanalysis helps to explain how children internalise notions of gender inferiority or superiority, and particularly the way in which *social* significance is given to *biological* differences. By being psychologically prepared for their different roles, girls and boys are predisposed to accept them. In an admittedly much simpler way than Mitchell, we will examine the process of the ideological reproduction of male domination or *patriarchy* in the next section.

Mitchell's general point about the importance of ideology has been taken up by D. H. Morgan. Just as in Marxist terms, the liberation of the working class is dependent on its members becoming conscious of their oppression, so too is the liberation of women dependent on their becoming conscious of their repression. Apart from a section on socialisation, we will not examine ideological oppression separately. Instead, we will analyse the relationship between structural and ideological oppression, particularly in respect of the family and work. In reality the two are inextricably woven together.

Another, more orthodox, Marxist should be mentioned. Sheila Rowbotham's *Woman's Consciousness, Man's World* (1973), studies the relationship of gender to class. She argues that gender oppression is distinct from class oppression but that in the case of working class women the two overlap. Their involvement she sees as essential to the creation of socialist feminism.

To summarise, then, feminist writers do not separate sexual and class oppression but try to understand how sexual oppression operates in a class structured society. It is not possible to quantify the relative effect of the two factors in any final way. In technical terms, it could be argued that there is a major element of *status stratification* about sexual inequality just as there is about racial stratification, although feminist writers tend to prefer more Marxist terminology. Sheila Rowbotham usefully summarises the position held by most feminists, certainly by most socialist feminists, on the relationship between sexual and class stratification:

> More relevant to us are the consequences of opposing a form of oppression which has taken a specific shape in capitalism, which nevertheless existed in precapitalist society. In order to act effectively we have to try to work out the precise relationship between the patriarchal dominance of men over women, and the property relationships which come from this, to class exploitation and racism.

The above books usefully present various feminist perspectives. Since their publication a vast range of feminist literature has been produced. Of the sociological works, three of the best are Ann Oakley's *Housewife, Housework* and *Women Confined*. In the first of these works, she argues that gender inequality is culturally, not biologically produced. In the other, she too examines particular instances of female subordination in, mainly, British society.

Interest has also developed in *men's liberation*. Two aspects of this need noting. Firstly, men are seen to need liberating from their oppressive or chauvinistic tendencies towards women – the reverse side of women's liberation. Secondly, socialist writers argue that men are *in their own way* the victims of capitalism and need liberating from this.

Gender Socialisation: The Ideological Reproduction of Male Domination

Family and Education

Gender behaviour is first learnt through *primary* or basic socialisation within the family and is reinforced later in practically every sphere of social life and particularly at school and work. Socialisation refers to the various ways in which a child learns to act in a manner acceptable within a given society. Gender socialisation is part of this process. Traditional patterns of socialisation in most Western countries distinguish sharply between male and female, although this has begun to change in the wake of the women's liberation movement. It is not too much to say that by the time they are 16, the majority of young men and women have been socialised into an ideology of male supremacy even if the forces of resistance to this ideology are stronger than they were. Broadly speaking, women are regarded as decorative, emotional and dependent, and men as practical, rational and dominant. Men are expected to earn a living and to support a family whereas women are expected to 'look after their men folk', and to produce children. Depending on its sex, a child is treated according to one or the other of these models and this prepares him or her for adult gender identity. Even before boys and girls can talk, they are spoken to in a different manner. Phrases such as 'he's going to be a big, strong boy' and 'isn't she a pretty little girl' trip easily off the tongue of family friends and relatives, and no doubt form the emerging self-identity of the child. Sue Sharpe quotes two classic examples of the sex stereotyping of males and females from birth congratulation messages:

Bet she's sugar and spice
And everything nice.
A pink and petite little treasure
Your new little 'she'
Who's certain to be
A wonderful bundle of pleasure!

A SON IS FUN!
He'll keep you busy
With blankets an' pins
And charm your hearts
With his boyish grins!
What's more he'll make you
Proud and glad
Congratulations mother and dad!

It is interesting that in parts of old Japan reinforcement of male children's sense of masculinity was even more extreme than has ever been the case in the West. The male child of four or five years old was allowed to treat his mother and other females more or less as he wished – even to the point of terrorising them. This was a rather crude preparation for male dominance in adulthood. It is less easy to find cultures which treat children of both sexes similarly and equally but in traditional Samoa this was substantially so until the age of five or six, when very noticeable differences in gender expectation did occur.

In most societies, as children grow older, they are increasingly type-cast into what sociologists term masculine and feminine *gender roles*. To play a social role is simply to act a given part. In contemporary British society, the role of housekeeping is still usually fulfilled by women, and that of main breadwinner by men. Boys and girls are prepared for future gender roles in a variety of ways. Boys are often given presents of cowboy suits, doctors' outfits and meccano sets, whereas girls are given dolls, nurses' uniform and cookery kits. The message could hardly be stronger. Jobs involving leadership and construction skills are for boys, whereas girls are expected to care for, assist and give service to others, either at home or at work. The basis of this division of labour is clearly laid down in childhood. This is most obviously so in families in which the jobs children are given to do around the house are based sex difference – say, cleaning and sewing for the girls, and mending broken plugs or furniture for the boys.

Some contemporary parents deliberately try to avoid socialising their children into traditional gender roles. One enterprising group of mothers in Liverpool, finding that the images of gender portrayed in available children's story books were too traditional, set about writing their own material. They rejected stereotypes in which the female is always weak and dependent and the male strong and dominant. Why shouldn't Princesses sometimes rescue Princes? If little Red Riding Hood had been trained in basic self-defence, perhaps she could have dealt with the wolf on her own account. Such notions may strike many as odd, but recorded interviews with some of the children who heard or read the stories showed they understood the point behind them. In small ways like this, social change can perhaps begin.

Gender socialisation within schools also plays a major part in conditioning males and females for future roles in the family and at work (see Chapter 5, pp. 120–2). When girls leave school at 16 or 18 they often get jobs that *are* as well paid as those held by boys of a similar age. Some office and secretarial work is particularly well paid, especially in central city areas. However, partly because women in general are less qualified than men and partly because they often leave work for several years to have children, opportunities for career advancement and salary increase are considerably less. The fact that almost as many females as males are involved in mainly part-time, *non*-advanced courses of further education rather demonstrates that females are expected and often expect themselves to do middle or low, rather than high, status work. As we shall discuss shortly this is, on the whole, an accurate impression of reality.

Gender Inequality and the Sexual Division of Labour

Gender, the Family and Work

So far we have described how gender identity is culturally created in advanced Western societies through socialisation and role-allocation. The question must now be asked why gender differentiation occurs at all. The answer is, as Mitchell and Oakley indicate, that a division of labour has developed in capitalist society by which women tend to be primarily involved in child nurture and domestic work and men in acquiring the basic means of livelihood. Socialisation prepares girls and boys for their future roles in the socio-economic system. Now, the only biologically inevitable feature of this particular form of sexual division of labour is that women give birth to children. The rest is open to gender adaptation. What follows, therefore, takes the broad perspective adopted by Mitchell and Oakley, rather than that of Firestone, that the sexual division of labour in capitalist society has taken a 'severe' form because this has been convenient for the capitalist system. The fact that in the last hundred years women have become increasingly involved in the economy illustrates rather than refutes the point – they have been needed in the expanding service sector. Nevertheless, the sexually based division of labour as described above is still powerfully entrenched in contemporary capitalist society, as was shown in the recession which began in 1979 when female labour was widely treated as more expendable than male. The sexual division of labour in capitalist society has resulted in a large degree of female dependency on males. This dependency has resulted in lower social status for women and correspondingly higher social status for men. As well as having less economic power and social status than men, women have also tended to be *politically* less powerful, because they are isolated and not organised. In short, although the social consequences of the sexual division of labour in capitalist society have tended to be disadvantageous to women and advantageous to men, this state of affairs is *not* inevitable. Both cross-cultural comparison and historical analysis of gender roles in our own society show that change is possible. We adopt the historical perspective next.

Changing Gender Roles Within the Family and at Work: Historical and Contemporary Perspective

Pre-industrial

One of the few generalisations supported by recent research into the pre-industrial family in Britain is that it was patriarchal at all social levels. Fathers had decisive power over their daughters and husbands over their wives. Young and Willmott suggest that brutalising their wives can rarely have been in the interests of husbands but wife-beating was an accepted way of asserting domination and, sometimes no doubt, mere ill temper. Most peasant families were units of agricultural production in which women took a full part. Women matched men in work if not in power. Anne Oakley states that 'in their role as agriculturalists, women produced the bulk of the family's food supply'. They managed dairy production, grew flax and hemp, milled corn and cared for the poultry, pigs, orchards and gardens. Men were primarily responsible for planting, cultivating and harvesting crops and for maintenance. Women allocated tasks, including household ones, to daughters, and men to sons. Textile work was second in national importance to agriculture and was shared between men, women and children: men doing the weaving, and women the spinning and allocating minor tasks such as picking and cleaning to the children.

Many better-off households had servants. Laslett calculates that 40% of children spent *part* of their lives as servants and 20% were raised in households with servants. As Harris puts it, the majority of members of such households were 'the dependents of some senior or more powerful person, usually of the male gender'. Laslett's thesis, endorsed by Harris, is that industrialisation broke up not the extended family (which was not, anyway the dominant family form) but the patriarchal family/household. For many modern feminists, however, the patriarchal family is a long time in dying!

The Nineteenth Century

Industrialisation disrupted traditional patterns of gender behaviour as it disrupted so much else. For a time, working class men, women and children worked together in industrial production and mining. Between 1802 and 1898, however, a series of Acts abolished child labour and gradually reduced female labour in these areas. Though many women found other work, often in the low-paid domestic service sector, a woman's place was increasingly considered to be in the home. In some ways the position of the working class woman in industrial society was worse than that of the peasant wife. In pre-industrial society most families produced some of their own food and clothes – largely under the wife's organisation – whereas in industrial society the wife was often wholly dependent on what money her husband chose to give her to buy these things. This was a position of striking inferiority. No doubt some of the above legislation was passed in a spirit of paternalistic protectiveness but it was also notably convenient to have the labour force adequately catered for domestically, (for a specifically Marxist interpretation of this point see Chapter 4, p. 63). In this way, it was both healthier and more productive.

Although the economic situation of middle class women was much better than that of working class women, they were similarly dependent on their husbands for money. In a wealthy family, servants might free 'the mistress of the house' from domestic toil and child-care, but there were limits to what she could then do with her time. Most professions, apart from teaching, were barred to women. In practice, middle class women were likely to spend their often ample leisure time in socialising, improving the decor of their homes and, sometimes, in charitable works.

The law put the lid firmly on the trap of female subordination. As we have already observed women were debarred from the best-paying working class and middle class jobs. Worse than that, women had no legal existence at all in early nineteenth century Britain. Before marriage a woman was the responsibility of her father, afterwards, she and her possessions belonged to her husband.

By the end of the nineteenth century a series of Acts had partly improved this situation. One of these, the Married Women's Property Act of 1882, gave a wife the right to own property and to dispose of it to whom she wished.

The Twentieth Century: The Growth of Feminist Consciousness

The decline of the Victorian patriarchal family has been a major feature of twentieth century social history. *Contraception* (the control of fertility) undermined the Victorian family and the position of male as patriarch as much as anything else. Given the choice, most women preferred to have two or three children rather than six or seven. Traditional taboos against contraception did not die overnight and, in addition, some socialist women were suspicious that population control might be used as an alternative to social reform. Even so, the practical advantages of birth control were too obvious to miss. 'Having a family' of six or seven was a lifetime's work for many women, and could be physically ruinous as well as intellectually severely limiting. In any case, the beginning of a steady fall in the birth rate occurred in the late eighteen seventies and this correlates with an increase in propaganda in favour of birth control. Certainly, in the long run, women have overwhelmingly accepted that family planning is a pre-condition of their own independence. Decrease in family size coupled with the development of efficient, time-saving household technology enabled many women to spend much longer as part of the labour force. In turn, experience of work widened women's horizons, boosted their confidence and whetted the appetite of some for more freedom and equality. The massive involvement of women in production, service industries and administration during the First World War strengthened this new mood.

The fight for female political and civil rights was substantially a middle class led movement, although as historian Sheila Rowbotham says, the tendency of accounts of the suffragette movement to concentrate on the Pankhursts as personalities has meant a lack of detailed work on the social composition of the movement. There were certainly many working class women participants, including the doughty Hannah Mitchell, who criticised the 'talk' of some of the middle class radicals whom she found better preachers than practitioners of sexual equality:

> Even my Sunday leisure was gone for I soon found that a lot of the socialist talk about freedom was only talk and these socialist young men expected Sunday dinners and huge teas with home-made cakes, potted meat and pies, exactly like their reactionary fellows.

It would be absurd to underestimate the importance of the acquisition of the vote for women. The vote is a basic right of modern citizenship. Nevertheless, merely having the vote in no way solved the problem of sexual inequality at work and domestically. More recent legislation has, not very successfully, attempted to deal with the former (see Chapter 12, pp. 330–1) but the latter, perhaps because it concerns the 'private area of life' has not been seriously dealt with by legislation and government policy in Britain. In Sweden and the major communist societies, however, legislatively supported policies in this area have been both pursued and enforced more effectively (Chapter 4, pp. 70–1).

Inevitably, family relations were gradually affected by the backwash of these changes in the economic and political spheres. Separate gender roles within the family, or segregated conjugal roles as we can more precisely call them, began to break down somewhat. If women went to work, then, the onus was on men to knuckle down and do some of the housework, although many failed to do so. Willmott and Young have referred to the gradual blurring of task segregation between spouses as the development of *symmetrical* or *joint conjugal roles*. It initially developed among middle class couples, and particularly when both husband and wife worked as professionals. As Rhona and Robert Rapoport, (a dual-career couple themselves), point out it is still among dual career families that symmetrical roles most frequently occur. With more women of all classes working, however, *role sharing* is necessarily also increasingly common among working class couples. One survey, by Hannah Gavron, actually found that working class husbands shared housework more than middle class husbands, but this goes against other findings. Ann Oakley is, in any case, sceptical about whether there has been a marked recent trend for couples to share housework at all.

Work has given many women a broader experience of the world and, perhaps most importantly, it has given them an independent source of income. The Victorian period clearly showed that as long as a woman depended entirely on a man for income, inequality between the sexes was virtually inevitable. The shadow of patriarchy is still strong but there is now more equality and democracy in family life than previously. Decisions about family expenditure and leisure activities are more likely to be shared now than in the past. Couples often 'do' more together. These days, if the man does go for a drink in the evening, as likely as not his wife will want to go with him. If children prevent that, it is an easy matter to buy in a few cans of drink and watch television. The car has made the family outing a feature of post-war social life. In short, the home itself, with its battery of consumer durables, has become a basis of leisure and entertainment. Why go to the cinema when 'the movies' can come to you?

Recently, an interesting strand of opinion has become more noticeable in the feminist movement. It cannot easily be labelled but it involves a re-assessment and upgrading of the traditional role of women, and a better appreciation of its variety and necessity. While insisting on policies of equal opportunity in the job-market, those who share this emerging perspective reject the notion that the success of women should be judged merely or even mainly by their achievements in traditionally male dominated areas (such as warfare or banking). Instead, two things are stressed. Firstly, that some domestic and child-rearing work can be creative and humanly very rewarding – this carries the rider that men could beneficially involve themselves in it more. Secondly, historically, in any case, women have borne a heavy and necessary burden of labour. We will examine these points separately, but first it is worth repeating Sheila Rowbotham's warning that attempts to idealise 'women's work' are invariably 'reactionary.' Ideals of motherhood tend to collapse before the distasteful reality of changing nappies and scouring toilets.

Ann Oakley severely questions whether the way towards women's liberation is simply to compete with men in the employment market. Yet she despairs that men will ever recognise or allow proper reward for the work women do. As long as this is so, the prospects are that women will continue to depend materially and psychologically (for security and identity) on men. As she says:

> Men and women cannot be equal outside the home if they are not equal partners inside it.

Paid housework, or a guaranteed right to a proportion of the main breadwinner's salary, are possible solutions to material dependency (although they do not appear to have much support). In reality, however, Oakley is thinking mainly of the need for a change, indeed, *a revolution in attitudes* – of both sexes – to the quality, dignity and humanity of child rearing and domestic labour – whoever does it.

Virginia Novarra's book, *Women's Work, Men's Work*, forcefully asserts that women's work makes a vital contribution to the survival of the race. It does so in the following major ways.

Through

1 *Reproduction*
2 *Agricultural Production (globally, more women are involved in agricultural production than men)*
3 *Clothing the Family (often making or mending clothes)*
4 *Tending the Family and others*
5 *Cultural Transmission*
6 *Caring for the Home and Home Environment (unpaid or lowly-paid work)*

Some years ago, feminist literature was characterised by such titles as *The Second Sex* or *The Female Eunuch*. A sense of grievance was, and remains, justified but a growing appreciation of the extent and quality of female work historically may throw as much light on how matters can be improved.

Changes in family life and gender roles have not taken place without some stress and individual confusion and suffering. The ever increasing divorce figures are proof of that. By the late nineteen seventies, in England and Wales, the proportion of marriages to divorces was virtually 3 to 1. Annually, about 150,000 couples were deciding that their marriage partnership was not worth continuing. Mostly, it is women who take the formal decision to petition for divorce: 70% of divorce petitions are filed by them. If more women than men do find marriage a disillusioning experience, it may be because they approach it more romantically and with higher expectations of personal fulfilment and happiness. Advertising and the media still largely conspire to create these hopes. The reality of housework and bringing up young children can be a shock, especially if the personal and sexual side of marriage fails to compensate as expected. A survey of 40 women with children found that a majority regarded housework as tedious and often felt isolated in the home. 'Getting a job' may help, but equally it can increase pressure on a woman if her husband should fail to respond by doing his share of domestic work. There is some evidence to suggest that marriage and family stress punish women more than men. Whereas before marriage more men than women suffer mental illness, afterwards very much the reverse is true.

Men, however, have also had problems in adjusting to changes in marriage and family. To lose control and privilege is rarely easy. However unreasonable it may be for a man to expect his wife to do for him what his mother used to, the tendency to make the comparison is understandable. Convenience foods probably do not compare very well to elaborate home-cooking, but this is part of the price both partners have to pay in a dual career family. Many men, too, must have found the anger and aggression of some women in the face of discrimination difficult to contend with. No liberation movement occurs without some explosion of rage against the dominant group, but this is little consolation to those in the firing line. On the whole, it is men who have benefited in economic and power terms from the sexual division of labour and it is inevitable that, sooner or later, female resentment should be expressed against them. There is no doubt that the sharp spur of female anger has stimulated many men to an appreciation of female exploitation. Of course, the sexual division of labour is not a product of a conscious male conspiracy but, historically, has been part of the way the basic functions of society have been fulfilled. Emotional rejection of what is now seen as an unfair and repressive division of labour will not in itself change things without the ultimate understanding and consent of both sexes.

In one very important sense, the sexual division of labour has affected men adversely and left them in need of a sort of liberation. The effort of working more or less continuously for forty or fifty years, which is the lot of many men, can take a tremendous physical and psychological toll. The health hazards of working down a mine or in a noisy, monotonous factory are well known. The fact that twice as many men as women under fifty have heart attacks⁻ may well be related to the demands of work. From the point of view of fuller self-expression, it is limiting for many men that their social identity and most of their time is so heavily bound up with their occupation. Given the variety of leisure pursuits available in the modern world, it is perhaps slightly ludicrous that for nine tenths of the average male's adult life he is thought of primarily in terms of his occupational identity. For the one tenth that he isn't, retirement, his physical and mental capacities are likely to be in decline. If this balance could be readjusted without significantly reducing their families' standard of living, many full-time working men would probably welcome it. The increase in female labour and in automation may make this increasingly possible. But for both sexes to make the most of these new developments, a change in traditional, rigid attitudes to gender indentity would also have to take place. The lyrics of the pop-group, the Kinks, may come to reflect a new social, though not, of course, physical reality:

> Girls will be Boys
> And Boys will be Girls . . .
> It's a mixed-up muddled-up
> Shook-up world . . .

Women and the Labour Market: 'Escape' or Exploitation?

So far, we have considered domestic and directly economic labour together because they are two sides of the same coin: one would not be possible without the other. It is necessary, however, to give a more detailed analysis of women's position in the employment market. Generally, increased job opportunities for women have been seen as part of their assumed 'liberation' and work has certainly often provided individual women with an escape from the tedium of domestic toil. Marxists and socialists point out, however, that there is considerable evidence of female 'exploitation' and accompanying under-achievement in employment, and that female employment and unemployment has varied with the economic need for it. Women have been the most expendable of workers. The increased use of female labour has, therefore, been a double-edged sword.

Even in the mid-Victorian era, when working class women were legally banned from working in heavy industry and mining, and middle class women were denied the right to qualify for most professions, women were by no means entirely excluded from the labour market. Working class women were 'needed' as domestic servants and a certain number of middle class women worked in lower status professions. Working class women often *had* to find work to supplement the wages of their husbands. They frequently did so as full or part-time domestic servants of whom there were well over half a million at this time. Hundreds of thousands of others were employed in textile production, an area of traditionally high female employment and low wages. Middle class women who needed to work, perhaps because they were spinsters or widows, could earn a living as elementary school teachers. By the 1890s, there were almost 150,000 female teachers. Nursing was also a major area of female employment. The 'semi-professions' of teaching and nursing were of much lower status and pay than the major professions of law and medicine (for instance) from which women were excluded.

The situation of women at work began to change towards the end of the nineteenth century and even more so in the twentieth century. Even allowing for population expansion, the increase in the numbers of women at work has been massive. Between 1911 and 1974, four million more women were added to the total labour force of about twenty five million. Of the six million people in part time work well over half are women.

Although most women who work probably want to do so, it would be a mistake to assume that the increase in female labour has been an unmitigated boon for them. Women in full time work have for a long time been paid less than men, even though the gap has narrowed substantially in recent years. Yet even though the Equal Pay Act of 1975 established the legal principle of equal pay for equal work, the average wage of women is only about 75% that of men. In successive years, 1978 and 1979, the average female wage fell slightly as a proportion of the male wage, after rising gradually since the middle nineteenth sixties. This is largely because, historically, women have been concentrated in low paid jobs. Clerical and secretarial work which became increasingly available to women from the latter half of the nineteenth century was often poorly paid.

Whereas, in 1977, 51% of employed women were in intermediate and junior non-manual work, only 5% were professionals, employers or managers. The latter figure compares to 21% of men in these occupations. Inequality of status between the two sexes is even more startling in the world of manual work. A majority of male manual workers is classified as skilled, whereas only 1 in 5 female manual workers are so classified. There is reason to believe that some jobs are classified as unskilled or semi-skilled precisely because they are generally done by women and not because of the real skill-content of the work. Throughout the occupational structure, then, men still tend to have more authority and status than women and to be better paid. Although there are more female accountants, police, barristers, doctors and even electrical engineers than ten years ago, in none of these occupations do women make up even 10% of the total, except in medicine where they represent 13.5% of the work force.

The areas of employment in which women are concentrated, cleaning, nursing, teaching and to a certain extent social work are the so-called 'helping' professions. It is almost as if the domestic role of looking after others is transferred into the work situation. Like domestic labour itself, work in these areas is comparatively poorly paid. The fact that teaching is sometimes said to be 'not badly paid for women' is perhaps more a reflection on the historically low wages of women generally, than on the great financial rewards offered by that profession. In any case, in teaching as in all professions, women tend to occupy lower scale, less well paid posts.

In addition to enjoying less authority, status and wages at work than men, women also tend to have less security. Although about 30% of female workers are now unionised, the majority still lack the strength and protection union membership gives. Part-time workers are in an especially weak position in the labour market. Of Britain's six million part-time workers, three and a half million are women. Part-time workers employed for fewer than sixteen hours a week are not entitled to redundancy payment, nor most other benefits under the Employment Protection Act. In effect, they can be hired and fired at the employer's wish. The traditionally weak position of women in the job market has led some commentators, including Hilary Wainwright, to suggest that women have been used as a 'reserve pool' of cheap labour in the expanding service sector. Women on the fringe of the job market could be employed when necessary in times of economic expansion and made redundant to save money in times of contraction. The law now protects women in full-time employment from this kind of treatment but those in part-time work are still vulnerable.

It would be superficial to suggest that employers alone have been responsible for the work situation of women described above. The fundamental weakness of most women as independent wage-earners lies in the fact that they also produce and are expected to bring up children. This means that they are not usually consistently involved in a career between, roughly, the ages of twenty-five and thirty-five, which is a crucial period for gaining experience and promotion. In practice, because of their dual commitments as housewives and workers, many women do not seriously attempt to compete effectively with men in the labour market. Many find 'temping' or part-time work fits in best with their domestic responsibilities. In addition, it is well established that large numbers of women welcome an 'escape' from the home, even into work that does not seem particularly fulfilling. Further, women who restart their careers at, say, thirty-five often do not have quite the same expectations as a similarly qualified man of the same age. In times of high unemployment, they are frequently glad to be able to get a reasonably suitable job at all. There is, too, a certain realism in the relatively low career expectations of many women in that the 'missing ten years' can constitute a severe disadvantage. On the other hand, those who have families and try to compete in career terms as well often put immense pressure on themselves – despite, sometimes, succeeding. A society which presents half its population with the above range of options seems to be profoundly flawed.

If, however, it would be wrong solely to 'blame' employers for the weak position of women at work, it would be even more short-sighted to suggest that lack of female ambition is the reason. The basic problem is that, as Hannah Mitchell put it, women compete 'with one hand tied behind their back' – the hand that 'holds the baby' and does the housework. That problem can only be solved either by relieving women of much domestic work or by rewarding them more substantially and securely for it. We now turn to the issue of policy and solutions.

Women's Liberation: Policy and Continuing Problems

We have seen the extent of gender inequality. We now ask what government has tried to do about it. The main measures of the 'equality package', as Ann Oakley calls it, are as follows. The Equal Pay Act (operative from 1975); the Sex Discrimination Act (1975); and the Employment Protection and Social Security Pensions Acts (1975). The 1967 Abortion Act and the Divorce Law Reform Act implemented in 1971 also have profound implications for women, though they are not specifically part of the 'package'. The first two focus largely on employment. It is too early to say how effective they will be but they do nothing *positively* about the concentration of women in low-paid occupations. A more *interventionist* policy might, for instance, involve guaranteeing women a minimum number of top and middle level positions in business companies and professional establishments. Sometimes, to achieve *actual* equality more than *legal* equality is required: after all, we are all legally entitled to eat at the Savoy Grill . . . The terms of the Sex Discrimination Act are more easily enforceable in education, and there are more signs of greater equality of achievement in that area, but the gap remains wide.

The Employment Protection Act contains the first legal entitlement to *maternity leave* for women in Britain. It bans dismissal on grounds of pregnancy and guarantees mothers their jobs for within 29 weeks of childbirth. Circumstances (and there are potentially many: the death of the child is one) in which paternity leave rather than maternity leave might be desirable are not recognised by the Act, and to this extent it has an element of chauvinistic protectionism about it. Still, 29 weeks 'grace' is better than nothing, although it could hardly have been much less. Further, the Social Security Pensions Act puts women's sickness and unemployment pay and pension rights on an equal basis to those of men.

Despite the above legislation and the seemingly not very effective Equal Opportunities Commission, women's status at work relative to that of men has not much improved over the last decade. We have already seen why this is so. Neither does the future look entirely hopeful. Noticeably more women are being educated to a higher level than previously, but still predominantly in subjects likely to lead to traditionally low-paying, 'female' professions.

The extent of female participation in politics may be taken as one measure of their influence on national life. On this basis their influence is low – notwithstanding Mrs Thatcher. In August 1978, only 5% of MP's were women, and only 6% were ministers.

Despite, therefore, the existence of *formal* or legal equality between the sexes, substantial *actual* inequalities persist. In the face of what are, from the feminist point of view, rather depressing facts, perhaps it is permissible to risk a note of optimistic speculation. It has occurred to some writers that certain qualities traditionally associated with women but which can occur in either sex – such as caring, gentleness and sharing – might provide a better moral blueprint for human conduct and survival than such traditionally 'masculine' characteristics as ambition, aggression and competitiveness. Ann Oakley, in the article quoted from above, cites a variety of feminist science fiction which speculates on precisely this possibility. Men are sometimes missing from this hypothetical future – their destructiveness is implicitly seen as both undesirable and dangerous. In the spirit of this literature, perhaps the nuclear bomb can be seen as a symbol of the male contribution historically: an achievement heavy with destructive potential. If so, it is perhaps time that the 'other' sex had a turn at, or at least more involvement in, the creation of a new social reality based on more positive and life-enhancing principles.

The issue of women's liberation is too urgent to conclude at the level of high speculation. At a more practical level, three positions on gender inequality can be distinguished. The first accepts an element of inevitability about gender roles but wants equality of status, rewards and security between them. A second viewpoint would like to see much more flexibility in the playing of gender roles. There would be more 'house-husbands' and more women operating as 'the main-breadwinner'. These two approaches are not incompatible, but to achieve either would require a massive change of outlook (among many women as well as men) and a substantial programme of legislation aimed particularly at improving the financial security of the houseperson. The third position seeks to abolish gender roles altogether. Instead, the two principles that would operate would be that people would do what they were best at and wanted to do and that, despite this, the needs of the community, and particularly children, should be met. It still seems a distant ideal.

In fact, in the nineteen eighties the feminist movement has continued to progress in terms of women's relations to each other and in their understanding of their own strategies and goals, rather than in persuading males to change their behaviour or in substantially penetrating patriarchal power structures (although these things are not incompatible). The logic of women concentrating on themselves is to clarify their own situation and intentions and to protect themselves from male hegemony and engulfment. For some women it may also be a rejection of males as a 'lost cause' – at least temporarily. Such qualified separatism may seem strange and even faintly unnatural to students who have not experienced it. Nevertheless, it is quite widespread particularly among the feminist minority working in the liberal professions and semi-professions. The women's peace camp at Greenham Common came to symbolise the new feminist mood, which is not to say that all feminists agree with every major aspect of it. First, the camp is a peace protest, and many feminists do feel an overriding commitment to preventing nuclear war and have little confidence that men of power will do what is necessary to achieve this. Second, the camp is separatist – for the reasons given above. Third, and related to the previous point, the camp organises along participatory, egalitarian and organic lines: the women seek to do jobs because they need doing and not for power, status or reward. Of course, all idealistic movements are subject to the threat of reaction, often violent, from both without and within, partly because they challenge conventional values, thought and behaviour and strain people's limits by demanding the best of them. However, a movement based on the vision of, potentially, a whole gender has greater strength in depth than most. We shall see.

Guide to Further Reading and Study

The continuing explosion of women's studies is apparent in that most large bookshops now have a section devoted to the area. Indeed there are some bookshops entirely devoted to it. There is plenty, therefore, to choose from. Pat Mayes, *Gender* (Longman,

1985) is a lively and wide-ranging starter. Ann Oakley, *Subject Woman* (Martin Robertson, 1981) covers the ground with authority and Michele Barrett, *Women's Oppression Today* (Verso, 1980) is also recommended. A well-organised collection of reading is Mary Evans, *ed, The Women Question* (Fontana, 1982). Hilary Wainwright's chapter in Philip Abrams, *ed, Work, Urbanism and Inequality* (Weidenfeld and Nicolson, 1982) is very useful. Sue Sharp, *Just Like a Girl: How Girls Learn to be Women* (Penguin, 1976) is an empirically based examination of gender socialisation. For a readable and thoughtful look at gender from a male point of view, see Andrew Tolson, *The Limits of Masculinity* (Tavistock, 1977). However, a truly convincing male statement on the gender question remains to be written.

Gender is a topic which lends itself to project-type work, especially as there is now a range of specialist studies within the area. Ann Oakley, *Women Confined* (Martin Robertson, 1979) on childbirth and Lisa Leghorn and Katherine Parker, *Women's Worth: Sexual Economics and the World of Women* on the global condition of women are good examples. The matter of methodology itself is covered by the following: Helen Roberts, *Doing Feminist Research* (Routledge and Kegan Paul, 1981) and Margrit Eichler, *The Double Standard: A Feminist Critique of Feminist Social Science* (Croom Helm, 1980).

Past Questions

1 'To classify working class marital relationships as *segregated* and middle class ones as *joint* is an oversimplification.' Discuss. (AEB, 1983)
(See also Chapter 4.)
2 'It's a girl!' 'It's a boy!' To what extent do such gender definitions determine life chances in different societies? (London, 1984)
3 'The idea of a universal division of labour by sex is but a patriarchal myth.' Discuss. (London, 1984)
4 'In talking of the division of labour between men and women, we are talking almost exclusively of gender roles rather than sex roles, determined by culture rather than biology.' (Rogers: *The Domestication of Women*). Explain and discuss this statement with reference to gender roles in the workplace. (AEB, 1985).

13 Race

Basic Terminology and Perspectives

This chapter focuses on racial and ethnic stratification and particularly their relationship to class stratification. Although race is a biological concept, it is not dealt with as such here – indeed, the precise biological basis of race is uncertain – rather, we analyse the responses of people to what they *perceive* as racial characteristics, and the meanings they attach to them. Thus, the real or supposed racial characteristics of Jews and Indians have sometimes been negatively labelled by others. Negative labelling or stereotyping of racial groups for prejudiced reasons is racist. Racist beliefs often function to justify racial discrimination as, for instance, in South Africa (see pp. 220–3). Closer to home, attitude surveys show that many white Britons are more or less racist (see pp. 345). At an apparently more scientific level, there are a number of academics, such as Arthur Jensen, who continue to argue that racial inheritance is a significant determinant of behaviour and so has major social consequences (see p. 123). However, such has been the admixture of races and the abuse of the concept of race, that many social scientists find more useful the concept of ethnic group. This refers to *cultural* rather than biological traits and is easier to demonstrate empirically. In practice, racism often reflects a mixture of racial and cultural prejudice. Finally, it is important to distinguish between prejudice and discrimination. The former refers to attitude, the latter to behaviour. Racist behaviour can be controlled by law but socialisation is the best approach to attitude change.

There are two basic perspectives on racial stratification: one has its roots in Weber, the other in Marxism. Weber considered that stratification distinctions based on race or ethnicity are status distinctions. In extreme cases separate castes might develop of which he suggested the 'Jews were the most impressive historical example'. No doubt he would have considered South Africa to be a caste society, as does John Rex who formerly lived in that country but who now lives in Britain. Rex uses the term *underclass* to describe the position of blacks in Britain and Douglas Glasgow has also used it in relation to blacks in the United States. Though not used by Weber, the concept is derived from him in that Rex sees the stratification position of the underclass as a product of status distinction based primarily on race (see pp. 346–7). Marxists typically analyse racial stratification within the context of

335

class stratification though they differ on the relative importance they attach to race. In *Immigrant Workers and Class Structure*, S. Castles and G. Kosack argue that racism has served to divide the working class, not least when practised by the workers themselves. These theoretical positions can be usefully borne in mind as we consider specific issues below.

The Historical and Economic Background of Racism in Britain and the West

Race is a crucial contemporary issue both in Britain and internationally. South Africa is the major focus of racial tension in the world, for it is only there that race is openly, and even proudly, proclaimed as the very basis of stratification. This system is known as *apartheid*, although it has recently been presented as 'separate development'. Apartheid involves the legally enforceable separation of whites and blacks in a way that ensures far higher material and status rewards for the former. In certain other countries, the lines of racial stratification are less sharply drawn but are still quite clear. In Britain and the United States, coloured (or black) minorities tend to hold low-paid, low-status jobs, to live in poor housing and to be less well-educated than the white majority.

a The Historical Background of Race Relations

The roots of contemporary racial division lie in the expansion of European empires, particularly during the eighteenth and nineteenth centuries when these empires straddled the world. The British Empire extended to the Far East, but more significant from our point of view was the occupation of India, Pakistan, large parts of Africa, and several islands in the West Indies. It is from these areas that coloured immigrants came to Britain after the Second World War. A key factor in laying the foundations for later racial conflict in Britain, the United States, and parts of Africa was the exploitation of Africans, especially West Africans. The major element in this exploitation was the slave trade. Slave traders, mainly from Britain, France, Spain and Portugal, bought and kidnapped Africans, and transported them to the southern United States and the West

Indies, where they were sold to work on plantations. In the southern States, a social structure based on slave labour developed, which left a legacy of bitterness, bigotry and exploitation, even after the formal abolition of slavery in the United States in 1863.

Between the two world wars, the major problem for Britain and other European imperial powers was to hold down discontent in conquered territories. By the early nineteen sixties, most British colonies had acquired independence, and already coloured immigration into Britain had begun. The focus of conflict shifted from the struggle for independence in the colonies to problems associated with the settlement of coloured immigrants in Britain itself. As early as 1958, race riots occurred in the Notting Hill area of London. After 1980, when Zimbabwe (formerly Rhodesia) became independent under majority rule, the only African country in which a minority of European extraction (in this case a large one) continued directly to dominate the black majority was South Africa.

The desire for economic gain is certainly a major motive for imperial expansion. The hope of acquiring political power and prestige, and of converting the conquered to, say, Christianity or Marxism, are others. Economic realities clearly underlie much twentieth century racial conflict – the spread of racial conflict in the United States is an example. From the late nineteenth century, there was a strong demand from Northern industrialists for cheap, black labour from the south. Later, this demand also occurred on the West Coast. As well as being cheap, black labour could be used to undermine the power of trade unions and to divide black and white working class people along racial lines. For their part, many black people were glad to leave the South, still darkened by the shadow of slavery, even though they encountered resentment and, sometimes, violence from the white working class in the urban areas of the North and West. In the early nineteen sixties, the big cities of the North and West were as torn by racial conflict and riots as the South.

b The Economic Background of Race Relations (with particular reference to Britain)

Economic factors also provide the major explanation for the pattern of coloured immigration in Britain and, to some extent, for the 'panic' about immigration in the late nineteen sixties and nineteen seventies.

Migration can be explained in terms of 'push' and 'pull' factors. The 'push' factors refer to conditions in the country of origin, such as unemployment and poverty, which persuade people to leave: the 'pull' factor is the demand for labour in the country of immigration. This is considered by Peach and others to be the dynamic influence behind British post-war immigration. A major personal motive for migration is, of course, to rejoin family and kin.

Immigrants to Britain went mainly into unskilled and semi-skilled jobs in industrial production. This enabled more of the indigenous population to move up into the expanding service sector – a fact which, at first, certainly sweetened acceptance of immigration. Not all immigrants, however, started at the bottom of the social hierarchy. Many thousands of doctors and nurses from India, Pakistan and the West Indies, were needed to support Britain's overstrained health system: even so, they tended to get the toughest and least prestigious posts, often in large, metropolitan hospitals.

In some areas where a shortage of labour existed, active recruitment occurred. London Transport recruited drivers in the West Indies and the Health Service also advertised widely. Official figures show that, in 1965 alone, Britain took 1,015 doctors from India, 529 from Pakistan and 182 from other Commonwealth countries. The Health Service is a striking, though not unique, example of Britain's dependence on the work of immigrants. In 1975, 35% of hospital doctors and 18% of family doctors came from outside Britain.

It is useful to draw a parallel between migrant workers in Europe and British immigrants. In the post-war period, the expanding economics of Western Europe needed foreign labour to increase production. Those countries which had colonies or former colonies, such as Britain or France, first recruited labour from these. Other countries which were without colonies, particularly West Germany, Luxembourg and Switzerland, had to recruit from elsewhere. They did so mainly from the poorer, non-industrialised countries of Eastern and Southern Europe – Greece, Turkey, Yugoslavia, Italy, Spain and Portugal. In 1974, it was estimated that 15 million immigrant workers and their families were living in Western Europe. A Common Market report for 1974 gives the proportion of immigrant workers in the labour force of the Western European countries as follows:

Luxembourg	35%
Switzerland	25%
France	11%
Germany	10%
UK	7%
Belgium	7%
Denmark	2%
Netherlands	3%

Source: *Our People,* Thames Television.

These workers are overwhelmingly concentrated in low-paid jobs with unpleasant and sometimes quite dangerous conditions (such as asbestos processing) and long hours (like the restaurant trade). They are also particularly vulnerable to redundancy during recession.

A vital difference, however, exists between Britain's immigrants and Europe's migrant workers. Immigrants to Britain who were Commonwealth citizens had a *right* to settle here with their families and to exercise full civil and political liberties, including voting. Most came believing that they would receive fair and equal treatment with white citizens. For many, these hopes have not been fulfilled.

Aspects of Racial Stratification in Britain

In attempting to assess the extent and causes of racial inequality, the workplace is an obvious starting point. Housing is perhaps the next most important point to consider. Racial inequality in education has already been considered in Chapter 5, and the relevant section might be read again, after those on employment and housing, as an example of inequality of cultural opportunity. The feelings and opinions of blacks and whites about one another are also presented as aspects affecting racial stratification.

a Race and Employment
The economic background to black immigration has already

339

been analysed. Here, we look at the job levels of the major black minorities compared with those of whites.

The data given in the table and chart below provide a snapshot of comparative employment/unemployment in Britain by ethnic origin and sex. Those of West Indian and Asian origin are disproportionately concentrated in manual work, males predomi-

Occupational Class by Sex and Ethnic Origin (1982)
per cent

	Men			Women		
	White	West Indian origin	Asian origin	White	West Indian origin	Asian origin
Professional, employer, manager	19	5	13	7	1	6
Other non-manual	23	10	13	55	52	42
Skilled manual and foremen	42	48	33	5	4	6
Semi-skilled manual	13	26	34	21	36	44
Unskilled manual	3	9	6	11	7	2

Source: *Employment Gazette*, Vol. 92 No. 6, June 1984, HMSO.

Percentage Unemployment by Ethnic Group

Source: Policy Studies Institute Survey as reprinted in *Social Studies Review*, Vol. 1 No. 4, March 1986.

nantly in skilled manual and females in semi-skilled manual and routine non-manual. The patriarchal complexion of the table across the ethnic groups is unmistakable. The table does not show that among Asians, the Pakistani/Bangladeshis are more concentrated in lower status occupations than Indians who, with African Asians, are the best represented among minority groups in professional and other non-manual work. A key question is whether the occupational status of the racial minorities has improved relative to whites. The Policy Studies Institute Survey (1982) gives a mixed answer. Between 1974 and 1982, the relative percentage of black to white employees in professional and managerial work increased markedly for both sexes except for Afro-Caribbean women; on the other hand proportionately far more blacks became unemployed and there was no relative reduction in the numbers occupying low status jobs. Arguably, a black 'bourgeoisie' and 'underclass' developed simultaneously.

Since 1975, minority unemployment has tended to be proportionately higher than that of the general population (it is about 13% of the work-force). The proportion of unemployed blacks has tended to rise in times of economic recession. This gives weight to the theory that, to some extent, minorities serve as a 'reserve pool' or marginal source of cheap labour which, within the limits of law, can be cut during a slump, and re-employed when expansion occurs. Minority unemployment is a particular problem amongst teenagers. In some inner city areas it has been estimated at 30% of the total, or even above. The consequences in personal and social terms can be easily imagined.

What factors account for the employment distribution presented in the table? One theory is that the relatively low occupational status of blacks is a result of the fact that they are recent immigrants. It is argued that, in time, they will move up the occupational hierarchy. This view seems to be drawn largely from the experience of immigrant groups in the United States. Each wave of ethnic immigrants into the United States took its place in turn on the bottom of the ladder and began to clamber up – sometimes on the shoulders of the next in-coming group. The British, Italians and Eastern Europeans have all done this. A version of the same process is happening now, as the American negro begins to edge significantly beyond the Hispanic elements (those of mainly Mexican and Puerto Rican origin) in the population. A problem in applying this model to

British coloured immigrants is that no further wave of immigrants is likely to replace them on the bottom rung of society's
ladder. In any case, it is doubtful if the post-war expansion of
white-collar employment will continue: opportunities for upward
mobility are, therefore, likely to be fewer.

Another explanation of the low occupational status of blacks,
not wholly incompatible with the previous one, is that they are
discriminated against in the employment market. This is certainly true. An objective assessment of the extent of discrimination in job applications was carried out by PEP. The job 'applicants' (some, in fact, were actors), were made up of West
Indians, Pakistanis and a group of white immigrants, who were
Greek. Their treatment by prospective employers was compared
with that of a group of white British 'applicants'. The research
is of great interest in terms of both its findings and method.
Recruitment to unskilled and semi-skilled manual jobs was
tested. The results of the various tests for discrimination in
manual jobs are given below:

Discrimination against each minority group for four situations combined

	West Indians		Indians		Pakistanis		Greeks	
No. of cases	104		111		109		84	
	No.	%	No.	%	No.	%	No.	%
Net discrimination	28	27	31	28	25	23	9	11

Note: doubtful cases are here *not* treated as genuine cases of reverse
discrimination.

Source: *PEP Report,* 1977, p. 111.

The tests for discrimination in manual jobs:

> ... show that there are still substantial levels of discrimination
> against Asians and West Indians ...; that (they are) mainly
> based on colour prejudice rather than prejudice against
> foreigners; and that levels of discrimination against Indians,
> Pakistanis and West Indians are much the same.

Some further discrimination for white-collar jobs occurred
against Asians and West Indian applicants in 30% of cases. At

junior levels there was more discrimination against men than women. There was a high level of discrimination against applicants for management traineeships (42%). Thus, discrimination closed that gateway to possible promotion to really senior positions for two in five coloured applicants.

Given the above situation, there is an obvious role for trade unions, not only in improving the pay and conditions of coloured employees but also in seeking to cut down on job discrimination. Trade union membership is rather higher amongst the minority groups than amongst the white population. The faith of Asians and West Indians in trade unionism has not met a very positive response. The official and repeatedly reaffirmed position of the Trades Union Congress is, of course, strongly against racial prejudice and discrimination, but the actual conduct of unions at local level has failed to live up to conference rhetoric. The PEP report gives several cases in which the local union directly supported discrimination or allowed discriminatory practices to develop through failure to oppose them. The most common justification given by union officials for the lack of a strong lead against discrimination from the unions is that it would not meet with the approval of their members. In practice, it seems that the membership has not been properly asked what its opinions are on this matter. John Rex's observations on the relations of coloured labour and the unions support the analysis of the PEP survey. Reviewing research in the area he states:

> In the long run the picture which may emerge is that, despite their trade union membership and their loyalty to the unions, the immigrants may confront unions which at best ignore their grievances and at worst positively support more privileged native workers in preventing the immigrants from breaking out of replacement employment into the main parts of the labour market.

The extent of discrimination against coloured minorities in the job market is so great that it must be considered a large additional burden to the normal problems of immigrant adjustment. It is true that coloured working class people also share the inequalities experienced by the white working class, but racial inequality as well as class inequality defines their structural situation.

b Race and Housing

Black people suffer from poor housing more often than others. Again, the *PEP Report* summarises the situation succinctly:

> Although Asians and West Indians are more in need of council housing than the rest of the population, because their housing conditions in the private sector are much worse, they benefit from council housing less.

Let us first examine racial inequality in housing in the private sector. Superficially, the housing situation of Asians and West Indians may seem no worse than that of the general population. According to 1981 census figures, 48% of West Indian heads of household are owner-occupiers – rather less than the general population. For Asians, the figure is even higher – 72%. But owner-occupation performs a completely different function for the minorities than for the indigenous population. For the minorities, home ownership is frequently not a sign of status and material comfort, nor a secure financial investment. They tend to live in older housing which often lacks basic amenities. PEP data shows that the number of black people living in houses built before 1940 is 86%, and that well over a third lacked exclusive use of bath, hot water and inside toilet. Some black people, particularly Asians, live in this kind of housing because they have no alternative. They are sometimes excluded from council housing because of length of residency requirements. Nevertheless, overall, the basic living conditions of most minority members did improve between 1961 and 1982.

The PEP report claims that there was a 'sharp decrease' in the levels of discrimination in purchasing and renting accommodation between 1967 and 1973, and implies that this may have been due, in part, to the Race Relations Act of 1968. Nevertheless, the figures presented on discrimination are disquieting enough. 27% of West Indian and Asian testers were discriminated against when telephoning for rented accomodation, 17% were discriminated against when attempting to purchase a house, and 12% received inferior treatment.

We now examine council housing. The last decade has seen improvements, 46% of West Indians and 22% of Asians now live in council houses. The PEP findings on race and housing are carefully and fairly represented. Housing allocation systems tend to disfavour minorities for a number of technical reasons, even where no racial discrimination takes place. Even so, evidence is produced to show that discrimination in allocation has occurred and still does occur in some areas. One indicator of discrimination is the relatively long time blacks sometimes remain on some council waiting lists compared with the general population. Encouragingly, however, the report sees a recent decrease in the extent of discrimination, although no cause for complacency is implied, and the analysis of housing ends with suggestions for policy improvement. One recommendation, sensibly enough, is that more large houses should be built or bought to house the larger black families.

It is obvious that the position of the minorities in the housing market is a result both of their limited financial resources and of some discrimination. Class and racial factors are, however, less easy to separate than this statement implies. Personal finance is an indicator of class but the relatively low income of blacks is itself, in some cases, due to discrimination. A problem as complicated as this will find no easy solution.

c Prejudice, Panic and Racial Stratification

We have already discussed the role of prejudice in two central areas of social life: employment and housing. There is no shortage of supporting evidence that many white Britons are racially prejudiced. Studies by Bagley and by Jowell and Prescott-Clarke are major relevant examples. Abram's research of 1966 showed that, of a sample of 2,500, 10% were prejudiced, and 17% prejudice-inclined. For what it is worth, this author's own intuition is that in a situation of close personal involvement, such as whether or not to date or take home a member of another race, an uneasy awareness of race (prejudice is, perhaps, too strong a term here) might figure prominently in most people's calculations. We are still far from a relaxed acceptance of racial equality in everyday affairs.

Unease can turn to panic and hatred in times of stress. In such periods, racial minorities may become scapegoats for wider discontent. This happened to the Jews during the Depression – not only in Germany but to a lesser, although noteworthy, extent in parts of Britain, too. Jews were blamed for everything from international Marxism to capitalist world conspiracy! They were abused and victimised, not least among minorities of working class unemployed in parts of the East

End of London. More recently, it is blacks who are the scapegoats of hard times. For some, they provide an outlet for frustration and an excuse to avoid analysing the real and complex causes of recession. As black sociologist, Stuart Hall, says with some irony:

> After all, who now wants to begin to explore and unravel the complex tissue of political and economic forces which have created and sustained the poverty of the inner-urban working class . . . Above all, is there a simple, obvious and more natural explanation at hand? Of course they are 'poor' because the *blacks* are *here*. That is not a logical proposition, but ideologists do not function by logic – they have a logic of their own. Race has provided, in periods of crisis and upheaval, precisely such a self-justifying circle of explanations.

Stuart Hall considers the tense national debate of the late nineteen-seventies about how many people of coloured descent there are in Britain and how many more might be allowed in as an irrelevance. In fact, in 1978 there were 1.9 million, out of a population of over 55 million. By that year, coloured immigration had been dropping continuously for some time and had reached a point where it was quite clear that fears of 'swamping' were completely unfounded; in fact more people were leaving Britain than arriving in it. It is difficult not to agree with Hall that continued obsession with immigration and further legislation to reduce it was more a symptom of panic and scapegoating than a measured attempt to deal with a real problem.

Prejudice and discrimination build barriers between people of different races. In Britain, these barriers have reduced the life-chances of members of minority groups. The result is racial stratification. We now discuss whether the position of black people in this country is such that they can be regarded as an 'underclass' beneath and adrift from the working class as a whole.

d Is There a Black 'Underclass'?
Defining the structural situation of the minorities is no mere academic matter. It is a necessary part of doing something about racial inequality. In summary, the evidence presented in this chapter shows that *the coloured minorities suffer from both status (racial discrimination) and class inequality.* It is easier to note the

potentially disastrous convergence of racial and class inequalities than to disentangle the two. Probably, they cannot be
fully disentangled.

In attempting to put a name to the distinct structural position of blacks, John Rex has suggested the term 'underclass'.
The word recalls Marx's term lumpen proletariat which refers
to the unemployed, and in some cases unemployable, mass
beneath the proletariat. Marx's term, however, had no particularly racial connotation. We can see four arguments for
using the term underclass, all of which differentiate blacks from
the working class and therefore prevent them from being fully
identified with it. Firstly, blacks are subject to racial discrimination and need to find ways of fighting it. Secondly, blacks as
a group tend to be poorer than the working class as a whole:
in that sense they are an 'underclass'. Thirdly, the trade union
movement and, perhaps to a lesser extent, the Labour Party,
has failed to adequately meet the needs of black people.
Fourthly, blacks have produced their own cultural and, to some
extent, political institutions, and it seems likely that these will
be further developed. Self-help is, perhaps, the first and last
line of preservation.

It may, however, still be premature to speak of a black
underclass'. Matters may not yet be quite as clear cut as this
term suggests. There are strategies for black advancement,
other than black community politics, which involve co-operation
with predominantly white organisations on a basis of *mutual*
interest and which might improve the conditions many blacks
live in. We examine the political solutions that may be open to
blacks in the next section and this should be regarded as an
extension of our discussion on whether or not blacks can be
regarded as an underclass.

e Ethnic Community Politics and Class Politics: The Black Response to Racial Discrimination and Inequality

The data given in the previous four sections shows, in the
words of John Rex, that 'the situation of the blacks is structurally distinct from that of the majority of the working class.' Initially, the structurally inferior position of blacks reflected the
problems of immigrant adjustment, but the *enduring reason* for it
is the extent of prejudice and discrimination in British society
coupled with the indifference and occasional hostility of the

unions. Racial discrimination is essentially a form of status stratification and it represents the major immediate problem of blacks in Britain.

ETHNIC COMMUNITY POLITICS In the absence of substantial help from the British working class movement, coloured people largely rely on *family and community self-help*. The following quotation is a perceptive and articulate personal account of what many immigrants must have felt as 'strangers in a strange land':

> My position was that of a young black Jamaican woman – an immigrant. I was not able to act as a detached observer, maintaining a value-free stance, and with emotions under strict surveillance. English behaviour was often unusual, and sometimes decidedly hostile, and I reacted to it with powerful feelings and protective strategies. It is not easy at first to distinguish the unpredictable and harmless from the really unpleasant. I had little understanding of the heterogeneous English society, and when I met an unusual situation I turned to my relatives and friends for help. Their advice, although not necessarily well-informed, gave me the support I so often needed in making sense of my experience.

Ethnic cultural identity is generated by the natural social ties of the ethnic community. The American immigrant experience provides a parallel to that of British immigrants. For instance, the Irish, Italian and Jewish communities formed organisations to defend and advance themselves in all areas of American life. The Irish were famous for their political social welfare 'machines', the Italians for their clannish and secretive business-criminal Mafia organisations, and the Jews are still well-known for their sense of ethnic loyalty and identity. The basic cell in these sprawling ethnic structures was usually the extended family. The same is true in many of Britain's immigrant communities. In the early period of post-war immigration, the typical immigrant was, however, a single person – usually a man. Nevertheless, his major aim was often to bring over his family and he sent money 'back home' for this purpose. Once the family had arrived, the next important step for many was to buy a house. To raise the money for this – and a surprisingly large minority of immigrant houses are fully paid for – required financial co-operation between family and, possibly, friends.

The need for everyday mutual assistance and sharing among

family, kin and friends as they settle into a new country and culture is obvious. Baby-sitting, gifts and loans assist over short-term crises, and friendly chats and advice are the stuff of daily life. Many immigrants are used to relying on family and friends for help rather than on the state, and may actually prefer to do so. A survey conducted in Birmingham, published in 1980, reported that elderly West Indians and Asians depend on state welfare less than elderly whites. Many, apparently, did not know of services like meals on wheels and home helps to which they were entitled, but most of those who did rejected them in favour of support from their families and neighbours.

Although much community life is informal, specific needs do produce the incentive to create more formal institutions. Some, of course, are more formal than others. At the humblest level is the ethnic shop or genuinely local ethnic restaurant. Beyond these are social clubs, discos and various places of pleasure and entertainment, with ethnic management and largely ethnic clientele. These may overlap, more or less, with the white world, although sense of separation is virtually inevitable.

Sometimes, particularly when an ethnic group feels threatened or spurned, ethnic identity expresses itself in political or quasi-military organisations. The core of the American civil rights movement of the nineteen-sixties was a coalition of black pressure groups. The Black Panther Party was, in part, a break-away from the non-violence of the civil rights movement into more aggressive, para-military politics. The Panthers explained their position partly in terms of the need to defend themselves against police victimisation of the black community. The immediate upshot was several bloody confrontations in which several Black Panthers were killed. In view of the American experience, what John Rex has to say about certain trends in black politics in this country deserves close attention: it is his second point that is significant: the riots of Bristol and Brixton already show him to be wrong on the first.

> I think that street battles and riots provoked by blacks are unlikely and I do not, though I am less sure here, think there will be any literal application of the slogan 'Burn baby, burn' in British cities . . .
> I do think, however, that the black political movements are moving toward a posture of defensive confrontation and that they are quite realistic in doing so.

Rex concentrates particularly on ethnic community politics although we can apply much of what he says nationally. He suggests three types of black political movements: *issue-oriented, personality-oriented* and *ideologically-oriented*. A major example of an issue-oriented movement is the protest against the number of black youths arrested on suspicion ('sus'). This a charge under the 1824 Vagrancy Act which allows the police to arrest, without warrant, a person whom they reasonably suspect to be 'loitering with intent to commit a felonious offence.' Police evidence alone can be sufficient to convict. Estimates of the percentage of coloured people making up 'sus' arrests vary from 44% (Home Office) to 80% for certain inner urban areas (Law Centres Working Group). The 'sus' law and the manner of its application have caused widespread concern within and beyond the black community. The 'sus' law has now been abolished but police relations with the black community remain fragile.

Issues need not be of long standing to cause conflict. On the contrary, those that suddenly arise are often the most inflammatory. Thus, the police raid on a restaurant in the St. Paul's area of Bristol in April 1980 sparked off one of the country's worst urban riots.

Education is another, quite different, issue which has provoked black action. In Redbridge and elsewhere, black parents and teachers have very positively involved themselves in supporting the school curriculum, with additional schooling in the evenings or at weekends.

We now consider Rex's second type of movement, the personality-oriented. An example of a nationally-known (though sparsely supported) personality-oriented movement in Britain was the Black Power Group led by Michael X during the nineteen-sixties. He was a mere shadow of the much better known Malcolm X who led the Black Muslim movement in the United States. Rex has in mind, however, local personalities who can manipulate incidents sometimes to further a cause but often for maximum personal publicity.

A more reliable basis for a political movement than the merely personal is ideological belief – Rex's third category. The American Black Panther Party, mentioned above, provides an example of this kind of movement. Within the British black community, there are a number of groups which are as much cultural as political, and which have distinctive ideologies. One example is the Rastafarian movement (see Chapter 13). Members of the group are disciples of the late former Emperor of Ethiopia, Haile Selassie, whom they believe to be divine. With varying degrees of conviction, Rastafarians subscribe to black separatism and some wed socialism to their religious beliefs. It has been said of this and of other 'back to Africa' movements that they represent an extreme defensive reaction by blacks against a white society which has already rejected them. A return to Africa is not, however, a realistic option, particularly as the majority of coloured immigrants have never been there in the first place. But the identity, confidence and expression that such movements provide should not be dismissed or underestimated. We develop this point at some length when discussing black and brown youth in the next chapter.

CLASS POLITICS Community politics alone are unlikely ever to be enough radically to change the position of Britain's black population. John Rex may virtually despair of an effective black and white working class alliance but he still recognises its ultimate desirability, if the massive governmental resources needed by inner city ethnic groups are ever to materialise. Community politics are necessary both to 'defend' and develop the community, but only government (arguably in combination with industry) can provide the means to lift 'ghetto' conditions – economic, housing and educational – much nearer to the acceptable national norm. In getting political support for such a programme blacks are not without some political muscle. At the lowest level, political parties need black votes just as unions require members. The Labour Party has already passed two important pieces of legislation, the 1968 and 1976 Race Relations Acts, attacking discrimination in major areas of life. They seem to have had some effect. Perhaps now the principle of *positive discrimination* on behalf of blacks – particularly in guaranteeing them adequate jobs and income – is an aim worth persuading the Labour Party to pursue. The 1968 and 1976 Acts seek to achieve equality under the law, but greater material equality is a harder ideal to attain and may require this different policy, which may *favour* black people. No doubt, too, many blacks will deem it expedient to continue to work in, and with the unions, in the hope of persuading them to support black interests more actively.

Conclusion

The violent urban disorders of 1985 seemed, temporarily at least, to reduce race relations in Britain literally and figuratively to a shambles. However that may be, they certainly compel a further re-examination of racial conflict and inequality in Britain. Three racially problematic areas can be distinguished: racism, racialism, and institutional racism. A distinction can be made between the concepts of racism and racialism, the former usually referring to belief and ideology, the latter, to behaviour which discriminates (disadvantageously to a given group) on grounds of race. Although racist ideology typically supports racial discrimination, this distinction between the two terms can serve to clarify policy goals. For instance, the anti-racist education movement clearly aspires to educate attitudes rather than merely change surface behaviour. However, the immediate need to stop racial discrimination has also to be met. The legislation reviewed above had this aim. In the long run, perhaps, the surest way to change behaviour is to change the attitudes that breed it. Marxists and other structuralists contend that attitudes and beliefs are unlikely to change unless the deeper circumstances that give rise to them also change. This brings us to our third point, institutional racism.

Institutional racism refers to the *systematic* disadvantaging of a racial group rather than to conscious, individual racism. Thus, it can be argued that the higher unemployment of blacks, their poorer housing and health, the fact that they generally receive less, and worse, education, reflects the institutional racism of British society. Their qualities, experience and (sometimes informal) qualifications are routinely underrated when resources are distributed. Institutional racism is, therefore, a structural rather than a conspiracy theory. Even if it is only a partially correct theory, its policy implications are enormous and as yet largely unfaced. If the riots are 'symptoms' of the deeper malady of institutional racism, then perhaps the price of failing to deal with it has become too high.

Guide to Further Reading and Study

Andrew Pilkington's *Race Relations in Britain* (University Tutorial Press, 1984) gives a useful overview of the field. Another general work for students is John Richardson and John Lambert, *The Sociology of Race* (Causeway Press, 1985). For a first hand feel of race relations problems, try Ken Pryce, *Endless Pressure: A Study of West Indian Life Styles in Bristol* (Penguin, 1979). Using the contrasting method of the social survey is the still very useful PEP Report by D. J. Smith, *Racial Disadvantage in Britain: The PEP Report* (1977). John Rex has published much of great usefulness in this field and I found his essay 'West Indian and Asian Youth' particularly illuminating. It is available in E. Cashmore and B. Troyna *eds.*, *Black Youth in Crisis* (Allen and Unwin, 1982). Probably still the most authoritative Marxists statement on race is S. Castles' and G. Kosack's *Immigrant Workers and Class Structure in Western Europe* (Oxford University Press, 1973). More recent and more theoretically eclectic is the collection of essays from the Centre for Contemporary Cultural Studies, *The Empire Strikes Back* (Hutchinson, 1982). Useful articles on the subject are, of course, constantly appearing: one such was John Benyon, 'Turmoil in the Cities', *Social Studies Review*, Volume 1, Number 3, January 1986. A recent and mildly more optimistic survey of the extent of discrimination in key areas is C. Brown, *Black and White in Britain: 3rd PSI Survey*, (Heinemann, 1984).

Past Questions

1 'Despite the concentration of immigrants in certain areas, strictly defined ghettos have not been produced, but there is a growing indication that they may well appear in the future.' (Allen) Discuss. (AEB, 1975)

2 Examine the contribution made by sociologists to the study of ethnic minorities and *either* (a) employment or (b) housing. (AEB, 1983)

3 Evaluate the major sociological explanations of why some social groups are disproportionately represented among the 'failures' of the education system. (AEB, 1984)

4 'Racial inequalities in contemporary societies are the direct consequences of those societies exploiting colonised peoples as cheap labour.' Discuss. (London, 1984)

5 To what extent does the concept of an 'underclass' or 'sub-proletariat' help to explain the high rate of unemployment amongst ethnic minorities in industrial societies? (AEB, 1985)

14 Age, Generation and Class

Guide to Further Reading and Study 388

Past Questions 388–9

Terminology and Overview

I have occasionally asked groups of students which form of stratification they regard as the most important: class, gender, race or age. As often as not, the majority reply age. Perhaps this reflects the particular importance of the peer group and age relations to adolescents. However, most people, regardlesss of age would probably agree with S. N. Eisenstadt's remark that 'Age and differences of age are among the most basic and crucial aspects of human life and determinants of human destiny.'

The term *age group* refers to a group of people differentiated from others according to age. The term *age grade* is commonly used to describe age groups which are clearly and formally established, especially in relation to those primitive societies stratified according to age. For instance, male aborigines pass through the age grades of hunter, warrior and elder. Age is best conceptualised in terms of the *life-cycle*. The life-cycle refers to those stages through which all who survive a full life-span pass. There is not complete agreement on the precise length and nature of the age-stages but Erik Erickson's eight-stage model is widely, if critically, used (see the table on page 356). His model is a developmental one and attempts to present the maturational relationship between biological/chronological, psycho-social and social aspects of development (columns 1, 2 and 3 respectively). As Eisenstadt suggests, the basic biological processes are probably more or less similar in all human societies although crucially the rate and quality of biological change is subject to wide individual variation for both genetic and environmental reasons. Freud was the first systematically to explore the notion that psychological development occurs in childhood partly through the resolution of certain tasks or crises – the first one of which is to establish a trusting relationship with the mother or mother substitute. Erickson extended the concept of central crisis to every stage in the life-cycle (see table).

The third aspect of Erickson's model describes the typical social context – in terms of relationships and institutions – in which

Eight Stages of Psycho-social Development

Stages	Psycho-social crises	Significant social relations	Favourable outcome
1 First year of life	Trust versus mistrust	Mother or mother substitute	Trust and optimism
2 Second year	Autonomy versus doubt	Parents	Sense of self-control and adequacy
3 Third through fifth years	Initiative versus guilt	Basic family	Purpose and direction; ability to initiate one's own activities
4 Sixth year to puberty	Industry versus inferiority	Neighbourhood; school	Competence in intellectual, social, and physical skills
5 Adolescence	Identity versus confusion	Peer groups and outgroups; models of leadership	An integrated image of oneself as a unique person
6 Early adulthood	Intimacy versus isolation	Partners in friendship; sex, competition, co-operation	Ability to form close and lasting relationships; to make career commitments
7 Middle adulthood	Generativity versus self-absorption	Divided labour and shared household	Concern for family, society, and future generations
8 The ageing years	Integrity versus despair	'Mankind'; 'my kind'	A sense of fulfilment and satisfaction with one's life; willingness to face death

Source: Erik Erickson, *Childhood and Society*, W. W. Norton, 1963, as modified in S. R. Hilgard *et al.*, *Introduction to Psychology*, Harcourt Brace Jovanovich, 1979.

development at given stages occurs. These contexts are very general and allow for great cultural variations. Even so, Erickson has been widely criticised for over-universalising the social and psycho-social aspects of his model. Judith Stevens-Long suggests that his enthusiasm for the institutions of monogamy and the nuclear family is somewhat ethnocentric, reflecting his own Western rather than any truly universal values and reality.

Childhood, youth and old age will be dealt with in detail here. It may seem that young adulthood and middle age are neglected stages of the life-cycle. This is partly so, although most sociology focuses on the family, work and leisure lives of mature adults. For young adults, the task is often to establish a career or family (or to decide not to) and for the middle aged it is to develop or perhaps change what has been established. There is a substantial body of social psychology which examines the various stresses and challenges of adulthood, including the imprecisely defined 'middle age crisis'.

The concept of generation occurs frequently in age group analysis although Erickson gives it scant attention. Mannheim distinguishes between generation as *location* and as *actuality*. The former refers to a group of similar age but the latter only applies when a generation shares a community of feeling or experience. Perhaps the world wars and the Vietnam war stimulated such communal identity for the youth of those times. Such widely shared experiences are rare and Mannheim used the term generational *unit* to describe a group within a generation which has a common view of events. Thus, there were pro and anti-war units among the 'Vietnam war generation'. Other social factors that affect given generations are structural change, such as that causing a big rise in unemployment (see pp. 164–5) and the size of a generational cohort itself (see p. 164).

Although Erickson's model remains a useful outline 'map', much historical, anthropological and sociological research and theory tends rather to stress the *different* ways age is perceived and structured between cultures. The works referred to in the following section illustrate this.

Childhood

The Social Construction of Childhood: Historical and Comparative Perspective

Ariès' *Centuries of Childhood* argues that 'in medieval society the idea of childhood did not exist' and that it developed from the fifteenth century as part of the modern preoccupation with family. In the middle ages the child was 'absorbed into the world of adults, soon after infancy'. The development of schooling was the factor that separated children and eventually adolescents from other age groups and provided them with their own age-specific experience (see pp. 363–4). Something of a romantic traditionalist, Ariès extols what he sees as the community-based sociability of the middle ages into which the young were expected to fit and deplores the obsession of the modern family with its younger members. Not surprisingly, de Mause and others have criticised him for minimising the evidence of neglect and brutality towards children in the medieval period as well as of a general indifference to children's welfare. Nevertheless, Ariès does introduce what has become a central feature of much contemporary social scientific analysis of age – that it is substantially a socially constructed phenomenon not merely a biological given.

The anthropological studies of Malinowski provide comparative data which further demonstrate that much of what we take for granted in the West about given age groups need not occur universally. Writing in the inter-war period, Malinowski describes the life of Trobriand children and adolescents as considerably freer and more open than that of similarly aged British contemporaries in terms of taking responsibility for their own activities, relations with parents and in sexual exploration. He contrasts the relationship of father to child in the two cultures: 'At the time when our father makes himself pleasant at best by his entire absence from the nursery, the Trobriand father is first a nurse and then a companion.' The prime responsibility for exercising authority over children lay not with the father but with the mother's brother. The paternal role in contemporary Britain is less rigid than it was, but other formidable structures of social control over children and adolescents still exist. Thus, the easy paced initiation of Trobriand youth into adult work contrasts sharply with the bureaucratically controlled and hierarchically administered Youth Training Scheme.

Childhood: Contemporary Issues and Policy

Reading through the vast literature on the family, it is not easy to get a sense of what it is like to be a child. Adolescents seem to speak much more clearly for themselves but the voices of young children come from a different world. Perhaps the long period of human maturation makes childhood dependency, powerlessness and vulnerability inevitable. What follows certainly demonstrates the power and control – for good and ill – of adults over children.

Ariès suggests that children were not so clearly differentiated from others until separated off by the system of compulsory education (see above p. 358). In traditional society they had worked with their parents, mainly in agriculture, and even in the early stages of the industrial revolution many young children were workers. Ronald Fletcher's insightful comment that both parents and the state have come to take an increasing interest in children suggests the framework within which modern childhood has been moulded. Let us take the involvement of the state with children first.

Throughout the nineteenth century a steady flow of legislation first restricted and then prohibited certain forms of child labour – notably in mines and factories – and the age limitation was steadily raised. In parallel, the state increasingly encouraged and financed the education of children until finally compulsory education was enacted. Why did the state take such a growing interest in children? First, as both Marxist and functionalist commentators have observed, basic education was seen as likely to contribute to the efficiency of the labour force. In addition, as the comments of some of the late nineteenth century educational inspectorate show, the teaching of moral conformity was also officially regarded as a goal of education. Second, more productive technology meant that child labour was not really needed. Third, some of the concern for children's education, health and moral welfare was undoubtedly motivated by philanthropic feeling of the kind expressed in literature by Charles Dickens and in politics by the Earl of Shaftesbury.

Modern families are often said to be 'child-centred'. Two trends – both well established since the start of this century have helped make this possible: first, parents have generally had fewer children and, second, the increase in leisure has given them more time to spend with those they do have. A considerable amount of time and concern is spent by parents, especially among the middle class, on their children's education. The fact that modern society is seen as open to talent and ability encourages this tendency. Parental relations with children must, of course, be seen within the context of the sexual division of labour. Historically, women have done most of the domestic work, including rearing children. As women moved back into the paid labour force from the late nineteenth century, the education system expanded to accommodate children for longer periods of time.

Arguably, state and parental interest in children has intensified in the Second World War period although this statement is not without qualification. Whatever the outcome, the needs and protection of children rather than the right of parents over children emerges as the dominant theme of post-war legislation in relation to children. Children benefited from the introduction of the National Health Service and other welfare measures, particularly child benefit. An important initiative was taken in 1948 with the formation of a child care service under the Home Office. The period of just over a decade between 1969 and 1980 was very significant in the field of child care legislation. B. I. Slomnicka describes the Children and Young Persons' Act of 1969 as 'a brave attempt to revolutionise the law relating to young people' by treating children in difficulty equally on the basis of need. This applied to delinquents as well as others with problems (such as the threat of physical or moral danger). Making the needs of the child paramount meant a parallel increase in the involvement of social workers and probation officers with children in difficulty. The recent trend, particularly since the 1975 Children Act, has been to take into care children at extreme risk from within their own families. However, as we shall see, this practice is not always pursued and the judgement to split a family cannot be an easy one. Indeed, just prior to the great publicity given to a number of abuse cases in the mid-eighties, there was a discernible trend back to keeping families together. It is worth quoting a key section of the 1980 Child Care Act to show the principles guiding local authorities when considering applying for a care order.

> In reaching any decision relating to a child in their care, local authorities shall give first consideration to the need to safeguard and promote the welfare of the child throughout his childhood; and so far as practicable ascertain the wishes and feelings of the child regarding the decision and give due consideration to them, having regard to his age and understanding.

An aspect of this clear emphasis on the interests of the child is the general duty laid upon local authorities to put more emphasis on the long term planning for her or his welfare.

These considerations provide a useful background against which to consider the problem of child abuse. Ruth and Henry Kempe divide child abuse into the following four types: physical violence, physical and emotional neglect, emotional abuse and sexual exploitation. Reliable statistics on the extent of child abuse do not appear to exist – reflecting perhaps, the hidden and shaming nature of the problem, the importance attached to family privacy and parental rights, and the relative powerlessness of most children to alert others to what is happening. According to the National Society for the Prevention of Cruelty to Children, 7,000 children were physically abused by their parents in 1984, 70% more than in 1979. However, these figures are merely based on the reports to the NSPCC's ten child protection teams, which only cover 10% of the child population. The increase probably reflects greater public awareness of abuse rather than a real growth in the crime. On the matter of sexual abuse, a Mori Poll conducted in 1985 indicated that one in ten children is victimised, often by a parent, sibling or other relative. Although cases of child abuse involving working class families come more often to law, it cannot be concluded that they are any less common among the middle class.

Sometimes children are killed as a result of abuse. Two cases were recently widely publicised. Jasmine Beckford died in July 1984 and Gemma Hartwell in March 1985, both killed by their fathers. The Blom-Cooper enquiry into Jasmine Beckford's death and the court reports on the Gemma Hartwell case show certain parallels. First, both fathers had substantial records of cruelty to their children. Second, and especially in the Beckford case, the judgement of the social workers involved tended to be sensitive to the parents' rights rather than children's rights and needs. The Blom-Cooper report provides a strong, clear directive to the contrary: 'Put the child first and if that means doing something that is disliked by the parents, that's what has got to be done.' Third, the question of adequacy of the training of many social workers is raised by these and other cases. Blom-Cooper recommends three rather than the usual two years' training for social workers, with more time spent on developing skills in specialist areas such as child abuse. Of course, this would require more public expenditure and tax payers and government may not support it. Not all authorities consider that the best approach to child abuse lies in the direction indicated above. In separate articles in the same edition of *New Society* (13 December 1985), both Bill Jordan and Tailgunner Parkinson express concern that the Blom-Cooper report may turn social workers into a frightened breed who live by the book. Jordan argues that 'social workers, like the police . . . bear the stigma of an unjust social order' and that more should be done to equalise the hard and squalid circumstances with which they often have to deal.

The matter of child abuse raises profound issues of social policy and sociology. Policy is concerned with solutions and some relevant suggestions are referred to in the previous paragraph. Sociology seeks a profounder understanding of phenomena and can feed back into social policy, making it better informed and more effective. Sociologically, what causes child abuse? A variety of factors, including stress and alcohol, have been found to be associated with it. Ruth and Henry Kempe claim that child abuse is less common in extended than in nuclear families – presumably because the chance of protective adult intervention is increased and because the strain of childcare can be more widely shared. From a macro perspective, it is probable that certain widespread cultural attitudes, particularly related to child rearing, may produce a climate more or less conducive to child abuse. In her article 'Why are Parents Tough On Children?', Valerie Yule enquires whether there is a pattern of behaviour among many British parents which begins with brusqueness towards their children and which can end in brutality. She observed 85 adult-child pairs each for a few minutes and found that for two-fifths of the sample, interactions were negative and in most of the other cases the adults took no notice of the child at all. Yule suggests that the freer expression of physical affection, on the part of parents for their children might make for greater happiness all round. Certainly, her small piece of research is thought provoking.

Another large-scale issue for consideration, is the relationships between child abuse (and general child welfare) and poverty. There is evidence that in both Britain and the United States children have replaced the old as the age group most at risk from poverty. Norman Fowler's green paper of 1985, 'The Reform of Social Security', commented that it is families with children that face the most difficult problems. It is too early to say yet, but many of his critics doubt whether his proposed reforms will much improve this situation. It is perhaps significant that in 1985 there were moral panics in both the United States and Britain about child abuse but not about child poverty. The very repugnance felt against the perpetrators of child abuse may serve to distract from the contribution that poverty can make to neglect and abuse. Is a society that tolerates widespread poverty among children blameless of abuse itself? When we talk of child neglect and abuse, we are not just talking about how *they* – the 'monsters' of the popular press – treat children, but about how *we* as a community treat them. This argument is even more uncomfortable if we apply it to the international responsibility for the condition of children in the Third World (see, pp. 172–7).

The Social Construction of Modern Youth

The view that childhood is socially constructed can be extended to youth and, indeed, to any age stage. Generally, the factors discussed below illustrate this point although, in some instances, the argument is raised that, for whatever reason (biological, psychological or social) certain characteristics of youth are virtually universal.

Universal Education

Universal education helps to shape the experience of modern youth just as much as it does childhood. At first, education was mainly an upper and middle class privilege – as described fictionally in *Tom Brown's Schooldays* – but it is now a universal right and legal requirement. Sharing a common structural situation for the purpose of formal socialisation, young people naturally develop a sense of shared interest. Yet, it is in the informal peer groups that intra-generational interaction is most free to flourish. As S. N. Eisenstadt observes, the peer group provides a means for experimentation and experience in roles, status and romance, and is generally an effective vehicle for transition between childhood and the complex demands of modern adulthood. In much the same way as universal education, though to a lesser extent, national service also provided a basis of collective experience and identity for many young. Sometimes, generational peer groups and even whole units turn against dominant norms and adopt delinquent and/or culturally deviant life-styles. Geoffrey Pearson points out that riotous behaviour by young people not constrained and motivated by either education or work, predates the nineteen eighties. Peer groups can form and operate on the streets – sometimes in a disorderly and criminal way. Finally, peer groups generated largely within the educational context or on neighbourhood streets reflect the influence of class, race, gender and individuality.

Modern Youth Culture or Sub-cultures?

In his pamphlet *The Teenage Consumer* (1959), Mark Abrams was one of the first to suggest that a new youth culture had been created in post-war Britain. As the title of the pamphlet suggests, the new culture was based on increased affluence enabling the purchase of such items as records, motorcycles, cosmetics and other recreational goods. Berger and Berger argued that '. . . international mass youth consumption and culture expanded further in the nineteen sixties', cutting, in their view to a considerable extent '. . . across class lines'. This is almost an embourgeoisement theory of youth culture, and British Marxist sub-cultural theorists, in particular, disagree with it. They find that the Bergers' concept of almost classless 'status spheres' of the young is belied by the continued impact of class, race and gender on youth subcultures which often survive and even undermine the powerful homogenising forces of what they prefer to call international capitalism.

Youth and 'Prefigurative Culture'

In her essay 'Culture and Commitment: A Study of the Generation Gap', Margaret Mead focuses on the problems of youth by distinguishing between three kinds of culture: postfigurative, cofigurative and prefigurative. A postfigurative culture gains its authority from the past and little change occurs. The young learn and apply traditional wisdom. A cofigurative culture is one in which change is occurring and the model of behaviour is that of contemporaries rather than elders. A prefigurative culture is one in which the speed of change is so rapid that culture must become anticipatory; the future of the child, rather than the knowledge of the parent or wisdom of the elder must become its guiding light. Undoubtedly, Mead's concept of prefigurative culture was affected by the idealisation of youth of the nineteen sixties and is tinged a little with bias (see, p. 365). However, it suggests two concrete observations. One, that the mental flexibility of the young may enable them better to cope with a rapidly changing world. This is apparent in the skill many young show in manipulating information technology but it may also apply to ideas and principles, (perhaps science fiction stories – widely popular among the young – are 'fairy tales' of the future). Second, the survival of the young is in the balance because of the urgency of the environmental, population and particularly the nuclear issue. Their future depends on the present solution to these problems. As Mead puts it, the future is now. However, in the period of conservative reaction of the nineteen eighties, it is clear that even if the young can envisage the future more clearly than adults, they do not appear to possess the power to do anything about it. Perhaps the example of Band Aid suggests that this is too pessimistic a conclusion.

The Psychology and 'Problems' of Youth

In the Western world, crime and suicide rates are relatively high among the young. A variety of mental disorders shows a sharp incline during the teenage years. According to data assembled by Michael Rutter, these include alcoholism, schizophrenia, anorexia nervosa and depression – although only a minority actually suffer from these illnesses. No single sociological explanation would precisely cover all these phenomena but, in general, the sociological perspective is that the complexities and pressures of modern adolescence are such that signs of difficulty and instability are to be expected. Poverty and joblessness, can make matters worse. A contrary argument, put forward, among others by Anna Freud, is that adolescence is naturally and universally a period of rebellion. Margaret Mead's *Coming of Age in Samoa* was an attempt to refute such theories by demonstrating that in Samoa 'adolescence represented no period of crisis or stress, but was instead an orderly developing of a set of slowly maturing interests and activities'. However, Derek Freeman's formidable critique of Mead's methodology in this study undermines her claim to have found a crucial 'negative instance' of the universalist view. Mead believed that her study of 50 Samoan adolescent girls showed that in general their adolescence was orderly and constructive thus providing a 'negative instance' to invalidate the proposition that adolescence is universally problematic. However, Freeman finds that of the 25 girls Mead studied in greatest detail, 4 were delinquent and 3 at odds with their kin: a percentage total of 28. His point that this suggests quite a high level of stress and conflict seems well taken.

Youth

Terminology and Perspectives

The interesting aspect of the sociology of youth lies in analysing and interpreting what young people do, think and feel. For instance: what did the young radicals of the sixties want? Why do some young people dye their hair orange? (A genuine mystery to some older people). What does all that football chanting mean? Sociological perspectives are useful only in so far as they explain behaviour: we will, therefore, keep this theoretical section brief and let the perspectives speak for themselves in practical application.

Three major perspectives on youth can be described. These are *functionalist, generational 'unit' and class-structural*. There are, of course, variations of each. Talcott Parsons and S. N. Eisenstadt present functionalist models. For them, youth is a period of training and preparation for adulthood. Personal difficulties in 'growing up' and even group rebellion are seen as dysfunctional, if predictable. Even so, they note that most young people do, in fact, successfully negotiate the transitional phase of adolescence. This functionalist model is not ahistorical (it does not lack historical awareness). Functionalists fully recognise that in modern society the period of youthful socialisation tends to be longer and that particular stresses accompany it. Weber's concept of the status group is also sometimes used in functionalist analyses of youth. Young people are considered to share the same pre-adult status and also to share similar problems of adjustment. Identity, security and much personal 'problem solving', as well as leisure activity, are based on the peer group.

Karl Mannheim's concept of the generational 'unit' has elements of functionalist perspective and the concept of separate generational consciousness that was popular in the nineteen sixties. Mannheim appreciated, as functionalists do, that the educational system cuts young people off from the work-centred life of adults. Within generational groups, particular units sometimes form. Thus, in higher education student movements emerge in certain circumstances. This is because students are frequently together and, as a result, are able to discuss and organise their response to major issues such as wars and racial discrimination. Sometimes their response takes the form of protest. No doubt because the nineteen sixties was a period of exceptional student activism, some commentators tended to overstress the separateness of the generations and the extent of generational conflict. Charles Reich in his book, *The Greening of America*, wrote as if a 'new consciousness', inspired by youthful imagination and idealism, was about to engulf America. He forgot that this radical consciousness was largely confined to middle class students in higher education, and was by no means adopted by all of them.

More recently, British sociologists, particularly the mainly Marxist group at the Centre for Cultural Studies in Birmingham, have argued that youth should be analysed in the specific class context of particular youth groups. Thus, student protest movements should be seen not just as the action of young people but of young, *middle class* people. Again, 'slum' gangs should be analysed not merely as 'young delinquents', but in relation to their class, neighbourhood and family environments, including the culture of working class adults. This approach, therefore, allows for the operation of generational factors within a broad framework of class, and we use it more than any other in this chapter.

Although we have already explained the meaning of the terms culture and sub-culture (see Chapter 3), it is appropriate to expand the definition here. *Culture refers to the way of life of a given group, for instance, of a particular society or class. Sub-culture refers to those aspects of the life of a group which distinguish it from the main or dominant culture.* Thus, we can speak of West Indian or Jewish sub-culture in Britain. *A counter-culture or contra-culture describes a sub-culture which is opposed to the dominant culture.* The term was widely used of the new radical life-style of the nineteen sixties.

Youth Conformity and Sub-Cultural Non-Conformity

Most young people conform, more or less, to society's norms. For them, peer group identity *complements* rather than *conflicts* with their roles in the family and at school or work. We explore *conformity* among youth shortly. Immediately, we examine the minority sub-cultures of non or less conformist young people. The only reason for preferring the term *non-conformity* to *deviance* here is that much youthful sub-cultural activity only *borders* on the deviant. (The explicitly deviant we examine in Chapter 18.) We have already explained how young people tend to be 'set apart' from the rest of society and we have mentioned some of the influences and stresses upon them. This section is more interpretist in that it analyses how certain minority groups of young people respond to their own experience, including the pressures of the media and the educational systems and, in doing so, often create original and interesting life-styles. We can roughly categorise these responses into three types: delinquent, pleasure seeking or political. Response is, however, mediated or influenced by social context – to express it crudely, either middle class, working class and/or ethnic culture. Differences in family, neighbourhood and educational experience deeply divide young people. We can put the above points in simple, diagrammatical form:

Youth (Minority) Sub-cultural Types

Type of Response	Social Base	→ Working Class	Middle Class
↓	↓	↓	↓
Delinquent		Strong	Weak
Pleasure-seeking		Strong	Less strong (except among a 'Bohemian' minority)
Political		Weak	Sometimes strong in Higher Education, otherwise not.

We will use these three types of sub-cultural response as a general guide (but no more than that), first to examine working class youth, then middle class youth. It must be noted that many young people opt in and out of sub-cultural activity and that between conformity and non-conformity there is a considerable 'grey' area.

Working Class Youth Culture and Sub-cultures

Working class youth culture is concentrated in areas such as the inner city and, more recently, public housing estates. It is a field of research that has been well studied both in Britain and the United States. The Chicago School of urban sociologists began the serious sociological study of this topic (see Chapter

18). Much of the best contemporary material has been published in Britain. Peter Willmot in *Adolescent Boys in East London* (1966), takes care to put the delinquent activity of a minority of working class adolescent boys within the context of working class youth peer group activity in general. We will examine working class youth in terms of activities rather than values. Nevertheless, it is worth listing some major underlying values as a reference point for what follows. These are: anti-authoritarianism; pleasure-seeking ('fun'); a strong sense of territory; masculinity and an admiration of physical strength and skill.

80% of Willmott's sample belonged to peer groups and enjoyed, with their friends, a variety of leisure activities such as dancing, going to parties and motor-bike riding, for instance which did not include their families. Significantly, though, the majority disapproved of gang violence and 'taking and driving', and it would be quite wrong to think of them as delinquents. The kind of things they 'get up to' – playing football (sometimes in the streets), watching football (with an eye to opposition supporters and the police), drinking and going to parties – can easily lead to 'scrapes with the law'. This is not the main point, however, as far as 'the lads' are concerned. Their aim is 'to have fun' and to 'get kicks'. It is mainly in terms of pleasure-seeking, therefore, that we analyse further working class youth culture.

One of the best ways of 'having fun' is to annoy authority. The artful mocking of it is a constant theme in the now vast literature on the activities of working class youth. Teachers, policemen and youth club leaders are the frequent butt of their ridicule and, less often, of their practical jokes. In an observational survey of a group of working class youths, Paul Corrigan found that a large number thought of teachers as 'big-heads'. We saw similar antagonism reported by Hargreaves and Willis (Chapter 5). Social workers and probation officers possibly escape more lightly because they usually work on a one to one basis with 'clients' rather than as obvious representatives of large and dominant institutions such as schools or the police force. At school, fun often takes the form of a rearguard action against being bored. The ultimate resort is to 'bunk off'. In all inner city areas, there are always a few working class 'kids' on the streets or at home during school time. They might be playing football, listening to records or just 'waiting for something to turn up'. In more official jargon, they might be referred to as 'at risk'.

It would be misleading to suggest that working class youth culture is exclusively or even mainly concerned with taking a rise out of authority. Much of it is positively motivated and energetically pursued. Mending, painting and decorating motor-bikes and scooters, playing football and being a football supporter, 'chatting up girls' can all involve great commitment and skill. There are many middle class teenagers relatively deficient in these areas compared with the working class. A minority of working class 'kids' play music and write songs, and many more take an intelligent interest in music, although the research of Murdoch and Phelps suggests that, for the boys, music is largely a matter of background noise or 'aural wallpaper'.

It is obvious that young working class people like spending time together away from adults. Nevertheless, they *are* working class and this shows in their activity. The skinheads of the middle and late nineteen sixties exemplify this point. Like other groups of young lads, no doubt the aggressive and occasionally violent behaviour of the skinheads can be explained in terms of a pursuit of excitement, but John Clarke, in a contribution to the collection of writings, *Resistance through Rituals* (edited by Hall and Jefferson), offers additionally a more thought-provoking explanation. He suggests that the behaviour and style of the skinheads, far from being random and irrational, closely reflects the realities of their lives. He points out that many features of the skinhead style – the short haircut, the wearing of braces over shirts, turning trousers up inches above the ankles, the wearing of cheap, heavy boots – were only slightly exaggerated and dramatised versions of traditional working class dress. Clarke suggests that, by dressing this way, the skinheads were, perhaps unconsciously, reasserting traditional class and community identity. This interpretation gains credibility when we remember that East End working class communities have been damaged and destroyed in the post-war period. Decline in employment opportunities, housing clearance programmes, near-chaos in parts of the Inner London Education Service must have caused disorientation, anger and despair in many lives, not least in those of the young. It is perhaps not surprising –

although deplorable in itself – that the skinheads frequently turned their aggression against immigrants rather than on the investors, developers and planners who were more responsible for their grievances and fears. Clarke, therefore, sees skinhead aggression and violence as largely defensive. He explains their behaviour as 'a symbolic defence of (threatened) territory' and as 'a magical attempt to recover community'.

Sociologists cannot locate all youth sub-culture so convincingly in class context as Clarke does the skinheads. This is partly because the media tends quickly to take up and popularise stylistic and creative sub-cultural aspects. Thus it may be that Punk music and style of dress was originally the product of unemployed, working class youth but, within a few months, the movement was being commercially exploited in the youth market generally. The Punk clothes worth hundreds of pounds, which were advertised in *Vogue* magazine, illustrate the point. In adopting sub-cultural forms, such as Punk music, for mass consumption, the commercial enterprises involved, and the media, both attempt to adapt the product for maximum acceptability and consumption. Thus the attempt to 'devulgarise' the Sex Pistols was rightly seen by the group as an attack on their freedom to produce and perform the material they wanted. When a sub-cultural symbol, like Punk rock music, is commercialised, instead of providing a long-term focus on which the movement can coalesce and identify, the symbol is 'stolen' by the pop industry, reprocessed and presented to a wider audience which does not seriously associate it with the protest and rebellion it may have originally represented. In contrast to the Punks, the skinheads did not produce anything saleable on the mass market, although some London and fashionable provincial boutiques attempted to market skinhead style clothes.

As well as providing ideas for the pop industry and media, youth sub-cultures also borrow freely from them and from other sources. The Teddy Boys of the nineteen fifties combined features of the style of London upper-class 'toffs' and American 'movie' gangsters to produce their own distinctive, swashbuckling, rather status-conscious style.

Underlying the above rituals is the desire to assert masculinity, often in a physical way. This is not exclusive to the working class, but it is chiefly in manual labour that working people have expressed themselves and physical toughness is particularly respected among them.

In the hard world of working class youth sub-cultures, the position of the female is very much that of pillion-passenger. Motor-bike 'burn-ups' and gang fights (real or mock) are forms of display, and all the better if girls are there to observe closely. As a *Sunday Times* newspaper analysis of a gang fight wryly states: 'excitement is heightened if police, press, TV – and girls – are in attendance'. The women's movement has, as yet, made few inroads into working class youth gender relations. It would be a mistake, however, to see the girls as mere status symbols and prizes in the social game-playing of the boys: the female peer-group has a distinct and important existence within the larger teenage peer group itself. Girls share much leisure activity. They are more likely than the boys to know details of the top twenty, to read teenage magazines, and to be familiar with the latest dance routines – which they perform, usually in protective togetherness, at discos. 'Going steady' is what detaches working class girls from the sex-based peer-group. If they can, they tend to marry early and their career aspirations, if any, are low. We reviewed these matters in our chapter on gender.

Working class youth sub-cultures are not usually consciously political. Nevertheless, when an issue affects their own interest closely, working class youth sometimes respond in a more or less political way. Two such issues are race and unemployment. Occasional clashes between groups of white and black youths have been a feature of urban life in this country since the nineteen fifties. A minority of white working class youths have reacted to what they see as the black 'alien' presence in or near their own communities with hostility and aggression. A number associated themselves openly with the fascist movement which underwent a revival in the late nineteen seventies. We examine the response of black youth to this in a separate section. In the late nineteen seventies and early eighties, unemployment was experienced by increasing numbers of young people, black and white. More and more sixteen year olds left school for their first year of 'non-work'. 'Dole-queue rock' – full of strident protest and youthful disillusion – was one response. What the long term result of large scale youth unemployment will be, is a matter for speculation. No doubt some public figures hope that competition for jobs will force young people to conform and 'smarten up'. What seems more likely to

develop among the unemployed is apathy and, among the employed, a determination to hang on to the jobs they have,
whether they like them or not. There is also the possibility that
this situation will prove fertile soil for the development of radical feeling among the young.

Two important groups of working class young people have
received little attention so far. We may term these the 'respect-
ables' and the 'real delinquents'. About one fifth of Wilmott's
sample were ambitious to leave the East End and, if possible,
obtain non-manual jobs. In addition to these, the majority of
the rest had satisfactory relations with their families and, to a
lesser extent, with their teachers. Only a hard core of about
10% were 'delinquent'. We study these in Chapter 18. They
are an interesting group and you may wish to read the relevant
section of that chapter now.

Middle Class Youth Culture and Sub-Cultures

Most middle class young people, like most working class people,
more or less conform. They do not, however, conform to the
same way of life. After all, they come from different backgrounds. A young middle class person of sixteen is much more
likely to receive further formal education than his working class
counterpart, and this is even more true of young males, than of
females. Homework takes up much of the time of young middle
class people. Even if they had the inclination, they would seldom have the opportunity to 'mess about' on the streets of
their neighbourhood. Research by Murdoch and Phelps, on the
other hand, shows that by no means all middle class teenagers
spend most of their out-of-school time doing homework. In
addition to the more academic ones, Murdoch and Phelps
observed a group of young, middle class males who, as well as
doing their academic work adequately, found time to pursue an
interest in 'progressive' pop music. Their taste was much more
likely than that of working class youth to include some folk and
pop music protest songs.

We will defer until a later chapter our consideration of
delinquency among middle class youth and concentrate here on
pleasure seeking and political sub-cultural activity. Their pleasure seeking is rather different from that of working class youth.
It needs to be understood in the context of higher education
because it often occurs on or near college or university cam-

puses. These campuses, particularly the residential ones, concentrate students, relatively free from financial worries, in a cloistered and tolerant situation. In Kenneth Kenniston's phrase, they are allowed a 'period of extended youth' which enables them to experiment with, and test, various values, attitudes and life-styles, as well as to acquire advanced formal education and training. Kenniston refers to this further as 'youth as a stage of life' which, for some, can continue into their late twenties. During these years, a minority of students sometimes adopt life-styles which may involve certain modes of dress, drug-taking, 'getting into' music, a free attitude to relationships and other behaviour foreign to the majority of the population.

We will examine a study by Jock Young of psychedelic drug-taking as an example of a mainly middle class youth sub-cultural form of activity. Of course, from a legal point of view, such activity is delinquent. Here, however, we are viewing it from the perspective of those involved, who see it as a way of acquiring desired experience. Over the years, members of such groups have been described as 'bohemians', 'beatniks' (or just 'beats'), 'hippies', or simply 'student-types'. We will tend to use the term *bohemian* for general reference. Following Matza, Young describes the pleasure-seeking, bohemian lifestyle in terms of *subterranean values*, although he is careful to point out that the use of psychedelic drugs is only one aspect of this way of life. Other subterranean values are short-term hedonism, spontaneity, excitement, and dislike of conventionally organised work. These contrast with *formal* values such as deferred gratification, planning future action, predictability and acceptance of productive work as virtuous. Broadly, subterranean values are concerned with pleasure and self-fulfilment for its own sake, and formal values with work and the necessary control that goes with it. Herbert Marcuse has seen the same contrast between subterranean values and formal work values in Freud's pleasure and reality principles. He expresses this as follows:

Pleasure Principle Values	Reality Principle Values
Immediate Satisfaction	Delayed Satisfaction
Pleasure	Restraint of Pleasure
Joy (play)	Toil (work)
Receptiveness (to pleasurable stimuli and experience)	Productiveness (in work)
Absence of Repression	Security (in return for self-repression/control)

Source: Herbert Marcuse, *Eros and Civilisation*, 1956, p. 12.

We will not argue the merits of the pleasure and reality principles here, but simply note that the former rules in the bohemian world, and the latter in the world of organised work.

Bohemians sometimes take psychedelic drugs, such as cannabis and LSD, because they believe that these improve their moods, and even enhance their perception of the world. Cannabis is a relatively mild psychedelic and is taken for its relaxing 'mellowing' effect. LSD is stronger, and some claim that under its influence new insights may be realised and joyful and profound states of awareness achieved. We must add that *any* psychedelic drug may also produce the opposite effect, especially amongst inexperienced or 'naive' users. Young suggests, however, that experienced users can often exercise considerable control over the effects of psychedelics, and the drug then becomes part of the whole way of life of the sub-culture rather than its main dominating influence. Psychedelic drug-taking may fit in with the kind of music, literature, leisure style and even personal relations preferred by the group. To get a 'feel' for bohemian sub-culture, it is best to read the novels of, say, the American 'beat' of the fifties, Jack Kerouac, or to listen to the 'sixties' music of the Grateful Dead or Jefferson Airplane. Of course, these artists belong to different 'moments' in the history of 'bohemia', but they are, nevertheless, part of the same broad tradition.

In general, political opinion amongst the young, including students, presents similar aspects to that of the rest of the population. Family and class are better indicators of a young person's political views than age. Two minor qualifications must be made to this. First, young people in Britain are somewhat more likely to prefer the Labour Party than other age groups, particularly the very old. This is usually attributed less

375

to youthful radical idealism and more to the fact that post-war generations have been socialised in a period when the Labour Party has been well established: for pre-war generations it was less a 'natural' alternative. Secondly, radical, usually socialist or communist groups, do attract a small minority of students. Others may join in when important issues, such as the Vietnam War, arouse their concern. As we shall see in the next section, however, neither the political nor the pleasure-seeking activities of a privileged minority of middle class young are likely, in themselves, to 'change the world'.

Middle Class Youth, 'Generational Consciousness' and Change

The idea that a new 'consciousness' or awareness was developing amongst the young was generated largely by the student movements of the nineteen sixties, and already it seems conceptually inadequate and dated. Young prophets of change advocated a heady mixture of bohemian alternative life-style and political idealism, as a recipe for improving what they saw as a corrupt world. Ironically, the notion of an alternative consciousness reached the height of popularity in such books as Charles Reich's *The Greening of America* and Theodore Roszac's *The Making of a Counterculture* when most of the student movements, including those in the United States, were in decline. The stated values underlying the 'new consciousness' were commitment to openness in interpersonal communication, and a willingness to share emotional, spiritual and physical experience generously. 'Ours is the radicalism of love', said a female student activist, in a phrase which sums up the idealistic aspirations of the movement. Charles Reich, in particular, argued that these values were beginning to dominate over the more conformist, work-based values of mainstream society – especially amongst the young. The 'pop' media, especially progressive music and underground newspapers, were the means by which the new values were disseminated. As well as citing the growth of youth 'pop' culture to support his case, Reich adduced the spread of the commune 'alternative society' movement and the emergence of less inhibited life-styles. This was to make great claims on the basis of slight empirical evidence, and sweeping conceptualisation. More measured analysis of the youth culture of the nineteenth sixties established that the 'new consciousness' existed almost exclusively amongst middle class youth, generally in higher education. Only the young in universities and colleges had the education and the time to reflect critically on American society at a period when racial tension and the Vietnam war provided serious cause for concern. But to move from disillusionment with American society to founding an 'alternative society' was a large step. In fact, few went so far as to set up new communes or to join existing ones, although several hundred of them, reflecting many different beliefs and values, mushroomed in the late nineteen sixties. Some failed rapidly although others have continued to exist. For most of the young, the 'new society' amounted to no more than a liberalisation of opinions and behaviour which manifested itself in style of dress, patterns of music-listening and reading, and a more open attitude to human relationships.

A survey by *Fortune* Magazine in 1969 showed, however, that a *large* minority of students identified to some degree with the progressive attitudes and behaviour associated with the 'New Left', a term which broadly covered the youthful cultural and political radicalism of the period. But, like the books which eulogised this new radicalism, the survey reflected a movement at its height and not, as the editors of *Fortune* thought, the beginning of a new, potentially dominant trend.

In retrospect, it is obvious that the middle class, frequently liberal and permissive background of the young radicals, and their privileged educational experience and leisure opportunities, deeply influenced the nature of the student movement. To speak of a 'generation in revolt' and of 'generational consciousness' on the basis of the behaviour of this limited group – as many contemporary commentators did – was to disregard the majority of youth who were at work or unemployed. These young people did not have then, any more than they have now, the opportunity to experience a 'stage of life' in which personal and intellectual development is a priority nor, as we shall see, do they share common cultural pursuits with those who do.

It would be a mistake to dismiss the bohemian life-style and political idealism of some middle class young as irrelevant self-indulgence. In a period of rapid technological and socio-economic change, they have more time and leisure than most to make sense of what is happening. Most importantly, they can contribute to the way change is interpreted and perhaps controlled in moral and human terms. This brings us back to the issue of the social effects of the new technology, and particularly its influence on the relationship between work and leisure (see Chapter 16). The ideal of a freer and more fulfilling society is as much that of Marx as that of youthful radicals. The difference is that he argued that the exploited and deprived, rather than the privileged, should be both the prime creators and the beneficiaries of such a society. Certainly, those that have borne the hardest burden of labour have as much right to enjoy such a society as those who have not.

Black Youth

Although most black youths are working class as measured by parental occupation, it is not appropriate to treat them exclusively under the heading of working class youth because of the importance of racial and cultural (ethnic) factors. As we saw in Chapter 13, the same argument applies to black adults. All young people have the problem of forging a workable identity, but for black youth it is particularly acute. They are presented with two potentially conflicting adult models. First is that of the British citizen, sharing equal rights and duties with whites: second is that of the black person, visibly distinct and with a cultural heritage that goes back to, say, the Punjab, Nigeria, Barbados or Hong Kong. Achieving a workable balance between these identities is possible but often difficult. There are two major reasons for this. Firstly, as we have just mentioned, it is bound to be difficult to bring into focus two separate national, historical identities. Secondly, the problem is made much worse by the experience of *prejudice* or *rejection*, since self-identity partly depends on what others think of you. Black immigrants and their children cannot avoid seeing themselves in the mirror of white people's eyes. What they often see there is suspicion and resentment, if not downright repugnance and hatred. (We studied this more empirically in Chapter 13.) The cultural life of immigrant groups, and particularly of the young, cannot be properly understood without bearing in mind the hurt and anger that racism can provoke. Equally, it must be remembered that Britain's minorities, including second and third generation 'immigrants' are proud of, and attached to, their ethnic cultural heritage. This is obvious in many ways such as literature, language, dress, food, religion, family tradition and so on. The phrase 'black is beautiful' captures both the pride and defensive self-assertion that has notably characterised ethnic groups in America and Britain since the nineteen sixties.

We will take West Indian youth sub-culture for more detailed analysis here. Love of music, religion and a liking for street based social activity are well known aspects of West Indian culture. Unemployment, or irregular employment, is also part of the familiar background of life, and young blacks, both here and in the Caribbean, are accustomed to dealing with it. The West Indian hustler in Britain has his parallel in the Jamaican 'rude boy' or 'rudie'. Rudies cope with the indifference of the job market by 'hustling' a living out of dealing in drugs, gambling, pimping or stealing. As a last resort, some may 'play the welfare system', but they have little taste for the bureaucratic 'hassle' this can involve. Often they live in some style, sporting smart cars and well-cut clothes with an easy air. Not altogether surprisingly, some 'rudies' prefer this life-style to the lower-level manual work that might occasionally be offered them. Still, we must be careful not to suggest that the 'rudie' is the typical figure of West Indian youth sub-culture. Many young blacks look hard for work and are demoralised and embittered if they do not find it. We simply do not have the empirical data available to say what is typical. All that we are doing here is describing some options available to West Indian youth.

The cool, worldly image of the rudie contrasts sharply with the religious fervour of another major West Indian youth sub-cultural figure, the Rastafarian. The 'Rasta' movement illustrates the defensive, retreatist trend which is an almost inevitable part of the cultural tradition of a group actually or potentially oppressed. Rastafarians trace their spiritual roots back to Africa: their plaited hair and, sometimes, their dress styles imitate African originals. They believe that the late Emperor Haile Selassie of Ethiopia will be reincarnated and will lead them out of 'Babylon' – a biblical reference to capitalistic society. From Kingston to Brixton, Reggae is the music of Rastafarianism. Reggae lyrics are heavy with biblical references, and the music's slow, moody rhythms reflect the influence of the 'sacred' drug, ganja (a type of marijuana).

379

Political movements are rarer than cultural ones among black youth; yet the politics of race, however simply they may be conceived, can hardly fail to be part of every young black person's consciousness. To be black in Britain is to risk prejudice and discrimination. That experience, or the possibility of it, unites black youth – rudies, Rastas and just boys and girls on the street – in a defensive awareness that can be broadly termed political. A single issue can suddenly kindle smouldering resentment into active hostility. In a time of rising unemployment among black youth, that possibility seems likely to be with us for a long while to come.

Is There a Generation Gap?

When discussing the question of whether there is a *generation gap*, the sociologist is frequently left with the feeling of grasping at empty air. All the detailed empirical evidence points to the conclusion that there is no wide gap between the generations. Yet, when talking to adolescents about this issue, one senses their mild discontent and feelings of being misunderstood by adults – even though they may be unable to cite substantial grievances. Similarly, adults are often inconsistent in their comments on 'the young', either over-praising or over-criticising. Such attitudes may mask uncertainty, and even insecurity, in relation to 'the coming generation'. After reviewing evidence about generational attitudes and behaviour, we will make an attempt to explain this latent antagonism in social structural terms.

We have already stated that a number of relatively small scale surveys stress that most young people, of whatever class, are fairly conformist and get on quite well with their parents. A well known larger survey confirms this. The National Children's Bureau conducted a survey of more than 13,000 sixteen year olds, in 1974. These teenagers were all those still able to be contacted who were born in a single week of March, 1958. Questions were asked on a wide variety of aspects of behaviour and attitude, but sex and drugs were excluded as topics, because answers were considered likely to be evasive. On questions relating to marriage and the family, teenagers emerged as thoroughly traditional. Only 3% rejected the idea of marriage and most wanted to have children. Four out of five respondents said that they got on well with both their parents. The main areas of conflict with them were over dress and hair, although in only 11% of homes was this a frequent source of friction. Stylistic conformity is a sign of peer group identification and some tension with parents might be expected in this area. Research carried out by Michael Schofield on the sexual behaviour of young people confirms the overall picture of relative conformity on the part of adolescents. Most young people associate sexual intimacy with personal, emotional involvement and do not regard sexual pleasure as an end in itself. Although Schofield's evidence and that of others shows a tendency for more young people to be willing to consider sex before marriage, this is in line with the growth of permissive values in society generally.

Another large scale social survey published by the National Opinion Polls (NOP) in 1978 confirms the broadly conformist pattern revealed by the NCB data. 66% of a sample of young people between the ages of 15 and 21 cited one or both parents as the most influential person, or persons, in their lives. Although listening to pop music was the most frequent non-energetic pastime for 85% of those questioned, pop musicians had fallen from favour compared with 1967, when NOP had conducted a similar survey.

There is no evidence that illicit drug taking, except drinking alcohol in pubs, is widespread among teenagers, although within specific sub-cultures certain drugs are sometimes used. It is arguable that this is a more intelligent, if still potentially dangerous, use of drugs than that of many adults who become, to varying degrees, dependent on medically prescribed drugs in order to 'cope with life'. In the nineteen seventies alcohol related offences, including drinking and driving offences, have increased among teenagers of both sexes; yet the flouting of the law prohibiting the drinking of alcohol in public places by those under 18 is widely tolerated by many sections of the community. It may be more useful to ask why this adult/teenage 'conspiracy' to ignore the law exists than simply to condemn those teenagers who drink while under age.

The suggestion that young people tend to be politically radical usually refers to the age group two or three years older than that surveyed by the National Children's Bureau – and even then it refers only to those within higher education. In fact, class and family correlate far more reliably with political identity than does youth, which provides no basis of prediction whatsoever.

Young people differ from adults to some extent in personal style and leisure pursuits, but tend to have similar attitudes of acceptance towards the family, marriage, and the social and political order. It is not surprising, then, as Smith points out in his book on adolescence, that most young people are ultimately successfully socialised into adulthood in the areas of work, family and citizenship. In a sense, Smith sees the problems that accompany adjustment to adult roles as adolescent 'teething pains'. This, is however, rather an *adult-biased* view. From the point of view of the young, perhaps an essential aspect of their experience is a sense of *powerlessness*. Weber has emphasised that power is a major aspect of stratification. Young people notably lack it – at school, at work and in the family. It is true that positions of power and authority exist within the 'alternative' world of the peer group, but this may not compensate for powerlessness in the 'real' adult-controlled world. Support for this interpretation comes from the National Children's Bureau survey. Far more resentment of school and teachers was expressed than of family and parents. 11% thought school was largely a waste of time; 15% said they never took school work seriously; 29% said they did not like school (a further 14% were unsure), and 54% found homework boring. Although some of this discontent may have been due to resentment at the raising of the school leaving age to 16, which this group of teenagers were the first to experience, a wider explanation is required.

The answer may lie in that being educated in modern society also requires being organised in terms of the allocation of group (academic and pastoral) membership, which classrooms a pupil is expected to be in, and the structuring of rest-break time. All this is done to achieve prescribed goals, notably examination success, which pupils may regard as necessary but often find irksome to pursue. In contemporary secondary schools, it is not so much resentment at traditional discipline but alienation at being a small part in predetermined and often impersonal organisation that may be the cause of pupil disillusionment and restlessness. Eagerness to earn money may be seen partly as a compensatory wish for independence.

Structural conflict between the young and adults occurs in other situations: with the police, for instance, who are required to enforce a large body of legislation restricting the activities of young people who, in the absence of family commitments, are precisely that group in society which has the leisure time to pursue many courses of behaviour, some of which are destructive. The family, too, is sometimes the focus of generational power struggle even when, as in many homes, family relationships are basically happy and reassuring. Conflict over such matters as personal style, pocket money or when to be back after an evening out, can cause tension in the home which in some instances can become chronic. Particularly unpleasant atmospheres can be created when parents use the financial dependency of a teenage son or daughter as a means of securing conformity.

Survey evidence on the attitudes of young people can be misleading. Frankly, one would not expect teenagers to have radically different attitudes from adults about politics, sex, and so on. But in terms of their everyday lives they are constantly in a position of subordination and, consequently, of low status. To explain the resulting friction as part of the syndrome of problematic adolescent behaviour smacks of psychological determinism and ignores real social structural tension and conflict.

In addition, the impact of various youth sub-cultures on the adult world should not be underestimated as a source of intergenerational tension. These sub-cultures, as presented by the media, are often seen by adults as representative of the young in general. Indeed, many young people not involved in them directly nonetheless pick up their fashions, language, attitudes and behaviour. Whereas youth often views such groups as the hippies, mods and punks with an eye to imitation, adults, especially parents, tend to regard them with strained tolerance, if not downright unease. Parents know that such sub-cultures provide models that may cause their children to stray from conformity into political protest, delinquency or bohemianism. In some ways, the straight and narrow road from youth to adulthood is the least interesting. It is not surprising, therefore, that a large minority occasionally deviate onto more adventurous and dangerous terrain. In doing so, some lose their way, but others acquire knowledge and experience that may be both personally valuable and of use to society.

Old Age, Population and Social Policy

We introduced the basic principles of demography in Chapter 7 pp. 157–8. That discussion provides a useful basis for understanding the position of the old in society. So far in this century, there has been a steady increase in the number of old people, both absolutely, and as a percentage of the total population. In 1901, the number of men over 65, and women over 60, was 2.4 million, and in 1976 it was 9.6 million. The figures, as a percentage of the total population, are 6% and 17% respectively. For a variety of reasons, mainly relating to the birth rate at particular times, this trend is not likely to continue much beyond the end of the nineteen seventies – but it will not go substantially into reverse, either. As a result, the working population must expect to have to maintain, for the foreseeable future, a largely dependent retired population of upwards of 15% of the total population. Within this group, it is projected that the very old, those aged 75 or over, will grow as a total percentage of the retired. For instance, the number of 85 year olds is expected to increase by 50%, up until 1995, to 700,000.

It is not surprising that concern for the elderly tends to be intermingled with an uncomfortable awareness of cost: care of the very elderly is the most costly. Inevitably, the old have been allocated a growing proportion of public expenditure, despite the claims of other needy groups. Yet the standard of living of pensioners, as a group, has declined relative to the rest of the population. Nicholas Bosanquet gives impressive evidence of this in his book, *A Future for Old Age.* As real incomes rise, people tend to spend more on transport, services and leisure, and less on food, shelter and heating. More is also spent acquiring cars and certain other consumer durables. Apart from a minority of old people who do have quite a high standard of living, the expenditure patterns of the elderly do not reflect these changes. In fact, they are much as they were twenty years ago. A proportion of 43.4% of income is spent on food, housing and heat by all households, whereas married pensioner couples spend 52.8% of their income on these three necessities, and single women pensioners 60.3%. Bosanquet gives a detailed picture of the relative poverty suffered by the old which reflects this basic inequality.

The economic situation of the old suggests the low social status they have in our society. Yet, contrary to the still popular myth, the British are not flagrantly neglectful of their elderly. Surveys by Townsend and others show that the majority of them are actively involved with relatives and friends: even among the bedridden, over half are looked after outside hospitals. In fact, only 5% of all old people are in residential institutions – about the same figure as in the early 1900's. Arguably, however, this is not the most telling statistic. An Age Concern survey of old people outside institutions found 38% living with just a spouse and 28% living with others. The fact that over 70% do not live with their children reflects the dominance of the nuclear family. In practice, this means that many old people are often lonely, even if they are seldom genuinely neglected.

Yet, in addition to relationships, and activity based on the family, old people, like other age groups, seem to prefer the company of their own generation. Many churches have old age pensioner clubs or other associations or activities, such as whist evenings, 'suitable' for old people. Most local political clubs and working men's clubs make similar provisions. Small groups of old people appear to meet frequently and informally at times of day when most of the rest of the population are at work. Old women are preponderant in these groups since women outlive men, on average, by about five years. In the post-75 year old population, the proportion of women to men is about 2 to 1. In addition, women are able to retire on a state pension at 60, whereas men work to 65. Amongst these facts is, perhaps, the basis of a case for an old men's liberation movement.

It is, perhaps, because modern societies value work so highly that the retired population suffers in status. Traditionally, a person's social identity has been derived mainly from his work and, implicitly, the old often seem to be regarded primarily as 'spent' workers. It is possible that if, as a result of unemployment, enforced leisure increases further, assumptions about the relationship between work and leisure and their relative value will change – and the status of worker, non-worker and past worker will change with them. These changes would, in turn, depend on the continuing substitution of machine labour for human labour, not only in the production of goods but also of services. Possibly, the working positions of the old and other

385

generations will not be so different if more people experience periods of non-work, enjoy even shorter working weeks and generally perhaps come to regard work less and less as the centre of their lives.

It is debatable, however, whether even a change in cultural attitudes of this kind would mean that 'the wisdom of the aged' would be more appreciated in contemporary society. By contrast, the old of 30 or 40 years hence will all have experienced mass education and will have been brought up in a technological society. Margaret Mead's statement, that in a post-figurative or fast-changing, future-oriented society, the knowledge and skills of the old become quickly dated, may no longer apply so forcibly to the old of 2000. All this is speculative and, for the present, the immediate issue is to help the elderly to deal with their material and human problems without patronising them, or seeming to regard them as a 'problem' in themselves. Christopher Lasch has suggested that the tendency of America to regard old age as a 'problem' reflects the selfish *individualism* or *narcissism*, as he calls it, of American society. We can entertain the same possibility of Britain. Lasch argues that the decline of belief in an after life and the identification of youth with beauty and success makes us dread old age. We push the thought of it to the back of our minds, just as we push old people into the sidings of society. When we do confront it, we often try to explain it away. Some pretend old age is exclusively a social category when clearly it has its roots in biological decline; others try to arrest the biological process itself by pills, potions or jogging. The refusal to face old age is a refusal to come to terms with our own mortality. Lasch, a radical and severe critic of American culture, offers no easy solution to what amounts to a national neurosis about old age. He insists that nothing but a re-ordering of work, education, the family and other major institutions will bring the old out of their redundancy and isolation back into the mainstream of society. For this to happen, we would need to believe that it is valuable for the old to be involved with us, and we with them. This would have to include a willingness to face with them the problem that ultimately comes to all – our own deaths.

Conclusion: Perspectives on Old Age

A variety of perspectives illuminate old age, as they do other age stages. Here we will briefly examine insights from comparative and historical perspective, interactionist and Marxist perspective. This should help both in interpreting and summarising the previous and other sections on old age in this book. One of the main advantages of the comparative perspective is that it can indicate what is a universal social fact and what is subject to cultural variation. Cowgill and Holmes found a number of *universals* and *variations* in their wide survey of old age. Among the universals are that old age is a separate social category in all societies; that some old people always continue to act as political, judicial and civil leaders; and that mutual responsibility between the old and their adult children exists. Among the important variations between primitive and modern societies are that in the former, the old tend to have higher status, more power, and do not retire merely because they are old. Historical perspective helps to explain why the old in modern society have become comparatively marginalised. One factor was the policy of removing the old from paid work. Another was the way the old have become targeted as a client group for practice (and profit) by professions such as medicine and social work – interestingly explored in Carole Haber's *Beyond Sixty-five: the Dilemma of Old Age in America's Past.*

Ageism is to view someone pejoratively merely because they are old. Like sexism and racism it is easy to be unconsciously ageist. Concepts such as stigma and stereotype are of obvious application in understanding ageist interactions. More broadly, as Christopher Lasch points out, to regard 'the old' as a problem group is itself implicitly ageist. Interestingly, a Harris poll on the so-called problem of old age, found that on every count the general public had a grimmer view of the problems of the old than did the old themselves (USA, 1975).

As its title suggests, Chris Phillipson's *Capitalism and the Construction of Old Age* supports Marxist analysis with insight from phenomenology. Phillipson argues that Capitalism 'is irreconcilable with meeting the needs of elderly people' – largely because as non-producers, they are marginal to its needs. He further contends that the old are particularly vulnerable to government cuts during economic recessions. Phillipson published well before the announcement in 1985 of the government's intention radically to cut back the State Earnings Related Pensions Scheme (Serps) and encourage private and occupational pensions. Whatever the eventual results for the old, this policy does seem as much a matter of financial economy as of social policy.

Guide to Further Reading and Study

My *Age and Generation* (Tavistock, 1985) covers the full life-cycle with the emphasis on youth and, to a lesser extent, old age. On childhood, P. Ariès *Centuries of Childhood* (Jonathan Cape, 1962) is a standard work. Simon Frith's *The Sociology of Youth* (Causeway Press, 1984) offers a general coverage of that age group. Mike Brake's *The Sociology of Youth Culture and Youth Subcultures* (Routledge and Kegan Paul, 1980) is comprehensive but demanding. Stuart Hall and Tony Jefferson's *Resistance through Rituals* (Hutchinson, 1976) remains a seminal collection of readings on youth subcultures from a Marxist phenomenological perspective. Dick Hebdige's *Subculture: the Meaning of Style* (Methuen, 1979) uses semiology effectively and covers the subcultural ground to the punks. Anything written on football hooliganism prior to 1984 now seems to have been overtaken by the scale and horror of events. However, P. Marsh, 'Life and Careers on Soccer Terraces' in R. Ingham *ed., Football Hooliganism* (Interaction Imprint, 1978) genuinely decodes the 'lads' behaviour. John Williams' 'In Search of the Hooligan Solution', *Social Studies Review*, Vol. 1 No. 2, considers more recent events.

D. Freeman's critique of Margaret Mead's work on Samoan adolescent girls raises major methodological and substantive issues: M. Mead, *Coming of Age in Samoa: A Study of Adolescence and Sex in Primitive Societies* (Penguin, 1971) and D. Freeman, *Margaret Mead and Samoa: The Making and Unmaking of an Anthropological Myth* (Harvard University Press, 1983, paperback).

M. Hepworth and M. Featherstone's *Surviving Middle Age* (Blackwell, 1982) and Chris Phillipson's *Capitalism and the Construction of Old Age* (Macmillan, 1982) are recommended.

The scope for using a variety of materials and research methods in this topic is considerable. These include content analysis of youth subculture via magazines, records and cassettes and a study of media stereotypes of any age stages.

Past Questions

1 *Either* (a) 'In many primitive societies age is institutionalised on the basis of authority; in modern UK society it is institutionalised on the basis of dependency.' Explain and discuss. (Abrams: *Work, Urbanisation and Inequality, UK Society Today*.) or (b) Explain and discuss the argument that youth represents a class or stratum with interests of its own in opposition to those of adults. (AEB, 1982)
2 'The twentieth century is the century of the child.' Explain and discuss (AEB, 1983)
3 Being 'old' or 'young' is not simply a matter of age, but also of role. How would you explain the differences in status given to the role *either* of the elderly *or* of youth in at least two different types of society? (London, 1984)
4 'We live in a child-centred society, yet relations between parents and children are weaker than ever before.' Discuss. (OLE, 1985) (See also Chapter 4 for material.)
5 Why do societies differ in the social significance they attach to age differentials? (London, 1984)

Section D **Work, Organisations and Alienation**

How to Use this Section

The pairing together of the themes Work, Leisure and Organisations is common enough not to require extended explanation. It is important, though to relate these matters to others of central concern. Above all, work and organisations are to be linked with stratification. Indeed, in an earlier draft of this book these two chapters were part of what was envisaged as a large central section on stratification: they are now separated out of convenience rather than theoretical conviction.

Whatever definition of class is accepted there is no doubt that work greatly affects it. Industrial conflict is a major dimension of class conflict and alienation at work is regarded by Marxists as a product of the capitalist division of labour. That there is a relationship between work and cultural and leisure activity will already be obvious to readers and this is examined in more detail in Chapter 15. It is only recently that organisational analysis has been rigorously related to stratification – yet to make this link is vital. Organisations are the practical, day-to-day context in which class and, for that matter, gender and racial inequality, are expressed and regenerated. Of course, organisations must be understood partly in terms of the useful functions they perform but they must also be seen as systems of power and potential conflict which benefit some more than others.

15 Work and Non-Work

391

Themes and Definitions

This chapter covers three major themes. It deals with the quality of people's *experience of work*, whether satisfying or otherwise. Secondly, it discusses *how working people organise themselves at work to pursue, mainly, better pay and conditions*. Finally, it examines *the relationship between work and non-work* and, in particular, how automation may be revolutionising our ideas about the normal and proper nature of that relationship. We look in detail at the *organisational structure* of work in the following chapter. It is enough to say here that the organisations people work in – factories, offices and farms – are by far the most important public institutions that affect their lives. Socialisation at work has an immense influence on values, attitudes and behaviour.

In addition to the above themes, we begin by again stressing the relationship of work to class. Stratification (the major social divisions) was the central theme of Section C, and class is the major example of it. Work and class are inseparable: the one produces the other (though this statement does not do full justice to the Marxist definition of class).

The Experience of Work

Broadly, there are three possible responses to work: *alienation, neutrality* and *satisfaction*, and we study these below. Beyond mere satisfaction lies the prospect of *genuine fulfilment* at work and we also consider what this might mean.

1 Alienation

It may seem unduly negative to begin our analysis of the experience of work with alienation but most sociologists seem agreed that work is not a very fulfilling experience for the majority. Mary Weir's remarks are representative in this respect:

> For millions of people work is the least rewarding aspect of life. The hours spent at the work bench or in the office are more likely to be hours of endurance than enjoyment, when people do jobs which provide few opportunities to use their skills and abilities. A sense of personal satisfaction and achievement is more likely to be associated with their lives outside work than within it.

Perhaps the central problem of work in this century is not physical exploitation but the sense of personal uselessness and meaninglessness produced by routine, repetitive work.

Marx and Weber
Two accounts of alienation must be distinguished. First is that of Marx: *he considered that workers in capitalist society are alienated from work because they own neither what they produce nor the means by which they produce it.*

393

He is quite clear about this:

> Finally, the alienated character of work for the worker appears in the fact that it is not his work but work for someone else, that in work he does not belong to himself but to another person.

A further aspect of alienation is apparent in the quotation. Because of the need to sell his labour, the worker loses his independence in work; he becomes alienated from his own activity and thus from himself. The contemporary Marxists, Bowles and Gintis, have attempted to relate the nature of the division of labour in capitalist society to the need of the ruling class to maintain control over the workforce. By daily repeating the same limited task(s), workers are prevented from understanding the whole of the process of production. What they do not understand they can hardly aspire to control. Bowles and Gintis do not, of course, regard the capitalist mode of production and the resultant alienation and mystification of the workforce as inevitable.

A second definition of alienation is widely used. To understand it we must first briefly describe what *bureaucracy* is. *Bureaucracy is a form of organisational structure characterised by a variety of roles, some of which have more authority and status than others.* Nearly all large-scale organisations in modern societies are organised in this way and we are so familiar with this form of organisational structure that we tend to think (wrongly) that it is the only type possible (for alternatives see the next chapter). This approach to understanding alienation rests on the work of Weber, although he himself seldom used the term. In this definition, *alienation is seen as caused by the effect on the work situation of the bureaucratic division of labour.* Weber considered that working particularly at the lower levels of bureaucracy, such as in a factory or an office, is alienating for two basic reasons. Firstly, doing the same thing over and over again, say, filing invoices, is boring to most people. Secondly, bureaucratic employees have little control over their work situation, and this is unsatisfying. Woodward, Touraine and Blauner have applied Weberian-type analysis specifically to industrial work and we examine their conclusions below. Weber himself was probably the first sociologist to appreciate that lack of identity, control and a sense of meaninglessness, in short, alienation, can equally affect the clerk, the typist, the soldier or anyone who fulfils a small role in a large, bureaucratic organisation. He stressed that alienation can occur as easily in state bureaucracies as in privately owned ones. Indeed, he anticipated that alienation would be a particular problem in socialist societies because of their inevitably (in his view) bureaucratic nature.

Despite the above major differences, Marx and Weber described the *psychological consequences of alienation* very similarly. The phrase 'feelings of alienation' refers to the same human experience for both. Writing of the industrial labourer, Marx says:

> He does not fulfil himself in his work but denies himself, has a feeling a misery, not of well-being, does not develop freely a physical and mental energy, but is physically exhausted and mentally debased.[7]

Etzioni summarises Weber's view and, usefully, links it with that of Marx:

> ... the worker, soldier, and researcher – and by implication all employees of all organisations – are frustrated, unhappy ... When asked, 'all said and done, how satisfied are you with your work?' about 80% of American blue-collar workers answered 'not satisfied'. Alienation is a concept that stands for this sentiment and the analysis of its source in Marxian-Weberian terms.

Despite their common understanding of what it means 'to feel alienated', Marx and Weber's difference over the origin of alienation is highly significant. Differing diagnoses lead to differing prescriptions. For Marx, the ultimate solution to inequality and alienation at work is to abolish capitalism and establish a communist system in which the means of production and what is produced are the common property. What is produced is then distributed on the basis of need, not purchasing power. This is a road down which Weber had no wish to travel – as we have noted, he anticipated that, whatever the theoretical ideal, communist societies would be very bureaucratic. He offered no solution to bureaucratic alienation, but regarded the march of 'rationality' as inevitable in all modern societies whether capitalist or socialist. He saw practical advantages in bureaucracy but feared its potential to alienate. Perhaps this accounts for the occasional pessimism and faint sense of regret for more romantic and less 'rational' times past in Weber's work.

Blauner, Touraine, Woodward and their Critics

About the early nineteen sixties, a succession of books appeared which examined *the relationship between technology and work satisfaction*. Notable among these were works by Touraine, Blauner and Woodward. The findings they presented were very much in accord. The French sociologist, Touraine, summarised three recent historical stages in production technology and worker involvement: flexible machines/craftworkers; standard machines/unskilled workers; automation/superintendents. He associated the first and third of these with relatively higher levels of satisfaction. Blauner's typology is similar though slightly more complex.

Technology and Alienation

Type of Work →	Craft	Machine Minding ↓	Assembly Line ↓	Process ↓
Type of Production/ Product	No → Standarised Product	Mechanisation and standard- isation	Rationalisat- ion Standardised Product	Rationalisat- ion Uniform Product
Level of Skill	→ High	Low	Low	Responsibility & understand- ing needed
Level of Alienation	→ Low	High	Highest	Low

Blauner's model is virtually self-explanatory. Machine-minding is usually required in *batch* production which is technically less efficient than assembly line *mass* production, but usually involves the worker in a slightly more varied way. Although the empirical basis of his work has been criticised as not very adequate, his conclusions find support not only from other sociologists but from common experience. Many artists have preferred the creativity and fulfilment of craft-work to the humdrum security and financial rewards of a safe but boring job. At the other end of the satisfaction-alienation spectrum is assembly line work. Of course, as we shall see, workers find ways of surviving and coping, but the phantoms of monotony, repetition and sheer tedium are never far away. In process work, by contrast, the worker is 'freed' from the machine. He oversees much, if not all, of the process of production and therefore has a closer involvement and identity with the whole. The brutal fracturing of the division of labour is partly healed.

Woodward's terms – unit, batch, mass and process production – cover the same area as Blauner's typology – craft, machine, assembly-line and process production. Like Blauner, she sees mechanisation as causing an increase in alienation until the onset of process production, which would show on a graph as the upside-down 'U curve' of alienation, takes a steep plunge. She also notes that in unit and process production, the dividing line between workers and technical and supervisory staff tends to be more blurred than in the case of batch and mass production. The situation was closer to what Burns and Stalker call the *organic model of organisation* involving more communication and democratic decision making. Thus, less alienation occurred through powerlessness.

Blauner's optimistic view of the effect of automation on work satisfaction has been sharply criticised by Duncan Gallie. He notes pointedly that the size of Blauner's sample of process workers was only 99, of which 78 were sampled in 1947 and 21 in 1961. Gallie himself, however, did not choose a sample survey method. Instead, he made four detailed case studies of workers in automated oil refineries, two in France and two in Britain. The point of this was to supply a *comparative cultural* frame of reference which he felt was missing in Blauner's work. In both cases Gallie found that *indifference,* not satisfaction, was the most frequently expressed attitude to work. On a whole range of other matters mainly affecting industrial relations, however, he found substantial differences between the French and British workers. He concludes that broad generalisations about workers' attitudes and about industrial relations, should consider variables relative to given cultures and not simply technological change. We can accept this basic point of Gallie's but it should be said that other work, including that of Wedderburn and Crompton, tends to verify Blauner, Woodward and Touraine's conclusion that automated labour is *in itself* relatively more satisfying than other forms of mechanised labour.

We earlier made an important distinction between Marx's and Weber's understanding of the major cause of alienation.

Blauner, Woodward and Touraine are closer to Weber in that they analyse alienation in terms of the technical organisation of production rather than in terms of the private ownership of the means of production. Blauner suggests four dimensions of alienation, which he contrasts with four non-alienative states:

Alienated States	Non-Alienative States
1 Powerlessness	Control
2 Meaninglessness	Purpose
3 Isolation	Social Integration
4 Self-estrangement	Self-involvement.

There is no need to explain the use of these terms at length. A little thought will make it clear why a fragmented, partial relationship to production tends to lead to alienation, and a fuller one to a more satisfied set of responses. 'Self-estrangement' can be regarded as the final stage of alienation in which the individual begins to lose self-respect and motivation. Blauner's list is a useful summary of what has already been said or implied about the psychology of alienation.

One point of Blauner's can usefully be taken further here. It is the contrasting conceptual pair of *self-estrangement* and *self-involvement*. The notion that work can alienate a person from himself is common to both Marxist and Weberian inspired literature on alienation. The idea presupposes that there does exist a self to be alienated from. The humanist psychologist, Abraham Maslow, has, as we have seen, attempted to define broadly what the fundamental, common properties of human nature are (see Chapter 3). He argues that whereas practically all jobs provide the means to satisfy basic social needs (food, shelter), fewer satisfy *egoistic* needs (status), and fewer still allow for relatively full *self-actualisation* (self-fulfilment, creativity). Others have elaborated on Maslow's simple scheme, but as a clear statement of the root social-psychological cause of alienation it is difficult to improve. *Alienation is the frustration of human potential as a result of unfulfilling work.*

2 Work Satisfaction and Neutrality: A Social Action Approach to Work Experience

Blauner's analysis of alienation has received criticism from

Goldthorpe and Lockwood in addition to that offered by Gallie. Goldthorpe and Lockwood's social action approach to this issue also leads them to reject the Marxist analysis of alienation. They point out that many of the workers in their sample did not have high expectations of work and were not therefore disappointed by their experience of it. They worked not for satisfaction, still less for fulfilment, but for money. Goldthorpe and Lockwood call this an *instrumental orientation* to work (the term orientation is preferred to attitude): it is used as a means or instrument to get something else – money. Their sample was mainly of young, married workers who, mindful of family commitments, may have been particularly 'money conscious', but other research bears out and extends this finding. Dubin shows that, for many industrial and white collar employees, work is not a major area of interest and self-expression. In a generally more representative sample of the male manual workforce than Goldthorpe and Lockwood's, Wedderburn and Crompton nevertheless confirm the latters' findings. The cumulative implication of these findings is that the workers are neither consciously alienated from, nor satisfied with, work but accept it *neutrally* as a means to an end. They work largely to finance their family and leisure life which does have personal meaning to them.

Another way of explaining this is to distinguish between *intrinsic* and *extrinsic* orientations to work. A person who works for intrinsic reasons does so for the satisfaction the job gives. Such people include craftsmen or vocationally motivated nurses. In this context, extrinsic means the same as instrumental. Most people appear to work for predominantly extrinsic reasons, and to have low expectations of what the job offers in itself. If dissatisfaction is the difference between expectation and experience, then, most are not dissatisfied, because they expect little in the first place. Thus, surveys suggest that women in routine office work are more satisfied than men doing work of a similar level of skill. A possible reason for this is that work is less of a central life interest for them than for men and so they are more easily 'satisfied' with it.

We seem, then, to have two almost contradictory perspectives on work experience: on the one hand, certain kinds of work are considered alienating and, on the other, the people who do these kinds of work may regard them as neutral but not alienating experience. We can easily reconcile the two views if we extend our understanding of alienation. Alienation is not just a description of *subjective* (personally experienced) feelings of many workers; it is also a more *objective* (more widely generalisable) statement about the waste of human potential that certain kinds of routine work, both manual and white collar, involve. In this sense, alienation is about lack of fulfilment, not just actual feelings of misery. It is quite possible to have many unfulfilled capacities without knowing it. Such a grossly unfulfilled person is alienated from his or her true potential. Marx argued that fulfilment at work is generally possible in socialist, but not in capitalist society. Weber thought fulfilment at work for the majority was incompatible with the extreme division of labour of large scale organisation, whether in capitalist or socialist societies. We need to look at the concept of fulfilment in greater detail because its use does imply the value judgement that some kinds of activity, including varieties of work, are more or less better (in the sense of more fulfilling) than others.

3 Fulfilment in Work

Abraham Maslow's theory of human needs can be usefully applied to the concept of fulfilment at work. Nearly everybody will expect to meet their basic needs of food and shelter through work, and most, too, will hope for some pleasant social interaction while at work. Fewer will acquire substantial esteem or prestige for the work they do though only the most humble will be outside the positive status hierarchy altogether. Only a tiny minority achieve self-actualisation or self-fulfilment through work. Very few are allowed to perform at a level of personal excellence that brings their best creative skills and abilities into play. Examples of some who can are people at the very top of our occupational elites, such as managing directors of large companies, star sportsmen and entertainers, and creative academics. Many others are perhaps haunted by what Gouldner calls 'the unemployed self' – a sense of potential underdeveloped and a life wasted in senseless work.

We have noted that Marx did not consider fulfilling, non-alienating work to be generally possible in capitalist society. Some Marxists regard with suspicion the limited industrial participation or *power-sharing* schemes involving workers, which have been adopted in Germany and Sweden, but others consider them a step on the road to a more socialist and less alienating society. Those who, unlike Marx, see alienation primarily as the result of technological and/or organisational factors, naturally look for solutions within these terms (we exclude of course, those who ignore the problem or believe it to be insoluble). We examine a variety of attempts to achieve relatively more 'human' systems of organisation and technology both later in this chapter and Chapter 16.

Informal Attempts to Deal with Alienation: An Interactionist Perspective

Reform and revolution aside, those who have to work in boring jobs are faced with the day-to-day need of 'getting by'. Here are some of the ways they use to do so.

The interactionist concept of *managing* self and others provides a helpful perspective on the many people who 'survive' monotony at work (and school). Apart from snatched conversational exchanges, day-dreaming is perhaps the most universal 'strategy', as Jason Ditton remarks in his participant study of work in a factory bakery:

> Although the workers looked as if they were doing the work automatically, one man, who had worked for twelve hours a day for two years in the 'dough' . . . pointed out that, underneath this, the mind never stops. Though giving the impression of working without thinking, he said that 'you think of a hundred subjects a day' . . .

Doubtless his 'hundred subjects a day' cover a similar range of musings as those in which you and I indulge.

Next to 'escaping into your head', the most common way of dealing with stress and monotony is probably by humour – 'having a laff'. In his authentic description of nineteen fifties working class life in Nottingham, *Saturday Night and Sunday Morning*, Alan Sillitoe gives us more than a few examples of 'laffs' through the actions of the novel's anti-hero, Arthur. Here is one:

> At a piecework rate of four-and-six a hundred you could make your money if you knocked-up fourteen hundred a day – possible without grabbing too much – and if you went all out for a

thousand in the morning you could dawdle through the afternoon and lark about with the women and talk to your mates now and again. Such leisure often brought him near to trouble, for some weeks ago he stunned a mouse – that the overfed factory cats had missed – and laid it beneath a woman's drill, and Robboe the gaffer ran out of his office when he heard her screaming blue-murder, thinking that some bloody silly woman had gone and got her hair caught in a belt (big notices said that women must wear hair-nets, but who could tell with women?) and Robboe was glad that it was nothing more than a dead mouse she was kicking up such a fuss about. But he paced up and down the gangways asking who was responsible for the stunned mouse, and when he came to Arthur, who denied having anything to do with it, he said: 'I'll bet you did it, you young bogger!' 'Me, Mr. Robboe?' Arthur said, the picture of innocence, standing up tall with offended pride. 'I've got so much work to do I can't move from my lathe'.

A tough sense of the ridiculous is at the heart of traditional working class life. In part, it is a way of coping with the absurdity and tyranny of work. We discussed working class humour and other cultural attitudes earlier (Chapter 10).

The ultimate escape at work is going to sleep. Quite often, night-shift workers are 'allowed' an informal 'kip' after they have finished their quota, but the British Leyland worker who was dismissed after bringing a bed to work was obviously considered to be taking things too much for granted. Apart from such arrangements, many workers have some recollection of occasionally going to sleep while working, either through monotony or fatigue, just as most students do.

An experienced foreman or sympathetic floor manager will not attempt to stop harmless attempts by workers to 'kill time' or, at least, make it pass more quickly. He may even extend a tea-break or stop to chat with an obviously tired, sick or stressed worker when the occasion seems to demand it.

All the daydreams, 'laffs', 'kips', and 'tea and sympathy', however, cannot make fundamentally boring work interesting. As we shall see, alienation is arguably the underlying cause of much industrial conflict and discontent as well as the milder, improvised 'escape attempts' described above.

The real escape, though, is *leisure* time. It is then that workers, starved of meaning and expression at work, can hope to 'do their own thing'. If, to use C. Wright Mills' image, people sell little pieces of themselves for money during week-days, they attempt to reclaim themselves in the evenings and at weekends with the coin of fun. Mills' tart irony rightly suggests that the problems of personal freedom, pleasure and leisure are more complicated than this simple division of time into 'work and fun' suggests. We examine these issues after the following section on industrial interest groups and conflict.

Industrial Interest Groups and Conflict

Industrial interest groups are formal organisations concerned with the interests of their members. There are two broad types, *employers' associations* and, for employees, *trade unions* and *professional associations*. In practice, employees make much more use of formal interest group organisations than employers. This is partly because employers are supposed to be in competition with each other and, indeed, the law discourages co-operation that might restrain trade or raise prices artificially. It is also because it is often easier and more convenient for employers to consult informally and in private. Both employers and trade unions are represented by national bodies, the Confederation of British Industry (CBI) and Trades Union Congress (TUC) respectively.

The Growth of Unionism

Whilst union membership grew from 7.83 million in 1945 to a peak of 13.3 million in 1979 (and was 11.3 million in `1983), the number of unions has declined from 186 unions affiliated to the TUC in 1951, to 112 in 1980. The net result has been the development of much bigger and, generally, stronger unions. As Jenkins and Sherman point out this trend to 'concentration and enlargement' matches the same process in industry itself.

The traditional and still the main purpose of trade unions is to protect and improve the pay and working conditions of their members. Recently, unions have frequently brought issues of job security, participation in management and even environmental and social policy issues within their range of concern. Nationally, the TUC is a powerful pressure group on major

403

matters of economic and social policy. It was the trade union-
ist, Jack Jones, who thought up 'the social contract', on the
basis of which the Labour government and unions attempted to
co-operate for over two years. At the local level, it is the
increase in the influence and power of shop stewards, who are
the immediate representatives of unionised workers, that has
been the striking development in the post-war period. Shop
stewards have often taken the immediate responsibility for
taking industrial action, although their decisions are usually
ratified by national leadership. Undoubtedly, there is some disagreement between those who support the 'shop steward
movement' as being both democratic and sensitive to the needs
of local unionists, and those who would prefer national union
leaders to have more power over union members as they do in
Sweden and Germany. This tension remains unresolved.

White Collar Unionism: Reasons for Growth

The growth in the unionisation of non-manual employees is the
major explanation of the recent increase in union membership.
In 1967 there were 2.5 million non-manual workers in TUC
affiliated unions. In 1977. there were over 4.6 million non-
manual members (this includes a minority in basically manual
worker unions). This increase exaggerates the extent of recent
white collar unionisation as several non-manual workers unions
had sizeable membership before affiliating to the TUC in the
late sixties or seventies. Of the white collar unions, the
National Association of Local Government Officers (NALGO) is
the fourth largest union in the country (709,000 members). The
teachers' unions, including polytechnic and university teachers,
and the Civil Service unions, both have well over half a million
members. In all, the percentage of white collar membership of
the TUC was 38% in 1977, and has been estimated at a possible 50% in 1985.

We now examine the reasons for the increase in white collar
unionism. These are: the increasing concentration of employees
in large buildings such as office blocks; the willingness of major
employers to recognise unions; government (mainly Labour)
promotion of union recognition; and, most importantly, the
desire to improve wages and other conditions of work. Writing
before the rapid increase of the nineteen seventies, George Bain
emphasised the first three factors at the expense of the fourth.

As most of the increase in white collar union membership has occurred in the public sector we would expect these three factors to be strongly apparent there. Both before and since Bain wrote, public sector employment has been becoming more concentrated and bureaucratised. Interestingly, Bain suggests that, as a result, white collar workers have been increasingly bound by rules made by remote management and that, in order to claw back control over their work situation, they join unions and indulge in collective bargaining. In explaining white collar unionisation, Bain puts the desire to be able to control their work situation more effectively ahead of the wish to obtain economic benefits. The evidence of the late nineteen seventies contradicts this assessment. Several white collar unions took industrial action in pursuit of (relatively) high wage claims during that period. In particular, Civil Service unions pursued a long and effective strategy of industrial action in 1979.

Writing almost a decade later than Bain, Jenkins and Sherman agree with his second point – that recognition of unions by employers is central in providing the stable and legitimate conditions in which they can develop. Above all, has been the ready acceptance of the *closed shop* by senior management. *A closed shop means that union membership is made compulsory for all employees.* Where it exists, it necessarily increases union membership. By 1979, over 65% of white collar workers belonged to closed shops (not much less than the percentage for manual workers). It may seem odd that management should actively promote union power, but there are good reasons for this. The closed shop brings stability and representativeness to collective bargaining. Simply, management knows who it is dealing with and that management-union agreements can usually be 'sold' to workers by union representatives. There are now 3,800 full-time shop stewards (representatives of the unions in places of work), paid by employers – more than full time trade union officials (about 3,000). Companies with closed shops normally pay individual union dues to the union before the worker receives his wages.

We now turn to the third factor accounting for the growth of white collar unionism. In addition to Bain's research, study at the Industrial Relations Research Unit at Warwick University further confirms that government policy has tended to stimulate union growth. The Trade Union and Labour Relations Acts of

1974 and 1975 provided statutory assistance to unions in securing recognition and collective bargaining rights. Partly as a
result, a big growth in the closed shop took place in
1976–1977, though the trend was, in any case, well established.

The fourth factor, the economic, seems the most important.
Whatever government and employers do, a white collar employee will not join a trade union unless he or she sees it to be
in his own material interest to do so. White collar employees
expect the same kind of services out of unions as do manual
workers. Jenkins and Sherman picturesquely refer to the following as 'the recruiting sergeants': reduced pay differentials
(the difference between high and low paid jobs), compared to
manual workers; redundancies and the effects of inflation on
the purchasing power of wages, in addition to the facts already
mentioned.

Simply because most people join unions for economic reasons
does not mean that all unions, whether manual or white collar,
will behave entirely similarly, or that all their members are
suddenly 'working class'. David Lockwood, using Weber's concepts, has pointed out that the *work situation* (authority, independence) *market situation* (qualifications, experience) and *subjective* class consciousness of white collar workers vary enormously. As the lower level white collar employee finds
work increasingly bureaucratised, and as he becomes more
remote from employers and management, he will define his own
interests as distinct from theirs and look to his union to defend
them. It may be that as the status rewards for white collar
work diminish, the monetary and other material rewards
associated with such employment will come to seem still more
important. Kenneth Roberts suggests that white collar unionism
means not that the white collar group are joining the working
class, but that they are trying to stay ahead of it. We have
already seen that instrumental collectivism is not in itself a
sound basis for class solidarity (Chapter 10). Indeed, it
could be regarded as institutionalised selfishness. At a higher
level, although some staff associations involving more senior
white collar staff adopt union membership, they may still perceive a harmony of interest between themselves and their employer. Such attitudes are perhaps especially strong in the private sector. Rosemary Crompton, from a specifically Marxist
perspective, has stressed the variety of white collar unions and

the motives of their members. In her view, this reflects the ambiguous class position of many white collar workers. They are neither productive workers nor do they control the means of production and profit. They stand between labour and capital and their behaviour at work reflects this ambiguous position.

The Professions

The expansion of professions is a further feature of the growth of the service sector characteristic of modern societies. In addition to managers and administrators, professionals make up a large proportion of what Halsey refers to as the 'service class'. Higher professionals include lawyers, scientists, engineers, doctors and dentists. Their market position is significantly stronger than that of lower professionals such as teachers, social workers and nurses and this shows in the much higher salaries they tend to command. Most lower professionals work for the government. Among higher professionals, private practice is becoming more rare and employment in the service of industry or the government increasingly common. This change in the market position of professionals has increased the possibility of conflict with other groups.

Until quite recently, sociological writings on the professions tended to assume both their high social status and that the contribution or 'service' of professionals to the community was qualitatively superior to that of 'lower' status workers. Marxists are an exception to this, as they have always placed the highest value on manual labour. Current analysis of the professions is much more inclined to use the concept of conflict in interpreting their relationship to society. This is apparent in two main ways. First, no necessary 'community of interest' is assumed between client and professional. On the contrary, their interests tend to be seen to be in *structural conflict*, regardless of the 'goodwill' of individual professionals. Secondly, because most professionals are now *paid employees*, their relationship to their employers is also regarded as a potential source of conflict similar to that experienced by other employees. Both are part of the general process by which work has become increasingly bureaucratised.

The Functionalist Approach and 'Trait' Analysis Approach
The work of functionalists such as Bernard Barber and Talcott
Parsons, typifies traditional sociological analysis of the professions. Quite simply, this perspective sees the professions as fulfilling useful social functions. They provide necessary medical,
legal, architectural or religious advice and service based on
specialised knowledge and competence. The key attribute of
professions is considered to be a primary commitment to community rather than self-interest. Terence Johnson distinguishes
between functionalist analysis of professions and 'trait' analysis
though the two approaches are highly compatible. *'Trait' analysis
is based on an attempt to list the basic characteristics of professions.*
'Trait' analysis has proved to be something of a blind alley.
On the basis of his own survey of the relevant literature,
Millerson points out that no two authorities agree precisely on
what the basic traits of a profession are. The following, however, are frequently mentioned: professional authority (over the
'layman'); the sanction by the community of the power and
privilege of professionals; the confidential nature of the professional client relationship; a code of ethics (rules) regulating the
profession; a theory of knowledge underlying the practice of the
profession (such as medical research/theory); and the existence
of a professional culture. A professional culture involves broad
consensus about how to behave as a professional, and is said to
be passed on to new recruits. Even today, barristers can still
participate in a quite ritualised common culture.

The 'trait' approach is so uncritical of official professional
ideology (the views professionals hold of themselves) that it is
almost 'pre-sociological'. Client response is assumed automatically to 'fit in' with the expert's view and the possibility of
conflict between professionals and other individuals and groups
is unexplored. The functionalist approach is hardly more sophisticated. Johnson charges that they do not examine the historical
development of professions and so fail to appreciate that professional practice is deeply involved with power relations in
society, including those based mainly on money. Consistently
enough, he illustrates his argument by reference to various historical stages in the development of professions, and, in particular, stresses changes in the professional-client relationship. In
the sixteenth and seventeenth centuries, professionals were
typically answerable to wealthy patrons. The professional's free-

dom was limited by this dependence and he certainly did not serve the majority of the community. Industrialisation changed the status of the professions. Their members and independence increased. The technical expertise of, for instance, engineers and specialist lawyers, was formidable and professionals achieved new status and power. Leading professions were able to persuade the general public of their own ideology – their own assessment of their skill and importance. It was at this time that professions developed into self-regulating organisations which were able to control their specialist areas of work, including the standard of entry to them. Control of entry enabled them to regulate the supply and therefore the price of professional services. Obviously, this was a very desirable position for professionals to be in. Medieval craftsmen similarly attempted to regulate occupational entry and the supply and price of services. No doubt members of most occupations would wish to do the same. The difference between professions and other occupations is that they have succeeded in convincing the public of their special skills and importance and of their need for corresponding privileges, whereas others have not.

A Power-Conflict Analysis of Professions

In contemporary society the traditional high status and autonomy (freedom) of professionals is less taken for granted, though they remain a relatively wealthy and privileged group. Modern professions can be usefully understood in terms of power-conflict. By analysing their position in the market and in the work place, we can get a better idea of their power and prestige relative to other groups. We consider professions in relation to three centres of power and control: central and local government, the client, and other colleagues. These centres of control apply somewhat differently to different professions.

a GOVERNMENT CONTROL During the course of the twentieth century, the government has become a massive employer of professional as well as lower white collar and manual employees. Government has not only become the paymaster of the great majority of 'semi-professionals' such as teachers, social workers and nurses, but also of doctors, dentists and various other specialist professionals. To a greater or lesser extent this has caused 'a crisis of identity' within these areas. The issue has been whether to respond to the power of government by organising as a union, or whether to maintain a more traditional professional image, even if this involves a less robust approach to industrial bargaining. The various industrial interest groups representing teachers illustrate the dilemma. Some, like the NUT, call themselves unions, and others, like the Assistant Masters Association, prefer the more professional sounding term Association – a preference that does indicate a more traditional and conservative attitude to their occupation, and industrial bargaining. Nevertheless, like other major groups employed by government, professionals have generally opted to use some of the means employed by unions to protect and promote the interests of their members even if they have not adopted the title of union. The British Medical Association is a good example.

As a result of the nationalisation of the health service most doctors and dentists became employees of the government. Both the British Medical Association and the British Dental Association have increasingly adopted the approach of trade unions in defending the pay and conditions of their members whilst still attempting to retain a professional ethos. The BMA ultimately altered its rules so that it could legitimately act as a trade union (even though it had actually been doing so for many years). On the other hand, professional aloofness was maintained by not affiliating the association to the TUC. The militancy of some junior doctors, which has included demonstrations, strikes and other forms of industrial action, suggests that the future of the BMA will be no less militant. Even so, it will continue to fulfil the traditional functions of a professional association as it has done since it was founded in 1851. This 'dual functioning' as both a professional association and as a trade union is not unique to the BMA. A number of other small professional associations, including the Council of Engineering Institutions, also operate in this way. This is a pattern that authors and trade union activists, Clive Jenkins and Barrie Sherman, dislike. They would prefer professional associations exclusively to carry out their traditional functions and, in addition, to leave their members to join large, national unions which would look after their interests as paid employees. The complex historical heritage, however, makes the achievement of so tidy a solution unlikely in the near future.

b CLIENT CONTROL It is helpful to divide client control of professionals into two categories depending on whom they work for: *control exercised by large scale organisations,* whether public or private, which employ professionals and *control exercised by the individual client largely through choice.* We will take the first type of control to begin with, as it closely relates to our previous discussion. Many professionals, including accountants, lawyers, engineers and scientists, are now directly employed by business corporations and so are also part of the new salariat. In organisational terms, this is often very similar to being employed by the state. The professional in this situation loses the freedom associated with independent practice and, usually, the opportunity to employ a broad range of expertise. He tends to do highly specialised work (in a sub-branch of law or accountancy) and, although his professional judgement is usually accepted within a limited area, has to submit to the overall authority of management. Several more recent commentators have rightly observed that Weber overlooked the potential for conflict between professional experts and management – whether in the public or private sector. In general, professionals are better qualified than management but have less authority within organisations. As Burns and Stalker point out, some managers deal with this situation by adopting more flexible, open-ended and democratic modes of decision-making. They use the term 'organic' to describe this tendency. A large-scale empirical study of the same issue led Peter Blau to conclude that this is, indeed, often the approach taken by management who have well qualified professionals on their staff. As Etzioni points out, however, professional and management functions are different, and the possiblity of conflict cannot be entirely removed. In ideal-type terms, professionals make recommendations on the basis of what seems 'right' by professional principles, whereas managers look for solutions that 'work' in terms of the rules and goals of the organisation. Stewart Clegg and David Dunkerly have commented interestingly on this issue and suggest that in practice, organisational and technical development have reduced the authority of professionals anyway:

> Increasing standardisation has taken place in the legal and

accounting professions. The popularity of 'do-it-yourself' house purchase and divorce is evidence of such routinisation; accountancy, largely through the effects of computers, has become more and more codified, standardised and routinised. In other words, not only clerical work but professional activities as well appear to be subject to an increasing division of labour characterised by routinisation.

Marxist Herbert Gintis, goes further and suggests that highly fragmented (specialised) and, therefore, alienated labour is as much a characteristic of bureaucracy as of industry. He adds that the division of labour in a hierarchical way ultimately favours those at the very top. These are not professionals, nor even managers, but members of the capitalist class.

It is not surprising that in the face of the above trends, many professionals 'hang onto' traditional notions of their status and power. The logical alternative might simply be to accept that they are merely very well paid workers. Most Marxists would argue that this is, indeed, so. From an action perspective it is easy to see that this ambiguity in the work situation of the salaried professional can produce a real personal dilemma. A corporate lawyer may be required to pursue a case by his employer-client which in his professional, personal and even moral opinion is a waste of time. But 'he who pays the piper calls the tune' – professional judgement can be overridden by top management. A teacher who is genuinely committed to his subject and education 'for its own sake' may find that 'exam pressure' forces him to teach in a way he dislikes. 'Exam pressure' is a term that can cover active control from the hierarchy and pupils in his own institution and, more remotely, parental, community and governmental opinion.

We now turn to the relationship of professionals to individual clients. If we except semi-professionals, the majority of professionals are still not employed by large institutions although a growing number are. In any case, the relationship between the professional and individual client continues to be of great importance. A frequently debated issue is the extent to which the professional can use his specialist knowledge to manipulate or 'mystify' the client (perhaps to 'get rid' of him quickly, avoid questions, or simply hide his own ignorance), and whether he should be prevented from doing so. We need to clarify this with an example. Some commentators feel that many doctors prescribe drug treatments too easily. This is felt to be particularly true in respect of psychological 'ailments' including, for instance, depression. The result is that, without proper counselling the client may think of the drug as a 'cure' rather than merely a treatment of symptoms. There is also the possibility of dependency. The real cause of depression is likely to be personal or social in origin and is likely to go undiscussed. To this extent the client's need is not met. Those who make these criticisms offer a number of related solutions, all of which involve the education of the public. If the client is to be recommended drug treatment, then he or she should be told more about what the drug is, how it works, and what its limits are. In addition, he or she should be told what positive steps can be taken to deal with the problem by means of, say, diet, exercise, or the handling of his personal and work relations. Given the limited time of doctors, the educational system and the media might be expected to play a role in this. Thus a culture in which people cared for their own health rather than relied on 'the expert' could further develop. The 'jogging' movement, and greater awareness of diet, suggest that this is already beginning to happen

Ivan Illich is one of the leading critics of 'professionalised knowledge'. He considers that often professional ideology functions primarily in the interests of professionals despite its supposed concern with standards and quality of service. He reacts against the wrapping up of knowledge in parcels labelled 'expert' because this produces a passive and even timid attitude to learning and makes the client unnecessarily dependent on the professional. He believes in as much open access to information as possible whether it be about medicine, the law or whatever. Underlying his suggestions is a belief that education, formal and informal, should be an active process in which the teacher or expert advises rather than dictates, participates rather than controls.

c PROFESSIONAL CONTROL OF PROFESSIONALS The third form of control, that of professionals over themselves continues to be important even though today it is often 'major' clients or employers who wield decisive power over the professional's life. Professional associations continue to regulate entry and, though they may often mean little in an everyday sense to their members, they can be a source of advice, support or, sometimes, censure, if things go wrong. They can also be a basis of leisure activity. Finally, because of the hierarchically organised division of labour, professionals themselves are frequently organised hierarchically in given organisations. A specialist surgeon or senior consultant is very much 'the boss' of 'his team' of junior doctors, various medical auxiliaries and nurses. In turn, these also occupy varying positions in the hierarchy. Thus, differential power and control manifests itself in the professional's working situation.

Recent analysis suggests that for the public to hold professionals in awe serves only to perpetuate the myth that their work is incomprehensible to most and deserves unquestioning respect. This sense of mystery serves as an ideological cloak beneath which professionals can pursue their own interests which need not coincide with those of others. Increasingly, clients are bringing professionals to account on the same practical basis as other occupations, that is, in terms of the quality of their work. Nevertheless, professionals do remain relatively wealthy and privileged partly because there is an objective basis to their claims to be especially competent in difficult skills. As far as professional power is concerned, we have noted several developments which challenge, even if they do not undermine, it.

Industrial Conflict: Factors Associated with Strikes

There are numerous forms of industrial conflict, of varying degrees of severity. The most important is the *strike*. Associated with striking is picketing – trying, within the limits of law, to persuade other workers to join a strike. Another form of action often used as an alternative to the strike weapon in industrial conflict is 'working to rule'. The sit-in involves the occupation or take-over of a factory by workers and is often a reaction to large-scale redundancies or closure. It usually occurs as a last resort but sometimes leads to a positive attempt by the workers to save the factory themselves.

Another form of conflict, industrial sabotage, can occur for a variety of reasons, from personal boredom or malice to opposition to management policies or even the capitalist system in general. Minor acts of sabotage sometimes have a comical aspect which helps to release tedium and frustration, as when a distinguished foreign client was delivered a new Mercedes complete with six coca-cola bottles clanking deep within its bonnet. Huw Beynon tells of the response of a line worker, who was prone to absenteeism, to the question of what it felt like to come into work on a fine, bright Monday morning. The answer was that he didn't know! The implication is, of course, that the worker found better things to do than work on fine, bright Monday mornings. Certainly, children 'bunk off' school because they find it 'boring' and 'a drag'. (see Chapter 5). Presumably some of 'the dads of the lads' indulge in similar practices for much the same reasons. Beynon also gives a number of examples of industrial sabotage which contain a serious message to perhaps otherwise inattentive management. Thus, workers who felt they were undermined or expected to work too quickly sometimes sabotaged cars to make their objection known. As Taylor and Walton imply, sabotage is a somewhat primitive method of communication, and it has been largely, though not entirely, superseded by trade union negotiation. Absenteeism is a form of escapism or even of rejection, rather than conflict. It mostly occurs in industries which take a severe physical and mental toll.

The damage that strikes do or do not do to the economy of Britain is a matter of recurrent controversy in this country. This often bitter debate is frequently conducted with only scant attention to relevant facts. The diagram below presents some data on strikes which we can use as a basis of our own discussion.

The graph shows that the general level of strike activity in the nineteen seventies was much higher than in any period since the last war. Between the wars only the short period between 1919–22 produced a higher average level. It was the *length* not the *number* of strikes that had increased.

Compared with other industrialised Western societies, however, Britain's recent strike record is *moderate* rather than exceptional. Between 1968–77 the average number of working days lost in Britain was 452 per 1000 workers, compared with 1187 per 1000 in Australia, 1893 in Canada and 1500 in the United States. Some of Britain's more immediate competitors did lose markedly less: West Germany, 24; Sweden, 18 and Holland, 36.

415

Italy, one of Europe's weaker economies, is an exception (1433 days lost per 1000 workers). Overall, Britain is about half way down the international strike table.

Days Lost in Strikes, (1945–1984)

aggregate number of working days lost in stoppages in progress in year to the nearest million

Source: *New Society*, 10 January 1980, p. 66, and *Social Trends*, 1986.

The sharp reduction in the number of strike days lost between 1980 and 1983 was equally sharply reversed in 1984, largely due to the miners' strike. In 1985 and 1986 the teachers and print workers' unions were involved in extensive strike action.

The Economic Motive

The most commonly stated motive for striking is *to improve pay* though we must immediately point out that research frequently demonstrates important non-economic underlying causes. Between 1965–74, 56.1% of disputes and over 80% of working days lost were the result of conflicts over pay. Most of the strikes during the so-called 'winter of discontent' of 1978–79 were mainly about pay, and were all the more intense as a result of the previous period of voluntary wage restraint. Between 1965–74, 80% of stoppages were about economic issues, and these involved 90% of the days lost. Even the steelworkers strike of 1980 was superficially about pay; relatively little was said about the British Steel Corporation's plan to reduce its workforce by approximately a third over a period of years – a strategy that might have been expected to result in industrial action. It may be that in times of high inflation unions feel they have to concentrate on pay in order to maintain, if not improve, the real value of wages. Sometimes strikes also concern working conditions or other matters affecting workers' welfare. The miners threatened to strike in early 1977 if the National Coal Board refused to implement early retirement plans for them.

Why has the importance of the economic motive apparently increased? Firstly, because of the growth in unionisation, people are better organised to take industrial action, including striking, than ever before. Secondly, rampant inflation has provided a persistent motive, or, at least, a justification, for strikes. Finally, there seems to have been a growth in consumer values the satisfaction of which requires high wages.

Underlying Motives (Non-economic): Control and Independence

The rather quantitative approach to explaining strikes in the previous section should not be taken entirely at face value. There is evidence that even though pay claims are the immediate cause of most strikes, other factors operate at a less obvious level. Here we cite two case studies to illustrate the point. First, is Alvin Gouldner's *Wildcat Strike: A Study of Worker-Management Relationship*. He finds that a strike for higher wages is just one event in a long chain of conflict between workers and management. The conflict stemmed from a change in management at the plant. Traditionally, worker-management relations were informal, friendly and based on trust. The new manager, an outsider, introduced new machinery and attempted to 'rationalise' the administration of the plant. This limited the, independence and offended the pride of the workers, particularly the miners. The relationship between workers and management was redefined in terms of conflicting interests, rather than a sense of mutual understanding and interest. It was in this context that the wildcat strike 'for higher wages' occurred, but to see it simply in terms of money would be sociologically unsubtle.

Lane and Roberts make a still more fundamental point than Gouldner about strikes. In their own case study of a strike at Pilkington's glassworks, they found that a strike occurred at the end of a period of quite good industrial relations in which most workers expressed no major grievances about pay or other matters. A strike also occurred in similar circumstances at the Vauxhall car assembly-line plant at Luton shortly after Goldthorpe and Lockwood completed their 'affluent worker' study. Lane and Roberts conclude that *strikes should be regarded as 'normal', in the sense that they are an accepted 'weapon' in the bargaining process between management and labour.* Their use in the context of industrial bargaining is not exceptional and usually requires no special explanation.

The desire of workers for some control and independence of their work situation and the need for effective power in industrial bargaining falls far short of a wish to 'take over' industry. Political motives of this kind are very rarely behind strikes although before the first world war they helped to inspire the syndicalist movement. Syndicalists took the view that revolution could best be achieved by a general strike followed by a seizure of power by the workers. More recently, politically motivated strikes have been rare. As Turner says, where an industrial conflict occurs, left wing activists may often take a lead in organising the workers but their ability to 'stir up' conflict that does not already exist seems marginal.

Structural Conflict between Capital and Labour

The previous points assume a certain 'in-built' conflict between capital and labour. Marxists stress this conflict particularly strongly. Hyman makes the general point:

> the confrontation within the workplace of two bases of control provides a constant source of instability and conflict.

Given that owners and management, on the one hand, and the labour force, on the other, want as large a share as possible of the profit of their mutual toil, disagreement and friction is virtually inevitable. Even the most optimistic personnel manager would hardly expect to do more than 'regulate' it in the context of modern large-scale industry. It is because they, too, see a day-to-day conflict of interest between capital and labour, that Lane and Roberts claim that strikes should be seen as 'normal' rather than labelled a 'problem' (once the public is presented with a 'problem' the next stage is often to look for the 'culprit' – not the most fruitful approach in industrial relations).

Marxists see a final solution to class conflict in industry only in the introduction of a socialist society. Others see a functional need to make the capitalist system operate more effectively. Thus, human relations theorists, Scott and Homans, argue that better communications between management and workers – for instance, through trained personnel managers – can provide a more constructive atmosphere and reduce disruption. Marxists consider this approach to be biased towards management and manipulative of workers. At worst it passes off deep problems of structural conflict and exploitation as personal or even psychological difficulties.

Causes Related to Specific Industries

So far, we have talked about the general causes of strikes. The extent to which strikes occur, however, varies between industries and between societies. We now attempt to account for these variations. We start by examining the strike record of different industries. James Cronin finds that highly unionised workers in industries crucial to the national economy, which tend to use incentive schemes to increase production, and which are subject to economic fluctuation, tend to be prone to strike. A recent study showed that, on average, miners, dockers, car workers, shipbuilders and iron and steel workers accounted for a quarter of strikes and a third of working days lost, even though they only cover about 6% of employees. With the possible exception of mining, these industries have tended to fluctuate within a spiral of decline and this may have contributed to their strike record. A second point is that the production technology in some of these industries is particularly alienating – for instance, the car industry – or the work is extremely hard and wearing as is mining and dock-work. In a sense, a strike can be a needed break or, to use Kenneth Boulding's words, it acts as a 'catharsis' and 'a release of tensions'. Finally, traditional industries such as these are often situated in areas with strong working class communitiès. Union strength and militancy and class solidarity are often the norm in such occupational communities. In some respects, however, this picture of the typical strike-prone industry is ten years out of date. Firstly, these kinds of communities are now in decline, and some of the workers involved in these industries conform more closely to the 'privatised' pattern of living observed by Goldthorpe and Lockwood, rather than the more open community life-style of the traditional working class. Secondly, the relatively strike-prone seventies saw a wider range of workers of all kinds and, not least, non-manual workers, using the strike weapon. Almost everybody, from civil servant to sewage worker, seems to have realised that union membership and action are the best way of maintaining or improving wages. This is true not only in Britain but also in many other countries.

It is, in any case, unwise to generalise too much about the strike records of particular industries because variations between societies are substantial, although the above pattern has some basis in international as well as national statistics. We turn now to this broader issue.

Industrial Relations Systems Analysis Applied to Different Societies

Although industrial relations systems analysis particularly reflects the sociological perspective of Talcott Parsons, its basic principles are more generally applicable, and need not embody his own conservative values. This approach links the particular factory or industry to the wider society. Strikes are seen in the context of the total national system of industrial relations, including workers and unions; management and government agencies especially concerned with the work place; the work community and, finally, the tradition of industrial relations in a given society. Industrial law is an important part of the 'environment' of industrial relations in most advanced countries and has often been a cause of dispute between labour and government in Britain. In the space of two years, between 1969 and

1971, both major parties attempted to introduce substantial legal changes in the position of the unions. Both failed, mainly because of the strength and effectiveness of union opposition.

Britain's system of industrial relations, once widely admired, has been traditionally conducted in an *informal* way without great reliance on the law. Undeniably, it has not stood up well to the economic stresses of the nineteen sixties and seventies. By contrast, the German system which is based on a more detailed structure of law, has recently enjoyed greater harmony, though this may have been as much due to economic prosperity as to their industrial law. In the Soviet Union, industrial peace is achieved by legal compulsion – a generally unpopular means in the West. Theirs is a system of industrial relations in which power is concentrated in the Government's hands. The opposite approach would be to adopt a system of real industrial democracy, that is, union participation or control. We consider this option after concluding our discussion of strikes, and that section can be regarded as a more detailed analysis of industrial relations systems in practice.

Multiple Motivations for Strikes

The major *stated* motive for strikes is the economic one. We have also suggested a range of other important contributory factors. As Hyman points out, however, it is a false dichotomy to assume that the causes of a given dispute must be either economic or *non-economic*. He adds that the relative importance of the various causes that contribute to the start of a strike may change as it goes on, and new reasons for continuing it may appear. The sheer determination 'not to lose' may increase as a strike goes on. Lane and Roberts point out that strikes can snow-ball. New grievances may become apparent as the strike continues and support may come from the previously uncommitted at the prospect of a good settlement. As the interactionist Silverman succinctly puts it, industrial relations must be seen as a changing *process* and not merely in structural terms. We must also reiterate that the broad social, political and legal structure within which a strike occurs (or is prevented from occurring) is of fundamental importance in comparing the strike profiles of different countries.

Beyond Industrial Conflict? Workers' Participation and Control

Most people do not control their work situation. Not only are their work roles defined by others, but they play no part in determining the goals and policies of the organisations for which they work. In Britain this statement is true not only of privately owned businesses but also of state run enterprises. Broadly, there are three opinions on this situation. The first is that the hierarchically (top downward) organised division of labour is inevitable and that 'both sides of industry' must accept their different roles and get on with the job of producing goods or services. This view accords with functionalist assumptions. A second view is that workers can usefully participate in some management decisions by means of elected representatives. Thirdly, is the view that the divide between ownership/management and labour must be removed by the introduction of socialism. We discuss these views more theoretically in Chapter 16 (pp. 454–61) but a few words are appropriate here.

The first view is probably the most commonly held. Rightly or not, most owners and managers think they should continue to 'run' industry and most workers, whether through lack of confidence and experience or otherwise, seem content to agree. A particularly conservative variation of this approach is to hold the view that the unions have become too strong and have 'upset the balance' of British industrial relations, and must therefore be curbed. This view inspired the industrial legislation of Margaret Thatcher's government.

High hopes are often attached to the principle of participation. Worker participation in management and ownership (by having shares in the company) occurs in Sweden and Germany, and is said by its supporters to raise productivity and to improve industrial relations. It is true that industrial relations in these countries are the most trouble-free in Europe. It must be stressed however, that other factors, not least growing prosperity, may be causal here. A further aspect of industrial relations in Sweden is that labour and government have consistently 'struck deals' involving, for instance, wage-restraint, on the one hand, and government commitment to social reform on the other. In any case, Swedish unions tend to be more restricted by law than are British. The arrangements broadly described in this paragraph are referred to as 'corporatism' and Sweden, in particular, is often cited as a corporate state. The German scheme received a positive assessment by a government commision in 1970. Most of the fears of German management about sharing responsibility and authority with labour had proved groundless and co-operation, not obstruction, had been the net result. In his thoughtful book *The Politics of Industrial Relations*, Colin Crouch argues that Britain would benefit from adopting a system of industrial relations similar to, though somewhat more flexible than, the German and Swedish models. He calls this approach 'bargained corporatism'. He sees a possibility that such a system might heal the divide in British industry:

> It is usually employers' representatives who bemoan the idea of 'two sides of industry' and who call upon workers to co-operate in the common good. But it is not workers who instituted the rigorous distinction between those who make decisions and those who receive instructions. Or, to put it another way, how can responsibility be demanded from those to whom responsibility is not given? The changes needed to induce more co-operation in British industry will have to be at the level of power and structure before they can be expected in workers attitudes.

Some socialists see participation as a 'half-way-house' to collective ownership and the running of industry. Others, however, consider that participation still leaves the balance of power and decision making too firmly in the hands of ownership and management, and are reluctant to see any change that would undercut the independent power to act of shop stewards. Some of these – particularly Marxists – favour a system of *workers' control* of industry rather than participation, and ultimately want the collective ownership and operation of industry in a classless society. No fair test of workers' control has yet occurred in Britain. Three of the best known cases – at Fisher Bendix, Meriden, and the *Scottish Daily News* – have been typical in that they were all 'taken over' by workers as a last ditch alternative to closure. Not surprisingly, they continued to struggle afterwards, particularly in terms of raising development capital. It is not easy to find a society in which workers' control has had a reasonable chance to operate. Clegg and Dunkerley argue that only a socialist society would provide the conditions that would enable worker-controlled enterprises to avoid the kind of isolation and difficulties experienced by British attempts. They dismiss the Soviet Union as too centralised in its economic management, and see the involvement of workers in Yugoslavia as participation rather than control. They settle on China during the cultural revolution phase as a closer example. For a time, many factories did operate with a high level of workers' involvement and in an anti-hierarchical way. Role-rotation symbolised in the slogan 'from the masses, to the masses', occurred widely, as did group-based methods of management decision making. Of course, such evidence is too scant to base any generalisation on, especially as more recent events in China have reversed the above trends. Equally, however, the ideals of socialism as applied to the organisation of work need not be shelved simply because they remain unachieved. If the principles of workers' participation or control become generally seen as humanly desirable, they would then be seen as humanly possible.

As far as Britain is concerned, such genuine commitment to industrial democracy does not exist, even within the mass of the Labour movement. Tom Forester is aware of this in the four reasons he gives for the failure of the movement towards industrial democracy in this country. These are lack of agreement on the precise definition and scope of industrial democracy among its supporters; inconsistent support from the trade unions and Labour party; employer hostility, and apathy among the rank and file. We can add the opinion that these attitudes reflect a culture that still socialises the majority to conform to authority rather than participate in policy and decision making. A. Halsey has said, the British are a deferential (awed by authority) nation. For the working class it is easier to obey or oppose capital and management than actively to share or take over responsibility, because most of them have never been educated otherwise. Still we concur with Forester's realistic rather than defeatist conclusion:

> To re-work a famous phrase, the spirit of man *is* straining to be free, but only after the mortgage has been paid. It will require a great deal more theoretical and propagandistic groundwork before the ideal of industrial democracy becomes a reality.

Work and Non-work

The division of existence into work and non-work time is very basic. However, these are better categories than work and leisure because much non-work time may be devoted to activities other than leisure. A number of attempts to develop the work/non-work categorisation have been made. Stanley Parker makes the following divisions: work; work obligations; existence time; non-work obligations; and leisure.

Parker defines work as earning a living – broadly, employment. Work obligations include activities done outside normal working hours which are associated with the job but beyond what is necessary to achieve a minimum level of performance; voluntary overtime and second jobs. The remaining three categories are, to a progressive extent, leisure categories. The third category, existence time, is the satisfaction of physiological needs such as 'sleep, eating, washing, eliminating'. Non-work obligations refers mainly to domestic duties. Finally, leisure is 'time free from obligations either to self or to others – time to do as one chooses'.

Elias and Dunning's categorisation of work/non-work can be matched fairly closely with Parker's scheme; private work and family management; rest; catering for biological needs; sociability; and 'mimetic' or play activities.

These types of categorisations are useful when considering the lives of males in full-time employment. They give a fair sense of the daily experience of necessity and pleasure. However, they are inadequate for understanding the work/non-work experience of those mainy involved in domestic labour, still overwhelmingly women. Sue McIntosh and her colleagues have criticised Parker sharply on this point. She takes each of Parker's categories in turn and shows their inadequacy when applied to housewives. First, she points out that in defining work as 'activity involved in earning a living', women in full-time housework are automatically excluded from Parker's framework. She observes that the work (domestic) activities of the housewife tend to overlap with and undermine the quality of her leisure. She gives a contemporary, feminist's slant to the old saw 'A woman's work is never done'. Again, she describes the distinction Parker makes in his category work and work obligations as 'fairly meaningless' for housewives. McIntosh's comment on the functions of existence time – eating, excretion, etc. – is that housewives often help others meet them – work, indeed! On the fourth category, 'the domestic part of work obligations', she observes that this is a large part of her total work in the home. She asks, 'Is women's work therefore to be equated with male "semi-leisure"?' About leisure itself, she states, 'Women have very little of this time.' Even the time a woman has may be defined by the choices her husband makes and she may be deterred from doing things on her own because of his possessiveness.

McIntosh, then, presents a typical work-leisure model of the housewife. The central feature of it is that domestic activity or concern virtually never ceases: there are few total 'escapes' into leisure, little real 'free time'. She pointedly raises the question of how women can gain more genuine leisure time and we will return to this later.

There are other variables besides gender which Parker's model does not adequately encompass. These include age, unemployment and race/ethnicity. Parker's view that work is the major influence on leisure is also of limited usefulness when applied to groups not in full-time work. In fairness, however, we ought to consider the group to which Parker's model best applies: people in full-time employment (mainly males).

Before presenting his own theory of work and leisure, Parker reviews existing work in the field. He classifies this into two schools of thought, segmentalists and holists. The former believe that work is separated from leisure and the latter that there is a tendency towards a fusion of work and leisure. Parker suggests that both approaches are too generalised and selective in their use of evidence. His own survey data found that both perspectives were relevant in relation to different, specific occupations. Consequently elements of these approaches appear in his own categorisation of the typical ways in which people relate their work and leisure: (1) the extension (holist) pattern; (2) the neutrality pattern; (3) the opposition (segmentalist) pattern.

(1) According to Parker:

> the extension pattern consists of having leisure activities that are often similar in content to one's working activities, making no distinction between what is considered work and what is considered leisure, and having one's central life interest in work rather than in family or leisure spheres.

He gives us examples of occupations in which this pattern is most likely to occur: 'successful businessmen, doctors, teachers, some skilled manual workers and social workers'.

Parker's observation about successful businessmen finds support from Young and Willmott's data on the work and family life of 190 managing directors. Work tended to dominate their lives and even leisure activities were shared with (usually) male business associates rather than with their families. Given the mainly instrumental attitude of many middle and lower level employees to their work, it is doubtful whether this pattern will diffuse down through the occupational system as Young and Willmott thought it might. However, it is worth speculating that as a result of the increase in high income earners in both Britain and the United States in the first half of the nineteen eighties, the extension pattern may become more common among higher social groups. Against this is the trend for more high income families to depend on a double income (indeed, particularly in the United States, children at school or college also often work part-time and thus add to the total income). Where women contribute substantially to the family income, they may be less willing to take total responsibility for the domestic side or to 'lose' their husbands to work and work-oriented pursuits to the same extent.

(2) Parker describes the neutrality pattern as:

> having leisure activities that are somewhat different from work, making a distinction between work and leisure, and having one's central life interest in family or leisure rather than in the work sphere.

He gives the following occupations as typically associated with this pattern: 'clerical workers, semi-skilled manual workers, and minor professionals other than social workers'. These occupations offer only low or medium autonomy at work, limited intrinsic satisfaction, but provide substantial leisure time for relaxation.

(3) Opposition pattern leisure activities involve:

> a sharp demarcation between work and leisure, and central life interest in the non-work sphere.

This pattern is 'to some extent exhibited by routine clerical workers' but 'seems more typical of unskilled manual workers, and those occupations such as mining and distant-water fishing'. The associated work factors are instrumental motivation, low autonomy in the work situation, limited opportunities for expression of abilities, and alienative attitudes.

427

Parker's analysis of the opposition pattern is based largely on two studies of extreme occupations: Denis, Henriques and Slaughter's *Coal is our Life* and Jeremy Tunstall's *The Fishermen*. For workers in these occupations leisure is recuperative and even escapist. Heavy drinking helps obliterate memories of harsh work and lowers inhibitions. Pleasure takes the form of release of pent-up energy in fun and macho fooling about and fantasy.

It is interesting to apply Abraham Maslow's model of human needs (see pp. 55–6) to Parker's analysis. Only those working in occupations associated with the extension pattern appear to have jobs which will greatly engage them in the process of self-actualisation (the achievement and expression of their highest needs). The neutrality and opposition patterns are associated with jobs unlikely to meet more than certain deficit needs. Some might provide such low status and public recognition that they might not even fully meet the need for self-esteem. Further, some work appears either so exhausting or intellectually blunting as to make the achievement of high levels of self-expression in leisure unlikely.

This trend of thought easily reconciles with Marxist analysis of the alienating nature of wage labour in capitalist society. Marx argued that the worker in capitalist society is alienated from himself and his species (human) being. In Maslow's terms his human potential is frustrated. However, Parker does not link his analysis of work and leisure to a critique of capitalism and Marxists would regard this as a criticism of his work. For them, both the production and consumption of leisure goods and services are alienated under capitalism. In particular, Bero Rigauer argues that the professional production of sport fragments and bureaucratises the experience of participants just as industrial production does that of workers. Similarly, the audience for commercialised sport may be distracted both from the exploitation and from a more active expression and development of their own talents – including, sometimes, sporting.

Culture, Class and Change

The debate about the relationship between work and leisure

has perhaps imposed too narrow a focus on the whole matter of cultural attitudes and pursuits whether at work or otherwise. Most critics would accept the observation that the quality of work and leisure life are both profoundly affected by technological change and by the nature of control and subordination at work and in society as a whole. The relationship between social control and culture is examined in detail in Chapter 20, and we have already raised important related issues in Chapters 3, 4, and 5. Here we will concentrate on technology and culture and, in particular, the effect of automation, including the influence of micro-chip technology, on social life as a whole, rather than on work or non-work taken separately.

Cultural change is, of course, not new, although the speed at which it occurs has increased since the industrial revolution. Some aspects of cultural change to which we have already referred are the break-up of traditional working class community, the forging of a common outlook between the surviving aristocracy and industrial elite, and the development of privatised nuclear family living among the majority of the working and middle class. The cultural effects of micro-chip technology are likely to be of comparable significance with these developments.

In the following analysis, it is important to remember the relationship between work, class and culture. This is a general, not rigid, relationship, but it is one which will help us to distinguish which groups are likely to benefit from the new technology and which not.

Automation: Opportunity or Disaster? An Exercise in Policy Speculation

We will follow Lilley's definition of automation which considers it to be the introduction of highly automatic machinery, or processes which largely eliminate human labour *and* detailed human control.

Optimists see a great potential for liberation from labour in the new micro-chip technology, whereas pessimists see it mainly in terms of the unemployment and accompanying social problems they believe it will produce. There is a further school of thought, expounded by thinkers like Hermann Kahn and Daniel Bell, which considers that as new technology replaces human labour, other jobs will be created that will not only

429

absorb those who have been displaced but will also service a higher standard of living. Even the last alternative, however, tends to assume a reduction in the working week and an increase in annual holidays. All these opinions relate to the future and all are sufficiently realistic to have a chance of being proved correct.

We will discuss the pessismistic view first. The major problem forseen is high unemployment (perhaps 5 million unemployed in Britain) coupled with psychological and practical failure to make the necessary social and economic adjustments. Already the word-processor has reduced the secretarial staff by half in some places in which it has been introduced, and large automatic warehouses need only one or two supervisory and technical staff. Michael Young's magnificent piece of sociological fiction, *The Rise of the Meritocracy*, first published in 1958, seems even more relevant now than then. Young did not regard his description of the future as inevitably destined to come true, still less, did he want it to. He merely warns us that it might. Young foresaw the emergence of a new elite of top scientists, technologists and professionals – men who have necessary *specialised* skills and reap high financial and status rewards as a result. This would happen together with a large mass of unemployed, or people employed in low grade work, such as domestic service or cleaning large buildings. He argued that the new 'masses' would include not only unemployed industrial workers but hundreds of thousands of clerical and office workers also 'laid waste' by new technology. Young pretends to be writing in 2034 but most of his projections appear to have already happened, or to be ominously close.

> More and more was demanded of the skilled men, less and less of the unskilled, until finally there was no need for unskilled men at all. Their work was merely routine, and so it could by definition be progressively taken over and performed by mechanical means. The more simplified a job became, the more easily could it be done by a machine which would feed itself with material, press the lever, and extract the finished article. Semi-automatic became fully automatic. Displacement of low-grade labour became very rapid after the Hitler war with the development of electronics, and especially of servo-mechanisms well-suited to direct industrial processes broken down into their simplest components. So marked was the progress that a new word – 'automation' – was coined for the old

business of mechanisation in the new form it was taking . . .

Many for whom there was no place in industry came to rest in routine clerical work, or in distribution. That was a happy solution, though not a permanent one. Mechanisation, starting in the factory, did not end there: offices and shops were also invaded. In the middle of the century book-keepers and typists were still common in offices; by the last quarter they had almost disappeared.

Though unnervingly right in his basic scenario, Young was wrong on an important point. He assumed for the purposes of his book, that educational reform would take the best to the top of society (his 'meritocracy') and ensure that the unintelligent would be left at the bottom. We have seen that social mobility patterns have not produced such a neat result. But it may well be a worse situation than even Young half-jokingly envisaged, to have large numbers of intelligent as well as less intelligent people unemployed or poorly employed and, perhaps, with little prospect of a better future.

Those who take what we have labelled a more optimistic view of the effects of the new technology usually do so on the basis of two qualifications. Firstly, they argue that the *social* effects of economic change must be planned for. Secondly, they contend that attitudes of guilt and humiliation associated with unemployment and 'the dole' must gradually disappear. Given this, the possibility of a much freer and more personally fulfilling culture can be built on the basis of the material affluence provided by technology. A number of socialists have been associated with this view, including Herbert Marcuse and Clive Jenkins. Marx himself must be counted among the optimists. He considered that technological invention provides the means of human liberation *if* it is collectively owned, controlled and used. This is what he said about automation and the social possibilities it creates:

> The human factor is restricted to watching and supervising the production process . . . The counterpart of this reduction is that all members of society can develop their education in the arts, sciences, etc., thanks to the free time and means available to all.

The material and the cultural aspects of 'liberation' are, in fact, closely linked. Socialist 'futurologists' like Marcuse and Jenkins, look forward to a time when wealth will be allocated by government on the basis of personal need rather than by the market on the basis of competition. This goes well beyond current conceptions of the welfare state. It means that people will have stopped thinking of wage-labour as the only generally respectable means of obtaining an income and accept that other bases of distributing wealth (such as need) are equally legitimate. In other words, a decline in commitment to the 'work ethic' must occur. The work ethic is based on the value that work is virtuous and should be rewarded and that, by corollary, unemployment is a sign of poor character. The point is that, in a time when there is not enough work to go around, this attitude itself becomes redundant. Nevertheless, it will not change easily. Those who are employed may well continue to pursue whatever rewards they can get, regardless of the needs of others. But it may be, as Jenkins suggests, that the power of the unions has a better chance of forcing through more egalitarian policies in the coming age rather than a more general appeal to charity and the goodwill of the community. Nevertheless, as he realises, they too, would have to be persuaded to act beyond their own immediate sectional interest and on behalf of the unemployed.

It is scarcely possible to exaggerate the change in cultural attitudes required before the liberated society envisaged by Marx can come about. In addition to the material rewards and sense of 'virtue' associated with work, it is also a prime source of *identity* and *status*. A society of greater leisure might offer, as Marx implies, a whole range of new identities and perhaps, instead of status, various forms of self-fulfilment. All this assumes that the new technology will be used substantially, if not exclusively, to create socially constructive commodities and services, and not destructively in, for instance, an expansion of armaments production. To hope for this is optimism in the extreme. It may be that our species will prove too afraid to make the most creative and liberating use of the new technology. To do so would require an unprecedented level of national and international trust, co-operation and sharing of resources.

It is possible that the ideas of hard-nosed liberal realist, Daniel Bell, will prove closer to the truth than those of socialist Clive Jenkins. Bell's idea of post-industrial society is not greatly different from what Young foresaw, except that he is confident that continued expansion in the service sector (including personal and social services) will provide both employment and the conditions of a better, more humane life than previously. He does not appear to share Young's concern with the possibility that post-industrial society will be sharply divided into meritocrats and masses or, simply, 'winners' and 'losers'. James Robertson sums this up well and puts the matter in to global context:

> It is best to be blunt about it. This approach to the future implies an ethic of elitism and domination in a class-divided world. Internationally it implies that, by becoming super-industrialised as the less developed countries become industrialised, today's industrialised countries will maintain their economic superiority. It implies that within each super-industrialised country there will be two sharply polarised classes – a responsible technocratic elite in charge of every important sphere of life, and the irresponsible unemployed masses . . .

Guide to Further Reading and Study

Work and non-work, like stratification, is an area of rapid change and I select this brief reading list to reflect this. The topics covered by the following books from Macmillan are clear from their titles: Richard Hyman and Robert Price, *eds, The New Working Class? White-collar Workers and their Organizations: A Reader* (1983); Rosemary Crompton and Gareth Jones, *White-Collar Proletariat: Deskilling and Gender in Clerical Work* (1984); Robert Taylor, *Workers and the New Depression* (1982); and Anna Pollert's *Girls, Wives, and Factory Lives* (1981). Two books from Fontana on industrial relations are useful: Hyman, *Strikes* (1977); and Colin Crouch, *The Politics of Industrial Relations* (1979). Work/non-work is interestingly covered in Alan Tomlinson, *ed, Leisure and Social Control* (Brighton Polytechnic, 1981) and Clive Jenkins and Barrie Sherman, *The Leisure Shock* (Methuen, 1981). See also the relevant reading lists at the end of Chapters 16 and 24.

Finally, many students have part-time jobs and tapping into their experience can bring alive many of the concepts and issues of this topic.

Past Questions

1 Striking represents one form of industrial conflict. What other forms are there and how can the varied levels of conflict in different industries be explained? (AEB, 1980)

2 Examine the view that conventional sociological distinctions between work and non-work, and between work and leisure, are increasingly inappropriate in contemporary society. (AEB, 1984)

3 'Where there is a separation of the work from home, work becomes the primary source of status. This is why those who cannot work are devalued, stigmatised and often see themselves as worthless.' Discuss. (London, 1984)

4 'The major effect of technological change is to increase the skill level of a small number of jobs, whilst reducing the skill level of a large number of jobs.' Discuss. (OLE, 1985)

5 'Whilst technology is an important determinant of work satisfaction, it is not the only determinant.' Discuss (AEB, 1985)

16 Organisations, Class and Power

Organisations are a personal issue as well as a public reality. The problem is, people often fail to see the personal importance of organisations. Students often profess boredom at the thought of studying them; yet, no topic has more to offer in the way of practical understanding. Most of us will spend our working lives with large or medium-size organisations and if we do not learn to 'manage' them, they will certainly manage us. Perhaps the feelings of alienation that many students experience at the very thought of studying organisations is a symptom of the fact that they can only conceive of being controlled and manipulated by them, and not vice-versa. This quiet desperation was given a voice by the nineteen sixties student radical, Mario Savio, when he urged fellow rebels at Berkeley, California, to stop the bureaucratic machine of the university by 'laying' their bodies on it. Partly to combat this pessimism, we will examine not only the structure and functioning of organisations but who has power and control within them, and also whether more democratic organisational systems are possible.

Both Weber and Marx were fully aware of the importance of the concepts of power and control in analysing organisation. They agreed that organisations are the instruments which 'run' modern life but disagreed about which groups had real control of them. Weber's organisational theory is linked closely to his analysis of the 'new class'. He had no doubt that top organisational officials had great power both in private industry and government departments. He anticipated the dictatorship not of the proletariat, but of the official. He felt that as bureaucracies expanded they would develop vested interests, and argued that even a democratically elected Parliament would have problems in controlling top civil servants and their departments (although he believed it should try). Marx, however, contended that in capitalist society the capitalist class controls the bureaucrats and uses them for its own ends. He argued that this was true not only of the salaried officials of private industry but, ultimately, of state bureaucrats as well, because he considered that the capitalist class also controlled the state. We have already met a modern version of this argument in the work of Dahrendorf and Giddens (Chapter 10, pp. 259–61) and will return again to it in this chapter.

Durkheim was not primarily interested in class control of organisations: rather, he took it for granted, as natural. He was more concerned with how a society, made up of complex organisations and characterised by an advanced division of labour, could hold together. As we have seen, he believed that this was possible because of organic solidarity – the interdependence of people and organisations in modern societies (see Chapter 6). Durkheim's point was a general one: later sociologists have had much more specific interests in the field of the sociology of organisations than he did.

Formal and Informal Organisations: A Preliminary Distinction

Formal organisations are operated by special officials on the basis of established rules, to achieve certain goals. Practically all the large organisations of modern society such as factories, office complexes, super-markets and schools, are formal structures. Their respective officials, rules and goals are familiar to us all. Although formal organisations are a particular feature of urban, industrial societies, certain examples such as armies and monasteries have existed for centuries. To an extent, formal organisations in modern societies have taken over or *supplemented* functions previously performed by family, kinship and community groups (see Chapter 4, pp. 75–6). Thus, state welfare as well as family help is available to the sick and needy through various organisational channels.

Informal organisations develop within all formal organisations. *Informal organisations are freely created social group relationships, not formally part of organisational structures.* It is difficult to imagine that even the most rigidly run prison or concentration camp does not have some form of 'underground' system of communication. The achievement of formal goals may depend on whether informal groups operate 'for' or 'against' the formal organisation. To put it in functionalist terms, they may be functional or dysfunctional. Thus, anti-school peer-groups are an example of informal organisations which are dysfunctional to the achievement of formal educational goals.

It would be misleading to leave the impression that informal organisations exist only within formal structures: friendship groups of peers and gangs occur outside them. Typically, perhaps, people find more meaning in their informal relationships than in their formal ones. The reservation widely felt about the 'over-organised' quality of modern life is partly based on the feeling that formal organisations seem to be intruding more and more into the private area of life. Even though more leisure time exists, it is largely 'organised' for us by the mass media rather than used imaginatively and intelligently. Obviously, this view is controversial and we assess it critically in Chapter 20, pp. 581–5.

Theoretical Perspectives on Organisations

Although there are many organisational theories that the student might come across, we can conveniently divide them into four main groups. *These are the bureaucratic or mechanistic; systems theories – particularly organic systems theory;* theories based on the concept of *interaction;* and *conflict theory.* Although these perspectives are frequently contrasted they are by no means wholly exclusive in all respects. Indeed, we will consider the bureaucratic and organic approaches together as much to show their complementary as their contradictory aspects.

We make no analytical distinction between industrial and other kinds of formal organisations in this section. The types of organisational structures described below can occur in both the industrial and non-industrial sectors such as central and local government departments.

1 Bureaucratic and Systems Theories

Bureaucratic or Mechanistic Theory and Organic Systems Theory

Max Weber laid down the classical or bureaucratic model of organisational theory. His model is a functionalist one. *He maintained that bureaucracy is the most functionally efficient form of organisation, even though it can sometimes operate in a rather 'inhuman' way.* Bureaucracies are formal organisations generally recognisable by certain characteristics. He constructed an ideal type of bureaucracy to show what these characteristics are. We can summarise them as follows:

1 The existence of different offices (or positions) governed by rules the purpose of which is to fulfil a specific, given function or functions
2 The hierarchical organisation of offices – that is, some positions have more authority and status than others
3 Management based on files and records used with the assistance of office staff
4 The appointment of trained officials to occupy roles in the bureaucracy

Weber saw the growth of bureaucratic organisation as a major example of the application of rational thought to practical problems. He regarded the triumph of rationality as a characteristic feature of the modern world. Another of its manifestations was the massive development of science and technology. Weber also described the nature of an official bureaucratic position. Above all, it involves a commitment to performing the functions the official is appointed to do and not to any powerful person or patron who might wish to interfere with the official's course of duty. It was necessary for Weber to make this point because, in the middle ages, this principle did not apply. When a king or lord appointed someone to a high position of service within his household, he expected his appointee to be loyal to him *personally* rather than merely to perform pre-determined and agreed functions. By contrast, a modern bureaucratic official is expected to do the job described in the terms of his *contract*. The contract defines his duties, establishes his salary scale and gives security of tenure subject to an agreed period of notice and good conduct. Most people reading this book will eventually take up a position of this kind. We live in a bureaucratic world! A classic example of a modern bureaucracy is the civil service. A pupil leaving school with a clutch of 'O' levels may begin as a clerical officer. In time, he or she becomes an Executive Officer and then, perhaps, a Senior Executive Officer: more remotely, the office of Principal Secretary beckons. Each office has its own functions and the further one progresses up the hierarchy, the more power and status accrue.

Criticisms of Weber's bureaucratic model will become apparent as we examine alternative organisational theories, and some dysfunctions of bureaucracy. One point is worth making immediately, however. There is an implicit contradiction in Weber's bureaucratic functionalism, and his more usual emphasis on conflict. Oddly, Weber did not fully develop the perspective that as well as fulfilling useful functions, organisations are also frequently the focus of conflict between groups. We develop this issue later in this chapter.

The organisational type that most obviously contrasts with the bureaucratic is what Burns and Stalker (1961) termed the *organic system*. They contrast organic systems with what they call *mechanistic systems* but, as the latter are in no way distinguishable from bureaucracies, this need not detain us.

Organic systems are characterised by a less rigid division of labour than mechanistic ones; they are less rule-bound, less hierarchical and more open to the influence of the informal group. The last point is crucial. The skill and experience of the individual can be communicated *laterally* (sideways) across the network of those involved in the task. The *team* as a whole shares power and responsibility. Overall, the organic approach shows a more subtle awareness of the complex nature and effects of interaction, formal and informal, than does the bureaucratic. Such an approach is often considered appropriate for relatively high level technical or scientific employees in, say, the electronics industry – for example, a team of computer programmers. Nevertheless, it has also been successfully tried with manual workers. At their Kalmar plant, Volvo broke down assembly work into 20 different functions. Each one is performed by a team of 15 or 20 workers. The cars pass from team to team on trolleys, allowing the worker considerable freedom of movement. The teams are not hierarchically organised, and solutions to problems are supposed to be reached through co-operation and not by authoritarianism.

Although the bureaucratic or mechanistic and the organic systems models of organisations are, to some extent, in competition with each other, there are circumstances in which one model may be more appropriate than the other. Burns and Stalker suggest that bureaucracy is often suitable for the pursuit of clear goals in stable conditions, such as producing a commodity for a safe and established market, and that an organic system is appropriate to less stable conditions in which precise goals may still be developing, such as electronics research.

Scientific Management, Human Relations Theory and Socio-technical Systems Theory
Frederick W. Taylor's theory of scientific management reflects

the same principles as Weber's bureaucratic theory, and, to a lesser extent, human relations theory and socio-technical theory bear comparison with organic systems theory.

Taylor, an American contemporary of Weber, reached his conclusions independently of the Austrian social scientist. Taylor was specifically interested in industrial organisations and particularly in developing ways to improve production. What he said about the role and function of the industrial worker was comparable with Weber's comments on the lower level white collar employee. Further, both recognised that higher level bureaucrats and managers had relatively more power. Like Weber, Taylor decided that efficiency was best obtained by task specialisation and standardisation, and the centralisation of decision making power at the top of the hierarchy. He argued that all mental work should be removed from the workshop, and put in the hands of management. He presented his ideas in a book entitled *Scientific Management*. An unadmitted guiding principle seemed to be to treat the worker as an extension of the machine or organisation and, indeed, this notion is, more or less, implicit in all bureaucratic structures. Among the advice he offered was that 'the two hands should begin and complete their motions simultaneously' and that 'proper illumination increases production'. In addition, he recommended that pay levels be closely tied to productivity. It seems appropriate that Taylor's approach is often referred to as *mechanical* or *mechanistic* theory.

Human relations theory originated as a reaction against Taylor's scientific management theory. From 1927 to 1932, a series of studies was mounted into worker productivity at the Hawthorne Works of the Western Electricity Company in Chicago. Initially, the researchers, led by Elton Mayo, were positively influenced by Taylor and their area of enquiry was actually suggested by his work. They wanted to find out the optimum level of illumination and other environmental factors to maximise production. There is more than a touch of comedy about the way they arrived at the 'results' of their research. They 'found' that the relation between the variables of illumination and production was virtually non-existent. In one of the studies in which the workers were placed in a control room in lighting conditions equivalent to moonlight, they still maintained a reasonable level of production: it fell off only when

441

illumination was so reduced that they could not see properly!

Ultimately, the Hawthorne experiments were of outstanding importance both because of the new theory of industrial relations they suggested, and by virtue of their contribution to a better understanding of social scientific method, specifically that of observation. We have already discussed the second of these, the effect of the researcher on the behaviour of the subject of research, in Chapter 2. We concentrate now on the first, the content of their findings. To put it simply, they found that *the productive performance of the workers was affected by social factors,* as well as material ones such as the level of illumination. The social factor at work in this case was the interest of the research team in the workers. Unexpectedly, this seemed to stimulate them to greater efforts than otherwise. The presence of researchers in a factory is, however, rare.

Follow-up studies by the Mayo team showed that the informal relationships of the workers themselves constitute the most important social variable affecting production. The role of informal groups was established by the notable Western Electric Company Bank Wiring Room experiment involving the wiring of switchboards. A group of 14 workers was set up separately and observed for six months. It was found that, although they were paid on the basis of a productivity bonus scheme, the men did not respond to this by individually trying to maximise their production, but established their own production norms as a group. Group disapproval was equally the fate of those who produced either more or less than the agreed norm.

Underlying the human relations approach is a more complex and more humanistic theory of human needs than that implied by classical theory. The latter assumes that *individuals* will work harder in improved material conditions and if they are given higher material rewards for more work. *Human relations theory argues that people also need the security, companionship, identity and guidance of the informal peer group.* These psychological needs are only capable of fulfilment with others. Taylor's attempt to treat the work-force as isolated individuals was based on the misleading fiction that workers are, in fact, isolated. In modern, large-scale organisations work is a collective experience.

The socio-technical systems theory attempts to combine both the technical and social factors affecting work so as to bring about the most effective overall performance. Mary Weir summarises three major points suggested by socio-technical system theorists to achieve this end: the individual must have some power to control and regulate his work; he should be able to adapt his own standards of work both to the expectations and demands of others and to the changing work situation generally; and the job should be both varied and have a coherent pattern. Finally, it should be linked meaningfully to the rest of the production process. It should also provide the worker with status in the community.

Both the human relations and socio-technical systems approaches have been criticised as merely 'making exploitation more bearable'. In a challenging critique of management theories the Marxist, Harry Braverman, attacks both Taylor's theory, and human relations and similar schools. He suggests that Taylorism did not last because it was too obviously crude and insensitive. The 'softer' theories provided the necessary ideological fig leaves to cover the still basically exploitative nature of capitalist production. But they fail to confront the private ownership and control of industry which Marxists traditionally regard as the root of alienation. Even given Braverman's premise, however, there remains the argument that it is better to be exploited in comfort than discomfort!

The Dysfunctions of Bureaucratic Organisation: Breaking the Rules

The arguments in favour of bureaucracy are considerable. Firstly, the bureaucratic division of labour combined with technological innovation has greatly increased the production of goods and services: to that extent it is efficient. Secondly, a bureaucracy usually ensures a degree of predictability: production quotas are pre-determined, people know how they are likely to be treated. Thirdly, partly because of its very impersonality, bureaucracy is often a condition of fairness. People are appointed to offices on the basis of qualifications and merit rather than patronage. Further, clients are dealt with by bureaucrats on the basis of equality and need, not favouritism. That, at any rate, is the theory, although several sociologists have criticised and modified it.

Arguing within a functionalist framework, Robert Merton points to several dysfunctions of bureaucracy which can lead to inefficiency. First, rigid adherence to bureaucratic rules may prevent an official from improvising a necessary response to unexpected circumstances. Thus, to offer our own example, a secretary in a production company, in the absence of superiors, may happen one day to find herself having to deal with an important client. Conceivably, by retreating behind her official role – 'I'm sorry, I'm only the secretary. I don't have the authority to deal with business matters' – vital orders may be jeopardised or, at a minimum, the client may feel he or she has not been well treated. In such a case, initiative, confidence and some imagination are needed. Bureaucracy does not always teach these qualities and can actually smother them. The results can be 'passing the buck'. Secondly, there is a danger that those rigidly trained to obey rules rather than to consciously achieve goals will become what Merton calls *ritualistic*. This means that they attach more importance to observing rules and procedures than in achieving the purpose for which they exist: this is referred to as goal displacement. As lower level bureaucrats are often not kept informed about general organisational goals, ritualism must be considered a potential fault of bureaucracy, rather than an individual failing. Merton classifies ritualism as a form of anomie (see Chapter 17, pp. 473–5). Finally, Merton argues that the sometimes alienating effect of bureaucracy on both bureaucrats and the public with whom they deal can be dysfunctional. Bureaucratic or ritualistic characters are not the most adaptable and efficient of people, and clients who have to submit to long bureaucratic procedure before, say, they can receive needed social security are unlikely to be very co-operative.

Merton argues within functionalist assumptions but, as we have seen, Burns and Stalker suggest that in certain circumstances it is more efficient to break with the bureaucratic method of organisation altogether. Broadly, this is when co-operative and organic rather than competitive and hierarchical structures are more suitable to organisational goal attainment. Arguing along similar lines, Peter Blau gives a number of examples in which formal bureaucracy proved inappropriate. One such instance occurred in an isolated American navy island base. Virtually cut off from external control, the formal organisation of the base broke down and natural leaders, who worked effectively but within an informal framework emerged. A better known study by Blau is of an American state employment agency. He compared two groups of job placement interviewers who operated on different organisational principles, the one highly bureaucratic, the other much more informal and co-operative. On balance, the second approach proved more effective in placing clients in jobs. Blau did not over-generalise from this case-study to the point of concluding that informal organisation is more efficient. Indeed, he found evidence to suggest that it sometimes operated in a biased manner as there were fewer bureaucratic checks to prevent officials favouring some clients at the expense of others. Rather, he suggested that what is often needed is balance, varying with circumstances, between formal and informal methods.

It is worth recalling two studies that we have already met which point to the limits of a rigidly bureaucratic approach. First is the pioneering Hawthorne study presented earlier in this chapter which established the importance of the informal social group in production. Second is Alvin Gouldner's case-study of a wildcat strike which showed that unrest can occur when workers, used to informality, responsibility and independence, have a bureaucratic regime imposed upon them.

Finally, there can be no clearer demonstration of the limited effectiveness of rigid rule-following in achieving goals than the fact that workers use the strategy of 'working to rule' (doing all tasks by the book) in the industrial bargaining process.

Refusing to work overtime is a common example. The result is often inconvenience to the public. Thus, transport workers can make chaos out of timetable schedules merely by working a 'normal' day. Strict and time-consuming adherence to safety check rules or a rigid refusal to allow more people on a bus than is officially stipulated can also be used as pinpricks in industrial campaigning. Put negatively, working to rule can be presented as a 'withdrawal of goodwill'. The National Union of Teachers (NUT) adopted this approach in their industrial action of 1979. In particular, lunch-time supervision of children was suspended. This was hardly lethal in its effect but it did result in a number of 'mad hatter's dinner parties' here and there. Clearly, then, relationships and goodwill, as well as rules are a part of organisation.

Talcott Parsons' Functional-Systems Theory

Parsons' organisational theory is interesting in that it combines

445

elements of Weberian functionalism with those of systems theory. He retains the notion that organisations have goals, but describes them as potentially much more flexible and capable of adaptation than does Weber.

Parsons treats organisations virtually as though they are small-scale societies, and his organisational analysis strongly recalls his social systems theory (see Chapter 3, pp. 47–8). The various parts of organisations are seen as interdependent; they have certain needs that have to be met for survival; they have goals; the whole is something more than the sum of all the individuals who are members of the organisation. The organic analogy is clearly apparent in all this; even so, there is nothing so far mentioned that adds substantially to Weber's analysis of bureaucracy. Parsons, however, goes beyond Weber in two important ways. Firstly, he pays more attention to the capacity of organisations to interact with one another and with the environment in general. The notion that, in order to function effectively, organisations must adapt their structure and goals to changes in the environment has certainly been of influence in modern management. In a fast-changing age the possiblity of 'being left behind' is ever-present. An organisation that cannot adapt is not likely to survive. An example of an organisation that has adapted to change is the House of Commons, a very different body now from that of several hundred years ago. British Leyland is an example of an organisation that is finding adaptation – particularly in its response to foreign competition and new technology – a struggle.

Secondly, Parsons recognises that organisations must, in some way, meet man's expressive as well as his instrumental needs. Even so, it is clear that he considers these needs are to be accommodated within the terms of the organisation's pre-set goals and certainly not as ends in themselves. This seems a deterministic and unconvincing way of reconciling personal needs with rational organisational goals. In reality, the individuals and groups that make up organisations often disagree much more than Parsons is willing to concede.

A well known application of functionalist systems theory is Peter Selznick's analysis of the Tennessee Valley Authority, set up in 1933 by President Roosevelt to help the region combat the effects of the Depression. The Authority was set up with the intention of involving local people in policy making. In practice, this did not happen and instead powerful local farmers were the major effective interest group consulted by the Authority's officials. Selznick suggests that the reason why this occurred was that for the organisation to 'survive' and its officials to retain their jobs, compromise had to be made with the major local power group. This may have been so but it is just as easy to see these developments in terms of interest group or class conflict as organisational survival.

2   Social Action and Interactionist Theories

Social Action Theory
David Silverman describes the meanings that individuals attach to, and find in, organisations, to be the major concern of action theory. People, not organisations, have goals. He is, however, appreciative of Parsons' attempt to conceive of organisations in terms of change and development, and he himself contextualises action within a wider institutional and social environment. He cites the previously mentioned study of Gouldner as an excellent example of an analysis that combines a sense of historical and institutional context with an understanding of the meaning actors attach to their behaviour (see Chapter 15, pp. 417–18).

Another excellent example of the importance of understanding how human behaviour, particularly in its emotional rather than its rational aspects, can affect organisations, is given by Ralph Glasser. In a television documentary (1980), Glasser tells how the olive producers of the Italian rural village of San Georgio refused to use a co-operative olive press – even though there existed good 'rational' economic arguments for doing so. Instead, they preferred to take their olives for pressing to the owners of private presses who were usually wealthy. Glasser suggests that the olive farmers acted in this way because they had a traditional relationship, based on established expectation and *fiducia* (trust) with the private press operators. By contrast, as Glasser points out, 'You can't have a relationship with a co-operative'. In fairness, it should be said that co-operatives do sometimes work well, and people do have relationships within them. Nevertheless, it is obvious that the producers did not *feel* that they could relate to the new situation. This feeling became the major operative factor in the above situation and accounts

447

for the failure of the co-operative. Glasser indulges in some conservative romanticism, but underlying this is a wise awareness of the texture of relationships and feelings woven over time, and a fear of what the brutal blade of technology and bureaucracy might do to them in the name of progress and rationality.

A better known example of a piece of research utilising action perspective, is Goldthorpe and Lockwood's affluent worker study. It will be recalled that they studiously avoided attributing motives to the workers but took the trouble to ask them what their motives were. It turned out that a majority had an instrumental orientation to work, or, simply, they worked for money, not satisfaction. (Chapter 15, p. 499).

Total Institutions: Interactionist Analysis of the 'Ultimate' in Bureaucracy

Social action theory and symbolic interactionism are compatible theoretical approaches, but whereas the former has been developed mainly in Europe, the latter was founded in the USA, and has its own characteristic concepts and vocabulary.

We may live in an increasingly bureaucratic world, but most of us can escape from it into our private lives and personal relationships. Most of us think of these 'escapes' as necessary to a balanced life and even to sanity itself. There are, however, some who live all the time, and for a long period, in highly bureaucratic organisations, in *total institutions*. How does the self – to use the interactionist term – adjust to omnipresent and 'permanent' bureaucracy? Before answering this question, we must briefly examine some different types of total organisations.

A major distinction between different types of total organisations is whether membership is *voluntary* or *compulsory*. Monasteries are an example of the former, prisons of the latter. Whether members belong to an organisation by choice or not will tend greatly to affect the quality of life within it – as a brief consideration of the difference between a monastery and prison should show. The voluntary-compulsory membership distinction does not, however, apply in every case: the members of some institutions, old people's homes and mental hospitals, for instance, may contain both types. A further way of categorising total institutions is simply in terms of the *purposes* they serve. Thus, goals may be *custodial* (prisons), *protective* (mental hospitals), *retreatist* (monasteries), or *task-oriented* (armies, boarding schools). Often a total institution may serve several purposes, for example, prisons protect the public and, sometimes, seek to reform their inmates.

Erving Goffman's *Asylums*, based on a field study carried out in a hospital in Washington in 1955–56, remains the best known study of a total institution. In order to see at first hand the personal and psychological effects on the patients of life in an asylum, Goffman undertook a participant observational study, playing the role of an assistant to the athletic director. We can divide what Goffman refers to as the *career* of the mental patient into two stages, the breaking down of the old self and the construction of a new self. Part of the second stage is the adoption of *modes of adjustment* which enable the individual to 'get by' on a day-to-day basis and perhaps to salvage some of his sense of individuality.

The first blow to a person's old or established sense of identity is when someone – often a close relative – complains of 'abnormality'. Identity is further broken down during the in-patient phase. Not all mental hospitals are equally bureaucratic, but the admission procedures Goffman mentions include photographing, finger-printing, number assigning, listing personal possessions for storage, and undressing. Not surprisingly, he refers to this as the process of 'mortification' of the self. In the second stage referred to above, the inmate attempts to build a new self centred on the institution. The system of privileges and rewards operated by the institution in return for obedience or, perhaps, for doing work around the hospital, focus the individual's attention and energy, and may give a sense of meaning and purpose and so help to reintegrate the personality. Despite the fact that total institutions are geared to standardise behaviour, inmates manage to adopt individual modes of adjustment. *Withdrawal* or *retreatism* is an extreme and often irreversible adjustment. Two forms of adjustment in which the institution tends to 'take over' the inmate are *conversion* and *colonisation*. Conversion is when the inmate accepts the institution's definition of himself as, say, 'emotionally immature' and tries to conform to the pattern of 'perfect inmate'; colonisation occurs when the institutional regime so engulfs the individual that it comes to seem preferable to the world outside. Prisoners, as well as mental patients, who prefer to have their lives 'run for them' sometimes adopt this mode of adjustment. Goffman uses the term, *playing it cool,* to describe a general posture of strategic adjustment. The mental patient may adjust to the bureaucratic power structure, and to other inmates largely as an attempt to improve his chances of discharge. In prisons, a similar adjustment is often rewarded with a remission of sentence. Goffman considers playing it cool to be the most common form of adjustment.

Some inmates *rebel* or, to use Goffman's precise term, take an 'intransigent line' rather than genuinely adjust, although he says relatively little of this possibility. The film, *One Flew Over the Cuckoo's Nest,* based on a novel by Ken Kesey, was a dramatised version of the rebellion of McMurphy, a patient in a mental hospital. McMurphy simply refused to accept the total planning and routinisation of his life. For him, the officially pre-programmed and controlled time-table – meal times, basket-ball games, television watching, lights out and, above all, day trips – provide opportunities for anarchic self-assertion. One episode in the film in which a bus-load of mental patients, led by McMurphy, take over a ship is a classic of comic absurdity. Finally, McMurphy ends up subdued by a brain lobotomy – the ultimate form of control. Lobotomies may be rare but electric shock treatment, the use of drugs, and manipulation of privileges, rewards and punishments to achieve conformity are common. The film does not moralise but, in the end, McMurphy's madness compares well with official thought and personality control. We are reminded that when 'society' defines someone as deviant, the consequent loss of that individual's freedom, and the tools used in reforging acceptable behaviour are formidable. Still, the film ends optimistically with McMurphy's friend, a previously subdued Indian, breaking out of the hospital in a bid for freedom.

A book very much in Goffman's style (although not uncritical of him) is *Psychological Survival: The Experience of Long-Term Imprisonment,* by Stanley Cohen and Laurie Taylor (1972). The authors frankly proclaim that one of their purposes is to provide a 'manual of survival' for long-term prisoners. Accordingly, they devote one chapter to 'making out and fighting back'. They find much more evidence of resistance in Durham prison – where they did their research – than Goffman did among patients in the Washington hospital. Accordingly, they write of *modes of resistance* rather than *adjustment*. They list five types of resistance: *self-protection, campaigning, escaping, striking* and *confronting*. Self-protection and campaigning are individual types of resistance. Cohen and Taylor spend little time on the material side of self-protection, for example getting more and better food. They concentrate on the protecting of self-image. They stress how prisoners reject the most damning 'labels' – 'killer', 'thug', 'brutal psychopath', – sometimes humorously and sometimes in anger. Campaigning, the most popular form of which was sending letters to MPs, was more often done as a way of 'getting back' at authority, rather than in any real hope of progress on given issues. Escaping, striking and confronting all involve a high degree of collective effort or connivance. The term 'confronting' needs to be explained. It describes any major collective effort to force the prison authorities, and sometimes a wider audience, to listen to the prisoners' complaints and opinions. There could hardly be a more conspicuous example of trying to draw public attention to grievances than, for instance, occupying a prison roof for a period – as has sometimes happened.

Cohen and Taylor show typical interactionist awareness that the differences between 'normals' and 'deviants' is generally one of degree rather than of kind. In a later book, *Escape Attempts: The Theory and Practice of Resistance to Everyday Life* (1976), they extend their concept of resistance to more conventional, as distinct from totally bureaucratic, situations. We have already seen how, at work and in schools, people attempt to 'manage' their own situations, despite the constraints imposed by the organised environment. In the first two chapters in the next section we examine further the tension between the demands of society for order and conformity, and the frequent tendency of individuals not to 'fit in'.

3 Conflict Theories

This section should be regarded as a direct continuation of the opening part of this chapter, in which the conflict perspectives on organisations of Marx and Weber were introduced. Whereas Parsons tends to see power as being used for 'necessary' purposes in the common interest, for example, in maintaining law and order. Marx and, to some extent Weber, sees it as being used by groups or classes mainly in their own interests. Thus, Weber feared the abuse of power by bureaucrats on their own behalf, and Marx on behalf of the capitalist class.

Clegg and Dunkerley remind us of what should really be obvious – that the reason for the existence of most organisations is the need to organise the labour process, and that this involves the control of workers by employers. Like Bowles and Gintis, they regard the extreme fragmentation of the labour process in industrial and office work as one means of controlling the working force, because it prevents them from understanding the nature of the whole production process. They differentiate not only between buyers and sellers of labour but also between working groups of different power in the market. Thus, they explain at length the reasons for the particular exploitation of female labour, as we also did in Chapter 12. Their discussion leads naturally to the question of different forms of organisational control (see next section), and to whom the product of labour rightly belongs, and how it should be shared. As they point out, their perspective is pertinent to organisations in both communist and capitalist societies. The most obvious difference between organisations today and in Marx's time is that many are now operated by the state. They show that a 'them and us' feeling in the workforce can occur in undemocratically run state enterprises such as those in the Soviet Union, as well as in capitalist ones. A state that simply gathers in profit or surplus value and redistributes it unequally is hardly likely to be perceived as any improvement on a capitalist entrepreneur.

Wallerstein's comments on organisations are comparable with those of Clegg and Dunkerley. He gives the broadest dimension possible to organisational analysis. He suggests that national societies are inadequate units for economic and social analysis and that they should be seen as only one organisational level within the *capitalist world economy*. Specific organisations, like the nation state or multi-national corporations, operate within the capitalist world system. This is generally true, but it should be realised that the political and organisational influence of the Soviet Union has provided an increasingly powerful challenge to capitalism since the war. We have examined this issue in the context of development (see Chapter 8, pp. 197–204).

One matter on which Clegg and Dunkerley say relatively little is how private troubles arising in organisations can be related to 'public issues'. An obvious example is how a corporation's policy of plant closures or cut-backs – perhaps the result of recession – can cause the personal misery of unemployment (Chapters 8 and 11). There is need for much more analysis of how individual and, indeed, national experience is formed by organisations operating in an unpredictable world system.

A number of liberal structural sociologists have applied Weber's concepts in a way that emphasises the functional aspect of organisations but shows an awareness of conflict. We have already seen that Weber considered that socialist societies were likely to become as bureaucratic, if not more so, than capitalist ones. More recently, this view has been presented as part of the broader, more controversial *convergence* thesis. In this context, convergence means that the economic and organisational structure of advanced societies, whether capitalist or socialist, are becoming increasingly similar. The view that such societies need central economic planning and large governmental bureaucracies to implement decisions is crucial to this idea. Another aspect of this thesis appears in the work of Daniel Bell and Ralf Dahrendorf. They argue that the complex problems of advanced societies require advanced management techniques. Political argument will not solve essentially technical problems, and may make them worse. Thus, national investment in energy may need to be planned years ahead, regardless of which government is in power. In their view, top managers and their technical advisers are vital in giving long-term continuity in both advanced capitalist and socialist societies. Dahrendorf, and, particularly, Bell, consider this new class of experts to be a highly influential elite (see Chapter 15, pp. 429–33 and this chapter). They see potential for conflict between this high status and well paid elite and the less privileged and well-off. Nevertheless, they consider this inequality to be inevitable and as much a feature of communist as of capitalist societies.

As we have seen, Marxists do not consider that managers have as much power as Bell and Dahrendorf suggest. In the West there is also the power of capital to consider and, we must add, in the Soviet Union, that of top communist politicians. Nevertheless, the massive extent of bureaucracy and the power of top management to use bureaucracy as their instrument are noteworthy and quite recent features of modern society.

Marxists can certainly learn from Weberian-inspired organisational analysis. Two points are apparent. Firstly, the 'new managerial class' is both highly paid and relatively powerful. In their eagerness to establish the primacy of capitalist power. Marxists tend to disregard this even though it is a fact that can be easily accommodated to Marxist theory and policy. Secondly, as Weber realised, the power of large organisations to control and alienate is immense because of their very size and of the remoteness of those who control them. The novelist, Kafka, caught the sense of how in modern societies organisations seem to 'run peoples' lives' almost without personal direction. This description is at least as applicable to the Soviet Union as to the West. Clegg and Dunkerley appear to have integrated this important insight into an essentially Marxist framework. They recognise that bureaucratically run organisations tend to produce alienation not only among lower level workers but even among professional employees as well. Crucially, however, they insist that it is still necessary to locate and analyse the major source of control behind organisations, whether it be capital or a political elite. Only then does it become possible adequately to relate organisational analysis to the issues of inequality of power and wealth. The basic question remains 'in whose interest is this organisation run?'

Control and Involvement, Oligarchy and Democracy in Organisations

We have already seen that Weber considered that modern organisations are best run along bureaucratic lines. For him, bureaucracy meant hierarchy and hierarchy meant oligarchy, that is, that power and control are concentrated at the top. More recent theorists have examined the issues of control and involvement in organisations and, as we shall see, have produced a more complex picture. The organic systems theory, mentioned above, has already introduced the notion that organisations can be run on somewhat more democratic lines than the bureaucratic model suggests. We now examine this matter more directly.

Etzioni takes three of Weber's major concepts, *power, authority* and *legitimation*, and applies them to the understanding of the way organisations work. Etzioni starts with the basic problem of how the majority of people, workers and employees, can be persuaded or forced to do what they might not freely chose to do – work for others. To understand Etzioni's answer, we must first know what Weber's three terms mean: *power is the ability to impose one's will* (for example by brute force); *legitimation is the acceptance of power because it is considered to be rightly exercised* (for example that of a king); and *authority is legitimate power*. Weber offered a three-part ideal-type model of authority: *traditional, charismatic,* and *rational-legal*. Traditional authority is 'hallowed with time', like that of a king, an established dynasty or a pope. Charismatic authority is generated by the personality of the individual, like that of Hitler or Martin Luther King. Rational-legal authority is established in law or written regulations. We have already said that it is this type of authority that characterises modern bureaucratic organisations.

Why is it that individuals accept the control and power of organisations and, specifically, of top organisational officials over their lives? Etzioni presents in turn, an explanatory typology of control: *coercive, utilitarian* and *normative* or *social*. Coercive power is control based on physical means, such as brute force. Utilitarian power is based on the use of material means, such as money payments: it embodies an element of positive incentive to conform, in the form of a reward. Normative power is based on morality and social conscience. When people conform for normative reasons they do so because they believe they *ought* to. Normative power and conformity are associated with legitimation because they occur when people accept that a given power is legitimate. Thus, a Catholic who accepts the authority of the Pope does so out of normative conviction. A citizen may obey the law from normative conviction although, for others, the threat of coercion may be necessary. Likewise, employees in an organisation, say a commercial one, may feel normatively disposed to accept its authority even though they originally joined it for ultilitarian reasons (to make a living). Bureaucracies are largely based on rules and often create an atmosphere of normative conformity. A little thought will make it clear that in many types of organisations, such as schools, two or even three kinds of control operate.

Etzioni matches three types of *involvement* with his typology of control. Coercion tends to produce *alienation*, utilitarian control is based on *calculative commitment*, and normative control on *moral commitment*. Calculative and moral commitment have, in effect, already been explained. Alienation is the opposite of commitment: it is the rejection by the spirit of what the body has to do, such as to serve a life-sentence in prison or to do endlessly repetitive and boring work. In part, Etzioni sees it as a leadership problem to decide what kinds of incentives are necessary to involve members in the organisation's goals. He also recognises, however, that workers and employees are likely to have their own ideas about the nature of their involvement, and that these will affect the running of the organisation. As we shall now see, there is perhaps more to this issue than Etzioni himself allows.

Is Democracy in Organisations Possible?

The most uncompromising statement of the inevitability of managerial elites is the so-called 'iron law of oligarchy' of Robert Michels. With the German Socialist Party chiefly in mind, he argues that popularly representative parties and unions, whose aim is to replace autocracy with democracy, are forced by necessity to develop a 'vast and solid' bureaucratic organisational structure themselves. In due course, the party bureaucracy itself becomes centralised and undemocratic. The vested interest of the organisation's elite rather than the needs of the people at large effectively becomes the most important consideration, despite professed democratic and socialist ideals. Ordinary people acquire no more power or control as a result of these movements. One set of masters replaces another. In that sense, Michels' 'law' is similar to Pareto's theory of cir-culating elites.

Alvin Gouldner criticises Michels' account as unbalanced. Michels emphasises only the ways in which organisational needs work against democratic possibilities. Tellingly, Gouldner suggests another need – ignored by Michels – that of the consent of the governed (or employees), to their governors. He sees a certain *recurrent* tension between the need for central leadership and authority and the desire of many people for more power, satisfaction and involvement at work than a rigid bureaucratic regime might allow. He says, with some poetic finesse, 'if oligarchical waves repeatedly wash away the bridge of democracy, this eternal recurrence can happen only because men doggedly rebuild them after each inundation'.

Gouldner's thoughts conveniently bring us to the nub of the debate about organisational oligarchy and democracy. Both democracy and oligarchy are possible in organisations and, for that matter, in the political system. What people get depends on what they want, and their power to obtain it balanced against that of others. Power-conflict is a process not an outcome. Thomas Jefferson, the second American President, counselled the people to be ever vigilant in the protection of their democratic rights, lest they be whittled away by central government.

Gouldner has rough words for Selznick as well as Michels. He refers to Selznick's 'dismal' catalogue of organisational needs. These are 'needs' for security; stable lines of authority; stable relationships, and homogeneity (similarity of parts). Gouldner, maintaining his emphasis on democracy, juxtaposes what he sees as an equally important set of needs: needs for challenge, for lateral communication, for creative tension, for heterogeneity (diversity) and the consent of the led. We return to the oligarchy-democracy debate shortly in the context of union organisation.

Gouldner, therefore, sees neither oligarchy or democracy as 'inevitable' but as alternatives to be championed and contested. Similarly, Rensis Likert offers a model of control-involvement which is more representative of the full range of possible management-worker structures than is Etzioni's. He identifies four important systems of organisation: *exploitative/authoritative; benevolent/authoritative; consultative* and *participative group management.* We can add a fifth: the *democratic/egalitarian* system of management favoured by some contemporary socialists but probably not fully achieved in any socialist regime.

In exploitative/authoritative systems, power and control are centralised and workers are treated exclusively in terms of their productive capacity. In the early stages of industrialisation in both Britain and America, powerful industrial moguls, such as Ford and Rockefeller, ran their industrial empires in this way. Frequently, this pattern became modified to the extent that the entrepreneur did begin to develop an interest in the general welfare of his workforce – the benevolent-authoritative pattern. Often this was for ulterior motives: a healthy workforce was a better workforce and, in any case, entrepreneurs often wanted to 'spike the guns' of unions which built up on the basis of working class discontent. Frederick Taylor was the theoretical philosopher of authoritative or, perhaps more accurately, authoritarian style of management. The consultative approach recognises that the workforce may have something to offer the management, at least in certain areas, in the way of experience and advice. Even where regular consultative meetings are established, however, ultimate decisions remain in the hands of ownership or management. Again, this system can become little more than decorative diplomacy. The concept of participative group management has had considerable support and success in parts of Europe in the post-war period. In Scandinavia and West Germany, workers have had substantial representation on the management boards of large companies for many years. In Britain, the Bullock report of the late nineteen seventies recommended that Britain's nationalised industries should implement a similar system of participation. The report's recommendations were rather complicated and their partial application to British Leyland and the Post Office petered out. The participation 'debate' continues, however.

The democratic-egalitarian model goes beyond the concept of the participation of 'both sides of industry' to that of abolishing the notion of 'sides' altogether. For a Marxist, this would first involve the abolition of class inequality. This does not, of course, mean that separate roles, such as manager or production worker, will cease to exist; rather, it is a question of making management democratic. Perhaps managers could be elected for a term of some years, as MP's are now, and positions on the board could rotate (as the American Presidency does in the sense that it can only be held for two four-year terms – for good democratic reasons!). To be genuinely egalitarian, this system would also involve a reduction, if not the abolition, of the differences in reward and status between management and workers. Obviously, this model would be barely acceptable within the limits of capitalist economic and social belief. The implementation of a democratic-egalitarian system would probably require socialism. We discussed this matter in some detail in Chapter 15, pp. 422–4.

It is appropriate at this point briefly to discuss whether, regardless of their capacity to participate in industrial democracy, unions can be successfully democratic themselves. This returns us to Michels' thesis. Lipset, Trow and Coleman, on the basis of a study of a printers' union in the United States, found that in certain circumstances democracy is possible. The printers' union had a thriving two party system. They put this down to the fact that the long and odd hours worked by the printers produced work-connected leisure organisations which, in turn, provided a basis of communication for, and involvement in, union politics. But Lipset's broader conclusion is more pessimistic. In most industries, the majority of workers quickly leave work for home, and it is only a minority which actively involves itself in union politics. This is certainly the case in Britain, where seldom more than a third of workers vote when given the opportunity to do so. Allen, however, points out that the formal machinery of union democracy is time-consuming and cumbersome to operate. In practice, the way union leaders are kept in check is more simple. If the workers disapprove of what they are doing, membership declines. Allen's argument is not entirely convincing. As early as 1949, C. Wright Mills pointed to the communication gap between national union officials and branch officials and between both these groups and the mass membership. These problems are by no means resolved today.

Gouldner perceives oligarchy and democracy as matters of preference and belief rather than 'inevitabilities'. This is not to deny that certain circumstances tend to promote oligarchy and others democracy. Professor Schumacher's book, *Small is Beautiful*, made the point that large organisations tend to require centralised power and that smaller ones can be democratically run. Nevertheless, given the intent, a measure of democracy is possible even in large organisations. At root, preference for organisational oligarchy or democracy depends on a view of human nature. Those who consider that people work best in a highly regulated structure will prefer classical or bureaucratic models: those who consider that people best express themselves in freer contexts will tend to support more democratic organisational structures. Even where democratic systems may be more time-consuming and less efficient, they may still be preferred, for human and moral reasons. But to leave the matter thus would be to mislead. Might, not right or need, usually determines the way organisations operate. Historically, there are almost no examples of democracy being achieved without struggle.

Towards a More Unified Sociological Theory of Organisations

A unified theory of organisations should not be attempted at the expense of ignoring significant theoretical differences between scholars of different perspectives. Nevertheless, several contributors to organisational theory have suggested that a framework of overall analysis, capable of sustaining certain differences in perspective, does now virtually exist.

Amitai Etzioni, who adopts a conflict structural approach, considers that it embodies the essential elements of both the classical and human relations perspectives. He clearly considers these to be two sides of the same coin – the rational and the personal-social. He also observes that conflict is a normal and, sometimes, a useful, feature of organisational life. For instance, a strike involves conflict, but it can lead to a settlement of differences and to a new period of organisational stability.

Etzioni is pursuing a promising approach in bringing together conflict-structuralism and micro-level sociology. However, Clegg and Dunkerley's more recent work, *Organization, Class and Control*, is a still more impressive attempt at synthesis. Whereas Etzioni draws mainly from Weber in presenting structural-conflict, Clegg and Dunkerley lean heavily towards Marx. They see class domination and conflict as *endemic* in both capitalist enterprise and state bureaucracy. They consider that the state bureaucracy in Russia is even more an 'engine' of repression, than the state in capitalist society, and in this analysis Weber's understanding of the oppressive burden of state bureaucracy is apparent. Yet they create no sense, as the structural-functionalists do, that the men and women who occupy small roles in large organisations are for that reason powerless. They understand that workers interpret and respond to their conditions and sometimes organise to change them. In this way conflict-structural theory and interactionism seem to complement each other in their work. Of course, Marxists appreciate with functionalists that organisations can function without conflict for long periods and sometimes almost indefinitely. The difference is that Marxists consider that structural division and, therefore, potential conflict is a permanent feature of capitalist society, whereas functionalists consider basic harmony and consensus quite possible. For Marxists such consensus is the result of the ideological conditioning of the working class to conform to a social and organisational order that exploits them and drastically limits their self-expression.

Guide to Further Reading and Study

Diagrams of bureaucracies, including schools, are easily obtainable or, alternatively, can be drawn up. A contrast between bureaucratic goals and 'actual' complex interaction can be made by asking students to compare the formal goals of educational establishments with what they, individually and as a group, 'get up to' at any given time. This can include daydreaming, 'bunking off', or whatever.

In their weighty tome *Organization, Class and Control* (Routledge and Kegan Paul, 1980), Stewart Clegg and David Dunkerley provide a fair summary of most perspectives on organisations as well as giving their own Marxist one. Their *Critical Issues in Organizations* (Routledge and Kegan Paul, 1977) is brief and designed for students. Max Weber's original piece, 'Bureaucracy' is reprinted in H. H. Gerth and C. Wright Mills, *eds, From Max Weber* (Routledge and Kegan Paul, 1948). Often the sociology of organisation is linked with work, and Graeme Salaman's *Class and Corporation* (Fontana, 1981) provides an example (see also the "Guide" at the end of Chapter 15).

For students, the study of organisations comes to life in participant observational studies: Erving Goffman's *Asylums* (Penguin, 1968) is a great original; Anna Pollerts' *Girls, Wives, Factory Lives* covers female experience from a radical-interpretist standpoint; Stanley Cohen and Laurie Taylor's *Psychological Survival: The Experience of Long-term Imprisonment* (Penguin, 1972) is a study of a total institution that goes well with Goffman's. E. F. Schumacher's *Small is Beautiful* (Abacus, 1974) puts the case for the small, human participatory but still efficient organisation with great eloquence. The concept of participation surfaces in a de-radicalised but interesting way in a number of popular American books of socio-cultural speculation, including Alvin Toffler's *The Third Wave* (Bantam Books, 1981).

461

Past Questions

1 What is a 'total institution'? Does this concept enhance our understanding of prisons *or* boarding schools *or* mental hospitals *or* shops? (AEB, 1980)

2 Sociological theories of the workplace include both 'scientific management' and 'human relations' theories. Explain why this is the case and discuss the consequences of basing such classifications on occupation. (AEB, 1983)

3 'In large-scale organisations, bureaucracy is the most efficient form of administration.' Do you gree? (OLE, 1983)

4 Why do bureaucracies find difficulty in accommodating change? (OLE, 1984)

5 Critically assess Michel's assertion that, 'who says organisation, says oligarchy'. (AEB, 1985)

Section E Social Order, Public Power and Personal Potential

How to Use this Section

The central theme of this section is the relationship between social order and individual potential and expression. This relationship is complex and contradictory. Social order normally ensures a stable context within which the individual can pursue his own ends, but this secure frame-work constricts as well as protects. The law itself embodies this ambiguity. Positively, it does establish some of the more important, formal rules of social order within which social interaction can take place. Negatively, it prevents individuals and groups from doing some of the things which, left to their own devices, they might want to do. The first chapter in this section describes *the nature of social order* and the various means of social control, such as the armed forces, the police and the courts, which may be used to enforce it. This chapter also introduces the concept of *deviance:* the term sociologists use to describe the breaking of social rules as norms. Chapter 18 is substantially a detailed examination of various types of deviance. It concludes, however, with a general review of theories of deviance and social order and suggests that the various sociological perspectives are more complementary in this area than is often realised.

Chapter 19 begins by examining more explicitly a concept that underlies the previous two chapters, that of *power*. Power, the ability to make someone behave as *you* want regardless of *their* will, is an aspect of all social relationships and institutions though those who have power may not always choose to use it. In this sense power operates, for example, in the family, the classroom and the workplace. The most familiar public context in which power-conflict takes place is politics. Laws are made by individuals or groups that have power. Marxists, however, consider that 'real' power in capitalist societies lies with big business, and not with political parties and government. The nature and distribution of power is an issue about which sociologists sharply disagree. In many ways this disagreement is a logical extension of the sociological debate on stratification discussed earlier (see Chapters 9, 10 and 11).

Chapter 20 discusses *ideology, culture and creativity*. This may seem an abrupt change from the central focus on the previous chapter, power. This is not so, however. There is no more important form of power than ideological power, the ability to influence and even control the ideas and beliefs of other men. We begin our analysis of ideologies or systems of belief by examining the social functions of religion. As it happens, this is an area in which Marx and Durkheim are in considerable agreement. We also examine the rather different perspective of Max Weber on religion. Despite the decline of traditional religion, there is no sign of an end to ideological belief in today's world. Communism is an example of a secular (non-religious) ideology. An analysis of the interests that control the media and the effects of the media on its audience continues the theme of ideological power.

The last section of Chapter 20, on the fulfilment of personal potential (self-actualisation), attempts to redress the structuralist bias of the preceding cultural analysis. The point is emphasised that the individual can interpret, change and even, in part, reject the culture he inherits. Though most people do not 'make history' in any public sense, many live their personal biographies much more originally and creatively than some arm-chair critics of popular culture suggest. Nevertheless, there is a real danger that 'mass culture', piped into the home and passively received, will undermine intellect and spirit. The final section of the chapter discusses this possibility.

17 Social Order, Social Control and Deviance

We have made the problem of stratification and equality the central pivot of this book, but the related issues of social order, social control and deviance can hardly be considered of less importance. Indeed, for functionalists, social order is the crux of sociological theory. As explained in Chapter 1, they regard social order as a precondition of the survival of society. Marxists treat this view with great suspicion. They consider that the relevant issue is not the necessity for social order, but the question of who benefits from such as does exist. In their view, social order in most societies does little more than provide opportunity for the powerful to exploit the weak. Despite these apparently incompatible starting points, we shall see that there are complementary as well as contradictory aspects in the way in which major structuralist theories treat this topic.

Neither symbolic interactionists nor ethnomethodologists have produced a distinctive general theory of social order, control and deviance. The macro-level has not primarily been their scale of concern. Instead, they have concentrated on the various 'actors' involved in behaviour 'labelled' as deviant. Some interactionists, particularly a number of British sociologists, have, however, attempted to link micro-level research with structural perspective.

Perspectives on Order, Control and Deviance

Functionalism

Social Order: Durkheim, Parsons and Shils

Functionalists regard social order as more normal and natural than disorder. Society, like the human body, depends for survival on the orderly functioning of its various parts. To understand this is to appreciate the fundamental point of the organic analogy.

The tradition which sees social order as natural goes back to Durkheim. Underlying social order was what he called social solidarity: we described what he meant by this term in Chapter 6. In essence, social solidarity depends on basic moral consensus. In turn, morality exists primarily to keep society together, Durkheim himself is quite clear on this point and it is the basis of his whole sociology:

Society is not a simple aggregate of individuals who, when they enter it, bring their own intrinsic morality with them; rather, *man is a moral being only because he lives in society, since morality consists in being solidary with (at one with) a group* and varies with this solidarity. Let all social life disappear, and moral life would disappear with it, since it would no longer have any objective.

The final sentence of this quotation makes it clear that, for Durkheim, morality is a *human* not a *divine* reality. Its purpose is to exercise control on man's instincts and wayward will. Durkheim does not trust human nature and sees a fundamental need for a system of moral order to constrain it:

> The totality of moral rules truly forms about each person an imaginary wall, at the foot of which the flood of human passions dies without being able to go further... if at any point this barrier weakens, (these) previously restrained human forces pour tumultously through the open breach; once loosened they find no limits where they can stop.

No less than Durkheim, Talcott Parsons sees a need for a system of norms and values to provide a framework of social order. He prefers the more neutral term *values* to morals (that is, he wishes to avoid any suggestion that given values are good or bad). (We examined his social system theory in some detail in Chapter 3.) For Parsons, underpinning the whole social system and providing the ultimate basis of all social integration are the fundamental values of society.

Edward Shils's thinking on the problem of social order is also well worth mentioning. He, like Durkheim and Parsons, stresses the role of values in creating coherent social order:

> The existence of a central value system rests, in a fundamental way, on the need which human beings have for incorporation into something which transcends and transfigures their concrete individual existence. They have a need to be in contact with symbols of an order which is larger than their own bodies and more central in the 'ultimate' structure of reality than is their routine everyday life.

This passage, typifies the almost reverential attitude of many functionalists to what they regard as the moral nature of society and, particularly, order and authority. A slightly more original feature of Shils's analysis is his emphasis on the role of the *central elite* in maintaining social order and consensus. The elite can do this only if its authority is generally accepted. Shils, like all major functionalist thinkers, appreciates that acceptance of

467

central authority and values does not occur equally in all parts of society. His interest, however, is in explaining the functional necessity of consensus, authority and order rather than in analysing why they are barely accepted or even rejected by some individuals or groups. As we shall see, Marxists and interactionists have far more to say on these matters and their views can be cited in criticism of functionalist theories of social order.

Social Control and Conformity

Before dealing with specifically functionalist thinking on social control, it will help to introduce the concept briefly in more general terms. Social control refers to the means and processes by which individuals and groups are persuaded or forced to conform to dominant norms. We can divide social control into *formal* and *informal* control. Formal means of control are the courts, the police and armed forces. Usually, these are subject to the major overall source of social control: the state. It is enough just to stress this essential point here, as we deal fully with the state later. On a smaller scale, specific organisations may have their own means of control. Thus, corporal punishment, 'lines', expulsion or detention may be used in schools. Informal means of control consist of less organised but often very powerful pressure to enforce conformity. Because functionalists consider that informal social control must be effective for society to work, we deal with it first.

Informal social control occurs largely by means of socialisation. We have examined in some detail how functionalists consider that the individual is wedded to the norms and values of society by means of socialisation within the family, educational system and in other ways. It is universally accepted by sociologists – not just functionalists – that socialisation is the major means by which moral and psychological commitment to society are brought about. By psychological commitment we mean that people become mentally predisposed to conform as a result of socialisation. The significant difference between functionalists and Marxists on this matter is that the former tend to emphasise the necessity of socialisation whereas the latter frequently stress its exploitative and repressive aspects.

Although functionalists prefer conformity to be underpinned by *moral consensus*, they accept that formal control, supported, if necessary, by coercion, must be the ultimate means by which it is enforced. That is why the courts, police and armed forces exist. Even so, when moral consensus breaks down, the problem of social order and control becomes much greater. In practice, elements of formal and informal control often operate together. The quotation below illustrates a combination of informal moral and more formal coercive persuasion of a kind more commonly found in traditional than in modern societies:

> The traditional community was able to compel individual family members to follow collective rules through a disciplinary technique called the charivari ... The charivari was, in its essentials, a noisy public demonstration to subject wayward individuals to humiliation in the eyes of the community. Sometimes the demonstration would consist of masked individuals circling somebody's house at night, screaming, beating on pans, and blowing cow horns (which the local butchers rented out). On other occasions the offender would be seized and marched through the streets, seated perhaps backwards on a donkey or forced to wear a placard describing his sins ...
>
> (In France) sexual offenders were often the targets of charivaris, such as married men in the village of Vaux (Oise) who got single women pregnant.

Contemporary Europeans rarely resort to such elaborate ritual to censure and control others; with the decline of traditional moral standards there is more tolerance of a variety of behaviour. Nevertheless, informal psychological coercion can be exercised against an individual who offends people morally or otherwise even if force, or the threat of force, is now less easily used outside a legal context. Consider, for instance, how it may be practised against someone who is known to be having an affair with a popular colleague's wife. He may suddenly find himself not invited out for 'a drink with the lads', to dinner parties, or to weekend sports outings. The 'atmosphere' may quickly change when he sits down with his colleagues for a chat or a game of cards; customary banter may begin to take on the quality of personal antagonism; those who already dislike the individual concerned, recognising the way the wind is blowing, may adopt an openly aggressive attitude ... the list of possible censorious responses could be continued almost indefinitely. At some time or another, most people will experience some of the above forms of social disapproval. The psychological effect on the censured individual is not pleasant and, of course, is not intended to be. Feelings of tension and pressure indicate that social constraint is biting. The need for group acceptance and approval is often enough to bring the individual 'back into line'. Although the above analysis of psychological coercion in a small group context is quite compatible with functionalist assumptions, there are few examples of such micro-level work in functionalist writing. Instead, functionalists tend to concentrate on the social system as a whole, leaving the understanding of small group behaviour to interactionists.

Deviance

We must begin by giving a basic functionalistic definition of deviance, to be qualified, it must be stressed, by other perspectives. Deviant behaviour occurs when an individual or group behaves in a way contrary to the normative consensus. Some authorities suggest that the term 'deviance' be reserved for those acts for which moral disapproval is likely to be generally felt, and that the term 'non-conformity' be used to refer to normative breaches which do not arouse moral censure. Whilst it is useful to bear this distinction in mind, it should not be regarded as rigid. Often behaviour which offends custom or polite practice is referred to as deviant even though no obvious immorality has occurred. There are a number of terms and analytical observations employed by functionalists which are also in general sociological use. We will deal with these before presenting some more controversial elements of functionalist deviancy theory.

a THE RELATIVE NATURE OF DEVIANCE Deviance is both culturally and historically *relative*. We will examine the cultural relativity of deviance first. An act can be judged deviant only by reference to a specific standard – usually the norms of a given group, and these vary from one group to another. Thus, to consume alcohol would be deviant in an orthodox Muslim community, but not in most Christian ones. To take another example, it is a Sikh tradition always to wear a turban in public, a practice continued by many Sikhs in Britain. Needless to say, within the general British population such an attitude to headgear is entirely foreign, and anyone other than a Sikh who adopted it would be considered highly abnormal. Deviance, therefore, is relative in that what is considered deviant changes from one cultural group to another.

The historical relatively of deviance merely means that definitions of what is deviant can change within a given society or group over a period of time. Changes and developments in normative attitudes towards deviance are part of what is meant by the term 'cultural change'. Changing attitudes to divorce and divorced people in Britain illustrate the point. In the Victorian period, divorce was generally strongly disapproved of, and virtually impossible to obtain except by the wealthy few. In contemporary Britain, divorce has become so common that the stigma attached to it has inevitably diminished greatly, and we would not now consider divorced people as deviant.

b THE VARIETY OF DEVIANCE A consequence of the relative and changing nature of deviance is that the variety of deviant behaviour is immense: this is easily demonstrable by reference to the field of deviant behaviour in just one society – Britain. In modern British society, deviance includes the following varied forms of behaviour: murder; having sexual intercourse under the age of sixteen; appearing nude in a public place; playing football in the outfit of a clown; wearing the clothes normally worn only by the opposite sex; attempting to fly without artificial aid. *All that the above factors have in common is that they contravene accepted norms.* We cannot even add that they all provoke moral censure. Some, such as attempting to fly without artificial aid, are likely to provoke amusement or pity depending on how seriously the intentions of the would-be aeronaut are taken. Finally, the variety of deviance is illustrated by the fact that any man or group is capable of taking an alternative 'deviant' position to the accepted one, although he may have to suffer unpleasant consequences for doing so.

c DURKHEIM AND DEVIANCE As well as sharing in the general view that deviance is relative, Durkheim further described it as *universal, normal* and *functional*. There is no problem in accepting the universality of deviance. No society can command total conformity from all its members. That Durkheim should consider deviance to be normal might seem a contradiction in terms: in fact, such a conclusion is implicit in

471

the universal nature of deviance. If it occurs everywhere, it must in that sense be normal, even though the precise forms deviant behaviour takes in a given society are regarded as abnormal in that society. The functionality of deviance raises more serious problems. How can socially destructive behaviour, such as vandalism or murder, be in any way functional to society? Actually, *it is not deviance itself but the reaction of others to it that Durkheim sees as functional.* Deviant behaviour gives society an opportunity simultaneously to condemn the type of behaviour in question and to reaffirm collective moral unity (remember, Durkheim was insistent on the reality of society as a moral entity and he considered any behaviour that focused moral sentiment as functional to the extent that it did so). Perhaps Durkheim's analysis of the social functionality of deviance caused him to ignore the stress, inconvenience and suffering that some deviant behaviour causes. In this instance, abstract functionalist argument formulated in social systems' terms seems to obscure the more urgent reality of human experience.

A highly controversial aspect of Durkheim's thought is his tendency to equate deviance with 'social pathology'. By this he means that deviants must be sick in a way comparable to, though obviously not identical with, the physically sick. In fairness, this exaggerated comparison is only really apparent when he adopts a strict version of the organic analogy. Consistent with his appreciation of the relative nature of deviance Durkheim pointed out that social normality and social pathology or deviance vary from society to society. He was in no doubt that social pathology tended to increase during times of great social change. In such times people are often left without clear rules or normative guidelines, and so become more prone to deviance. In particular, the decline of religious certainties could undermine security and confidence in traditional morality. Durkheim referred to this state of 'normlessness' as *'anomie'*. We analyse his detailed application of this concept to suicide in the next chapter. He considered that the rapid change of the late nineteenth century generated a climate of anomie characterised by increasing rates of suicide, homicide, drunkenness and other signs of pathological desperation. He believed that the major problem in modern society is to find a new basis of moral solidarity. He did not believe that overlapping self-interest, the basis of organic solidarity, was quite enough.

d ROBERT MERTON Robert Merton, writing just before the Second World War, made the most significant contribution to functionalist deviancy theory since Durkheim. Merton used the term 'non-conformity' instead of deviance, but we may assume that what he is talking about is, in fact, deviance. As can be seen from the diagram below, Merton juxtaposes conformity and four types of non-conformist adjustments.

	Culture goals	Institutionalised means
1 Conformity	+	+
2 Innovation	+	−
3 Ritualism	−	+
4 Retreatism	−	−
V. Rebellion*	±	±

* This fifth alternative is on a plane clearly different from that of the others. It represents a *transitional* response which seeks to *institutionalise* new procedure-oriented toward revamped cultural goals shared by members of the society. It thus involves efforts to *change* the existing structure rather than to perform accommodative actions *within* this structure, and introduces additional problems with which we are not at the moment concerned.

Source: Taken from Peter Worsley, *ed, Modern Sociology,* 1978, p. 619.

For him, conformity lies in accepting the 'culture goals' of society – material success is such a 'culture goal' in the USA – *and* in pursuing them by legitimate 'institutionalised means' – that is, within the limits of normative and legal acceptability. Correspondingly, three of the four forms of adjustments lie in rejecting either or both culture goals and the institutionalised means by which they can be pursued. The fourth, rebellion, involves both a rejection of the goals and means of the old order (− −) and an attempt to assert new ones (+ +).

There is much to quarrel with in Merton's model, as we shall see when we examine his analysis of 'innovation' (his major concern) as applied to criminal deviancy, but he does map out the chief areas of deviancy in a way that is interesting and suggestive of possibilities for further research. Merton himself has developed the concept of ritualism as applied to bureaucratic work. He points out that people involved in such work can become so dominated by rules of procedure and routine that they lose sight of the purpose of their work. Thus, a social security official who delays urgently needed assistance until every bureaucratic check has been made on a client is indulging in ritualistic behaviour. Merton feared that such 'bureaucratic characters' might become something of a plague in large-scale, highly organised modern societies. Merton's retreatist category provides a useful perspective. It is arguable, however, that the retreatists he mentions – such as some out-casts, vagrants, chronic drunkards and drug addicts – *drift* into deviancy for a variety of complex reasons. Generally, Merton's plus and minus signs tend to oversimplify the complexity of real life, although his model has some value as a basis of departure for classifying deviancy.

Marxism: Social Order, Control and Deviance

Social Order

There is good reason for making this section shorter than the one which preceded it. Marxists do not 'see' society in the way suggested by the group of concepts with which this chapter is concerned. They understand society in terms of conflict rather than order. Marxists barely pause to acknowledge the practical necessity of social order. Where order exists, they see it in terms of the control of one class by another, not as the product of genuine consensus. They primarily concern themselves with capitalist society but recognise the same principle – class domination – in other, more traditional societies. The dominant class seeks to establish and maintain a social order based invar-iably on its own interests, at the expense of others. Class con-flict is always likely to undermine order imposed by the ruling class.

It will be remembered that, when analysing social stratifica-tion and conflict, we spent longer on the Marxist than the functionalist perspective. Now, in dealing with social order and control, we make the reverse emphasis. Seen from the Marxist perspective, the law and the various control agencies that enforce it are tools of class exploitation rather than bulwarks of justice. The law is not regarded as a neutral instrument that provides equal justice for all, but as something protecting the property rights of the wealthy few at the expense of the rest. The law is certainly functional, but for the privileged minority, not the majority. *Individual* property rights are seen as much more firmly established in law than, for instance, the *collective* rights of the trade unions. These are regarded as insecurely established, and always likely to be whittled down by government or disadvantageously interpreted by the courts. Marxists virtually turn the concept of legal justice in capitalist society on its head. The fact that the statistics appear to show that proportionately more working class people than middle class people commit crime is taken to illustrate the biased, class nature of bourgeois justice, rather than greater working class criminality. To take an extreme example – if someone in poverty steals from a wealthy person or institution, the injustice is seen to lie with the society which tolerates poverty, not with the individual.

Marxists argue that not only does the law protect inequality but that people have unequal access to the law. Having money to hire a good lawyer can mean the difference between being found innocent or guilty. At a more subtle level, the ability to present a respectable image in court might appeal favourably to the sentiments of predominantly middle class magistrates, judges and jurors. These points may well explain why there is some evidence to suggest that working class people are more likely to be found guilty than middle class people for the same offence.

By citing such examples, and there are plenty of them, Marxists are able to throw back the ideals of liberal justice at those who profess them. Does freedom under law simply mean freedom to be unequal? Can freedom exist without a much greater degree of equality? Does equality under the law really exist when the content and operation of the law seem to favour the middle class? Of course, these are Marxist questions based on controversial Marxist assumptions, but they are serious enough to warrant consideration regardless of personal ideology.

Social Control, Ideology and Repression

Marxists agree with functionalists that socialisation plays a crucial part in social control, but whereas functionalists tend to accept the necessity of this, Marxists are highly critical of the dominant values and norms of capitalist society which they equate with 'capitalist ideology'. They consider that the working class is often ideologically deluded or 'mystified' into conforming to a social order that is against its 'true' interests. Marxists generally regard in this light attempts by sections of the media to persuade the working class that strikes are irresponsible and 'bad for the country'. Similarly, Marxists are much more critical than functionalists of the role of the ruling class in formulating central values and ideas. They would agree with Shils that the ruling ideas of a society are those of the ruling class (Shils prefers the term *elite*), but they stress that these ideas benefit those at the top of society rather than those at the bottom. Thus, if the working class practises the values of hard work and conformity to the law, the bourgeoisie will be able to enjoy its wealth, power and status in peace. Working class people who avidly pursue personal success (a 'bourgeois' value in the Marxist view), weaken the collective strength of the working class while not seriously challenging the power of the bourgeoisie which, in any case, can usefully absorb a limited number of able working class people. So what is called by functionalists the 'central value' of economic individualism, is, in Marxist terms, an example of some members of the working class being misled by bourgeois 'individualistic' ideology.

If socialisation is the soft edge of social control, the hard edge is represented by the army, police, courts and custodial system – what Althusser calls the 'repressive state apparatus'. Marxists see these as instruments of class rule. Some also consider that teachers, probation officers and social workers play a similar role: 'soft cops' is how they are sometimes described. Members of these professions or semi-professions are largely concerned with persuading frequently rebellious or alienated youth to conform to what, in the Marxist view, is an exploitative society.

'Deviance': A 'Dirty Word'

Because Marxists do not recognise the legitimacy of capitalist social order, they generally have little use for the concept of 'deviance'. The response of the majority of Marxists to working class deviance amounts to 'Well, what can you expect? Some might have more than a sneaking sympathy for, say, the working class thief: a few might even regard his theft romantically as a form of property redistribution – incipient socialism! But no Marxist would regard crime as a substitute for organised economic and political action by the working class, or even as a significant form of support for it. In any case, Marxists condemn explanations of working class crime based on assumptions of inferiority or pathology. For them, blame lies with the system and, perhaps, those who benefit from it, not with its victims.

Those Marxists who have taken a more active recent interest in deviancy theory have tended to focus their attention on the upper end of the class system. Frank Pearce's book, *Crimes of the Powerful*, is a notable contribution of this kind (see Chapter 18). Pursuing a different theme, Colin Sumner has suggested that Marxists try to analyse how definitions of normality and deviance in class-divided societies are produced, and how they serve the system. This could be a very interesting line of analysis. To what extent, for instance, do the media form standards of normality and deviance? Who controls the media and in whose interest? Sumner leaves us with a strong sense that these and related questions are well worth pursuing.

Interactionism: Deviance, Social Order and Control

It might seem perverse, at this stage, to depart from the order in which we have been considering the topics of this chapter. The nature of interactionist theory, however, demands a quite different treatment from that given to functionalism and Marxism. Historically interactionalists have been much more interested in deviance than in social order. Interactionist research on social control has been more vigorous, and since the late nineteen sixties several major studies of specific agencies of control have been published. Yet, these studies reflect the characteristic interactionist assumption that those who control deviance must first define what it is. It is, therefore, with deviancy theory that we can most logically start our analysis. For reasons given there we reserve detailed consideration of interactionist social control theory until the next chapter.

Primary and Secondary Deviance – Labelling
Whereas functionalists stress normative consensus, interactionists argue that modern societies are characterised by a great variety or *plurality* of values and norms. This diversity of attitude exists in most areas of human activity, including religion, sex, politics and race. Conformity to the law is seen not as a product of moral consensus but either as the ability of some groups to impose rules or, as a matter of practical necessity.

Until recently, interactionists have paid more attention to *how rules are applied and the effect of their application or non-application on the deviant person,* rather than why and how some groups and individuals, such as employers and headmasters, make the rules and others, such as employees and pupils, have to obey them. We return to this issue, essentially one of power, shortly. On the practicality of rules, Lemert points out that much modern legislation is justified in terms of organisational requirement, rather than morality. For instance, many traffic offences are not immoral in themselves. Travelling at 32 miles per hour in a 30 mile per hour zone would not cause genuine moral indignation in any but the most authoritian personality: even so, the practical necessity to enforce the speed limit remains.

Interactionists do not, then, analyse deviance simply as rule breaking, but equally in terms of how and to whom the rules are applied. This is the basis of Lemert's distinction between *primary* and *secondary deviance.* According to him, primary deviance is the initial commission of a deviant act. Secondary deviance is the effect that 'societal reaction' has on the conduct of the deviant subsequent to the commission of the initial deviant act. 'Societal reaction' means the reaction of society, or specifically of any group within society, such as the police, the courts, the family and acquaintances of the deviant, the media and, through the media, the public. Lemert's relative silence on primary deviance is a matter we will return to, critically, later.

Primary and Secondary Deviance

Primary Deviance (Rule Breaking) for example, Speeding	**Label** (Societal Reaction) → Charge, Conviction ↓ *or* **No Label** for example, Ignored, Not Noticed Rationalised (Seen as a 'Mistake')	**Secondary Deviance** That is, → Deviant Status In this case, 'Traffic Offender' (Minor Criminal)

He and other interactionists have overwhelmingly given their attention to secondary deviance. If, as Howard Becker claims, 'an act is deviant when it is so defined', (an act is deviant when societal reaction declares it to be), then it is what happens in the life of the deviant *after* the social definition has been made that is the focus of interactionist analysis. We can illustrate the distinction between primary and secondary deviance in schematic form.

Learning, Meaning and Societal Reaction

We can use Howard Becker's study of marijuana users to illustrate two further points about interactionist deviancy theory. These are that deviant behaviour, like most other human behaviour, including conformist, is *learnt,* and that people become deviant partly because they find such behaviour meaningful that is, to oversimplify somewhat, *they become deviant because they want to.* Becker also explores the labelling process or societal reaction in some detail. The idea that deviant behaviour is learnt is implied in the title of Becker's key essay 'Becoming a Marijuana User', and is consistent with Mead's theory of socialisation. Becker points out that to smoke marijuana enjoyably, first, the technique has to be learnt; then it is necessary to learn how to perceive the drug's effects and, finally, the user has to learn to enjoy them. It perhaps needs to be explained that, without this learning process, taking the drug can be both unpleasant and, seemingly, without effect. (We gave a fuller account of the meaning of psychedelic drug use in pleasure-seeking sub-cultures in Chapter 14.) Learning and meaning are linked in Becker's analysis. *People only voluntarily learn what seems meaningful to them.* Like Mead, Becker fully allows for the influence of 'significant others', in this case dance musicians who use marijuana, on the individual. Using it is part of their way of life; it fits in with their style and they naturally offer 'established newcomers' the opportunity to try it. Becker notes that the individual is likely to drop or cut back on marijuana smoking when he or she leaves this environment, and the habit ceases to have much cultural meaning.

Becker introduces a concept termed *deviant career,* which he relates to societal reactions. Like any career, that of a deviant is affected by a variety of unpredictable factors which he calls *career contingencies.* The first contingency, a precondition of a deviant career, is that the action or actions of the individual be labelled as deviant. To draw examples from beyond Becker's particular study, labels such as 'mentally ill', 'socially handicapped' and 'juvenile delinquent' may trap a person within an

479

identity from which it may be difficult to escape. Thus, a *stigma* is attached to him which may damage his self-image and affect the response of others to him. For example, a person labelled 'mentally ill' or 'criminal' may be discriminated against when trying to get a job, or rent lodgings.

Social Order and Control

Interactionists reject the functionalist theory that order rests on a consensus of values. Instead, they offer a *power model* of conformity and deviance. *The norms and laws of a society are invariably the product of conflict between groups.* Becker is quite clear on this:

> People are in fact always *forcing* their rules on others, applying them more or less against the will and without the consent of those others.

He goes on to give several examples of this. Rules are made by the old for the young and, to a great extent, by men for women, and by whites for blacks. To take the last example, in the southern States of the USA, the segregation laws preserved the interests and prestige of whites, and subjugated and exploited blacks. But Matza, in particular, has recognised that in reality norms and values are more changeable and ambiguous than either the functionalist or a simple power-conflict model might imply. We can illustrate this from our previous example of black-white relations. For over a century, and particularly in the last 25 years, race relations in the United States have been changing and legislation has fully reflected this. Normative change always brings ambiguity: people don't quite know where they stand. Thus, as segregation in the southern states was challenged and increasingly discredited, the laws upholding it were increasingly ignored in 'liberal', often urban areas. Normative change and ambiguity also illustrate the relative nature of social norms and values which interactionists fully accept. They are not timeless commandments etched in stone, but matters that may be contested, changed, undermined or even ignored.

Matza has further pointed out that the deviant's self-definition might not accord with the neat categories of law and convention and that definitions may be contested. For instance, what is the 'correct' label for women or, for that matter, men, who receive 'gifts' from those with whom they have more or less casual sexual relations? Some might readily call them 'prostitutes', but it could be that the individuals concerned have taken great pains to preserve their self-respect by not behaving precisely as they think prostitutes do. Perhaps the gifts are meant to be occasional, and not thought of as payment for favours given. In this way, personal acceptance of the identity of a prostitute can be plausibly resisted. Difficult though it may be to appreciate this distinction, as far as interactionalists are concerned, if a distinction genuinely exists in an individual's mind, it exists as a fragment of reality.

We examine interactionist analysis of social control in the next chapter. Here it is enough to say that interationists do not consider that agencies of control simply enforce the will of successful interest groups as expressed in the law. They, too, have their own interests and ideology which prevent them from being neutral instruments of enforcement. We will consider this proposition in relation to both the police and the courts.

An Assessment of the Interactionist Theory of Deviance

Two major criticisms of the interactionist approach can be made. Firstly, it does not offer an explanation of primary deviance. Secondly, it is said, particularly by Marxists, that it fails to explain adequately the relationship between power, especially class power, and deviance. We take these points in order. Even Lemert hurries past primary deviance on his way to analysing secondary deviance which is clearly his main interest. Becker, with engaging frankness, agrees that 'stick-up men' do not 'stick people up' simply because somebody has labelled them 'stick-up men', but he still leaves unexplained why some men and women behave in this way whilst others do not. It is true that interactionists do not claim fully to explain why deviance occurs in the first place, but this does result in certain weaknesses in their general theory. In particular, the notion that certain social environments – perhaps those which are in some way 'deprived' – may be associated with certain sorts of deviant behaviour is, apparently, of little interest to them. Yet, this view is not necessarily incompatible with interactionist perspective and, if it were explored by interactionists, might even be found complementary to it.

We now turn to the second criticism commonly made – that it deals inadequately with the relationship between power and deviance. More precisely, this is a specifically Marxist criticism that most interactionists do not sufficiently link their analysis of law and deviance to class theory. In the Marxist view the law and the state ultimately operate in favour of the ruling class. Marxist sociology of deviance is, therefore, concerned with showing how this is so. Many interactionists do not subscribe to a Marxist class conflict theory of society. Rather, they see the power structure in terms of a contest between all sorts of groups – including ethnic, religious, feminist – as well as classes which seek to establish their own interests and moral values. Becker's own case study of the interests behind The Marijuana Tax Act of 1937 (aimed at stamping out use of the drug) does not mention class at all, but concludes that the Federal Bureau of Narcotics was the major influence or 'entrepreneur' in getting the Act passed.

The above Marxist-interactionist disagreement in no way invalidates basic interactionist labelling theory nor its associated concepts. Indeed, many Marxists, particularly younger ones, are freely using interactionist concepts and notably so in the area of sub-cultural analysis. We have already come across examples of this in the work of Paul Willis and Jock Young. Further, when interactionists deal with class and power, they often reach conclusions compatible with Marxism. Thus, the proposition that white collar crime might be under-recorded in official statistics because of police and judical bias in favour of the middle class is commonly found in Marxist and interactionist literature.

Conclusion: The 1980s, Public Order and Social Justice

To many, the first half of the nineteen eighties seemed unusually violent, both nationally and internationally. 1985 itself was a year of great violence. It ended with civilians being indiscriminately slaughtered at Vienna and Rome airports by a Palestinian terrorist faction and the new year began with the IRA blowing up two members of the Ulster Constabulary to remind us that '1986 was going to be another year of violence'. These incidents might provoke reflections on the nature of political violence, but our concern in this chapter is rather more with other forms of deviance and disorder. In the late summer of 1985, urban riots occurred in Brixton and Tottenham, London, and in Handsworth, Birmingham, on a scale comparable with those in 1981. Earlier in the year there had been fierce confrontations between police and some striking miners. At a more personal level of violence, there was an outbreak (at least of media reportage) of child abuse. Generally, the rates of most major categories of crime increased (see p. 487). The Conservative government's response to urban disorder and street crime was to introduce the Public Order Bill designed to decrease intimidation of citizens and to enable the police to intervene to defuse potentially riotous situations. At about the same time a report, *Faith in the Cities*, was published under the auspices of the Church of England, and this took a different tack. Whilst in no way justifying the urban crime and disorder, the Report linked these trends with inner city economic and social decline. It was also suggested that government social and economic policy favoured the better off rather than the disadvantaged. Going beyond the Report, it is worth raising the traditional principle of the social contract. People are only likely fully to observe the law if they have a fair stake in the order it upholds. To say that people must compete to acquire a stake is insufficient. In the United States, where this principle has been rather harshly applied, it has helped to produce what Michael Harrington called 'the other America', an underclass of losers or rather, because of their disadvantages, virtual non-starters. A social contract is a two-sided bargain: the even-hand of government ensures a minimum level of decency to all its citizens who in return conform to the law, thus ensuring a minimum level of social solidarity.

Guide to Further Reading and Study

The problem of order is well covered from the functionalist and conflict structuralist points of view in Cuff and Payne, *eds*, *Perspectives in Sociology* (Allen and Unwin, 1984). The first two chapters of Anthony Giddens' *Durkheim* (Fontana, 1978) give a clear account of the latter's thought on the matter. Charles S. Suchar's *Social Deviance: Perspectives and Prospects* (Holt, Rinehart and Winston, 1978) is a clear and comprehensive survey of deviancy theory. Jack D. Douglas and Frances C. Waksler, *The Sociology of Deviance: An Introduction* (Little, Brown and Company,

1982) presents a variety of approaches beyond the 'usual' perspectives. Howard S. Becker's seminal work *Outsiders* (The Free Press, 1963) remains one of the best statements of interactionist deviancy theory.

See end of Chapter 18 for Further Reading and Questions.

18 Types of Deviance

Guide to Further Reading and Study   518–19

Past Questions   519

Students are often disappointed when they come to study deviance. The topic promises more than it seems to deliver. Crime, sexual deviance, drug addiction – the labels all sound enticingly sinful. In practice, the topic is so theoretical that the appealing decadence of these activities becomes lost. Immersion in theory seems to smother the initial, exciting whiff of evil and, sometimes, student interest in the topic, too. This chapter is, in part, intended as a sympathic response to this problem. By now a certain knowledge of theory can be taken for granted; thus we can look at a specific area of deviancy in more detail without becoming too involved in abstractions.

1 Crime and Delinquency: Theories

What causes crime? This question has become increasingly urgent as far as Britain and most Western European countries are concerned, because of the large officially recorded increase in certain kinds of crime since the end of the Second World War, and particularly since the late nineteen sixties. The rise in the number of notifiable (more serious) offences known to the police has been greatest in the areas of violence against the person (1977 – 82,200; 1983 – 111,300), and in various forms of stealing. We will question the precise accuracy of official criminal statistics, but clearly recorded increases of this size are likely to be correct at least in the *trend* they indicate. (See table below.)

Six broad explanations of crime are considered below: the urban sociological; the functionalist and strain perspectives; the biological; the interactionist; the Marxist; the multi-factoral. These perspectives need not be regarded as mutually exclusive, though some obviously are. There is no real distinction between the terms crime and delinquency: both refer to the breaking of the criminal law. The term juvenile delinquency, however, describes violation of the law by someone less than seventeen years old.

a Crime as 'Inbred'

The view that some individuals are psychologically predisposed to crime as a result of their biological inheritance is not, of

Notifiable (to 1978 Indictable) Offences Recorded by the Police

England and Wales			Thousands
	1969	1971	1973
Total (1)	1,498.7	1,665.7	1,657.7
Violence against the person	37.8	47.0	61.3
Sexual offences	23.5	23.6	25.7
Burglary	420.8	451.5	393.2
Robbery	6.0	7.5	7.3
Theft and handling stolen goods (2)	911.5	1,003.7	998.9
Fraud and forgery	78.9	99.8	110.7
Malicious and criminal damage (1) (3)	14.7	27.0	52.8
Other offences	5.5	5.6	7.8

	1975	1977	1983	1984
Total (1)	2,105.6	2,636.5	3,247.0	3,499.1
Violence against the person	71.0	82.2	111.3	114.2
Sexual offences	23.7	21.3	20.4	20.2
Burglary	521.9	604.1	813.4	897.5
Robbery	11.3	13.7	22.1	24.9
Theft and handling stolen goods (2)	1,267.7	1,487.5	1,705.9	1,808.0
Fraud and forgery	123.1	120.6	121.8	126.1
Malicious and criminal damage (1) (3)	78.5	297.4	443.3	497.8
Other offences	8.4	9.7	8.7	10.4

Source: Compiled from *Social Trends*, 1979 and 1986.
Precise comparison of figures before and after 1980 is not possible because of the introduction of new counting rules in that year.

course, sociological, although sociologists must consider its validity against sociological explanations. The recent origins of this view are traceable, in crude form, to Cesare Lombroso, an Italian doctor whose ideas were influential around the turn of the last century. Lombroso believed that certain 'primitive' physical characteristics, including large jaws, acute sight and a love of orgies(!) indicated a criminal type, but empirical research by Charles Goring established no such correlations. More recently, it has been suggested that men possessing an extra male sex chromosome (Y) are more likely to commit violent crime than others. This is so, but such men still account for a very small proportion of all violent crime.

Hans Eysenck is the champion of the hereditarian argument in this as in other fields. He claims to have established a link between certain genetically based personality traits, such as *extroversion,* and criminal behaviour, although he prudently describes this as a *predisposition*, not a necessarily causal factor. Sociologists tend to react sceptically to such arguments. It can never be finally proved that a given action is primarily the 'result' of genetic predisposition rather than either the influence of social environment or individual choice. Sociologists are, however, more favourably inclined to psychological arguments which explain behaviour as a response to social or, for that matter, physical environment, rather than heredity. Thus, the Chicago school of sociologists, whose work we discuss next, appreciated that the material deprivation, physical decay and tough cultural environment of the inner city influenced children in such areas towards delinquency. Sociologists also accept that extreme conditions of this kind might produce mental illness, including criminal pathology (acute material or mental deprivation, or both, could make someone criminally insane). Nevertheless, few sociologists, if any, see such unusual circumstances as the basis of a general explanation of crime. What they do accept is that certain social conditions might produce a given kind of response, such as delinquency, but such resultant activity is certainly not regarded as mentally abnormal. Some sociologists are occasionally accused of being sympathetic to deviants. If true, this is perhaps less dangerous than regarding them as mentally aberrant, for what solutions to crime does this explanation lead to? Drug treatment? Brain surgery? A course of behaviourist psychotherapy? To some, these treatments seem more insane or, to be consistent, more criminal than the behaviour they seek to control.

b Urban Ecology and Crime

The inner city is the major location of crime associated with deprivation, and the *Chicago school attempted to establish links between environment, deprivation and crime, both theoretically and empirically.* Mainly by the use of official statistics, they attempted to demonstrate empirical correlation between high rates of crime, numerous other forms of deviancy, such as alcoholism, mental illness, prostitution and suicide, and the conditions of life prevailing in what Burgess called the 'zone of transition' of the urban area. Both the transience of the inner urban population (that is, its unsettled, mobile nature) and the physical decay of the environment were conditions conducive to deviance. The Chicago sociologists, when referring specifically to the physical environment, tended to use the terms 'zone of deterioration' or 'twilight zone' and when referring to population mobility, 'zone of transition'. Decaying conditions helped to create stress on the family, to weaken community relationships, and to isolate the individual, thus giving rise to anomie. Such circumstances could predispose individuals towards deviant behaviour. The fact that these areas were already generously populated by more than their share of assorted crooks, pimps and conmen made the possibility of 'picking up' a criminal 'trade' all the more likely.

The Chicago theorists, like Durkheim before them, contrasted the high crime rates of the inner city with the much lower crime rates of rural and suburban areas. They found an explanation for this, to some extent, in the thinking of Durkheim and Tönnies on the break up of traditional community and the growth of anomie. Small, rural communities can 'police and protect' their own, but in cities, both property and people become impersonal. Cars and luggage, for example, can be stolen in full view of the public who may have no idea of what is going on. Related to this is the vast growth in the *amount* of property, both personal and public, during this century and particularly since the war. When 'nobody' seems to own, say, a lamp-post or a telephone kiosk, it becomes, psychologically, easier to hurl a brick at it. A further point is that the sheer mass and variety of conflicting interests in the city makes community control difficult, and generates friction conducive to crime.

An overview of studies of delinquency in Britain by John Barron Mays seems to support the conclusions of American research. Studies in Liverpool dockland, in Croydon, in a mining town in the Midlands, and in old and new areas of Bristol all appear to agree that delinquency is a larger part of the way of life of such areas than elsewhere, and has survived the coming of greater prosperity. Mays' work, however, is more contemporary by some 30 years than that of the Chicago school, and he considers more recent explanations of deviance in the urban context. The Chicago school itself did little more than develop that part of Durkheim's anomie theory dealing with social disorganisation in modern urban society.

c The Functionalist and Strain Perspectives

The functionalist, Robert Merton, concentrates on the effect of the social system on the deviant, rather than the way in which immediate physical environment influences behaviour. He emphasises how the potential criminal is excluded from the legitimate opportunity structure (conventional career success), and so is pushed towards crime in order to get what he wants (desired goals). A reference back to Merton's model of conformity and non-conformity will show that he contextualises non-conformity within the normative structure of the *social system as a whole*. He classifies criminal deviance under 'innovation', that is behaviour which accepts socially prescribed goals (+), but which uses normatively unacceptable means (−) to obtain them. Specifically, in the USA the culture goal of material success is accepted by some who nevertheless lack the legitimate means – for example, skills, qualifications and connections – to obtain it. Crime provides a major alternative means by which material success may be obtained; so much so, in fact, that Daniel Bell entitled an article 'Crime as Part of the American Way of Life'. Because the dominant norms that guide and constrain people in pursuits of material success are of little use to those excluded from the legitimate opportunity structure, Merton refers to their situation as anomic. This is a valid, if somewhat elastic, application of Durkheim's term.

Underlying Merton's analysis is the assumption that the desire for economic gain lies behind much crime. This view was held, albeit in much simpler form, by Victorian social reformers such as Charles Booth who believed that once poverty had been abolished there would be no 'need' for crime. In fact, relative (or comparative) deprivation continues, even though extreme poverty is rare in the West. Although thieves may have 'enough', they steal because, like the rest of us, they want *more*. Crudely, greed has replaced need as a dominant motive. The strain theorists, to whose work we now turn, develop these notions to a more sophisticated theoretical level.

Sociologists who have followed and extended Durkheim's analysis have sometimes been referred to as 'strain' theorists, no doubt because Merton's model poses a strain between the goals of the potential criminal and the structure of the legitimate opportunity. Whilst generally agreeing with Merton that the desire for economic gain motivates such crime, Cloward and Ohlin (1960) make a more detailed analysis of the possible forms of criminal reaction to lack of legitimate opportunity. Some criminals may adjust with spectacular success and rise to the criminal world's equivalent of the top managerial level: the 'godfather' figures of the Mafia are an example. At a lower level is the 'skilled craftsman' who may work for himself, or for an organised gang. In the latter instance, he would expect high 'wages' or a substantial 'cut' from the job. Less organised crime provides an alternative for those without access to the criminal elite: haphazardly planned and sometimes risky street crime is a common example. Perhaps the near-pointless violence sometimes associated with this type of crime reflects the sense of 'double failure' of the low-grade criminal, a 'loser' in both the 'straight' and criminal worlds. Another group still, 'the retreatists' (see Merton's model) seek to negate their sense of failure by taking drugs.

Albert Cohen, another strain theorist, emphasises the 'status frustration' felt by lower class youths in explaining their delinquent behaviour. As we have seen, they tend to 'fail' at school and often drift in and out of unsatisfying, low-status work. He uses the term 'reaction formation' to describe how delinquent gang members rebound from conventional failure and seek to create their own alternative status hierarchies based on their criminal achievements. Committing a daring offence or even having a criminal record may become matters to boast about. Yet the desire for status is not, in itself, deviant. Thus, delin-

491

quent behaviour is seen as a distorted mirror-image of normal behaviour – an unpleasing glimpse of what anyone might do in the absence of legitimate alternatives of self-expression and esteem. A. K. Cohen provides a link between functionalist-strain and sub-cultural theory (discussed below). The latter approach, however, tends to see deviant sub-cultures not so much in reactive terms but as a positive assertion of lower working class values.

d Sub-cultural and Interactionist Theories

SUB-CULTURAL THEORIES We discuss the sub-cultural and inter-actionist perspectives together, although they are distinct, because an increasing number of authors use concepts and insights from both.

The sub-cultural theorist, Walter B. Miller, reacted against the analysis of the strain theorists, discussed above. He was the first to make a clear analysis of gang delinquency in terms of positive lower class values such as toughness, smartness, excitement and freedom from authority. It is this conformity to lower working class culture rather than rejection of middle class values that is the key to understanding delinquency. A very similar analysis to this was independently adopted in Britain during the nineteen fifties by both Terence Morris and J. B. Mays. Lower working class kids were often free to roam the streets in search of 'kicks' and were inconsistently, and there-fore ineffectively, punished by their parents if their 'fun' hap-pened to break the law. Indeed, their parents might well be criminal themselves. In a study of East London in the early nineteen sixties, David Downes noted relatively little difference between the values of youthful delinquents and those of the adult lower working class. A study by Willmott of the same kind of area suggested that about 10% of working class youth were delinquent-inclined and that this inclination was formed by social environment. (See Chapter 14, p. 369.)

In part, the work on sub-cultures of Downes and others, provided the basis on which the Birmingham Centre for Cul-tural Studies has produced an impressive body of work analysing youth, particularly working class youth sub-cultures. It needs to be clearly stated that most of this research is not concerned primarily with working class juvenile delinquency as such, because most working class juveniles are not delinquents.

Nevertheless, there is often a thin line between legitimate excitement on the streets and breaking the law: the search for fun does not necessarily stop at the point of illegality. On the contrary, the enjoyment of motor-bike 'burn-ups', soccer 'hooliganism', and minor acts of vandalism is probably sharpened by the fact that they involve cocking a snook at law and authority. *Delinquescent* (delinquency prone) behaviour is not too strong a word to describe the tendency of much working class youth sub-cultural activity. We described these sub-cultures at some length in Chapter 14 and the student should re-read the relevant section (pp. 367–80), bearing in mind that there our concern was with pleasure-seeking, whereas here it is with delinquency. As was also pointed out in Chapter 14, some black youngsters also have life-styles that border on the delinquent. A 'black' song expresses the point more eloquently than a sociologist could, although the words lose much without the music:

Many rivers to cross
But I can't seem to find my way over
Wandering, I am lost
As I travel along the white cliffs of Dover

Many rivers to cross
But where to begin . . . I'm playing for time
There've been times
I find myself thinking of committing some dreadful crime.

The interactionist, Matza, has criticised sub-cultural theorists for over-stressing the difference between sub-cultural and dominant values. Instead, he sees adolescents, particularly from the lower class, as drifting into crime out of a sense of fatalism and lack of something else to do. More recent sub-cultural theorists have accepted that this can often happen, but they still maintain the importance of distinct sub-cultural identity and values.

INTERACTIONIST THEORIES In the previous chapter we highlighted, mainly through Howard Becker's analysis of marijuana users, three major elements of 'labelling' theory: its explanation of deviancy as learnt; the stress given to the meaning of deviant behaviour by the actors involved; and the role of societal reaction. We pursue these points further here.

The American sociologist, Edwin H. Sutherland, insisted that delinquent behaviour is learned. Sutherland can be seen as an intermediary figure between the Chicago school of the inter-war period and modern interactionists on both sides of the Atlantic. Like the urban sociologists, he recognised that a socially disorganised environment is conducive to delinquency, but he wanted to understand more about the personal and psychological experiences that lead an individual into delinquency. After examining virtually all possible explanations, Sutherland arrived at the hypothesis that people commit crime because they learn to do so. He refined this into the theory of *differential association*. The difference between those who do, and those who do not, commit crime is that the former have been associated with criminals and the latter have not (or not to the same extent). In support of his thesis, Sutherland pointed out that crime is often concentrated in particular areas, streets and even families. This fitted in well with the ecologists' emphasis on the adverse influence of deteriorating neighbourhoods on children's behaviour. On the other hand, Sutherland's emphasis on the role of 'significant others' (in this case, criminals) in deviancy socialisation shows the influence of the symbolic interactionist, George Mead, on his ideas.

Undoubtedly, differential association is the joker in the pack of theories of crime and delinquency. As a statement of the obvious it is not easily matched, even in a discipline noted for such pronouncements. It is, of course, true that all social behaviour that is not entirely instinctively preprogrammed involves some element of learning and habituation. What Sutherland fails to explain convincingly is why only *some* individuals with apparently the same 'associational' experience of crime become criminals. We are back where we started! On the credit side, he did help to undermine crude explanations of delinquency as *merely* unsocial or maladjusted behaviour and, instead, explained it as 'normal' *within the context of the deviant's own experience and environment*. This approach has influenced both policy and theory. Practically, it directs the reformer's attention to changing the social situation rather than the individual – a common enough approach in Europe but one which, perhaps, needed more vigorous assertion in individualistic America. Theoretically, Sutherland's admittedly schematic attempt to understand delinquency from the delinquent's point of view has been fully shared by modern interactionists. We have already analysed how Becker describes the regular use of marijuana as a learned habit. David Matza incorporates the same idea into his concept of *affiliation*. Deviants drift, but they drift towards activities that interest them and about which they want to know more. Both Becker and Matza seem to allow for rather more choice in the matter than Sutherland, as Becker's example of marijuana *use* (a positive emphasis) shows.

There is no need to expand here on the importance of the meaning attached by actors – in this case delinquents – to their behaviour: that point has been frequently made already. In particular, the sub-cultural studies of the Birmingham group, presented in Chapter 14, show a strong interactionist influence in their concern for the feelings, motives and experience of 'the kids'.

MORAL PANICS, MORAL CRUSADERS AND THE MEDIA The insight that deviance is 'constructed' by a combination of individual action and societal reaction is central to interactionism. We use Stanley Cohen's book, *Folk Devils and Moral Panics* to provide a detailed analysis of this process which rests squarely on Lemert's concept of secondary deviance.

Interactionists frequently argue that societal reaction can actually increase or 'amplify' the deviant behaviour of the labelled individual or group. Stanley Cohen has used the example of the rival 'Mod' and 'Rocker' youth factions of the mid nineteen sixties to illustrate the point. The dramatic pre-publicity given to their expected confrontations almost certainly attracted many more young people than might otherwise have been present. In this way, the media helped to create the events it anticipated or, as Cohen says, 'these predictions played the role of the classic self-fulfilling prophecy'. Similarly, over-reporting of what did (or did not) happen at a confrontation could help attract more people on another occasion (don't we all like 'being in the papers'?) In turn, over-reporting could provoke excessive public reaction. Once a 'spiral of amplification' of this kind is generated, it can acquire an artificial momentum of its own: when this happens, what is 'real' and what is imagined is not easy to disentangle.

Given that the media does not consciously seek to popularise deviant activity, why does this over-reporting take place? There is, of course, the sound commercial reason that deviancy stories make good copy and sell newspapers. A more sociological explanation is offered by Cohen. It is suggested in the title of the book itself: *Folk Devils and Moral Panics: The Creation of the Mods and Rockers.* In what sense, then, were the Mods and Rockers 'devils' and what was the nature of the 'moral panic' they precipitated? To answer this question, Cohen uses the concept of 'boundary crisis'. Post-war Britain was relatively affluent, but the majority had not yet adjusted psychologically to the new prosperity. The frank pleasure-seeking and instrumental attitude to work of some groups of young people seemed to undermine the work ethic in a dangerous and uncomfortable way. Although most people had experienced a shift in the balance between work and leisure in their own lives, commitment to the values of hard work and self-discipline prevented them from entering the newly-discovered pleasure gardens with the gay abandon of the Mods and Rockers. The activities of the latter could be tolerated to a greater degree than would have been imaginable in the thirties, but even so morality dictated that 'there had to be limits'. The press presented 'the need for limits' as 'self-evident' and a matter for 'common sense', but such terms should not be taken at face value by the sociologist. Whatever their moral validity, their effect is to tend to close down a debate in favour of the dominant consensus. No doubt this is partly because an open discussion on some of the issues raised by the behaviour of the Mods and Rockers, including attitudes towards drugs and sex, would by definition bring into question majority consensus on such matters.

Those who seek to organise and orchestrate ritual condemnations of 'folk-devils' are referred to by interactionists as 'moral crusaders' or 'moral entrepreneurs'. They 'make it their business' to see that morality is defended and that justice is done to those who offend it. Often, some of the more popular Sunday newspapers take on this task, although perhaps they do so because deviancy stories boost sales, rather than as a result of deep commitment to traditional morality. Lord Longford and Mrs Mary Whitehouse have been more obviously sincere moral crusaders in what they sometimes call 'the fight against pornography', and Mrs Whitehouse, as chairperson of the pressure group, The National Viewers and Listeners Association, has opposed the way sex and violence have been presented on radio and television.

e Marxism, Crime and the Law

In *Crimes of the Powerful*, Frank Pearce offers more than a critique of white collar crime. He outlines and, in part, empirically illustrates, a full Marxist theory of the law, crime and power of what Marxists call the ruling class. Central to his argument is the concept of 'ideology' which he treats, in traditional Marxist terms, as the ideas of the ruling class (which are sometimes also believed in by sections of the working class). To a large extent, the idea of 'law and order' in capitalist society is regarded by Marxists as simply an ideological tool of the ruling class, intended to make sure that the working class conform. Public moral concern with lower class crime and the money, time and energy spent on controlling it diverts attention from the exploitative activities of the ruling capitalist class, whose leading representatives would not creditably survive close legal scrutiny of their own business or professional lives. Generally, they have the wealth and power to ensure that such examination seldom occurs, but gradually a body of research on upper class crime is being produced. Pearce himself quotes a American Federal Trade Commission estimate that *detectable* business frauds accounted for over fifteen times as much money as robbery. William Chambliss' detailed study of organised crime in Seattle, Washington, reached the conclusion that leading figures in the business, political and law enforcement fields made up the city's major crime syndicate and worked together for massive criminal gain in gambling, prostitution and drug trafficking. Much illegally made profit was then ploughed back into legitimate business. Chambliss contends that crime occurs among all classes, but that the types of crimes committed and the extent to which the law is enforced varies between classes. The crimes of the powerful are likely to be more lucrative and to escape prosecution. It is important to get Chambliss' work in perspective. He does not show that the majority of the local upper class in Seattle is criminally corrupt, and still less that the majority of the upper class in the United States is corrupt. Nor does he or any Marxist have to do so to prove that capitalists control the capitalist system. They do this, according to Marxists, whether they break the law or not. If the rules of the game are weighted in their favour, they may not need to break them. Perhaps the point of Pearce and Chambliss' research is that if the needs or convenience of the upper class require criminal behaviour, then it is often forthcoming.

Just as Marxists do not accept the law in capitalist society at face value, neither do they accept the categories of crime and deviance as fair or objective. On the contrary, many so-called criminals and deviants in capitalist society are seen as 'victims of the system'. Yet the plight of the lower class criminal and deviant has never concerned Marxists to the extent that it has liberals. This is because Marxists see the hope for social change in a revolutionary movement of the 'solid' working class, certainly not in the criminal fraternity. By contrast, it is central to liberal philosophy to seek to 'reform' and improve the conditions of marginal groups, including criminals and deviants, rather than to wait for social transformation brought about by a revolution they neither want nor expect.

Two aspects of the Marxist analysis of criminal deviance are of great interest. Firstly, there is a considerable need for the general public to be more precisely informed about the 'crimes of the powerful' and particularly about the relationship between powerful economic interests, the law and political power. The Watergate scandal and aspects of the Jeremy Thorpe 'affair', concerning the relationship between business and politics, hardly fill the public with confidence. Similarly, the large sums shown to have been illegally paid by many international companies to help create favourable trading relations with given countries make petty theft look very petty indeed. To what extent do these cases, however extreme they may seem, throw light on what is typical? Here is a tangled but fascinating web for researchers to trace and explain. Secondly, the Marxist analysis of law as a form of ideology is also of immense potential interest. David Gordon argues that *'selective'* enforcement of the law which penalises the working class and favours the upper class creates a misleading impression of who is 'guilty' in capitalist society. As Frank Pearce and Jock Young point out, a full analysis along these lines would require careful qualification. It is undeniable that many laws do work for the day-to-day convenience (traffic laws) and protection (laws prohibiting violence against the person) of most citizens. Despite this, the thesis that the powerful few are able to use the law as an ideological smokescreen to confuse the majority whilst they themselves get on with the business of business, is certainly worth further exploration.

f The Empirical Approach: An Example

The final approach to criminal and delinquent behaviour considered here is empirical rather than theoretical in nature. It is an attempt to establish what social facts or factors correlate with criminal and delinquent behaviour. Of course, neither facts nor factors can exist in a theoretical vacuum, and must be presented within some structure of meaning; nevertheless, the multi-factoral approach is noted for producing profuse data rather than profound theory. Explanations are offered in a piecemeal way, which may be termed pragmatic, and with careful reference to the empirical findings which are considered to substantiate them. Often, the theoretical perspectives that are adopted tend to be interdisciplinary or taken from other, more conceptually grounded work. The empirical, pragmatic and interdisciplinary approach is typical of traditional British criminology and has found a major expression in the work of the Cambridge Institute of Criminology and particularly in the writings of D. J. West. Research at the Institute predates the development of interactionist and Marxist deviancy theory in Britain, and still continues vigorously. The major, if somewhat remote, intellectual influence on the Institute is Durkheim.

Perhaps West's best known work is his contribution to a longitudinal study of delinquency. The original sample was 411 eight year old boys from 'deprived' urban backgrounds. The third report of the study team, *The Delinquent Way of Life*, written by West and Farrington, was based on interviews with 389 of the original group, then in their mid-teens, between 1971 and 1973. 101 of these youths had official convictions by the time of the interview. The content of the previous two reports is well summarised by West and Farrington:

> Our previous work demonstrated that a constellation of adverse factors present at an early age, notably large families, low intelligence, poverty, unsatisfactory parental child-rearing behaviour and criminality, increased very significantly the likelihood of a boy acquiring a juvenile delinquency record.

It is probably correct to say that the average newspaper reader would be well aware of all this – certainly, the Chicago urban sociologists of the inter-war period were. To spend large sums of money 'demonstrating' the above perhaps does little more than suggest that sociology is, indeed, sometimes the science of the obvious.

In its analysis of the boys' behaviour at primary school, the report claims that 'troublesome' behaviour is seen as 'a particularly powerful indicator of future juvenile convictions'. In a review of the book, Laurie Taylor, a leading interactionist, wrote of this particular 'finding':

> Being called 'troublesome' (or 'intelligent' or 'queer') has social and cultural consequences. It may actually impel individuals towards particular cultural groups with specific values, ideas and behaviour'.

In other words, the label 'troublesome' may push a child into becoming a 'trouble-maker' whereas another label – let us say a more positive one – might affect his behaviour quite differently. For West and Farrington to fail at least to mention this is, as Taylor points out, to by-pass a considerable body of research relevant to their conclusions.

In the third report, West and Farrington's main 'finding' is that certain 'antisocial characteristics' tended to occur together in the delinquent. Here, their work depends on psychological as well as sociological perspectives. The antisocial characteristics are 'self-reported aggression, unstable work record, anti-establishment attitudes, driving after heavy drinking, heavy gambling, drug use, involvement in antisocial groups, sexual activity, immoderate smoking, hanging about and being tattooed.' Again, none of this is surprising. West and Farrington conclude by claiming that they have clearly demonstrated 'the close connection between officially recorded delinquency and particular attributes of character and life style – the delinquent way of life'. Whether these 'attributes of character' are considered by the authors to be inborn or to be the result of the deprived childhood experience of most of the delinquents described in previous reports, we are not told. The former – in effect an argument that there is a criminal personality-type – would align West and Farrington with the behavioural psychologist, Eysenck. The latter – that it is social environment or even a repressive social system that 'causes' lower class crime – is a radical, if not revolutionary one, and might lend support to policies of massive social reform. The conclusion is inescapable that a fuller theoretical contextualisation of West and Farrington's work is necessary. A purely empirical approach is impossible because both the selection and interpretation of facts require a theoretical framework. We return to the general problem of criminal and deviancy theory at the end of this chapter.

g Crime Perspectives

It is necessary to be sensible about interpreting crime. Clearly, some interpretations and factors can be used in explaining some kinds of crime, but not others. Thus, material or status deprivation might help explain the crimes of the poor but not those of the rich. Further, certain theories are more compatible than others. Again, in explaining the crimes of the poor, socio-economic, urban ecological and Marxist interpretations cover common ground in a similar way: so, too, do the interactionist and Marxist interpretations of white-collar crime. In so far as the empirical approach is theoretically 'neutral', the data it produces can be interpreted variously. In practice, however, this approach is frequently linked with reformism – for the 'help' or 'correction' of deviants – and steers clear of the criticism of the system employed by Marxists and some radical inter-actionists.

We now examine two other major types of social deviance: suicide and political deviance.

2 Suicide

Suicide occurs when a person intentionally kills himself. Suicide in Britain has declined since the early nineteen sixties, when over 5,000 suicides per annum were regularly recorded. In 1976, 4,300 people committed suicide. The suicide rate showed a slight upturn in 1979 and was again almost 5,000 in 1983.

The best starting point for the study of suicide is still Durkheim's *Le Suicide*, first published in 1897. Although recent sociologists have convincingly criticised Durkheim's statistical method, his typology of suicide remains fruitful ground for analysis. He divided suicide into *altruistic, egoistic* and *anomic.*

Altruistic suicide occurs when an individual sacrifices his life for what he believes to be a higher cause. This type of suicide has much in common with martyrdom; indeed, it might be considered as self-inflicted martyrdom. The most spectacular recent example of altruistic suicide is the action of the Japanese pilots who dived their planes into enemy shipping, thereby committing *kamikase.*

501

It is best to think of egoistic and anomic suicide together, as opposite sides of the same coin. If we explain anomic suicide first, it will become clear how egoistic suicide fits into Durkheim's general pattern of explanation. *Anomic suicide occurs in its typical pattern when economic change so disrupts the fabric of society that the norms and beliefs by which people once lived no longer seem to apply.* We can illustrate the point by taking an example which, again, occurred after Durkheim's own death in 1917. The Wall Street Crash of 1929 caused an outbreak of suicide among the American rich or, more precisely, the previously rich. It can be argued that they were driven to suicide not only by material loss but also because of stress in the face of the psychological and normative adjustment to the different life style that loss demanded. Durkheim's own nineteenth century research substantiated the view that economic change, whether for better or worse, tended to increase the suicide rate.

Viewed in a wider theoretical context, Durkheim's research into suicide should be regarded as an attempt to illustrate that social facts (in this case, economic change) explain individual behaviour (suicide). It is the major example of his use of the positive method. More recent work by Henry and Short has provided qualified support for this approach. They showed that business cycles could be correlated with suicide rates. Unlike Durkheim, however, they use psychological as well as sociological theory and data in their analysis. This is a welcome recognition of the complexity of the issue.

Ervin Stengel goes too far when he says that 'Durkheim's concept of the collective state of society and its suicidal inclination is only of historical interest', but there are various emotional and personal factors invariably involved in the committing of suicide which cannot be adequately explained and understood as mere correlates of social facts 'measured' by statistical trends. The ethnomethodologist, Jack Douglas, goes further, and insists that suicide must be understood as an act fraught with personal *meaning*. That personal meaning, he considers, can never be understood in statistical terms. We return to his criticisms of Durkheim in a slightly different context later.

We now explain egoistic suicide. This is more likely to occur *when a society is so unstable that the individual may be unable to find meaningful guidance and security in times of moral uncertainty.* Durkheim cited evidence to show that Catholic communities provided a stronger focus for personal identity than Protestant ones, and therefore tended to have lower suicide rates. It is also in the absence of stable identity and social conditions that anomic suicide occurs. In practice, modern sociologists have tended to use the term anomic suicide to describe *suicide occurring in unstable or fast-changing social conditions, whether these are caused by economic change or other factors. Thus, the term anomic suicide can cover egoistic suicide as well.*

It is worth including in this brief survey of suicide a reference to P. Sainsbury's study of suicide in London (1955). This work is theoretically unsophisticated, but it makes the important point that suicide can occur for a variety of different reasons and not always simply because of strictly social factors. The following illustrates the point. As Stengel points out, Sainsbury's categories and his allocation of individual cases within them are 'somewhat arbitrary and artificial', but some such distinctions are necessary if the various factors contributing to suicide are to be understood.

Causative factors in 390 cases of suicide in North London 1936–8. Modified after P. Sainsbury, *Suicide in London,* 1955

Factors	Contributory in % of cases	Principal in % of cases
Social factors	60	35
Personal	20	14
Physical illness	29	18
Mental disorder	47	37
Personality abnormal	17	17

Source: *Stengel,* 1977, p. 47.

We now examine suicide and parasuicide in contemporary British society. Parasuicide is a broad term which describes attempted suicide, or apparently attempted suicide. It is necessary to include apparently attempted suicide within the meaning of the term because every year many hundreds and even thousands of people, particularly young people, use a suicide gesture as a thinly veiled cry for help. By the late nineteen seventies, the annual parasuicide rate in Britain was well over 100,000 – about 20 times more than the figure in the early nineteen fifties. What has caused this spectacular rise? No doubt the increased availability of drugs, both on prescription and on the black market, has something to do with it, but for a more convincing sociological explanation, it is helpful to refer again to Durkheim's concept of *anomic suicide*. Anomic suicide is only one example of anomic behaviour which is caused by anomie. Durkheim defined anomie as feelings of normlessness or rootlessness due to social change and instability. Other examples of anomic behaviour besides suicide are crime and drunkenness. Durkheim argued that as society changes from the traditional to the modern, anomic behaviour would increase. There is considerable evidence to support his case. In particular, the high rate of parasuicide among the young indicates a sense of meaningless and despair. In the comments of social workers and of young parasuicides themselves are to be believed, this is certainly true. 'A feeling of absolute loneliness' often inspires parasuicide, according to one involved observer. Other signs of anomie among parasuicides are drug-taking, high rates of venereal disease, illegitimate pregnancies, abortions, and frequent address changes. Even Durkheim did not foresee problems of this scope, but his concept of anomie does enable us to understand social change, fragmentation and decay much more profoundly than might otherwise have been possible.

3 Political Deviance

We end our discussion of deviance and social control with a brief analysis of political deviance, partly in order to conclude on a note of optimism. In certain cases, though by no means all, political deviance can be an expression of great personal idealism and morality. It is this aspect we wish to stress here. Firstly, however, it is necessary to explain what political deviance is. *It is political action or belief which goes beyond the limits of political behaviour allowed by the existing regime.* Examples of political deviants are the Russian dissidents against the Soviet Regime, of whom the author, Solzhenitsyn, is outstanding. The generals who conspired to overthrow Hitler in 1944 are another example. Closer to home, the IRA provides a less comfortable example. The issue of the individual or group versus the state which is raised by the question of political deviancy is of general social interest. We began our analysis of order and deviance by talking of the practical necessity of norms, and the various ways, including socialisation, by which people are taught and persuaded to observe them. We have suggested all along, however, that the individual may use his own will and imagination to negotiate and adapt society's rules. In rare instances he may reject them altogether. This may happen where an individual considers that it is his moral duty to do so. Thus, a pacifist who refuses to accept call-up papers is pitting the authority of his own conscience against the authority of the state. In many lesser instances, an individual may feel that he must at least protest before obeying a particular rule. Of course, this is unlikely to occur with most day-to-day norms; yet, bearing in mind the apparent ease with which people can be persuaded to follow evil and destructive authority, it is worth ending with the observation that each individual has the option of trying to change or, in the last instance, even of rejecting, the norms and rules that frame his life – as well as obeying them.

Power, Social Control and the Definition of Deviancy

By now, the reader will be aware that defining who is deviant is no simple matter. It is true that functionalists see the matter as fairly unproblematic: for them, deviants are those who break society's rules. The state makes the formal rules of society, and various control agencies, such as the police and the courts, enforce them. Interactionists and Marxists see the matter in more complex ways. From what has already been said, it will be clear that they both consider that agencies of control implement rules that favour some at the expense of others, although this is not equally true of all rules. We can take this as our starting point for more detailed analysis.

Interactionism
Recent interactionist deviancy theory has tended to concern itself particularly with the way agencies of social control process potential deviants and administer or withhold labels. Not only have the police and courts been scrutinised, but also probation officers, teachers and social workers. Ethnomethodologists have

been especially active in studying social control. They even go beyond interactionists in searching out the *meanings* that social actors give to the events. To understand why a policeman arrests a 'suspect' or why a magistrate convicts on given occasions, *situationally specific* studies of each case must be made. Motives for action vary and although observation may show that consistent patterns exist, no absolute generalisation about conduct is possible, because people change.

Paul Rock offers a model of the police as a law enforcement agency. He bases his analysis mainly on American material because the sociology of the police has been largely an American pursuit. Four related issues underlie his model:

1 *The Police as Inhibitors (Preventing/Controlling) of Deviancy.*
2 *The Police as Transformers of Deviancy*
3 *The Police as Translators of Definitions of Deviancy into Enforcement.*
4 *The Police as Creators of the Reality of Deviancy in the Public Mind – that is, how the public perceive deviancy.*

Before explaining what the above issues mean, it is worth pointing out that Rock brings them into a common focus by envisaging the police system as an organisation which interacts with society. This study is, therefore, an example of an interactionist organisational analysis. The police must achieve, or at least appear to achieve, the primary and externally prescribed goal of enforcing law and order, but they also have certain secondary goals which relate chiefly to maintaining themselves as a strong, efficient, respected and well-paid organisation. To a great extent, the achievement of primary goals depends on the achievement of secondary ones. Thus, a poorly paid police force with a low morale would not be expected to be very successful in the enforcement of law and order.

We turn to Rock's four issues. There is no difficulty in understanding the role of the police in inhibiting deviancy. This is not an impartial activity, however, as they have to *select* which areas of deviant behaviour merit most skill, effort and resources. A drive against vandalism may mean that less manpower is directed towards, say, stopping business frauds. Decisions of this kind *transform* deviancy: crudely, the pattern of deviant behaviour is, to some extent, structured by what the police 'allow' to happen or not happen. In turn, this may be affected by police manpower and resources as well as decisions about which crimes are more, or less, important. This leads us to the issue of the police as *translators*. They translate the law into action (or not) partly on the basis of the content of the law itself, partly in response to variations in public opinion and partly in terms of their own understanding of the importance of a given law. Thus, a certain stand in public opinion favouring community policing seems to have contributed to its adoption in some areas, such as Devon and Cornwall. Skolnick particularly stresses the power of the police to define the 'operative legality of the system of administering criminal law' that is, to choose which laws to enforce. An excellent example occurs in the Manchester area. There, Chief Constable Anderton has proclaimed freely that he finds prostitution and pornography repugnant. Undoubtedly, he has required the law to be enforced against them much more rigorously than is usual elsewhere. Of couse, he has a legal right to do this, but his decision is (inevitably) political in the limited sense that he is enforcing principles clear to himself though not necessarily to everyone else. Finally, we consider the police as creators of the 'reality' of deviancy as perceived by the public. This is a result of their power to operate certain policies of enforcement both at a senior level, and on the beat. To a greater or lesser extent, such policies *may* involve real discrimination as well as necessary selection. Thus blacks, the working class or young people *may* be relatively discriminated against. Skolnick also points out the relevance of practical and routine factors in affecting police behaviour. A policeman may decide that it is 'about time' he made an arrest, or he may believe that it will help his career to achieve 'a high score'. The result of all this is that statistical 'facts' about deviancy presented to the public are, in ways both profound and trivial, created by the police. We examine this point in more detail in the next section.

The same essential argument that the agency of control itself partly determines who is labelled deviant applies also to the judicial system. Pat Carlen's aptly titled book, *Magistrates' Justice*, shows the magistrate to be as impressionable and even as partial in judgement as others.

THE COURTS – MAGISTRATES AND JURORS Carlen's study, and a number of other interactionist and ethnomethodological ones concentrate on the actors in the courtroom drama itself, usually with due attention to what happens 'behind the scenes'. The variety of accidental contingencies that can affect the outcome of a trial is striking. The kind of support a defendant gets from key figures, such as probation officers and social workers, can often greatly influence and even determine the nature of a sentence. If, for instance, a probation officer decides that a client has finally 'gone too far' (admittedly a crudely unprofessional response) and makes this clear in his report to the court, a harsher judgement may be likely. The 'plea-bargaining' system, prevalent both in Britain and the United States, is a practice which would seem to lend itself to abuse. Plea-bargaining involves the accused obtaining more favourable treatment in return for an admission of guilt. Firstly, the interrogation of suspects in police custody can involve 'deals' in which, say, a lesser charge is 'traded-off' for a statement admitting an offence. Secondly, judicial officials sometimes give more lenient sentences in return for guilty pleas. When justice is put into the market place like this, the possibility of a 'bad deal' for the poor and less well-informed seems correspondingly greater. Needless to say, this trade-off process can facilitate police and court business and sometimes gains prestige for the police and prosecution; that is, presumably, the justification for it.

The kind of detailed, closely observed study we have been describing is frequently favoured by the ethnomethodologists, although such an approach is by no means their monopoly. Harold Garfinkel, one of their chief exponents, was led to his conclusions partly by his attempts to analyse the deliberations of a group of jurors. In the following taped comment, he appears to be saying that the jurors used their own common-sense knowledge of society to arrive at what seemed to them a fair verdict:

> What I mean is that it was for them a matter that somehow or other in their dealings with each other they managed, if you will permit me now to use it (commonsense), to see. (*Author's brackets*).

Garfinkel further suggests that it is the job of sociologists to describe and understand what this commonsense knowledge is and how it is applied in a particular context. The application of this view to control theory is that jurors arrive at verdicts not merely on the basis of legal considerations but by calling upon a much wider fund of general knowledge, including an acquired idea of justice. Functionalists tend to consider that the process of legal enforcement is relatively unbiased. Ethnomethodologists make the point that even though people are, to some extent, guided by mutually accepted standards of conduct, behaviour is diverse, different and not wholly predictable. This includes the process of normative and legal enforcement. To put the matter extremely, in a given case justice can be what jurors and judges decide it is, rather than something more objective.

Marxism, Social Control and Deviancy Definition

We can deal briefly with the topic indicated under this heading because the concept of social control summarises and focuses all that we have said so far about Marxist theory in the last two chapters. Ruling class control of the social order and of definitions of deviancy is the crux of Marxist analysis in this area.

Capitalist ideology affects the various agencies of social control as it does all other institutions in capitalist society. The police 'automatically' concentrate on working class rather than middle class crime because this is what they have been taught to look for and expect.

Stuart Hall has made an interesting Marxist analysis of what he calls 'policing the crisis' of contemporary British capitalism. He considers that British capitalism is experiencing severe difficulties. In order to divide and distract the working class from criticising and organising against capitalism, the capitalist media and leading politicians create a 'panic' about immigration and immigrants. This has the effect of putting working class whites at odds with working class blacks (nearly all blacks in Britain are working class) and obscuring from both that the real cause of unemployment lies in the nature of the capitalist system itself. The generally racist climate affects the police. Assisted by increased government expenditure on law and order, they concentrate more attention and resources in black areas and particularly against black youth (see Chapter 13). This has the result of ensuring high crime figures for blacks and stigmatising the black community further in the eyes of the public. This brief summary inevitably fails to do full justice to Hall's argument, but his analysis amounts to a very comprehensive structural explanation of how one ethnic group comes to be defined as 'deviant'.

Control Agencies and the Social Creation of Statistics

So far, we have quoted official statistics with the occasional hint that they may not be quite as 'factual' as they appear. We will now explore this possibility further. Criminal and suicide statistics are those chosen for discussion here, although similar considerations apply to court and government statistics generally.

What are criminal statistics? Or rather, what do they purport to be? Two main units are measured: the offences and the offenders. Given that not all offences known to the police and officially recorded as having been committed are solved, the figure for offences is always larger than that for offenders in any given year. Thus, in 1976 the total number of all recorded offences in England and Wales, indictable and non indictable, was 3,792,000 and the number of persons found guilty of offences was 2,072,000.

Some of the inadequacies of official statistics are of a technical nature and are not a matter of controversy. First, there is a 'dark number' of undiscovered crimes. There are various possibilities that explain why a crime might go undiscovered: a victim of blackmail may be afraid of his blackmailer; a shoplifter may persuade the shop management not to prosecute; a neighbourhood quarrel involving minor crime may be adequately controlled without calling the police; a victim of assault who knows his assailant might block legal proceedings for friendship's sake. An accurate estimate of what the sum total of such 'offences' might be is impossible, but few criminologists would be surprised if they exceeded the number of recorded crimes. One Chief Constable has 'guestimated' that crime reported to the police is only 10% of all crime, although a very much higher percentage of serious crime does come to police attention.

Several other variables can affect the accuracy of official statistics. Updating of police equipment, especially in communications and in information filing and retrieval methods, and improvements in training would be expected to increase detection rates. Expansion of the police force should achieve the same result. Between 1974 and 1978, the police force in England and Wales increased by 7,000, and it may be that the apparent 'increase' in crime during this period was in some part actually an increase in the *detection* of crime. If the police decide to 'crack down' on a particular kind of crime, then the statistics for that crime would be expected to show an 'artificial' increase during the relevant period. For example, in November 1978, the Tokyo police made a massive temporary switch of manpower and resources to achieve the arrest of members of motor bike gangs who had previously been able to break traffic laws with near impunity. Clearly, traffic offences involving motor bikes would go up for November of that year though, if the policy of deterrence worked, not for December. Similarly, when the police respond to 'moral panics' by concentrating more effort to combat 'the evil' in question, fluctuations in the statistics relating to that crime correspondingly occur.

Statistics can be made to seem misleading simply by being used badly. The selective use of statistics to support subjective generalisations is a particularly common form of misuse. Vague statements referring to 'the increase in sexual crimes and crimes involving violence' are an example. Sexual crimes actually decreased between 1969 and 1977 – (see the table on p. 487). There had, of course, been a massive increase in crimes of violence in that period, but it does not include murder and the non-indictable offence of assault (a less serious category of crime than violence against the person). Confusion also sometimes occurs because the statistical implications of legislative change is not always properly appreciated. For instance, as a result of the Theft Act of 1968, the figure for theft and the handling of stolen goods before and after the Act's implementation are not comparable.

The queries so far raised in relation to the validity and use of official statistics have been mainly technical and, as such, are amenable to technical solution. A number of interactionists and ethnomethodologists, however, have raised a more fundamental question about the accuracy and meaning of official statistics. It is best to approach their argument through a specific case: that of juvenile delinquency. In his book, *The Social Organisation of Juvenile Justice,* ethnomethodologist, Aaron Cicourel examines how two towns, with almost identical populations, experience quite different rates of juvenile crime as recorded in official statistics. He gives two explanations: the different organisational policies pursued by the police in the two towns, and the different way police policy towards delinquency was interpreted *'via the background expectancies'* of officers dealing directly with juveniles. In the first town, a loose attitude to recording delinquent acts and an informal approach to dealing with delinquents made the problem *appear* small, and vice-versa in the other town where much 'tighter' practices and stricter assumptions prevailed. In the first case what came to be regarded as a small problem seemed to require progressively fewer officers to deal with it, whereas in the second case the problem became amplified and so more manpower and resources were deployed to 'solve' it. All this, of course, affected the statistics of delinquency in the two towns in opposite ways, decreasing them in the first instance, and increasing them in the second. Cicourel's general conclusion for sociological research is:

> A researcher utilising official materials cannot interpret them unless he possesses or invents a theory that includes how background expectancies render everyday activities recognisable and intelligible.

Cicourel's point that statistics are partly created, and not simply collected, has been applied in much wider contexts than his own limited comparative case study. In particular, the validity of the statistically 'typical' criminal – the young, urban working class male – is considered as a partly misleading abstraction by some interactionists. It is worth noting that in a number of self-report studies of young people (that is, research based on descriptions by young people of their own conduct), the ratio of working class to middle class delinquent activity drops from the 5 or 6 to 1 of official statistics to about 1.5 to 1. Further, in 1977 and 1978 a relatively large proportion of black youths were arrested on 'suspicion' or 'sus' as the youths called it. Many felt themselves to have been discriminated against. Clearly, this is a sensitive area and not one about which to make wild generalisations, but on the basis of television investigations alone there is evidence that sometimes this is so. Perhaps this adds a further characteristic to the criminal stereotype in inner urban areas – colour.

It is not only the young working class male who may be

grossly over-represented in criminal statistics. We have already cited a range of studies by both interactionists and Marxists which seek to demonstrate an in-built (though not necessarily always conscious) bias of the social and legal systems in favour of the upper and middle classes and against the working class. As early as 1940, Edwin Sutherland produced evidence that white collar crime might be substantially under-estimated in official statistics. He found that often the petty crimes of pilfering or major crimes of bribery passed unnoticed or, were dealt with 'within the firm'. Even the flouting of commercial and industrial law was more likely to be the subject of governmental reprimand than legal action. A study by W. S. Carson of 200 firms in south east England, some 25 years later, found similarly that only 1.5% of officialy detected breaches of factory legislation were prosecuted. To these we must add the more far-reaching allegations, made by those Marxists to whom we have already referred, of crime involving local ruling elites and, internationally, large corporations (pp. 497–8).

The work of Anne Campbell on female juvenile delinquency goes some way towards undermining the statistical basis for the view that far more males commit crimes than females. Official statistics put the ratio of male to female crime at about 7 to 1 – the precise ratio varying with age groups. In a self-report study of 105 adolescent girls, Campbell found that in an overall average of offences, the male to female self-admission rate was 1.12 to 1. She attributes this to paternalism on the part of the police who favour what they consider to be 'the gentle sex' in matters of law enforcement. As a result, they issue far more informal and unrecorded cautions to females than males. Campbell's research cannot be considered conclusive, although other evidence also exists to suggest that female crime is under-represented in official statistics. Certainly, the view that men are 'naturally more aggressive' than women and, consequently, more prone to crime needs to be treated with caution. As more women have moved into the labour force and have received 'tougher' socialisation, the ratio of female to male crime has tended to narrow – even as measured by official statistics.

The views put forward by Cicourel and other ethnomedologists and interactionists have not gone without criticism. Barry Hindess has made a sharp analysis of their critique of official statistics. He comments in turn on two possible versions of their position, both of which he finds supported in their writings. The first position is that because we can never 'ultimately' know precisely why and how individual policemen, magistrates and others select the causes that 'make up' official statistics, these statistics are virtually useless. This is because although the individual cases may appear in the same statistical category, they may not in fact refer to the same phenomenon. Hindess refutes this conclusion whilst agreeing with the observation that provokes it. He argues that this kind of 'ultimate' uncertainty is a feature of all aspects of life and not just a problem for sociologists. They, like the practitioners of other disciplines, must simply make sure that, as far as possible, their data, including statistical data, is representative and internally consistent (that is, that each unit that is supposed to refer to a given phenomenon actually does so). Admittedly, this is more easily said than done, but it *must* be done if sociology is to be practised at all. The second or 'weak' version of the interactionist position as construed by Hindess is that because the 'everyday understandings' of police, magistrates and others help to 'create' official statistics, these must be taken into consideration when evaluating and interpreting a given set of statistics. Hindess agrees with this but considers it to be a statement of the obvious. In effect, it is the position he himself takes in refuting the first, and in his view more typical, version of the interactionist position. In putting forward the view that the 'everyday misunderstandings' of those who create statistics must be considered in this way, Hindess also refutes the simplistic positivistic position: that official statistics can be used unquestioningly to 'prove' a given case.

The same issues about the use of official statistics are at stake in two well known interactionist critiques of the statistical basis of Durkheim's analysis of suicide. Both Maxwell Atkinson and Jack Douglas criticise Durkheim for assuming that all coroners used the same criteria in deciding what was or was not suicide. They are easily able to give evidence to the contrary. Douglas points out the example of one coroner who would decide that suicide had occurred only if the evidence of a suicide note could be produced. Other coroners accepted less conclusive evidence. Ultimately, this meant that different coroners were contributing a different range of 'facts' to the 'same' statistical category, with the result that 'statistical reality' could be imprecise and misleading. Let us take a more serious example of this point: the validity of the statistical basis supporting Durkheim's claims about the distribution of egoistic suicide. Durkheim explains the relatively 'low' rate of suicide in Catholic societies as compared to Protestant ones, in terms of the greater integration of the former. But another explanation can be given for the differences in the recorded rates of suicide between the two types of society. The Catholic religion condemns suicide as a mortal sin, something which merits eternal damnation. In many cases this cultural attitude towards suicide might very well influence coroners to return a verdict other than suicide. Pressure of this kind would not generally be put on coroners in Protestant societies where moral condemnation of suicide tended to be less. In view of this, uncritical acceptance of official suicide statistics for the purposes of comparative social analysis would be poor methodology.

Making Sense of Deviancy Theory

The various theoretical approaches to social order and deviance are often presented as mutually exclusive. Certainly, it would be ludicrous to imagine that 'sticking them all together' would somehow result in a complete theory satisfactory to all parties. Nevertheless, in some ways the major theories can be seen as complementary rather than contradictory. Further, in some instances, differences in terminology obscure a larger measure of agreement than might at first be apparent.

Even on the subject of social order, control and integration, it is possible to uncover elements of agreement between the two major structural theories about how society functions. Functionalists argue that conformity and consensus are necessary for the orderly functioning of society, but Marxists, too, need to explain why, in many capitalist societies, the majority accept the system, and appear to have no taste for revolution. Marxists believe that the many working class people who accept and even support the capitalist system have been deluded by 'bourgeois ideology' into a state of 'false consciousness'. Both theories are describing the same phenomenon: what differs is the terminology and the underlying political values: functionalists tend to support and want to conserve bourgeois, liberal society, whereas Marxists do not. Not surprisingly, these preferences often seep into their theoretical analyses.

There is also a considerable measure of unstated agreement between Marxism and functionalism about social deviance. Merton thought of criminal behaviour as a result of exclusion from the legitimate opportunity structure of society, and strain theorists examined what this meant in terms of economic and status deprivation. There is a clear implication in all this that 'society' bears at least some responsibility for crime simply because the gateways to legitimate achievement are wide open for some and almost closed for others. Marxists observe the same unequal access to material and status reward hierarchies but condemn it more comprehensively. To them, theft is just the distorted mirror image of capitalism's already ugly face. The convergence between the two perspectives is even apparent sometimes at the level of moral evaluation. The Marxist 'what can you expect?' response to the high crime rate in Western Europe and the USA expresses a sentiment comparable with that of the liberal, Daniel Bell, when he refers to crime as 'part of the American way of life'.

The major achievement of interactionism has been to rediscover for sociology the notion that the central social reality is individual meaning and experience. In view of the tendencies towards determinism within both structural theories, this is a crucial contribution. As an account of how people behave in everyday life in relation to the legal and normative order, interactionism seems closer to what actually happens than the functionalist conformity-deviance model. Life is more complex than the functionalists allow. Marxists argue, however, that interactionism is inadequate in its analysis of how the power of institutions and the class interests behind them affect and even control individual lives (see Chapter 16). The laws, rules or norms of institutions are powerful means of regulating behaviour, and this is notably true of the institutions that constitute the 'bourgeois' state. Moreover, institutional frameworks often survive the coming and going of individuals. In their different ways, Marxists and functionalists appreciate better than interactionists that it is the institutional structure of society that both limits and provides opportunities for individual and group action.

Perhaps interactionism would be more effective if, as well as concerning itself with individual meaning, its protagonists also attempted to develop it more vigorously as a 'linking theory' between the concept of the 'creative' individual, and the 'formative' institutional structure of society. We have already noted some efforts in this direction, though these have been more a matter of Marxists using interactionist perspective than the other way around. Despite the limits of the interactionist approach, many would feel that amidst such abstract concepts as order, social control and deviance, individual meaning and reality should be retained. If that makes sociological generalisations more difficult, then so be it.

Deviancy Perspectives, Methods, Policy and the Future

Having examined some similarities between the various perspectives on deviance, here we briefly explore the practical consequences for policy formation of the different approaches. The functionalist stress on the need to control deviance leads to superficially uncomplicated solutions: control requires punishment or treatment or, at least, a warning.

Both Marxists and interactionists have been 'accused' of sympathising with deviants, rather than the social order against which they offend. Young sociologists, alienated from society to various degrees, may, indeed, find it easy to identify with 'outsiders', such as juvenile delinquents, who are more obviously at odds with 'the system' than themselves. Certainly, the choice of observational or participant observational methodology brings close involvement with groups studied. Jock Young, Paul Willis, Paul Corrigan and, before them, William Foote Whyte, chose this method. Becker himself shows how close to the point of identification deviancy researchers sometimes get:

> To develop and test my hypothesis about the genesis of marijuana use for pleasure, I conducted fifty interviews with marijuana users. I had been a professional dance musician for some years when I conducted this study and my first interviews were with people I had met in the music business. I asked them to put me in contact with other users . . .

It would be a mistake, however, to lump together interactionist and Marxist sympathy for the 'underdog' without reference to their broader positions. The American Marxist, Gouldner, has attacked interactionists sharply on the grounds that they approach deviancy in a spirit of sentimental romanticism. Practically, they accept that there must be limits to deviance, but emotionally they are attracted by it. They incline to favour more tolerance to deviants or even to 'turn a blind eye'; hardly a comprehensive programme. It is certainly true that Marxists have recently made more strenuous efforts than interactionists to envisage a wholly different approach to deviance from that generally adopted in Britain and America. Ultimately, they hope for a society in which freedom and justice will combine to make the category of deviant obsolete. As Ian Taylor, Paul Walton and Jock Young state:

> The task is to create a society in which the facts of human diversity, whether personal, organic or social, are not subject to the power to criminalise.

Perhaps, after all, this is simply a more organised way of saying what many interactionists feel but do not believe is possible. Will there not always be rules and, if so, will there not always be some who break them?

Speculation aside, both Marxists and interactionists stress the need for a fairer system of law and order. The concept of *community justice* in which the law is interpreted and administered by local people has had some currency but, as Stanley Cohen has pointed out, there is no guarantee that such justice would be any more humane than at present, and some chance that it might be less so. The policy of expanding free legal aid and advice is widely acceptable to radicals. For the Marxist committed, such policies would also provide a basis to educate clients about the nature of justice in capitalist society and could be linked, tactically, to the more distant goal of bringing about the fundamental change necessary to achieve a just society.

Guide to Further Reading and Study

In addition to the more general works mentioned at the end of the last chapter, the following are useful in specific areas. E. Durkheim's *Suicide* (Routledge and Kegan Paul, 1970) is, of course an original classic whilst Erwin Stengel's *Suicide and Attempted*

Suicide (Penguin, 1977) is a useful general work. When first published in the early nineteen seventies, Stanley Cohen's *Folk Devils and Moral Panics: The Creation of Mods and Rockers* (Martin Robertson, 1980) was partly responsible for popularising interactionist concepts among some British sociologists. The 1980 edition contains a preface overviewing theoretical developments in the area of deviance. Of similar ilk and period is Jock Young's *The Drugtakers* (Paladin, 1971); chapter 6 gives an excellent account of the values and life-style of a deviant, hedonistic subculture. More recently Stanley Cohen's interests have turned to social control, see his *Visions of Social Control* (Polity Press, 1985) and he has edited a collection of readings with Andrew Schull, *Social Control and the State* (Basil Blackwell, 1983). Edwin M. Schur's *Labeling Women Deviants: Gender, Stigma and Social Control* (Random House, 1984) is up to date and comprehensive on the gender aspect. Recently Marxist and critical theory in this field has moved away somewhat from deviancy theory to social policy issues; see, for instance, Ian Taylor, *Law and Order: Arguments for Socialism* (The Macmillan Press, 1981), and Tony Platt and Paul Takagi, *eds*, *Crime and Social Justice* (The Macmillan Press, 1981). Paul Rock and Mary McIntosh, *eds*, *Deviance and Social Control* (Tavistock, 1974) is collection of interactionist and Marxist articles.

Past Questions

1 'Durkheim was not interested in individual cases of suicide. . . . Rather he wanted to show that the cause of rates of suicide was wholly social.' How far was he successful? (AEB, 1978)

2 Many cities have 'problem areas' near the centre. Why is this? (AEB, 1979)

3 Discuss the uses and limitations for sociologists of official statistics on crime and delinquency, and give an account of how sociologists have responded to these limitations. (AEB, 1983)

4 The law is only one form of social control in society. Assess the importance of other forms of social control, using examples from different types of society. (London, 1984)

5 'Both as an organisation and as individuals, the police have considerable choice about . . . which crimes and criminals to prosecute, how to allocate what number of men to different law enforcement tasks and so on.' Discuss (J. Lambert: *The Police Can Choose.*) (AEB, 1985)

19 Power, Politics and People

520

Power and Authority

According to Max Weber, power is 'the probability that one actor within a social relationship will be in a position to carry out his own will despite resistance, regardless of the basis on which this probability rests'. In more ordinary language, power is the ability to get one's way – even if it is based on bluff.

Although we think of *power* as being associated particularly with politics it is, in fact, an aspect of all, or nearly all, social relationships. As Weber writes, positions of power can 'emerge from social relations in a drawing room as well as in the market, from the rostrum of a lecture hall as well as the command post of a regiment, from an erotic or charitable relationship as well as from scholarly discussion or athletics'. We can add that power plays a part in family and school relationships also. If Weber's sociology has a single central concept, it is that of power. It is as important in his perspective as is conflict in that of Marx, and order in that of the functionalists. He considered that economic and social goals as well as political ones are achieved through power-conflict. People compete for limited resources and status: for every one who achieves fortune and fame, there are thousands who do not. Nevertheless, it was characteristic of Weber that he stressed the importance of the political sphere. Political decisions, such as changes in taxation

521

or social welfare, could be taken, and these could have great effect on the economic and social life of a country.

Weber distinguished *authority* from power. Authority may be thought of as *legitimate power* (power that is accepted as being rightfully exercised). He divided authority into three broad types: *traditional, charismatic* and *rational-legal*. We have already examined authority in the context of organisations. Here, our interest in it is as a form of political power: accordingly, we choose our examples from the political sphere. The sense of the inevitability of traditional political authority is well illustrated by an established dynasty, such as the centuries-old Habsburgs of Austria. By contrast, charismatic authority is generated by personality and the myths that surround it. Hitler, Martin Luther King and the Cuban revolutionary leader, Che Guevara, are all examples of charismatic leaders. The fact that they are all recent figures shows that charismatic authority is still a feature of modern politics. In advanced industrial countries, however, rational-legal authority tends to be the predominant type and has, in particular, replaced traditional authority. This type of political authority tends to be the predominant type and has, in particular, replaced traditional authority. Rational-legal political authority is established in law. The American system of government provides the best example of it because, unlike Britain, it has a written constitution (articles of government). This establishes the relationship between the legislature (which passes laws), the judiciary (which can determine if these laws are constitutionally allowable), and the executive (which, under the law, runs day-to-day government). Britain is often considered to have an 'unwritten' constitution but this has never been codified in a single, rational-legal document.

Politics: Power, Policy, the State

Politics is about power and purposes. It is the struggle to achieve the means to do certain things or, more precisely, to implement policies. Sometimes, what politicians want to do becomes obscured in the struggle to get the power to do it, but we must recognise, at least analytically, both these aspects of political activity.

Firstly, we deal with the means of power. The major means of political power is government and we can conveniently discuss the chief types of government here: *democracy, oligarchy* and *dictatorship*. We will consider each in turn.

Democratic systems can be divided into three broad types: *representative* or indirect democracy; *participatory* or direct democracy, and *delegatory* democracy. In representative democracy, the people do not rule directly but elect representatives to rule for them. Representative democracy is associated with parliamentary institutions to such an extent that it is often referred to simply as parliamentary democracy: Britain and America are major examples. In addition, representative democracies tend to be characterised by what are termed *civil liberties*. These include freedom to organise politically, freedom of speech and of the press, and the equal status of citizens under the law. In practice, these freedoms except – arguably – the last are not absolute. They are established in, and limited by law. Thus, freedom of the press in Britain is limited by the laws of libel and contempt (which cover what can legally be written about other people), and the Official Secrets Act. In the USA the comparable legislation is less strict and, to that extent, it has a freer press than Britain. The principle that freedom, like anything else, has to be balanced against other principles, applies in both countries.

The crux of our concern with democracy is the debate between liberals and Marxists about the nature and extent of democracy in advanced capitalist countries. Liberals consider that, for instance, Britain, West Germany, Italy, Australia and the United States are *genuinely* democratic. Marxists disagree: they argue that, at best, these countries are 'bourgeois democracies' which deny 'real' freedom to the majority of their population. For Marxists, a greater degree of freedom depends primarily on greater equality. For instance, freedom under the law may not seem very meaningful to someone who cannot afford a lawyer. This liberal-Marxist debate is the main recurrent theme of this chapter.

Participatory or direct democracy strictly means that people represent themselves and take their own decisions. The term 'participatory', however, is often used to mean some degree of personal involvement in decision making, short of direct democratic control. It has been in small communities, such as ancient Athens and medieval Geneva, that something approaching direct democratic self-government has proved most feasible. Nevertheless, in modern Tanzania and China, both large countries, popular involvement in day-to-day affairs has been found possible at the local or village level. In neither country has this replaced central government and bureaucracy (such as the civil service), often of a rather authoritarian kind, at the national level. The Russian revolutionary, Lenin, hoped and believed that a socialist revolution would replace the capitalist state with a proletarian state largely run by, or at least answerable to, direct democratic institutions called *soviets* or *communes*. At first, there were some signs that this might happen during and after the revolution of 1917. The fact that it did not, and that an authoritarian government developed instead, poses problems for modern socialists, who continue to seek more direct forms of democracy than are common in parliamentary democracies.

Delegatory democracy is a form of 'half-way house' between direct and indirect democracy. *Delegates are mandated (told) by those who elect them to carry out specific orders and are, therefore, much more 'tied' to the wishes of their constituents than are undelegated representatives.* In the late nineteen seventies and early eighties there was a fierce debate in the Labour Party which focused on the extent to which MPs should be representatives or delegates.

Oligarchy is government by the few: the term is usually used to describe government by an unrepresentative few. Frequently, the basis of oligarchical power is military. Thus Greece, the ancient home of democracy, was recently ruled by a junta (group) of colonels for several years. Although it is theoretically possible to talk of representative oligarchy, different terms are usually preferred. Liberal political theorists use the terms 'representative elite' or 'democratic elite'. Marxists deny that what liberals call democratic elites are, in fact, genuinely democratic; instead, they use the term 'ruling class'.

Dictatorship is government by a single individual responsible only to himself. Hitler and Stalin were dictators, each man professing different political ideologies, Fascism and Communism, respectively. Yet it is for the similar *way* in which they both concentrated total power in their own hands, and the great inhumanity with which they exercised it, that they are remembered. rather than for their ideological differences. The term 'totalitarianism' is often associated with dictatorship, but has a rather wider usage. Totalitarian regimes are those in which power is wholly concentrated in the hands of a few people or of a single person.

The State

At this point, the important concept of the state must be more fully introduced. Governments, whether democratic, oligarchical or dictatorial, generally exercise power through the state. The state includes the government itself – of whatever kind – both in its capacity as the maker of law and of policy. It also includes the civil service – a vast bureaucracy of many thousands of people. The judiciary and magistracy are also part of it. Local government is, by definition, not part of the central state apparatus but is often greatly influenced and, in some respects, even controlled, by central government. Local government can, therefore, sometimes be a powerful arm of central government: (The Labour governments of the nineteen sixties and seventies persuaded most local authorities to accept and implement some form of comprehensive education.) In addition, local governments have their own bureaucracies. As we have seen already, when referring to the work of Althusser, Marxists have a much more extensive conception of the state than the minimal description given here. Their view will be fully discussed shortly.

Politics is not only about power struggle. It is also about *policies, or the purpose to which power, once attained, can be put.* We will say something of the general beliefs and goals (or ideologies) of the major parties in Britain and the United States shortly. Here, it is enough to indicate the wide range of issues that can become questions of political conflict. In Third World countries, these could include starvation, land reform, population control and literacy; in Western countries, women's rights, immigration, taxation and public spending policy have been recent issues. It is worth noting that the political struggle does not always take place *within* the existing political system. For instance, totalitarian regimes do not allow organised opposition to exist: those who oppose the government are virtually forced to establish illegal political groups to have their opinions heard, and to achieve their goals. Such groups existed in both Hitler's Germany and Stalin's Russia, as they do in present day South Africa and Czechoslovakia.

People

The struggle for power and the implementation of policies come to little if they do not benefit people. Politics and history no longer merely concern the exploits of famous men if, indeed, they ever really did. Modern politicians have to occupy themselves with the public good and to respond to the promptings of the public itself. How 'the people' are organised and how they organise themselves in the form of parties and national and local pressure groups is discussed below, as is the extent and limits of popular political participation.

Voting Behaviour and Political Socialisation

The Labour and Conservative (Tory) Parties have dominated British politics for most of the period from 1918 until the present day. In 1918, the Representation of the People Act was passed, which extended the vote to all men over twenty-one and all women over thirty. The act enfranchised millions of working class people and helped to make it possible for the Labour Party to take over from the Liberals as one of the two major parties. A majority of the working class increasingly saw the Labour Party as their 'natural' representative political organisation. The key questions in this section are, therefore, 'Who supports the two major parties, and why?' The answer to the first question is a matter of empirical fact, but the answer to the second requires theoretical explanation. We now examine the two questions.

Class and Voting

OBJECTIVE AND SUBJECTIVE CLASS The major variable associated with voting behaviour is *class*. Most working class voters vote Labour and most middle class ones Conservative: in fact, a consistently higher proportion of the middle class votes Conservative than those in the working class who vote Labour. Only about one fifth of the middle class vote Labour, whereas about one third of the working class now vote Conservative. Because the working class is larger than the middle class, the working class Conservative vote is about half of the party's total vote. Obviously, all the proportions given in this paragraph tend to vary up or down depending on who wins a given election. For instance, working class support for the Conservatives increased in 1979 when they won the election, and decreased in 1964 when they lost.

The above broad correlations between class and voting patterns are based on generally accepted definitions of class, such as that offered by the Registrar General. Widely used definitions of this kind are referred to as *objective*. Objective class may or may not coincide with *subjective* class, the class that a person *thinks* he belongs to. The distinction between objective and subjective class is of great interest to us here because the relationship between *subjective* class and voting behaviour is even stronger than that between *objective* class and voting behaviour. Evidence from a number of sources, including Butler and Stokes, has shown that about 80% of those who are both objectively *and* subjectively working class vote Labour, whereas the objective working class vote *as a whole* never rose above 67% between 1952 and 1962. The strength of subjective class image and voting patterns is further illustrated by the behaviour of the minority of unskilled workers who, for some reason, think of themselves as middle class. According to Butler and Stoke's data, 55% of this group voted Conservative in 1959. The tendency for those at the top of the occupational hierarchy who see themselves as working class to vote Labour is not quite as marked, but is still statistically very significant.

It should not surprise us that people behave consistently with their own view of things (subjective class self-image) more than in accordance with how some external indicator might lead us to expect they would behave (objective class). Weber was right to insist that the sociologist must seek to understand the subjective motives for action. Translated into the terms of this discussion, the insight that what people *believe* to be real becomes real in its consequences, means that if people believe they belong to a given class, they tend to vote for the party normally considered to represent that class. Nevertheless, we still seek an answer as to why people's subjective class, especially that of the working class, should so frequently vary from what might objectively be expected. Firstly, however, we briefly explain 'normal' or conformist voting behaviour.

CONFORMIST VOTING BEHAVIOUR Conformist voting behaviour is

527

defined as voting for the political party that, by general agreement, most represents the given voter's class interests – that is, the Conservative party for the middle class and the Labour party for the working class. Put this way, conformity is what is to be expected: most people vote in terms of class and self-interest (which are perceived as generally coinciding). To vote in this manner is considered to be politically *rational* behaviour although the actual variety of voting behaviour makes the definition seem somewhat arbitrary. It is, however, highly significant that Labour voters tend to hold *images* (impressions or views) of both society and the political parties as *more divided along class lines* than do Conservative voters. This is clearly apparent from the diagram below which is worth detailed study.

Party images in Bristol North East, 1955 (percentages)

Images of the Labour Party	by Labour supporters	by Conservative supporters
For the working class	68	32
For the Welfare State	18	12
For the country as a whole	5	4
For full employment	4	2
For nationalisation, controls	4	32
Impractical, extravagant	1	18
	100	100

Images of the Conservative Party	by Labour supporters	by Conservative supporters
For all classes	6	30
For free enterprise, for business	7	26
For the rich, big business	85	8
For individual freedom	—	14
For denationalisation	1	5
For full employment	—	9
Capable, experienced leaders	1	8
	100	100

Source: Jean Blondel, *Voters, Parties and Leaders*, 1969, p. 82.

Thus, 68% of Labour voters of the Bristol North-East constituency thought of Labour as 'for the working class' and 85% of them thought of the Conservatives as 'for the rich, big business'.

Frank Parkin has written with great illumination on working class voting patterns, and his work helps to explain the strong element of class awareness in the *traditional* working class Labour vote. He suggests that, given the generally Conservative nature of British society, what is surprising is that a majority of the working class *do* consistently vote Labour. He contends that the traditionally dominant institutions of our society – the established church, the monarchy, the military, legal and civil service elites, the public schools and ancient universities, the institutions of private property and the media – embody values which are both middle class and closely in accord with conservatism. Conservatives have for a long time appealed to communal values, such as nationalism, monarchy, religion and imperialism to 'unify' the country. It would seem almost inevitable that this powerful and pervasive conservative influence would encompass all classes. How is it, then, that a majority of the working class resist its full import? Simply, various 'shields' or 'barriers' exist against it, which allow socialist values to be fostered. These protective barriers are formed by working class sub-cultures which generate different values from the dominant culture. The major source of these values is the work-place. There, the working man may experience both the collective strength of his peers, and conflict with his employer. Thus, the work-place is the cradle of socialist values. Parkin also sees the traditional working class community as an additional basis of working class and socialist solidarity. Where occupational communities such as mining towns and dock areas exist, solidarity is likely to be especially strong. These areas, however, are on the decline (see Chapter 6, pp. 139–41).

Goldthorpe and Lockwood have reached similar conclusions to those of Parkin. They divide the working class into two groups: *traditionalists* and *instrumental collectivists*. The former is divided into *proletarian* traditionalists and *deferential* traditionalists. The proletarian traditionalists are more radical and class conscious, and correspond to the socialist-inclined group described by Parkin. The more conservative, deferential working class need not concern us here. The instrumental collectivists are, however, of immediate interest. These are workers who are committed to a collective approach to unions and the Labour party, not out of loyalty or solidarity but because of what they can get out of them. In a quota survey that is now almost twenty years old, Goldthorpe and Lockwood found that affluent workers tended to support Labour, to an even greater extent than the working class as a whole, for precisely these instrumental reasons. This analysis does, however, allow for the possibility that instrumentally motivated workers will switch their vote if it seems in their interest to do so. More recent evidence suggests that this is exactly what some of them do.

With reference again to the figure, we now discuss the 'normal' middle class Conservative vote. The fact that Conservative voters entertain a wider variety of predominant images of their own party and of the Labour party must be carefully interpreted. It needs to be reconciled with the fact that the middle class votes Conservative *more solidly* than the working class votes Labour. The explanation is that Conservatives tend to believe that they vote Conservative not for class reasons, but because they consider that the Conservative party is 'better for the country' or is the party which 'governs in the national interest'. These motives are only implicitly apparent in the figure, but further evidence for them can be derived from a recent study of the social and political attitudes of farmers, a traditionally-minded group, in Newby *et al., Property, Paternalism and Power* (1978). The farmers interviewed claimed to dislike class conflict, but voted and generally behaved in other ways very much in terms of their own class interest. They regarded their support for the *status quo* (society as it is) as in everybody's interest, not merely, or even particularly, in their own. No doubt they were sincere in this, but given that their income is typically five or six times greater than that of farm labourers, it is legitimate to ask whether or not they are 'right'.

DEVIANT VOTING BEHAVIOUR

a MIDDLE CLASS DEVIANT VOTERS There are fewer middle class than working class deviant voters, both absolutely and as a proportion of their class. Raynor suggests that the relatively few middle class Labour voters can be divided into two extreme groups, and we will add a third that recent research at Oxford has uncovered. The first group is those with considerable experience of higher education: these can be referred to as the 'intellectual left'. They include, particularly, some academics, journalists and 'media people' and members of vocational or 'helping' professions, such as social work or teaching. Slightly controversially perhaps, it can be argued that the wide education and knowledge of these people enables them to see beyond their own interest and to sympathise with the disadvantaged. They vote Labour because they see it as the party which better represents the disadvantaged.

Raynor's second group is those with low status within the middle class. Unlike the first group, they do not vote Labour for idealistic reasons, but more out of pique and insecurity. Typically, they rank higher in education and qualifications than in social status: they find outlets for the resulting resentment in the phlegm of radical politics. (It is worth noting that the analysis of radicalism in terms of status deprivation has been influential in recent American sociology and history, where it has been criticised as both conservative and speculative.) Certainly, this approach employs a highly cynical interpretation of motive. In refuting it, Frank Parkin argues that low status jobs are a *result* of radical ideals and not vice-versa. He suggests that the political attitudes of middle class radicals are formed before they start work, and that they choose work which is most compatible with their radical values. This tends to be vocational and of relatively low pay and status.

The third group for consideration are numbers of first generation white collar employees, or 'the sons of affluent workers' as John Goldthorpe calls them. It seems that some of these continue to support the Labour Party even after their rise in socio-economic status. No doubt this partly reflects loyalty to their 'roots' but it also suggests that, as the traditional working class shrinks, the Labour Party may have succeeded in presenting policies that potentially widen its basis of support.

b WORKING CLASS DEVIANT VOTERS The number of non-Labour working class voters is so large that it is almost misleading to categorise them as 'deviant'. It is certain that there must be profound reasons to account for so substantial a phenomenon. The most convincing explanation of the large working class Tory vote, and one which is echoed in most writings on the subject, is that the dominant institutions of our society embody conservative and middle class values. As a result, the working class as well as the middle class becomes socialised into conservative values *unless* more radical socialisation cuts across this central flow of influence (see Parkin, above). In functionalist terms, this simply means that a 'consensus around the central value system' is created by institutions such as the monarchy and the church, which exist partly for that purpose. Marxists agree, but consider that this process misleads or 'mystifies' the working class into conforming, sometimes enthusiastically, to a social system that exploits them.

Detailed study of the working class Conservative vote supports the above analysis. As we have seen, Goldthorpe and Lockwood have given the term deferential traditionalists to one group of working class Tories. Referring to the same group, McKenzie and Silver use the term 'deference voters'. These are people who prefer ascribed 'socially superior' leaders to those who have risen by their own efforts. McKenzie and Silver found these attitudes among some of the urban proletariat, although they are more usually associated with farm labourers. Often it seems that isolated, individual workers, such as caretakers of prestige, private establishments or personal and domestic employees of the wealthy, adopt deferential attitudes.

McKenzie and Silver suggest that what they term secular voters may be superseding deferential voters as the major working class basis of Conservative support. Compared to deference voters, secular voters are young and well-paid. In general secular voters seems to describe the group referred to by Goldthorpe and Lockwood as instrumentalists. The latter, of course, deny that this group is tending to become more Conservative and, in doing so, refute the embourgeoisement hypothesis. Nevertheless, the strong swing (11.5) of affluent workers from Labour to the Conservatives in the 1979 election suggests that the embourgeoisement hypothesis may have more long-term mileage in it than Goldthorpe and Lockwood suspected. In any case, they themselves point out that instrumentalists are more likely than traditionalists to change their voting habits to suit their perceived interests – a point also made by McKenzie and Silver. The latter also point out that instrumentalists tend to be less attracted to Labour by socialist values than of the benefits of practical policies. If such benefits are not apparent they may change their vote (see also pp. 558–9).

Variables other than Class Associated with Voting Behaviour

Besides class, other variables which correlate with patterns of voting behaviour are age, region, gender, religion and race. All of these are, in some measure, class-related. Thus, young people and women vote more according to their class background than any other factor: a young working class person will *tend* to vote Labour and a middle class woman will *tend* to vote Conservative. Nevertheless, these and other factors mentioned above seem to exercise a certain effect on voting behaviour relatively independently of class. We will briefly discuss these factors now, taking age first.

There is a tendency for the old to vote Conservative and for the young to vote Labour. Whilst most middle class young voters vote Conservative and most working class old voters vote Labour, in neither case is the normal class pattern of voting reflected *quite* as strongly as in the rest of the population. Why is this? The view that it is because the old are 'naturally' more Conservative and the young 'naturally' more 'left' or radical has been convincingly queried by both Goldthorpe and Lockwood and Butler and Stokes. The alternative explanation is made in terms of 'political generations'. Anthony King summarises this research succinctly:

> On this view, the preponderance of Conservatives among the over 65s is the result ̄not primarily of their being old as such but of their having matured politically at a time when the Conservatives were the dominant party, and when Labour was only beginning to emerge as a political force (that is, in the first 20 years of this century – *author's brackets).*

Equally, young people since the Second World War have seen Labour either in government or as the major opposition party. What is true, however, is that the old change their vote, whatever it is, much less easily than young people. This difference in political constancy is well illustrated in the following diagram:

Voting Constancy and Age

	Pre 1918	Inter-War	Post War	Post 1951
Time when first able to Vote				
% Supporting the same Party in 1959 and 1964	86	81	79	58

Source: Anthony King, 'A Sociological Portrait of Politics,' in *New Society*, 13 January, 1972, p. 58.

Change is particularly likely to occur when a young person's parents vote contrary to their class and he reverts to class-party allegiance, but the best general explanation may be that young people simply take time to make up their minds and to develop settled patterns of political allegiance.

Support for political parties varies widely from region to region even *within* social classes. Thus, a manual worker in the south west is twice as likely to vote Conservative as one in Wales. The 1979 election was particularly notable for the strength of regional voting trends. For instance, the depressed north remained generally Labour whereas the affluent south eastern commuter zones swung strongly towards the Conservatives. The general principle seems to be that in regions in which one class and party is predominant, members of the other class tend to be more easily drawn away from 'normal' class-party allegiance towards the majority. The same is often true of towns and neighbourhoods of this kind.

Women are more conservative than men. If men alone had the vote, Labour would have been in power virtually all the post-war years. Research in this area is limited, but one line of speculation is that women are less likely immediately to experience the radicalising effects of industrial conflict than men and are, consequently, less likely to develop the related political affiliation to the Labour Party. Second, in an ageing population, there are more old women than men (over 1½ million more over 65 in 1977) and the old, as we have seen, are disproportionately conservative.

'Even religious history still matters in politics', Anthony King tells us. He goes on to say that 'the Church of England is still, to a most remarkable degree, the Tory party at prayer'. Surveys consistently show that Anglicans are much more likely to vote Conservative than members of other major churches. Butler and Stokes found in 1963 that, among Anglicans who went to church at least once a week, 72% were Tories. Interestingly, church attendance is, in general, associated with conservatism but this association is particularly strong among Anglicans. Catholics provide an exception to this trend in both Britain and America where, historically, they have favoured the more radical of the two major parties, the Labour Party and the Democratic Party, respectively. In Britain, the link between religion and politics is now on the wane, and is difficult to distinguish at all in younger voters. Northern Ireland, of course, is a complicated exception to this trend. Further afield, the 'Muslim revolution' in Iran suggests that, in the more traditional Third World, religion can be as powerful a source of political motivation as any other. Race is now an issue of considerable importance in British as well as in American politics (see Chapter 13). In both countries coloured ethnic groups have tended to vote left of centre.

All the above factors tend to correlate with class and, in some cases, with one another: even gender and religion correlate. Women are more religious than men, and both factors correlate with voting Conservative. Where two or more predisposing factors occur together, as in this case, the tendency they are associated with is more likely to occur. But it is crucial to note that it *may not* occur. There exist Conservative miners in working class areas and Labour company directors who regularly attend Anglican services. As political behaviour cannot be wholly predicted, this presumably indicates that it has an element of individual choice about it. It might be thought that this would be most apparent in the case of 'floating' or uncommitted voters. The evidence is, however, that this group is amongst the least educated and worst informed part of the electorate. They often appear to vote almost at random rather than after profound consideration. Nevertheless, the point stands. The possibility of political choice is real, and its likelihood is increased the better educated and informed the electorate is. Bryan Heading interprets the recent erosion of the reliable basic support for both major parties as an indication that more of the electorate are choosing to vote for whichever party seems to offer them most at a given time rather than simply to follow traditional allegiance. Perhaps prematurely he associates this apparant decline in the class basis of party support with increased affluence and applies it particularly to better-off Labour voters.

Parties, Pressure Groups and Government: The Liberal Model of the Democratic Society

Those who contend that liberal democracy 'works' argue that parties and pressure groups effectively represent people and

535

influence government. Further, they believe that political government, reflecting the will of the people, is the supreme state power. The civil service is seen as the 'servant' of government: the judiciary is regarded as independent of government, but is not expected to concern itself with political matters. The liberal model of democracy is examined below. In addition to the term 'liberal democracy', that of 'liberal pluralist' or, simply, 'pluralist' is often used. Pluralist refers to the many groups – notably parties and pressure groups – that liberals believe participate meaningfully in democratic politics.

Parties, Political Elites and the State

Political parties existed in Britain well before universal manhood suffrage (that is, the right of all males to vote). Parties, therefore, predate democracy. Nevertheless, the party system has adapted well to the demands of liberal democracy. The major parties attempt to appeal consistently to certain broad groups of people. The Labour Party seeks support mainly from the working class and certain sections of the middle class, such as members of the new professions. The Conservative Party is traditionally the party of the middle and upper classes. There is, however, as we have seen, much overlap in the class basis of party support and, in particular, among the upper working and lower middle classes. Even so, a major party seems to require a solid basis of class support to survive. The Liberal Party rapidly declined as a major party when it ceased to appeal to an identifiable section of society. The suitability of the two party system to liberal democracy is further suggested by the American example. Two competing parties quickly established themselves after the Americans had won their independence from Britain. In time, these developed into the present day Democratic and Republican parties. Like the chief British parties, these also tend to represent major sectional interests, although not to the same extent.

Political parties have ideologies or certain principles and beliefs which usually reflect quite closely the values and material interests of those groups and classes from which they draw most of their support. The British Conservative Party is strongly committed to capitalism, whereas the Labour Party believes in socialism – although the majority in neither party would wish to fundamentally change the 'mixed' nature of the economy. It is still probably true that the Conservative Party is the party of tradition, whereas the Labour Party identifies with progressive change and reform. For liberal-democratic theorists these are very significantly different ideological positions, but Marxists argue that, rhetoric aside, *the two major parties actually behave rather similarly when in government.* By contrast, liberal-democratic theorists consider that philosophical differences can lead to *practical policy differences.* Thus, various measures of the Labour government of 1945–50 would be considered distinctly socialist, and in sharp contrast to the clearly pro-free-enterprise policies of the Thatcher government elected in 1979. In fairness, this example is selected to suit the argument and most Labour and Conservative governments have been more similar to one another than these. In any case, it is a tacit assumption of liberalism that no major party will seek to overthrow the basic social and political 'consensus'.

Liberal democracy is, in part, a theory about the *the relationship between the majority of the poeple and their leaders, the political elite.* This relationship has balancing elements: the elite is *representative,* and yet it also *leads.* We will deal with these two aspects separately.

Historically, elite theory has tended to be undemocratic. Of the two major early twentieth century elite theorists, Pareto and Mosca, it was the latter who argued that the political elite *could* be generally representative of the people or 'masses', to use the term preferred by elite theorists. The party system, free elections and pressure group activity were means to ensure representativeness.

An important related issue to the representative nature of elites is the extent to which, once elected, they remain under democratic control. Is democracy 'real' only once every five years when people cast their vote? Robert Dahl believes that elections play an important part in controlling government and he also cites a second major means by which leaders are made answerable to the people:

> The election process is one of two fundamental methods of social control which, operating together, make governmental leaders so responsive to non-leaders that the distinction between democracy and dictatorship still makes sense. The other method of social control is continuous political competition among individuals, parties or both. Elections and political competition ... vastly

increase the size, number and variety of minorities whose preferences must be taken into account by leaders in making policy choices.

Above all, elections, or the certainty that an election must come, means that a governing party must always conduct itself in a way that will ultimately appeal to the majority of the electorate. There is evidence that widespread retrospective voting does occur: many voters do remember major features in the overall performance of administration and this acts as a check upon it. As Dahl points out, however, many particular policies may be concerned with the interest only of a minority, such as farm subsidies for the agricultural interest, though this does not necessarily mean that they therefore alienate the rest of the electorate. Many policies which please a minority are non-contentious to the majority. When the election comes, nevertheless, the government knows that, to win, it must have the backing of a 'majority of minorities'. This, according to Dahl, keeps it in check.

Liberal elite theorists have stressed the necessity of *leadership* by the political elite almost as much as its representative nature. In large societies, only a minority can be involved in leadership. Further, competitive political selection should ensure that the elite leads on merit. The prime general function of leadership is to create social consensus and establish social order. Edward Shils believes that, in doing this, the elite protects its own interests, as well as those of the majority. Whilst agreeing that the process of consensus production does occur, Marxists deny that in capitalist society it works for the common good. On the contrary, it merely misleads the working class. Class conflict tends not to be stressed by democratic elite theorists. The alternative term to classes, 'masses' – which obscures classes and class conflict – sounds too contemptuous to modern ears to be used by liberal theorists. Instead, they stress the need for the political elite to weld these into a working consensus.

We can link Dahl's democratic theory with the functionalist view put forward by Talcott Parsons of how power operates in a democracy. Parsons argues that leaders *use* power for the general good or, more precisely, for collective goals. Leaders are 'honest brokers' in power. Defence of the country and maintenance of law and order are two examples of the necessary use of power for the general good. It is crucial to Parsons' theory that *how much* power political leaders use ultimately depends on the will of the people. In war-time, the representative of the people in Congress or Parliament may sanction the use of greater powers by the government. Emergencies aside, the use of power is controlled by the processes described by Dahl. Parsons, therefore, conceives of power rather as economists think of money: more or less can be created as the situation demands.

The Liberal View of the State

Liberal theorists tend to regard the relationship between government and the rest of the state as relatively unproblematic. The government rules and the civil service implements its policies. The Marxist idea that the capitalist class is the 'real' controller of the state is simply not taken seriously. Weber, however, raised an important question in relation to the civil service. He considered that, like all bureaucracies it created its own vested interests and tended to be slow-moving. Civil servants, for reasons of their own, *may* give partial advice to ministers or take too long in producing it. Weber regarded a powerful Parliament as the best protector against an oppressive civil service bureaucracy.

Pressure Groups

Pressure groups, as well as parties, are parts of the liberal-democratic model. If parties are the bulwarks of democracy, pressure groups are the supports and buttresses. They are an essential part of the pluralist vision in which power is seen as widely shared and exercised. Like parties, pressure groups pre-date democracy but like them they have become part of liberal democracy. Jean Blondel, who shares the pluralist perspective, sees parties and pressure groups as equally involved in the democratic process, although in different ways:

> Interest groups differ from political parties by their aim, which is not to take power but only to exert pressure. They differ from parties by their objects, which are usually limited in scope. They differ from parties by the nature of their membership, which is often limited to one section in society.

There have always been groups sharing a common interest which have collectively pressed their case to the powerful. The

Wolfenden Report states that in the period since the war the number of pressure groups has increased considerably. From the liberal point of view, pressure groups provide a *necessary* means of *limited* conflict on specific issues but this takes place within a *context of fundamental consensus.*

We can classify pressure groups into two broad types: *sectional* (or protective) and *promotional.* Sectional groups are those whose membership has some common factor, such as occupation. It is to defend the common interest of their membership that such groups exist. Trade Unions and professional associations provide the best known examples of sectional pressure groups. The biggest union is the Transport and General Worker's Union (TGWU), and a well known professional association is the British Medical Association (BMA). Sectional groups are usually economic but can also be produced by, for instance, religious and ethnic divisions. The National Association for the Advancement of Coloured People (NAACP) and the Congress of Racial Equality (CORE) are two traditional Black Rights pressure groups in the United States.

Promotional groups seek to promote a cause. One example is Amnesty International which seeks to aid and assist political prisoners throughout the world. Political prisoners are, roughly, prisoners of conscience as opposed to ordinary criminals. Amnesty International is an organisation for which there is likely to be a long-term need. By contrast, other promotional groups achieve their aim, and can then disband. For example, a variety of anti-Vietnam war groups sprang up in the nineteen-sixties but dissolved when the war came to an end.

We need to distinguish between pressure groups in terms of the time-span of their existence, as well as on the basis of their interests or the causes they champion. The anti-Vietnam war groups were examples of *ad hoc* groups, formed to contest a specific issue, whereas Amnesty International and, still more obviously, the Trades Union Congress (TUC) are *permanent* groups. (see diagram). Blondel also makes the important point that certain organisations which are not strictly speaking interest groups may occasionally use their *influence* in the political process. Thus, the Catholic church makes its official (though not necessarily representative), opinion felt on such matters as divorce and abortion legislation.

540

	Sectional Groups	**Promotional Groups**
Permanent	Trades Union Congress	Campaign for Nuclear Disarmament
Ad Hoc	Archway Road Campaign	Various Anti-War Groups

Pressure groups use a variety of means to influence public opinion, such as advertisements, demonstrations and meetings. Sometimes they focus more directly on Parliament or the executive government. Often this means lobbying a powerful or influential individual such as an MP. Our interest, however, is less in the detail of the methods of pressure group activity than in whether or not the results of this pressure are effective. Pluralists would say that they are, Marxists that they are not. At least, that is the essence of the argument, although both positions require some qualification. Christopher Hewitt has attempted to test which of these two cases is more correct by reference to empirical data. He examines the roles of a variety of interest groups in relation to twenty-four major post-war crisis issues which cover the area of foreign, economic, welfare and social policy. The issues he analyses include the debate and struggles over the Suez crisis, the nationalisation of steel, the National Health Service Act and the Commonwealth Immigration Act of 1962. He includes interest groups from all major sections of national life in his study, including trade unions (blue and white collar); business organisations; religious organisations; local government bodies; research organisations and various promotional groups. He concludes that policy making in Britain is not elitist in the sense that any single elite or interest is dominant, but that different interests succeed at different times. Statistically, the unions are particularly successful in that issues are most frequently resolved as they wish. The Marxist response to this argument is that issues dealt with in national politics are within the national consensus and that genuinely alternative (Marxist) principles and policies are not discussed. This view is examined in the next section.

There are other arguments put forward by liberal democrats in support of the pressure group system. Pressure groups provide an accessible, day-to-day means by which popular opinion and influence can be expressed. They act upon political parties but are not necessarily part of the party system. In practice, however, the two major industrial interest groups tend to be tied into the party system. The unions and the TUC, and business and the CBI tend overwhelmingly to support, respectively, the Labour Party and the Conservative Party. It is significant, although seldom stressed by pluralists, that in a society noted for its class system, the two major parties and the two major interest groups should divide along class lines. Nevertheless, the major groups which support and, in part, finance the political parties exact a 'price' for loyalty: in return, they expect their interests to be protected and advanced. If, in their opinion, this does not occur, then, on a given issue, they may oppose the party they normally favour. Thus, the proposals to change the legal position of the unions, put forward by the Labour government of 1966–1970, were opposed with great determination by the union movement.

A further criticism of interest group politics, in addition to that put forward by Marxists referred to above, is that it tends to leave out or, at least, to leave behind, those who are least able to organise themselves: these people are found in the overlapping categories of the poor, the old, and the chronically sick and disabled. Immigrant groups also have tended to be less organised than their needs require. This is partly because they are financially and materially disadvantaged, and therefore have difficulty in affording the cost of organisation, and partly because it takes time for a group to accumulate the knowledge and experience to deal with the complex structure of institutionalised power in this country. It is a feature of British and American politics that, in the nineteen sixties and seventies, the disadvantaged have become increasingly organised and vociferous. Instead of assuming that the welfare state will 'take care of them', the deprived have formed groups such as Claimants Unions (concerned with supplementary benefits) and Tenants Associations and squatters rights aimed at *obtaining* what they see as their rights. Even pensioners have been seen to converge on Parliament Square to lobby MPs. Often the deprived have been assisted in pursuing their interests by community social workers or radical professional people and, occasionally, students. Sometimes this link has taken an institutional form. Des Wilson and Frank Field, the charismatic former directors of Shelter (the pressure group concerned with housing) and The Child Poverty Action Group, respectively, exemplify this kind of alliance. Of course, the involvement and concern of radical intellectuals with the poor is by no means new, but it did receive fresh stimulus in the nineteen sixties, and this impetus remains apparent even in the early nineteen eighties. The increased number of pressure groups, particularly among the disadvantaged, may suggest that pluralism works; equally, however, the need for these pressure groups may indicate that the way liberal capitalism functions fails to satisfy the wants of large numbers of people.

It is not easy for people living in a Western democracy to evaluate the extent and quality of the political and civil 'freedom' that liberals claim exists in these countries. This freedom is manifestly not absolute. Freedom of speech and freedom of the press is limited by law. The party-pressure group political system seems to favour the loudest voices: certainly political rights have not led to a radical reduction in material inequality. But it would be very foolish to undervalue the freedom that does exist. Within broadly defined limits, people can speak their minds, even if some have far easier access to a public audience than others. People *are* able to organise for a cause even though some, by virtue of greater knowledge, wealth or influence, can do so more easily than others. Private lives are largely left private by the State – in their own homes, at least, people can 'be themselves'. These freedoms might not seem so substantial or so precious if we did not have before us the bloody alternative of totalitarianism practised in Germany and Russia in the nineteen thirties. Perhaps the major argument in favour of liberal democracy is that attempts to improve on it have usually resulted in something much worse and in the reduction of political, civil and personal freedom. In the post-Second World War period a cautionary, even defensive, note has characterised liberal statements about democracy. Ageing liberals remember pre-war Germany and Russia as far worse than any liberal regime and are now inclined to settle for and defend what they know and value rather than to experiment and try to improve. By contrast, socialists and Marxists argue that a fundamentally freer, more equal and more just society than exists in liberal democracies is possible. While legitimately disagreeing with liberals, they can learn from them that creating such a society is fraught with dangers and that, if the attempt fails, far more may be lost than gained. To regard liberal warnings of this kind as 'mere moralism' is to show a gross ignorance of the failures and cruelties of recent European history.

Representative Political Elite or Ruling Class?: The Liberal/Marxist Debate

The Marxist View of the 'Capitalist State'

Most Marxists would deny that the model of democracy described in the previous section represents 'real' democracy. For them, it is merely 'bourgeois democracy', a smokescreen behind which the capitalist class pursues its own interests. Parliament and political government are not considered to be the major source of power. *Capitalists make the important decisions: economic man rules political man.* Although many contemporary Marxists would modify this view, many also retain a firm commitment to it in its classic form.

We have discussed in sufficient detail already Marx's view of society as fundamentally divided by class conflict. Of more relevance here is the issue of *how* Marxists consider that the ruling class rules. Both Tom Bottomore and Anthony Giddens make the point that, if capitalists do rule, they do so indirectly. They cannot do so directly as they are in a minority, both in the legislature and the executive in most capitalist countries. In feudal society, there was a much more precise correspondence between economic and political power. The feudal lords were the ruling class in the sense that they occupied the major political as well as economic positions. The landed nobility fulfilled the most important positions in central and local government. That is not true of capitalists today, although they are well represented in politics. If capitalists rule at all, therefore, they do so indirectly. Because of this, Marxist attempts to 'prove' the existence of a ruling class have often tended to be either circumstantial (relying on suggestive rather than conclusive evidence), or rather abstract and theoretical. Ralph Miliband's book, *The State in Capitalist Society,* appears to fall into the first group, although Miliband himself would claim that he more than demonstrates his case. As the title of his book suggests, he is concerned with the control and operation of the state in capitalist society. He considers the state to be made up of the following institutions: the government, the administration (the civil service), the judiciary and parliamentary assemblies. State power lies in these institutions. In addition to what Miliband says, it is useful to bear in mind Althusser's concept of state apparatuses. The capacity of the state to control the armed forces and police as well as the major means of communication, notably the media, is crucial to its power. This control is open to challenge and, in any case, it is fiercely argued between liberals and Marxists precisely how much power the state in capitalist societies has over the ideological state apparatus. Obviously, the relationship between the government and media differs somewhat in different capitalist countries but, generally, Marxists argue that there is relatively limited freedom of expression, whereas liberals take the opposite view.

The Upper Class Background of Occupational Elites

A major part of Miliband's book examines two related questions whose answers, taken together, determine whether or not there is a ruling class in British and other European capitalist societies. Firstly, is the state actually operated by people from the same upper class social background? Secondly, if so, do these people run the state in their own interest and at the expense of other classes? Miliband's answer to both questions is 'yes', although he has an easier time answering the first than the second. On the common social background and experience of those who dominate the command positions of the state, Miliband is unequivocal:

> What the evidence conclusively suggests is that in terms of social origin, education and class situation, the men who have manned *all* command positions in the state system have largely, and in many cases, overwhelmingly, been drawn from the world of business or property, or from the professional middle classes. Here, as in every other field, men and women born into the subordinate classes, which form of course the vast majority of the population, have fared very poorly . . .

Although Miliband is primarily concerned with Britain, he cites considerable empirical evidence to show that the same situation prevails in other Western European 'democracies'.

Miliband's book was published in 1969, but substantially the same argument was presented in 1979 by Anthony Giddens who, in fact, makes a broader claim than Miliband – that there is *no* major institutional sector in Britain where less than half of those in top positions are of public school background, and, by implication, also of upper or upper middle class background. (For details, see Chapter 10.) Drawing on a study of elites carried out at Cambridge, Giddens concludes that over 80% of Anglican bishops, of principal judges and of army officers over the rank of major-general were from public schools, as were 60% of chief secretaries in the civil service, and 76% of Conservative MPs (1951–70). In contrast, only 26% of Labour MPs had a public school background.

Giddens emphasises especially the upper class dominance of industry, which, from the Marxist point of view, is particularly important because the economy is seen as the ultimate basis of power. In a sample taken from the Cambridge survey, 73% of the directors of the industrial corporations and 80% of the directors of financial firms proved to be of public school background.

Giddens cites other work which shows that directors of industrial and, especially, financial companies very often have kin 'within the trade'. The phenomenon of interlocking directorships is a point emphasised in both British and American literature on industrial elites. The term 'industrial elites' refers to the way in which various individuals hold directorships in more than one company so that the same individuals may sit together on several different boards. Accordingly, they may influence and even co-ordinate the policy of two or more companies: indeed, this is often precisely the intention of interlocking directorships. The Cambridge study showed an increase in directional connection between large companies. At the beginning of the century, fewer than half of the 85 corporations studied were linked by shared directorships, whereas in 1970, 73 out of 85 organisations studied appeared in the network of connections. Potentially, this provides an impressive basis for control of industry.

Is the Upper Class also a Ruling Class?

We come now to Miliband's second area of enquiry. Does the upper class rule in its own interest, and at the expense of others? As Miliband and Giddens are well aware, to demonstrate upper class dominance of major elites does not prove either that the upper class is the 'real source of political power' or, still less, that it *rules in its own interest.* In particular, the powerful position of the upper class in industry does not automatically mean that it can control the political process or that, 'in the last resort', its economic power is more decisive than the political power of government. These issues require further examination.

In attempting to determine whether the upper class is also a ruling class, it is helpful to establish what links exist between business and politics. If these are considerable, we can conclude that there is at least the *potential* for business to influence the political process and, perhaps, even to *control* it in its own interest. A study by Roth and Kerbey shows that, between 1960 and 1966, MPs held, in total, 770 directorships and 324 positions as chairmen, vice-chairmen or managing directors. It is highly significant that 90% of these positions were held by Conservative MPs. Insofar as the economic-political flow of influence does express itself through personal links of this kind, it is, therefore, far more likely to be found in the Conservative Party than in the Labour Party. The upper class is well represented in both industry and the Conservative Party. As we have seen 76% of Conservative MPs over the period 1951–70 went to public school, a major purveyor of upper class culture, compared with only 26% of Labour MPs. Few Marxists, however, regard the Labour Party as the likely means by which capitalism will be abolished and socialism established. Why is this so?

Marx himself held out little hope that socialism could be successfully introduced through Parliament, although there is evidence that he thought that the arrival of universal male suffrage (voting rights) might make the system more responsive to socialist demands. In the event, Marxists are able to point out that, despite seventeen years of Labour government, since 1945, the fundamental facts of inequality have not changed very much. Everybody has become better off, but the relativities have not changed significantly. Marxists tend to consider that the welfare state has partly 'humanised' but not fundamentally changed the position of the working class and the poor. Writing in the late nineteen-sixties, but expressing a perennial mood among Marxists, Miliband says:

> Social-democratic parties (Labour parties) or rather
> social-democratic leaders, have long ceased to suggest to anyone
> but their most credulous followers (and the more stupid among
> their opponents) that they were concerned in any sense whatever
> with the business of bringing about a socialist society. (author's
> brackets).

In qualification of Miliband's remark, it should be said that
there is still a sizeable socialist, if not Marxist-inclined, group
within the Labour Party, which continues to work for fundamental change through the parliamentary system, despite its
dissatisfaction with the performances of the Labour government
of the nineteen sixties and seventies.

Nicos Poulantzas

Further analysis of the role of the ruling class in capitalist society is presented by Nicos Poulantzas, a French Marxist. In a
celebrated exchange with Miliband, Poulantzas criticises him for
concentrating too much on details about the social background
of various occupational elites and of the ruling class as a
whole. For Poulantzas, these factors are not particularly crucial.
In his view, it would be possible for large numbers, even a
majority, of people of quite humble social background to
administer capitalist society – *but it would still be capitalist society*
and therefore run in the interests of the capitalist class and not
the proletariat. This brings us to Poulantzas's central point and
the one on which he considers that he differs, at least in
emphasis, from Miliband. Poulantzas contends that it is the
structure of the capitalist system and not the social background
of the various elites which is the major factor for Marxists to
consider when analysing the state. According to him, what matters is the relationship of the parts, including the state, to the
social totality (the whole of society). Thus, it comes as no surprise to Poulantzas that socialist parties with a wide basis of
popular support and even, perhaps, with leaders of working
class origins, should find it difficult to implement socialism
when, supposedly, 'in power'. The British Labour Party might
be elected 'to power' but what it can actually do is limited by
the rest of the system. It would almost certainly be afraid to
introduce policies that would lose the confidence of international financiers and stock exchange investors. To do so
would probably cause a major economic crisis. There might
even be the possibility that radical policies would turn the

military against the government. This threat, however, is most easily demonstrated in relation to underdeveloped countries. Thus, the popularly elected (although not with an absolute majority) President Allende of Chile, a Marxist, was overthrown by a conspiracy involving some of the parliamentary opposition, members of the armed forces and the American Central Intelligence Agency. The implication is that when legality fails to protect the interests of capital, then illegal means may be used.

The above does not mean that Poulantzas dismisses the state as unimportant – far from it! Some years after his debate with Miliband, he wrote: 'The state plays a decisive role in the relations of production and the class struggle'. But Poulantzas warns that what a socialist party could actually *do* with state power, if it were to obtain it, would be conditioned by the relationship of the state to the rest of the system at that time. This would include such matters as the strength of capital and the extent of socialist support among the working class.

There is a element of 'shadow boxing' about Miliband's and Poulantzas's disagreement, because the former insists that his work is a structural critique of the state in capitalist society and not just a collection of loosely interpreted empirical data. In any case, Poulantzas's point that an adequate *theory* of the state must relate coherently to the rest of the social system is valid.

It is worth briefly exploring the wider implications of Poulantzas's remark that 'the state plays a decisive role in the relations of production and the class struggle'. In saying this, he is rejecting the deterministic interpretations of Marx's base-superstructure model of society. He denies that capitalism will inevitably collapse as a result of its inherent economic 'contradictions' as some Marxists still believe. (Whether Marx himself ever believed this, in any simplistic sense, is debatable.) For Poulantzas, the capitalist nature of society and class relations arising from relations to the means of production do *structure* class conflict – both in the economic and political context – but they do not pre-determine its outcome: socialism has to be achieved through political struggle. With some reservations, the American Marxist sociologist, Erik Wright, supports this position in his book, *Class, Crisis and the State*. In particular, he offers a sensitive discussion of the issue of whether socialism can be achieved through the "bourgeois' democratic system or whether it requires violent revolution. We have already referred to some of the problems of the former approach: the difficulties in relation to the second are perhaps greater. Firstly, the human cost of violent revolution needs to be profoundly considered. Can it be justified? Secondly, modern governments have at their disposal such powerful and centrally controlled arsenals of destruction that they seem virtually unassailable.

Ideology and Power

A crucial question that Marxists need to explain is why the majority, who are not the prime beneficiaries of capitalism, do not oppose the system more vehemently. Miliband and Poulantzas are agreed that the dominant ideology plays a vital role in securing the compliance of the majority to the power and position of the ruling class. We have already discussed how the educational system can teach people to conform – even to a society in which they have relatively little material stake – and the role of the mass media in this respect is worthy of much more space than we can give it here. For the moment, a single quotation from Miliband will serve to represent the Marxist perspective:

> Given the economic and political context in which the mass media functions, they cannot fail to be, predominantly, agencies for the dissemination of idea and values which affirm rather than challenge existing patterns of power and privilege, and thus be weapons in the arsenal of class domination.

Ideological control involves power over men's minds. As Bachrach and Baratz point out, an aspect of this is the ability to decide which issues should be allowed to become publicly debated and which should not be, for instance, control of the press. Steven Lukes takes this point further by frankly recognising that the values, attitudes, and even wants of the majority can be moulded by the power of a few. Marxists are unimpressed by exercises such as that carried out by Hewitt (discussed earlier) which seem to support a pluralist model of power, because they argue that the issues that really matter are seldom discussed publicly, anyway. For Marxists, such issues would include whether a society based on private property (including that of the ruling class) *can* be socially just, whether violence is necessary to destroy the capitalist system and what a 'liberated' socialist culture might be like. The limits of the political debate are reflected in decisions taken and not taken (for example, issues of pollution and poverty may be disregarded and defence-law and order and immigration policy vigorously pursued). Marxists, then, agree with functionalists that ideological consensus can be achieved in capitalist society: the difference is their evaluation of it. Functionalists see it as necessary; Marxists regard it as an element in class exploitation. For them, there is no more telling illustration of the power of the ruling class than their ability to persuade the working class to accept and even morally approve of their own subjection. The consolation for Marxists is that they see the possibility of an end to inequality and the power of the ruling class.

Power Elite versus Ruling Class Theory: A Radical Disagreement

Before summarising the merits of the pluralist and Marxist views of democracy, we must briefly analyse the power elite theory of the American radical sociologist, C. Wright Mills. Mills was a conflict theorist but was much less of a Marxist than the other authors so far discussed in this section. He probably owed more to Weber than to Marx. He was a severe critic of post-Second World War American society. His fierce but measured language broke across the bland face of functionalist orthodoxy like a fire-cracker. A startled Talcott Parsons compared him to a gun-happy outlaw, free with the trigger but not very accurate in his aim. It is true that Mills began more than he was able to finish, but by the time of his death in 1962, he had sown the seeds of a radical revival in American sociological scholarship, and provided an intellectual starting point for the emerging political radicalism of the American New Left. His best known and most influential work is *The Power Elite*, first published in 1956. It is typical of Mills's intellectual inventiveness that he reworked traditionally conservative elite theory within a radical perspective. He argued that there are three popularly *un*representative elites at the top of American society: the political elite, the military elite and the industrial elite. Together, these made up the power elite. The relative power of the three elites could vary. In his own time, when the Cold War was at its height, he believed that the military was the most powerful of the three. He insisted, however, that members of the elites shared common material interests as well as, frequently, a common upper class background. Individuals such as President Eisenhower moved easily between the elites, and thus helped to fuse more closely identity of ideology and interest. Mills was in no doubt that the power elite 'ran' America to its own benefit and against that of the majority of people. He considered that the American Congress operated only at the middle level of power and was unable to check the power elite. It was influential mainly on those issues that did not fundamentally affect the structure of society or the essential interests of the power elite. Thus, it might legislate for a little more or a little less welfare aid but not for a fundamental redistribution of wealth. Below the power elite was what Mills did not hesitate to describe as 'the masses'. They comprised the middle and working classes and the poor. He regarded the middle class as fragmented and generally concerned with its own various sectional interests, and the working class as sufficiently 'well-fed' to be thoroughly deradicalised and uninterested in change. Mills's comments on the working class had plausibility in relation to the relatively unorganised and non-socialist American labour force but they were rejected by European Marxists as much less applicable to that continent. The poor consisted of such groups as the unemployed, the old and disproportionate numbers of coloured minorities. Mills saw little prospect that this group would become an effective agency for change, but he did refer, in passing, to the 'moral idea of a counter-elite' and to 'images of the poor, the exploited, and the oppressed as the truly virtuous, the wise and the blessed'.

As we shall shortly describe, this notion had considerable appeal to the young American radicals of the nineteen sixties to whom Mills became something of a folk hero and intellectal father figure. In turn, Mills regarded young, radical intellectuals as the best, if still unlikely, chance for change in America.

Liberal Pluralist and Marxist Theory: Summary
Pluralist theorists take liberal democracy more or less 'at face value'. They believe it works, and consider that political parties and interest groups adequately represent the people. Marxists present a variety of arguments to demonstrate that pluralist claims are incorrect and that power in capitalist societies is, in

reality, in the hands of the ruling class. They point to the dominance of the upper class in various major elites and, in particular, to the overlap between Parliament and industry. Even Labour governments have been seen to pose only a minimal threat to the ruling class and to have made no fundamental change in inequalities of power, wealth and prestige. The power of the ruling class in the area of ideological control helps to explain, for Marxists, the acquiescence of large sections of the working class in their own 'exploitation'. Mills's mixed legacy defies categorisation, but he caught the ascendant mood of the emerging American and European New Left of the nineteen sixties. The popular slogan of that decade 'Power to the People,' is not so distant an echo of Mills's inspirational rhetoric.

People, Participation and Power
Pluralist democratic assumptions, as well as being attacked from a Marxist point of view, have received criticism from another perspective. The phrase 'participatory democracy' describes this perspective which was presented particularly forcefully by radical American activists in the early nineteen sixties, although the concept has deeper roots both in America and Europe. The terms 'position' and 'perspective' perhaps suggest more precision and sophistication than actually existed in the thinking of those who supported participatory democracy in the sixties. The concept represented a commitment to the idea that people should have some control and involvement in the organisations and decisions that affect their lives. It was as much a matter of sentiment as of ideology, of action as of theory. In the late nineteen fifties and early sixties a strong feeling had grown up among some students and intellectuals, both in Europe and America, that power had become remote from ordinary people who typically played out their working lives in small roles within large organisations run by the powerful few. Groups of young radicals began to try to change this state of affairs by working with the poor and deprived in various community action projects. At first, the student activists were not clear about the relationship between their own local efforts and the change they hoped to effect in the central power structure of American society. As we shall see, ideas about this eventually did develop.

Although the new radicals were not very precise about their own theoretical position, they were able to articulate their criticism of pluralism. Firstly, they regarded power and inequality as issues that went far beyond merely *formal* political processes and institutions into every part of American life. They wanted to make participatory democracy real in every major institutional system from education to welfare organisations. Secondly, they considered that the poor were handicapped within competitive, pluralist democracy, as they have fewer resources and less knowledge than other groups to publicise and achieve their aims. Therefore, they needed help in these matters.

The practical expression of the new radical sentiment took the form of a 'return to the people'. An American student organisation, Students for a Democratic Society, established several community development projects in a number of depressed urban areas. It was hoped that, with help, the poor would begin to control the organisations that presently controlled them. The immediate purpose was to educate the poor in dealing with the power structure as well as to win specific 'battles' over such matters as welfare claims, housing conditions and official 'neglect' of the environment. The resolution of one such issue in Newark, New Jersey – putting a traffic light at a dangerous point on a road – took several months, but those involved learned much about the functioning of local government and administration. In Britain, two officially funded ventures, the Community Development Projects and the misleadingly named Young Volunteer Force Projects, to a certain extent pursued a simiar philosophy to the SDS.

Many of those involved in such schemes soon began to feel that their effectiveness was likely to be very limited. They realised, too, that in trying to help the poor in this way they were tacitly accepting the pluralist assumption that the poor really can compete successfully with other groups even in unequal, capitalist society. They began to appreciate that, in practice, their efforts were likely to make little difference to the fundamental causes of inequality and powerlessness. John Benington of the Coventry CDP expresses an opinion commonly arrived at by radical community organisers in Britain and America:

> A growing awareness of 'the flaw in the pluralist heaven' has forced a number of the CDPs towards a structural class-conflict

554

model of social change. This is based on the assumption that social problems arise from a fundamental conflict of interests between groups or classes in society. The problems are defined mainly in terms of inequalities in the distribution of power and the focus of change is thus on the centres of organised power (both private and public).

Benington's emphasis on fundamental as opposed to reconcilable conflict puts him firmly in the socialist camp. Indeed, the concept of popular participation, especially in industry, has long been a theme in socialist thought. Because of this, some critics, such as Tom Bottomore, do not regard participatory democracy as a new idea at all and would certainly deny that it provides the basis for a new political ideology. The fact that this principle of participation has also been enthusiastically accepted by the British Liberal Party as well as by many socialists, indicates that Bottomore is correct in regarding it as an inadequate basis for a distinctive political philosophy. Equally, it might be argued that any political philosophy that does not encourage and develop participation is itself inadequate. There is an increased awareness of this point among contemporary Western Marxists: they frequently argue for the development of socialist *and* democratic practice on the left, even 'before the revolution'. Genuinely democratic socialism will not suddenly appear without such practice.

To a limited extent and, often, grudgingly, the principle of participation has gradually gained more acceptance in British society. In the past twenty years, participation in education, planning, housing, transport and, marginally, in industrial decision making has tended to increase. The process, however, is slow and uncertain. Raymond Williams was right when he wrote of the emergence of democracy as 'the long revolution'. For this 'revolution' to be successfully established, democratic participation and (to accept the full logic of democracy) control, must exist in all major areas of social life. This includes the economic and social as well as the political. Democracy at work will probably affect the daily lives of people much more profoundly than do present political rights. Indeed, democracy cannot be properly understood in merely political terms. Families, peer groups and relationships can be more or less democratic. We saw earlier that power exists in virtually all social interactions. Democracy means sharing power by popular involvement and, by involvement, generating meaning and identity.

Power, People and Sociological Theory

In this final section we examine more deeply the underlying principles behind the theories of power and politics to which we have already referred: liberal democratic, Marxist and Weberian. Finally, we make a point which is inspired by American populist or popular democratic tradition.

Liberal-democratic theorists, such as Robert Dahl, believe that power is much more diffuse or 'spread out' than Marxists believe. The political elite, according to them, is ultimately answerable to the people and this is a constant contraint on its actions. Yet the belief of liberals in *popular sovereignty,* that power comes from the people *is* simply a belief. This idealism is tempered by a recognition of the need for leadership. Finally, political power is regarded by liberals as generally dominant over the power of economic groups. To a large extent, liberals echo Weber in this point of view. The implication of this belief is that political rights, especially the right to vote, are very important.

Marxists, on the other hand, argue that power is primarily a function of the control of resources. To explain this, let us first take an example from outside the political arena. As a rule, large, athletic people have more physical power than small, unathletic people. This is the direct result of the physical resources at their disposal – their bodies. Similarly, rich people have more power than poor people because they control more economic and, therefore, other resources. Power might extend as far as 'buying the time' (employing) of poor people and, to that extent, controlling part of their lives. Even ideological power involves the control of the means of communication – such as the mass media or, historically, the pulpit. To put the matter more technically and specifically, the roots of power relations are in the relations of classes to the means of production (whether the production of things or ideas). In capitalist society, the bourgeoisie own the means of production and are therefore the most powerful class. This does not mean that the proletariat is without power; it, too, has a relationship to the means of production. After all, it operates them! This gives it a strategic advantage in class conflict. The collective withdrawal of labour is an immensely powerful weapon. Indeed, syndicalists, though not Marxists, have argued that a general strike is the most effective means of bringing down the capitalist system. Marxists consider that this could not happen and that a transition to a communist society could not take place without the guidance of a Marxist political party.

Marxists assume, then, that power will normally be exercised for self or *class* interest. This is to see power in terms of conflict rather than as a resource for *general* use, as the functionalists tend to see it. Even the pluralists who stress the existence of many 'mini' conflicts pay service to the ultimate predominance of basic consensus. Weber recognises both these elements but inclines towards a conflict view of power. In his distinction between power and authority, however, and in his organisational theory, he moves us on to the *institutionalisation* of power. 'Rational', institutionalised power he considers to be a dominant feature and, to some extent, a plague of modern times. Even so, he seems to bow before the necessity and inevitability of such power – a typically functionalist posture.

A less reverent view of power suffuses the American political tradition, even if this attitude has not appeared in functionalist sociology. Modern America was founded upon revolution against British imperialism. Americans have tended to remain watchful and, often, distrustful of their own leaders – sometimes with good cause. It was because Thomas Jefferson believed that politicians should be subject to the people that he, an American President, said 'God forbid we should be twenty years without a rebellion'. Jefferson exaggerated to make a point – which was that, left to themselves, those in power will probably try to acquire more power, and possibly abuse it. The more power they acquire, the greater the abuse can be. Democracy is largely about preventing this from happening. Modern examples of totalitarianism have re-emphasised Jefferson's wisdom. In this view, democracy is part of a process, almost cyclical in nature, in which government becomes over-powerful and is then brought down to size and shown to be the servant, not the master of the people; at least, for a time. And then the process begins again. For Marxists, a major challenge is to achieve a much greater degree of equality than exists in capitalist societies and to combine it with real democratic freedom. That this is possible still requires to be convincingly shown, both theoretically and practically.

Conclusion

Two very important and connected developments have occurred in British politics during the 1980s. First, the class-voter-party linkages described earlier have largely broken apart as far as the working class is concerned. Second, British politics in the 1980s has been the age of Thatcherism.

In 1966, the proportion of the manual working class voting Labour was 69% and in 1979, perhaps a fairer basis of comparison than the debacle of 1983, it was 50%. Probably of most significance in the 1983 election, was the impressive performance of the Third 'Party', the Alliance, which took votes from *both* Labour and Conservatives in *all* major occupational categories. However, the haemorrhage from Labour to the Alliance was much greater and the Conservatives received only 2% less of the total poll than in 1979. Interestingly, a frequent previous trend in which more women than men voted Conservative did not occur in either 1979 or 1983. Ironically, the basis of the Thatcher majority is not particularly female.

What has caused the above trends? First, by most definitions, the working class has become smaller. Heath et al. estimate that it was 47% of the electorate in 1964 and 34% in 1983 (on the basis of an admittedly narrow definition of workng class). This explains perhaps half of Labour's lost votes. Second, a smaller proportion of the (remaining) working class currently votes Labour. This is the harder fact to explain and the literature does not do so entirely convincingly. If class is less important, have issues and personalities become more important? Surprisingly, in their survey of electoral attitudes, Dunleavy and Husbands find that, judged on the major issues alone, Labour and the Conservatives tied for support in 1983. That leaves personality, and certainly, the opinion polls consistently showed Margaret Thatcher well ahead of Michael Foot, the Labour leader, in the 1983 election. Perhaps a re-reading of the 'deviant' voting behaviour of earlier elections will suggest further explanations (see pp. 530–2). Could it be that as (or if) class wanes, the 'natural' deference of the British people will favour Conservatism? Or, more likely, is individual choice (subjective voting in the old model) emerging as a more important matter? Indeed, Himmelweit et al. replace the class model of voting with a consumer model – voters give their support to the party that offers them most.

Thatcherism has focused as well as benefited from some of the above developments. It may be that it is less the ideological content of Thatcherism and more the conviction and ideological style of Thatcher that explains Conservative success under her leadership. Others prefer a more pragmatic style of politics but perhaps she has shown that pragmatism, however necessary, is not enough to mobilise and sustain support.

Guide to Further Reading and Study

Several studies of voting behaviour fully consider the results of the 1979 and 1983 elections. These include Anthony Heath *et al*, *How Britain Votes* (Pergamon Press, 1985) and Patrick Dunleavy and Christopher T. Husbands *British Democracy at the Crossroads: Voting and Party Competition in the 1980s* (Oxford University Press, 1985). A slightly earlier book which sets up a helpful model of recent voting behaviour is Hilde T. Himmelweit *et al*, *How Voters Decide* (Academic Press, 1981). Still a useful introduction to most of the main issues raised in this chapter is Jean Blondel's *Voters, Parties, and Leaders* (Penguin, 1969). For a Marxist balance to Blondel's liberal inclinations see Ralph Miliband, *The State and Capitalist Society* (Quartet Books, 1969). For those who can obtain it, Anthony Giddens' 'An Anatomy of the British Ruling Class', (*New Society*, 4 October 1979) is a good outline (reprinted in my *New Introductory Reader in Sociology* (Nelson, 1983)). C. Wright Mills' *The Power Elite* (Oxford University Press, 1956) is a classic and original study and T. B. Bottomore's *Elites and Society* (Penguin, 1964) covers broader ground in a highly accessible way.

Past Questions

1 Compare and contrast pluralist and Marxist theories of the distribution of power in advanced societies. (AEB, 1984)

2 'The major development affecting political life since 1970 has been the changing pattern of support for the traditional political parties.' Discuss. (OLE, 1984)

3 'The Labour vote remains largely working class; but the working class has ceased to be largely Labour.' (Ivor Crewe, commenting on the 1983 General Election.) Explain and discuss this statement in the light of recent election results. (AEB, 1985)

4 What have sociologists identified as the role of the state in advanced industrial societies? (AEB, 1985)

5 How relevant is the concept of 'political elite' to the study of British politics? (OLE, 1985)

6 Using evidence from at least two societies, assess the claim that in Western industrial societies power is widely dispersed. (IMB, 1985)

20 Culture and Ideology: Religion and the Media

Culture and Ideology

If we make a useful, though artificial, distinction between culture and social structure, culture is the dynamic and communicative aspect of social life, and structure refers to the institutions that form and constrain us. In reality, social process and social structure do not exist separately, and phenomenologists tend to collapse the distinction between them on the grounds that all social life, including its institutional side, is simply the ongoing product of peoples' (inter)actions. However, even viewed in a more restricted sense, culture includes socialisation, education, and aspects of class, ethnicity, race and gender, as well as religion and the media. As such, culture and sub-culture have been recurrently considered throughout this book.

The central cultural issue is the creation and communication of meaning. We all try to create meaning in what we do or we let others create it for us. When workers 'lark about' or students 'daydream', they are defining the situation as they want rather than as authority intends. Much more seriously, dissidents in totalitarian regimes are staying true to their own beliefs or meanings and rejecting those imposed upon them. So, despite external pressures, people do respond in their own way to experience. This is not to say that everybody thinks originally but, at some level, most people do think for themselves.

In Chapter 3 we discussed how both Marxism and functionalism emphasise the power of society to shape the cultural meanings and behaviour of members. As a result, people generally conform to what Functionalists refer to as 'roles' and Marxists as 'class position'. Many contemporary thinkers within both perspectives adopt the Freudian view that once patterns of feeling, belief and behaviour have been established, people do not change them easily. Arguably, Functionalism is weak in explaining how individuals and societies change, and strong on how social conformity, stability and solidarity are maintained. Functionalist analyses of social breakdown and conflict tend to be conceptualised in terms of deviance rather than politics, whilst Marxists see them much more in terms of class and political struggle.

Marxism is an ideology of liberation, although sometimes the opposite has been practised in its name. Much contemporary debate within Marxism has focused on how the liberation of the working class will take place and particularly what the respective roles of culture and ideology and structural change will be. Will ideas, persuasion and individual initiative play the major role or will a structural breakdown in capitalism make socialism virtually inevitable? Marx gave indications in both directions and whilst few Marxists are simplistic enough exclusively to adopt either view there have been severe disagreements on emphasis and political strategy. E. P. Thompson has argued for a strategy of persuasion and that a peaceful socialist future is there for the 'making'. Though no crude 'breakdown-of-capitalism' theorist, Louis Althusser has, in contrast, stressed that ideology serves socio-economic realities. He concedes only a limited independent effect or, as he calls it, 'relative autonomy' for ideology. Indeed, the structuralist theory of Althusser, Bourdieu and Poulantzas seems barely to allow for the development of widespread ideological opposition to capitalism, so formidable is its system of cultural reproduction as they describe it (see pp. 97–101).

Acceptance of the need to persuade means accepting the possibility of losing the argument. The thought that the culture of liberal capitalism may be popular and well entrenched, is not palatable to Marxists. Yet the revival of capitalist ideology in Britain and the United States in the early 1980s was undeniable. Margaret Thatcher and Ronald Reagan presented their own philosophies of freedom and liberation to their electorates with marked success. In Britain, the Conservative victories occurred not particularly against Marxism but against the Labour Party and the Alliance – both predominantly social democratic in ideology. In the early 1980s the government's emphasis was on economic individualism and laissez-faire but in the mid-1980s it showed some intention to focus on issues of culture and value. In a major speech in 1985, Norman Tebbit, then the Chairman of the Conservative Party, saw the future and the recent past as follows:

> Above all, I believe that by the 1990s we shall see the effects of a revulsion against the valueless values of the permissive society . . . Permissiveness compounded by the economic failure and personal irresponsibility engendered by the socialist state leads inevitably to the violent society.

Whether 'the socialist state' can be reasonably held responsible for the big rise in reported crime during the Conservative period in office is as open to debate as are the other propositions of Mr Tebbit. Debate there will be, for what is being frankly and

563

aggressively offered is an attempt to change British culture and society in a particular direction. The main ideas and policies in this debate are extensively reviewed in Chapter 22. It is not easy to opt out of a debate that will radically affect the kind of society we live in.

What has all this to do with religion and the media? Simply, that they are the main means by which cultural values and ideology are communicated. For this reason it is important to try to understand the media. Who controls the media? Is the media biased? If so, whose bias does it reflect and is this bias conscious or unconscious? Does the media cause some people to behave violently? Is a democratic or, at least, a widely participatory media possible? Whatever its precise nature or quality, it is through the media that a crucial engagement of values, ideology and policy has occurred.

Culture and Ideological Control: Religion and the Media

There is no more powerful weapon than influence over people's minds. To influence thought is the surest way of influencing behaviour. Such influence depends on access to the communications media. In the past, the church was the major public means of ideological communication. The local gentry also played an influential role in the community. Their message to the people was generally to conform and to obey.

The modern mass media has largely replaced the church as a form of cultural expression and communication. Sociologists, however, find it far less easy to generalise about the influence of the modern media than about that of the medieval church. Politicians, on the other hand, have been less uncertain. Hitler and, his henchman, Goebbels, were convinced that control of the mass media by the state would provide a major means of establishing their ideas and securing their rule. They secured similar control over the educational system. Other totalitarian rulers have equally taken it for granted that social control can be achieved partly through control of mass communications.

The issue of ideological control is the major theme in our discussion of religion and the media. It is not, however, the only aspect of these matters explored. People are certainly not passive receptacles of centrally produced and administered ideas. Many interpret religion and the products of the media in a lively and creative way and we will attempt to do justice to this in what follows.

Religion

a RELIGION AS IDEOLOGY The most frequently observed function of religion is that of *integration*. In their different ways, both Durkheim and Marx were agreed on this. We are familiar, by now, with Durkheim's belief in the need for moral consensus in society. In traditional societies, religion was the major means by which this was achieved. For Marx religion is 'mere' ideology. For centuries it had misled and 'mystified' ordinary people into conforming to social orders in which the majority were exploited by the few. Happiness eternal was the promised reward for accepting their lot in the here and now. The following few lines from a well-known popular hymn, illustrate the kind of religious sentiment scorned by Marx:

> The rich man in his castle,
> The poor man at his gate,
> God made them high and lowly
> And ordered their estate.

Marx himself referred to religion as 'the opiate of the masses' and latterday Marxists have pilloried it as 'pie in the sky when you die'. Neither description could possibly be taken as a compliment. It is worth including a quotation from Durkheim at this point, which shows just how close he is to Marx on this matter:

> Religion instructed the humble to be content with their situation, and, at the same time it taught them that the social order is providential: that it is God himself who has determined each one's share. Religion gave man a perception of a world beyond this earth where everything would be rectified; this prospect made inequalities less noticeable, it stopped men from feeling aggrieved.

Whereas Marx saw this as repressive, Durkheim saw it as necessary.

Both Marx and Durkheim used 'primitive' religion to illustrate their analyses. Durkheim wrote a major work on the topic, *The Elementary Forms of Religious Life*. In particular, he examined the significance of religious symbolism. He regarded the totem pole as a focus of collective tribal unity. Religious worship and ritual provided occasion for the reaffirmation of community. We can see similar symbolism in some contemporary religion. Catholics sometimes refer to their church as 'the body of Christ on earth'. There could be no more powerful image of collective unity than that: Marx's examination of 'primitive' religion goes straight to the heart of what he regarded as its ideologically exploitative nature. Priests and witch-doctors conspired to relieve ordinary tribal members of their surplus wealth by claiming that they needed to be supported in order to practice magic and to communicate with the gods. Often contributions were such that they were able to do so in some style.

One of the most interesting and challenging applications of Marx's analysis of religion as ideology was to the role Protestantism has played in justifying capitalism. Marx argued that merchants and industrialists of the sixteenth century and later, preferred the Protestant to the Catholic religion because the former satisfied their commercial requirements more than the latter. Whereas Catholicism forbade usury (lending money at exorbitant rates), it was acceptable under Protestantism. Whereas Catholic theologians regarded great interest in acquiring wealth as greedy, Protestants, and particularly Calvinists (members of a Protestant sect) looked upon material success as a sign of God's grace and favour. Protestant philosophy offered a further bonus to practical minded capitalists. Hard work and industry were at the core of Protestant moral practice and these virtues applied as much to the working class as to the bourgeoisie. Credit in the heavenly bank account rather than a hefty wage-packet was to be the reward of labour. This view had much to commend it to industrialists concerned with profit, accumulation and investment rather than the standard of living of the working class.

b RELIGIOUS IDEAS: CAUSE OR CONSEQUENCE OF SOCIAL CHANGE? In one of the most celebrated of historical-sociological encounters, Max Weber took issue with Marx on his analysis of religion as ideology. Superficially, the debate is about a question of empirical fact, but at a deeper level it concerns the cause and nature of historical change. The factual issue is itself profound enough:

was Protestantism primarily the product of capitalism or did it, on the contrary, help to produce capitalism? Marx takes the former view, Weber the latter. Marx's position has, in effect, already been explained. He argued that, like other forms of religious ideology, Protestanism helped to justify certain social relations – in this case the exploitation of the proletariat by the bourgeoisie. For Weber, the matter was less simple. He argued that Calvinism, a particular form of Protestantism, had played a major role in creating a cultural climate in which the capitalistic spirit could thrive. It would be too crude to say that Weber thought that Calvinism 'caused' capitalism, but he did consider that there was a certain *correspondence* between Calvinist ideas and the qualities required to be a successful capitalist. Calvinism provided favourable conditions for the development of capitalism. For instance, Calvinism preached hard work and frugality, the Protestant ethic – very useful virtues to a businessman. Weber cited many examples of Calvinists who became businessmen, while, however, fully recognising that factors other than the spiritual content of Calvinism contributed to the rise of capitalism. An important one was the development of new machine technology which massively increased production potential. We are not here concerned with the detail and precise accuracy of Weber's argument (though, commendably, many historians have been) but with his general explanatory approach. At this point we must make explicit the wider issue of which the 'capitalism/Calvinism' argument is one example.

Weber's major point here is that ideas can change history, and in so doing, can contribute to changes in the material context of life. It will be remembered that the whole trend of Marx's analysis of religious ideas is in the opposite direction. He sees them primarily as justifying existing social and economic circumstances, and certainly not as providing a major source of historical change. On the contrary, religion was an ideological pall intended to obscure new and different ideas. But Marx did recognise that new ideas *could* be developed. Man's consciousness is able to react thoughtfully and creatively to experience, particularly everyday work experience. Socialism itself had to be 'thought of' before it could become a reality. However, for Marx, ideas are formed within, and structured by, socio-economic material reality. Socialism only becomes possible or practically 'thinkable' when society is economically and socially developed to the point where socialist ideas are seen to be realistic.

C THE 'DECLINE' OF RELIGION IN MODERN SOCIETIES (SECULARISATION)
Following David Martin, we can distinguish two complementary aspects to *secularisation*. Firstly, it refers to the decline in voluntary involvement in formal religious activities such as church attendance or regular worship at home, and to any decline in the power, wealth and influence of the church as an institution. Over the centuries this decline of the church's wider influence has been apparent in, for instance, politics, the arts, medicine and social welfare. Secondly, secularisation applies to thought and attitudes and we examine this matter in the next section.

S. S. Acquaviva has charted the decline of Christianity in a wide range of countries, and the corresponding emergence of a more secular way of life. This has been nowhere more marked than in Britain now, reputedly, 'the most secular nation in Europe'. The decline in formal religion has been comprehensive This has been especially true of the Church of England. The number participating in the rites of passage – baptism, confirmation and church marriage – has declined, as has that of Easter communicants. In 1950, two thirds of the children born alive in England were baptised in the Church of England; in 1973 the figure was well under half. In 1953, some 6.5% of the population took Easter communion in the Church of England. In 1973, fewer than 4% did so. In 1976, only 120,000 marriages were solemnised in the Church of England, compared with 194,000 in registry offices. The Church of Scotland and the Roman Catholic Church were both growing in membership in the nineteen fifties, but have both gone into decline since. The same story is true, to varying extents, of Methodists, Baptists, Congregationalists and Presbyterians.

The decline in institutional prestige of the church is well illustrated by Bryan Wilson in his article 'How Religious are we?' Half humorously, he remarks that religion 'is no longer news, except when a clergyman commits a moral misdemeanour'. He sees the role of religion in school and at the workplace as now almost negligible. Religious instruction in schools has often become a travesty: many teachers using the periods for current affairs. He suggests that the workplace is perhaps the environment 'most alien' to religious values.

Mechanical principles of organisation, whether in factory or office, seem almost the antithesis of religious myth and values. The remoteness of contemporary religion from political life is worth more space than Wilson gives it. In the reign of Henry II, the major political opponent of the King was the Archbishop of Canterbury. Recently, we have seen the occasion when the Prime Minister was too busy to see the Archbishop.

The irrelevance of religion to practical and political affairs is, however, only generally true of the *internal* life of advanced, historically Christian nations. Religious issues often remain of major importance elsewhere and particularly in the relations between traditional, but modernising Muslim states, and advanced, western countries. The religious element in the conflict in Northern Ireland, with its various international ramifications, reminds us that religion can still fuel the fires of political and social conflict and that secularisation is by no means a universally accomplished fact.

Still, the process of secularisation has been steadily progressive in what was once Christendom. We must now explain why Weber's thoughts on the matter are an informative starting point. For him, secularisation was an aspect of the wider process of *rationalisation*. He considered that the underying principle behind modernisation is rational, scientific thought. Applied to technology and to organisation, rational thought has restructured the social world. Equally to the point, applied to man's understanding of himself and his place in the universe, rational thought has undermined religion and replaced it with various secular and, largely, materialistic explanations of his existence and relationship to nature. Darwin, Freud and Marx were major contributors to the replacement of religious explanations of human behaviour by scientific ones. Loss of intellectual authority and status helped to erode the moral authority of the church. Further, the urban, industrial proletariat was physically as well as spiritually more cut off from the church than the rural peasantry had been: the mill-tower rose larger than the church steeple. Although there were religious responses to the new industrial age, such as Methodism, the long term movement was away from religion. Partly in material consumption men found other sources of comfort and consolation, as well as other explanations of the meaning or lack of meaning of life.

d DESACRALISATION, 'DISENCHANTMENT' AND SPIRITUAL SURVIVAL
Desacralisation is the loss of the capacity to experience a sense of sacredness and mystery in life. In its way, it is quite as important as the more practical process of secularisation to which it is related.

The medieval world in which God was Creator, 'His' mother a virgin, and in which spirits, good or evil, were believed to intervene in everyday life must have been perceived in a qualitatively different way from that in which secular man sees the world today. Belief in mystery and miracle has largely gone, apart from the imaginings of children. 'Disenchantment', to use Weber's term for this, has set in. The triumph of science and reason has been at the cost of myth, fable and spiritual romanticism.

Yet there is ample evidence in the modern world that man's spirit or emotions, if that term is preferred, continue to demand a kind of satisfaction that neither science nor material prosperity can bring. This can be illustrated by the undoubted fact that religion as a *source of personal meaning and fulfilment* survives much more widely and with greater vitality than institutional religion. Interestingly, Thomas Luckman considers that the primary function of religion is to give personal meaning to life. Although few in Britain go regularly to church, the vast majority believe in 'something', even if no more than a vague force behind the universe. What is more, according to David Hay, 'well over a third of all women and just under a third of all men in Great Britain claim to have had some sort of religious experience'. To use Hay's own terms, almost half of these 'wouldn't touch the church with a bargepole'. It is worth giving a brief extract from one of the examples of 'mystical' experience cited by Hay:

> Then it happened. 'I lost all sense of time, of my own body and 'ego'; it was as if I became one with the natural world . . . for an unthought passage of time I was filled with the certainty and knowledge of the meaning of life'. Previously he'd been cynical about religion . . .

It is surely beyond the scope and means of sociology, however defined, to understand and explain such experiences, but it is essential to acknowledge them as profoundly meaningful in human terms. There is a vast amount of creative art attesting to this, including the writings of poet-mystics, such as Blake and Coleridge, and some of the music of such groups as The Grateful Dead. Controversially, some of this work has been influenced by drugs. Psychedelic drugs are sometimes considered to be a short-cut to mystical experience, but others take the view that the dangerous and usually uncontrolled nature of the experience they induce amounts, at best, to 'counterfeit infinity'.

The yearning for spiritual and emotional fulfilment beyond everyday reality is further evident in the popularity of religious sects, particularly apparent since the nineteen sixties. These have included such movements as the Jesus People, the Divine Light Mission, the Moonies and the Scientologists. Some sects have contained elements of the crackpot and the exploitative, if not the downright sinister. Nevertheless, their considerable appeal, especially to the young, indicates that they do answer a real need – however, inadequately. One organisation, the Transcendental Meditation (TM) movement, has helped to spread the practice of meditation to many individuals and groups throughout the world. TM and other quasi-religious movements have been notably popular in the United States. It is worth remarking that religion has, in any case, declined less in the United States than in most European countries. This may be because religion there has never been as formal and institutionalised as in, for intance, Britain; nor has it been as closely identified with an upper class establishment. It has been rather more a matter of personal experience and expression.

Even those countries which have adopted communist or Fascist ideologies have not entirely escaped from the shadow of religion. For instance, the virtual deification of the Chinese leader, Mao, in his own life-time was a semi-religious phenomenon. Perhaps, the same can be said of the worldwide adulation among radicals of the 'martyred' Cuban revolutionary, Che Guevara – adulation that was sometimes given on the scantiest of knowledge of his achievements and beliefs. It may be that both Mao and Che provided a focus of identity and unity that many need. If so, their role in this respect is very similar to what Durkheim described as the social function of religion.

The Structure of the Media

Before presenting the sociology of the media, it is helpful to know what it is and how it is controlled. *The media consists of printed, audio and audio-visual systems of communication.* Major examples of each are, respectively: books, newspapers and magazines; records, radios and audio-tapes; the cinema, television, and video. The broadcasting media, particularly television, has replaced the press as the major media.

The media can be roughly divided into non-commercial and commercial. The non-commercial media is almost entirely publicly operated. The commercial broadcasting media and, to some extent, the press are also subject to public regulation. There is debate about the degree of public involvement that there should be in the media. Peter Golding divides publicly regulated media into three types. Firstly, is the goverment controlled media, whose explicit function is to convey government information (propaganda). This form of media organisation is associated with modern totalitarian states, but often occurs in poorer countries in which the government is the only body capable of finding and organising a national press or broadcasting service. The second type of public mass media organisation is the semi-official statutory (established by Parliament) body. The BBC is a non-profit-making corporation which comprises a Chairman, Vice-Chairman and Governors. The Corporation is not directly responsible to a minister, but its members are, in effect, appointed by the government. The closeness or otherwise of the BBC to the government has always been a matter for dispute. The third sort of public regulating agency is concerned with allocating contracts for programmes and, unlike the BBC, only minimally with making them. The major body of this kind is the Independent Broadcasting Authority which oversees both commercial television and radio. The commercial press includes the 'quality' newspapers – the *Guardian, Times* and *Telegraph*, the 'middle-brow' *Daily Mail*, and the 'mass' circulation, *Express, Star, Sun* and *Mirror*. To these must be added many scores of magazines and journals.

Who, then, controls the mass media? For the moment, we will say no more about the BBC than that, under the Board of Governors, it is run by salaried professionals. The commercial media presents a quite different picture. The press is, in effect, run by those who can afford to buy and keep going a newspaper or magazine. 'Afford to' is an operative phrase as news-papers are often money-losers rather than money-makers. They are often *status* rather than economic investments, as the *Times* and *Sunday Times* were to Lord Thompson. The situation in respect of the commercial broadcasting media is slightly more complex. Groups or consortiums of people put in offers or *tenders* to run a local station as it becomes available, and the IBA decides who is sucessful.

Three points can be made about the commercial media. First, it *is* commercial. This means it is run for profit, even though an element of public service may also be involved. Later, we ask what effect commercial motivation has on the content of broadcasting. Secondly, is the extent to which the media in Britain is *concentrated* in a few companies. The follow-ing table, from Peter Golding, shows this very clearly. Thirdly, is the process of diversification which is characteristic of media-oriented companies. This means that they often have many other investment interests besides those in the media or are themselves part of larger companies. Thus, the Inter-national Publishing Corporation (IPC) which owns the *Daily Mirror, Sunday Mirror* and *Sunday People* is part of a larger com-pany, Reed International which has interest in wallpaper, paints, DIY products, fabrics and building products, as well as publishing.

Proportion of total market accounted for by the five leading companies in each medium, 1972

	%
National morning newspaper circulations	86
National Sunday newspaper circulations	88
Commercial television: % television homes served	73
Paperback books: % domestic production (estimate, 1971)	86
Mid-price LP records: % market	69
Cinema: % box office takings (top four circuits)	80

Source: Peter Golding, *The Mass Media*, 1974, p. 49.

Theories of Media: Control and Effects

In order to understand a topic it is often helpful to give an historical summary of research in the area. The history of research on a given area can amount to a précis of the consen-sus of knowledge about one topic. Because of the perspectives division this is sometimes less true of sociology than of the natural sciences. In the case of media-research, however, it is hardly true at all. Past and current research trends frequently have little connection with each other. This is largely because media research in the first twenty post-war years tended to ask questions that were too limited in scope. Further, the answers to many of the questions that were asked often depended on the answer to other questions that were not asked! Thus research into media effects on audiences was sometimes conducted with little regard for those that the programme makers intended to produce. In addition, the part played by the owners of the commercial media in attempting to influence audiences was seldom considered. As a result of this piecemeal approach, much of the best media research in the last ten years has been concerned to find a new, more comprehensive framework for analysis. This has meant building better models and constructing more far-reaching hypotheses about how the media operates in a wider social context.

a LIBERAL OR LAISSEZ–FAIRE PERSPECTIVE The view that, within generous legal limits, the media in capitalist democracies is free is widely held. Certainly, those commentators, such as Robert Dahl and Jean Blondel, who believe that liberal democracy 'works', consider that the media does provide access to a wide range of opinion. Perhaps because this is the dominant view in Western societies it tends to be assumed rather than proved. It is part of 'taken for granted' ideology. It has, however, been strongly criticised from Marxist perspectives. We will set aside these criticisms until later, and present only the liberal case here.

What, then, is the basis of the view that the media is 'free'? First, is the argument that freedom to set up newspapers, magazines and other publications ensures that a wide range of opinion will, in fact, be represented, even though not everybody can *afford* to establish a publication. Secondly, the principle that editors and, under them, journalists, rather than proprietors, decide the content of a newspaper is considered to be generally effective. Thirdly, the public has access to print through letters and, occasionally, through more substantial pieces. Fourthly, the broadcasting media ensures a wide and balanced expression of opinion by providing access to or, at least, fairly representing the opinions of, all major groups, including significant minorities. It will be remembered that freedom for minorities – as long as they stay within the law – is equally a principle of political liberalism. Groups that are so far beyond the social consensus that they wish to overthrow the existing order of society are less likely to have access to the media or to obtain favourable media coverage than other groups. 'Freedom within consensus' is perhaps a fair summary of the liberal view of the media. Fifthly, is the argument that the public can control the media by using its market power; it can refuse to buy or switch off and thus force the particular media enterprise to change or go out of business.

Journalists often hold a liberal or *laissez-faire* view of their own activities. In stereotype, they are tough, independent-minded people determined to 'get the facts'. The media audience appears in the liberal picture via free-market economics. Audience response is considered to have a major effect on whether a programme continues or not, and on the content of future programmes. The belief that the media is responsive to public opinion is crucial to the liberal view of the way it operates.

b MARXIST PERSPECTIVE *The strength of Marxist analysis of the media is that it puts the media in socio-economic context.* Its weakness derives from the fact that this context is so huge that it becomes difficult to prove conclusively any significant proposition made.

Marxists generally consider that the media operates in a way that helps to maintain the capitalist system. Althusser's notion of the ideological state apparatus which includes the media is not, perhaps, the best way of conceptualising the issue. After all, the state has relatively little directly to do with the running of the commercial media. The BBC would claim virtual autonomy from the government in most matters, although in France, Althusser's own country, the relationship between government and the media is closer. Herbert Marcuse, the American based Marxist cultural critic, provides a different, and perhaps more subtle, framework of analysis of the relationship between the media and the socio-economic system. He considers that the media diverts the masses away from an awareness of their *true* exploitation, just as religion did in the past. In this view, the source of this exploitation is the inequality of the work situation. Trivial but amusing entertainment, the prospect of consumer satisfaction that advertisements forever promise, dull the edge of any doubt about the social order. As Marcuse sees it, the message of the media is that all can hope to achieve material success and should strive to do so. He considers this message to be *illusory*, a form of ideological mystification. For him, cultural exploitation of this kind is as much part of the capitalist system as economic exploitation and social inequality.

Writing in similar vein Pierre Bourdieu criticises the liberal view that freedom of choice exists in media consumption. He says, in essence, that choice comes only with understanding. The majority cannot *really* choose to listen to, say, difficult programmes on philosophy or sociology, because they lack the linguistic means (or *interpretive codes* as Bourdieu calls them) to understand them. Only a minority are educated to be able to interpret this kind of material and, as long as this is so, the majority will not have access to it. Frank Parkin comments similarly on differential aesthetic or artistic appreciation. Manual labourers whose experience is of practical situations and who have little formal education may well be intellectually cut off from much worthwhile cultural achievement. It is simply not part of their experience or world view. But this should not produce contempt for working class culture. In fact, some of the most appreciative and affectionate descriptions of working class culture have come from socialists such as Richard Hoggart, Raymond Williams, (both of working class origins), and the historian, E. P. Thompson. These pen-portraits are often tinged with nostalgia, because the culture is dying along with communities that produced it. Population dispersal and the emergence of the mass media are major causes of this decline (see Chapter 10, pp. 271–6). Later we briefly look at what Marxists think might replace both working class culture and the largely commercially inspired culture of the mass media. Although Marxists, in principle, therefore, prefer non-commercial media, they are critical of how it actually works in Britain. BBC1, they say, has to compete effectively with ITV, and consequently produces a similar range of programmes. If BBC 2 is able to be more adventurous, it is before smaller and usually more privileged audiences. As well as having to live with market forces, the non-commercial media sometimes has to respond to government pressures as well. Even in Britain overt political involvement sometimes occurs. This happened in the case of the programme 'Yesterday's Men' which was radically critical of a number of politicians. Reflecting on the experience, its producer said:

> I would never try to do it again . . . Better to be safe than imaginative.

Still, it is the economic system rather than the intervention of politicians that influences the content of the media. In a comment on 'Yesterday's Men', Philip Abrams puts the point well:

> Actually 'Yesterday's Men' was something of an exception in that it evoked control through political power. The more normal constraint is economic. As Eliot concludes, the typical situation, in Britain anyway, is not that variation occurs within a context of political toleration but rather that such variation as there is 'takes place against a ground base provided by the commercial logic necessary for the economic survival of (the) organizations of cultural production'. It is after all a market society.

Two largely empirical studies, *Bad News* and *More Bad News*, must be added to the more theoretical Marxists' works referred to above, although it cannot be assumed that all those involved in the research are Marxists. Their evidence is that the media is far from unbiased and objective in its presentation of news. In particular, they found that the language used by newscasters and reporters in describing situations of industrial conflict reflected favourably on employers rather than employees. Thus initiatives of the former tended to be termed 'offers' or 'pleas', whereas those of the workers were described as 'threats' or 'demands'. A substantial body of quantified evidence of this kind suggested not conscious conspiracy, but systematic bias reflecting pre-existing attitudes.

c INTERACTIONIST PERSPECTIVE Compared with the broad views of the liberal and Marxist perspectives, interactionist analysis is less complete but more detailed. It attempts to tell us rather less about the role of media in the total social context but more of the day-to-day processes involved in the production of media material and of the variety and complexity of response to it. Three major strands of recent interactionist work in the area have been chosen for presentation. These are *the consensus-producing role of the media; the production of media material, by particularly, 'news people', and audience response.*

Interactionists have frequently illustrated the consensus-maintenance role of the media by reference to its treatment of deviance. We analysed this approach in some detail in Chapter 16. Content analysis of popular newspapers such as the *Sun* and the *News of the World* does show an extraordinarily high average of deviancy stories. These are reported against a background assumption that the majority are normal and moral, thus making the supposed abnormality of the stories' characters appear sensational and worthy of condemnation. Stanley Cohen gives a very useful ideal type model of how the process of deviancy selection, condemnation, and consensus-affirmation can occur. He titles the model, the 'signification spiral' (that is, the labelling of deviance) and it is only slightly adapted here.

The Signification Spiral

1 Identification of specific issue: eg, student political 'extremism'.

2 Identification of culprits: eg, 'subversive minority', 'lunatic fringe'.

3 Convergence: Linking of issue to other problems eg, lack of discipline and control of the young.

4 Notion of thresholds – once they are crossed, further escalation must result – 'slippery slope to anarchy'.

5 Explaining, warning and prophesying – 'Look what happened elsewhere'.

6 Call for firm steps – clamp down hard leads to the effect of reinforcing consensus.

Interactionists also link the production of media material with consensus reinforcement. They certainly see the restrictions on the freedom of journalists, broadcasters and others creatively involved in the media as much more considerable than do the more simplistic versions of the liberal model. Some of these are of a practical, organisational nature. When deadlines have to be met, it can be easier to go to an 'official' or 'accredited' spokesman, or 'expert' on a topic, rather than others who may be equally involved. The Glasgow Media Group established in their book, *'Bad News'*, that during a strike of Glasgow garbage collectors it was Council representatives rather than the strikers who appeared in the media, though political bias as well as organisational convenience must be considered as a factor in explaining this. At the most mundane level, a politician who has the sense to give a speech in time for the main editions will be likely to get more coverage than one who does not – even though his speech may not be 'worth' more reportage space.

We now discuss the third point, audience response to the media. From what has already been said, it will be clear that many interactionists share with Marxists the view that the media tends to produce consensus and conformity. But they also observe that a genuine *interaction* between individuals and the media can, and often does, take place. We examined this in the context of youth culture, when we saw that members of youth groups sometimes borrow and adapt styles of dress and behaviour that they see on the media. Equally, the reverse sometimes happens. The folk and rock musical revival of the nineteen sixties began at the grass roots before it happened on the media. It should be noticed that these points are further examined in the next section which reviews a wide, but not easily categorised, range of media research.

d SOME EMPIRICAL WORK ON MEDIA EFFECTS Much quantitative work on media effects is fragmentary, lacking in adequate theoretical conceptualisation, and contradicting other similar research. The following is a brief attempt to summarise the more interesting issues raised by this body of empirical work and its more coherent findings.

A repeated finding is that the media *reinforces* already existing attitudes and patterns of behaviour rather than causes entirely new ones to be formed. Work by Klapper and by Winnick established that audiences tend to *select* programmes or parts of programmes that confirm their established preferences. Thus Winnick showed a film about drugs, 'The Man with the Golden Arm', to a group divided between those who favoured drug-taking and those who did not. Both groups tended to find that the film confirmed their existing views. A further aspect in selection is the role of *reference group*. Few programmes attract a blanket audience. Age, sex and class are factors that affect selection. The media rarely seems to uproot the effects of primary socialisation by family and peer group but is itself 'mediated' by these agencies and the social context of which they are a part.

Work by Dr William Belson, by H. J. Eysenck and D. K. Nias largely contradicts the above findings on the specific question of the effect of violence on the media (Eysenck and Nias also examine the effect of sex on the media). Belson compared the behaviour and viewing habits of 1565 London boys aged between 13 and 16, between 1959 and 1971. Markedly less violence was admitted by those who watched less television. Of those who had watched a lot of violence on television, 7.5% confessed to having engaged in serious violence themselves. Belson's findings clearly need to be taken seriously, but they are certainly open to criticism. It cannot be proved that watching more violence on television was the factor that 'caused' more violence. Other variables may have been operative. Watching a lot of television is itself associated with lower socio-economic status. Perhaps it is some other factor or factors associated with lower class culture that produces violent behaviour. It is almost impossible to separate the effect of television from other variables affecting behaviour.

Eysenck and Nias, in their own laboratory research into violence and the media, attempt to isolate the effect of violent films on behaviour from that of other factors. Groups – both adult and children – exposed to televised violence consistently behave more aggressively than control groups. If – and they do not show this – these effects were duplicated in real life then they would have proved their case. But before rushing to conclusions, it is prudent to mention some critical comments on Eysenck and Nias' work. As Anthony Smith points out, comparative cultural data complicates the apparently simple truth of their findings. Japan, for example, has a very substantial degree of violence in its television, but a very low level of social violence. It seems that the Japanese emphasise the suffering caused by violence, rather than the aggression that caused it. This observation leads Smith on to a wider point. He suggests, in effect, that society gets the media it deserves. A violent society will tend to produce violence on the media – no doubt many will even *want* violence on the media. Though Smith does not say this, he seems to imply that what first needs reducing is real violence, then, perhaps, people will want less violent make-believe. This is not at all the conclusion of Eysenck and Nias, who ask for a degree of censorship of media violence and pornography. In so doing, they have the support of the National Viewers' and Listeners' Association, the 'brainchild' of Mrs Mary Whitehouse. Liberals and radicals alike tend to resist this. If entertainment, even art, can be censored today, who knows how far censorship may go tomorrow? The issue is important enough in itself but, for our more immediate academic purposes, it is worth noting how social scientific research can easily become a part of political and social policy debate. So much for the ivory tower!

e MEDIA: CONTROL AND EFFECTS: SUMMARY There is agreement among liberals, Marxists and interactionists that the media must be seen in the context of the rest of society. To varying degrees it is also accepted that the media tends to reflect and uphold the *status quo*. Marxists see the *status quo* as an exploitative capitalist one, whereas liberals consider that both majority consensus opinion, and a considerable range of minority opinion is expressed on the media. The range of views expressed helps to form and change opinion. Marxists see commercial control of much of the media as an illustration of ruling class power, whereas liberals regard it as essential to the preservation of a free media. Interactionists also stress that the media tend to reinforce consensus, but are less specific about which group or groups consensus benefits. Much interactionist and straight empirical work illustrates the active role of audiences in selecting from the media. Selection seems to reinforce existing attitudes and preferences which further suggests that the key to understanding media lies in analysing its relationship to the social system as a whole.

Culture: Society and the Individual

The purpose of this section is to engage in a little, tentative 'futurology'. We try to imagine what sort of society Britain might become, seen first through liberal, and then through Marxist eyes.

The view that many liberals share of the future can be easily grasped and fairly stated. After all, Britain and the United States are liberal societies now. The future is conceived in terms of continuity and evolution, not radical change. Writing of liberal societies in general, Edward Shils argues that the life of the mass of the people has already improved compared to the past. He has no time for historical sentimentality:

> The proletariat of these past societies, except for a few skilled occupations with elaborate traditions of their own, were a poor, besotted lot; the peasantry were clods, sometimes woodenly pious, sometimes simply woodenly dull.

Things have got better, but Shils is moderate in his claims:

> A significant proportion of the population in every society lives in a fairly vegetative routine, withdrawn and unresponsive except for occasional patches of harsh aggressive expansiveness. In the mass society of the present century, the proportion seems smaller, the period of sensitivity in the individual's course of life longer.

Other liberals are more positive than Shils. The welfare state has improved the material side of life, provided free education, and raised the general level of culture. Equality is regarded as neither practical nor desirable but these improvements can be built upon providing that the economy produces the wealth to pay for them. Further progress must occur only within a framework of authority and order. Change must not be allowed to jeopardise civil and political liberties as it did in inter-war Germany. The spectre of totalitarianism has tempered liberal reforming idealism to the point where liberal ideology has become tinged with conservatism.

In contrast to the qualified and cautious idealism of liberalism, Marxism is unashamedly an ideology of liberation. Communist society requires a 'new man'. We have already met, in the work of Abraham Maslow, the idea that it is only when man's basic material and psychological needs are assured that self-actualisation can occur. The social dimension of this is that a society which provides this fundamental security for all will have a framework for cultural advance. Marxism goes further. It *insists* that capitalism cannot provide a framework for the full expression and development of human potential because it treats human beings; as commodities (in the 'free' market) and alienates them from the product of their work (through wage-labour). Only when collective ownership of the means of production is established and when the product of labour is shared more fairly will men identify with work and gain the confidence and self-respect to develop their potential. Until greater equality and fairness exist, conflict, not community, will characterise our culture. But if collectivisation simply means that the state takes over the operation of industry from capitalism, then little will change in the day-to-day life of ordinary people. In comparison with liberal capitalist societies, they may gain a little materially and lose some freedoms. Socialism without democracy is simply another form of tyranny. So what is the necessary democratic element needed in order for a democratic socialist society and culture to flourish? Democracy involves the individual having the power to participate meaningfully in the decisions and processes that affect his or her life, whether at work, in the family, at school, in respect of the media, and otherwise. That might seem to some to be almost too much democracy . . . But let us hold criticism of this view for a moment and explore it further. To those Marxists, socialists and others who favour a more participatory society, the alternative seems to be more alienation. To have no more power at work than to be hired or fired, for a woman always to have to see 'her man as boss', for pupils always 'to have to be told what to do', for the so-called 'masses' to sit passively 'watching the box' – rarely even stirring to change channels – is repressive. These situations prevent the development of intelligence and personality. Only through participation can these qualities develop more fully. Participation is, then, a learning process but it must be based on a reality (people learn better in 'real' situations), a reality in which power is *genuinely* shared. Men and women must have more involvement in work than that of expendable wage-labourers (here today, gone tomorrow, but the computer goes on the same). Women must no longer be dominated by men. That requires economic equality between the sexes. For children, it is slightly different. They are not fully mature and need adult protection and guidance. But within a secure framework they can learn better by *doing* than by being told what to do. Further the media should be more accessible to the people and localities it is supposed to serve.

It is, of course, easy to outline blueprints. To make the, perhaps unavoidably, large-scale institutions of advanced society more democratic requires great imagination and effort. It requires the imagination to envisage how it can be done, and the effort to do it. Some Marxists, probably a small minority, say it requires violent revolution. The vast majority of Marxists and many other socialists and radicals disagree and settle for change by means of 'the long, slow march through the institutions'. The best way to change people's minds is not, after all, to chop off their heads! Open-minded debate and persuasion is the alternative course. The fact that the organs of opinion are generally on the side of the *status quo* makes the task difficult but, perhaps, not impossible. Further, the nature and outcome of ideological clash is greatly influenced by the economic and social context in which it takes place and to which it must be addressed.

It is not a purpose of this book fully to explain Marxist policy except in so far as Marxism, as well as being a sociological perspective, is also a political belief. Marxism remains the major ideological carrier of ideas about a possible alternative or 'new' culture and society. We have touched on this already in many contexts including the family, work, and stratification. Here we provide a final illustration of the link between Marxist sociology and politics by reference to the work on broadcasting of Raymond Williams. He starts from the belief:

> that men should grow in capacity and power to direct their own
> lives – by creating democratic institutions, by bringing new
> sources of energy to human work, and by extending the
> expression and exchange of experience on which understanding
> depends.

These values guide his suggestions for change. He argues that the commercial media and, in his view, the too centralised and paternalistic BBC, should be dismantled. Instead, four or five independent, publicly funded, regionally dispersed corporations should be set up. *Publicly representative* intermediate bodies with powers to grant money to make programmes should be established. Groups and individuals who want to produce programmes should within the limits of scarcity, be given the means to do so. Williams is aware that allocation of resources must not be used as a form of control:

> it is of the nature of democratic culture that it keeps the
> channels of growth clear. It is a public duty to see that
> individuals or groups offering new kinds of work are given at
> least a fair chance.

In any case, he says, there should be no ban on people raising their own resources to make programmes. Now, these suggestions, even in the much fuller form they are given in Williams' book *Communications,* do not amount to a complete blueprint for a democratic socialist media. But they perhaps show that such a thing is possible.

Guide to Further Reading and Study

John Berger's *Ways of Seeing* (Penguin, 1973) could provide a 'different' start to the study of culture, challenging as it does taken-for-granted perspectives and assumptions. Raymond Williams' *Culture* (Penguin, 1981) has obvious relevance to the themes of this chapter but many will find the final chapter of his classic *Culture and Society* (Penguin, 1961) more accessible. No easy read either, is the Centre for Cultural Study's *Ideology* (Hutchinson, 1978). The CCC's *Culture, Media and Language* (Hutchinson, 1980) is a livelier more empirically grounded collection of papers. A wide selection of readings on religion and belief is provided in Kenneth Thompson and Jeremy Tunstall *eds, Sociological Perspective* (Penguin, 1976). The process of secularisation is reviewed in P. Glasner's *The Sociology of Secularisation* (Routledge and Kegan Paul, 1977). A basic 'A' level text on the media is David Glover's *The Sociology of The Mass Media* (Causeway Press, 1984). J. Fiske and J. Hartley's *Reading Television* (Methuen, 1978) is inexpensive and covers a wide range of issues. Len Masterman's *Teaching About Television* (Macmillan, 1980) is aimed mainly at teachers of under-sixteen-year-olds, but the introduction provides a useful discussion of the ideological content of television, and how to present and stimulate analysis of this in the classroom. Of the various and influential publications of the Glasgow Media Group, *Really Bad News* (Writers and Readers, 1982) is the cheapest and most recent. Martin Harrison *TV News: Whose Bias?* (Policy Journals, 1985) is a critique of the work of the Glasgow Media Group. Jeremy Tunstall's *The Media are American: Anglo-American Media and the World* (Constable, 1977) gives the important global perspective. Geoffrey Barlow and Alison Hill *eds, Video Violence and Children* (Hodder and Stoughton, 1985) explore a sensitive issue about which much more will no doubt be written. H. J. Eysenck and D. K. B. Nias *Sex, Violence and the Media* (M. T. Smith, 1978) pursues a similar theme.

Past Questions

1 'Western industrial societies are undergoing a process of secularisation.' Explain and discuss. (AEB, 1983)

2 'The decline of organised religion has been accompanied by the growth of "alternative" religions.' Discuss. (OLE, 1985)

3 Discuss the relationship between ownership, control and production in the mass media. (AEB, 1977)

4 'Reporting "news" is inevitably partial, selective and biased.' Discuss, with reference to the reporting by the media of areas such as industrial relations, race relations, deviance and political issues. (AEB, 1982)

Section F Sociology, Knowledge and Social Policy

How to Use this Section

The main purpose of Chapter 21 is to extend the introduction to theory and method begun in Chapters 1 and 2. We discuss what kind of discipline sociology is and critically review the major sociological perspectives. Chapter 21 also contains an essay on the sociology of knowledge. Sociology cannot adjudicate between various claims to knowledge and truth but it can establish the social factors that influence particular systems of knowledge and ideology – this is quite large enough a task! The reader is referred elsewhere in the book for applied examples of the sociology of knowledge. Implicit especially in Chapters 21 and 22, but throughout this book, is the question 'by what right does sociology make its pronouncements' on systems of knowledge and ideology or whatever? The brief answer is that it is bound by the rules of (social) scientific enquiry and of the humanities which illuminate social causation and meaning (a rather longer answer is given in the text!).

Chapter 22 links the sociology of knowledge to what we *do* about social problems (social policy). As there is no firm agreement about the nature and relative importance of social problems, it is necessary to discuss them in terms of various sociological theories – mainly within the three major perspectives. Despite their differences, these theoretical approaches do help us to see why certain interest groups perceive and define problems in a given way, and each draws on the methodology of the sociology of knowledge and particularly the concepts of relativity and subjectivity. Sometimes, of course, there may be wide agreement about a particular 'problem', such as murder. The second part of

Chapter 22 changes direction and discusses the ways in which various political groups have tried or would like to try to deal with 'social problems'. Their policies are presented as political ideologies, i.e. as subjective viewpoints and solutions. This central perspective on policy as 'applied' ideology – a practical commitment to achieving a particular outcome or vision – is maintained through Chapters 23 and 24 which deal with health and education policy, mainly in the British context. However, both chapters also contain sections which examine the social construction of health and educational 'knowledge' in broader terms.

21 Sociology and Knowledge

Is Sociology a Science?

We have already examined this question in the first two chapters of this book, and before adding further comment we will summarise what was said there. If science is defined broadly as the accumulation of verifiable knowledge, then sociology is a science. If it is defined narrowly as the testing of hypotheses by positivistic methodology, then sociology can hardly claim to be a science. (See Chapter 1, pp. 24-31). Such a definition would also exclude much observational work in other disciplines. It is true, however, that sociology rarely produces results that are as precise and repeatable as those produced by the natural sciences. Nevertheless, Durkheim, Marx and Weber never stopped trying to be as scientific as possible and their work laid a rich theoretical and methodological basis for the further development of the discipline along scientific lines. More recently, the complex and rigorous empirical research of professional sociologists, such as John Goldthorpe and A. H. Halsey, goes far beyond the competence and commonsense understanding of the layman in its methodological basis and findings.

In contrast to self-consciously scientific approaches to sociology, interpretive sociology is often less concerned with causal explanation or factual description than with human understanding. Perhaps such work is closer to the humanities than to sciences. This does not make it *un*scientific but, perhaps, it is essentially *non-scientific. Unlike functionalists and many Marxists, interpretive sociologists have often shown no great desire to have their work classified as scientific.* C. Wright Mills, a sociologist who does not admit to a simple label himself, refers disparagingly to the 'cook-book' appearance of some scientifically oriented sociological text-books. Erving Goffman compares traditional positivist methodology to the instructions on a child's chemistry set: 'follow the rules and you, too, can be a real scientist'.

Interpretive sociologists willingly embrace what embarrasses the positivists: the subjective element in society and in sociological research. Subjectivity cuts two ways. Firstly, the researchers have their values: secondly, those being studied behave individually and therefore in a way that cannot be precisely predicted. Ethnomethodologists, such as Cicourel and Garfinkel, claim that it is impossible for sociologists to be passive observers of 'truth'. What they 'see' is bound, in some sense, to be the result of the interaction between themselves and what they study. Yet ethnomethodologists *also* claim to be in the business of discovering and describing how people act and interact. Given their emphasis upon the subjective element in perception, how can they be confident of the accuracy of their own observations and reports? The answer seems to be that they, at least, are aware of the problem and so better able to deal with it than positivists, who may naïvely believe that they can 'phase themselves out' of their work. On the matter of the individuality of the subject of social research, Schutz, the phenomenologist, is relevant, and goes further than the ethnomethodologists. He points out that, whereas the natural sciences have concepts about objects, the social sciences have concepts about objects which have concepts about objects (including, perhaps, the researcher himself). In other words, people can think and, we must add, choose. They may even decide deliberately to mislead the researcher. Because of this, the level of accurate prediction in the social sciences can never be as high as in the natural sciences. Schutz, however, also points out that groups of people share common patterns of thought and behaviour, and that the researcher is able to check his descriptions of these with those of other observers. If there is agreement about what is observed, this, perhaps, is as close to achieving objectivity as is possible.

So much for what sociologists themselves think about the nature of their discipline. We now examine the opinions of two major philosophers of science upon the same issue (a philosopher of science is somebody who systematically attempts to clarify the principles underlying science). On the whole, these commentators from outside sociology have tended to take a reproving tone. Karl Popper's particular 'bogey man' is Marx. It is, however, Marx 'the prophet of revolution' that Popper admonishes – not Marx the sociologist – although, in fairness, Popper's argument is that the two are inseparable. He says that in 'prophesying' proletarian revolution, Marx is essentially unscientific in taking as given something that has not yet happened. In Popper's view, 'prophecy', religion and ideology have no place in science and, therefore, he declares Marxism to be unscientific. We do not have to accept Popper's conclusion to agree that Marxists' sociological theory and concepts must be open to the same criticism and testing as those of other perspectives. The fact that a Marxist sociologist is likely to be politically Marxist does not free him from the constraints of the discipline. No sensible Marxist sociologist would want the kind of illusory freedom in which mere assertion replaces argument based on reason and evidence. It is Popper's soundest and central point that social science, like natural science, must

591

constantly test and re-test its theories. The most rigorous way to do this is for the researcher to attempt to *falsify*, rather than verify, his or her own hypothesis – Popper's famous principle of falsification. He argues that Marxism cannot be scientific because many of its major theories refer to the future and are not, therefore, open to falsification. It is impossible to prove definitely that there will not be a proletarian revolution because the future is unknown. Such a statement is, therefore, unscientific. In their own defence, many modern Marxists would argue that their immediate concern is less with proving or falsifying propositions than with providing a theoretical critique of capitalist society and with developing theoretical alternatives to it. Most of them would also dissociate themselves from the supposed prophetic element in Marx's writing and, to that extent, Popper's criticisms become redundant.

A further point made by Popper is of particular interest to sociologists. It is that no hypothesis can be considered finally proven. For example, although thousands of white swans have been sighted, there remains the possibility of coming across a black one. Similarly, to do the same experiment 999 times with the same result may *seem* to prove something, but the thousandth experiment *may* produce a different result. The practice of science involves a sort of industrious scepticism and Popper would frankly like to see more evidence of it among social scientists. More research and less theorising seems to be his advice. In view of how difficult it can be to 'set up' sociological research, this is perhaps not an encouraging view.

Ernest Gellner is a recent writer in the tradition of Popper. His particular objection is Garfinkel's ethnomethodology. He condemns its obsession with subjectivism as mere romanticism and, like Popper, he advocates a staunchly empirical approach to the understanding of society. Although the Marxist, Barry Hindess, has little else in common with Popper and Gellner, he also attacks extreme ethnomethodological subjectivism in his critique of statistics (Chapter 18, pp. 513–14).

There is much commonsense – if this is not too odd a word to use of such sophisticated work – in the thought of Popper and Gellner. Theoretical cloud castles in the sky must be brought to earth and examined for substance and content, a comment that applies to functionalism as much as to Marxism. Similarly, those who are so 'hung up' on subjectivism that they allow little hope of meaningful sociological discourse hardly help to further the development of the discipline as a collective enterprise. (For a further discussion of this point, see later in this chapter, p. 610).

Until now, we have tended to regard science as a standard by which to take the measure of social science. Apart from a simple distinction between a broad and narrow definition of science, we have assumed the concept of science itself to be unproblematic. In so doing, we are in danger of giving it the status of a sort of sacred cow, divine and inscrutable. The work of Thomas Kuhn, however, attempts to 'debunk' such a reverential view of science and to ask not only how true it is to its own professed principles of empiricism and objectivity, but also whether these principles are the ones by which the natural sciences actually operate. Subjectivity may be a spectre that haunts science as well as social science.

What is Science?

Kuhn dismisses the notion that science is merely a collection of theories, methods and factual findings. Instead, he suggests the view that scientists, like sociologists, make use of *paradigms* or perspectives about their specialist fields which influence the *direction* and *nature* of their experimental research. Thus, Einstein's theories can be said to have provided the basis of a new working paradigm for astro-physics. Many of his ideas were speculative, partial and unproven, but they have since *inspired* more detailed research into problems concerning space and time. To this extent, Einstein's thought seems to provide much the same function as a sociological perspective.

A central feature of Kuhn's argument is that scientific paradigms change radically at given periods in history. Thus, his book is entitled *The Structure of Scientific Revolutions*. This revolutionary change occurs when a discovery cannot be made to fit into the dominant paradigm. We need an example here. For centuries, it was believed that the earth was the centre of the universe and that the sun revolved around it. This paradigm survived despite the increasing difficulty of accomodating newly discovered facts to it. Eventually, Copernicus produced evidence that overturned it. A new paradigm, that the earth revolves around the sun, became accepted.

Given paradigmatic changes and revolutions within the sci-

593

ences, similar disagreements in sociology, expressed through the perspectives, appear less crippling to the claims of the subject to respectability and even scientific status. It is true that the natural sciences generate a greater 'sense' of consensus about theoretical and methodological approach than sociology does, but it is still a young discipline and it is possible that greater 'paradigmatic unity' may yet develop.

A further criticism may be offered against the notion of science as a monument to objectivity. Science, too, is haunted by the problem of subjectivity. First, a relatively minor point. Heisenberg's *uncertainty principle* points out that the light required to observe tiny particles will affect the way they behave. Thus, to a small degree, the scientist causes the behaviour he observes! That is a classic example of the dilemma of subjectivity. Second, a serious ethical point. Scientific research, like social research, takes place *in* society. Research provides knowledge which may be used constructively or destructively. Scientists who allow their skills to be used in a cause they believe to be morally wrong are in the same position as soldiers, administrators and others who do the same. Research findings do not exist in a social vacuum – some power is likely to use them. Einstein believed passionately that scientists should take responsibility for the work they do and its possible application to human life.

What is Sociology?
By way of a long detour, we come again to this question. Sociology is the study of human social life by any means that are effective. These may be more or less scientific, depending on how that term is defined, or even non-scientific. *All that is necessary is that their application contributes to our knowledge and understanding of social life.* To do this, 'findings' must be presented sufficiently intelligibly to be communicable to the body of professional sociologists (and, ideally, via them to the interested public). C. Wright Mills is surely correct when he argues that sociology is better practised with imagination and flexibility than with rigid adherence to the models of natural science. *Sociology is a craft to be judged by its product: what works best is best.* Whilst not rejecting the broadly scientific basis of sociology, Nisbet caps Mills in stressing the role of the creative imagination in sociology. This, he says, gives it the quality of an art

form. Nisbet's observation brings the wheel full circle: *sociology is both science and art.* Given the complexity of its subject matter, it needs to be.

The Sociology of Knowledge

We said in the first chapter that there can be sociology of everything. Perhaps this statement receives its most demanding application in respect of the sociology of knowledge. Actually, the matter is much simpler than the phrase 'sociology of knowledge' might suggest. This branch of sociology seeks to study the influence of social context on ideas and beliefs. *Why* is it that people become, say, Communists, Catholics or Muslims?

Although the emphasis of the sociology of knowledge is on the ideas and beliefs of groups, it is helpful to begin our explanation of it by reference to the individual. The concept of individual socialisation is a particularly useful starting point. We saw in Chapter 3 that the norms, values and beliefs of a person are greatly influenced by the childhood socialisation she receives. What a child comes to *know* is largely the product of the particular society she is born into. A child brought up in a strongly Muslim culture will have a Muslim outlook, and one brought up in a communist culture will perceive life from a communist point of view. Yet both are likely to insist that *their* way of seeing things, their 'knowledge', is closer to 'the truth' than that of others. The sociologist of knowledge will not take sides in this dispute. His purpose is to establish why people come to believe what they do believe.

It is a simple matter to make the transition from the analysis of the social basis of individual knowledge to that of group knowledge. The same process of socialisation is at work in helping to create the outlook of groups as of individuals. *Educational systems, the culture of the workplace and the media all generate or reinforce values, beliefs and normative attitudes which contribute to the general stock of assumptions or knowledge, as we are calling it, of given societies or groups.* Thus, we would expect the media in communist societies to present a different view of the world from that in liberal Western societies, both in its selection of facts and in its processing and treatment of them. The way 'the world' is presented will obviously affect the consciousness of the receiving audience (though this does not imply that people cannot and do not resist the influences and interpretations that may be dominant within their national media).

Two concepts are especially important in the methodological armoury of the sociologist of knowledge: *relativity* and *ideology*. *In order to establish the social influences on cultural knowledge, the sociologist must proceed on the assumption that such knowledge is relative, not absolute. Relative* means, therefore, that the knowledge of, say, a Christian, Hindu, or whoever, owes something to the social context in which the beliefs developed. It is the sociologist's business to explore this connection. Thus, as we have seen, Weber explianed the growth of Calvinism in terms of its 'fit', or compatibility, with capitalism. To overstate the case slightly, people believed in Calvinism at least partly because it suited their economic interests to do so, whether they realised this or not. Now such a proposition may seem directly at variance with the claim of Calvinists that their beliefs represented the will of God. If we generalise the point to the effect that *all* religions or other systems of belief are, in part, socially (including economically) rooted, the potential for conflict between the sociology of knowledge and such religions appears to be very great. This should not be so, however. Sociologists may observe, with Pascal, that truth on one side of the Pyrenees is falsehood on the other, but they are not competent to deliver a final verdict on competing claims. They should not play God nor, *as sociologists*, should they deny God, (though their personal beliefs are, of course, their own business). They are concerned with the much more humble and limited task of *tracing the social links between systems of knowledge and the societies in which they develop.*

The second concept referred to above, that of ideology, has already been frequently used in this book and requires only brief reference here. The term refers to *ideas* and carries the particular implication that *the ideas people hold serve the purpose of justifying their own interests, even though they clothe them in the language of idealism.* The specific use of the concept in the sociology of knowledge will become apparent shortly.

So far, we have demonstrated that systems of knowledge do, indeed, differ and we have also shown how they are introduced (through socialisation and communication). We have not yet clearly stated what the social functions of knowledge systems are. We can do this best by referring to various perspectives on the sociology of knowledge: the functionalist, Marxist, Mannheimian, and the phenomenological. Again, despite the vocabulary, it is all much simpler than it sounds.

Curiously, *functionalist* contributions to the sociology of knowledge are seldom referred to. Yet it is in this area that Durkheim's insight was perhaps at its greatest. He dismissed from consideration the claims to objective truth of competing religions and argued that *the major function of all religions is to integrate people into particular societies by creating moral consensus.* For him, this is the hidden or *latent* purpose of the passion, commitment and intolerance that often accompany religion itself, or any other powerful system of belief. The disbeliever in the creed, whether political or religious, is seen as a potential threat to social solidarity. It is for this reason, no doubt, that nonconformity is so harshly treated in totalitarian communist and fascist societies. Durkheim particularly stresses the importance of the educational system as a purveyor of knowledge (in the sense of moral values and attitudes as well as facts and skills). He perhaps overestimated the value of teaching conformity at the expense of the development of an independent and critical outlook.

In *Marx's* writings, the sociology of knowledge is subsumed into his concept of ideology. In turn, his use of ideology is firmly located in his class analysis of society. This contrasts with the funcionalist emphasis on the general belief system of a given society. Dominant classes produce ideologies – which they may or may not believe themselves – which justify or obscure their domination and mislead the exploited classes. Put into different words, dominant ideology legitimates the position of the ruling class. Marx argued that, in any age, the ruling ideas are the ideas of the ruling class. Thus, in a capitalist society, capitalist ideas prevail. We have studied many applications of Marxist approaches, particularly in the context of politics, religion, the media and education (see, especially, the contribution of Marcuse, Chapter 20, pp. 575–6 and Bourdieu, Chapter 5, pp. 97–101). Marx argued that only one form of knowledge is scientific, as opposed to ideological: the theory of *scientific socialism.* *As a materialist, however, he insisted that its truth could become apparent solely through practical application and the eventual creation of a classless society in which self-interested ideology would be unnecessary.*

Karl Mannheim, in his influential work, *Ideology and Utopia,* extended Marx's analysis of ideological knowledge to Marxism itself, and to other revolutionary traditions. For him, there was no escape for Marxism from relativism into 'scientific objectivity'. The Marxist 'utopia' was no different in kind and no more historically inevitable than any other dream of the future. *Mannheim, however, did distinguish between bodies of ideas that support the status quo, which he called ideologies, and those that seek to change it, which he termed utopias.* He included Marxism among the latter. Both ideologies and utopias reflect historical circumstances. Thus, Marxism itself was generated by the realities of capitalist industrial society. Mannheim also related intellectuals' ideas to the social climate. Rather like Kuhn, he considered that the direction of development of knowledge in the natural sciences and mathematics, as well as other academic areas, was subject to social influence, although he did consider their content to be more objective. Less controversially, he pointed to the self-interested basis of much professional ideology (an issue we have discussed in some detail in Chapter 6). Yet Mannheim allowed that intellectuals have a greater range of awareness than others and thus are in a favourable position to develop alternative ideologies or utopias. This idea was adopted by C. Wright Mills in the nineteen fifties, who argued that intellectuals and students, not the proletariat, offered the best hope for change.

All the sociologists referred to above recognise that the religions, ideologies and subject disciplines that form men's minds and shape their knowledge are also created by men. Their emphasis, however, is on the former, rather than the latter, aspect. *Phenomenologists,* likewise, recognise both the socially formative and humanly created aspects of knowledge, but they begin their analysis with the latter. Arguably, the key emphasis in the title of Berger and Luckman's book, *The Social Construction of Reality: A Treatise on the Sociology of Knowledge* is on the 'construction'. *As far as they are concerned, all social reality, including knowledge, begins with subjective experience of it. Knowledge is not something that exists 'out there' that 'happens to' people.* The major means by which people communicate is language. In the last chapter, we saw that interactionists, with whom phenomenologists have much in common, stress the flexibility and developmental potential of language and, consequently, of knowledge. The exchange and development of knowledge occurs as much, indeed more, in everyday communication than in academic environments. Berger and Luckman stress that it is the understanding of everyday life that is the major focus of sociology: virtually all spheres of human life involve the communication of information, attitudes or values and, in that sense, the sociology of knowledge is an aspect of all sociology.

We conclude by returning to the problem of relativity and knowledge. Perhaps it is not quite so clear cut as we indicated above. There are two contrasting traditions within sociology which claim to be able to achieve rather more than to lay bare the relative aspects of knowledge. The first is the *positivist tradition*. Although positivism is based on the principle of relativity, it aspires to such a definitive statement on the nature of knowledge that it can be regarded as a distinct theory of knowledge. Going back to Comte, this tradition contends that scientific knowledge is 'truer' than theological (religious) or metaphysical (idealistic in the sense of purely philosophical) knowledge and will, indeed, replace them. Comte argued that scientific or 'positive' sociology would eventually provide a complete explanation of human existence. Ironically, this was to claim the sort of absolute status for positivistic sociological knowledge that he denied to religion and philosophy, although it is doubtful if he was aware of this paradox. Durkheim also believed that although primitive societies were characterised by myth, legend and religion, modern society might achieve a truer understanding of social reality through scientific sociology. As we have seen, this belief is also present in Marx's thought. The two, however, did not agree about the nature of the 'reality' they perceived. *'Scientific' sociology, like traditional religion, has become pluralistic* – it offers no one version of the truth and can hardly, therefore, claim to be the key to it. Further, apart from the disagreements among positivists, there remains the possibility that there are other kinds of knowledge about social life than that based on the analysis of cause and effect, the fundamental principle of positivism. Berger's analysis of 'meaning' is one such example, and we give another below.

The second tradition within sociology that aspires to offer something approaching a comprehensive account of the basis of knowledge is the critical sociology of *the Frankfurt school of Marxists* (although Marx is only one, and perhaps not the greatest, influence on them). The best known critical theorist is Jurgen

Habermas (1929–). In his work, *Knowledge and Human Interests*, Habermas has argued that there are three forms of knowledge, the *empirical-analytic* (positivist), the *historical-hermeneutic* (interpretist), and *self-reflection* (a form of philosophical knowledge). In other words, Habermas accepts that the two forms of knowledge studied, respectively, by scientific and interpretive sociology are both valid but, interestingly, he adds a third. We can discern two elements in self-reflection, or critical, knowledge. Firstly, man uses his unique attribute of self-consciousness to examine critically his own social life. Unlike positivistic or interpretist knowledge, this involves consciously going beyond what is actually 'there' in external social reality by commenting critically upon it. Secondly, *Habermas suggests that there actually is an 'ideal' or objective standard by which we can criticise social reality – otherwise, what would the meaning be of such words as 'exploitation' or 'cruelty'? The basis of this standard of objective criticism is man's awareness of truth and this comes from within himself, not from society.* Truth involves saying what we 'really' mean and expressing what we 'really' feel. Societies often *repress* (a key concept in critical theory) our freedom to do this by making us afraid of the consequences (a form of control), Habermas wants to move towards a freer and more truthful society. But can we accept his 'objective' criteria for truth and freedom? They are remarkably attractive. We must extend to them, however, the same scepticism that the sociology of knowledge applies to all religion and social philosophies whilst recognising that, at some higher idealistic, or even human, level, Habermas may be right.

Does this sociological scepticism mean that there is *no* reality out there', or merely that, for some reason, people disagree about what it is? Karl Mannheim offers a helpful, if limited, suggestion on this matter. It is that *people's different perspectives on society (or on anything else, for that matter) are often complementary in nature. They can be used together to build up a fuller, more precise version of the object of study (in our case, society).* This comment has particular application to contemporary sociology, given its fragmented state. Of course, there is no guarantee that a more *unified sociological paradigm* – perhaps based on an integrated and developed structural-phenomenology – will more closely reflect 'social reality' than do any of the present perspectives. But perhaps the time is ripe for sociologists to make this constructive effort. The insights of phenomenology should be used to enrich sociology, not to destroy it. Admittedly, a collective enterprise of this kind would be painful and would involve laying to rest numerous sociological fables and exorcising not a few sociological ghosts. (Three 'worked examples' of the sociology of knowledge are given later in this section: the sociology of social problems, pp. 627–45, the sociology of health knowledge, pp. 671–9, and the sociology of educational knowledge, pp. 719–21.)

Is a Unified Sociological Paradigm Possible?

Limited Perspectives?

Sometimes students express impatience with 'the perspectives approach' to sociology. Their impatience is based not only on the growing number and complexity of the perspectives themselves but also on the feeling that there ought, after all, to be more agreement on the nature of social life and how to study it. Reflecting on the disagreements among sociologists, a distinguished non-sociologist once remarked sardonically that sociology is a sub-committee set up by philosophers which has not reported back yet. I have some sympathy with the sentiment behind this jibe. As I have been writing this book, the sense has increasingly grown on me that there is an element of shadow-boxing about many of the sociological fisticuffs I have described, and that there is a much greater measure of potential agreement amongst sociologists than they have yet learnt to admit. Here, in a creative spirit, I want to suggest some elements of common, or complementary, ground between the perspectives and, unavoidably, to indicate certain approaches which no longer seem very useful. Ironically, this means that I must relax my text book writer's attempt to hold the ring neutrally between contesting perspectives and adopt for myself the sharper weapons of commitment.

Concern that sociological theory has become excessively fragmented has been widely expressed by sociologists themselves in recent years, despite a passive and often uncritical acceptance of 'the perspectives approach' within teaching circles. The functionalist, Ronald Fletcher, has been forthright in attacking this approach to teaching sociology: indeed, he refers to it as an 'entirely fallacious orientation' that is 'being imposed on each new generation'. He believes that there are certain fundamental principles accepted by the founding fathers which provide a sound basis for the study of society and, presumably, that the elucidation of these principles is what the teaching of sociology should be about. We will return to this shortly.

The radical, Anthony Giddens, likewise refuses to accept that the discipline of sociology is no more than a collection of differing perspectives. He explains the current 'seemingly disoriented situation of social theory' in terms of the post-war breakdown of the consensus around functionalism. He discerns three tendencies within sociology which have emerged during the 'post-consensus' period. First is the *perspectives approach* itself: an enthusiastic, 'Let the thousand flowers bloom' attitude to the subject. Second is a return to a would-be 'purely empirical' orientation to sociology which dismisses, or disregards, larger issues of theory in favour of *'getting on with research'*. Third is *a reversion to rigid orthodoxy*. Giddens has in mind crude Marxism, but crude functionalism represents the same search for simple certainty. Actually, Giddens' list is hardly exhaustive, and his selection of current trends a little pessimistic. As he is aware, other tendencies, including ethnomethodology and less crude varieties of Marxism, have emerged besides those he mentions. I agree, however, with his statement that 'social theory stands in need of systematic reconstruction'. We will now look at the various sociological perspectives with this need in mind. It should be said that what follows assumes that the major theoretical points made elsewhere in this book have been substantially absorbed by the reader.

Functionalism: How Adequate is the Organic Analogy?
In the first chapter, we introduced the functionalist comparison of society to a biological organism. In later chapters, we examined several applications of the organic analogy. The application examined in greatest detail was the way in which societies are considered to develop from the simple to the complex, just as growing bodies do. This approach stresses the evolutionary aspect of the analogy, and is apparent in the work of Durkheim and Parsons, but can be traced back to the British sociologist, Herbert Spencer (1820–1903), who was substantially influenced by Darwin's theory of biological evolution. We will consider shortly whether the concept of evolution manages to provide an adequate basis for understanding social change.

Apart from applications of the organic analogy based on

evolutionary perspective, others reflect the view that society is structured and functions like an organism. This emphasis finds its strongest expression in the writings of the British anthropologist, Radcliffe-Brown, (1881–1955), but it also partly underlies the more sophisticated social systems theory of Talcott Parsons. The basic notion here is that the various parts of society work in relation to one another (see the family-society model, Chapter 4, p. 61) and that society can best be understood by analysing these inte lations (see Parsons' social systems model, Chapter 3, pp. 47–8). Functionalists consider that just as some parts of the body are functionally more important than others so, too, must society be hierarchically arranged for functional purposes. This view is apparent in the work of Davis and Moore (Chapter 11, pp. 304–7) and Michels (Chapter 16, pp 456). Another major functionalist concept is that of social equilibrium by which society is assumed to seek balance and orderly functioning in the same way that the body does. Consensus on norms and values is considered a necessity for healthy functioning, although the analogy is rarely pursued as literally as this. Deviant behaviour, however, is often compared to physical 'pathology' by functionalists, not least by Durkheim himself.

We now turn to a critical appraisal of functionalism. *Firstly, organs do not think, whereas people do, or, to put it more technically the organic analogy contains no parallel for intentional social action. Biological processes are not achieved through the use of will, reason and imagination but invariably take place below the level of conscious awareness.* Although Talcott Parsons claimed to have developed a 'theory of social action', he has been widely and effectively criticised for failing to do so. As Giddens remarks, with some elegance, 'recognisably human agents seem to elude the grasp of his scheme: the stage is set, the scripts written, the roles established, but the performers are curiously absent from the scene'. The result of this is that functionalism presents what Dennis Wrong calls an oversocialised conceptualisation of man. We, too, made this very point in Chapter 3 and used symbolic interactionist theory to balance functionalist analysis of socialisation.

A second criticism frequently made of functionalism is, as we have seen, that *it exaggerates the role of consensus and underestimates that of conflict in the functioning of society.* It should be added that the concepts of consensus and equilibrium are linked, in that functionalists regard the former as a precondition of the latter. This emphasis on stability and order is reflected in the organic analogy itself, although functionalists stress these as much because they accord with their conservative political views, rather than in slavish imitation of the analogy. It is true that organic bodies, particularly animals, strive to maintain internal balance (partly through an often complex process of homeostasis or adaptation) but there is no proof – indeed, it is most unlikely – that societies as entities are inherently endowed with similar adjustment mechanisms. Social order and equilibrium may be maintained through the conscious action of individuals and groups, but that is a different matter. Although consensus does contribute to social order it, too, must in part be intentionally created and maintained. It certainly cannot be regarded as automatically self-regulating or perpetuating. In other words, *social equilibrium and consensus occur in a different way from organic equilibrium.* There is no adequate explanatory parallel between the organic and social fields. Again, the biological analogy breaks down in practice.

A third criticism of the organic analogy is that *it produces a misleading separation of structure (society's parts or institutions) and system (society's functioning).* In particular, it leads only to a partial conceptualisation of the problem of social change. By contrast, this division seems to work well in the natural sciences. In biology, it helps to examine the structure of a plant or animal (anatomy) and then to describe how the various parts function in relation to one another and the whole. In a limited descriptive sense, the same approach is useful in sociology although, significantly, society cannot be similarly 'laid out' anatomically for examination. In real life, society 'functions' through the more or less organised actions of individuals and groups, not in the manner of an unreflecting organism. Nor does change occur solely through evolution and adaptation, although it may to some extent. Equally important in the history and development of nations and cultures are revolutions and drastic breaks with the past. Parson's notion of dynamic equilibrium, by which social balance adjusts to accomodate new phenomena within the system, still stresses continuity at the expense of change and severance. It also woefully underestimates the role of people in making history. For him, systems change and almost 'make' people, not the other way around. (See also pp. 47–8.)

In retrospect, Robert Merton's attempts to use the concept of function to embrace a wide variety of social events looks like the death throes of a theory stretched beyond its inherent capacity. In particular, his concept of *manifest* function which he uses to describe intended, as opposed to unintended (*latent*) consequences of institutional functioning is a notably impoverished attempt to allow for the role of choice in social life. The basic problem is that it is not possible to provide an adequate account of consciously directed action within a framework that takes as its model the unconscious functioning of the organism.

A final criticism of functionalism is that it is teleological, or tautological, as Chris Brown has called it. In other words, *because functionalists see certain functions being performed by given institutions, they conclude that there must be need for these functions –* that is, they explain causes by their consequences. Actually, many institutions exist, the 'need' for which can be doubted. Inevitably, opinions will differ as to which institutions qualify: some will suggest the House of Lords, others the trade unions. Further, men create organisations and institutions not only to fulfil social needs but to pursue their own purposes and interests – sometimes at the expense of others. As far as 'needs' are concerned, beyond basics, 'one man's meat is another man's poison'.

Finally, although nobody can take exception to a descriptive account of the functions institutions perform, including those many of us may not be aware of, this is only an aspect, and a rather obvious one, of sociological analysis. *Who made things as they are, and in whose interests,* are equally important questions which functionalists tend to ignore.

The issue is not whether functionalism is an 'incorrect' perspective but whether it is the most useful and illuminating available. It is certainly helpful as a descriptive, if uncritical, account of what institutions 'do' – and, as such, it has some appeal to students. Further, the functionalist analysis of socialisation warns us, usefully, of what is 'done' to us individually in order to make us conforming members of society. Both these aspects of sociological analysis, however, are fairly obvious and well dealt with in other perspectives. Functionalism must stand or fall on the fruitfulness of its central concepts as presented in the biological analogy, or in Talcott Parsons' more recent, and, admittedly, more sophisticated systems theory. Assessed on that basis, I suggest that functionalism is an outmoded, essentially nineteenth century perspective which is likely soon to be superseded.

Criticisms of 'Crude' Marxism and the Revival of Marxist Thought

The criticisms of structural-functionalism are persuasive enough to recommend a search for an alternative sociological paradigm. Marxism comes to mind although it, too, has been the subject of serious criticisms. We need to examine these before we can assess the merits of Marxism as a convincing basis for a unified sociological paradigm. I have taken the view that Marxist sociological theory is informed by, or learns from, Marxist political practice and, therefore, I have not rigidly separated the two here. The Marxist heritage is profoundly ambiguous: Marx has left two legacies, although it is unlikely that he intended to do so. The first is based on the belief that class conflict and socialist revolution are historically inevitable, and the other is based on the view that, to achieve a social revolution, it is necessary to work for a change in the consciousness of the working class. (As they come to realise the nature of capitalist exploitation, they will surely organise to end it). It is the first of these two legacies of thought which has been the most severely criticised.

The belief that a revolution of the proletariat is inevitable on account of certain economic 'contradictions' in capitalism, has been criticised repeatedly as crudely deterministic. This means that its adherents consider that 'the future is known from the past', and, they state, certain major future events are bound to happen because of 'the laws of history'. We have examined Karl Popper's comments on this issue earlier in this chapter. Marx's application of dialectical theory to historical change is sometimes cited as an attempt to uncover such laws. The principle of the dialectic is that opposite elements (thesis and antithesis) combine to produce a synthesis (new phenomenon). The concept comes from natural science, but as applied by Marx to recent history, it means that the clash of the capitalist class with the proletariat will produce a new synthesis: the classless society. It is doubtful whether Marx intended this model to be accepted as rigidly inevitable, but if he did, it is, indeed, an example of crude determinism. Perhaps Marx has suffered as much from the ideas of some of his followers as from his critics. No wonder he once said 'I am not a Marxist'. The major refutation of determinism, which modern Marxists do generally accept, is that, *within the structural realities of their time, people make their own history and, for that reason, the future cannot be predicted.*

A second criticism of Marxism is that it is *idealistic in theory and cruel and repressive in practice.* When commentators say this they have in mind primarily the example of Soviet totalitarianism and imperialism. They argue that the Russian record of human rights and foreign policy is not attributable simply to the wickedness of the Soviets, but is a basic feature of Marxist 'dogma' itself. They contend that 'in the real world' it is not possible to combine material equality with a high level of personal freedom and expression. When the state is controlled by an unrepresentative group, it may use its power to repress not only political opposition but also to organise, control or repress a wide range of other activities, not least those of a cultural kind. Many European and American Marxists accept these criticisms, but deny that the Soviet regime represents a fair picture of Marxism. We now examine some of their ideas on the subject.

First is the trend towards *Marxist humanism.* This aspect of Marxism concentrates on the repression of human potential in capitalist society and the prospect of its release in communist society. The sources of humanism within Marx's own works are his early writings on human potential and his analysis of alienation, discussed in the last chapter. In Britain, Raymond Williams and E. P. Thompson are major representatives of Marxist humanism (see Chapter 20), and in the United States C. Wright Mills and the German exile, Herbert Marcuse (see Chapters 10 and 20 for both) achieved international influence.

At the risk of oversimplification, we include critical theory within the broad trend of Marxist humanism (see pp. 568-9 of this chapter). Critical theory, as its name suggests, raises the possibility of criticising the way things are from another point of view. Marcuse himself was a critical theorist until his death in 1979. He attacked capitalist 'reality', particularly from the point of view that it is culturally repressive – especially, although not exclusively, of the working class (see Chapter 20, pp. 374-5). Before fleeing to America from Nazi Germany, Marcuse worked at Frankfurt University, the 'home' of critical theorists. Like other philosophers and sociologists of the Frankfurt school, Marcuse was greatly influenced by Freud as well as by Marx, and effected a synthesis of the two that captured the imagination of many student radicals of the nineteen sixties. He took Freud's concept of psychological repression and applied it to capitalist society. He argued that capitalism is not interested in full human expression and development, but primarily in exploiting labour. In doing this, it represses human potential and reduces people to the level of a machine. Because, like Habermas, Marcuse holds out the possibility of more liberated human life, we class him as a Marxist humanist. His work, as well as that of Williams, Thompson and Mills, shows that the interest of Marxist humanists is not narrowly sociological but extends to the whole range of cultural expression.

A second contemporary trend in Marxism is *Marxist structuralism,* associated particularly with the French Marxists, Althusser and Bourdieu. We discussed their thinking in the context of socialisation, especially education, and referred again to Althusser in Chapters 19 and 20. Structuralists tend to see a rather tight fit between the base and the superstructure. In other words, they see culture less as free expression and more as an area in which ideological conformity to capitalist society is created. In this sense they are rather like structural functionalists, although whereas the latter generally approve of conformity to capitalist society, Marxist structuralists certainly do not.

Thirdly, developments in Marxist thought have also been forged in *political practice* as well as in the studies of academics. Lenin, Mao and the Cuban revolutionary, Che Guevara, were men of action as well as intellectuals. They were all successful revolutionaries and it is not surprising that they emphasised the need for Marxists to organise in order to create the change they wanted rather than to assume that history was inevitably on their side. They stressed the role both of the revolutionary party and of committed leadership in helping to bring about revolution. The danger in this was that the leadership would lose touch with the majority of the people on whose behalf revolution was supposed to take place. Having 'imposed' revolution, post-revolutionary change might also have to be imposed on a population whose 'consciousness' might be far from communist. Marxists differ on whether such imposition is justifiable. The alternative is to seek fundamental change only with mass support, either gradually or through revolution. The difficulty here is that the forces of the system preventing the growth of such support are immense; one way of measuring support is through the ballot box. Zimbabwe has an elected Marxist government, but it remains to be seen whether it can survive the opposition of the powerful countries and international business interests ranged against it. The elected Marxist government of Allende in Chile was prevented from doing this.

It is not easy to classify neatly the theoretical contributions of Marxist activists. The three revolutionaries mentioned above all stressed the need for men to force the historical issue in order to bring about socialist change. To that extent they were humanists. Whether the violence they used in pursuit of change contradicts their humanism is a point that could long be debated.

Contemporary Marxism is in a ferment of debate; yet some issues are becoming clear. Few Marxists now are historical determinists, although a case could be made that the French structuralists have merely substituted cultural mechanics for economic. But the broad trend to reconcile the immense power of social structure to form people with their capacity ultimately to change the repressive nature of their own social environment is extremely positive. We return to this theme in our final section which deals with the possibility of a unified sociological paradigm.

Interpretive Sociology: Is it Compatible with a Structural Perspective?

Since Mead, symbolic interactionism has progressed theoretically as much through practical application as through abstract thought isolated from research. Accordingly, we have been able to examine in some detail recent interactionist analyses of work, deviance and organisation. There is no need to review this research now. Instead, we will discuss the criticism frequently made of interactionism – that it lacks a structural dimension. In particular, we will assess Tom Goff's comparison of Mead's sociology to that of Marx. In his book, *Marx and Mead,* Goff attempts to show that the work of Marx and Mead is, essentially, complementary rather than contradictory. To the extent that he is successful, his analysis has profound implications for the theoretical reconstruction of sociology called for by, among others, Anthony Giddens. In what follows, I will not attempt to prove propositions already extensively discussed earlier, but will simply restate them in order to outline a fuller argument.

Firstly, both Marx and Mead emphasised that the individual is formed in society, and give comparable emphasis to the influence of social structure on people. Mead went into far greater detail of how this takes place and his social psychology has been very useful in much practical interpretist research. Recently, Marxists such as Jock Young and Paul Willis appear to have been influenced by it or, at least, by other compatible currents within phenomenology. Secondly, both Marx and Mead describes people as conscious beings with the potential to change and recreate their own social environment: neither the individual human being nor the group is ever 'reduced' to society. If Mead conveyed much more of the psychology of individual choice and understanding than did Marx, Marx presented a much more urgent message of emancipation from social repression and an alternative and freer way of life. A third point of convergence can be derived from the other two. For both of them, social structure and human creativity are not separate, but dialectically related – that is, man and environment interact with each other and can change each other. This leads to the fourth agreed point – that human thought is located in a social context, and informed by experience. In that sense, it is practical in nature and, for Marx at least, can be directed most rationally towards radically improving the quality of human life.

Goff has indicated Marx's concept of alienation as a major possible area of difference between him and Mead. Certainly, Mead had no particular sense that the division of labour in capitalist society was especially alienating: in fact, he was inclined to argue that the process of productive fragmentation was likely to continue and seemed none too distressed by it. He did, however, have a vivid appreciation of the way social institutions can smother individuality – a sentiment which accords with a Marxist-Weberian notion of alienation (see Chapter 16, pp. 393–6). The following quotation shows this:

> Oppressive, stereotyped and ultra-conservative social institutions – like the church – ... by their more or less rigid and inflexible unprogressiveness crush or blot out individuality or discourage any distinctive or original expressions of thought and behaviour in the individual selves or personalities implicated in and subjected to them ...

It is not too much to conclude, therefore, that Mead's framework of social analysis can be adapted to accommodate the concept of alienation.

Although the above considerations indicate that Mead's social thought is compatible with, and even complementary to, the structural aspects of Marxist theory, it remains true that the former is more suited to the micro-level of analysis and the latter to the macro-level. It is unquestionable that Mead developed the more detailed conceptual tool-kit for small-scale interaction and Marx the more detailed one for institutional analysis and class conflict, although in so far as these two levels inevitably overlap there is room for synthesis. But accepting that different levels of social analysis exist, and that theory and research will reflect this, it is objectionable to present the two perspectives as radically opposed: the above shows that they need not be.

Whether ethnomethodology is inherently compatible with structural perspective is open to more doubt and depends on how exactly it is defined. In the first chapter, ethnomethodology was referred to as an attempt to describe how individuals make sense of, or give explanatory accounts of, their experience. We need to extend this point here before returning to the broader issue of the relationship between ethnomethodology and structural perspective. Two concepts used by ethnomethodologists need to be introduced. Unfortunately, both reflect the extreme verbosity with which ethnomethodology is commonly associated, but they are capable of simple definition and illustration. The terms are the *documentary method* and *indexicality*. The documentary method is employed by all of us and involves the assumption that a given event or occasion can be made sense of by seeing it as just one example, or document, of a general type. Thus, to take Cicourel's previously cited study of delinquency, a police officer may see a particular youth with *what he regards* as delinquent characteristics and accordingly place him within the general category of delinquent, that is, he reacts to the 'documentary' evidence, perhaps a skinhead haircut and tattooed arms. He could, of course, be mistaken. The concept of indexicality means that sense can only be made of any object or event by relating it back to its context, or the circumstances of its occurrence. Thus, the word 'five' makes sense as an answer to the question,'What time is it?' but not as an answer to

611

'How many players are there in a cricket team?' Similarly, to continue with the kind of example that appeals to Harold Garfinkel, the founder of ethnomethodology, a policeman in the outfit of a clown would make sense in the context of a fancy dress ball but not in the context of a drugs raid. We can agree, then, that meaning depends on context. The interrelatedness of meaning and event – almost to the point of equation – is referred to as *reflexivity* by ethnomethodologists, and is a third key concept of the perspective. Because of their respect for the uniqueness and unpredictability of personal meaning, ethnomethodologists examine social activity with careful reference back to context and the various verbal descriptions (conveyors of meaning) given of it by social actors. Study in this depth of detail has, necessarily, to be on a small scale, as was Cicourel's study of the social organisation of juvenile delinquency, and Atkinson's research into coroners' definitions of suicide.

Both structural perspectives and symbolic interactionism offer theories of social order and structure. For the former, order and structure lie in the institutional framework which constrains members of society, and for the latter order is negotiated and structure created through interaction. Ethnomethodologists go a stage further back, as it were, by examining *how individuals cope with, and make sense of, existing situations* (whether 'orderly' or not). This interest need not, in my view, be incompatible with structural perspective. Presumably, it is not unlikely that the underlying patterns and taken-for-granted assumptions which individuals seek and find reinforced in experience (reflexivity) can be widely *shared*. If so, this fact structures interaction. Otherwise, there would be chaos. Yet some ethnomethodologists seem to object to the concerns of other perspectives. Perhaps this is partly a territorial dispute which will be resolved once ethnomethodologists have defined their areas of research interest in a way that is more comprehensible to other sociologists.

Towards a Unified Sociological Paradigm

In this section, I want to make three major points in support of the thesis that I have consistently urged in this book – that sociology has, and needs to have, an essential underlying theoretical coherence and unity. The first point is that *the methods of sociology, although highly diverse, can be regarded as a unify-ing factor in that they are the common property of all practitioners of the subject.* The second point is that the *major concepts in sociology pro-vide a basic sub-structure to the discipline* (Nisbet's term) despite dif-ferences in definition and usage within perspectives. The third point is that, leaning heavily on Anthony Giddens, I want to explore briefly some emerging possibilities for the *systematic recon-struction of sociological theory* that he deems necessary. Such a reconstruction, however, is likely to be a matter of synthesis rather than complete innovation.

The first point is perhaps the least important and can be briefly made. I differ from what still seems to be a prevailing assumption of some sociologists that qualitative methods are overwhelmingly associated with interpretist theory and quantita-tive methods with functionalist theory (and perhaps, too, mere empiricism). Clearly there are substantial links of this kind – some of which we pursued earlier (Chapter 2, pp. 24-40). However, I believe that these were stronger, say, fifteen or twenty years ago than now. Today, sociologists seem increas-ingly to use whatever method suits their purpose best, and this is not always 'one or the other type'. Stan Cohen, David Har-greaves and many feminist sociologists have used a wide variety of methods in the course of a single piece of research. As the work of these authors suggests, sociological methods are perhaps better thought of as a varied tool-kit of analysis rather than ideological appendages of various perspectives.

The second point is also a relatively simple matter. It is not difficult to study sociology with the help of a more explicit emphasis on concepts, even though this approach to teaching the discipline appears to have declined in recent years. Witnes-sing chaos in the subject, sociologists have sometimes appar-ently mistaken the subject itself for chaos and have conceived of it almost exclusively in terms of disagreements between the perspectives. Indeed, some teachers of sociology go to great lengths to invent differences that they imagine may exist bet-ween perspectives, presumably because they think either that by doing so they are practising sociology, or because they believe it is a stimulating intellectual exercise. Using the major con-cepts as a framework of presentation provides a way out of this confusing sophistry and fragmentation. It is true that a given concept may carry a variety of interpretations and meanings, but these are usually logically compatible and often complementary.

We will briefly recap on some of the major concepts used in this book. They are self; socialisation; culture; ideology; structure; stratification; power; order; change; agency and community. The above do not make up a complete list of all the major concepts I have used here: still less do they comprise all the major concepts in sociology. The point is, however, that the systematic exploration and application of such concepts can provide a coherent basis both for sociological teaching and, to some degree, research, which is certainly not achieved by excessive and exclusive emphasis on the perspectives. The perspectives are usually taught in relation to topics (often in no particular order) with theory and method slotted in somewhere. An alternative approach is to use concepts or, better, clusters of related concepts, which have a particular relevance to a given topic or series of topics as more explicit tools of analysis. Thus, the concepts of socialisation and culture have special application to the topics of family and education and can provide part of the focus for studying these topics. Similarly, stratification is a concept that applies to the topics of class, race, gender and generation. It is not, however, necessary to fit topics into clusters of concepts to give them due importance – this is merely a method of approach. Concepts do, of course, recur throughout topics: my point is that giving more weight to the basic concepts of sociology and rather less to the perspectives can produce a more coherent basis for approaching sociology and give a truer reflection of the fundamental concerns of the discipline than simply pursuing topics via perspectives. Looking beyond 'A' level sociology, I would also argue that an approach to social science which stresses concepts and methods will have more to contribute to a core curriculum than one based primarily on the perspectives. The proof of the pudding must be in the eating, however, and I want to illustrate my point about the importance of concepts by referring to some detailed examples – most of them used earlier in this book.

First are the concepts of self, socialisation and culture which we treated as a cluster in Chapter 1. For several reasons these related concepts are an excellent vehicle for presenting sociology to 'A' level beginners. Firstly, they are not too abstract and can easily be given personally meaningful illustration. The basic idea that the self or individual is socialised into a given culture can be explained by reference to any student's own biography. Secondly, the concepts lend themselves to cross-cultural comparison. Margaret Mead's work can be used to show just how much of what is taken for granted in a given society is, in fact, culturally influenced. Thirdly, they can be used as a natural platform for coming to terms with the basic ideas of Parsons and Mead in a way that does not make their thought seem confusingly contradictory (as it is frequently made to appear). Conflict theory can also be initially approached by linking the concepts of socialisation and class culture. Early in an 'A' level course, it is enough to appreciate the 'them and us' attitudes of the traditional working class and the more individualistic 'society as a ladder' orientation of the middle class. Admittedly, this is a sparse introduction to conflict theory, but in the first month or so of a course it is enough. Perhaps the above example shows that giving due emphasis to fundamental concepts does not involve disregarding the perspectives. On the contrary, it helps to establish them on a sound and comprehensible academic basis within the discipline.

Before turning to other concepts, it is worth dwelling further on the central importance that culture should have in the theory and teaching of sociology. Culture is an analytical tool too important ever to have gone out of usage, but it has recently been given particularly powerful application by leading Marxists on both sides of the channel. For Raymond Williams and Pierre Bourdieu, it is the focal concept around which they organise much of their material, although they do so in different ways. Further, culture defined as the transmission of values and norms has always been central to functionalism (reflecting particularly the influence on the perspective of anthropology through Malinowski and Durkheim). Whereas functionalism stresses the apparently 'neutral' but essentially conservative concept of socialisation, Marxists extend cultural analysis into the area of ideology – another concept used recurrently here. No sociologist would argue that social structure and culture are separate entities: on the contrary, the point is that they fuse and interact. To analyse structure and ignore culture would be to perform an autopsy on the corpse of society. That is why cultural themes flow through our treatment of class, gender, racial and generational stratification. Nevertheless, a specific concept may be particularly appropriate in the analysis of a given topic. Thus, culture is especially applicable to topics involving socialisation and communication, such as education and the media.

I want now to turn to the concept of social structure, possibly the most important in sociology. I shall link structure with a number of other concepts, including power. I hope to show that the somewhat different ways these concepts are treated within given perspectives need not preclude a coherent analysis and understanding of their meaning and application. Marxism, functionalism, and social action perspective are all broadly structural. George Mead also fully recognised the powerful influence of social institutions, although he staunchly resisted the idea that this is a totality. Stratification is the major structural concept and is most commonly applied to class, gender, race and generation (although, in theory, it can be applied to any form of distinction which results in social inequality). I don't deny that, in the analysis of stratification, emphasis must be given to the *various perspectives. Equally, however, there is a great deal of common ground* – acknowledged and partly unacknowledged – between them, particularly between the conflict structuralism of Marx and Weber. Take the examples of racial and generational stratification: racial and generational groups often experience status stratification on the basis of, say, colour and age, as a Weberian might contend. This approach, however, can be accommodated within a broader theory of class conflict in a way acceptable to Marxists. Although age groups may share a common generational experience, class is probably a greater influence on young people's lives. Similarly, most blacks are members of the working class as well as of a racial group and therefore the concept of class as well as status is important in understanding their structural position. Many sociologists, of course, prefer to recognise these complexities rather than try to live within some rigidly orthodox version of a perspective. John Rex, for example is prepared to work with both Weberian and Marxist concepts, even though it is also obvious that he has no relish for the more obscurely theoretical Marxist formulations. A similar open-mindedness seems to characterise the work on stratification carried out by John Goldthorpe. The conceptual framework of the *Oxford Mobility Study* may be broadly Weberian, but Goldthorpe's own comments on class inequality and conflict should please any Marxist.

The links between the concepts of stratification and power are too well-known to require pursuing in detail here. Broadly, Marx located the source of power in class relations and Weber saw it more diffusely as the possible product of class, political, military, personal, ideological or other factors. For some sociologists, that is that: never the twain shall meet. Yet, under the guise of a very different terminology from Weber's, Marxists as different as Althusser and E. P. Thompson have argued that power is generated not exclusively at the economic level, but also, to a significant degree, at the political and superstructural level. Of course, there are important qualifications to be made, but that position does not seem to be basically incompatible with what Weber says.

It will not have escaped notice that I have said nothing so far of functionalist analysis of stratification. I do not wish to pursue my case beyond reason, and the fact is that functionalist and Marxist stratificational theory are in contradiction. Functionalists regard stratification as inevitable, whereas Marxists consider that, in certain circumstances, class inequality – the major form of stratification – could be abolished. I object, however, to the current sociological vogue of regarding this and similar differences as primarily ideological. Unless sociology is to be regarded as a mere mish-mash of personal opinion, these issues need to be treated as theoretical differences which require to be tackled and, as far as possible, resolved at the theoretical and empirical level. That is what sociology is supposed to do. We all know that personal values and ideology play a role in scientific and social scientific inquiry, but that should not preclude professional communication and co-operation in developing theory among sociologists of different political viewpoints.

My examination of the concepts of culture and structure should have given a clearer idea of the basic point I am trying to make here. I am not attempting to sweep the perspectives under the carpet in a stubborn attempt at achieving sociological unity nor, indeed, am I denying that it is partly in treating concepts differently that differences in the perspectives show themselves. The issue is one of emphasis and approach. First things first: concepts should have a larger share in the presentation of sociology than they usually do, and explanation of them should, if possible, be handled in a way that avoids logically contradictory notions of what the concepts mean. The perspectives ought not to involve such radical contradiction or, if they do, something is badly wrong somewhere, and students would have every right to be sceptical of, if not downright disillusioned with, the subject.

I want, finally, to examine the question of whether the development of a unified sociological paradigm is desirable or possible. Given that the theories which help to make up a paradigm are built upon concepts, the issue of a unified sociological paradigm is an extension of the problem of conceptual analysis. However, the scale and complexity of the matter is unique in sociology – it is very much the $64,000 question of the subject. Perhaps it is sensible to think in terms of paradigmatic unity as a useful *ideal* to focus constructive work rather than as some sort of static and stultifyingly final theoretical consensus. At best, the alternative to this seems to be to accept several partly contradictory sociological paradigms as a permanent feature of the discipline and, at worst, to consider that these various paradigms or perspectives can reasonably be based on mere ideology or personal opinion. In my view, neither of these positions is logically or scientifically tenable. Perhaps a third position is that, in Althusserian terms, the various perspectives are concerned with different 'problematics'. I take this to mean that they pose different questions, and so examine somewhat different areas of social inquiry. I can accept that sociologists will pursue distinctive interests using methods of their own choosing, but I can see no reason why their analyses should not be accessible to the comprehension and criticism of others.

It is only possible here to examine one or two theoretical issues of relevance to the question of paradigmatic unity. I must, however, first briefly outline the scope of the problem. I suggest that two major theoretical areas on which 'paradigm building' requires to concentrate are those of *structure, change* and *agency* (who or what causes change) and *culture* and *community*. The last two are paired because the understanding of community as shared culture is recurrent in sociology, not least in functionalism and Marxism. What we have already said about structure and culture can be considered to support what follows. Firstly, then, we review some problems that the concept of structure currently presents in sociological theory. I agree with Giddens that conflict structuralism, particularly Marxism, provides a better basis for understanding how social groups, including classes, relate to one another than does consensus structuralism. In particular, the organic analogy applied to society as a whole obscures more than it illuminates. But it can be added that the assumption of stable social and political consensus and equilibrium in the West made by intellectuals, including leading sociologists, in the nineteen fifties, was thoroughly undermined by the turbulence and conflict of the next decade. Still more decisively, consensus assumptions should never be applied to the cauldron of world politics or to understanding the emergence of Third World countries; in fairness, they seldom were. As well as Marxists, labelling and interactionist theorists have produced a whole range of arguments against a simple consensus-deviance model (see Chapters 17 and 18, especially pp. 477–82). At this stage, it hardly seems premature to declare broadly in favour of the conflict theorists on the long post-war debate about the balance of conflict and consensus in modern societies. The notion of consensus must, however, retain a major place within sociological theory, but it requires to be linked to the concept of ideology (and, via ideology, to culture). When national consensus does exist, the questions to ask are why and how it was brought about and, particularly, in whose interest it operates. In other words, consensus must be viewed in ideological terms. Simply to assume value consensus as 'normal' misses important issues, and reduces the sociologist's role to attempting to describe the processes by which conformity is achieved or not (an essentially conservative contribution).

On matters of structure and power Marxists can learn much from Weber. Exploitation and domination are not exclusive features of capitalist society: indeed, the most totalitarian of power structures probably lie outside capitalist societies. Weber's analysis of power and bureaucracy helps to explain why. (See Chapter 16, pp. 438–40). I would argue, nonetheless, that Weber's assumption of the inevitability of bureaucratic hierarchy and elitism needs to be balanced by a more positive sense of democratic alternatives.

Probably more sociological brawls have occurred over the issue of social change and agency than over any other. There is no need to repeat in detail our review of the Thompson-

Althusser debate (Chapter 21, pp. 607–8) or the remarks about historical determinism made earlier in this chapter. What I conclude, optimistically, from these discussions is that there is an emerging consensus that regards both traditional structural-functionalism and crude Marxism as unacceptably deterministic. The alternative is to see man as the agent of his own destiny, despite the obstacles he places in his own path.

Anthony Giddens has pointed out a theoretical issue of considerable interest concerning structure, agency and system. He remarks that functionalism tends to collapse the distinction between structure and system to the point where the two terms are used·interchangeably. This is the result of regarding the operation of the social system as merely the functionings of social structure (the fundamental functionalist tautology) and, in the process, disregarding the contributions of social actors. It becomes impossible, however, to amalgamate the two if we take the contrary view that people, not institutions or structures, are the dynamic agents of social systems. In order to 'bridge the gap' between structure and system, Giddens proposes that the term *structuration* be used. If I understand him correctly, he intends to use it to synthesise two elements: (1) *that people – individually or in groups – are the active forces in social systems and* (2) that *they work within structured (or normatively defined) situations.* Thus, structure and system meet dynamically at the point of social action. Most illuminatingly, Giddens compares structuration to the process of linguistic communication of meaning (systems operation) and, in the process, it (language) can be changed and expanded (agent activity). It is not difficult to imagine how the concept of structuration could be applied to the analysis of normative structures and creative activity within organisations and social situations. It seems to go some way towards reconciling the two sides of the agency-structure debate within sociology.

We now finally examine the problem of culture and community with a view to showing that both concepts are at the heart of all structural sociology. It is sometimes said that community is of concern to functionalists but not to Marxists. Functionalists regret the 'loss' of traditional community whilst Marxists invest too much hope in the future to idealise the past. Further, functionalists often seem to be concerned to 'preserve' whatever remnants of community that do survive in modern society whilst Marxists want to drive a wedge between any 'false' solidarity of the classes. This radical difference conceals an even deeper shared concern. Marxists, too, desire community, but whereas functionalists seek for it in the past, Marxists project it into the future and, specifically, see it as a feature of 'classless' society which will be achieved sometime after the demise of capitalism. At least this suggests a common goal of social harmony and thus provides a starting point for theoretical dialogue. The concept of culture is relevant here because, without shared values, the basis of community does not exist. What functionalists have steadfastly failed to accept is that, as long as society is deeply divided along class lines, culture and community will reflect this fracture. The material and cultural inequalities that class systems produce fuel conflict and discontent. They preclude stable community (assuming that the enforced 'community' of totalitarian societies, which represses class conflict, is unacceptable).

As I begin to conclude, I recall a lecture delivered in September, 1979, by Ronald Fletcher. His thesis was that there is a 'shared universe of discourse' within sociology – substantially arrived at by the founding fathers – which is merely obscured by the current over-emphasis on perspectives within teaching circles. There is a case for this view. Even functionalists accept, in theory, the possibility of creative social action and, further, have made attempts, however cumbersome, to build the concept of conflict into their theoretical framework. Unlike Fletcher, however, I consider neither functionalist theory based on organic analogy nor Parsons' social systems model adequate to the task of utilising the concepts effectively either in empirical research or theoretical exposition. That said, his fundamental premise stands – that the founding fathers conceived of the social world in a broadly complementary and compatible way, rather than a contradictory one. Enough is shared in the way of basic concepts and categories to make progressive discourse possible. All the better, if, within a coherent framework, great diversity exists. It is intriguing to find Marxist, Tom Bottomore, and functionalist, Robert Nisbet, displaying a similar sentiment to that of Fletcher in their preface to a book which they jointly edited, *A History of Sociological Analysis* (1979). They, too, suggest that sociology is bigger than, and something more than, the differences that occur within it. Particularly arresting is the notion that Marxist sociology can be more positively viewed as a movement *within* sociology in general, rather than as alternative to it:

> But there is today no Weberian nor Durkheimian sociology, and even in the case of Marx a considerable gap exists between Marx's own theory of society and the various forms of present-day Marxist sociology, with the development of the latter, we would dare to suggest, embodying advances in, 'sociological' rather than 'Marxist' thought.

Despite the sense that a broad sociological framework does exist, Bottomore and Nisbet recognise that modern sociology contains a variety of different strands of interest, including a vital phenomenology of interaction. They are certainly a long way from concurring with Comte's narrowly positivistic ambition that sociology should develop the means 'to know in order to predict, to predict in order to control'! Yet they are also far from uncritically according equal status to all perspectives. To do so would be virtually to accept that sociological research is simply the organised presentation of subjective feeling, and the teaching of sociology merely the purveying of this indulgence to a wider audience. On the contrary, sociological research, like the perspectives themselves, must be assessed on the soundness of its theoretical and empirical content. Analysing the influence of personal or political ideology on research is simply one factor in this task and not, as has sometimes seemed to be the assumption, the major concern of teaching sociology. All disciplines finally face the problem of whether we can objectively 'know' anything, but some sociologists have tended to revel in this essentially philosophical problem at the expense of the pursuit of more practical matters of theory and method. I might add that such metaphysical obsession is particularly inappropriate for offering at 'A' level.

Happily, there is a growing body of sociological research that is well able to bear scrutiny in terms of rigorous standards of assessment. As we have seen, given that the methodological basis of quantitative and qualitative research is different, the basis of assessing it varies accordingly. The upsurge in highly empirical work, such as Townsend's *Poverty Report* and the *Oxford Mobility Study*, and the burgeoning of Marxist phenomenology are contrasting examples of current trends. Yet, there is no reason why this work should not be broadly complementary rather than contradictory. Despite its variety, it should produce a sounder basis for building general sociological perspective than mere speculation and subjectivism.

As we move into the second half of the nineteen eighties, a reaction against 'the perspectives approach' is asserting itself. This is most obvious in academic circles and increasingly so at 'A' level. In particular, the major textbooks are sometimes seen as ritualising and oversimplifying sociology and what sociologists do. My own initial voicing of these arguments was in 1979 in 'Limited perspectives: some reflections on the "perspectives approach" in 'A' level sociology' (*Social Science Teacher*, vol. 9, no. 2) and they were also reflected in the first edition of this book. Currently, an alternative to the perspectives approach is to use sociology to illuminate social problems and social policy. The advantage of this is that it strives to make sociology relevant – precisely what many students have always wanted but felt they never got. For this reason, the current trend is fully reflected in this section and, in its more internationalist implications, in Section B. Another response to textbook dominance has been the introduction of more original material into teaching by means of topic books, readers and otherwise.

Sociology is notoriously a discipline (some would even deny it is that) of fad and fashion, and it is important we gauge the genuine potential of the new intiatives rather than turn them into an enthusiastic crusade. First, neither greater emphasis on social policy nor increased use of original sources in themselves directly affect the state of sociological theory. The theoretical problems remain. Second, there is a danger that the new trends will serve as an escape from the problems of theory. Ostrich-like we will bury our collective disciplinary head in the sand because it has all got too difficult. Third, and worst, is that the new emphasis on problems and policy will generate a new sociological positivism, a spurious science of society. Interpretist insight should have laid this ghost to rest but the contemporary *zeitgeist* is so 'crackpot realist' that a new social mechanics could just take over, or, if we are spared that, a well meaning but directionless problem-solving approach could come to dominate.

Finally, on the question of theory/method proper, I see two significant trends. First, is the pluralism described above. The three major perspectives are just a part of this and, certainly, in the case of Functionalism, a decreasingly important part. Charles

623

Wright Mills wrote eloquently of the theoretical diversity of sociology in 1960 without, of course, feeling the need to use the term perspectives. Given tolerance, the variety of sociology can be seen as an advantage rather than a disadvantage. Thus, stripped of their claims to be exclusively right, both Durkheim and Max Atkinson can each be seen as right in their way. Second, efforts to synthesise the variously fragmentary and complementary aspects of sociological theory are continuing and will continue. However, there is no fear that any final overview will be achieved, resulting in mass redundancies among sociologists. People keep changing and society changes with them. Ours is not a stable discipline. There is always something new to explain and to enjoy.

Guide to Further Reading and Study

Assuming a reasonably advanced level at this point, the following general texts can be recommended: David Berry's *Central Ideas of Sociology* (Constable, 1974) and Stephen Mennel's *Sociological Theory: Uses and Unities* (Nelson, 1980). The following two books are intelligent presentations of respectively positivist and phenomenological approaches: Ronald Fletcher's *Sociology: The Study of Social Systems* (Batsford, 1981) and Jack. D. Douglas, *The Understanding of Everyday Life: Towards the Reconstruction of Sociological Knowledge* (Routledge and Kegan Paul, 1974).

Past Questions

1 'The history of sociological theory has been the story of a continuing debate with Marx's intellectual inheritance.' Discuss with reference to one or more sociological theorists with whose work you are familiar. (OLE, 1983)

2 Outline the nature of positivism and explain which research techniques in sociology most closely reflect positivist principles. What might a research sociologist do to avoid the alleged problems within positivist methodology? (JMB, 1985)

3 'When choosing a topic to study and deciding how to approach it, a sociologist will inevitably be influenced by moral and political values.' Explain and discuss. (AEB, 1985)

4 'Physical and natural science is governed by agreed rules of procedure whereas social science is characterised by competing perspectives.' Explain this statement and consider its relevance to the argument that sociology is a science. (AEB, 1985)

22 Social Problems and Policy

Sociology and Social Problems

Many people study sociology because they expect the subject will give them a better understanding of social problems. This expectation is often not quickly met and is sometimes not met at all. The relevance of the subject to practical issues can get lost in a welter of theory. However, I believe sociology can deliver on its promise to provide insight into social problems and inform the policies designed to solve them. I will set aside the issue of definition until later and for the moment simply regard a social problem as a matter perceived as causing difficulty by the general public or by a given group.

The first way in which sociology can illuminate social problems is by clarifying the link between social structure and personal experience. This connection has been most eloquently expressed by Charles Wright Mills:

> Perhaps the most fruitful distinction with which the sociological imagination works is between 'the personal troubles of milieu' and 'the public issues of social structure. . .'
>
> *Troubles* occur within the character of the individual and within the range of his immediate relations with others; they have to do with his self and with those limited areas of social life of which he is directly and personally aware. . .
>
> *Issues* ('problems' in the terms of this chapter) have to do with matters that transcend these local environments of the individual and the range of his inner life . . . An issue is a public matter: some value cherished by publics (organised groups) is felt to be threatened.

Having distinguished between personal troubles and public issues, Mills then goes on to argue that very often they *both* have a social structural dimension. Major social events and changes such as high unemployment, war and urban decay are public issues but they are, of course, experienced in a personal way by many individuals. The fundamental causes of these problems cannot be dealt with by personal adjustments but must be tackled by major public response.

627

A second contribution sociology can make to the understanding of social problems is to demonstrate the problematic but hidden consequences of certain social practices and conditions. Robert Merton calls this making manifest (public) latent (hidden) social problems. By way of illustration, he refers to the body of research which has increased, awareness of the human, economic and social cost of sexual and racial discrimination. Writing in almost Millsian language, Merton states:

> Sociologists who demonstrate the waste of socially prized talent that results from great inequalities of opportunity bring to focus what was diffusely experienced by many as only involving personal troubles rather than constituting a problem of society.

Indeed, Merton's point is really a particular application of Mills' analysis.

A third contribution of sociology to the study of social problems is that it can show how certain matters come to be defined as social problems and can locate the assumptions made by interested parties. The key concept here is power – the power to identify and promote (or suppress) a given matter as a social problem. Both Marxists and interactionists have made notable contributions to our understanding of this process. Marxists argue that the wealthy and powerful are generally more able to define social problems and affect policy towards them than the poor and less powerful. In the area of social problems, Marxist class analysis is complemented by the middle and micro range perspectives of interactionists who have examined how professions and interest groups such as the police and the judiciary have affected public perception of social problems. We can take drugs as an example. Marxists typically point to the commercial and advertising interests which seek to romanticise the public's image of cigarette smoking and to inhibit more robust policies of control. The interactionist, Howard Becker, has studied the contrasting case of marijuana – a drug seemingly no more dangerous than tobacco. The use of marijuana was legal in the United States until the passage of the Marijuana Stamp Tax Act of 1937. Becker argues that the Federal Bureau of Narcotics campaigned to make marijuana use illegal partly to expand its own social and organisational power. In 'getting the rules changed' on marijuana, it succeeded in doing this. Separately, but particularly taken together, Marxist and interactionist perspectives make a major contribution to our understanding of public attitudes and policy towards drug use. Functionalists also readily accept the element of group conflict in social problem definition and policy formation. As Robert Merton puts it, 'one group's problem can be another group's solution'. Nevertheless, the focus of Functionalism typically remains on those problems about which there is a broad consensus of concern and which seem to them to be dysfunctional to the operation of society.

Fourthly, by helping to explain the causes, context and perception of social problems, sociology can give direction to the humanistic concern that many people feel about issues such as poverty, unemployment and violence within the family. As Becker puts it, sociology helps to discover strategic points of intervention in the social structures and processes that produce the problems. The Head Start programme was one such strategic intervention supported by sociological analysis (see Chapter 24). Informed by structural perspective, many workers in the 'helping' professions take up political positions in support of, for instance, more resources for the poor, more jobs and policies to reduce stress on the family.

What sociology cannot do is give an absolute definition of the content of a social problem or provide a comprehensive list of social problems. With few exceptions, sociologists would agree with Howard Becker that 'social problems are what people say they are'. We have to decide for ourselves, in the light of our values and understanding, what we regard as social problems and what, if anything, we are gong to do about them. But sociology can provide the perspective and data to sustain alternative moral points of view to those widely supported and publicised.

Social Problems: Definitions and Perspectives

Social Problems Seen as Individual Deviance: conservative perspective

Nineteenth and early twentieth century writers on social problems in both Britain and the United States commonly sought their causes in individual pathology or weakness of either a physical, mental or moral kind. Belief in self-help and the survival of the fittest gave support to the view that the deserving succeed and the weak and worthless fail. This philosophy is indicated in the title of

629

Charles Henderson's textbook on social problems published in 1906: *An Introduction to the Study of Defective, Dependent and Delinquent Classes*. Religious and moralistic motives were common among those who helped the poor and the urge to uplift them spiritually was as strong or stronger than the desire to assist them materially. At this time few envisaged that the state would largely take over 'charitable' activities from the churches.

Individualistic explanations of social problems flourished again in the nineteen seventies and eighties. Such approaches have always had some popular currency but in this period they gained substantial political and academic support. Both Ronald Reagan, the American President and Republican Party leader, and Margaret Thatcher, the British Prime Minister and Conservative Party leader, vigorously adopted philosophies of individual enterprise and reward and cut back on many welfare programmes. Thus, Thatcher stated 'Let our children grow tall, and some grow taller than others'. More down to earth was her then Minister of Employment, Norman Tebbit's advice to the unemployed to 'get on your bike'. To those who argue that poverty in modern capitalist society is largely social structural in nature, such comments minimise and individualise poverty and inequality.

One of President Reagan's advisors, Charles Murray, attempts in his book *Losing Ground, American Social Policy 1950–1980*, to provide intellectual and empirical support for the above philosophy and related policies. Murray argues that in the post-war period in the United States, the most marked improvement in the condition of the poor occurred throughout the 1950s and early 1960s *before* the War on Poverty of the Johnson administration and the continued massive welfare programmes of his successors prior to Reagan. Ironically, after two decades of relatively steady progress, improvements in the condition of the poor, as measured by a number of indicators, slowed in the late 1960s and stopped altogether in the late nineteen seventies. In other words, poverty got relatively worse as programmes to reduce it increased. According to Murray, this is because many found it preferable to be 'on welfare' (i.e., in poverty) than to work: they took advantage of what he calls 'the generous (welfare) revolution'. This view, of course, has also frequently been voiced on this side of the Atlantic. However, critics of the individualistic approach tend to turn the argument on its head and attack the 'system' that offers to millions only the choice of welfare or low pay.

The above perspective on social problems links directly to the social policies of the New Right and these are described in detail later (pp. 656–62).

The Functions and Dysfunctions of Social Problems

THE INFLUENCE OF DURKHEIM The major contemporary statement of Functionalist perspective on social problems is probably Robert Merton's introduction to *Contemporary Social Problems* edited by himself and Robert Nisbet. Like much Functionalist theory, Merton's piece greatly reflects the thinking of Emile Durkheim. The latter's analysis of deviance has deeply influenced the Functionalist approach to social problems. The basic characteristics Durkheim associates with deviance were given earlier (pp. 466–7). Functionalists define many social problems as deviant and for that reason the concept of deviance is prominent in this section.

Durkheim's view that deviance is functional (because it enables the majority to reaffirm their moral unity) needs qualification in the present context. He regarded, as functional, only a 'normal' level of deviance. His attitude to abnormally high levels of deviance is clear in his book *Suicide*. Having dealt with other types of suicide, he begins his treatment of anomic suicide with the statement that '[i]n normal conditions the collective order is regarded as just by the great majority of persons' but that 'when society is disturbed by some painful crisis or by beneficient but abrupt transitions' moral and normative uncertainty tend to result. He refers to this state of 'de-regulation' as 'anomie'. Anomic conditions are likely to be characterised by a rise in deviant behaviour, including suicide. Durkheim clearly regarded such periods as problematic and often confusing for those living in them. For instance, he wrote as follows about the 'crisis' that can result from 'an abrupt growth of power and wealth' of the kind he had witnessed in Europe in his own lifetime:

> The scale is upset; but a new scale cannot be immediately improvised. Time is required for the public conscience to reclassify men and things. So long as the social forces thus freed have not regained equilibrium, their respective values are unknown and so all regulation is lacking for a time. . . . Since the relations between various parts of society are necessarily modified, the ideas expressing these relations must change. Some particular class especially favoured by the crisis is no longer resigned to its former

lot, and, on the other hand, the example of its greater good fortune arouses all sorts of jealousy below and about it.

Durkheim went on to argue that the industrial revolution had generated such rapid change and deregulation in trade and industry that anomie was chronic to these areas.

We can now briefly summarise the influence of Durkheim on functionalist perspectives on social problems. First, Durkheim's analysis of social problems of deviance is structural-functional; major changes in the social structure can produce social problems and these problems and people's response to them can feed back into the social system (or parts of it). Second, Durkheim sought to demonstrate that the functional consequences of social problems are not always apparent (or manifest) – a point given central importance by Robert Merton. Third, the concept of anomie has been widely used in functionalist analysis of social problems – again, notably in modified form by Merton. Fourth, Durkheim introduces the concept of social equilibrium. He links this to the concepts of normal and abnormal social states. Abnormally high rates of deviance (and perhaps, by extension, other social problems) are associated with lack of equilibrium (or disequilibrium). Some Functionalists have treated this complex of concepts cautiously but they have had a powerful influence on the work of Talcott Parsons. Fifth, like Durkheim, many Functionalists regard modern society as particularly prone to generate social problems because of the extent and rapidity of change.

ROBERT MERTON We now turn to Robert Merton's work on social problems. First, Merton locates his analysis of social problems within the total structure and functioning of society. The very way society is institutionalised and organised is likely to produce particular kinds of problems:

> The same social structure and culture that in the main make for conforming and organised behaviour also generate tendencies towards distinctive kinds of deviant behaviour and potentials of social disorganisation. In this sense, the problems current in a society register the social costs of a particular organisation of social life. . . .

To suggest an example, perhaps the pressures to respectability and moral behaviour in Victorian Britain created the need for a deviant underworld of indulgence and promiscuity.

As the quotation indicates, Merton divides social problems into two main categories, those caused by social disorganisation and those caused by deviance. These will be examined separately after Merton's general analysis of social problems.

Like most sociologists in this field, Merton distinguishes between the objective and subjective aspects of social problems. The former is the social condition itself – poverty, unemployment or whatever – and the latter is the perception of it as a problem. Like the interactionist Howard Becker, Merton points out that people do not always agree about what is a social problem: 'one group's problem is another group's solution'. However, he seeks to emphasise the objective rather than subjective aspect. He counters the interactionist wisdom that 'if men define situations as real, they are real in their consequences' with the caution that 'and if people do *not* define *real* situations as real, they are nevertheless real in their consequences'. He insists that subjective failure to define real conditions such as inferior housing and overpopulation as problems may result in 'dysfunctional' consequences for society. He argues that sociologists have a special role in revealing the 'latent dysfunctions' of given situations, including those unintentionally caused by government policy. To give an example, sociological research might establish that social security cuts aimed at reducing public expenditure have the unforeseen consequence of undermining the health of certain groups and so raise health costs. Such a finding could influence future policy formation.

A second way in which Merton implicitly attacks the subjective emphasis of the interactionists is by reference to evidence that in modern societies there is substantial agreement about how to rank the relative seriousness of many social problems of deviance. Thus, Sellin and Wolfgang found that judges, police and college students in the United States similarly evaluated the seriousness of crimes. Comparable studies of broader sections of American and other modern societies 'consistently found a wide consensus on the seriousness of actions traditionally defined as criminal': crimes of violence against persons ranked ahead of crimes against property and attitudes to victimless crimes were particularly tolerant. So, whilst Merton accepts a necessary subjective element in the definition of social problems, he prefers to emphasise objective factors by employing the concept of latent dysfunction and by reference to normative agreement on ranking social problems.

To return to Merton's division of social problems into problems of disorganisation and problems of deviance, these are broad groupings and we have already devoted two chapters to one of them, deviance. Merton states that social disorganisation 'refers to inadequacies in a social system that keeps people's collective and individual purposes from being as fully realised as they could be'. So, Merton sees any failure of social organisation which frustrates goal achievement as a problem. This seems uncontroversial. But Merton's view of the major sources of social disorganisation suggest a conservative drift in his Functionalist model. Thus, he regards conflicting interests and values and faulty socialisation as major sources of disorganisation. As an example of the former, he describes a society which does not provide an effective way of settling the disputes of management, workers and stockholders as disorganised. His argument illustrates the familiar Functionalist concern with consensus. By contrast, Marxists consider such institutionalised attempts to deal with industrial conflict as little more than a papering over of the cracks of class antagonisms. For them fundamental conflict, not functional efficiency, is the norm of capitalist society and for most of them, to intensify it is their immediate goal. Merton's use of the term 'faulty socialisation' to describe a second main source of disorganisation seems unfortunate, though it is typically functionalist. It suggests that there is a 'correct' or 'right' form of socialisation to which people 'ought' to be subjected. Unintentionally, Merton evokes an image of a society of well-processed conformists of the kind that Charles Wright Mills found so alarming but which he regarded as a sinister possibility given the tendency of modern bureaucracies to standardise and routinise individual behaviour.

Merton's categorisation of deviance as a major form of social problem gives the opportunity to review some of his more recent observations on the subject (1976). He states that deviant behaviour 'involves significant departures from norms socially assigned to various status and roles' and that it usually constitutes a social problem.

Merton makes a major distinction between two types of deviant behaviour which, were it to become more widely accepted, could have a significant impact on deviancy theory. He differentiates 'nonconformist' and 'aberrant' deviant behaviour. The following summarises the five differences he gives between them:

1 Nonconformists are open about their dissent, aberrants try to hide their departures from social norms.
2 Nonconformists challenge the legitimacy of social norms whereas aberrants accept it.
3 Nonconformists seek to change norms, aberrants seek to escape sanctions for breaking norms they accept.
4 Nonconformists are acknowledged by conformers to break norms for reasons of value, aberrants for self-interest.
5 Nonconformers appeal to a higher morality and may lay claim to legitimacy by drawing upon society's ultimate values whereas aberrants seek to satisfy their private interests and cravings.

Merton finds examples of nonconformity in 'race, ethnic and gender liberation movements as well as other forms of collective social protest' and mentions crime, alcoholism and drug abuse as principal forms of aberrant behaviour. Merton's distinction seems very useful. The term deviance serves to indicate a wide category of behaviour – viz. rule-breaking – but there is a need systematically to distinguish the crucial issue of intent. It makes little sense equally to define the rule-breaking of Martin Luther King and a shop looter as deviant. In terms of moral intent, they are at the opposite ends of the continuum. Merton's fifth point particularly emphasises this and is consistent with Lawrence Kohlberg's view that the highest form of moral choice transcends conventional social norms. Given the high moral status Merton attributes to nonconformity, it is difficult to see why he categorises it as a social problem except, of course, that great nonconformers from Jesus to Ghandi can be a 'problem' for the social order they live in.

Another aspect of Merton's 1976 version of his essay on social problems, is his attempt to take into consideration certain criticisms of previous versions and of Functionalist perspective generally. This applies particularly to his treatment of deviance. Thus, as indicated above, he finds labelling theory helpful in understanding the subjective side of social problems and in analysing secondary deviance (see p. 633). He attempts to reconcile Functionalist anomie theory with labelling theory by arguing that the former tries to explain the social origins of deviant behaviour whereas the latter focuses on how stigmatisation can perpetuate it. More broadly still, he argues that differential association, anomie, labelling, and conflict theories 'have a potential for being complementary' partly because they apply to different aspects of social deviance. However, he does not then go on to offer even in outline a unified theory of deviance to support his claim.

Despite Merton's attempt to embrace concepts and insights from other perspectives, his analysis remains classically functionalist and is therefore open to the classic criticisms of Functionalism. First, from social action and interactionist perspectives, his analysis envisages social problems in terms of systems rather than people. It can be argued that the 'dysfunctions' of systems are often better seen as the problems caused by some for others (e.g. by polluters for those polluted) or by the persistence of outdated and injurious cultural beliefs (e.g. that large families are a good economic investment). To focus on people as the producers and victims of social problems means writing about the topic in a different way from that of Merton and the Functionalists: it involves stressing the intentions and purposes of people rather than the functions and goals of systems. Second, the limitations of Merton's aspirations to theoretical synthesis are shown in his scant analysis of radical conflict and social problems. For him, social problems are the dysfunctions of a *given* social system. Nowhere does he engage the possibility that a social system might be fundamentally problematic, i.e. prone to conflict rather than harmony. To do this would draw him into a discussion of social legitimacy and change of the kind that Functionalists tend to avoid.

The Social Construction of Social Problems

In a memorably simple statement, Howard Becker defines social problem as follows: 'Social problems are what people think they are.' This definition parallels the one he gives for deviance: 'deviant behaviour is behaviour that people so label'.

Becker, like Merton, recognises that there is an objective and a subjective aspect to social problems: the former being the condition or behaviour itself, the latter being the definition of it as a problem. Whereas Merton's emphasis is on the objective aspect, Becker is more concerned with the subjective which for him is the starting point of any understanding of social processes, problematic or otherwise. Becker scrutinises the notion of objectivity as closely as Merton does that of subjectivity. He stresses that the moral and political concern that often surrounds social problems means that sociologists must carefully establish details about objective conditions and indeed check whether these exist at all. He points out that 'People . . . *can* define non-existent conditions as a social problem.' He gives the witch hunt at Salem as an example of when many members of the community imagined that they were infested with witches and 'took stern measures to deal with the supposed social problem'. Such moral panics can, of course, do great damage to their victims. It is consistent with Becker's thinking to point out that even the response to real social problems can contain elements of moralistic excess. Thus, the wave of concern in the United States in 1984/85 over the deeply serious issue of child abuse involved some hysterical and inaccurate accusations.

Becker develops the interesting concept of the 'natural history' or 'career' of a social problem first introduced by Fullers and Myers. They describe three stages in this history: awareness, policy determination and reform. Becker illustrates these stages in the case of his own detailed study of the rise of marijuana as a social problem (see pp. 479–80). According to his account, the Federal Bureau of Investigation played a major role in moulding initial awareness of the issue. The FBI was also prominent in the debate and policy determination phase as was the media which, Becker argues, tended to take an alarmist line about the drug. The emotively titled film *Reefer Madness* (1937) was a near propaganda piece of the period. The reform stage, when a 'solution' becomes institutionalised, occurred with the passage of the Marijuana Stamp Act of 1937 which made the drug illegal in the United States for the first time. History does not stop at this point, of course, and the marijuana issue came to the fore again in the nineteen sixties. The current situation is that it is generally illegal but very widely used.

It is thought-provoking to compare the histories of marijuana and tobacco use in the United States (and Britain) and to speculate on why one is illegal and the other not. In this respect, Jack Douglas and Frances Waksler suggest that part of the opposition to legalising marijuana is based on a dislike of the bohemian, pleasure-seeking lifestyle still vaguely associated with it. By contrast, tobacco smoking is 'healthily' associated with the work ethic, either as an aid to concentration or as legitimate and earned relaxation. Douglas and Waksler also comment on the high and growing rate of heroin use. Controversially, they argue that public perceptions of the drug and its effects are generally confused and misinformed. They attribute many of the behaviours associated with the drug not to its chemical effects but to the processes of secondary deviance. Thus, the addict is virtually labelled an outcast and may turn to theft or prostitution to sustain the habit. Similarly, a London doctor recently argued that the legal prohibition of heroin has driven its use underground and out of control (*Guardian*, 30 September 1985). Dr Marjot found inconsistency and bigotry in public attitudes towards drugs, with alcohol and tobacco receiving favoured treatment. He urged the need for a public debate on the whole issue including the question of legalising heroin use in order to gain some control over it.

The interest of interactionists in how people come to perceive and define 'problems' has resulted in a body of work analysing how the media 'constructs' and even 'creates' social problems. Several of these studies have already been referred to here, including Stanley Cohen's now classic *Folk Devils and Moral Panics: The Creation of Mods and Rockers*, which describes how news reporters and processors, various 'moral entrepreneurs', and the Mods and Rockers themselves, created what was largely a media event (see pp. 495–6). More recently, Marxists have employed interactionist concepts to analyse media presentation of 'problems' of racial and industrial conflict and have attempted to relate media bias to the structure of racial and class inequality and domination (see pp. 576–7).

Two criticisms of interactionist perspective on social problems may be considered. First, the approach is sometimes thought to exaggerate the subjective element in social problems at the expense of the objective. Merton, for instance, denies that 'social problems exist *only* if many people declare them to exist' because they may be latent but real and damaging. However, my own view favours Becker who argues that research may be required to identify a given condition but 'its problematic character would arise from how people defined its consequences'. A second criticism of interactionist social problem theory tends to be made by Marxists. They criticise interactionists for adopting a pluralist model of power conflict in explaining the emergence, definition and solution of social problems. Marxists argue the need for class analysis and there have in fact been several Marxist studies of social problems/conflict synthesising interactionist concepts with class perspective, including those referred to below.

The 'System' as the Problem: Radical Structural and Marxist Perspectives

As understood here, radical structural and Marxist perspectives agree on one central point: that capitalism produces fundamental social problems. The classic free enterprise system, so praised by conservative individualists, is seen as inherently incapable of producing social justice and stability. The pursuit of profit and the exploitation of labour results in severe inequality. Radical structural and Marxist theorists tend to regard inequality not so much as *a* social problem but as *the* core social issue of capitalism, out of which other problems and issues are generated. Thus, Marxists in particular consider that problems relating to freedom of expression cannot be solved adequately unless the issue of inequality is first dealt with. So, whereas the two other major perspectives tend to present social problems in terms of social order and deviance, for Marxists inequality is the key social issue.

The above approach is, of course, more than a perspective on social problems, it is an analysis of a system – the capitalist system. Though theorists adopting this broad analysis agree on the basic cause of social problems in capitalist society, they do not necessarily agree on the solution. Some argue that social justice, equality and freedom can be achieved by the reform of capitalism whereas others consider that these goals cannot be attained unless the system is abolished. I refer to the former as radical structural theorists and the latter as Marxists. The disagreements between the two groups become more apparent in the section on policy, though not all writers take a clear position.

The Marxists, John Westergaard and Henrietta Westergaard adopt a structural analysis of inequality in *Class in Capitalist Society: A Study of Contemporary Britain.* They prefer the term inequality to poverty because the latter can so easily be (mis)-explained as an individual or group problem. They wish to focus on inequality as a product of the capitalist system. Inequality cannot be dealt with simply by making efforts to get certain groups above the poverty line. Reforms gained in times of expansion may be lost during a recession, or economic and technological developments may put new groups into poverty. For them, poverty or rather inequality is a class rather than an individual or group issue. All wage-workers, employed or unemployed, are potential victims of the capitalist system. Their solution lies in collective action to change the system, not in merely supporting fragmented 'remedies' which 'are not designed to produce wholesale change in the general structure of inequality'.

Similarly, Stuart Hall and his co-authors analyse the problem of racism in Britain by means of Marxist structural analysis. In *Policing the Crisis, Mugging the State and Law and Order*, they argue that blacks in Britain have frequently been made the scapegoats of economic crisis, particularly rising unemployment. Political and media attention on the race issue whipped up a series of moral panics which distracted attention from the failure of capital to generate economic growth and high employment. The 'mugger' was a particularly negative stereotype of young, black urban males which aggravated racial tension and hampered the development of class solidarity across racial lines.

During the first fifteen post-war years in the United States, Charles Wright Mills did more than anyone to keep alive the structural perspective linking personal problems to public issues, when most of his leading contemporaries were proclaiming that affluence and scientific progress and management had provided the means to solve the country's remaining social problems, thus making radical political debate redundant. However, by the time of Mills' death in 1962, there was a new generation of sociologists eager to debate social problems in structural and political terms. In 1970, Alvin Gouldner in *The Coming Crisis of Western Sociology*, argued that openly declaring and pursuing political values in sociological analysis was more responsible and humanistic than the supposed value neutrality of the Functionalists. This approach was sometimes referred to as reflexive or critical sociology.

Crisis in American Institutions, a reader on social problems edited by Jerome Skolnick and Elliot Currie, was also published in 1970. The book fully reflects the basic contentions of Mills and Gouldner. In their introductory essay, revised through several editions, the editors have kept up a running debate with Functionalists Robert Merton and Robert Nisbet, editors of *Contemporary Social Problems*. They deny that a neutral 'theory of social problems in the sense Merton implies' is possible. Dismissing his charge that they indulge in 'moral rhetoric' they emphasise their own commitment to a 'critical perspective', focusing 'most heavily on the fundamental social processes of the American system and on the institutions in which these processes are encountered'. Thus they divide the contributions into two parts: 'systemic problems' and 'institutions in crisis'. Fundamental problems of the system include 'economic crisis' and 'inequality' and institutions in crisis, 'the family' and 'the workplace'. Elliot Currie's co-authored contribution *The Fading Dream: Economic Crisis and the New Inequality* explores some facets of contemporary inequality in the United States which are of particular interest to Britain as the Americanisation of the British Economy continues and a range of social problems similar to those in the United States develops here. Between 1973 and 1979, 13 million more jobs were created in the United States. Many of these were low-paying service jobs which attracted mainly women, whereas better paying jobs in heavy manufacture which employed mainly men decreased. As a result the average discretionary income (income after necessities are met) of the American worker declined by 16% in real terms. For many families this decline was offset because with the job expansion they had become dual-income families. However, there was a substantial increase in poverty in families with only one earner and single parent families. It is worth adding that a similar trend to the loss of high-paying and the increase in low-paying (often part-time) jobs is also occurring in Britain, as is the partly compensatory trend to dual-income families. However, the creation of jobs is proceeding much more slowly in Britain and the proportion of unemployed to low-paid in poverty is relatively higher than in the United States. What is significant, however, is the attempt to create large low-pay sectors in both economies (at a time when trade unions are weak). This trend is complemented by the rise of a small, high-salaried group. Indeed, Currie writes of a new expanding 'superclass' of high earners in the United States – especially in the case of high dual-income families. In Britain in 1985 the enormous wage increases granted to so-called 'top people' already on high salaries dwarfed those received by other occupational groups in both absolute and percentage terms.

It is a merit of Michael Harrington's *The New American Poverty* (1984) that he puts some of the above and many other important trends pertaining to inequality within a coherent, structural context. A reforming socialist rather than a Marxist, he nevertheless offers an analysis that would be broadly acceptable to many Marxists. Again, his comments are almost as applicable to Britain as the United States. He begins by locating 'a deep structural source of a new poverty that could persist into the indefinite future' – the 'internationalisation of the economy [and]

641

of poverty' by the multinational corporations. The power of the multinationals to switch investment and production around the globe has weakened the bargaining power of labour in developed capitalist societies and has tended to lower wages and increase unemployment. Labour itself has become internationalised and far more disorganised and weak as a result. He refers to the millions of un-documented migrant labourers in the United States who are very low-paid and who may also depress the wages of indigenous workers by their willingness to work for so little. We examined the same process in relation to European migrant and many black workers in Britain in Chapter 13. As Harrington puts it, '[t]he Third World is . . . not simply out there, it is within and at the gates'. Like Currie, Harrington points out that most of the service jobs that are replacing those in heavy manufacture in both Britain and America are relatively low-paid. He also dispels the myth that there will be many 'high-tech' jobs available. In fact, far more routine 'low-tech' than high-tech jobs are being produced and far more non-technical jobs in the low paid sector, such as fast-food and janitoring, than either.

Partly as a result of the above trends, Harrington sees a new 'underclass' developing, largely cut off from the materially good life available in various degrees to other Americans. The use of the term underclass will not recommend Harrington's analysis to Marxists, most of whom prefer that of lower working class, but there is little doubt that he has located an empirically real phenomenon however we conceptualise it. He uses the term underclass primarily to indicate those in long-term structural poverty among whom are disproportionate numbers of the unemployed, the low-paid, ethnic minorities, the 'rootless' mentally ill or retarded, the less educated young, and one parent families. The rise in the number of one parent families – most of whom are headed by women – living in or at the margin of poverty and of low-paid working women leads Harrington to refer to the 'feminisation' of poverty. In 1960, 65% of poor families were headed by men under 65 years of age, and 21% by women, whereas in 1979 the respective figures were 42.4% and 43.7% – a profound change and an ironic commentary on the position of women in the supposed age of female emancipation. This figure also explains why 20% of America's children are in poverty according to the estimate cited by Harrington.

Britain is even more vulnerable to international economic trends than the United States. Indeed, Andrè Gunder Frank has suggested that Britain may be the first advanced capitalist country to 'underdevelop' (see p. 200). Joanna Mack and Stewart Lansley's social survey, *Poor Britain* (1985) gives a detailed account of poverty in Britain that is much more up to date and in some ways methodologically superior to Peter Townsend's which was published in 1979 but drew on data gathered up to a decade previously. Although it would be unfair to pin a particular political or theoretical label on Mack and Lansley's work (originally presented in a television documentary series, *Breadline Britain*) the tone and presentation of the book is certainly more likely to appeal to the political left than to the right. Mack and Lansley establish that there is a considerable degree of consensus among the British public on the necessities required to maintain 'a minimum standard of living on socially established criteria and not just the criteria of survival or subsistence'. Over 90% of people (from a representative quota sample of 1174 respondents) agree on the importance of the following for basic living in the home: heating, an indoor toilet (not shared), a damp-free home, a bath (not shared), and beds for everyone. A further range of 21 items – from having enough money for public transport to possessing a warm waterproof coat – was regarded as necessities by more than one-half of respondents. This list of 26 necessities, established by the majority of respondents, is the basis on which they measure poverty. They find that 'all those with an enforced lack of three or more necessities are in poverty. . . . All fall below the minimum way of life laid down by society as a whole.' On this measure, 5 million adults and 2.5 million children are in poverty. The table below shows the varying depths of poverty in Britain as measured by lack of necessities. The authors comment on those in intense poverty: 'their lives are diminished and demeaned in every way, so far do they fall below the minimum standards of society today'.

Mack and Lansley find five main groups whose living standards are too low: the unemployed, single parents, the sick and disabled, pensioners and the low paid. There are roughly as many in poverty who are in low-paid work as there are unemployed but the unemployed are almost twice as likely to suffer intense poverty. The authors argue that the impact of the recession – particularly the very high level of unemployment – and government social policy which has resulted in an increase in

The Depths of Poverty (in millions)

	In or on the margins	In poverty	Sinking deeper	In intense poverty
Adults	7.9	5.0	3.3	1.7
Children	4.2	2.5	1.4	0.9
Total (millions)	12.1	7.5	4.7	2.6
Percentage of the population	22.2	13.8	8.6	4.8
Lack of necessities (number of)	1/2	3	5/6	7+

Some Missing Necessities

- approximately 3 million people in Britain today cannot afford to heat the living areas of their home
- around 6 million go without some essential aspect of clothing – such as a warm waterproof coat – because of lack of money
- some 1.5 million children go without toys or, for older children, leisure and sports equipment because their parents do not have enough money.
- nearly 3.5 million people do not have consumer durables such as carpets, a washing machine or a fridge because of lack of money
- around 3 million people cannot afford celebrations at Christmas or presents for the family once a year
- at least 5.5 million people cannot afford basic items of food such as meat or fish every other day, a roast joint once a week or two hot meals a day
- nearly half a million children do not have three meals a day because their parents are so short of money

Adapted from J. Mack and S. Lansley *Poor Britain*, Allen and Unwin, 1985, pp. 184 and 90.

income for the super-rich and a decrease for the poor are the main causes of current renewed concern about poverty. Their survey also noted, however, a waning in the backlash against 'welfarism' which partly swept Margaret Thatcher to power and they found a majority (57%) who thought the government was doing too little to help those lacking necessities. It seems that the tide of opinion is changing somewhat in favour of the poor, though at what point this may be reflected in electoral returns and government policy remains to be seen.

Social Policy

Definitions

As Michael Hill suggests at the beginning of his book *Understanding Social Policy*, one way to answer the question 'What is social policy?' is to list the areas of public policy included under the heading. The areas that Hill himself deals with are social security, the personal social services, the health service, education, employment services and housing, and together these constitute the substance of the British Welfare State. However, as Hill emphasises, this simple definition of social policy will not suffice. Nor, any longer, will T. H. Marshall's classic statement that 'the avowed objective of twentieth century social policy is welfare'. Marxists and others argue that the objective of certain social policy measures is to control disaffected groups in the population rather than to act out of concern for their welfare. Indeed, the whole subject of social policy has been 'blown open' in that it is now widely accepted that social policy is generated through political conflict and debate and that its study must encompass this. Social policy analysis, therefore, must consider political ideology and the effect on social policy of other policy areas, especially economic (since economic factors greatly influence social policy). Hill suggests three things for consideration in defining social policy: first, that social policy may not only be concerned with welfare; second, that other policies (such as economic) may affect welfare more than social policy; third, that public policy should be seen as a whole and that social policy is related to other policies.

Finally, Hill does not give a single, brief definition of social policy. However, the following statement by Peter Townsend summarises the broad view of social policy now widely adopted:

> If social policy is conceived of as the institutional control of services, agencies and organisations to maintain or change social structure or values, then what is at stake is not just the social division of welfare or the management of public, fiscal and private welfare, but the allocation of wealth, the organisation of

645

employment, the management of the wage system and the creation of styles of living.

In short, social policy is about the kind of society people want to create and what they do to create it.

Social administration refers to the means by which social policy is implemented. Given that analysis of policy goals involves political issues, then so must analysis of administrative means. Naturally social policy makers seek to shape their administrative machinery – say the social or education services – to their purposes. There are, of course, a variety of administrative skills but in so far as we are directly concerned with administration, it is as a tool of policy. Administrators may intentionally or unintentionally hamper the goals of policy makers and this is a relevant point to study in policy outcome analysis. Indeed, the civil service is often criticised in this respect not least in the celebrated television series ironically titled 'Yes, Minister'.

The Welfare State

Although the emphasis is now changing somewhat, much modern social policy analysis has focused on the welfare state. Debates have ranged from fundamental matters of ideology to practical issues of cost and efficiency. Asa Briggs defines a welfare state as one which modifies the effects of market forces to provide citizens with a minimum income, to protect them against a range of problems such as sickness and homelessness, and to ensure equal access to a range of services such as education. Of course, what this comes down to in practice is a matter of public intent and political decision. As A. N. Rees points out, it can be far more difficult and humiliating to be 'on welfare' when the consensus is moving against welfare than when it is more favourable. A welfare state securing the citizen's accepted right to certain minimum provisions cannot be assumed.

The British welfare state was largely established by the Labour government of 1945 to 1950. The major exception was Butler's 1944 Education Act. The mood in support of social reform to achieve greater security and opportunity for the majority developed strongly as a result of wartime experience. Many felt that they had earned a fairer society by virtue of their efforts and deprivation over the war years. In addition, war often has a somewhat egalitarian effect by throwing the social classes together in a common cause. Personal value, including one's own, can become more important than status and wealth. Politicians recognised the new climate of opinion and a variety of government reports on a number of social issues were carried out during the war. The most important of these was the Beveridge Report (1942) often thought of as the blueprint for the welfare state.

Beveridge proposed an attack on the five giant evils of want, disease, ignorance, squalor and idleness. It helps to group these five evils into a triad of (i) ignorance (ii) disease and (iii) want, idleness and squalor. Ignorance was attacked by the Education Act (1944) and disease by the National Health Act (1946) although it was the Conservative, Butler, and the socialist, Bevan, rather than the Liberal Beveridge, who were respectively most responsible for them. Beveridge's name is associated with the National Insurance Act (1946) which (along with the National Insurance Act of 1944) established a compulsory flat-rate system of contributions covering basic social needs, primarily sickness, injury, unemployment and old age pensions. Beveridge, then, led the attack on want. A. M. Rees refers to the above three pieces of legislation as the 'three pillars of the British welfare state'. A fourth could be added in the form of the National Assistance Act of 1948 which was also inspired by Beveridge. This provided assistance for special cases who slipped through the national insurance safety net. Both the National Insurance Act and the National Assistance Act have been superseded by later legislation. Insurance contributions and major benefits now have an earnings related element and national assistance has been replaced by supplementary benefit (1966).

Idleness, in the sense of unemployment, and squalor, in the sense of inadequate housing, are forms of want. It was part of Beveridge's thinking that the government would take economic planning measures to ensure a very high (if not full) level of employment. This view reflected the Keynesian consensus of the period which followed John Keynes' view that the government could 'fine-tune' the economy to achieve a buoyant labour market. In part, the government used its control of the nationalised industries to do this. The Thatcher administrations from 1979 broke with the Keynesian consensus, believing that job creation occurs as a result of the expansion of the private sector. In reality, however, it intervened with a series of schemes and subsidies to stimulate the private sector comparable in scale to those adopted

647

by previous governments to assist both the public and private sectors. Beveridge's fifth evil 'squalor' is usually taken to refer to housing and, more recently, to the environment. Squalor was attacked by both the Labour and Conservative Parties by substantial programmes of house building, programmes which have been severely cut back by the policies of the Thatcher government. The New Towns Act (1946) was aimed at providing new and thriving environments for the inhabitants of deprived and decaying inner city areas (see pp. 142–3). The Act is characterised by a sensitivity to environmental issues perhaps ahead of its time.

The Welfare State and Equality: An Assessment

Beveridge was no revolutionary and the welfare measures of the war coalition and post-war Labour government did not amount to revolution. Rather, they represented the height of a long evolution of liberal or social democratic reform. Each of the major areas of reform – education, health and welfare – was characterised by a long period of increasing government involvement. The nature of capitalist industrial society stimulated this concern, raising as it does problems of inequality and insecurity, and of social order and control. Education to the age of ten years was made compulsory in 1880 although a national infrastructure of elementary education had been established ten years previously. The Public Health Act of 1875 was a legislative landmark, establishing a national system of local health authorities, yet, typically of the British reformist tradition, it codified and developed existing tendencies rather than established an entirely new system. Lloyd George's National Insurance Act of 1911 first established a contributory system of national insurance against unemployment and sickness. Prior to this the poor had been variously treated as objects of charity or control, depending on whether humanitarian or punitive sentiments were uppermost. The Victorian workhouse reflected a tough, almost penal attitude to the poor, who, in the individualistic ideology of the period, were often blamed for their own condition. More recently, something of the same attitude was widely expressed in sections of the media and public opinion in the anti 'social security scrounger' campaign of the first Thatcher administration (see p. 294). The National Insurance Acts of 1944 and 1946 greatly expanded the application of insurance which Beveridge envisaged as a citizen's right. Similarly, the liberal policy analyst, Thomas H. Marshall wrote of the three rights of modern citizenship: political, civil and social. Within the liberal/social democratic tradition, Beveridge is considered to have made a major contribution to establishing social rights.

So far, the immediate post-war years have been the most productive period of welfare reform but many developments and refinements of the Beveridge heritage have occurred since. Changes in the national health and education system are described elsewhere (Chapters 23 and 24). Perhaps the most significant change in national insurance has been the introduction of an earnings related element, initially by the Conservatives (1959) and extended by Labour (1966). In itself, this is less egalitarian than Beveridge's original scheme, involving only an equal contribution and equal benefits dependent upon need, but for many it removed the incentive to join private insurance schemes.

To what extent has the welfare state brought about greater equality in Britain? Again, this point is discussed in relation to education and health elsewhere (pp. 706–15 and 684–92). In brief, in respect to education, formal equality of opportunity does not compensate for class disadvantage and the result is that increasing inequality of outcome occurs from primary to higher education. Gender and racial inequality in education persist (see pp. 120–5). As far as the NHS is concerned, a relatively high degree of equality of class access has not resulted in the outcome of equal health across the classes (see pp. 686–92). This is largely because members of the middle class use the NHS more effectively and adopt healthier lifestyles – partly because they can afford to.

The contribution of the rest of welfare to social equality is a large and complex matter. Most commentators agree that the relatively small component of the welfare state involving cash transfers – such as rent rebates and one parent family allowances – are broadly redistributive. The charge that the welfare state is inegalitarian is generally aimed at the social services and, particularly, the universal services, i.e. those subsidies and services available to all. These include public transport, public libraries, tax relief to owner-occupiers (as well as most of the NHS and educational systems). Summarising his own work on the matter, Julian Le Grand states that 'the better off almost invariably used such services to a greater extent than the poor, and . . . such services have failed to achieve equality, however defined'.

Arguably, the attack on housing squalor and inadequacy has been the most successful aspect of welfare state policy since the war although in the mid-nineteen eighties major problems are again apparent. As Donnison and Ungerson point out, there is now greater equality of housing assessed by most basic standards of measurement. Thus, there are more houses per household, more rooms per person, and a higher proportion of baths and toilets per person. Most, but by no means all, of the improvements have gone to those in need. Ironically, perhaps the major area of welfare achievement in equalising resources currently seems to be faltering in this respect. First, the relative position of those in rented council and private property in relation to owner-occupiers is generally worsening. The Conservatives' rate-capping and economic rent policies have reduced housing benefit whilst the substantial system of tax concessions for mortgage holders remains intact. Alan Murie argues that a highly polarised and segregated housing market is the most likely consequence of continuing neglect of policies beyond the encouragement of owner-occupation. Second, the policy of selling council houses has reduced both the number and quality of public housing stock. Third, and related to the last point, the number of homeless families and families on council waiting lists has been increasing. This may be another indication of the development of a growing underclass or, in Marxist terms, lower working class, substantially worse off than the rest of the working class. Of course, policies change and it may be that government will again make the remaining housing problems of this country an urgent priority for public action.

If the attack on squalor is a relative success story of the British welfare state, the ideal of full employment has become its Cinderella. The widespread belief that the levels of unemployment seen in the nineteen thirties would never be approached again has proved an illusion. In 1985 the number of unemployed (as conservatively measured by the government) exceeded the peak of the nineteen thirties although the pecentage figure (13%) was still lower. International economic factors certainly played a part in this and throughout Europe governments of a variety of political complexions struggled to stem the rising tide of unemployment. However, in Britain what was new in 1979 was a government which disclaimed primary responsibility for reducing unemployment and which, by its monetarist policies, was widely considered to have exacerbated it. In any case, the British unemployment rate became the second highest in Europe.

In assessing how egalitarian is the welfare state, we need to consider who pays for it as well as who benefits. This involves a brief review of the British taxation system and particularly the extent to which it is progressive, i.e. taxes the rich more, or, regressive, i.e. taxes the poor relatively more. Two recent developments have made the British tax system more regressive. First, the proportion of income on which tax is paid has been increasing steadily during the post-war period. In other words, the tax threshold – the point at which people start paying income tax – has got much lower and non-taxable earnings allowances much less (in percentage terms). As a result, quite low paid employees are taxed on more of their income than previously. Second, the introduction of Value Added Tax, and particularly the raising of this to 15% in 1979, has proved regressive. A higher percentage of the incomes of the poor than the rich goes in VAT, though, of course, in absolute terms a rich person pays more than a poor person. In addition, there are a great variety of ways in which the better off, and the corporations from which they derive much of their wealth, can avoid taxation. Overall, Westergaard and Resler conclude that, apart from the lowest paid who are taxed relatively less, the British taxation system is barely progressive. So whilst the burden of paying for the welfare state is *relatively* evenly shared across the classes, the middle class is the prime beneficiary. Further, whilst since 1979 the top 1% have been getting a relatively larger share of post-tax income (from 3.9% to 4.6% 1981/82), the bottom 50% have been getting relatively less (from 26.2%–25.2% 1981/82). To put it mildly, this does not amount to a situation remotely suggesting social equality.

The question of whether the welfare state has increased equality can be applied to gender, particularly to whether it has improved the situation of women. Beveridge's support for family allowances which were adopted during the war had been widely campaigned for by feminists in the inter-war years. However, reflecting the general view of his time, Beveridge did not question the sexual division of labour and by channelling family and other welfare benefits mainly through the male, probably strengthened patriarchy. With Beveridge's familist ideals partly in mind, feminist Elizabeth Wilson suggests that his plan 'now reads as deeply conservative'. Many contemporary feminists seek a system –

supported by the state – which will secure the *individual* welfare of women and children, i.e. income and benefits without dependency on males.

The above review clearly indicates that the welfare state has not achieved equality of access (availability) or equality of outcome (use) in relation to key services, though the situation varies greatly between them. Neither is the financing of the welfare state very egalitarian. Growing realisation of this has brought about what is widely referred to as a welfare state 'crisis'. There are a variety of views about how to respond to this, each reflecting ideological preferences. It is to these matters of policy and ideology that we now turn.

Ideology, Social Policy, and the Welfare State

The three major ideologies underpinning social policy positions are liberalism/social democracy, Conservatism (including the 'New Right') and Marxism. I shall also make brief reference to Functionalist theory on social policy although this is a sociological perspective rather than a political ideology. These ideologies have already been described in some detail in the context of development/underdevelopment. The liberal/social democratic view dominated political and public opinion for the 30 years following the war. The liberal consensus involved an acceptance of a mixed economy and of the welfare state. Most members of both major parties subscribed to this consensus. A portmanteau word – Butskellism – made up of the surnames of a leading Conservative, Butler, and of the leader of the Labour Party, Gaitskell, was even produced to describe this approach of moderate reformism.

Liberalism/Social Democracy: The Original Vision
Nevertheless, significant differences of emphasis existed among both politicians and scholars within this generally liberal approach. A key issue that emerged was the extent to which welfare should be provided *universally* or *selectively*. Universalism is based on the principle of providing a service to all citizens as a matter of right. Selectivity involves establishing criteria of acceptability for a given welfare service and means-testing applicants accordingly. A parallel distinction is that between *institutional* and *residual* concepts of welfare. In the words of Harold

Wilensky and Charles Lebeaux: 'a residual system, provides that social welfare institutions should come into play only when the normal structures of supply, the family and the market, break down', whereas an institutional system sees 'the welfare services as normal, "first line" functions of modern industrial society'. Beveridge recommended a system of national security that was universal and compulsory. Aneurin Bevan set up a national health service free to all. Yet, the principle of universalism has been eroded in both cases and by both parties, in the former case by introducing a two tier system of payments, and in the latter by introducing now quite substantial prescription charges.

We now consider the arguments put forward in favour of a universal/institutional system. First, it provides services on the basis of right and equality and therefore fosters a sense of common community. This amounts to a considerable social vision. Second, social democrats typically considered that a more socially secure society would be a more orderly one – a belief that parallels Smelser's Functionalist argument that the development of welfare has promoted social integration. Similarly, a healthier labour force was widely perceived as likely to be more productive. The major argument against universalism is cost – the more comprehensive the system of free services, the higher taxation. In addition, the related charges of abuse of services, dependency and loss of work incentive are made, mainly from the political right. More broadly supported was the view that emerged of the welfare bureaucracy as too large, inefficient and alienating. Richard Titmuss was committed to a basic 'infrastructure of universalist services' but tried to meet the above criticisms by suggesting that other services might be available only to certain 'categories, groups and territorial areas' on the basis of specific need. In this way, he hoped to avoid the means testing of individuals which had caused great bitterness in the nineteen thirties. In fact, in the post-war period, the drift of the British welfare state has been away from universalism towards selective means testing. Since Margaret Thatcher came to power in 1979, this drift has been given a sharper sense of direction.

The main argument in favour of the selective/residual model is that it is cheaper and resources go to those who 'really need' them. It is also seen by its supporters as less likely to spawn bureaucracy. Against this is the increase in humiliating means testing and the possibility that once a service is no longer regarded as a universal right it can be qualified and reduced indefinitely. We will return to the universalism versus selectivity debate when dealing with the rise of New Right (Conservative) social policy alternatives.

The Ideological and Institutional Crisis of the Social Democratic Welfare State

The crisis in the British welfare state preceded by several years the coming to power of Margaret Thatcher in 1979. Underlying the crisis of welfare was (and is) the long relative decline of the country's economy. This endemic problem was intensified in 1974 by the quadrupling of the price of oil following the action of the OPEC cartel. Against a background of world economic recession, the Labour governments of Harold Wilson (1974-76) and James Callaghan (1976-79) struggled to maintain intact the welfare state and a policy of near full employment. However, the crisis was to test the post-war social democratic compromise between capitalism and socialism – basically accepted by all parties – almost to the limit.

Ten years previously, there was little appreciation of the crisis to come. In his professorial inaugural lecture of 1962, F. Lafitte expressed the optimistic orthodoxy that a well-managed mixed economy would supply the wherewithall for a gradual expansion of the welfare state – particularly its 'communal services'. As late as the mid-nineteen seventies, Ramesh Mishra was still commenting unproblematically on the need for a balance between the values of 'fraternity and collectivity' of the welfare ideal and of 'liberty and individuality' of the free market. In reality, however, the 'balance' or compromise was already under severe stress. This was because the free market itself failed to produce a reliably expanding surplus with which to finance the welfare state. Social democrats of all parties were therefore faced with an unpleasant choice which few of them had foreseen: should government policy be directed mainly at taking pressure off the free market by trying to reduce taxation and expenditure, primarily welfare expenditure, or should it continue to support and even expand the welfare state by squeezing the private sector? On the horns of the dilemma, social democracy split, letting in the Thatcherite New Right which, without a qualm or ambiguity, opted for the first solution.

Just how deep social democracy split is illustrated by comparing the currently (1985) very different position of David Owen and

Peter Townsend who, in the nineteen sixties, were both members of the Fabian Society, a reformist group within the Labour Party. Convinced of the fundamental need for a strong private sector and alienated from the growing Marxist inclined element with the Labour Party, Owen broke with Labour and helped found and now leads the Social Democratic Party. He particularly stresses the need for a strong private sector. In contrast, Townsend stayed firmly on the left of the Labour Party, without, however, accepting a Marxist label. His current policy proposals (1981) are radically socialist. Bearing in mind that unanticipated economic crisis plunged social policy into near chaos in the nineteen seventies, he argues that the Labour Party must more closely link economic and social policy. Thus, he contends that policies to achieve full employment and a minimum wage should be pursued. On the issue of income redistribution, he favours, in the short term, a wealth tax, and in the longer term, a 'ceiling of say, £100,000 (1981) ... on the wealth (other than owner-occupied home) which, from a chosen date, any individual could own or inherit'. He also wants 'substantially higher' income – through a range of benefits – for the non-employed. Overall, his proposals are tuned to help particularly the disadvantaged, the disabled and women. In contrast to the social democrats of the nineteen fifties and sixties, his emphasis is on the direct redistribution of income and wealth rather than the provision of universal services. He concludes by stating that the 'reconstruction of society ... deserves to become the primary object of social policy in the last two decades of the twentieth century'. Despite the split from Labour and the formation of the Social Democratic Party, there are still those within the Labour Party who are perhaps closer to David Owen's viewpoint than Townsend's. There are also a number of Marxist inclined Labour politicians both inside and outside Parliament, who stand to the left of Townsend, though he himself now challenges the previous boundaries of social democratic ideology.

No doubt in response to the ideological and policy turmoil of the late nineteen seventies and eighties, Ramesh Mishra has critically reviewed his own previously rather blandly, if eloquently, stated social democratic perspective. In *The Welfare State in Crisis* (1984), he presents a qualified case in favour of a particular form of social democratic welfare state – the corporatist welfare state. He believes that this model – relatively successfully practised by Austria and Sweden – more effectively integrates economic and social policy than any other. The corporatist welfare state retains the mixed economy, with a strong private sector, but is managed by a mixture of Keynesian demand stimulation and supply side economics (often associated with the New Right) to encourage production and labour mobility. On the social side, a 'social partnership' of capital and labour is encouraged by government, in which high levels of social welfare and of industrial productivity are pursued as mutually beneficial and compatible goals. As Mishra himself points out, such an approach can only deal with social problems at a national level whereas, in fact, many are now caused at the international level (see Chapter 8, pp. 200–4).

As the work of Townsend and Mishra shows, the social democratic perspective on welfare has not been destroyed but it has been severely savaged from both right and left. We now turn to consider alternative ideologies.

The New Right: Thatcherism

In both Britain and the United States, it was the political right which primarily benefited from the problems of social democracy. In 1979 Margaret Thatcher became Prime Minister for the first time and in 1980 Ronald Reagan was elected President. Both were returned for a second period of office in 1983 and 1984 respectively. What the New Right stands for on a global scale has already been described (see Chapter 8, pp 206–9), and these principles apply to domestic policy.

The primary goal of the New Right is to enable the private sector to flourish by reducing taxation and by lowering the rate of inflation through control of the money supply (monetarism). Both these measures, especially cutting taxation, tend to reduce the amount of money available for government expenditure. Both Thatcher and Reagan preferred to cut welfare rather than defence expenditure. This was not merely a matter of reluctant choice, however, for both believed that welfare bureaucracy had become wasteful and inefficient and that among some recipients, welfare was eroding the will to work. Their social programmes were aimed not only at saving money but at providing a more motivated and disciplined work force for a (hopefully) revitalised private sector. The new Conservative ideology had a tough logical consistency and, in the conditions of the late nineteen seventies, a considerable popular appeal.

The social policy measures of the New Right fall into the selective/residual model of the welfare state. Let us take council housing as an example. In 1979 government policy was to keep council house rents generally low by means of a *general subsidy*. In fact, in 1979 council rents were at their lowest post war level. The 1980 Housing Act gave the Secretary of State strong powers to push up rents in areas receiving the central subsidy. Between 1979 and 1982, rents more than doubled. However, for those who met the means test criteria, protection was provided by increased rent rebate and supplementary benefit payments. A problem with such schemes is low take-up, particularly amongst the most needy. Only 50% of eligible one-parent families and 46% of two-parent families took up rebates compared to 82% of childless households. To what extent this was due to inadequate publicity of the scheme, too little time on the part of harassed parents, or repugnance at the stigma of means testing, is a matter for speculation. Further, those just above the eligibility line would have been particularly hard hit by the doubling of rents. The above and other aspects of Conservative housing policy lead Alan Murie (from whom the above data is taken) to term it 'a thoroughly residual policy'.

In the many cases where means tested schemes already existed in 1979, the Conservatives have frequently reduced benefits and/or eligibility. Thus, between 1979 and 1980, about 174,000 children lost entitlement to free school meals for which the government, in any case, gave up responsibility for nutritional quality. The number eligible has since increased due to the rise in unemployment. It is not easy to quantify the reduction in social security benefits under Thatcherism, let alone to trace their human cost. However, writing of the first administration, Ruth Lister and Paul Wilding refer to the 'cuts, nicks and slices which have in three and a half years taken some £2000 million away from those dependent on social security'.

Figure A below, presents the expenditure record of government on major areas of welfare between 1959 and 1984. Like many such diagrams, it obscures as much as it illuminates but it provides a useful basis on which to begin to assess the trend of welfare state expenditure. Figure B below, puts British welfare expenditure in comparative perspective. Interestingly, although Britain is often cited as an example of a welfare society, its social welfare expenditure pattern is much closer to that of the United States – the bastion of private enterprise – than to the more truly social democratic Sweden.

A How UK Spending on Social Welfare Divides Up

£ billion at 1984 prices

Social Security*

Education

Health

Housing

Personal Social Services

1959 64 69 74 79 84

*including unemployment benefit

Source: CSO as reprinted in *New Society*, 25 October 1985, p. 145.

B How Spending on Social Welfare Programmes has Grown

as % of gross domestic product

Sweden

United States

United Kingdom

1960 1975 1981

Source: OECD

The following are some points to note in interpreting Figure A, above. The fall in the rate of increase in expenditure on education and science must be seen in the demographic context of falling rolls. However, real cuts have been made in higher education, in primary education, and in teachers' pay. Great controversy surrounds the increase in expenditure on health and personal social services. Again, demography plays a key role in interpretation because it is the expanding population of the elderly which has mainly caused the increase. Government ministers emphasise the increased expenditure but within the NHS it is widely regarded as insufficient to meet new needs. The government's major expenditure saving has been on housing and its policy is clearly residual. The massive increase in social security is accounted for by the equally massive rise in unemployment; most benefits have been cut in real terms.

The policy of de-institutionalisation, pursued by both the Reagan and Thatcher governments, provides an interesting example of the dovetailing of economic expediency with ideology. De-institutionalisation means directing certain dependent groups out of public institutions and into the family and community. It has been practised mainly in relation to the mentally ill and handicapped but also in relation to the old. Clearly the policy has potential advantages, but for it to work, substantial support for the concerned families and communities (however that term may be defined) must be provided. Without this, two groups tend to suffer – as has been apparent in the de-institutionalisation of many of the mentally ill. First, are those who traditionally carry the burden of care – overwhelmingly women, often with many other commitments. Second, are members of the dependent groups – as was seen by the apparently increased numbers of mentally ill people wandering the streets in the mid-eighties. To attempt to save money at the risk of 'dumping', say, a middle aged, long-institutionalised psychotic on his elderly mother is the kind of sad consequence that can result from under-financing de-institutionalisation. Yet, it is in these 'small' corners of human misery that the cost of cuts must be sought.

The privatisation of welfare is another aspect of the social policy of Reaganism and Thatcherism. Le Grand and Robinson indicate that it applies in three areas: the provision, subsidy and regulation of services. Examples of a reduction in state provision are the closing of local authority residential homes (some of which are now privately run) and the sale of council houses. Examples of state subsidy reduction are the reduction of the general subsidy to council house tenants and the increase in NHS prescription charges. An example of decreasing regulation is the lifting of restrictions on competition between private and public bus companies.

A policy that covers so many situations is not easy to generalise about, but the main issues are clear and vital. Those in favour of privatisation argue that it is more efficient than the public provision of services. Research on this point varies from case to case but, on balance, does not sustain this generalisation. Thus, Millward's review of the evidence found that the private collection of refuge tended to be more efficient, but that this was not the case with the provision of water or electricity. The privatisation of British Telecom in 1984 should give most readers a chance to make their own judgement in one area. Second, supporters of privatisation tend to argue that it increases liberty both by releasing intiative and increasing choice. However, it is as logical to argue that the welfare state increases the liberty of the disadvantaged by providing them with the basic means of life, without which they could not make significant choices (whereas private enterprise does not seek to guarantee this). Third, critics of the welfare state argue that it has failed to produce equality and that a combination of privatisation and income subsidies for the 'truly needy' would be more effective. The key issue here is how big the redistribution of income would be. In the absence of public services, it would have to be very substantial to increase equality. In any case, to do so is not the goal of Conservatives although a number of social democrats, including Peter Townsend, are now (1985) examining the policy of substantial income redistribution as an alternative or supplement to universalism as a means to achieve greater equality.

The document that most significantly embodies the social policy principles of the New Right is the bill on Britain's social security system presented to Parliament in January 1986 by the Secretary of State, Norman Fowler. The details of the proposals may change and, should the Conservatives lose the next election, these will not become law at all. Were the proposals to pass into law, they would be the most radical restructuring of social welfare since Beveridge although they represent a very different philosophy and purpose than his. It is the ideology underlying the white paper, not its ultimate destination that interests us here.

The following summary of the proposals will be brief. First, the State Earnings Related Pension Scheme (SERPS) will be cut back so as to almost halve the cost by the year 2033 (just about the time when most readers of this book will be coming up for a pension!). This will enormously increase the need and, presumably, the demand for personal pensions organised via the private sector. Second, supplementary benefit will be abolished, to be replaced by income support, and some discretionary help will be available from a Social (loan) Fund. Third, housing benefit will be cut from £4.3 billion to £3.85 billion. All, including the poorest, will be expected to pay a minimum of 20% of their rates. Fourth, a new Family Credit will help 200,000 more low-paid families than did Family Income Supplement which it replaces. However, both these and the slightly better-off poor will lose other benefits (see proposal two, above). Fifth, birth and death grants will be replaced by means tested help.

The Fowler package fully illustrates New Right ideology. First, we said that a primary purpose of New Right policy is to reduce public expenditure and taxation to stimulate the private sector – the primacy of economic over social policy. Estimates of the sum that the cuts involved in the proposals would save run up to £1 billion. The price of this, in the government's own figures, is that whereas 2.2 million claimants would gain under the proposals, 3.8 million would lose, including 2.2 million pensioners (seemingly to reverse the relative improvement in this group's position during the last twenty years). Second, the proposals firmly pursue the principle of selectivity. This is shown by targeting of the very low paid for help (even at the expense of larger numbers of other poor) and by the abolition of the birth and death grants. The selection of the low paid for help rather than the unemployed seems to be to encourage work rather than unemployment. Third, the very important pension reforms powerfully illustrate the government's preference for private rather than state solutions to social problems.

The following comments on the white paper are tentative, and reflect various shades of opinion. First, the white paper is transparently not concerned to redistribute income and wealth (except mildly within the poor themselves). If the savings from the cuts are used to finance cuts in higher or standard income tax, the overall effect will be to redistribute upwards (i.e. in line with the general effect of Conservative government policy from 1979). Second, the unemployed, who in a particular way may be considered the responsibility of the Thatcher governments, get little or nothing through these proposals. Third, the widely hoped for increase in child benefit is not scheduled – presumably because of cost. Fourth, the problems of the low take-up of selective benefits are not convincingly met in the white paper. A. B. Atkinson suggests that 'the take-up problem will remain severe' (*New Society*, 20/27 December 1985). Fifth, within their own limits the proposals represent a clear philosophy. They take the country in a particular direction. Equally, they implicitly challenge the opposition parties to respond with comparably coherent and committed policies at a time when they are still reformulating their own ideologies in changed and difficult circumstances. No doubt, the opposition will seek to define and struggle for their own versions of the good society, but immediately the initiative lies with those who subscribe to the version presented above.

In criticism of New Right policies, Le Grand and Robinson argue that a strong welfare state promotes community:

> For many people, the concept of the welfare state embodies a principle of collective provision and finance that they find preferable to individualistic forms of behaviour encouraged through private market systems. Thus the welfare state serves to develop a sense of communal interest rather than self-interest.

This view is compatible with both Marxist and liberal/social democratic values and ideology. The vision of the New Right is based on a very different moral and theoretical framework. Yet, some Marxists maintain that the structure of modern capitalism forces both social democracy and Conservatism down a similar path of compromise – the one having always to accommodate the needs of free enterprise, the other not daring to reduce the welfare state much beyond the point where social disorder might result. Marxists maintain that only they offer a radically different alternative.

A final point deserves consideration when assessing the social policy of the New Right and, indeed, Thatcherism generally. It is simply whether or not you respond to the spirit of Thatcherism, to her and her followers' attempts to change the culture of the British people. Despite assertions to the contrary, there are, of course, alternatives.

Marxist Perspectives on Social Policy

Marxists have always faced a dilemma in relation to the liberal welfare state. On the one hand, elements of the welfare state benefit the working class and have been won partly by the efforts of the trade union movement, the Labour Party and other predominantly working class organisations. On the other, Marxists commonly view the welfare state as a means of reducing working class militancy and demand for socialism. This conflict has produced some ambivalence in Marxist perspectives on the welfare state.

One of the most influential recent Marxist works is James O'Connor's *The Fiscal Crisis of the State* (1973). The crisis to which he refers lies in a contradiction between what he describes as the two main functions of the state: accumulation (of wealth through capitalist enterprise) and legitimisation (partly through the pacificatory effects of the welfare state referred to above). The crisis is that the cost of legitimisation is becoming more than private enterprise can support – thus, the budget deficit. In commenting on O'Connor's work, Ramesh Mishra concedes that

O'Connor focuses on a potentially contradictory *tendency* in liberal capitalism. However, Mishra argues that it is only a tendency and that, in general, the welfare state supports rather than weakens capitalism. Whatever the general merits of Mishra's observation, there is no doubt of the current relevance of O'Connor's analysis when most social democracies do appear to be struggling with the contradiction he indicates.

Whereas O'Connor concentrates on the fiscal crisis of capitalism, more recent writings by Ian Gough and other Marxists analyse in addition the broader aspects of the economic crisis of the seventies and particularly its consequences for the working class. These writings agreed that capital would try to make labour pay the price of this crisis in lower wages and reduced welfare. Nevertheless, Ian Gough in *The Political Economy of the Welfare State* (1979) argues that working class organisations should continue to press for reform. The state of the political left in the nineteen eighties was one of much greater disarray than Gough anticipated but his contention that socialists must distinguish between reforms that promote 'welfare capitalism' and those that promote 'welfare socialism' continues to generate interest and controversy. Ramesh Mishra's response is that, in practice, such a distinction is not possible: the aim of many social reforms is both to improve conditions (socialist-inclined) and to adjust beneficiaries to 'the system' (capitalist-inclined). My own view favours Gough because any political movement must struggle to bend change in its own preferred direction. In fact, several Thatcherite issues require a carefully discriminating response: examples are community versus institutional care, and the intention and impact of educational initiatives such as the Youth Training Scheme and the Certificate of Pre-Vocational Education (see pp. 715–21). More broadly, Gough sees potential for such groups as the Claimants' Union and Women's Aid, supported by the trade union movement, to defend and ultimately extend the more socialist aspects of the welfare state.

Whatever the room for manoeuvre of the kind Gough indicates, Marxists consider that no major party has yet attempted to introduce a genuinely socialist welfare state in Britain. Similarly, they point out that the Labour government preceding the first Thatcher administration had already begun to make cuts in welfare – largely to defend the capitalist economy. Accordingly, in *Public Opinion, Ideology and State Welfare*, Peter Taylor-Gooby, argues that 'the view that the welfare state is currently the victim of a sudden attack by the new right is somewhat misleading'. In support of Taylor-Gooby, it is arguable that even before 1979, the British welfare state was barely better than minimal, certainly when compared to those of the Scandinavian countries. In practice, Thatcher found it difficult to cut 'fat' without flesh and has made most of her savings through privatising nationalised industries rather than reducing welfare expenditure. Even so, whatever the long-term estimates of the Thatcherite cuts, it is worth recalling Harold Wilson's comment on unemployment and applying it to social welfare reductions: "If it happens to you, it's a hundred per cent." Taylor-Gooby goes on to state:

> The vision of the history of the welfare state as a decline from the golden age tends to mask the conflicts and continuities that have always existed in policy. The contemporary problems of the welfare state arise from the failures of policy to meet the demands of changing circumstances – from inertia rather than the radical development of policy.

The 'radical development of policy' Taylor-Gooby considers necessary is, of course, socialist. However, publishing in 1985, he is well aware that few, even of the working class, are Marxist (indeed, in the 1983 general election, the majority of them did not even vote Labour!). Norman Ginsburg in *Class, Capital and Social Policy* examines the wider problem of why the consciousness of the working class is not more socialist. He considers that it is seduced by capitalist commodities into obsessive consumption (commodity fetishism) – a behaviour which is strongly expressed and regenerated within the family. Partly as a result, class solidarity is fragmented. Patriarchy is also obscured by commodity fetishism and by the individualisation of collective family concerns into 'accepted' roles. The welfare state is widely presented and perceived as another mechanism for distributing commodities rather than as a potential instrument of socialism. Interestingly, the social democrat, Ramesh Mishra, argues that Marxists uselessly lament the consumer tendencies or, applying O'Connor's term to workers a well as capitalists, accumulative tendencies of the working class. Its members merely share these desires with other classes and Marxism must provide for them if it is to have political appeal. Whilst Mishra's point may be valid, it is worth commenting that socialism is not merely concerned with material

664

consumption but with the quality of human relations and culture. Thus, in theory, consumption as well as production would be organised and experienced differently under socialism than capitalism.

Whilst Gough cautiously draws attention to the socialist potential of the welfare state, Taylor-Gooby and Ginsburg tend to stress its limits and, indeed, its services to capitalism. One conclusion from this is that any Marxist or socialist party needs to be quite clear on what it can realistically expect to achieve through the welfare state, given a situation of influence or power. Clarity of vision would be especially necessary in a situation of transition towards socialism.

Gender and Social Policy (with Particular Reference to the Family)

The Marxist/socialist 'wing' of the contemporary feminist movement appears to have reached a generally clear analysis of female oppression within capitalism and a clear programme of change. The purpose of this section is critically to present the latter, but it will help first to recall how they conceptualise women's oppression. Mary McIntosh's article *The State and the Oppression of Women*, argues that in capitalist society the family household has two basic functions – 'it serves (though inadequately) for the reproduction of the working class and for the maintenance of women as a reserve army of labour, low-paid when they are in jobs and often unemployed.' The point is that women's labour is made cheap in capitalist society: domestic labour is unpaid except by grace of the husband and their paid work is more poorly rewarded and more easily expended with than men's.

McIntosh argues that within capitalism the family household has been 'importantly structured and constrained by state policies' to ensure that it achieves its functions. The form of marriage encouraged by the state has involved a 'dependent-breadwinner' structure. This family structure provides unpaid maintenance of male labour (the reproduction of labour) and systematises biological reproduction. Family policy, in particular, and welfare policy in general, such as unemployment and supplementary benefit, support this situation (see pp. 651–2). Women who do not fit into the system may suffer as a result. Women living with their husbands or lovers, and school leavers cannot claim supplementary benefit and can only claim unemployment benefit if they have

Social Problems and Policy

paid full contributions. McIntosh suggests that policy towards one parent families has provided the means to survive, whilst seeking to avoid encouraging the practice. McIntosh is aware of the 'Marxist functionalist' nature of the argument but strongly differentiates it from classical Functionalist perspective by insisting on the 'contradictions' between the family and state within capitalist society and within the family itself. A central contradiction is that the role of women as cheap reproducers of (male) labour and as a reserve army of labour themselves can conflict – thus forcing substantial direct state intervention in the supposedly 'private sphere' of the family, as notably occurred, for instance, during the second world war.

C. C. Harris sharply criticises the kind of Marxist Functionalist arguments used by McIntosh on the grounds that they may explain *how* but not *why* institutions function in a given way. Thus, no historical explanation is offered as to why women rather than men perform domestic labour (though see pp. 62–3). Harris also seems to regard the focus on oppression as emotive and unscientific. However, it is hardly surprising that women should focus on this matter and suggest policies to relieve it.

Anna Coote's article 'Labour: The Feminist Touch' assumes that women have been domestically oppressed and that the main strategy for dealing with this is for women increasingly to penetrate the labour market and to achieve equality within it and otherwise. Publishing seven years after McIntosh, in 1985, she suggests that the figures of women in paid work (60%) 'suggest that we are no longer a "reserve army of labour"; we are regulars'. What remains to be done, however, is for women to gain equality at work whilst the needs of children and people (men or women) doing domestic work are met. The programme she offers is bold but perhaps no bolder than is necessary to achieve the end she seeks:

> The strategy focuses on the spheres of reproduction *and* production, but starts with the former, on the grounds that this is the primary sphere, from which production springs.
> The strategy would give priority to breaking down the traditional division of paid and unpaid labour, so that responsibility for children would be shared equally among men and women, and between home-based parental care and community-based collective care. It would mean a much shorter working week for men and women, vastly improved child-care provision outside the home, and

a restructuring of family income, by increasing female earning power and child benefit, and improving the 'social wage'.

The shorter working week Coote refers to is to provide more jobs for women and more time for men to do domestic work (including caring for their children). She also suggests extended parental leave, on an equal basis for men and women. To protect low-paid workers, a disproportionate number of whom are women, she emphasises the need for a statutory minimum wage.

How does the socialist feminism of McIntosh and Coote relate to other strands in the feminist movement? Neither appear to want to be at odds with the libertarian wing of the movement as represented by, for instance, the Americans, Leghorn and Parker (see pp. 212–15). However, they clearly consider that the localised, network-based activities of feminists must be complemented and supported by central government action. Neither McIntosh nor Coote seek to improve the situation of women by attacking only patriarchy. Coote's programme blends an attack on patriarchy with an attack on certain main aspects of capitalism. Whilst recognising that men are unlikely, voluntarily, to relinquish power, she nevertheless attempts to make a feminist-sensitive programme of social reform appealing to them (e.g. in its job creation and leisure aspects). Nothing as specific or coherent as this has emerged from those feminists who regard patriarchy as the sole source of female oppression (referred to by Juliet Mitchell as Radical Feminists). Indeed, arguably the equality package of the mid-seventies has largely established the framework that they want for fair and open competition between the sexes (see pp. 330–2). McIntosh and Coote seek a framework of equality and co-operation founded on mutual independence between the sexes, rather than competition.

To summarise, the socialist feminist programme seeks to restructure the family household both in terms of functions and roles. The family will continue to reproduce children but the rearing of them will be shared more equally between the sexes and much better public child-care facilities will be established. All modern movements to release women from domestic bondage – from the Kibbutz to Soviet socialism – have attempted to find means other than the mother to rear children. Britain has not seriously done so. Even progressive local authorities such as Camden in London have only a small number of publicly provided nursery places relative to need. For instance, the children of many single parent families are not provided with places – virtually making it impossible for their mothers to work. Coote argues that better nursery and pre-school facilities and more male involvement in child rearing will better enable women to achieve the equality that decently paid work brings. Thus, the era in which women are 'second bested' at home and in paid work could begin to draw to a close.

Social Problems and Policy: Conclusion

High unemployment, poverty, racial and gender disadvantage, urban disorder – these are social problems by almost anybody's definition and Britain has its share of them. There is limited agreement between the major ideological/policy perspectives discussed above on how to deal with these problems although supporters of each have increasingly come to stress that wealth has to be produced before it can be distributed. There is also potential for overlap between radical social democrats and Marxists. It is quite possible that given favourable circumstances, each of the above approaches could be made to work effectively and to improve social conditions – at least, within the terms of its own frame of reference. When we choose to support a particular approach to social policy, we are making a statement of value as well as of practicality. Of course, policies must be workable. Passionate statements of value and goals are useless unless related to effective solutions. Currently, we are perhaps moving into an era of greater openness and discussion in relation to means. Some of the problems of both universalist and selection solutions are now much more obvious. Positive alternatives and compromises are hard to find but lively efforts to do so both among politicians and theorists are certainly occurring.

Guide to Further Reading and Study

The prominent appearance of Social Problems and Policy on 'A' level syllabuses indicates a trend to relevance and practicality which seems to spark a positive response in many students. The topic is a wide one and individual students can gain from more intensive study of one area – e.g. housing, urban disorders, 16 to 19 education policy – which can be presented in the form of a paper to the rest of the class (a change from the weekly essay format). This would be a convenient way of 'dividing up' the various chapters in the following two standard texts on social policy: Michael Hill's *Understanding Social Policy* (Basil Blackwell and Martin Robertson, 1983) and K. Jones, J. Brown, and J. Bradshaw *eds, Issues in Social Policy* (Routledge and Kegan Paul, 1983). A book much more in the perspectives mould is Ramesh Mishra's *The Welfare State in Crisis: Social Thought and Social Change* (Open University, Harvester Press, 1984). Mishra is fair, if critical, to other perspectives but also argues his own case in a chapter titled 'Towards the Corporatist Welfare State: the Way Ahead?'. Peter Townsend's *Sociology and Social Policy* (Penguin, 1975) is authoritative and passionately concerned. There is a growing flood of topic books broadly within this area of which I found particularly lively and informed Hilary Graham's *Health and Welfare* (Macmillan, 1985). A good collection of Marxist and feminist readings is: M. Loney, D. Boswell and J. Clarke *eds, Social Policy and Welfare* (Open University Press, 1983). One of several widely used Marxist analyses is N. Ginsburg, *Class, Capital and Social Policy* (Macmillan, 1979).

Past Questions

1 'There is disagreement among sociologists concerning the nature of social problems, and about how and why they should be studied.' Examine the major areas of controversy. (AEB 1982)
2 'Social science provides neutral information for benevolent policy makers.' (Specimen Question 1982 AEB syllabus)
3 'The Welfare State provides more effectively for the under-sixteens than the over-sixties.' Discuss. (OLE 1983)
4 'The establishment of the Welfare State represents the single most important attempt to change the social structure of British society this century.' Explain and discuss. (AEB 1984)

23 The Sociology of Health and Health Policy

Themes and Definitions

There are two main and recurrent themes in this chapter. The first is that there are different paradigms or frameworks for perceiving and organising health. Cultural anthropology is the discipline best suited to exploring these different frameworks. Accordingly, the chapter begins with a survey of cultural paradigms of health and illness: magical, religious (briefly), modern scientific, and holistic medicine. A particularly narrow form of scientific medicine – 'mechanistic' or positivistic – is subject to criticism from a more humanistic medical perspective (of which holistic medicine is an example). Mechanistic and humanistic approaches to medicine are also contrasted in the sections on mental health and illness and on gender and health. The sociology of knowledge examines the relationship between paradigms and social factors and, along with the later section on the sociology of educational knowledge, our examination of health paradigms is a main example of the sociology of knowledge in this book. The second major theme is the unequal distribution of health and it explicitly or implicitly occupies most of the chapter. It includes an analysis of health inequalities in relation to gender and the Third World as well as social class. The chapter concludes with a review of sociological perspectives on health and relates these to social policy perspectives.

Webster's Dictionary gives a commonly accepted definition of health: it is 'the condition of being sound in body, mind or soul; esp: freedom from physical disease or pain' (1965). The Constitution of the World Health Organization presents health as more than freedom from disease but in addition as 'a state of complete physical, mental and social well-being': a quality of life as well as a material issue. Such generalities aside, understanding of health and illness, perhaps especially mental illness, varies

671

significantly from culture to culture and even within cultures. The terms illness and disease will be used interchangeably here although a useful distinction is sometimes made between them.

L. G. Moore *et al.*, present disease as 'a reflection of failure to adapt to the environment . . . usually manifested by abnormalities in the structure and function of body, organs and systems'. Illness, however, relates to the *'experience'* of such abnormal conditions and 'thus includes those social psychological aspects of disease that not only affect the ill person, but may also affect the person's family and friends'. How we respond to disease is an important aspect of being ill.

Cultural Paradigms of Health

A paradigm is 'the entire constellation of beliefs, values, techniques, and so on shared by members of a given community' (Kuhn, 1970). Without using the term, James Frazer, in effect, presented the evolution of human knowledge in terms of the paradigms of magic, religion and science (*The Golden Bough*, 1922). More recent research has shown Frazer's scheme to be over-simple, but he does usefully indicate the major cultural paradigms of explanation and belief.

Magical and Religious Paradigms of Health and Illness
Health and illness can usefully be understood within wider cultural paradigms or belief systems, particularly those of magic, religion and science. Magic involves the manipulation and control of the natural world by certain individuals such as witches, sorcerers and shamans. These powerful figures were considered able to cause or alleviate much misfortune, including illness. Two forms of magic are witchcraft and sorcery. Witchcraft is generally regarded as an in-born ability to generate misfortune, whereas sorcery requires conscious effort and often involves the ritual manipulation of items belonging to the object of the sorcery.

Edward Evans-Pritchard carried out an anthropological study of the African Azande, including their understanding of death and illness as a result of witchcraft and sorcery. Whereas disease is generally regarded as a materialistic phenomenon in the West, for the Azande it is generated psychically and spiritually. The Azande believe that witchcraft is a substance in the bodies of witches, the 'soul' of which may leave the witch and take possession of the victim at any time but especially at night. The 'resulting' illness is seen as the production of witchcraft and often a witch hunt follows.

Accusation plays a key role in the response to witchcraft. From the perspective of the Azande and cultural groups with similar beliefs, accusation is part of the process of explanation and reparation. From a more detached sociological perspective, we can see that the practical affirmation of the belief system strengthens social solidarity. Accusation is the vehicle for this as it labels and stigmatises deviant behaviour. In Durkheim's terms, accusation helps to redraw normative boundaries. Conflict theorists point out, however, that certain groups may benefit more than others from ritual reaffirmation of the social *status quo*. Andre Singer and Brian V. Street adopt this approach in *Zande Themes*. They note that the beneficiaries of witchcraft are invariably the wealthy and powerful. Members of the princely class are not accused of witchcraft but by successfully accusing others they can acquire forfeits and thus extend their wealth and power.

Not all examples of witchcraft and sorcery lend themselves so easily to explanations of self-interest or social systems maintenance (solidarity). In any case, respect is due to magical belief systems simply because they may in certain ways be true and powerful. This is the impression left by Carlos Castaneda's long and continuing study of the magico-religious beliefs of the Yacqui Indians and of M. J. Harner's research on the Jivaro Indians of the Ecuadorian Amazon. Even the anthropological detachment of Evans-Pritchard seemed on one occasion to falter into affirmation of magic when he became a 'witness' himself: 'I have only once seen witchcraft on its path. . . .'

I will deal very briefly with the relationship between religion and health and illness because what has been said about magic applies equally to religion. Frazer's key and still useful distinction between magic and religion is that the former is controlled by human beings and the latter by God or spirits. In practice, this distinction is not always so clear. For example, powerful religious intermediaries have something in common with shamans or benevolent sorcerers, especially in their roles as healers and interceders with the divine. More fundamentally, despite the fact that they are different systems of knowledge, both magic and religion are non-scientific (though not illogical in their own terms).

673

Just as magic explains illness in terms of witchcraft and sorcery, so many religions explain it at least partly in terms of 'God's will'. Like magic religion is sometimes used as ideology to justify self or group interest (see pp. 565-6). There is a potential, but not inevitable conflict between the religious and scientific explanation of illness.

Modern Scientific Medicine

Lorna G. Moore *et al*, present two major defining assumptions of modern scientific medicine: first is the germ theory of disease and the need to cure infection to restore health; second, is the efficacy of preventive medicine. The two arms of modern scientific medicine are, then, the curative and the preventive. All scientific theory depends on the empirical demonstration of causal relationships and it was the work of Louis Pasteur on germ theory, particularly germ contagion, in the mid to late nineteenth century that established the basis of modern medicine. Criticisms of modern scientific medicine tend to focus on (a) a limited approach to curative medicine that has developed, based on drugs and surgery and (b) a corresponding failure to emphasise the role of prevention. Few, however, would oppose the use of science in medicine, it is the abuse that is criticised.

The great advantage of Moore's broad definition is that it highlights the common assumptions underlying certain traditions of treatment within scientific medicine. Moore states that allopathy, homeopathy and naturopathy share the two core assumptions mentioned above. There are also significant differences between them. Allopathic medicine is based on the principle of finding a means to counteract disease. Drugs are the main counteractive agents used. Because of the successful use of drugs in combating germs, Western medicine is often identified with allopathic medicine to the neglect of other systems of treatment. Homeopathic medicine is based on the principle that a particular sickness can be treated by administering minute doses of a remedy that produces the same symptoms as the disease. The homeopath regards symptoms of disease as an attempt by the body to restore homeostasis (balance), a process which treatment seeks to stimulate. Reactions to disease vary and individuals rather than diseases are treated. In so far as homeopathy reaches out to the whole person, it shares the principles of holistic medicine (see pp.

677–9). Naturopathy is based on the principle that a natural, mainly fruit and vegetable diet, provides the body with the ingredients it needs to avoid disease. Similarly, herbal remedies are used when disease does occur. Naturopathy can also include regular exercise, a healthy environment, avoidance of and techniques to deal with stress.

Although allopathic medicine remains dominant in the West and is increasing in influence elsewhere, serious criticisms of the way it is practised are now widely made. The essence of these criticisms is that a machine-like, dehumanising model of health and illness has come to dominate allopathic medicine and there is, in addition, much surgery and 'high-tech' medicine. Elliot Mishler refers to this approach as the biomedical model and he identifies four assumptions which underly it. First, disease is seen as deviation from normal biological functioning. A criticism of this assumption is that effective biological functioning varies somewhat from person to person. Second is the doctrine of specific aetiology or causation, i.e. a specific germ causes a given disease. A problem here is that individuals do not respond to germs in the same way so that other factors in disease causation must exist – presumably related to the individual's health and ability to maintain health. Third is the assumption of generic diseases which means that the same kinds of diseases occur in all human societies. Despite its analytical usefulness, this perspective tends to ignore the variety of cultural interpretation given to disease. Fourth is the assumption that medicine is scientifically neutral. In fact, as we shall see, the practice of medicine has profound personal and social implications which the attitude of scientific 'objectivity' can obscure.

In essence, the above criticism of the biomedical paradigm is that it is too mechanistic (sometimes it is referred to as the bio-mechanical model) and fails to take account of either individual variety and need, or of cultural diversity. A particularly sharp critique of the bio-medical model is given in 'The Machine Metaphor in Medicine' by Samuel Osherson and Lorna Amara Sigham which appears in Elliot Mishler's edited volume, *Social Contexts of Health, Illness and Patient Care*. I shall use their discussion of the influence of the mechanical metaphor on the management of death to illustrate their main points. They present three dimensions of a machine metaphor which they find expressed in contemporary medicine.

Dimension of Machine Metaphor	Expression in Medicine
1 Machines are reducible to their component parts	A mind-body split (body as spirit-free)
2 Machines are without emotion	An exclusion of emotion (body as affect-free)
3 Machines are instrumental (means, not ends in themselves) and non-purposive, and as such are not guided by considerations of value.	Inattention to considerations of value (body as value-free)

As a result of mechanistic thinking, hospitals rarely provide the atmosphere and rituals in which the individual's spiritual and emotional feelings about death can be freely and fully expressed and discussed. Medics and paramedics do not see this as their 'job': they are not trained and sensitised to help deal with this 'side' of death. Thus, this is one nurse's idea of role-appropriate behaviour at the impending death of a patient, quoted by Glaser and Strauss:

> A stern face, you don't have to communicate very much verbally, you put things short and formal. . . . Yes, very much the nurse.

Osherson and Amara Singham's primary message is that 'to understand medicine truly, we must look beyond it'. Personal and cultural meaning and context are relevant to the consideration of health, illness and death. They are certainly not opposed to scientific medicine or even to all applications of mechanistic medicine, but they see a need for a broader perspective. There are, of course, others who are opposed in principle to the major forms of treatment of 'mechanistic' medicine, drugs and surgery. However, complete rejection of the biomedical paradigm is not the only response to the critique of it presented in this section.

IVAN ILLICH'S CRITIQUE OF MODERN SCIENTIFIC MEDICINE Although sometimes couched in obscure rhetoric and jargon, the brunt of Illich's critique against modern medicine is clear enough. Based in the Third World, in Mexico, the immediate object of his attack in *Limits to Medicine* is the medical establishment of the industrialised countries. Illich pitches his critique widely. He argues that medical iatrogenesis (illness caused by medicine itself) extends beyond the clinical, such as ill-advised drug use, to the social and cultural. Social iatrogenesis refers to the injury – much of it psychological – caused by the bureaucratic and impersonal way in which modern medicine is organised: it occurs when the language in which people could experience their bodies is turned into bureaucratic gobbledegook; or 'when suffering, mourning, and healing outside the patient role are labelled a form of deviance'. Cultural iatrogenesis describes the widespread acceptance of 'managed health' and failure to accept personal responsibility for one's own health.

As the Marxist Vicente Navarro acutely observes, Illich's critique of modern bureaucracy in *Limits of Medicine* and other works is based on a disillusionment with industrial society. He echoes the scepticism of Tönnies and Simmel about the 'bigness' and impersonality of modern society which they saw as undermining individual and local power and involvement in many aspects of life. These populist sentiments were revived in the nineteen sixties and early seventies when not surprisingly Illich became something of a cult figure among radical activists. From his own socialist perspective, Navarro suggests that Illich offers no real alternative principle of social organisation to capitalism. Illich's reply might well be that most socialist systems are as open to his criticisms as capitalism: democracy and participation are readily found in socialist theory and authoritarianism and bureaucracy more easily in practice.

Holistic Medicine: A Humanistic Alternative

Holistic medicine understands health and illness not merely in biomedical terms but in total personal and cultural terms as well. Moore *et al.* refer to holistic medicine as a biocultural (which embraces personal/social factors) rather than simply a biomedical approach. There is wide agreement in the literature about the nature and goals of holistic medicine. The following comments by Kenneth R. Pelletier define holistic attitudes to health and illness and express the humanistic emphasis of holistic medicine. By emphasising the integration of mind and body, he rejects the dualism of the bio-medical model:

> Holistic medicine recognises the inextricable interaction between the person and his psychosocial environment. Mind and body function as an integrated unit, and health exists when they are in harmony, while illness results when stress and conflict disrupt this process. These approaches are essentially humanistic and re-

677

establish an emphasis on the patient rather than upon medical technology. Modern medicine has tended to view man as a machine with interchangeable parts, and has developed sophisticated procedures for repairing, removing, or artificially constructing these parts. . . . Consideration of the whole person emphasises the healing process, the maintenance of health, and the prevention of illness rather than the treatment of established disorders.

The title of Pelletier's book is *Mind as Healer, Mind as Slayer: A Holistic Approach to Preventing Stress Disorders.* He contends that stress-induced disorders have substantially replaced infectious disease as the major medical problem of advanced industrial nations. In Western Europe, the United States and Japan, cardiovascular disorders, cancer, arthritis, and respiratory diseases are prime causes of ill-health and death. Pelletier argues that mental processes play a part in the contraction and management of these diseases. In making his case, he conducts an interesting incidental 'dialogue' with the language of scientific medicine in which he attempts to 'rehumanise' it. Thus, he rejects the dominant definition of 'psychosomatic' as a disorder which persists in the absence of clearly diagnosed organic pathology (and which is sometimes thought of by practitioners as 'imaginary'.) Instead, he uses the concept 'to convey . . . a fundamental interaction between mind and body which is involved in all diseases and all processes affecting health maintenance'.

Pelletier describes a number of techniques for controlling stress, including meditation and biofeedback. An important aspect of both is the active involvement of the individual in maintaining his/her own health. Yet, Pelletier emphasises that it is possible to measure scientifically the effectiveness of this subjective involvement. He refers to '(n)umerous research projects (which) have demonstrated that meditation is psychologically and physiologically more refreshing and energy restoring than deep sleep'. Among the measurable indications of this in an experiment with Indian Yogis are the extreme slowing of respiration to four to six breaths per minute and a predominance of alpha brain-wave activity (associated with the absence of stress). Biofeedback is the monitoring of bodily functions to establish the effect of given factors on them. Pelletier refers to research and clinical practice which show that a large range of bodily functions normally thought to be involuntary can be brought under conscious control. These include heart rate, muscle tension, body temperature, and more experimentally, stomach acidity and white blood cells. The potential here for taking personal responsibility and action for one's own health is obvious.

There is today a wider awareness than say 30 years ago of the importance of a range of factors in health and illness among people, many of whom have barely heard of holistic medicine. This awareness gained impetus from the humanistic and naturalistic movements of the sixties. There is now greater understanding of the importance of exercise, as illustrated by the popularity of jogging, aerobics and various other workouts. The same is true of diet and stress-control. Pelletier, writing soon after the sixties, speculated that a 'profound transformation of human consciousness' was fuelling these developments. In the tough, 'realistic' eighties, it is not easy to feel that this is still so, but there has certainly emerged a lively and developing health movement that looks beyond 'mechanistic' medicine.

Political Economy and Health Policy

How health services are organised in a society is a central issue of social policy. Disagreements about the organisation of health services reflect differences of political and economic ideology and values, thus the title of this section. I have already described principles of conservatism, Marxism, and social democracy in the context of social policy and these same principles underlie health policy. It might be helpful to note that some of the standard texts on social and health policy use somewhat different terminology to refer to these ideologies. Thus, G. Room in *The Sociology of Welfare* refers to what I call conservatism as market-liberalism, a term which reflects the roots of the ideology in eighteenth/nineteenth century *laissez-faire* capitalist thought. Marxism he refers to as neo-Marxism – an acceptable way of indicating that Marxist regimes differ not only among themselves but sometimes apparently from the views of Marx. His use of the term social democracy to refer to what I sometimes term modern liberalism is common practice.

The health systems of different societies naturally reflect varying outcomes in the conflict of health policies and underlying economic and political interests. In Britain, the health services are predominantly, but not exclusively, public – a social democratic compromise. In the United States, health is mainly provided through the private market but with important elements of public involvement. The health service in Marxist China is almost entirely public and reflects elements of traditional as well as Western health care. The point of mentioning these three cases is not to suggest precise, 'ideal types' of given health policies. The outcome of real political struggle and the imperfections of policy implementation is almost always more messy than model descriptions of ideologies, as our detailed discussion of the British system will show.

The British System of Health Care

Historical
Important improvements in the health of the British people had occurred well before the setting up of the national health system in 1946. Indeed, some of these developments can be traced back to and probably beyond the mid-eighteenth century. Progress in prevention rather than cure accounts for the gradual improvement of the health of Britons up to the time when the use of new curative drugs (notably, antibiotics) became widespread in the mid-twentieth century.

First, improvements in the quality and cleanliness of the environment contributed substantially to health improvement. This was (and remains) a fundamental matter as Disraeli's reference to the need for good 'air, light and water' when speaking for what became the 1872 Public Health Act indicates. This Act codified over a century of fragmented central and local government initiative in the health field and required all local authorities to appoint medical officers of health and sanitary inspectors. Sewage, drainage, the construction of pavements, roads and housing, street-lighting, and the quality of food production, storage and distribution, all continued to improve. A second factor, improvement in personal and family nutrition and hygiene, is complementary to the first. Clearly the availability of running water and the existence of adequate sewage and drainage helped people to a more hygienic lifestyle. Better quality and availability of cleansing agents and utensils was also a factor as was the contribution of health education in schools, attendance at which became compulsory to the age of ten in 1880.

Third, the government took steps to improve the quality of professional health care. Thus, in 1858 the Medical Act established a Medical Register administered by the Medical Council with the purpose of establishing and monitoring professional standards among doctors. The Certification of Midwives Act of 1902 did the same for that group and improving standards of midwifery and this no doubt contributed to the fall in child mortality in the immediately ensuing period.

Fourth, the role of government, obvious in points one and three, deserves separate mention. Both Tory and Liberal governments, often against their preferred *laissez-faire* principles, had repeatedly passed reforming legislation to reduce the rigours and ill-health of industrial, urban life. In the early twentieth century, the (then) major parties were further stimulated in this direction by the rise of the Labour Party. The Liberal government, elected in 1905, passed a series of measures which foreshadowed the post-Second World War welfare state. Acts were passed which used the school system to improve the nutrition (school meals) and health (medical inspections) of children. The National Insurance Act of 1911 was highly significant in the history of popular health provision. It provided financial benefits and free doctor's services for the poor. Government employers and employees made weekly contributions to pay for the scheme which was run by private insurance companies. The Liberal package made a fundamental contribution to the basic security of the lives of millions of working people but was partly motivated by the hope of buying off socialist revolution and gaining the party working class support.

The decline in the death rate and general improvement in the population's health occurred before the invention and widespread availability of most modern 'wonder' drugs. However, these further improved matters. The infectious diseases that were the main killers before the nineteenth century, such as the 'plague', smallpox and typhus, are now curable. Instead, diseases of physical and mental degeneration such as cancer, which modern medicine has been less successful in treating, increasingly take their toll. Even so, the spread of AIDS in the nineteen eighties reminds us that new types of infectious diseases which are difficult to cure can still develop.

Finally, it is worth noting that the steep decline in infant mortality lagged behind that of adults and older children. This decrease did not occur until the birthrate itself began to drop sharply. The lesson seems to be that fewer children generally get more and better resources and attention. In addition, services for

681

mothers and children expanded rapidly during the first quarter of the twentieth century.

The National Health Service

The National Health Service was established in 1948. It was organised into three separate parts, a 'tripartite' structure: the hospital sector, the executive council sector, and the local health authorities. Hospitals were not run by local authorities but by regional hospital boards on which consultants were strongly represented. Consultants retained the right to do some private as well as national health service work. Primary services to individuals and families were to be the responsibility of General Practitioners, dentists, opticians and pharmacists who were answerable to the executive council. The Local Authorities were to take care of a range of remaining health concerns including environmental health, maternity services, home helps and school services. All National Health services were to be free. In 1974, the tripartite structure was unified into a single hierarchical system: Secretary of State for Social Services, Department of Health and Social Security, Regional Health Authorities and Districts. Unfortunately, the level at which a (rather weak) degree of popular participation was built in – the Area level – has proved virtually redundant. Increasingly, the Districts carry out the functions originally intended for the Area Authorities.

The National Health Service was introduced to the accompaniment of much idealistic rhetoric. The setting up of the service had been one of the major recommendations of the Beveridge Report of 1942 which had been enthusiastically received by a wide public. Considerable national support for and pride in the NHS remains – making a cool assessment of its achievements difficult. Even many critics of the service's limitations and failures make it clear that they support it in principle. In any case, the achievements of the NHS are substantial. These include a much fairer distribution of General Practitioners and certain other medical services to women on a comparable basis with men – which the 1911 Act had conspicuously failed to implement, and notable comparative cost effectiveness. However, there remain substantial inequalities of health care and the NHS continues to be a highly centralised and undemocratically administered service.

Two continuing issues – the dominance of the hospital sector of the NHS and the continuing role of private medicine – were apparent in the negotiations leading to the setting up of the system. The consultants effectively established their claim to a substantial share of resources, for research as well as practice, and to the right to practise a limited but highly lucrative amount of private medicine within NHS premises. Many consultants, therefore, seem to get the best of both worlds. More broadly, the power and prestige of the hospital sector is a prime example of the triumph of curative rather than preventive medicine in the NHS. The allocation of a large share of resources to high-level, 'scientific' medicine occurs at the expense of preventive medicine and the delivery of mass services. Another important penetration of the NHS by private profit is the operation of the drug companies. Their return on capital has typically been twice as much as that for manufacturing industry as a whole. Doctors are often bombarded with advertising for new products which are in many cases little different from existing lines. Recently, the government has promoted the buying of generic drugs (as opposed to 'brand' names) to cut costs.

After a detailed review of opinion and debate before the NHS was set up, Vivienne Walters concludes that 'the NHS was not so much a response to the difficulties working class patients experienced in obtaining care, as an attempt to rationalise an inefficient health care system and provide it with a stable financial base'. Before 1948 many were not covered by insurance and frequently could not afford treatment. This, of course, affected the earning potential of doctors and other medical practitioners. The NHS extended their clientele and guaranteed their income. A second point is that though the NHS functioned to improve the quality of the existing and future labour force, it certainly did not deliver control or extensive participation in the health service to working people. Government, professional, managerial and commercial interests remained dominant. These comments do not seek to detract from the immense personal benefit many, especially women and children, obtained in gaining access to free primary and hospital care for the first time.

Walters does not suggest any conspiracy about the way the NHS was set up. Indeed, she emphasises that neither the TUC nor the Labour Party pressed for a genuinely democratic socialist health service but broadly supported the NHS as it was set up. Lesley Doyal who, like Walters, writes from a Marxist perspective, argues that British medicine is best thought of as 'nationalised' rather than 'socialised'. She suggests that a socialist system of health care will not be achieved in the absence of powerful working class demand and organisation for it. As it stands, the NHS is a social democratic compromise in which the state mediates the interaction of classes and interest groups in the health field within the framework of a mixed economy.

Continuing Inequalities in British Health Care: Sectoral, Regional and Social Class

Lesley Doyal examines three aspects of NHS resource allocation – between different sectors of the NHS, between geographical regions and, most importantly, between social classes. I will follow her analysis, occasionally supplementing it with data and comment from the government commissioned report, *Inequalities in Health* (1979) and other sources.

As was mentioned above, the hospital sector is the dominant one within the NHS. In 1948 it accounted for 55% of total NHS expenditure and in 1974, 65%. This inequality is increased in the case of those teaching hospitals which have private endorsements. Resource allocation between different medical specialities shows a complementary pattern. More resources are available for the acute sick, the major client population of such hospitals, and less for the chronic sick, particularly the mentally ill and handicapped, who are typically treated in non-teaching hospitals (which also receive relatively fewer resources for acute patients).

As far as geographical differences in resource allocation are concerned, the south fares better than the north and the richer areas better than the poorer. Despite this, matters have improved since 1948 and, according to the *Inequalities in Health Report*, England has a more even regional distribution of doctors than other industrialised Western countries. However, the rough correspondence between the unequal geographical distribution of health resources and social inequality generally, leads Julian Tudor Hart to suggest the 'inverse care law': the more a social group has need for medical resources, the less likely it is to find them locally available.

As Doyal notes, ever since the inception of the NHS, there has been a continuing debate about whether working or middle class patients use it most. Simplifying somewhat, it seems that the working class use curative services more than the middle class but not to the extent that their need implies, given their higher morbidity and mortality rates. However, the middle class use a broader range of services particularly of a preventive kind such as mass miniature radiography, cervical cytology, and antenatal and postnatal care. On the issue of quality as distinct from quantity of service, the middle class appear to be at an advantage. This is largely because facilities and availability of services tend to be better in middle class areas.

The comparative quality of social relationships requires consideration as well as the material and technical quality of health care. Interactionist as well as structural perspective is helpful here. Structural perspective suggests that middle class patients may come to medical practitioners with a number of cultural advantages such as language skills and greater self-assurance. As David Tuckett puts it, the absence of these in working class patients 'may hinder a relationship of mutual participation', leaving power and decision-making entirely in the practitioner's hands. Interactionist perspective is helpful in understanding the detail of the doctor–patient relationship, particularly in the matter of negotiation or lack of it. Negative labelling may occur for a variety of reasons in addition to social class. Irving Zola gives an interesting example of the negative labelling of Italians resulting in the self-fulfilling prophecy of illness in a comparative study of the treatment of various ethnic groups in Boston. He found that in cases where no organic basis for illness was discovered, Italians were consistently diagnosed as having some psychological difficulty such as personality disorder or tension headaches, whereas Irish and Anglo-Saxon were usually diagnosed as having nothing wrong with them. Zola suggests that doctors were able to prise symptoms out of the more voluble and dramatic behaviour of the Italians in a situation in which illness was being looked for. I am not aware of any comparable study of the possible labelling of ethnic groups in the NHS but the much higher diagnosed rates of mental illness among the Afro-Caribbean community suggests that the issue might be worth researching in that context.

Whatever the precise facts about comparative class usage of the NHS, the stark truth is that the health of the working class remains generally much worse than that of the middle class. The roots of this lie in social inequality itself rather than with the NHS, although different national health policies could improve matters. We now discuss the extent and causes of health inequality between the social classes.

Social Class and Health Inequality

The facts of health inequality between the social classes are well-documented. Mortality and morbidity rates are higher among the working class, especially social class V, than among the middle class. As Vivienne Walters points out, infant mortality rates 'are among the more sensitive indicators of class inequalities in health' and '(s)tatistics published since the turn of the century have consistently shown higher death rates for lower social classes and though the rates for all classes have declined, the differences between them have not narrowed'. The table below illustrates this point.

Early Neo-natal, Late Neo-natal and Post Neo-natal Mortality Rates per 1,000 Live Births by Sex and Social Class, England and Wales, 1970–72

Social Class	Early neo-natal deaths[a] males	females	Late neo-natal deaths[b] males	females	Post neo-natal deaths[c] males	females
I	8.89	6.31	1.23	0.99	3.47	2.32
II	9.73	7.43	1.39	1.29	4.09	3.22
III Non-manual	10.70	7.60	1.64	1.27	4.57	3.11
III Manual	11.04	8.27	1.81	1.53	6.20	4.99
IV	12.70	9.14	2.02	1.84	7.31	5.97
V	17.06	12.64	3.06	2.41	14.61	11.62
All classes	11.59	8.58	1.84	1.57	6.48	5.11
Per cent excess V/I[d]	92	100	149	143	321	401

Notes: a Deaths under 1 week
     b Deaths between 1 and 3 weeks
     c Deaths between 4 weeks and 1 year
     d The difference between classes I and V expressed as a percentage of the rate for class I.

Source: Office of Population Censuses and Surveys, *Occupational Mortality. The Registrar General's Decennial Supplement for England and Wales 1970–72*, HMSO, London, 1978, p. 157. Reprinted in Walters, V, *Class Inequality and Health Care; The Origins and Impact of the National Health Service*, Croom Helm, 1983, p. 119.

Mortality rates among children and adults show a similar pattern of class inequality as the figure below shows.

Mortality by Social Class of Children and Adults

Children (1-14 years)

Adults (15-64 years)

*The standardised mortality ratio is a measure designed to correct for differences in the age structure of the population, so that the actual number of deaths is expressed as a percentage of the number that would be expected if the age structure had remained unchanged from a base year.

Source: *Occupational Mortality 1970–72*, London, HMSO 1978, © Crown copyright 1978; reproduced with the permission of the Controller of Her Majesty's Stationery Office.

As Lesley Doyal remarks, these continuing differences in mortality arise both from the greater incidence of 'new' diseases such as lung cancer and of 'older' diseases such as TB and bronchitis which are 'traditionally associated with poverty'. Not surprisingly, class patterns of sickness or morbidity follow the same trend as the mortality rate.

Lesley Doyal's comment after analysing much of the relevant data on morbidity and mortality has fundamental, indeed, revolutionary implications for health care:

> These class differences in morbidity and mortality, ... provide strong evidence to support the argument that social and economic factors remain extremely important in determining the ways in which people live and die.

Relative ill-health, then, seems largely to be a product of socio-economic inequality and could be reduced with the reduction of inequality.

Vivienne Walters similarly attacks narrow approaches to health and illness and suggests that the NHS represents a definition of health by the state largely in terms of access to care. This approach has been at the expense of a more thorough exploration of 'the links between health, the organisation and delivery of health care and the nature of class relations in British society'.

Echoing Althusser, she goes on to say that '(t)his suggests that the state has served an ideological function in so far as it has legitimised medical definition of health and failed to address class inequalities in health and the political bases of these'. Marxists make similar arguments to these about the operation of social welfare generally (see pp. 662–5).

What is it about social class that generates the health inequalities presented above? The *Inequalities in Health* report identifies poverty and the relatively poor access of lower social-economic groups to the knowledge and resources which help to maintain health. So both the cultural and material disadvantages of the working class are indicated as causal factors, with the latter considered to be the more fundamental. Health inequality is simply a function of basic social inequality. The health of the working class, particularly the lower working class, would improve if it had 'sufficient household income, a safe, uncrowded and unpolluted home, warmth and hygiene, and means of rapid communication with the outside world'.

There are potentially as many explanations of the poorer health of the working class and of solutions to it as there are of poverty itself. The 'Inequalities' report itself takes a radical social democratic line, arguing for a significant increase in income, resources and services (including health services) for the needy and especially for children. The most fatalistic is the Conservative version of the culture of poverty thesis, which locates the causes of inequality in the values, attitudes and behaviour of the lower class which are passed on from generation to generation (see pp. 296–7). Perhaps reflecting this view, the Conservative governments of 1979 onwards have provided free health care only on a *selective*, means tested basis and have raised prescription charges for others. One of its most stated goals in relation to social and health services has been to cut costs. An example of cost cutting – although no doubt its advocates also feel genuine ideological support for it – is the policy of promoting family and community, rather than institutional care of the mentally ill and handicapped and, to some extent, of the ailing aged. There are good arguments for 'mainstreaming' such potentially marginal and stigmatised groups but only if the policy is fully supported with resources and expertise. Thirdly, early in the second Thatcher administration, it was rumoured that her government would like to privatise large sectors of the health service. This was officially denied although such a policy would be consistent with the free enterprise principles of Thatcherism. In fact, cost-cutting *preceded* the first Thatcher administration of 1979 and Lesley Doyal comments as follows: 'In attempting to reduce the cost of the NHS during a period of recession, the state can be seen as facilitating the interests of capital as a whole'. In her view, the poorer and less healthy are made to bear most of the cost of economic recession.

Marxists, such as Doyal, consider that health inequality is reproduced throughout the major institutional areas of capitalist society. The system of private profit generates this inequality and she traces health inequality through the processes of *production* and *consumption*. She shows that health inequality does, indeed, begin at the point of production. Industrial accidents and disease tend to occur more often in traditional working class occupational areas such as mining, construction and railways. In part, this is due to the nature of heavy manual work but more could be done to secure a safer working environment. For instance, in 1975–76, 59 miners were killed at work, 538 seriously injured, and 52,946 injured and off work for more than three days. The toll of industrial disease among miners is particularly high. About 30,000 still suffer to some degree from lung disease and in 1973, 367 deaths were officially declared to be caused by the lung disease pneumoconiosis. Doyal argues that the two major potential defenders of the working class – trade unions and the state – have not been very effective in achieving adequate enforcement of industrial health and safety legal regulations. For example, there are still very few factory inspectors for all the workplaces to be visited and even when successful prosecutions do occur, penalties are often very light.

Doyal states the problem of the production/consumption of unhealthy items sharply:

> Commodities are being produced for sale and consumed at an ever-increasing rate, and a great many of these products are not 'useful' according to any commonsense definition of the term. More than this, they may actually damage the health of consumers.

For discussion of the issue of consumption I will adopt Doyal's examples of tobacco and certain processed foods, though I am responsible for the detailed commentary. Despite the known correlation between tobacco smoking and lung cancer, the government allows a situation in which the public is overwhelmingly encouraged rather than discouraged to smoke (for instance, in 1975 between £50–70 million was spent on the former, and £1 million on the latter). It is not only the massive quantity of tobacco, particularly cigarette advertising, but the insidious nature of it that seems to be effective. Appeals are variously made to status, masculinity, femininity, and 'coolness' depending on the brand and the 'bright ideas' of the 'creative' (advertising) department. Members of the public sometimes claim that they are 'not affected' by such advertising beyond being amused or entertained in passing. One wonders, however, whether if the proportion spent on encouraging and discouraging tobacco smoking were reversed tobacco consumption would remain stable.

There are social class and gender dimensions to tobacco consumption. As information has spread to the public about the unhealthy effects of tobacco, rates of consumption have fallen among higher socio-economic groups but not among lower. Speculatively, it may be that working class people are more aware of and affected by pro-tobacco television advertising than even the popularised versions of scientific evidence on its harmful effects. It may also be that 'having a smoke' or 'a fag' is more deeply embedded in the culture of working class relaxation. Smoking may be *felt* as a necessary release from the stress of hard, physical work (even though, *in fact*, it increases stress in the long run). The rapid growth in tobacco consumption among working class women may also be related to the increasing number who work in the occupational as well as the domestic economy. Smoking may be experienced as a crutch against the pressures of dual roles.

A variety of reasons are cited for the government's tolerance of the above situation. First, the government relies for a significant part of its tax revenue on the sale of tobacco – rather less than 5% in 1975. Second, the tobacco industry is a powerful and well organised lobby. It has presented an appearance of compromise such as developing 'safer' cigarettes and acquiescing in the banning of cigarette advertising in cinemas whilst managing to retain the bulk of its commercial freedom. Third, Britain is predominantly a capitalist society and to control an established area of free enterprise may be ideologically repugnant to some and seem to set an undesirable precedent. Finally, perhaps a society as well as an individual can become addicted to a bad habit. Apparently, the collective will to 'kick it' is not yet here.

There have been several significant changes in dietary patterns in Britain over the last 150 years. Whilst food is more abundant and usually more sanitary, there is often cause for concern about its content – or lack of certain content. Between 1860 and 1960, it is estimated that the average annual consumption of refined sugar doubled, while that of fat increased by 50% whereas the consumption of fibre decreased by 90%. Increasingly, dietary experts regard these developments as unhealthy especially where there is little balancing intake of fresh vegetables and fruit which is more likely to be the case among the working class. The processing of food is a significant feature in the above trends. Processing creates homogeneous (consistent) and long-lasting products, i.e. the product always tastes the same and has a long shelf-life. Processing also forms and even stimulates taste and consumption by, for instance, adding sugar or other sweeteners. There is obvious commercial advantage in all this. This is achieved mainly by chemical and other additives but what is taken out of many natural products must also be considered. Thus, refined sugar and processed bread lose many natural nutrients (which may or may not be artificially replaced). Sometimes, what is removed is sold as a separate product to increase profit.

Nicky Hart uses the comparative method to criticise Doyal's linkage of ill-health to the capitalist system of production and consumption. She cites data which show that the rates for death caused by industrial accidents are somewhat higher in the socialist societies of Czechoslovakia and Hungary than in Britain, and that whilst lung cancer causes a higher proportion of deaths in Britain the rate for circulatory disease is rather lower. Hart argues that the 'drive for industrialisation' and the lack of workers' freedom to protect themselves may account for these rather higher rates. She also observes that a substantial improvement in the general level of health has occurred in Britain under capitalism.

However ill-health may be caused, the health-food movement is an attempt to avoid it. Nevertheless, it would be naive to assume that everything sold under the name of health food is good and that processed food is less nutritious. In capitalist society, movements which begin at the grassroots are often turned into big businesses if they show signs of being able to generate a popular market. There are now many health food chains whose owners' primary motive appears to be profit rather than health. Thus, some of the products and business methods of Herbalife, possibly the biggest of the international "health" companies, have sparked controversy and legal action. In 1985 a joint lawsuit was filed against Herbalife International by the California Attorney General and others, charging that the company misrepresents the effects of its products in its promotions and uses an illegal 'pyramid' marketing scheme to sell its products. The consumer needs to be aware of a possible combination of greed and quackery in the big business health movement.

Health in capitalist society is partly a social product and partly a matter of personal awareness and responsibility. Some public issues such as pollution unavoidably affect the individual and have to be dealt with collectively. Still, there is much that can be done by the individual to achieve healthier diet and lifestyle. Often it is at the personal level that larger institutional and social changes begin.

Gender and Health

The dimension of gender cuts through health as it does through other aspects of life. In general, health services are managed by men and 'manned' at the lower levels by women. According to figures published in 1975, women occupied only eight seats out of 253 on the major committees of the British Medical Association and only four out of 46 were members of the General Medical Council. Although nearly 80% of employees in medical and other health and veterinary services are female (1983) only about 25% of doctors are female – well reflecting the 'doctors and nurses' stereotyping of childhood. Yet there is nothing 'natural' in these figures as comparative data show. In the USA women make up 8% of doctors, in Finland 24%, in Poland 46% and in the USSR 74%. In the Eastern European socialist societies childcare and health are associated areas, heavily supported by the state, which present women with a wide range of career choices. Even though women are much less well represented at the policy-making level in the socialist societies, the general pattern in the health professions is much less patriarchal than in Britain and the United States.

We now consider the quality of care provided by the health services. Health care can intrude into what is normally regarded as core personal space – the body (and, in the case of mental

692

health, the mind). Quite obviously, sex differences can play a major part in the dispensing and experience of health care. Female fertility is the key differentiating factor. A pregnant female, whether she gives birth or terminates, embarks upon a series of experiences unavailable to the male. Yet, it is usually males who attempt to manage these experiences. Let us take the case of childbirth. In *Women Confined: Towards a Sociology of Childbirth*, Ann Oakley identifies five features of what she refers to as the 'medical frame of reference' which she describes as 'a qualitatively different way of looking at the nature, context and management of reproduction' from that of mothers. These are the five features:

(a) the definition of reproduction as a *specialist* subject in which only doctors are experts in the entire symptomatology of childbearing

(b) the associated definition of reproduction as a *medical* subject, as exactly analogous to other pathological processes as topics of medical knowledge and intervention

(c) the selection of *limited criteria of reproductive success*, i.e. perinatal and maternal mortality rates

(d) the *divorce* of reproduction from its *social* context, pregnant parenthood being seen as women's only relevant status

(e) the restriction of women to maternity – their derived *typification* as 'by nature' maternal, domesticated, family-oriented people.

After an extensive critique of the above 'medicalised' model of childbirth, Oakley tries to establish the subjective reality of childbirth. It is a complex human experience, involving losses and gains and often un-met expectations. Her proposals for changes in the management of birth indicate the direction of her argument: an end to unnecessary medical intervention in childbirth, the re-domestication of birth, a return to female-controlled childbirth and the provision of therapeutic support for women after childbirth. It will be clear from the above that as well as attacking the medical framework of childbirth, she also seeks to demolish popular romantic conceptualisations of childbirth (and motherhood).

Significantly, Oakley's arguments are applicable to the general paradigm of 'mechanistic' medicine as well as to the particular case of medicalised childbirth. Male domination and scientific domination (though *not* science itself) are presented as twin partners in the repression of not only womankind, but of humankind. Accordingly, her proposals for change extend beyond birth to the bringing up of children and to the wider social context. These proposals have much in common with those offered in Anna Coote's social policy package described in the previous chapter (pp. 665–8).

Health in the Third World

For far more people in the Third World than in the West, health is an urgent matter of life and death. As we have seen, the people most at risk are children (see pp. 172–7). It was probably the death and threat of death of children, particularly, that sparked the worldwide response to famine in Ethiopia in 1985. I have attempted to cover the main policy issues concerning the health of Third World children in Chapter 7; here the emphasis is on the broader theories linking development or underdevelopment with health.

Modernisation theory provides limited insight into this matter and a better starting point is the free-market theory of Peter Bauer and the new Conservatism. His comments on birth control and population are pertinent to health. He criticises internationally-funded birth control programmes in the same terms that he criticises international aid – they interfere with the processes of choice and with the real limitations of circumstances which for him define socio-economic life. A first criticism of Bauer is that many (probably millions) of preventable deaths will occur if what he regards as natural forces are left to work themselves out. The chances of wage and subsistence economies sustaining the population of poorer 'developing' countries, particularly in sub-Saharan Africa, are remote. Second, there is nothing essentially natural in the economic and social relations of the developed and undeveloped world. The contrary is equally arguable. The impact of the West on many primitive and traditional societies has been chaotic and often destructive, as well as sometimes beneficial (see below). Third, it is entirely subjective (though germane to his theory) to regard help organised by governments and international agencies as somehow unnatural and interfering.

What differentiates liberal social-democrats from Bauer and his ilk is the acceptance of the last three points. The *Brandt Report*, for instance, takes a broadly capitalist world economy for granted but seeks to modify the negative effects of its distortions and failings. Thus, it advocates help for those exploited by or struggling within the capitalist world economy – ultimately as a matter of 'mutual interest' (see pp. 209–12). Clearly these arguments apply rather more urgently to health than many other matters. On the matter of hunger and food, Brandt says simply: 'there must be an end to mass hunger and malnutrition': mainly by a combination of improving the food producing capacity of developing countries and by increasing food aid.

Marxist scholars argue that historical and contemporary capitalism has grossly exploited the health as well as the labour of the peoples of the Third World. Authors such as Teresa Hayter and Lesley Doyal amply illustrate that the spread of disease, slaughter and massive social and psychological disruption were typical products of European expansion. The slave trade is perhaps the most vivid example, although it was not only the enslaved whose lives and health were threatened through contact with Europeans. In the nineteenth and early twentieth century, the migrant labour system in sub-Saharan Africa resulted, in Lesley Doyal's assessment, in a deterioration in the health of the workers involved. Contact with Europeans and European diseases, the unhealthy living and working conditions imposed on the labour force, and the disruption of the traditional rural economy undermined the health of men, women and children. The argument that the economic interest of employers favoured a healthy labour force hardly applied – a common pattern was to send unhealthy workers back to their villages and simply recruit more. The break-up of families and communities, the isolation of males in labour compounds and the frequent poverty of women and children, resulted in an increase in alcoholism and prostitution. Ironically, some colonialists saw the poor and unhealthy life they had created for Africans as proof of black inferiority.

Although Marxists welcome the achievement of political independence by colonial nations, they stress that in the 'post-colonial era', the economic dependency of much of the Third World continues. Vicente Navarro's *Medicine Under Capitalism* is a study of health inequality in the Third World which complements Gunder Frank's broader theory of underdevelopment. Like Frank, he takes Latin America as his area for detailed study. In countries such as Colombia, Peru and El Salvador, he typically finds urban

695

enclaves of privileged bourgeois consumption and largely poor and exploited rural areas. In health terms, this translates into the consumption of largely private, curative medicine for the urban rich and a lack of investment in preventative measures, such as water and sewage projects that would benefit the rural majority. Nor is the wider development that might ultimately benefit the standard of living and health of the majority occurring:

> The industrial sector ... is controlled by and functions for the lumpen-bourgeoisie and its foreign counterparts, not for the benefit of the development of the whole of the individual country.

Communist China provides an interesting example of a socialist solution to the health problems of a developing nation. When the Communists came to power in 1949, they were faced with widespread famine and disease and a broken-down and inadequate system of medical care. Emphasis was put on sanitation and other forms of prevention such as inoculation and the Chinese also developed a tiered medical system which has been an influential model to other developing socialist societies. The base of the system is made up of the tens of thousands of 'barefoot' doctors who provide a basic medical service designed to reach all the peasantry. They receive a maximum of 18 months training which combines Western medicine with traditional Chinese medicine, particularly herbal treatment and acupuncture. In addition, the doctors stress the role of personal and communal responsibility for health. A similar system of grassroots medical care operates in urban areas, but here more developed and professional facilities are usually available. Medical problems that cannot be treated by a 'barefoot' doctor can be referred to more fully trained doctors and nurses. Hospitalisation is also possible where necessary. Part of the cost of the Chinese health system is financed by individual payments or insurance, nevertheless, it seems broadly egalitarian and effective.

Mental Health and Illness

Psychiatry

The biomedical model of medicine is perhaps most sternly tested in its application to mental illness. The classic example of this model in mental health is the psychiatric hospital which commonly relies on drug-based treatments. First, the organic basis, if any, of a mental illness is much harder to establish than in physical illness. Thus, chemical changes in the brain seem to accompany schizophrenia, but precisely what relationship these have to the values, attitudes and behaviours of schizophrenia is quite unclear. Second, partly because the etiology (causes) of mental illness are so unclear, effective scientific treatments of mental illnesses have proved particularly difficult to develop. Third, the very label mental illness has been called into question in a way that reference to physical illness could hardly be questioned (see below). Fourth, there is evidence that those who claim to be able to recognise scientifically (diagnose) the symptoms of mental illness cannot do so reliably.

The last point requires substantiation as it implies scepticism of a body of 'expert' opinion which is widely, though far from universally, accepted. D. L. Rosenhan's *On Being Sane in Insane Places* reports two experiments which test the claims of scientific psychiatry on its own traditional territory, the psychiatric hospital. The first experiment describes how eight sane people gained secret admission to twelve different hospitals. Apart from alleging certain symptoms, and falsifying name, vocation and employment, no further alterations were made. After admission – which was gained in every case – the pseudopatient ceased simulating any symptoms of abnormality. Despite their normal behaviour following admission, none of the pseudopatients were detected. All, apart from one, were admitted with the diagnosis of schizophrenia, and each was discharged, not as wrongly diagnosed, but with a diagnosis of schizophrenia 'in remission'. Length of hospitalisations ranged from 7 to 52 days, with an average of 19. Rosenhan comments:

> The label 'in remission' should in no way be dismissed as a formality, for at no time during any hospitalisation had any question been raised about any pseudopatient's simulation. Nor are there any indications in the hospital records that the pseudopatient's status was suspect. Rather, the evidence is strong that, once labelled schizophrenic, the pseudopatient was stuck with that label.

As Rosenhan observes, whereas labels of physical illness are not commonly pejorative, psychiatric labels are. The failure of the psychiatrists to change their diagnosis contrasts vividly with the observations of many ward patients that the pseudopatients were normal (35 out of 118 patients made comments to this effect on the first three cases, when accurate counts were kept).

The reports of the pseudopatients also provided data on the experience of being in a psychiatric hospital. The fact that patients appear to have made more accurate observations than psychiatrists on the conditions of the pseudopatients indicates that their experience in relation to the hospital power structure was profoundly de-personalising. In this respect, the findings complement those of Erving Goffman's study *Asylum* to which Rosenhan sympathetically refers (see pp. 448–50).

In critically scrutinising his own findings, Rosenhan raises the possibility that there may be a tendency in psychiatry, as in medicine, to diagnose illness rather than health – 'to be on the safe side' (referred to by statisticians as the type 2 error – a false positive). An experiment was therefore arranged to test the reverse tendency – to diagnose the (supposedly) insane as sane. The staff at a research and teaching hospital were told that in the course of the next three months, one or more pseudopatients would attempt to gain admittance. Staff were asked to rate each patient according to likelihood of pseudopatient status on a scale of 1 to 10, with 1 and 2 reflecting high confidence that the person was a pseudopatient. Judgements were obtained on 193 patients from all staff with whom they had contact – attendants, nurses, psychiatrists, physicians and psychologists. Forty-one were considered with high confidence to be pseudopatients by at least one member of staff, 23 judged suspect by at least one psychiatrist, and nineteen suspected by one psychiatrist and one member of staff. In fact, no pseudopatients from Rosenhan's group presented themselves during this period. Rosenhan comments:

> The experiment is instructive. It indicates that the tendency to designate sane people as insane can be reversed when the stakes (in this case, prestige and diagnostic acumen) are high. But what can be said of the 19 people who were suspected of being 'sane' by one psychiatrist and another staff member? Were these people truly 'sane', or was it rather the case that in the course of avoiding the type 2 error the staff tended to make more errors of the first sort – calling the crazy 'sane'? There is no way of knowing. But one thing is certain: any diagnostic process that tends itself so readily to massive errors of this sort cannot be a very reliable one.

Psychoanalysis

Psychoanalysis provides a different tradition of treatment from that of psychiatry. Like psychiatrists, Freud, the founder of psychoanalysis, considered himself to be scientific in his study and treatment of mental disorder. However, he differs from the psychiatrists in two critical ways. First, he put the *relationship* between the analyst and patient at the centre of the therapeutic process. Despite the vast proliferation of psychoanalytic theories and techniques, this viewpoint has remained basic to psychoanalysis and even psychotherapy (a catch-all term to describe the many forms of mental healing not strictly wedded to the analytic method originated by Freud). Second, Freud strongly emphasised familial and more broadly cultural contexts in understanding mental illness, especially sexual disorders and hysteria. This gives his work a social psychological and even sociological quality.

The role of the social in contributing to individual mental disorder was also paramount in the work of the radical psychologist R. D. Laing throughout the nineteen sixties. His early works such as *Self and Others* and his book with A. Esterson, *Sanity, Madness and the Family* emphasised the role of significant others in 'driving people mad'. Thus, crudely, mad people tend to come from mad families. To this extent, Laing's work may be considered supportive of the family therapy movement. In the late sixties, Laing went on to criticise what he saw as the greed and militarism of capitalist society. Like many others at the time, he was partly motivated by the horrors of the Vietnam War. Now he seemed to be suggesting that individual madness was an understandable reaction to a mad society. A second theme in Laing's work, which complements his social awareness, is his concern for the meaning that patients attach to their experience. He seeks not to explain symptoms but to understand what the patient is trying to say. Immediately, he draws on the existential and phenomenological traditions for this perspective, but more remotely, the insight that there is 'reason in madness' – and the reverse – can be found in Shakespeare and other writers (see especially, *King Lear* and *Hamlet*).

In entering upon a serious dialogue with the mad, R. D. Laing began to demythologise madness, to bring it within our common experience. In his two books, *The Myth of Mental Illness* (1960) and *The Myth of Psychotherapy* (1985), Thomas Szasz rejects altogether the labels mental illness (and the accompanying stigma) and psychotherapy (and the accompanying mystery of cure). He replaces them with the proposition that people have problems in living about which they may have conversations (i.e., seek solutions). In rejecting the biomedical model of mental illness, he insists that complexities of behaviour and communication should not be reduced to the organic level. He argues that the label mental illness obscures what in fact is a normative judgement: people call others mad when they do not like or when they disagree with their behaviour. In his view, normative disagreements should be stated and resolved not in medical terms but in social, legal and ethical ones. Thus chronic hostility should not be seen as a mental problem but as an ethical and social one. In surveying the vast and various range of 'psychotherapies' in his more recent book, Szasz argues that most of them are of no more than *some* help in solving problems, rather than the comprehensive cure-alls some claim to be. At worst, some of these therapies are bogus 'rip-offs' as well as confusing and confused 'mumbo-jumbo'.

In comment, Szasz's work leaves more than a doubt that there are certain conditions and related behaviours for which the term mental illness may still be appropriate, viz., those for which no apparent rational explanation exists. Thus, the notion of mental illness could be relevant in the case of a 'schizophrenic' who murders his mother for no apparently 'rational' motive, whereas it would not apply to an otherwise 'normal' person who murders his mother for a comprehensible motive such as to speed his inheritance. Of course, to take this view, is to make a judgement about what is rational, which Szasz would consider subjective. Szasz's own argument attempts to restore to normality a huge range of problems frequently regarded as instances of mental illness – depression, chronic hostility and repression. He attacks the almost religious mystique that has developed around therapy, at the centre of which is the psychotherapist as priest or guru – the only one with sacred access to the temple of psychic mysteries. Instead, he suggests that people talk about their problems – to friends or to others who may help, including, sometimes, psychotherapists.

A key perspective of much recent social scientific work on mental illness is that it is substantially a relative rather than an absolute phenomenon. This approach is apparent in the work of two otherwise very different scholars, the American interactionist Thomas Scheff, and the French cultural historian Michel Foucault. In his introduction to *Mental Illness and Social Processes*, Scheff suggests that the various contributors share, not perhaps a common theory of mental illness, but a common method of studying it:

> The authors seek what might be described as an anthropological perspective: to avoid the explicit and implicit assumptions that members of the society make about mental illness, they approach the topic as outsiders. This approach is known in anthropology as the study of 'folk medicine'.

Scheff goes on to observe that suspension of commitment to one point of view or another extends to whether or not 'mental illness' is in fact an illness. An adaptation of Becker's definition of deviance would seem to capture his point: 'mental illness is behaviour which is labelled as such'. This perspective releases the sociologist to study the social construction of mental illness: why, for instance, blacks are labelled schizophrenic more often than whites and women diagnosed as depressive more often than men.

Michel Foucault's 'archeological' approach to the 'history of madness' in *Madness and Civilization* also treats mental illness in a non-judgemental way. Foucault's method is to ignore current and recent writings on madness in the past and to immerse himself in primary sources. Just as an archeologist reassembles artifacts from the past, so Foucault reassembles cultural attitudes and ideas. He deliberately avoids defining madness because what is regarded as mad and reactions to madness vary from period to period. Thus, the medieval world maintained an uncertain but persistent dialogue with madness. Madness was not without meaning as the influential figure of the court 'fool' indicates. The 'Age of Reason' incarcerated the mad and madness as the unwanted opposite of its own rationality. Foucault extended his scepticism to the positivist approach to mental illness in our own time. Madness becomes the alienated object of science with which there is no meaningful discourse.

The view that contemporary treatments of mental illness may be subject to cultural limitations is sometimes seen as radical. Certainly, the above perspectives suggest that the claims to expert status and reliable knowledge of psychiatrists and psychotherapists merit close examination. Drugs and gurus may provide temporary escape, but finding answers to problems requires a more demanding but simpler personal and social inquiry.

Sociological and Social Policy Perspectives on Health: A Review

The emphasis of this chapter has been on health policy. As a result, the political perspectives of free-market conservatism, liberal social-democracy, and Marxism have been more prominent than sociological ones. The second major emphasis of the chapter – on paradigms of health – was presented mainly in comparative historical and cultural terms rather than on a sociological perspectives basis. It might be helpful, therefore, to summarise the various sociological perspectives on health.

Marxism

In the case of Marxism, political and sociological perspective are closely related: The analysis of what 'ought to be' is implicit in the analysis of what 'is'. Marxist analysis of health begins, as with other matters, with the economic system and particularly relations to the means of production. Thus, Lesley Doyal explains the poorer health of the working class in historical and contemporary capitalist society by reference to the exploitation of their labour. Both she and Vivienne Walters then analyse the whole complex of working class health and ill-health – including the workplace, housing, the environment, commodity consumption, use of and access to health facilities – in terms of social class inequality. In her analysis of British colonial Africa, Doyal shows how the exploitation of labour and resources led to a disruption of local cultural and environmental stability, leading to widespread ill-health. In the post-colonial period, the multi-national company is seen by both Doyal and Vicente Navarro as the main agent of Western domination of the Third World. Navarro, in particular, argues that the structure of health inequality in the Third World (Latin America is his example) is a product of underdevelopment. Foreign and domestic capitalists and the upper middle class consume quality health care whereas the peasantry and the poorest elements in the urban population suffer scarcity. Neither foreign nor domestic capitalists are primarily committed to development which would benefit the majority. The former seek resources and cheap labour but their products are sold mainly in the advanced countries whereas the latter are more concerned with their own consumption than developing mass domestic production and markets. Thus, underdevelopment, including health underdevelopment, occurs. According to Navarro, Rostow's 'take-off' stage of development which requires mass domestic consumption and would improve the general quality of life, including the level of health, is hampered by the economic domination of the multinationals.

Navarro's disagreement with modernisation theory extends even to a sharp critique of the radical populist, Ivan Illich. Problems that the latter attributes to modern science and organisation, Navarro attributes to capitalist control of these areas.

Functionalism

Functionalist perspective on social welfare indicates that the 'mass' health policies of modern societies represents 'adjustments' to popular pressure for an improved environment and health facilities and also serve the function of maintaining a healthy labour force. However, it is Talcott Parsons' analysis of the *sick role* that has been the seminal Functionalist work of the post-war period in this field.

He defines sickness as a form of deviant behaviour which, like crime, requires a social response (1951). He presents four cultural expectations which he felt the sick person typically understands and accepts when adopting the sick role:

1 relief from normal duties
2 non-responsibility for own condition and cure
3 that the condition is undesirable and the patient must want to get well
4 medical help should be sought.

By structuring the sick role in this way, society asserts control over and copes with sickness. Left to themselves, the sick might be a considerable source of havoc and hamper the well functioning of society. Acceptance of the sick role contains the problem and implies an intent to 'get back to normal'.

Parsons' concept of the sick role has generated much research and comment. He himself observed that not all ill people accept that they are sick. Some 'fight it', literally until they drop, and such behaviour can obviously cause problems. Various studies have examined whether all 'sick' people do, in fact, accept the four expectations. Thus, the notion that the sick person must want to get better (3) does not appear to be accepted in the case of those with chronic afflictions. Similarly, reliance on others for cure (2 and 4) has limited applicability to those seeking psychoanalysis because most analysts require clients to participate in their own recovery. Arguably, this expectation is becoming more widespread in most branches of medicine and to that extent Parsons' model of the sick role is beginning to date.

Two further criticisms can be made of Parsons' model. First, his tendency to describe the sick role as rather helpless and dependent on the medical 'expert' lays him open to the now familiar criticisms of over-scientific medicine. Second, in presenting the social structuring of the sick role primarily in terms of society's need for maintaining order and stability, he fails to explore the links between capitalism and ill-health. Rather, he assumes that the relationship between (capitalist) development and health is positive. As we have seen conflict theorists provide contrary analysis and evidence.

Interactionism

The premise of interactionism is that people create meaning through symbolic communication. This perspective is helpful in understanding the various paradigms of health presented in the first section of this chapter. Thus, the magical and scientific paradigms of health describe two very different, but internally consistent, frameworks of thinking and action. Interactionists explore the idea that people create their own reality at the micro level of interaction as well as at the macro-cultural level. As this chapter has illustrated, concepts such as negotiation, labelling and self-fulfilling prophecy illuminate the doctor–patient relationship as much as, for instance, the teacher–student one. Analysis of negotiational dynamics is most effective when important variables such as the class, gender and ethnicity of the participants are considered.

Despite the insight interactionism provides into cultural processes it is not a fully developed theory of social structure. This is because it does not directly address the issue of power. Often, interactionists are a little vague about who has power and how it is used or, they adopt liberal-pluralist, Functionalist or Marxist theories of power. In the area of health and health policy, as in others, interactionist can supplement (and sometimes humanise) the major structural perspectives.

Guide to Further Study

Lesley Doyal and Imogen Pennell *The Political Economy of Health* (Pluto Press, 1979) can be recommended both for the extent of its coverage and the clarity of its style. It deals with historical and contemporary health issues in Britain and in the underdeveloped world. A good balance in Doyal is Nicky Hart *The Sociology of Health and Medicine* (Causeway, 1985). The Marxist Vicente Navarro's *Medicine under Capitalism* (Prodist, 1976) is stimulating and jargon-free and covers mainly health and medicine in the United States and Latin America. Two useful collections of readings, both presenting especially interactionist perspectives, are David Tuckett, *ed, An Introduction to Medical Sociology* (Tavistock Publications, 1976) and Elliot G. Mishler, *ed, Social Contexts of Health, Illness and Patient Care* (Cambridge University Press, 1981). Kenneth R. Pelletier's *Mind as Slayer, Mind as Healer* (Allen and Unwin, 1979) is a committed account of holistic medicine from a doctor who is also sociologically informed. None of the books mentioned in the text provides a good start to the study of mental illness. Ken Kesey's novel, *One Flew Over the Cuckoo's Nest* (Pan Books, 1973) is more accessible and sharply dramatises many of the points made here. Doyal and Hart cover Feminist perspective, and particularly worth reading is Ann Oakley, *Women Confined: Towards a Sociology of Childbirth* (Martin Robertson, 1980).

Past Questions

1 *Either*: (a) 'Social services ... do little to equalise the distribution of rewards flowing from the institutions of market, private property and inheritance.' (Mishra, *Society and Social Policy*). Explain and discuss. *Or* (b) Outline and evaluate any *one* sociological contribution to the study of mental illness. (AEB, 1982)

2 Outline and evaluate the sociological insights provided by viewing *either* childhood and youth *or* health as social constructs. (AEB, 1984)

3 'Patterns of health and illness can be understood only in the wider context of social and economic systems.' Examine this view. (AEB, 1985)

24 Educational Policy

Introduction

The main education policy issue of the first 30 post-war years was equality of educational opportunity. Although later widely seen as inegalitarian, the grammar/secondary modern school system as well as the comprehensive system were generally envisaged as expanding educational opportunity. Compensatory education was a specific targeting of disadvantaged children to improve their educational opportunities. In the mid-seventies the political and

706

educational mood began to change. New themes emerged including excellence rather than equality, the relevance of education to the needs of industry and, though less explicitly, the firmer control and socialisation of the young. Perhaps it was the quadrupling of oil prices in 1974 that sent a chill realisation through the West, including Britain, that affluence could not be taken for granted but might have to be struggled and competed for. The need for achievement rather than support for the disadvantaged became the dominant concern.

However, some 40 years earlier it did appear that the major issues in respect of primary and secondary education had been largely settled by the Butler Education Act of 1944. There was a sizeable political and public consensus behind this Act. It stated the government's commitment in principle to providing an educational system which enabled each person fully to develop his or her abilities. In pursuit of this objective, local authorities were required to organise education in three progressive stages; primary, secondary and further (most post-school education *excluding* higher education, which was based mainly on universities). Although this was not specifically laid down in the Act, most, though not all, local authorities divided secondary education into grammar, secondary modern and technical schools. This threefold division became known as the *tripartite system*. Grammar schools were for more 'academic' children and secondary modern schools for virtually all the rest. Nationally, only a very small percentage of students went to technical schools which provided practical, vocationally-oriented courses. Most local authorities used an 11+ examination to select pupils for specific types of schools. Very few offered grammar school places to even as much as thirty per cent of their secondary intake and many offered far fewer.

The three problems and related policy debates which we deal with below must be understood in the above educational context. Of course, the broader social context is also relevant, particularly the class nature of British society. It became clear in the nineteen fifties and early sixties that the educational system as it had developed under the 1944 Act was not ensuring equality of opportunity between social classes and was failing to bring out the potential of many children, particularly those from disadvantaged backgrounds. Halsey's early work with Floud and Martin, and Jackson and Marsden's study already

707

referred to were significant sociological contributions to this growing awareness. The major issue at secondary level focused on the 11+ exam and the system to which it paved the way.

The alternative secondary school system suggested by opponents of the tripartite was the *comprehensive system*. The comprehensive debate is our first· policy issue. Secondly, we consider efforts made to compensate children from 'disadvantaged' social backgrounds *before* they entered the educational system. The aim here was to try to put to rights the cultural imbalance that young lower working class children were thought to suffer from. Thirdly, we look at a still continuing debate about the content of the 16 to 19 curriculum. This debate has been intensified by the introduction of a series of radical educational reforms particularly in the area of vocational and pre-vocational education. The sense of turmoil in the educational system was reflected in unprecedented industrial action among teachers in support of a pay claim.

The Comprehensive Debate

The major criticism against the tripartite system, put forward by the Labour party, was that the 11+ examination discriminated against working class children. Research showed that relatively few working class children passed the exam, even among those who were of comparable intelligence to successful middle class children. But so difficult was the 11+, that inevitably many middle class children also failed it. Unless their families could afford to send them to private school, these children, too, had to share the common fate of 'failures' – and 'failure' *was* the term used. An educational system that had many more 'losers' than 'winners' was likely to cause widespread resentment. It was not long before specific and detailed arguments against the tripartite system began to be presented. Criticism also focused on the content of the exam itself, as well as on the divisive effects of the tripartite system. Some authorities cast doubts on the validity of the aptitude and attainment tests frequently used in the exam. In local authorities in which teachers' reports were also used as a basis of selection, it was an easy matter to suggest that unfair and subjective judgement might decide a child's future. 'Deciding a child's future at eleven' was at the nub of the debate: eleven was widely considered to be too early to determine this issue. A child might have an 'off day' during the 11+ examination period; might not realise the importance of the exam, or be a 'late developer' ... For those who accepted them, these arguments suggested the alternative to tripartite of a non-selective or comprehensive system of secondary schooling. Those who favoured comprehensivisation did so because they believed that it would remove the damaging and unfair stigma of 11+ 'failure.' Further, by enabling pupils of different social backgrounds to mix with each other, it was thought that a cultural 'rub-off' effect would occur, of particular benefit to working class children. The Labour government elected in 1964 issued Circular 10/65 inviting those local authorities which had not yet done so – still, in 1965, the large majority – to draw up schemes for comprehensive education. By the end of 1978, just over eighty per cent of state secondary education was organised along comprehensive lines although some observers seriously doubt whether much more than sixty per cent are 'genuinely' comprehensive.

In assessing the performance of the comprehensive system, it must be realised that the term comprehensive covers many different types of schools. The Leicestershire system, for instance, involves separate institutions for the 11 to 14 age group and for the 14 to 18 age group. More typically, South East Essex has 10 schools for 11 to 16 year olds which 'feed into' a single-site sixth form college. Despite the growing popularity of the sixth form college and of other '16+' colleges, the most common form of comprehensive is still the school for 11 to 18 year olds.

More important in judging whether a school is genuinely comprehensive is its internal system of academic organisation. These vary widely. Some schools 'stream' pupils rigidly – 'tripartite under the same roof' as their critics would say – whilst others use mixed ability teaching for most, if not all, classes. Many would say the former are not really comprehensive. Similarly, pastoral or tutor systems (concerned with general pupil welfare and discipline) can vary greatly in quality. Tutor groups which contain children from a variety of social and, where relevant, racial backgrounds are closest to the comprehensive spirit.

It is still early days to compare the academic results produced within comprehensive and tripartite education areas. The occasional foolish and misleading comparison in recent years of results in socially quite different areas has not helped. Sounder general assessments remain much the same as John Eggleston's of 1975. He summarised the evidence available to the effect that the results from comprehensive schools and the aggregated (added together) results of secondary modern and grammar schools in similar areas were about equal. Precisely the same conclusion was reached by a report published by the National Children's Bureau in 1980. The NCB survey gains greatly in authority because of its *longitudinal* nature. Whereas other studies simply compare attainment levels in a group of comprehensive and grammar/secondary modern schools at a single time, this study examines relative performance at the time of entry (11) and at 16. Its basis of comparability is therefore much stronger. 8,700 children, some of whom went to grammar or secondary modern schools and others to comprehensives, were tested at the ages of 11 and 16. It was found that those in the latter group did as well as children of similar ability in the former group. High ability children in comprehensives did as well in mathematics and reading tests as those of equivalent attainment at 11 who went to grammar schools. The least able seemed to do rather better in comprehensives than in secondary moderns. Despite these generally reassuring findings, the fact that the comprehensive system has not yet brought about a clearly demonstrable improvement in the performance of working class children relative to middle class children is certainly a disappointment to its supporters. A firmer conclusion on that point, however, must wait until the system is widely established on a stable basis, and the disruptive effects of reorganisation on pupils, parents and teachers have passed.

A controversial early study by Julienne Ford on the effects of the greater social mixing that the comprehensive pastoral and (sometimes) academic systems promote, produced findings that were not encouraging to supporters of comprehensivisation. In the three schools where Ford made her case study, she found that an attempt had been made to achieve social mixing through the pastoral system by placing children of different social backgrounds in the same form and house, whereas academic groupings tended to reflect class divisions more sharply. Ford found that it was the academic group which generally provided the basis for friendship. Middle class children, who were a majority in the upper academic groupings, tended to associate with one another, and the same applied to the working class children in the lower academic groupings. It must be noted, however, that a single limited study does not provide a valid basis for generalisation though it can certainly alert people to the problems that can arise in a given type of institution. Ford herself points out that the achievements of comprehensivisation can better be assessed by detailed longitudinal studies (of which the NCB survey is an early example).

In the absence of really convincing evidence against it, the comprehensive system is not likely to be abandoned because of minor defeats in a war of facts about results. Less tangible and measurable characteristics of the system are also important. In our less formal and less status conscious age, the separation of children at 11 on a hierarchical basis would be repugnant to many simply in terms of basic values and feelings. Further, the comprehensive system at least allows teachers (and parents) to work with children of a greater variety of social backgrounds and ability in the same institution. Under the tripartite system this was less possible. In that sense, the comprehensive system is potentially a more flexible instrument of policy. As we shall further illustrate, however, those who expect education to 'change society' may have to look elsewhere for a more reliable tool. Even Halsey, a committed reformer, says: 'Education('s) ... capacity is essentially not to create but to recreate society.' To achieve fundamental social change, if that is the aim, more than educational reform is needed.

Compensatory Education: An Example of the Principle of Positive Discrimination

The principle behind compensatory education is to provide additional educational or education-related help to those who are socially disadvantaged. Given the obvious goodwill and apparent commonsense behind such a policy, it is perhaps surprising that it has proved to be so controversial in practice.

Like many recent progressive initiatives in post-war education and social work, compensatory education was first tried in the United States. There, the major motive was to compensate those who had been deprived for racial reasons, whereas in Britain, the focus has been on compensating for general social disadvantage (though in the inner cities this has included large numbers of black and brown people). Neither country has adopted educational policies to compensate females for the historical disadvantage they have widely experienced.

As early as 1956, a 'demonstration guidance project' was established in New York, to provide extra educational support for intelligent children of the deprived racial minorities. It was reckoned a success and similar programmes followed but with the difference that they included the whole ability range. In 1965, the Johnson government included a 'Head Start' programme in its policies of social reform. As its name suggests, the purpose of 'Head Start' was mainly to prepare disadvantaged minority children for school by giving them special pre-school help.

Assessments of Head Start vary. The principle criteria used in the follow-up studies in evaluating success were gains in I.Q. and improvement in academic performance. On both counts the results of the *initial* follow-up studies were disappointing. I.Q. gains tended to be short-term, and there was little difference in attainment between the Head Start children and others of similar background. The hereditarians in the nature-nurture debate have cited this as evidence that intelligence and even educational performance cannot be significantly improved by 'environmental engineering.' Others have viewed the matter differently. Hunt argues that some schemes in the Head Start programme were inappropriate to the needs of the children they were supposed to help. Apparently, the curricula adopted often *assumed* considerable competence in the verbal and numerical skills that it was the object of the programmes to teach! This was because available curriculum material reflected the needs and attainment of middle class children who normally had virtually exclusive access to pre-school education. Several better designed pre-school programmes have, in fact, achieved lasting gains. A prominent feature of some of these has been the close involvement of the children's mothers, but Bereiter and Engelmann report several successful projects not involving direct maternal participation. Frequently, these involved a special stress on developing linguistic skills. A later (1976–77) and more comprehensive follow-up of Head Start by Lazar and

Darlington showed an average reduction of academic failure in project children of 36.4%. It must be noted, however, that their findings were based on better pre-school projects, and not from a random sample of Head Start projects. They are not, therefore, representative of the whole original Head Start population.

In a useful review of the evidence relating to Head Start, Harry McGurk adds a cautionary note. He points out that both mothers and children often got considerable pleasure out of Head Start schemes and increased their confidence as a result of being involved in the programmes. This is important in itself. As McGurk says, our society professes other values than simply improving I.Q. scores.

The Educational Priority Area (EPA) programme, has been Britain's major effort in the field of compensatory education. The EPA's embodied the principle of *positive discrimination* (that extra help should be given to the socially disadvantaged) advocated by the Plowden Report of 1967. The EPA projects were set up by the Labour Secretary of State for Education and Science, Anthony Crossland. They were located in London, Birmingham, Liverpool and the West Riding of Yorkshire. On the basis of their exploratory work, they recommended positive discrimination, especially in the form of pre-schooling, in their report to government in 1971. Plowden aside, the main propagandist and theorist of positive discrimination in Britain has been A. H. Halsey. The policy of positive discrimination has not been short of critics however and we will briefly review their comments before returning to Halsey's defence.

First is a powerful criticism of the *limited scope* of positive discrimination based on analysis initially put forward by Barnes and Lucas, but later reiterated by Peter Townsend. They correctly point out that although particular areas of geographical concentration of poverty do exist, the majority of the poor are scattered throughout the country and outside these areas. As a result, positive discrimination can miss the needs of the majority and serve as a smokescreen for penny-pinching by government. Barnes and Lucas refer to the 'ecological fallacy' underlying the EPA approach: a policy that is generated through area analysis rather than the needs of specific social groups.

The above observations partly provide the basis for a more fundamental criticism by Townsend. He argues that policies of positive discrimination tend to be merely cosmetic whilst the real causes of disadvantage and poverty remain untouched. In his view, these causes are national in scope and structural in nature. He demands industrial, employment, housing and land policies which will radically redistribute wealth and systematically reduce, if not abolish, poverty. In order to illustrate his point, he draws on the experience of an exercise in positive discrimination outside education, the Community Development Project. In particular, the Coventry CDP group argued that in the face of national or, even, international factors which affected the local context in which they worked, they could do relatively little. For example, a few community workers could not deal with the consequences of thousands being thrown out of work as a result of a recession in car production. They contended that only a national policy of economic redevelopment and social justice could cope. This kind of analysis has received distinguished support from the American, Christopher Jencks, in his book *Inequality*.

Basil Bernstein's controversial article, 'Education cannot Compensate for Society' (1970), was concerned with the cultural aspects rather than socio-economics of positive discrimination. The essence of his criticism is that compensatory education implies that working class culture is in some sense inferior. The policy implications of this are to direct attention away from the quality of schools and curricula towards supposed inadequacies in working class families. Bernstein suggests that is the wrong emphasis. He argues that it is more important to put right the mainstream of the educational system than to over-concentrate on marginal 'compensatory' reforms. He argues that curriculum reform is needed to take into account the way working class children live their lives – the 'conditions' and 'contexts' of their culture should affect everyday education as much as do those of the middle class. Bernstein is surely correct in this central point. Educational change that does not affect the central curriculum is likely to be of only peripheral influence. On the other hand, there is no reason why both major reform and special help for the acutely disadvantaged should not occur.

A. H. Halsey has consistently defended compensatory education against its critics. The starkly assertive title of an article he published in 1980 is 'Education can Compensate,' and it is clearly intended as a reply to Bernstein's piece of ten years before. He especially emphasises the reassuring American evidence of Lazar and Darlington. He stresses that, given enthusiasm and careful organisation, a pre-school programme of compensatory education can be a 'crucial weapon' of government policy. He fully accepts, however, that the mainstream of the educational system must also be fair and effective as well. Thus, he continues passionately to support comprehensive education. For their part, his Marxist critics continue to wonder whether educational reform can significantly help the disadvantaged in the absence of fundamental social and economic change.

Education and Training Policy for the 16 to 19 Age Range

Reorganisation: Description and Critique

In the first half of the nineteen eighties, a substantial reorganisation of the provisions for the education and training of the 16 to 19 age range occurred. We will first describe these changes and then consider their causes and consequences.

The change at 16+ requires only brief mention here. The new curricula and modes of assessment generally appear progressive. However, replacing 'O' level and GCE with GCSE seems unlikely to affect the subsequent stratification of students into 'academic' and 'non-academic' which is a major concern of this section. Indeed, performance at 16+ will continue to be the basis on which this stratification is made. So far, the main change in vocational education has been the introduction of the New Training Initiative announced in 1981, the major programme of which is the Youth Training Scheme (YTS). YTS offers some further education and preparation for work to all 16-year-olds who want to embark on it – generally those who would otherwise be unemployed. Very broadly, it takes on the majority of school leavers who, in the early nineteen seventies, would have gone into manual or routine service work. Most YTS schemes (75% or more) involve on the job experience or training. A less vocationally oriented initiative, the Certificate for Pre-Vocational Education (CPVE) was first taught in 1985–86. This course is school or college based and is aimed at students who are uncertain of their vocational future and/or who may want to take 'O' levels after CPVE – though the latter tend to be of a small minority. CPVE provides experience of a greater number of vocational areas than the more specialised YTS. CPVE also allows for a much wider educational content than YTS of a kind that might encourage the development of critical judgement and aesthetic taste as well as functional competency. Thus, whilst the ten core competency areas required to be taught in CPVE are mainly practically oriented, competency areas such as industrial, social and environmental studies and creative development (but see below) are promisingly open-ended and permit teachers and students to explore these areas well beyond minimal levels of skills and understanding. Despite these two new schemes, some of the previously established vocational courses are still provided. 'A' level continues to be the course that the majority of the top 20% of 'O' level candidates take. About half of these will go on to higher education. A new but so far not widespread scheme that cuts across the 16–19 curriculum framework is the Technical and Vocational Initiative for 14–18 year-olds.

The above framework reflects the policies of the first and second Thatcher administrations inspired by the new conservatism (see pp. 656–62). The government claimed that its policies were aimed at providing more vocationally relevant courses which would meet more effectively the needs of British industry for trained manpower. These concerns pre-dated the return of the first Thatcher government and were expressed by James Callaghan, her Labour predecessor. Another commonly stated aim of the reforms was to achieve greater cost effectiveness in education and to impose upon it some of the 'disciplines' of private enterprise. Within education the argument is often made that the more vocationally relevant courses appeal to 'certain types' of students – variously described as 'work-oriented', 'practically-minded', or 'non-academic'. This form of labelling seems particularly open to patronising manipulation.

A frequently stated political argument against the Thatcher 16–19 package is that it was introduced hurriedly and with inadequate consideration of content to reduce embarrassingly high unemployment figures. Whatever the initial merit of this argument, it is now true that both the Labour Party and the Alliance favour educational provision for this age group on at least as extensive a scale as that introduced by the Conservatives.

However, in both cases, the content would be significantly different. A second criticism of the Conservative initiatives put forward mainly by the political and intellectual left is that their main purpose is to exercise social control over otherwise unemployed and potentially restless youth. Educational sociologist, Denis Gleeson, puts the case bluntly:

> The push toward training reform may have little to do with equipping labour with specific technical skills to make it more employable, but perhaps more to do with establishing 'substitute criteria' (vocational preparation, work experience, further education, and so forth) for controlling the aspirations of disaffected young people.

Linked to this criticism is the view that YTS is a means of providing cheap labour both by reducing the money teenagers get for their work and by undercutting the wages of older workers. The fact that some YTS schemes seem to involve very little training gives support to this proposition.

An observation made by Morris Kaufman, in principle a supporter of vocational training, can be interpreted to support the social control argument. Kaufman comments that whilst there has been a growing number of inspections of YTS courses based on FE colleges there has been a complete absence of comparable inspections based on companies. It appears that the 'heat is on' education to come into line and to bring the young into line.

A serious criticism of YTS – though it applies less to CPVE – is that it sacrifices the development of critical thinking and humanistic feeling in order to provide training in job-related and, to a lesser extent, social skills. The accusation is that the YTS curriculum offers little stimulation to make rational and informed judgements and to feel and care about people and issues – moral, political, social, aesthetic or whatever. Several explanations for these imputed deficiencies may be offered. Perhaps the government does not think that vocationally-oriented young people are capable of critical thought or perhaps it merely considers they are not interested in it. Or perhaps, with the example of the disaffected youth of the sixties in mind, the government wants to contain their education within narrow practical limits. If so, in my view, a fundamental mistake is being made, because, whether trained to think or not, young people will think anyway. The danger is that without wide stimuli to critical thought, they will indulge mere opinion and prejudice and will become indiscriminating dupes of the mass media. In Maslow's terminology, everyone, or virtually everyone, has the potential to develop towards high levels of creativity and critical thought. It is a basic purpose of education to help them to do so. There is far less reason to fear young people who have developed rationality and sensitivity than to fear those who haven't. Irrational and perhaps violent mass movements of young people are more likely to be bred by authoritarianism than by a humanistic curriculum. The comments in this paragraph are not sociological, nor are they inspired by commitment to any single discipline. They reflect the traditional educational value, that, along with a mastery of the basics of communication, the core of education is humanistic understanding. This can be stimulated by a vast variety of means from a study of the classics to classroom discussions of contemporary problems. The point is, it needs to be stimulated by something. Those who believe 'the kids aren't interested in ideas' have given up education in favour of human mechanics. There is a need to blend the new emphasis on skills with the old emphasis on thought and sensitivity. As Richard Pring eloquently put it:

> There are ways of behaving that need to be learnt, that do make life easier, and that a teacher can, through the use of various strategies, train young people in ... [but] The moral life is more than skilful behaviour; and maturity as a person requires a slow process of development that transcends any training programme.

Finally, the charge is sometimes made that the currently emerging (1986) framework of 16–19 education is likely to be very socially divisive. Thus, Headmaster John Swallow, sees a 'developing stratification' which 'threatens to destroy the comprehensive principle'. Swallow is concerned with the segregation and inequality of esteem that a highly streamed post-16 system of education generates. Just as relevant, however, are the wider issues of equality of opportunity and of the role the educational system plays in the reproduction of class and gender inequality. Existing research shows that social disadvantage has an adverse effect on the educational performance of many working class young people (see pp. 113–16). The new 16–19 system, with its tendency to sharp segregation, would seem to reduce the odds of a late second chance for 16+ 'failures'. The first report on gender and patterns of job placement within YTS suggests that traditional roles which disadvantage females are being reinforced. Judith Parris, Hilda Brown and Hilary de Lyon's *The Class of '84, A Study of Girls on the First Year of the Youth Training Scheme* gives relevant data. Whilst 64% of girls receiving training are on administrative/clerical and sales courses, only 6% are being trained in maintenance and manufacturing. The figures for boys are 15% and 40% respectively.

The New Curricula and the Sociology of Educational Knowledge

Before considering alternatives to it, we will look at the British system of 16–19 education, from the perspective of the sociology of educational knowledge. In the collection of readings, *Knowledge and Control*, Michael Young suggests that the power to define what passes as legitimate knowledge is not wholly objective but reflects social forces, including those of class, race and gender. The influence of these factors on curriculum content and organisation may be more or less obvious. In the same book, Bourdieu and Bernstein argue that in Western capitalist societies the culture (or 'knowledge') of the middle class is favoured over that of the working class (see pp. 97–101). Similarly, gender and race and ethnicity deeply affect the hidden and formal curriculum (note, for instance, the moves towards multi-cultural and more recently, anti-racist education). How, then, is educational knowledge being organised for 16–19-year-olds in terms of content and assessment? First, there is the matter of content, and particularly the worrying division between the 'A' level academic and YTS vocational commented on above. The CPVE appears to offer a more balanced academic and vocational programme but in general the new reforms seem to be intensifying the traditionally rigid separation of academic and vocational education at 16 in Britain. Such educational separation must have socially divisive consequences, creating a minority of 'winners' (drawn mainly, but not exclusively, from the middle class) and a majority of 'losers' (drawn mainly from the working class).

Second, is the question of modes of assessment, a matter which can have important effects on the unconscious as well as the conscious mind and character. *How* people are evaluated affects their self-image and esteem, i.e. it becomes part of what they 'know' about themselves. Thus, on completing YTS or CPVE, the student receives a profile detailing the level achieved over a range

719

of (centrally prescribed) competencies, including job-related and social skills. The profile has a number of potentially positive features. It clearly gives more information to all concerned than a series of number or letter grades for particular subjects. The fact that the profile is negotiated between student and instructor(s) is both a useful learning device and should teach democratic procedure. There is also considerable scope for project work on both courses which could pave the way for more individualised curricula and resources-based learning (other than textbooks!). These seem to be innovations in the direction of good educational practice. However, a serious question overshadowing both YTS and CPVE relates to the detail and quantification required for profiling the personal and social competencies. Thus, CPVE divides the core area of creative development into ten factors (each for assessment on a five point continuum) ranging from 'Can appreciate the need for good product design', through 'Can apply own creative and expressive skills', to 'Can make an original contribution to a group creative activity'. One wonders if creative people would really want to be assessed in this way. First, to reduce matters of quality, beauty and value to numbers is both anti-humanistic and, ironically, imprecise (in that it gives a spurious appearance or objectivity to an assessment that involves an irreducible element of subjectivity). Second, to assess the bulk of a course in this way risks what Claude Grignon calls 'accumulative fragmentation'. This means that things or qualities that merit appreciation in their totality such as the products of labour or an aspect of personal character are seen primarily in terms of the separate 'parts' that make them up. Whether all, or even most, human 'competencies' can be meaningfully divided in this fashion is open to doubt. To do so perhaps represents the attempted triumph of positivism over humanism.

Finally, on the matter of educational knowledge, it is worth raising the question of who has power over the curriculum. The general tendency in the new reforms has been for the government to promote (though not itself directly to lay down) national criteria in given subjects (at 16+) of courses (YTS and CPVE). However, as far as CPVE is concerned, within these criteria, scope exists for school or college and even community involvement in curriculum development and in assessment. Some argue that this principle should be more fully extended and applied to other courses, such as 16+. Much assessment would then be school based, though monitored either centrally or by local or regional panels of competent experts (mainly experienced teachers). To move seriously in this direction would release British education from the stultifying and rigidifying effects of its centralised public examination system. The effects of the current reforms on who controls curricula is complex but, on balance, the outcome is likely to result in more centralisation than democratisation.

Education at 16 plus in the United States: Comparative Perspective

Impressed by the arguments against educational segregation at 16, there is a body of opinion which opposes the division of 16+ education/training into separate streams or groupings along the lines of the 'A' level/YTS/CPVE arrangement. There is nothing magical about the age of 16 any more than the age of 11 that requires young people to be evaluated and stratified into separate and distinct groups. Making telling use of a wide comparative frame of reference, Kenneth Roberts attacks common British assumptions about 16+:

> The main structural reform required to unblock British education's mainstream is the public examination at 16 plus. These exams were designed to weed out all but a talented few. It is inevitable that the majority fail and are left with nowhere to travel up the educational ladder. As Wilby (1979) argues, the main problem with Britain's comprehensives is that their standards are artificially high rather than too low. The most radical proposals for opening opportunities at 16 plus would abolish public examination at this age and design curricula on the assumption that young people will remain in education until age 17 or 18. Other proposals would merge 'O' levels and CSEs, then replace 'A' levels with an examination within the majority's capacities. Sweden and the USA have broad-based mainstreams that encourage all young people to remain in full-time education at least until age 18. Having opened the mainstream it will be possible to inject some of the relevance that the vocational track's supporters seek by revising traditional notions of ability, rewriting curricula, and ceasing to treat the abstract as more worthy than the applicable.

It is worth taking up Robert's reference to the United States' high school system in which the majority go through to 'graduation' at 18 without any special examination at 16 or any radical change in the content of the curriculum post-16. Students share a common core curriculum which universally includes English, history/social studies, maths, science and increasingly (modern) technology and health/physical education. More often than not English, maths and science are taught in groups selected on the basis of previous attainment but frequently mixed ability groupings predominate in the other subject areas. The rest of the curriculum – usually between a third and a half – is made up of 'electives' which, as the term indicates, are chosen by students themselves with the help of a counsellor. Electives can range from driver education to Latin but usually contain substantial numbers of vocational options (some of which may be taken at separate vocational centres).

The advantages of the American high school system reflect its essentially comprehensive nature. First, a common core curriculum, some of it typically taught in common, provides a shared experience and frame of reference. This would seem to generate a better basis of community than a more highly differentiated curriculum and segregated teaching groups. Second, is the corollary, that the less obvious stratification of students in terms of success and failure seems to result in less damage to self-esteem than occurs in the British system where the large majority 'fail' at 16 in a very obvious way, i.e. they cannot go on to take 'A' levels. By contrast, the majority of American students receive their high school diploma at 18 (or 19, or 20!) and the majority (about 60% of any given year group) go on to experience some form of higher education (though 'only' about 30% obtain degrees). The emphasis is on finding ways to achieve – rather than providing formidable obstacles to doing so. The ethos is one of success rather than fear of failure. Third, because of the relative openness of the United States' educational system, the possibility of achievement, and of compensating past disadvantage or failure, remains available longer.

Of course, it would be quite misleading to idealise the American high school system. As with other matters, its virtues are its vices and in the early nineteen eighties there was widespread national concern and debate about allegedly low general standards and lack of excellence which some saw as the product of the public system's egalitarian and comprehensive principles. It is interesting to note the widely accepted conclusions of this debate from the point of view of evaluating recent reforms in British 16–19 education. The National Commission on Excellence in Education called for an expanding and tightening of the core and argued that teaching of the basics should not suffer in order to provide vocational preparation which could often take place more effectively in employment or higher education. Similarly, the influential Carnegie Report emphasised the importance of the basics and recommended an expanded core but was somewhat kinder to vocational education. The Report argued that *all* students could benefit from a limited amount of vocational preparation or, at least, work orientation whilst in high school. It implied an erosion of the barriers between academic and vocational education, recalling an old educational ideal of combining theoretical and practical knowledge.

Conclusion

It is perhaps appropriate to end a book written primarily for teenagers and young adults with a chapter on educational policy. That, after all, is what touches you as closely as anything else. At the beginning of this book I stated, in fairness, my own values but it would not worry me if by now you have forgotten what they are. The aim of education is not for students to come to hold the same values and views as a given teacher but to choose and clarify their own – or, at least, to make a start on this. To be able to do so is an important part of what Maslow referred to as self-actualisation. It is perhaps unfortunate that when presenting the purposes or functions of education, sociologists tend to emphasise imposed socialisation and often omit self-actualisation or, simply, self-development. Socialisation is necessary and can provide a basis for fuller self-development, but if we are talking about education we should also be talking about self-development.

These comments prompt some concluding reflections on the major phases of educational policy since the last world war. Despite their great differences, the tripartite and comprehensive phases did share some notion that equality of opportunity was a desirable and attainable ideal. True, the former system was cramped by stereotypical concepts of practical (secondary modern) and academic (grammar school) students but the ideal of enabling talent and intelligence was there. Indeed, the aim of enabling each individual fully to develop his or her capacities was stated in the 1944 Education Act. With comprehensivisation and the parallel schemes of compensatory education came the slow realisation that schools alone cannot fully compensate for social disadvantage. Nevertheless, schools can make some difference and often a crucial one. The onus is on educationalists to further improve schools and not to collapse into despair or elitism. It is not yet clear where the reforms of the 16 to 19 curriculum will lead us. At best they could produce a better balanced education all round, with more academic and vocational options and greater ease of transfer between courses. At worst, they could result in a narrow 'vocationalism' for the majority and an equally narrow, elitist 'academicism' for the minority. But the outcome, whatever it is, is still for the making. It is hard enough for teachers to identify and effect the main changes taking place and it must be even more so for students. Nevertheless, perhaps the stakes are high enough for us to try.

Guide to Further Reading

Much educational sociology is directly or indirectly concerned with policy and this is true of several of the books mentioned at the end of Chapter 5 (especially Halsey *et al, Origins and Destinations*). Stephen Ball's willingness to draw practical implications from his *Beachside Comprehensive: A Case-Study of Secondary Schooling* (Cambridge University Press, 1981) makes it a valuable general contribution to the comprehensive debate. The study of educational policy allows for specialisation in an area of particular interest, such as gender or anti-racist education. 16 to 19 education, particularly vocational education, is an area singled out for more detailed treatment in this chapter and the following is a brief bibliography: D. Gleeson, *Youth Training and the Search for Work* (Routledge and Kegan Paul, 1983); K. Roberts, *School Leavers and their Prospects: Youth and the Labour Market in the 1980s* (Open University Press, 1984); and A. G. Watts, *Education, Unemployment, and the Future of Work* (Open University Press, 1983). J. Parris, H. Brown and H. de Lyon, *The Class of '84: A Study of Girls in the First Year of the Youth Training Scheme*, is available from the National Joint Committee of Working Women's Organisations (NJCWWO), 150 Walworth Rd., London SE17 1JT.

Past Questions

(These questions should be answered with reference to Chapter 5
as well as Chapter 24.)

1 The sociology of knowledge attempts to relate knowledge to
social structure. Offer a critical account of any *one* approach to
this branch of sociology. (AEB, 1982) (Refer also to Chapters 21
and 23.)

2 The British educational system has been described as operating
according to a 'sponsorship' rather than a 'contest' model. What
do you understand by this statement, and has its validity been
changed by the comprehensive reorganisation of secondary
education? (OLE, 1983)

3 Have post-war changes in educational policy and provision
brought Britain closer to realising the 'vision' of the meritocratic
society? (AEB, 1983)

4 'The expansion of educational provision in Western industrial
societies is a direct consequence of the demand for an increasingly
skilled work-force.' Explain and discuss. (AEB, 1985)

Bibliography of Books and Articles
from which quotations have been taken

ABRAMS, P. (1979) 'A Power within a World of Power,' in *Times Higher Educational Supplement*, 2 September 1977.

ARIÈS, P. (1962) *Centuries of Childhood*, Jonathan Cape.

ATKINSON, A.B. (1985) 'Norman Fowler isn't Scrooge,' in *New Society*, 20/27 December 1985.

BANFIELD, E.C. (1977) 'The Imperatives of Class,' in J. Raynor and E. Harris eds, *Urban Education: The City Experience*, Ward Lock.

BARAN, P. and SWEEZY, P. (1966) *Monopoly Capitalism*, Penguin, 1968.

BAUER, P. (1975) *Dissent on Development*, Harvard University Press.

BECKER, H. (1963) *Outsiders: Studies in the Sociology of Deviance*, The Free Press.

BECKER, H. (1966) *Social Problems: A Modern Approach*, John Wiley and Sons.

BENNINGTON, J. (1977) 'The Flaw in the Pluralist Heaven,' in J. Raynor and E. Harris eds, *Urban Education: The City Experience*, Ward Lock.

BLONDEL, J. (1969) *Voters, Parties, and Leaders: The Social Fabric of British Politics*, Penguin.

BOTTOMORE, T. (1964) *Elites and Society*, Penguin.

BOTTOMORE, T. and NISBET, R. (1979) *A History of Sociological Analysis*, Heinemann.

CHESTER, R. (1985) 'The Rise of the Neo-Conventional Family,' in *New Society*, 9 May 1985.

CHEVANNES, M. and REEVES, F.W. (1979) 'Footprints in the Sand,' in R. Meighan, I. Shelton and T. Marks eds, *Perspectives on Society*, Nelson.

COHEN, R. (1982) 'The Emergence of Wage Labor,' in C. Allen and S. Williams eds, *The Sociology of Developing Societies: Sub-Saharan Africa*, Macmillan.

CICOUREL, A. (1968) *The Social Organisation of Juvenile Justice*, Heinemann.

CLEGG, S. and DUNKERLEY, D. (1980) *Organisations, Class and Control*, Routledge and Kegan Paul.

COOPER, D. (1973) 'Being Born into a Family,' in Phil Brown ed, *Radical Psychology*, Harper Colophon Books.

COOTE, A. (1985) 'Labour: The Feminist Touch,' in *Marxism Today*, Volume 29, Number 11, November 1985.

CROUCH, C. (1979) *The Politics of Industrial Relations*, Fontana.

DAHL, R. (1968) *A Preface to Political Theory*, University of Chicago Press.

DELMAR, R. (1977) 'Looking Again at Engels's "Origins of the Family, Private Property and the State",' in Juliet Mitchell and Ann Oakley *eds, The Rights and Wrongs of Women*, Penguin.

DITTON, J. (1972) 'Absent at Work: or How to Manage Monotony,' in *New Society*, 21 December 1972.

DOYAL, L. (1979) *The Political Economy of Health*, Pluto Press.

DOUGLAS, J.W.B. (1968) *All Our Future*, Panther.

DURKHEIM, E. (1972) from Anthony Giddens *ed, Emile Durkheim: Selected Writings*, Cambridge University Press.

DURKHEIM, E. (1897) *Suicide*, Routledge and Kegan Paul, 1970.

EISENSTADT, S.N. (1956) *From Generation to Generation*, Collier-Macmillan.

ETZIONI, A. (1964) *Modern Organisations*, Prentice-Hall.

EVANS-PRITCHARD, E. (1937) *Witchcraft, Oracles, and Magic among the Azande*, Oxford University Press.

FORESTER, T. (1980) 'Whatever Happened to Industrial Democracy?,' in *New Society*, 17 July 1980.

FOSTER, M. (1985) 'Cold Turkey,' in *New Society*, 18 October 1985.

FRANK, A.G. (1975) *On Capitalist Underdevelopment*, Oxford University Press.

FRANK, A.G. (1981) *Crisis: In the Third World*, Holmes and Meier.

FREIDMAN, M. and FREIDMAN, R. (1981) *Free To Choose*, Avon Books.

GARFINKEL, H. (1974) 'The Origins of the Term "Ethnomethodology",' in Roy Turner *ed, Ethnomethodology*, Penguin.

GEORGE, S. (1977) *How the other Half Dies: The Real Reasons for World Hunger*, Penguin.

GIDDENS, A. (1977) *The Class Structure in Social Theory: Action, Structure and Contradiction in Social Analysis*, Macmillan.

GLEESON, D. (1983) 'Further Education, Pedagogy and Production,' in Gleeson D., *ed, Youth Training and the Search for Work*, Routledge and Kegan Paul.

GOLDTHORPE, J.H. (1980) *Social Mobility and Class Structure in Modern Britain*, Clarendon Press.

GOULDNER, A. (1965) 'Bureaucracy is not Inevitable,' in Peter Worsley *ed, Problems of Modern Sociology*, Penguin, 1978.

HALL, P. (1985) 'The Social Crisis,' in *New Society*, 22 November 1985.

HALL, S. (1978) 'Racism and Reaction' in *Five Views of Multi-Racial Britain*, published by the Commission for Racial Equality.

HALSEY, A.H. (1979) 'Bernstein on the block,' in *The Times Educational Supplement*, 16 December 1979.

HALSEY, A.H. (1978) *Change in British Society*, Oxford University Press.

HARRINGTON, M. (1984) *The New American Poverty*, Holt, Rinehart and Winston.

HAY, D. (1979) 'The Spiritual Experiences of the British' in *New Society*, 12 April 1979.

HAYTER, T. (1985) *Aid: Rhetoric and Reality*, Pluto Press.

HILL, M. (1983) *Understanding Social Policy*, Basil Blackwell and Martin Robertson.

HYMAN, S. (1972) *Why Do Strikes Occur?*, Fontana.

JENCKS, C. *et al*, (1977) 'Schooling and cognitive inequality,' in P. Raggat and M. Evans *eds*, *Urban Education: The Political Context*, Ward Lock.

JOHNSON, R. (1979) 'Three problematic elements of a theory of working-class culture,' in J. Clarke *et al*, *eds*, *Working Class Culture: Studies in history and theory*, Hutchinson.

JORDAN, B. (1985) 'Children in Care,' in *New Society*, 13 December 1985

KERR, C., DUNLOP, J., HARBISON, F. and MYERS, C. (1960) *Industrialism and Industrial Man: The Problems of Labor and Management in Economic Growth*, Harvard University Press.

KINCAID, J.C. (1973) *Poverty and Equality in Britain*, Penguin.

KING, A. (1972) 'A Sociological Portrait: Politics,' in *New Society*, 13 January 1972.

KUHN, T.S. (1970) *The Structure of Scientific Revolutions*, University of Chicago Press.

LAING, R. (1973) 'The Mystification of Experience,' in Phil Brown *ed*, *Radical Psychology*, Harper Colophon Books.

LEGHORN, L. and PARKER, K. (1981) *Women's Worth: Sexual Economics and the World of Women*, Routledge and Kegan Paul.

LENIN, V.I. (1909) in Henry Christman *ed*, *Essential Works of Lenin*, Bantam

LE GRAND, J. and ROBINSON, R. (1984) *Privatisation and the Welfare State*, Allen and Unwin.

MACK, J. and LANSLEY, S. (1985) *Poor Britain*, Allen and Unwin.

MARX, K. (1844) in T.B. Bottomore and M. Rubel eds, *Karl Marx: Selected Writings in Sociology and Social Philosophy*, Penguin, 1967.

MARX, K. (1859) in David McLellan *ed*, *Grundrisse*, Macmillan, 1971.

MARX, K. and ENGELS, F. (1888) *The Communist Manifesto*, Penguin, 1981.

McINTOSH, M. (1978) 'The State and the Oppression of Women,' in Kuhn, A. and Wolpe, A., *ed*, *Feminism and Materialism*, Routledge and Kegan Paul.

McINTOSH, S. and Work Group (1981) Work and Leisure in Alan Tomlison *ed*, *Leisure and Social Control*, Brighton Polytechnic.

MEAD, G.H. (1934) *Mind, Self, and Society*, The University of Chicago Press, 1962.

MEAD, M. (1971) *Coming of Age in Samoa: A Study of Adolescence and Sex in Primitive Societies*, Penguin.

MERTON, R. and NISBET, B. (1976) *Contemporary Social Problems*, Harcourt, Brace, Jovanovich Inc.

MILIBAND, R. (1969) *The State in Capitalist Society*, Quartet Books.

MILLS, C.W. (1956) *The Power Elite*, Oxford University Press.

MILLS, C.W. (1959) *The Sociological Imagination*, Oxford University Press.

MISHRA, R. (1977) *Societies and Social Policy: Theories and Practice of Welfare*, Macmillan.

MITCHELL, J. (1971) *Women's Estate*, Penguin.

MOORE, L.G., VAN ARSDALE, P.W., GLITTERBERG, J.E. and ALDRICH, R.A. (1980) *The Biocultural Basis of Health*, C. V. Mosby.

NAVARRO, V. (1976) *Medicine Under Capitalism*, Prodist.

NISSEL, M. (1980) 'The family and the welfare state,' in *New Society*, 7 August 1980.

NYERERE, J. (1979) 'The Rational Choice,' in A. Coulson *ed*, *African Socialism in Practice: The Tanzanian Experience*, Spokesman.

OAKLEY, A. (1979) 'The failure of the movement for women's equality,' in *New Society*, 22 August 1979.

OAKLEY, A. (1980) *Women Confined: Towards a Sociology of Childbirth*, Martin Robertson.

PARKER, S. (1972) *The Sociology of Industry*, Allen and Unwin.

PARSONS, T. (Fall, 1959) 'The School Class as a Social System: Some of its Functions in American Society,' in *Harvard Educational Review*, XXIX.

PELLETIER, K.R. (1979) *Mind as Healer, Mind as Slayer*, Allen and Unwin.

PHILLIPSON, C. (1982) *Capitalism and the Construction of Old Age*, Macmillan.

POULANTZAS, N. (1978) *State, Power and Socialism*, New Left Books.

PRING, R. (1985) 'A Form of Life,' in *Times Educational Supplement*, 14 June 1985.

REID, I. (1977) *Social Class Differences in Britain: A Sourcebook*, Open Books.

REES, A.M. (1985) *T. H. Marshall's Social Policy*, Hutchinson.

REX, J. (1979) 'Black Militancy and Class Conflict,' in R. Miles and A. Phizacklea *eds, Racism and Political Action in Britain*, Routledge and Kegan Paul.

ROBERTS, K. (1984) *School Leavers and their Prospects: Youth and the Labour Market in the 1980s*, Open University Press.

ROBERTSON, J. (1978) 'Technology—master or servant,' in *New Scientist*, 23 November 1978.

ROSENHAN, D.L. (1978) 'On Being Sane in Insane Places,' in Swartz, H.D. and Kart, C.S. *eds, Dominant Issues in Medical Sociology*, Addison-Wesley.

ROSTOW, W. (1960) *Stages of Growth: A Non-Communist Manifesto*, Cambridge University Press.

ROWBOTHAM, S. (1973) *Women's Consciousness, Man's World*, Penguin.

ROWBOTHAM, S. (1977) *Hidden from History: 300 Years of Women's Oppression and the Fight Against It*, Pluto Press.

SAMPSON, A. (1981) *The Money Lenders: Bankers in a Dangerous World*, Hodder and Stoughton.

SCHEFF, T.J. (1966) *Being Mentally Ill: A Sociological Theory*, Aldine.

SHILS, E. (1961) 'Centre and Periphery,' in Peter Worsley *ed, Modern Sociology*, Penguin, 1978.

SHILS, E. (1963) 'The Theory of Mass Society,' in Philip Olson *ed, America as a Mass Society*, Collier-Macmillan.

SHORTER, E. (1977) *The Making of the Modern Family*, Fontana.

SILLITOE, A. (1958) *Saturday Night and Sunday Morning*, W.H. Allen.

SIMMONS, O.G. (1983) *Development Perspectives and Population Change*, Papers of the East-West Population Institute.

SKOLNICK, J. (1966) *Justice without Trial*, John Wiley.

SLOMNICKA, B.I. (1982) *Law of Childcare*, Macdonald and Evans.

SMITH, D.J. (1977) *Racial Disadvantage in Britain: The PEP Report*, Penguin.

STENGEL, E. (1977) *Suicide*, Penguin.

TAYLOR, I., WALTON, P. and YOUNG, J. (1976) 'Towards a New Criminology,' in Paul Willis *ed, Crime and Delinquency in Britain*.

TAYLOR, L. (1977) 'No More Flags,' in *New Society*, 31 March 1977.

TAYLOR-GOOBY, P. (1985) *Public Opinion, Ideology and the Welfare State*, Routledge and Kegan Paul.

THOMPSON, E.P. (1968) *The Making of the English Working Class*, Penguin.

TOWNSEND, P. (1981) 'Poverty in the 80s,' in *New Socialist*, September/October 1981.

WALTERS, V. (1980) *Class Inequality and Health Care: The Origins and Impact of the National Health Service*, Croom Helm.

WEBER, M. (1920) *Economy and Society*, Bedminster, 1968.

WEIR, D.J.H. (1977) 'Class Consciousness among Clerical Workers,' in E. Butterworth and D. Weir *eds, The Sociology of Modern Britain*, Fontana.

WEIR, M. (1976) from the Introduction of Mary Weir *ed, Job Satisfaction: Challenge and Response in Modern Britain*, Fontana.

WEST, D.J. and FARRINGTON, D.P. (1977) *The Delinquent Way of Life*, Heinemann.

WILENSKY, H.L. and LEBEAUX, C.N. (1958) *Industrial Society and Social Welfare*, Russell Sage Foundation.

WILLIAMS, R. (1961) *Culture and Society*, Penguin.

WILLIAMS, R. (1968) *Communications*, Penguin.

WILLIS, P. (1978) *Learning to Labour*, Saxon House.

YOUNG, M. (1958) *The Rise of the Meritocracy*, Penguin.

Author Index

Subject Index